READING & WRITING
COMMUNICATING IN COLLEGE

EAC 150

Custom Edition for Seneca College

CONTRIBUTORS

Katherine Yuk
Shirley Turchet
Jim Howes
Anthony Dayton
Sobia Zaman
Lidia Petrone
Melanie A. Rubens

With material from:

Strategies for Successful Writing:
A Rhetoric, Research Guide, Reader, and Handbook
Third Canadian Edition
by James A. Reinking, Robert von der Osten, Sue Ann Cairns, and Robert Fleming

The Ready Reference Handbook: Writing, Revising, Editing
Third Canadian Edition
by Jack Dodds and Judi Jewinski

PEARSON
Custom Publishing

Taken from:

Strategies for Successful Writing, Third Canadian Edition
by James A. Reinking, Robert von der Osten, Sue Ann Cairns and Robert Fleming
Copyright © 2007, 2004, 2000 by Pearson Education Canada
Published by Prentice Hall
Toronto, Ontario

The Ready Reference Handbook: Writing, Revising, Editing, Third Canadian Edition
by Jack Dodds and Judi Jewinski
Copyright © 2005, 2001, 1998 by Pearson Education Canada
Published by Allyn and Bacon
Toronto, Ontario

Printed in Canada

10 9 8 7 6 5 4 3 2 1

ISBN 0-536-27820-2

2006240330

AG/KL

Please visit our web site at *www.pearsoncustom.com*

PEARSON CUSTOM PUBLISHING
75 Arlington Street, Suite 300, Boston MA 02116
A Pearson Education Company

CONTENTS

RHETORIC

WRITING STRATEGIES: A WRITING PROCESS

WRITING STRATEGIES: RHETORICAL APPROACHES

CHAPTER 1

Writing:
An Overview

Why write? Hasn't the tempest of technology swept all of us into a brave new electronic world? Aren't email, voice mail, cell phones—all the magical devices of our new electronic estate—fast dooming ordinary writing? Not long ago, some people thought and said so, but events haven't supported those predictions. Although electronic devices have made some writing unnecessary, the written word flourishes both on campus and in the world of work. Furthermore, there's evidence that writing will become even more important in the future.

Writing offers very real advantages to both writers and readers:

1. It gives writers time to reflect on and research what they want to communicate and then lets them shape and reshape the material to their satisfaction.
2. It makes communication more precise and effective.
3. It provides a permanent record of thoughts, actions, and decisions.
4. It saves the reader time: We absorb information more swiftly when we read it than when we hear it.

Many people will expect you to write for them. Instructors ask you to write reports, summaries, reflective journals, research papers, and essay exams. Job hunting usually requires you to write resumes and cover letters. And once you're hired, writing will probably figure in your duties. You might be asked to discuss the capabilities of new computer equipment, report on a conference you attended, or explain the advantages of new safety procedures to supervisors or staff. Perhaps you'll propose that your organization install a new security system, conduct a market survey, or develop an alternative traffic flow pattern. The ability to write will help you earn better grades, land the job you want, and advance afterward in your career.

Writing also yields personal benefits. Sometimes people find that private writing, as in a journal, can help them sort out their emotions and come to greater clarity about decisions. At university, taking notes in class or writing summaries of lecture and notebook material can help you understand, remember, and integrate information. Informal, exploratory writing can help you uncover ideas you didn't know you had. In your personal life, writing can bring social and even financial benefits. Or you might have to write a tactful letter of apology to mend a broken relationship. On a more practical level, you might need to defend a reimbursement claim that you filed with your dental insurer or document a request to replace a faulty product. Skill and comfort with writing helps you handle these matters.

Although we may write for ourselves in order to explore ideas, to make knowledge our own, or to communicate privately with our inner selves, we more commonly write in response to a situation that involves other people. Situations often determine the purpose and audience of our writing as well as its content, style, and organization. Whether we are writing a text-message, an application letter, or an analytical academic essay, we usually write in a specific cultural context according to certain conventions. We write differently depending on whether we are dashing off emails to friends or writing academic papers. We follow different conventions when writing journal entries, emails, instant messages, policy briefs, memos, letters of reference, reflective critiques, and formal research-based essays. To write effectively in different social, business, or academic contexts, we need to be aware that readers have different expectations and values in different situations.

THE PURPOSES OF WRITING

Whenever you write, a clear purpose should guide your efforts. If you don't know why you're writing, neither will your reader. Fulfilling an assignment doesn't qualify as a real writing purpose, although it may well be what sends you to your desk. Faced with a close deadline for a research paper or report, you may tell yourself, "I'm doing this because I have to." An authentic purpose, however, requires you to answer this question: What do I want this piece of writing to do for both my reader and me? As you might expect, purpose grows out of the writing situation.

Here are four common *general writing purposes,* two or more of which often join forces in a single piece:

To Inform Presenting information is one of the most common writing purposes. The kayaking enthusiast who writes about how to manoeuvre a kayak plays the role of teacher, as does the researcher who summarizes the results of an investigation for co-workers. In school, you will often be asked to demonstrate your understanding of concepts in exams and papers so that instructors can gauge how well you have mastered the course material.

To Persuade You probably have strong views on many issues, and these feelings may sometimes impel you to try to sway your reader's views. In a letter to the editor, you might attack a proposal to establish a nearby chemical waste dump. Or, alarmed by a sharp jump in provincial unemployment, you might write to your MLA and argue for a youth employment program.

To Express Yourself Creative writing includes personal essays, fiction, plays, and poetry, as well as journals and diaries. Self-expression has a place in other kinds of writing too. Almost everything you write offers you a chance to display your mastery of words and to enliven your prose with vivid images and fresh turns of phrase.

To Entertain Some writing merely entertains; some writing couples entertainment with a more serious purpose. A lighthearted approach can help your reader absorb dull or difficult material. Satire lets you expose the shortcomings of individuals, ideas, and institutions by poking fun at them. An intention to entertain can add savour to many kinds of writing.

Besides having one or more *general purposes,* each writing project has its own *specific purpose.* Consider the difference in the papers you could write about herbal medicines. You might explain why readers should take herbal medicines or argue why these medicines should be federally regulated.

Having a specific purpose assists you at every stage of the writing process. It helps you define your audience; select the details, language, and approach that best suit their needs; and avoid going off in directions that won't interest them. The following example from Celia Milne's essay, "Pressures to Conform," has a clear and specific purpose.

> Unhappiness with body image seems to be a national preoccupation. According to statistics compiled by the National Eating Disorder Information Centre in Toronto, 90 percent of Canadian women are dissatisfied with some aspect of their bodies. One of the main battlegrounds in the fight for improvement, of course, is eating. According to *Maclean's* year-end poll published in late December, 43 percent of Canadian women—compared with 33 percent of men—believe they are overweight. The eating disorder centre says that its surveys show that fully 70 percent of Canadian women are preoccupied with their weight, and 40 percent are yo-yo dieting. "For most women, when they get together in a group a common topic is trying to lose weight," says Dr. Christine Davies, a family physician in Saint John, N.B., who is concerned about how that may rub off on their daughters. Margaret Beck, acting director of the eating disorder centre, affirms that danger. "The research," she says, "does seem to suggest that mothers who are food- and weight-preoccupied tend to have daughters who are the same."

The topic sentence that begins Milne's paragraph clearly focuses on her claim that dissatisfaction with "body image" is a widespread concern in Canada. The subsequent four sentences provide statistical evidence from the National Eating Disorder Information Centre in Toronto and a *Maclean's* poll reinforcing her specific argument that the majority of women are unhappy with their weight or appearance. The final three sentences further corroborate Milne's argument by introducing statements from medical experts who confirm that weight and body image concerns among Canadian women are prevalent and likely to continue.

Now examine the next paragraph, which does *not* have a firmly fixed specific purpose:

> Community is a sea in which people swim unconsciously, like fish. We fail to recognize our neighbours as fellow humans, and they show the same lack of fellow feeling for us. A complete lack of concern for one another is evident in today's complex society. What is community? Is it a plant? A building? A place? A state of being? Knowing what it is, we can see if such a place exists. To know community, one must realize who he or she is. Identity of a person is the first step in establishing a community.

This student writer can't decide what aspect of community to tackle. The opening sentence attempts a definition, but the next two veer onto the shortcomings of the modern community. Notice how aimlessly the thoughts drift. The vague leadoff sentence asserts "Community is a sea . . . ," but the later question "What is community?" contradicts this opening. Also, if community is a plant, a building, or a place, why must we realize who we are in order to know it? This contradictory and illogical paragraph reveals a writer groping for a purpose.

The paragraph, however, isn't a wasted effort. These musings offer several possibilities. By developing the first sentence into a full paragraph, the writer could show some interesting similarities between community and a sea, so that instead of taking community for granted, readers could see it in a new light. By pursuing the idea in the second and third sentences, the writer might show the callous nature of modern society and thus encourage readers to act more humanely. The last two sentences might lead the writer to discover a connection between personal identity and one's place in community. Thus, a specific purpose can sometimes emerge from preliminary jottings.

THE AUDIENCE FOR YOUR WRITING

Everything you write is aimed at a particular audience—a person or group you want to reach. The ultimate purpose of all writing is to have an effect on a reader (even if that reader is you), and therefore purpose and audience are closely linked. Whether you are writing to inform *someone* of something, to persuade *someone* to believe or do something, to express feelings or insights to *someone*, or to entertain *someone,* you will write better if you know or can at least imagine a particular someone, the audience for your writing.

Moreover, in both personal and academic writing, you can't assume that the reader is able to read your mind and understand what you really meant to say. In face-to-face conversations, you can observe your listeners' reactions and instantly respond to signs of confusion, boredom, or anger. You can clarify your meaning by offering examples. Or you can alter your tone, ask a question, or even change the subject. You can even use gestures and facial expressions to emphasize your main points. But when you write, the words on the page are all that represent you and carry your meaning. Once written or sent into cyberspace, your written work is on its own, even if the tone is wrong and the message garbled or incomplete. Readers will not charitably fill in any gaps in meaning. Of course, when you write to friends or someone else you know well, you can usually anticipate how they might respond to what you say. But when you write for people you know only casually or not at all, such as employers, customers, or the general public, you need to assess your audience before starting to write. The more you understand their assumptions, expectations, needs, and desires, the more strategically you can tailor your writing to them, and the more they will understand.

A good way to assess your readers is to develop an audience profile. This profile emerges gradually as you answer the following questions:

1. What are the educational level, age, and economic status of the audience I want to reach?
2. Why will this audience read my writing? to gain information? learn my views on a controversial issue? enjoy my creative flair? be entertained?
3. What attitudes, needs, and expectations do they have?
4. How are they likely to respond to what I say? Can I expect them to be neutral? opposed? friendly?
5. How much do they know about my topic? (Your answer here will help you gauge whether you're saying too little or too much.)
6. What kind of language will communicate with them most effectively?

Assignment instructions sometimes ask you to envision a reader who is intelligent but not an expert, someone receptive to new ideas but unwilling to put up with boring or confusing material. Another assignment may ask you to write for a certain age group, especially one with particular interests. At other times, you'll be asked to write for a specialized audience—one with some expertise in your topic. These differences affect what you say to each audience and how you say it.

The Effect of Audience on Your Writing

Let's examine how audience can shape a paper. Suppose you are explaining how to take a certain type of X-ray. If your audience is a group of lay readers who have never had an X-ray, you might explain at the outset that taking an X-ray is much like taking an ordinary photograph. Then you might explain the basic process, including the positioning of the patient and the equipment; comment on the safety and reliability of the procedure; and describe how much time it takes. You probably would use few technical terms. However, if you were writing for radiology students, you might instead emphasize exposure factors, film size, and required views. This audience would want technical terms and detailed explanations of the procedure. You would speak to these readers as colleagues who appreciate precise information.

Audience shapes all types of writing in similar fashion, even your personal writing. Assume you've recently become engaged, and to share your news you write two letters: one to your clergy, the other to your best friend back home. You can imagine the differences in details, language, and tone of each letter. Further, think how inappropriate it would be to accidentally send the letter intended for one to the other. Without doubt, different readers call for different approaches.

Discourse Communities

Professionals often write as members of specific communities that have their own conventions, shared assumptions, and specialized language or discourse. For example, environmental biologists with similar interests might exchange information about their research into the effects of environmental policies related to global warming. The members of a community share goals, values, concerns, background information, and expectations, and this shared knowledge in turn affects how they write. Because such writing is closely tied to the interests of the community, professional articles often start with a section linking the content to previous research projects and articles. In addition, custom often dictates what information must be included, what pattern of organization should be used, and what style the paper should follow. For example, in formal academic writing, documentation of sources follows different conventions in the humanities (such as English) than in the social sciences (such as psychology).

In addition, different academic disciplines may emphasize different writing structures and may have different approaches. For example, in a marketing class, you might be asked to do a case study; in a communications class, you might be asked for a technical report and PowerPoint presentation; and in an economics class, you might be asked to identify an economic problem and explore a hypothetical solution to the problem. A chemistry instructor might expect you to write a lab report in such a way that someone with your background could repeat the experiment exactly as you did. In a literature class, an instructor will probably be more interested in your in-depth analysis or interpretation of a story than in your exact recounting of the plotline. So throughout your studies, you will discover that learning to write well means becoming familiar with the values and customs of different discourse communities. To do this, you need to read carefully in a particular field, acquainting yourself with its current issues and concerns and learning how to write about them. Ask yourself these questions as you start reading in any professional area:

1. What are the major concerns and questions in this discourse community?
2. What seems to be common knowledge?
3. To what works do writers regularly refer?
4. How do those in the field go about answering questions?
5. What methods do they follow?
6. Which kinds of knowledge are acceptable? Which are not?
7. What values seem to guide the discourse community?
8. What kinds of information must writers include in papers?
9. How are different writing projects organized?
10. What conventions do writers follow?

Of course, we all belong to many different communities; but the more comfortably you can move from one discourse community to another, the more you will be in a position to exert influence in your world. At university, as you gain familiarity with the language, conventions, and expectations of different academic audiences in psychology, philosophy, or economics, you will find it easier to write papers in these different discourse communities.

EXERCISE *The three excerpts below deal with the same subject—antigens—but each explanation is geared to a different audience. Read the passages carefully; then answer the following questions:*

    a. What audience does each author address? How do you know?

    b. Identify ways in which each author appeals to a specific audience.

1. The human body is quick to recognize foreign chemicals that enter it. "Foes" must be attacked or otherwise got rid of. The most common of these foes are chemical materials from viruses, bacteria, and other microscopic organisms. Such chemicals, when recognized by the body, are called *antigens*. To combat them, the body produces its own chemicals, protein molecules called *antibodies*. Each kind of antigen causes the production of a specific kind of antibody. Antibodies appear in the body fluids such as blood and lymph and in the body's cells.

            L. D. Hamilton, "Antibodies and Antigens," *The New Book of Knowledge*

2. [An] *antigen* [is a] foreign substance that, when introduced into the body, is capable of inducing the formation of antibodies and of reacting specifically in a detectable manner with the induced antibodies. For each antigen there is a specific antibody, the physical and chemical structure of which is produced in response to the physical and chemical structure of the antigen. Antigens comprise virtually all proteins that are foreign to the host, including those contained in bacteria, viruses, protozoa, helminths, foods, snake venoms, egg white, serum components, red blood cells, and other cells and tissues of various species, including man. Polysaccharides and lipids may also act as antigens when coupled to proteins.

            "Antigen," *Encyclopaedia Britannica*

3. The substance which stimulates the body to produce antibodies is designated antigen (antibody stimulator). . . .

Most complete antigens are protein molecules containing aromatic amino acids, and are large in molecular weight and size. However, it has been demonstrated that other macromolecules, such as pure polysaccharides, polynucleotides, and lipids, may serve as complete antigens.

However, certain other materials, incapable of stimulating antibody formation by themselves can, in association with a protein or other carrier, stimulate antibody formation and are the antigenic determinants. These determinants are referred to as *incomplete antigens* or *haptens*, and they are able to react with antibodies which were produced by the determinant-protein complex.

However, before an antigen can stimulate the production of antibodies, it must be soluble in the body fluids, must reach certain tissues in an unaltered form, and must be, in general, foreign to the body tissues. Protein taken by mouth loses its specific foreign-protein characteristics when digested in the alimentary tract. It reaches the tissues of the body as amino acids or other altered digested products of protein. Consequently, it no longer meets the requirements for antigenic behavior.

Orville Wyss and Curtis Eklund, *Microorganisms and Man*

Level of Diction

How does a writer choose the right level of diction, or word choice, for a particular audience? It depends on the writer's purpose, as well as which discourse community the writer is addressing. Think about a safety engineer who investigates a serious industrial accident on which she must write two reports, one for the safety director of the company, who represents a technical audience, and another for the local newspaper, which represents a general audience. Although the two accounts would deal with the same matter, they would clearly need to use very different language: specialized and formal in the first case, everyday and more relaxed in the second. In both cases, the language would have to reflect the background of the audience. As you write, always choose language suited to your audience and purpose.

Edited standard English follows the familiar grammatical rules maintained in most formal and academic writing. Generally, everything you write for university or college courses or on the job should be in edited standard English. *Nonstandard English* refers to any version of the language that deviates from these rules. Here is an example from Dionne Brand's short story, "Blossom: Priestess of Oya, Goddess of Winds, Storms and Waterfalls":

This was Blossom's most successful endeavour since coming to Canada. Every once in a while, under she breath, she cursè the day she come to Toronto from Oropuche, Trinidad. But nothing, not even snarky white people could keep Blossom under. When she first come it was to babysit some snot-nosed children on Oriole Parkway. She did meet a man, in a club on Henry Street in Port-of-Spain, who promise she to take care of she, if she ever was in Toronto. When Blossom reach, the man disappear and through the one other person she know in Toronto she get the work on Oriole.

As this example shows, nonstandard English does have a place in writing. Fiction writers use it to narrate the talk of characters who, if real, would speak that way; journalists use it to report eyewitness reactions to accidents and crimes; and people who compile oral histories use it to record the recollections of people they interview.

Edited standard English includes four levels of usage: formal, informal, formal–informal, and technical. Another commonly recognized category is colloquial language and slang.

Formal Level The formal level, dignified and serious, is suitable for important political, business, and academic occasions. Its vocabulary is marked by many abstract and multisyllabic words but no slang or contractions. Long sentences and deliberately varied sentence patterns help give it a strong, rhythmic flow. The more formal rhythm or cadence of these sentences comes, in part, from the relatively complex and varied sentence patterns. Overall, formal prose impresses the reader as authoritative, stately, and graceful.

The following excerpt from the introduction to the third edition of Susanna Moodie's *Roughing It in the Bush* illustrates the formal level:

> In most instances, emigration is a matter of necessity, not of choice; and this is more especially true of the emigration of persons of respectable connections, or of any station or position in the world. Few educated persons, accustomed to the refinements and luxuries of European society, ever willingly relinquish those advantages, and place themselves beyond the protective influence of the wise and revered institutions of their native land, without the pressure of some urgent cause. Emigration may, indeed, generally be regarded as an act of severe duty, performed at the expense of personal enjoyment, and accompanied by the sacrifice of those local attachments which stamp the scenes amid which our childhood grew, in imperishable characters upon the heart. Nor is it until adversity has pressed sorely upon the proud and wounded spirit of the well-educated sons and daughters of old but impoverished families, that they gird up the loins of the mind, and arm themselves with fortitude to meet and dare the heart-breaking conflict.

In this address to the readers of the third edition of her journals recounting expatriate life in Canada during the nineteenth century, Susanna Moodie formally expresses her sense that "emigration is a matter of necessity, not of choice." This initial parallelism is characteristic of the contrast throughout the passage as Moodie notes the dire circumstances of life in the colony, removed from "the protective influence of the wise and revered institutions" of Europe. All of the sentences use complex causal relationships and modification. The sense that the European emigrant performs a noble task in an ignoble place is reinforced by elevated diction—longer words such as *educated, protective, revered, sacrifice, imperishable, impoverished*, and *fortitude*, along with shorter abstract words like *duty, proud, spirit*, and *mind*. The carefully controlled language and syntax lend an earnest, altruistic tone to this passage directed toward a largely European audience.

Informal Level Informal writing resembles orderly, intelligent conversation. Earmarked by relatively ordinary words, loose sentences (sentences in which the main clause comes at the beginning), and numerous shorter, less varied sentence structures than formal prose, informal writing may include contractions or even slang, and it is more likely than formal writing to use the pronouns *I, me, my, you,* and *yours.* Casual and familiar rather than dignified and rhythmic, informal writing does not usually call attention to itself. Nevertheless, the language is precise and effective. Here is an example:

> There was a distressing story in the paper a few months ago. I wish I'd clipped it out and saved it. As it is, I can only hope I remember it fairly accurately. There was a group of people who wanted a particular dictionary removed from the shelves of the local library because it contained a lot of obscenity. I think they said there were sixty-five or so dirty words in it. Some poor woman who was acting as a spokesman for the group had a list of offending words, which she started to read aloud at a hearing. She managed to read about twenty of them before she started sobbing uncontrollably and couldn't continue.
>
> Thomas H. Middleton, "The Magic Power of Words"

Unlike the Moodie excerpt, this paragraph has relatively uncomplicated sentences. The passage also includes two contractions (*I'd* and *couldn't*), one casual expression (*a lot of*), and the pronoun *I.* Most of the words are very short, and none would be out of place in an ordinary conversation.

Formal–Informal Level As life has become less formal, informal diction has become increasingly widespread. Today many articles and books, even ones on relatively serious topics, mix informal and formal elements. Here is an example:

> Faith in sports has been vigorously promoted by industry, the military, government, the media. The value of the arena and the locker room has been imposed on our national life. Coaches and sportswriters are speaking for generals and businessmen, too, when they tell us that a man must be physically and psychologically "tough" to succeed, that he must be clean and punctual and honest, that he must bear pain, bad luck, and defeat without whimpering or making excuses. A man must prove his faith in sports and the American Way by whipping himself into shape, playing by the rules, being part of the team, and putting out all the way. If his faith is strong, he will triumph. It's his own fault if he loses, fails, remains poor.
>
> Robert Lipsyte, *Sports World*

Although a few expressions in this excerpt—*bear, the American Way, triumph*—echo formal diction, most of the words have an informal ring, and two expressions, *whipping himself into shape* and *putting out all the way,* skirt the edges of slang.

Technical Level A specialist writing for others in the same field or for sophisticated nonspecialists writes on the technical level, a cousin to the formal level. Technical language uses specialized words that may be unfamiliar to a general audience. Its sentences tend to be long and complex; but unlike formal diction, the writing doesn't lean toward periodic sentences, parallelism, and balance. Read this example from the field of entomology, the study of insects:

The light organs of fireflies are complex structures, and recent studies using the electron microscope show them to be even more complex than once supposed. Each is composed of three layers: an outer "window," simply a transparent portion of the body wall; the light organ proper; and an inner layer of opaque, whitish cells filled with granules of uric acid, the so-called "reflector." The light organ proper contains large, slablike light cells, each of them filled with large granules and much smaller, dark granules, the latter tending to be concentrated around the numerous air tubes and nerves penetrating the light organ. These smaller granules were once assumed by some persons to be luminous bacteria, but we now know that they are mitochondria, the source of ATP [adenosine triphosphate] and therefore of the energy of light production. The much larger granules that fill most of the light cells are still of unknown function; perhaps they serve as the source of luciferin.

Howard Ensign Evans, Life on a Little-Known Planet

Note the specialized vocabulary—*granules, uric acid, mitochondria,* and *luciferin*—as well as the length and complexity of the sentences. Five sentences make up the passage, the shortest having twenty-four words. None is periodic, and none has a parallel or balanced structure.

Every field has *jargon,* specialized terms or inside talk that provides a convenient shorthand for communication among its members. For example, for an audience of biologists, you may write that two organisms have a *symbiotic relationship,* meaning "mutually beneficial"; for psychology majors, you might use *catalepsy* instead of "a temporary loss of consciousness and feeling, often accompanied by muscular rigidity." As a general rule, use technical terms only if your audience will know their meanings. If you must use technical words when writing for a general audience, define them the first time they appear.

Colloquial Language and Slang   *Colloquial* originally meant "the language of ordinary conversation between people of a particular region." *Slang,* according to *The Canadian Oxford Dictionary,* is defined as "words, phrases, and uses that are regarded as very informal and are often restricted to special contexts." These two categories shade into each other, and even authorities sometimes disagree on whether to label a term *colloquial* or *slang.* The word *bender,* meaning "a drinking spree," seems firmly in the colloquial camp, and *bummer,* a term recently used by young people to mean "a bad time," is just as clearly slang. *Break a leg* is theatre slang used to wish a performer success. But what about *guy* and *kid*? Once they were slang; but so many people have used them for so long that they have now become colloquial.

Regardless of their labels, colloquial and slang terms are almost never appropriate in formal writing. They sometimes serve a useful purpose in informal writing by creating a special effect or increasing audience appeal. Even so, careful writers use them sparingly. Some readers may not understand some colloquial language, and slang usually becomes dated quickly. The following paragraph uses colloquial and slang expressions successfully:

When I was just a kid on Eighth Avenue in knee pants . . . [Big Bill] was trying to get himself killed. He was always in some fight with a knife. He was always cutting or trying to cut somebody's throat. He was always getting cut or getting shot. Every Saturday night that he was out there, something happened. If you heard on Sunday morning that somebody had gotten shot or stabbed, you didn't usually ask who did it. You'd ask if Big Bill did it. If he did it, no one paid much attention to it, because he was always doing something like that. They'd say, "Yeah, man. That cat is crazy."

Claude Brown, Manchild in the Promised Land

Kid, yeah, and *cat* reflect the speech of Brown's characters and thus add authenticity to his account. Despite the informal diction, Brown uses parallelism in the second, third, and fourth sentences; repetition of *he was always* emphasizes the single-minded self-destructiveness of Big Bill's behaviour.

EXERCISE *Identify the level of diction in each of the following passages. Support your answers with examples from the passages. Point out slang or colloquial expressions.*

1. We may now recapitulate the reasons which have made it necessary to substitute "space-time" for space and time. The old separation of space and time rested upon the belief that there was no ambiguity in saying that two events in distant places happened at the same time; consequently it was thought that we could describe the topography of the universe at a given instant in purely spatial terms. But now that simultaneity has become relative to a particular observer, this is no longer possible. What is, for one observer, a description of the state of the world at a given instant, is, for another observer, a series of events at various different times, whose relations are not merely spatial but also temporal.

   Bertrand Russell, The ABC of Relativity

2. In some ways I am an exceptionally privileged woman of thirty-seven. I am in the room of a private, legal abortion hospital, where a surgeon, a friend of many years, is waiting for me in the operating room. I am only five weeks pregnant. Last week I walked out of another hospital, unaborted, because I had suddenly changed my mind. I have a husband who cares for me. He yells because my indecisiveness makes him anxious, but basically he has permitted the final choice to rest in my hands: "It would be very tough, especially for you, and it is absolutely insane, but yes, we could have another baby." I have a mother who cares. I have two young sons, whose small faces are the most moving arguments I have against going through with this abortion. I have a doctorate in psychology, which among other advantages, assures me of the professional courtesy of special passes in hospitals, passes that at this moment enable my husband and my mother to stand in my room at a nonvisiting hour and yell at each other over my head while I sob.

   Magda Denes, In Necessity and Sorrow: Life and Death in an Abortion Hospital

3. I have just spent two days with Edward T. Hall, an anthropologist, watching thousands of my fellow New Yorkers short-circuiting themselves into hot little twitching death balls with jolts of their own adrenalin. Dr. Hall says it is overcrowding that does it. Overcrowding gets the adrenalin going, and the adrenalin gets them queer, autistic, sadistic, barren, batty, sloppy, hot-in-the-pants, charred-in-the-flankers, leering, puling, numb—the usual in New York, in other

words, and God knows where else. Dr. Hall has the theory that overcrowding
has already thrown New York into a state of behavioral sink. Behavioral sink is a
term from ethology, which is the study of how animals relate to their environment. Among animals, the sink winds up with a "population collapse" or "massive die-off." O rotten Gotham.

Tom Wolfe, *The Pump House Gang*

Whether you choose a relatively formal or casual level of diction depends on
your audience, purpose, and situation. Moreover, it goes without saying that, as you
shape your paper, the writing must please you as well as your audience—it must satisfy your sense of what good writing is and what the writing task requires. You are,
after all, your own first reader.

THE QUALITIES OF GOOD WRITING

Three qualities—fresh thinking, a sense of style, and effective organization—
help ensure that a piece of prose will meet your reader's expectations.

Fresh Thinking   You don't have to astound your readers with something never
before discussed in print. Genuinely unique ideas and information are scarce
commodities. You can, however, freshen your writing by exploring personal
insights and perceptions. Using your own special slant, you might show a connection between seemingly unrelated items, as does a writer who likens office
"paper pushers" to different kinds of animals. Do not strain too desperately for
originality, because far-fetched notions spawn skepticism.

Sense of Style   Whatever context you are writing in, once you have figured out
what you want to say, say it as clearly as you can. Sometimes students think that
vague, mysterious writing intrigues readers; however, most readers do not want
to play guessing games. Write to communicate, not to impress. Good writing is
clear, with a style appropriate for the particular situation, audience, and purpose. It may be quite appropriate to write without capital letters or apostrophes
in an online chat room, but not in an academic essay. In technical, scientific, or
legal documents, readers expect a neutral tone. If you are writing a narrative
essay or persuasive argument, well-chosen verbs and nouns, and vivid examples
or metaphors can help to draw your reader in. Your style should be suited to the
writing situation, whether informal or formal.

Effective Organization   While some personal writing and cyber-writing does
not have a linear structure, readers expect academic papers to have a beginning,
a middle, and an end—that is, an introduction, a body, and a conclusion. The
introduction sparks interest and acquaints the reader with what is to come.
The body delivers the main message and exhibits a clear connection between
ideas so that the reader can easily follow your thoughts. The conclusion ends the

discussion so the reader feels satisfied rather than suddenly cut off. Overall, your paper should follow a pattern that is suited to its content.

WRITING AND ETHICS

Accuracy, fairness, and honesty in your writing help inspire trust in your readers. Like you, readers expect that what they read contains dependable information. If you are writing a report, a brief or abstract, or a review or recommendation, you do not want to skew your conclusions by failing to mention important evidence that contradicts your conclusions. In research writing, which is addressed in Chapters 13 and 14, you establish credibility when you give credit to authorities and clarify sources of your information. Few readers would bother with a carelessly presented or even deliberately deceptive piece of information.

Think for a minute about how you would react to the following situation. You decide to vacation at a Canadian country resort after reading a brochure that described its white-sand beach, scenic trails, fine dining, and peaceful atmosphere. When you arrive, you find the beach overgrown with weeds, the trails littered, and the view unappealing. The gourmet restaurant is a greasy-spoon cafeteria. Worse, whenever you go outside, swarms of vicious black flies attack you. Wouldn't you feel cheated? In addition, think how you'd feel if you decided to attend a university because of its distinguished faculty members only to discover upon arrival that they rarely teach on campus. The university uses the researchers' reputations to attract students, even though these researchers are usually unavailable. Hasn't the college done something unethical?

Ethical writing, which is accurate, fair, and honest, reflects the integrity of the writer.

The Principles of Ethical Writing

Accuracy Writing perceived as truthful should *be* truthful. Granted, a writer may use humorous exaggeration to make us laugh, and some sales pitches may stretch the truth a bit in order to entice buyers ("Try Nu-Glo toothpaste and add sparkle to your life"). But most readers recognize and discount such embellishments as harmless. However, deliberate distortions and falsehoods may hurt not only the reader but the writer as well. If you were angered by misrepresentations in the vacation brochure, you would likely warn your friends against the resort; you might even take legal action.

No Deliberate Omissions To be perceived as truthful, a document should tell the whole truth, omitting nothing the reader needs to know in order to make an informed decision. The text should not be deliberately incomplete so as to mislead. Suppose a university's recruitment brochure stresses that 97 percent of its students get jobs upon graduation, but omits the fact that only 55 percent of these jobs are in the graduates' chosen field of study. Certainly these brochures are deceptive, perhaps attracting students who would otherwise choose schools with better placement records.

Clarity Writing should be clear to the reader. All of us know the frustration of trying to read an important legal document that is impossible to comprehend. Moreover, a person who writes instructions so unclear that they result in costly or harmful mistakes is partially (and often legally) responsible for the consequences. An annual report that deliberately obscures information about its yearly losses is not fair to potential investors.

Honest Representation Writing should not present itself as something different from what it is. It would be unethical for a drug company to prepare an advertisement in the form of an unbiased news story.

No Intentional Harm Writing should not be intended to harm the reader. Certainly it is fair to point out the advantages of a product or service that readers might not need. But think how unethical it would be for a writer to encourage readers to follow a diet that the writer knew was not only ineffective but harmful. Think of the harm a writer might cause by attempting, deliberately, to persuade readers to try crack cocaine.

Good writing is also ethical writing. A good test of the ethics of your writing is to determine how you would react after you had read your own work and acted on the basis of the information. Would you feel comfortable with it, or would you feel cheated, manipulated, belittled, or deceived? By practising the principles of ethical writing, you show respect to your readers and to yourself.

CHAPTER 2

Strategies for
Active Reading

Effective reading is not the passive process that many people imagine. On the contrary, it requires the ongoing interaction of your mind and the printed page. Bringing your knowledge and experience to bear on a piece of writing can help you assess its events, ideas, and conclusions. For example, an understanding of marriage, love, and conflict, as well as experience with divorce, can help readers comprehend an essay that explores divorce. As you read, you must also understand each point that's made, consider how the various parts fit together, and try to anticipate the direction the writing will take. Successful reading requires work. Fortunately, you can follow specific strategies to help yourself read better.

ORIENTING YOUR READING

Different purposes require different approaches to reading. When reading for pleasure, you can relax and proceed at your own pace, slowing down to savour a section you especially enjoy, speeding up when you encounter less interesting material, and breaking off when you wish. But reading for information, solid

understanding, or critique calls for a more methodical approach. Before starting, ask yourself these questions:

- **Why am I reading this material?** Is it for long-term use, as a reference for
  a project, or as a building block to understanding more material?
- **How well do I need to know the material in the article?** Can you look back
  to the article as a reference? Is there only one main point you need to
  know? Are you going to be tested on much of the material in depth?
- **Is some material in the article more important to me than other
  material?** Sometimes in doing research you may be looking for a specific
  bit of information that is only one paragraph in a long article. If so, you
  can skim for the information. In most documents you read, certain sections are more important than others. Often you can read to get the main
  points of the article and not focus on all the details. But other times, of
  course, you need to understand all the material in depth.
- **What will I do with the information in the article?** If you are looking
  for ideas for your own writing, you might read quickly. If you are responsible for writing a critique of the article, you need to read carefully and
  critically.
- **What kind of reading does the material suggest?** The significance, difficulty, and nature of the writing all can influence how you read. An easy
  humorous narrative can be read in a more leisurely fashion. But an argument for or against an important issue merits careful attention to the
  main points and the evidence and may even require you to outline the
  argument.

EXERCISE

Reading Activity *Look briefly at "The Appeal of the Androgynous Man." Identify three
purposes you could have for reading this essay. Identify how these purposes would affect
how you would read the essay and what you would look for in the essay.*

A FIRST READING

When going on a trip or an outing, you don't just jump in your car and take off.
Usually you take some time to think about where you want to go. Sometimes you
even have to check your route. The same is true of effective reading. Because of
the challenging nature of most college- and university-level reading assignments, you should plan on more than one reading. The goal of the good first
reading is just to orient you to the material.

Orient Yourself to the Background of the Essay   Before you begin, examine
information accompanying the essay for clues about the essay's relevance. Scan
the accompanying biographical sketch (if available) to determine the writer's

expertise and biases on the topic. Read any notes by the author or editor about the process of researching or writing this essay. For professional essays, look for an abstract that provides a brief summary of the article. At this point, you may want to judge the credibility of the source, a topic discussed in Chapter 13.

Use the Title as a Clue   Most titles identify the topic and often the author viewpoint as well. Thus, "The Sweet Smell of Success Isn't All That Sweet" suggests that the author isn't overly impressed with the conventional attitudes toward success. In addition, some titles signal the writer's primary strategy such as a comparison, definition, or argument.

Skim to Get the Gist of the Article   Sometimes you can just read the introductory and concluding paragraphs and the topic sentences (often the first or last sentences of paragraphs) to get the overall meaning of the article. Other times you will need to read the whole essay quickly. In your first reading, you can skim the more difficult sections without trying to understand them fully. Just try to get an idea of the essay's main thrust, the key ideas that support it, and the ways that they are organized.

Make Connections   When you've finished skimming the essay, think about what you have learned, and then, either by saying it to yourself or jotting it down, express it in your own words. Until you can state its essence in your own words, you don't really understand what you've read, and you will be unlikely to remember it. Then make connections between the ideas. Go back and underline the thesis statement, or, if there isn't any, try to formulate one in your own words. Identify the main strategy the writer uses. Identify what you already know about the topic, and examine your personal connection with the topic. You will read more effectively if you can connect what you read to your own knowledge and interests. Finally, jot down questions that the first reading raises in your mind.

EXERCISE
Reading Activities

1. Using the author bio statement at the beginning of the article "The Appeal of the Androgynous Man," identify what you can about the author's background, interests, and biases.

2. Before reading, write what you expect to be the essay's main idea, based on the title.

3. After skimming the essay, identify the main points of the essay and the thesis. Jot down at least two questions you have at the end of your first quick reading.

SECOND READINGS

If the material was difficult, or thorough comprehension is essential, a second or even third reading may be necessary. On the second reading, you read more slowly than the first reading so that you can carefully absorb the writer's ideas.

Read Carefully and Actively Read at a pace suitable to the material. Underline significant topic sentences as well as other key sentences and ideas or facts that you find important, but keep in mind that underlining in itself doesn't ensure comprehension. Restating the ideas in your own words is more effective. Depending on your purposes, you may also want to write down the main points in your own words or jot down ideas in the margins. As you proceed, examine the supporting sentences to see how well they back up the main idea. Keep an eye out for how the essay fits together.

Consider Reading as a Kind of Conversation with the Text Develop the habit of asking questions about facts, reasons, ideas—practically anything in the essay. Jot down your queries and their answers in the margins. You can see how a student interacted with the first page of Amy Gross's essay, "The Appeal of the Androgynous Man.") Good writers anticipate questions and answer them somewhere in the essay. Moreover, because you have posed the questions yourself, you are more likely to see the connections in the text. If the author hasn't answered your questions anywhere in the essay, then you have discovered some weaknesses in the writing and research.

Master Unfamiliar Words At times, unfamiliar words can hinder your grasp of the material. Whenever you encounter a new word, circle it, use context to help gauge its meaning, check the dictionary for the exact meaning, and then record it in the margins or some other convenient place. If the writing is peppered with words you don't know, you may have to read the whole piece to figure out its general drift, then look up key words, and finally reread the material.

Take Conscious Steps to Understand Difficult Material When the ideas of a single section prove difficult, write down the points of those sections you do understand. Then experiment by stating in your own words different interpretations of the problem section to see which one best fits the writing as a whole.

Sometimes large sections or entire texts are extremely difficult to understand. Use these strategies to improve your comprehension:

- State the ideas that are easier for you to understand and use them to unlock more difficult (but not unintelligible) meanings in related sections. Save the most difficult sections until last. But don't assume that you have to understand everything completely. Some works take a lifetime to fully understand.
- Discuss the essay with other students who are reading it.
- Read simpler material on the topic to get a basic knowledge of the topic.

■ Ask your instructor for help. He or she may help you find background material that will make the selection easier.

Pull the Entire Essay Together   Whenever you finish a major section of a lengthy essay, express your sense of what it means. Say it out loud or write it down. If you have difficulty seeing connections between the ideas, try representing them visually. You might make an outline that states the main points followed by subpoints. For a comparison paper, you might create a table with the main points of the comparison side by side. In addition, you can draw a diagram, list chronological steps, or write out main facts.

You can also use special techniques to strengthen your grasp of material that you may need to remember for a long time. Try restating the main points a couple of days after the second reading to test your retention. Sometimes it is helpful to explain the material to a sympathetic listener; then, if anything has become hazy or slipped your mind, reread the appropriate section(s). But if you must learn the material very thoroughly, make up a test and give it to yourself.

MASTERING READING PROBLEMS

Master the Problems That Interfere with Reading   Many environmental and personal factors influence the effectiveness of your reading. If your environment is too noisy, you are too tired, or you have something on your mind, you can have difficulty reading. Do your reading at the time of day when you are most alert. Be sure you are in a well-lit environment that allows you to concentrate. Try to be rested and comfortable. If you get tired, take a short break or go for a short walk. If something else is bothering you, try to resolve the distraction or put it out of your mind. To avoid boredom, read more actively by connecting the topic and your interests and goals.

If you have extensive problems with your course reading, ask for help. Most universities and colleges offer courses in reading and provide tutors and workshops. Higher education usually requires a lot of reading, so take the steps necessary to become the most effective reader possible.

EXERCISE
Reading Activities

1. Reread "The Appeal of the Androgynous Man." Write more questions and notes in the margin as you deepen your understanding of the main points.
2. Create a table with two columns comparing the author's points about the "all-man" and those about the "androgynous man."
3. Find three difficult or unusual words in the essay. Determine their meaning from the context before checking them in a dictionary.
4. Try explaining the main ideas of the article to a friend or roommate.

READING TO CRITIQUE

In university and college, you usually read not only to understand but also to evaluate what you read. Your instructors want to know what you think about what you've read. Often you are asked whether you agree or disagree with a writer's argument. Sometimes you are asked to write an explicit critique of what you have read.

Your instructors want to see if you can distinguish facts and well-supported arguments from opinions and assumptions. Merely because information and ideas are in print does not mean that they are true or acceptable. For example, an essay might have faulty logic, unreasonable ideas, suspect facts, or unreliable authorities, despite its professional look. Don't hesitate to dispute the writer's information. Ask yourself these questions:

- Does the main point of the essay match your experience or prior learning about this subject?
- Does the evidence support the claim?
- Do the ideas appear reasonable?
- Do other works contradict these claims? Has the author omitted other pieces of evidence that might contradict the main points?
- Do the ideas connect in a logical way?

By knowing the principles of argumentation and various reasoning fallacies, you can critique any piece of writing. These issues are discussed in Chapter 12.

EXERCISE

Reading Activities *Prepare your critique of "The Appeal of the Androgynous Man" by doing the following:*

1. Identify where and how the claims fail to match your experience.
2. Indicate where the evidence does not support the claims.
3. Indicate at least three places where the ideas do not appear reasonable.
4. Identify any evidence that seems to contradict the author's claims.
5. Evaluate whether the ideas connect in a logical way.

READING AS A WRITER

If you write, you can use reading as a springboard for improving your writing. Reading the views of others, the experiences they relate, and the information they present often deepens your understanding of yourself, your relationships, and your surroundings. In turn, this broadened perspective can supply you with writing ideas. When possibilities surface, be sure to record them. Some writers keep a reading journal in which they summarize what they've read and jot down writing ideas that come to mind. In addition, you can take down specific ideas, facts, and perhaps even a few particularly interesting quotations. You may want to incorporate this material into your writing later on. But be sure to record the source so that you can document it properly in order to avoid plagiarism.

When you read several sources that explore the same topic or related topics, you may notice connections among their ideas. Since these connections can be fertile ground for a paper of your own, don't neglect to record them. Once you have jotted down these ideas, circle or label the ideas they connect to. You can also draw lines linking different thoughts to each other and back to the main point. Then express your view of how these ideas fit together as a thesis statement. Interacting with multiple sources and using their ideas to advance the purpose of your writing is a form of synthesis. When you synthesize ideas into a new paper, review your information, determine the points you want to make, and experiment until you find the order that works best. As you write, use the material from your sources, but be careful to credit the authors properly in order to avoid plagiarism.

You can also learn new techniques and strategies from other writers. If you find an introduction, an organizational pattern, a transition, a certain description or comparison unusually engaging, then study the writer's technique. Perhaps you can use it yourself. Similarly, observe when a piece of writing fails and try to determine why.

EXERCISE
Reading Activities

1. Identify at least two strategies used in "The Appeal of the Androgynous Man" that you would find useful.
2. Identify at least two phrases that you found effective.
3. Identify at least two ideas that sparked ideas you could use in your own writing.

Does she favour androgynous men? What kind of appeal?

She will give a woman's perspective. She writes for and edits women's magazines.

Amy Gross

both male and female in one

The Appeal of the Androgynous Man

Amy Gross, a native of Brooklyn, New York, earned a sociology degree at Connecticut College. Upon graduation, she entered the world of fashion publishing and has held writing or editorial positions at various magazines, including Talk, Mademoiselle, Good Housekeeping, Elle, *and* Mirabella. *She is the newly appointed editor-in-chief of* O, *the Oprah Magazine. In our selection, which first appeared in* Mademoiselle *in 1976, Gross compares androgynous men favourably to macho "all-men."*

1   James Dean was my first androgynous man.[1] I figured I could talk to him. He was anguished and I was 12, so we had a lot in common. With only a few exceptions, <u>all the men I have liked or loved have been a certain kind of man: a kind who doesn't play football or watch the games on Sunday, who doesn't tell dirty jokes featuring broads or chicks, who is not contemptuous of conversations that are philosophically speculative, introspective, or otherwise foolish according to the other kind of man.</u> He is more self-amused, less inflated, more quirky, vulnerable and responsive than the other sort (the other sort, I'm visualizing as the guys on TV who advertise deodorant in the locker room). He is more like me than the other sort. <u>He is what social scientists and feminists would call androgynous: having the characteristics of both male and female.</u>

2   Now the first thing I want you to know about the <u>androgynous man is that he is neither effeminate nor</u> hermaphroditic. All his primary and secondary sexual characteristics are in order and I would say he's all-man, but that is just what he is not. He is more than all-man. ╲both male and female sex organs

3   The merely all-man man, for one thing, never walks to the grocery store unless the little woman is away visiting her mother with the kids, or is in the hospital having a kid, or there is no little woman. All-men men don't know how to shop in a grocery store unless it is to buy a 6-pack and some pretzels. Their ideas of nutrition expand beyond a 6-pack and pretzels only to take in steak, potatoes, scotch or rye whiskey, and maybe a wad of cake or apple pie. All-men men have absolutely no taste in food, art, books, movies, theatre, dance, how to live, what are good questions, what is funny, or anything else I care about. It's not exactly that the all-man's man is an uncouth illiterate. He may be educated, well-mannered, and on a first-name basis with fine wines. One all-man man I knew was a handsome individual who gave the impression of being gentle, affectionate, and sensitive. He sat and ate dinner one night while I was doing something endearingly feminine at the sink. At one point, he mutely held up his glass to indicate in a primitive, even ape-like, way his need for a refill. This was in 1967, before Women's Liberation. Even so, I was disturbed. Not enough to break the glass over his handsome head, not even enough to mutely indicate the whereabouts of the refrigerator, but enough to remember that moment in all its revelatory clarity. No androgynous man would ever brutishly expect to be waited on without even a "please." (With a "please," maybe.)

4   The brute happened to be a doctor—not a hard hat—and, to all appearances, couth. But he had bought the whole superman package, complete with that fragile beast, the male ego. The androgynous man arrives with a male ego too, but his is not as imperialistic. It doesn't invade every area of his life and person. Most activities and thoughts have nothing to do with masculinity or femininity. The androgynous man knows this. The all-man man doesn't. He must keep a constant guard against anything even vaguely feminine (i.e., "sissy") rising up in him. It must be a terrible strain.

5   Male chauvinism is an irritation, but the real problem I have with the all-man man is that it's hard for me to talk to him. He's alien to me, and for this I'm at

[1]James Dean (1931–1955) was a 1950s film star who gained fame for his portrayals of restless, defiant young men.

Seems as if she is going to talk about the advantages of androgynous men as compared to other men. Sees them as better.

Attempt to counter stereotype? Can't androgynous men also be effeminate?

Suggests "all-men" men reject behaviours and interests they consider feminine, but isn't she stereotyping? Are all these men like this? She seems to be exaggerating.

least half to blame. As his interests have not carried him into the sissy, mine have never taken me very far into the typically masculine terrains of sports, business and finance, politics, cars, boats and machines. But blame or no blame, the reality is that it is almost as difficult for me to connect with him as it would be to link up with an Arab shepherd or Bolivian sandalmaker. There's a similar culture gap.

6   It seems to me that the most masculine men usually end up with the most feminine women. Maybe they like extreme polarity. I like polarity myself, but the poles have to be within earshot. As I've implied, I'm very big on talking. I fall in love for at least three hours with anyone who engages me in a real conversation. I'd rather a man point out a paragraph in a book—wanting to share it with me— than bring me flowers. I'd rather a man ask what I think than tell me I look pretty. (Women who are very pretty and accustomed to hearing that they are pretty may feel differently.) My experience is that all-men men read books I don't want to see paragraphs of, and don't really give a damn what I or any woman would think about most issues so long as she looks pretty. They have a very limited use for women. I suspect they don't really like us. The androgynous man likes women as much or as little as he likes anyone.

7   Another difference between the all-man man and the androgynous man is that the first is not a star in the creativity department. If your image of the creative male accessorizes him with a beret, smock and artist's palette, you will not believe the all-man man has been seriously short-changed. But if you allow as how creativity is a talent for freedom, associated with imagination, wit, empathy, unpredictability, and receptivity to new impressions and connections, then you will certainly pity the dull, thick-skinned, rigid fellow in whom creativity sets no fires.

8   Nor is the all-man man so hot when it comes to sensitivity. He may be true-blue in the trenches, but if you are troubled, you'd be wasting your time trying to milk comfort from the all-man man.

9   This is not blind prejudice. It is enlightened prejudice. My biases were confirmed recently by a psychologist named Sandra Lipsetz Bem, a professor at Stanford University. She brought to attention the fact that high masculinity in males (and high femininity in females) has been "consistently correlated with lower overall intelligence and lower creativity." Another psychologist, Donald W. MacKinnon, director of the Institute of Personality Assessment and Research at the University of California in Berkeley, found that "creative males give more expression to the feminine side of their nature than do less creative men. . . . [They] score relatively high on femininity, and this despite the fact that, as a group, they do not present an effeminate appearance or give evidence of increased homosexual interests or experiences. Their elevated scores on femininity indicate rather an openness to their feelings and emotions, a sensitive intellect and understanding self-awareness and wide-ranging interests including many which in the American culture are thought of as more feminine. . . ."

10   Dr. Bem ran a series of experiments on college students who had been categorized as masculine, feminine, or androgynous. In three tests of the degree of nurturance—warmth and caring—the masculine men scored painfully low (painfully for anyone stuck with a masculine man, that is). In one of those experiments, all the students were asked to listen to a "troubled talker"—a

person who was not neurotic but simply lonely, supposedly new in town and feeling like an outsider. The masculine men were the least supportive, responsive or humane. "They lacked the ability to express warmth, playfulness and concern," Bem concluded. (She's giving them the benefit of the doubt. It's possible the masculine men didn't express those qualities because they didn't possess them.)

11   The androgynous man, on the other hand, having been run through the same carnival of tests, "performs spectacularly. He shuns no behavior just because our culture happens to label it as female and his competence crosses both the instrumental [getting the job done, the problem solved] and the expressive [showing a concern for the welfare of others, the harmony of the group] domains. Thus, he stands firm in his opinion, he cuddles kittens and bounces babies and he has a sympathetic ear for someone in distress."

12   Well, a great mind, a sensitive and warm personality are fine in their place, but you are perhaps skeptical of the gut appeal of the androgynous man. As a friend, maybe, you'd like an androgynous man. For a sexual partner, though, you'd prefer a jock. There's no arguing chemistry, but consider the jock for a moment. He competes on the field, whatever his field is, and bed is just one more field to him: another opportunity to perform, another fray. Sensuality is for him candy to be doled out as lure. It is a ration whose flow is cut off at the exact point when it has served its purpose—namely, to elicit your willingness to work out on the field with him.

13   Highly masculine men need to believe their sexual appetite is far greater than a woman's (than a nice woman's). To them, females must be seduced: Seduction is a euphemism for a power play, a con job. It pits man against woman (or woman against man). The jock believes he must win you over, incite your body to rebel against your better judgment: in other words—conquer you.

14   The androgynous man is not your opponent but your teammate. He does not seduce: he invites. Sensuality is a pleasure for him. He's not quite so goal-oriented. And to conclude, I think I need only remind you here of his greater imagination, his wit and empathy, his unpredictability, and his receptivity to new impressions and connections.

WRITING ABOUT WHAT YOU READ

Often in university and college, you are asked to write about what you read. Sometimes this assignment is a major research paper, which is discussed in Chapters 13 and 14. However, sometimes you have to write shorter summaries and critiques. Though similar to the research paper, these shorter assignments test your ability to understand what you read.

Writing a Summary

A summary states the main points of an essay in your own words. A good summary lets someone who hasn't read the essay understand what it says. It can be one or more paragraphs. It should

- provide a context for the essay,
- introduce the author of the essay, and
- state the thesis.

These first three elements often form the introduction of a multiparagraph summary. Then

- state the main points of the essay (sometimes but not always based on the topic sentences), and
- conclude by summarizing the author's final point.

To prepare to write a summary, follow the steps in effective reading. Briefly outline the main points that make the writing easier. But avoid using the author's exact wording unless you use quotation marks. Also, don't interject your own views. A summary should reflect only the author's ideas.

A Sample Single-Paragraph Summary of
"The Appeal of the Androgynous Man"

What kind of man should appeal to women? According to Amy Gross, the editor-in-chief of O magazine, in "The Appeal of the Androgynous Man," the ideal is the "androgynous man," a man who shares the personality characteristics of both male and female. To make her point, Amy Gross contrasts the all-man man and the androgynous man. She believes that the all-man man does not share in activities like shopping, has no taste in the arts, is imperialistic, resists anything feminine, and is interested only in exclusively male topics. Worse, she points to studies that show that more masculine men are less creative. Further, she argues that the all-man tends to see women as something to conquer rather than as partners. The androgynous man, by comparison, is very different. He does not resist things that are feminine and so shares in domestic activities, is comfortable with the arts, and can share interests with women. He is shown by studies to be more creative. Further, according to Gross, "The androgynous man is not your opponent but your teammate." As a result, she concludes that the androgynous man has the qualities that women should really look for in a man.

Writing a Critique

Often instructors ask you to give your views on an essay, indicating where you agree and disagree with the author's position. Keep in mind that you can agree with some points and still disagree with others. A critique combines a summary of the article with your thoughtful reaction. Most critiques consist of several paragraphs. A critique usually includes

- a description of the context of the essay
- an introduction of the author
- a statement of the essay's thesis
- the thesis for your critique
- a summary of the essay's main points
- a statement of the points with which you disagree
- a statement with reasons and evidence for your disagreement
- a conclusion

You are well prepared to write a critique if you follow the steps for reading effectively and reading critically.

A Sample Multiparagraph Critique of
"The Appeal of the Androgynous Man"

1   What kind of man should appeal to women? According to Amy Gross, the editor-in-chief of *O* magazine, in "The Appeal of the Androgynous Man," the ideal is the "androgynous man," a man who shares the personality characteristics typically considered masculine and feminine. But matters are not so simple. Amy Gross falsely divides men into two stereotyped categories. In fact, real men are much more complex.

2   To make her point, Amy Gross contrasts the all-man man and the androgynous man. She states that the all-man man does not share in activities like shopping, has no taste in the arts, is imperialistic, resists anything feminine, and is interested only in exclusively male topics. In addition, she points to studies that show that more masculine men are less creative. Further, she argues that the all-man tends to see women as something to conquer rather than as partners. The androgynous man, by comparison, is very different. He does not resist things that are feminine and so shares in domestic activities, is comfortable with the arts, and can share interests with women. He is shown by studies to be more creative. Further, according to Gross, "The androgynous man is not your opponent but your teammate." As a result, she concludes that the androgynous man has the qualities that women should really look for in a man.

3   Gross would be correct if the all-man male were as she described him, because he would truly be undesirable. No woman should want a partner who takes her for granted, doesn't share her interests, or treats her simply as someone to conquer. But is that really what men are like? My brother plays football and loves to watch it on television. He also hunts and fishes. However, that isn't all he does. He plays with kittens, loves to cook, plays the guitar and sings, and secretly likes "chick flicks." As far as I can tell, he treats his girlfriend well. He

seems genuinely concerned about her, will spend hours shopping with her, goes to events that interest her, and generally seems sensitive to her needs. Is he an "all-man" or an "androgynous man"? Equally a man can write poetry, love Jane Austen, cook gourmet meals, and still take women for granted.

4   Gross presents evidence from psychological studies that show that more masculine men are less creative than more feminine men. But she doesn't provide enough evidence for the reader to assess the studies. How did the researchers actually measure masculinity and femininity? How many people were tested? What did they count as creativity? Certainly, the author, who was writing in the mid-70s, would have been influenced by the first wave of feminism, and by the rhetoric of the women's liberation movement. At this time, people were just beginning to question financial and social inequalities between men and women. However, much has changed since then. What was relevant in Gross's time is not necessarily relevant today.

5   Moreover, the fundamental mistake Gross makes is that she believes that women should select men according to types. They shouldn't. Women should date, love, and marry individual men. As a result, a woman should really be concerned about whether the man shares her interests, treats her well, has qualities she can love, and will be faithful. Where the man fits in a chart is far less important than the kind of man he is, regardless of whether he is "androgynous."

CHAPTER 3

Strategies for Planning and Drafting Your Writing

Many students believe that good essays are dashed off in a burst of inspiration by born writers. Students themselves often boast that they cranked out their best papers in an hour or so of spare time. Perhaps. But for most of us, writing is a process that takes time and work. Better writers are not born with their gift but learn through informed practice how to incorporate their ideas into a paper.

Although popular writers sometimes describe their favourite formula for success, writing isn't a fixed process. No one order guarantees success, and no one approach works for every writer. For example, some writers establish their purpose and draft a plan at the start of every project, while others begin with only a tentative purpose or plan and discover their final direction as they write. Writers can proceed in an orderly, straightforward sequence, but more commonly they leapfrog backward and forward. Partway through a first draft, for example, a writer may think of a new point to present, then pause and jot down the details needed to develop it. Similarly, part of the conclusion may come to mind as the writer is gathering the details for supporting a key idea.

Regardless of how the writing process unfolds, it consists of six stages. If you have no plan, or if you've run into snags with your approach, advancing through each stage will help you get your essay under control. Once you're familiar with these stages, you can combine or rearrange them as needed.

> Understanding the assignment
> Zeroing in on a topic
> Gathering information
> Organizing the information
> Developing a thesis statement
> Writing the first draft

UNDERSTANDING THE ASSIGNMENT

Different instructors give different kinds of writing assignments. Some specify the topic; some give you several topics to choose from; and still others offer you a free choice. Likewise, some instructors dictate the length and format of the essay, whereas others don't. Whatever the case, be sure you understand the assignment before you start.

Think of it this way: If your boss asked you to report on ways to improve working conditions at your office, and you turned in a report on improving worker benefits, would you expect the boss's approval? Following directions is crucial. So if you have any questions about the assignment, ask your instructor to clear them up right away. Also make sure that you understand the instructor's expectations and the emphasis for a particular assignment. For example, some assignments require formal academic writing, while others may need a more informal and personal style. An essay for a sociology class will follow different conventions than an essay for an English class. Don't be timid; it's much better to ask for clarity than to receive a low grade for failing to follow directions.

Once you understand the assignment, consider the project *yours*. Whether you are writing for a local newspaper, for a friend, or for your instructor and classmates, here is your chance to inform others about a topic that is important to you. By asking yourself whom you are writing for, and what the assignment allows you to accomplish, you can find your purpose.

ZEROING IN ON A TOPIC

A subject is a broad discussion area: for example, sports, academic life, or Canadian culture. A topic is one small segment of a subject: for example, testing athletes for drug use, rising tuition fees for university education, or changes in health care. If you choose your own topic, pick one narrow enough that you can develop it properly within the length limitation. Avoid sprawling, slippery topics that result in a string of trite generalities.

In addition, choose a topic you can learn enough about in the time available. Avoid overworked topics, which repeat information that most people are already familiar with. Instead, select a topic that lets you draw upon your unique experiences and insights and offer a fresh perspective to your reader.

Strategies for Finding a Topic

Students sometimes prefer having a larger, more general area to write about than a more focused topic. However, writing is usually easier—and more interesting for you and your reader—if you take on a topic that is more specific and manageable. Would you be more interested in an essay entitled "Hockey in Canada" or one entitled "Why Hockey Is No Longer Canadian"? Whenever your instructor assigns a general subject area, you need to stake out a limited topic suitable for your paper. If you're lucky, the right one will come to mind immediately. More often, though, you'll need to resort to some special strategy. Here are six proven strategies that many writers use. Not all of them work for everyone, so experiment to find those that produce a topic for you.

Tapping Your Personal Resources Personal experience furnishes a rich storehouse of writing material. Over the years, you've packed your mind with memories of family gatherings, school activities, movies, concerts, plays, parties, jobs, books you've read, TV programs, dates, discussions, arguments, and so on. All these experiences can provide suitable topics. Suppose you've been asked to write about some aspect of education. Recalling the difficulties you had last term at registration, you might argue for better registration procedures. Or if you're a hopeless TV addict who must write on some advertising topic, why not analyze video advertising techniques?

Anything you've read in magazines or journals, newspapers, novels, short stories, or textbooks can also trigger a topic. Alice Munro's short story, "Boys and Girls," in which a girl growing up in rural Canada comes to accept the gender role she is assigned, might suggest a paper on gender socialization, or another on farm work. An article reviewing the career of a well-known politician might stir thoughts of a friend's experience in running for the student council. Possibilities crowd our lives, waiting for us to recognize and seize them. But one word of caution: When using personal experience, ensure that it fits the assignment. Formal academic papers don't have a place for opinions and reflections.

EXERCISE *Select five of the subjects listed below. Use your personal resources to come up with one topic for each. Then for each topic, list three questions that you might answer in a paper.*

City life	An aspect of nature
A particular field of work	Contemporary forms of dancing
Drugs	Youth gangs
Concern for some aspect of the environment	Fashions in clothing
Saving money	Trendiness
Home ownership	Human rights

Keeping a Journal   Many writers record their experiences in a journal—a private gathering of entries accumulated over a period of time. In addition to helping writers remember and reflect on their experiences, journal keeping provides an abundance of possible writing topics as well as a valuable opportunity for writing practice.

The hallmark of the journal entry is the freedom to explore thoughts, feelings, responses, attitudes, and beliefs. In your own private domain, you can express your views without reservation, without concern for "doing it right." *You* control the content and length of the entry without being held to a specified topic or number of words. Journal writing does not represent a finished product, but rather an exploration. In addition to personal journals, learning journals—where you reflect on what you've learned in your classes—can help yield interesting topics for formal research papers.

A few simple guidelines ensure effective journal entries:

1. Write in any kind of notebook that appeals to you. The content, not the package, is the important thing.
2. Write on a regular basis—at least five times a week if possible. Avoid writing by fits and starts, cramming two weeks' entries into one sitting.
3. Write for ten to twenty minutes, longer if you have more to say. Don't aim for uniform entry length (for example, three paragraphs, or a page and a half). Simply explore your reactions to the events in your life or to what you have read, heard in class, or seen on television. The length will take care of itself.

Let's examine a typical journal entry by Sam, a first-year composition student. This journal entry could spawn several essays. Sam might explore the causes of residential deterioration, define sportsmanship, explain how Mrs. Wynick made learning a game, or argue for stricter pollution control laws.

Last week went back to my hometown for the first time since my family moved away and while there dropped by the street where I spent my first twelve years. Visit left me feeling very depressed. Family home still there, but its paint peeling and front porch sagging. Sign next to the porch said house now occupied by Acme Realtors. While we lived there, front yard lush green and bordered by beds of irises. Now an oil-spattered parking lot. All the other houses on our side of the street gone, replaced by a row of dumpy buildings housing dry cleaner, bowling alley, hamburger joint, shoe repair shop, laundromat. All of them dingy and rundown looking, even though only a few years old.

Other side of the street in no better shape. Directly across from our house a used-car dealership with rows of junky looking cars. No trace left of the park that used to be there. Had lots of fun playing baseball and learned meaning of sportsmanship. To left of the dealership my old grade school, now boarded and abandoned. Wonder about my Grade 5 teacher Mrs. Wynick. Is she still teaching? Still able to make learning a game, not a chore? Other side of dealership the worst sight of all. Grimy looking plant of some sort pouring foul smelling smoke into the air from a discoloured stack. Smoke made me cough.

Don't think I'll revisit my old street again.

EXERCISE *Write journal entries over the next week or two for some of the following items that interest you. If you have trouble finding a suitable topic for a paper, review the entries for possibilities.*

Pleasant or unpleasant conversations	Cultural or sporting events
Developing relationships	Academic life: myth vs. reality
Single or married life	Public figures—politicians; movie,
Parents	rock, or sports stars
Reflections on English readings	Thoughts about another course

---

Sorting Out a Subject All of us sort things. We do it whenever we tackle the laundry, clear away a sinkful of dishes, or tidy up a basement or garage. Let's examine how we might handle a cluttered basement. To start off, we'd probably sort the contents according to type: books in one place, clothing in a second, toys in a third. That done, chances are we'd do still more sorting, separating children's books from adults' and stuffed animals from games. As we looked over and handled the different items, long-buried, bittersweet memories might start flooding from our subconscious: memories of an uncle, now dead, who sent this old adventure novel . . . of our parents' pride when they saw their child had learned to ride that now battered bicycle . . . of the dance that marked the debut of the evening gown over there.

Sorting out a subject is similar. First, we break our broad subject into categories and subcategories, and then we allow our minds to roam over the different items to see what topics we can turn up.

As you'll discover for yourself, some subjects yield more topics than others; some, no topics at all.

EXERCISE *Select two of the following subjects, and then subdivide them into five topics each.*

Advertising	Movies	Transportation
Computers	Occupations	Sports
Fashions	Popular music	Television programs

Asking Questions   Often, asking questions such as those below can lead you to a manageable topic:

How can this subject be described?
How is this subject accomplished or performed?
What is an example of my subject?
Does the subject break into categories?
If so, what comparisons can I make among these categories?
If my subject is divided into parts, how do they work together?
Does my subject have uses? What are they?
What are the causes of my subject?
What is the impact of my subject?
How can my subject be defined?
What case could be made for or against my subject?

Let's convert these general questions into specific questions about a broad general subject: telescopes.

Narration:	What is the story of the telescope?
Description:	How can a telescope be described?
Illustration:	What are some well-known telescopes?
Process:	How does one use a telescope?
Analysis:	What are the parts of the telescope, and how do they work together?
Functional analysis:	How is a telescope useful?
Causal analysis:	Why did the telescope come about?
Analysis of effects:	What effects have telescopes had on human life and knowledge?
Classification:	What are the different kinds of telescopes?
Comparison:	How are they alike? How are they different?
Definition:	What is a telescope?
Argument:	Why should people learn to use telescopes?

Each of these questions offers a starting point for a suitably focused essay. For example, Question 3 might be answered in a paper about the Hubble Space Telescope and the problems experienced with it. Question 10 might launch a paper that compares reflecting and refracting telescopes.

EXERCISE   *Convert two of the general subjects below into more manageable topics. Then, drawing from the list of questions suggested above, ask specific questions about the topics. Finally, come up with two essay topics for each of the two subjects.*

Results of Sorting Out the Subject Public Transportation

Land			Water		Air	
Buses	Taxis	Trains	Seagoing	Lake, River	Airplanes	Helicopters
Local bus services for the handicapped	Rights of passengers	The Orient Express, the Twentieth Century Limited	The Titanic	Barge cruises	Delays from security checks	Air taxis
Bus tours	Preventing crimes against drivers	Subways	Luxury liners		Airline strikes	Cargo
City buses		Via Rail	Theme cruises		Overbooking flights	Search and rescue
Improving bus terminals		Japan's high-speed trains	Modern sea pirates		Making air travel safer	Hospital transfers
Designing buses to accommodate the handicapped		Deterioration of railway track beds	Travelling by freighter		Threats from terrorists	
			The impact of overseas flights on ship travel		Causes and prevention of jet lag	
					Noise pollution around airports	

Example: Take a general subject, such as Music, and then narrow it to a more manageable topic, such as "Downloading Music from the Computer." After running through the list of questions above, you might choose two essay topics, such as "How to Download Music from the Internet" and "The Advantages of Downloading Music."

Tourism	Games	Health
Sports	Free Trade	Business Schools
Languages	Television	

Freewriting   The freewriting strategy snares thoughts as they race through your mind, yielding a set of sentences that you then look over for writing ideas. To begin, turn your pen loose and write for about five minutes on your general subject. Put down everything that comes into your head, without worrying about grammar, spelling, or punctuation. What you produce is for your eyes alone. If the thought flow becomes blocked, write "I'm stuck, I'm stuck . . . " until you break the mental logjam. When your writing time is up, go through your sentences one by one and extract potential topic material. If you draw a blank, write for another five minutes and look again.

The following example shows the product of one freewriting session. Jim's instructor had assigned a two- or three-page paper on a sports-related topic; and since Jim had been a member of his high school tennis team, his thoughts naturally turned toward tennis.

> Sports. If that's my subject, I'd better do something on tennis. I've played enough of it. But what can I say that would be interesting? It's very popular, lots of people watch it on TV. Maybe I could write about the major tennis tournaments. I'm stuck. I'm stuck. Maybe court surfaces. That sounds dull. I'm stuck. Well, what about tennis equipment, clothing, scoring? Maybe my reader is thinking about taking up the game. What do I like about tennis? The strategy, playing the net, when to use a topspin or a backspin stroke, different serves. I'm stuck. I'm stuck. Maybe I could suggest how to play a better game of singles. I used to be number one. I can still remember Coach harping on those three C's, conditioning, concentration, consistency. I'm stuck. I'm stuck. Then there's the matter of special shots like lobs, volleys, and overheads. But that stuff is for the pros.

This example suggests at least three papers. For the beginning player, Jim could focus on equipment and scoring. For the intermediate player, he might write on conditioning, concentration, and consistency; for the advanced player, on special shots.

Brainstorming   Brainstorming, a close cousin of freewriting, captures fleeting ideas in words, fragments, and sometimes sentences, rather than in a series of sentences. Brainstorming garners ideas faster than the other strategies do. But unless you move immediately to the next stage of writing, you may lose track of what some of your fragmentary jottings mean.

To compare the results of freewriting and brainstorming a topic, we've converted our freewriting example into this list, which typifies the results of brainstorming:

Popularity of tennis	Equipment
Major tournaments	Clothing
Court surfaces	Scoring
Doubles strategy	Conditioning
Singles strategy	Concentration
Playing the net	Consistency
Topspin	Special shots—lobs, drop volleys,
Backspin	overheads
Different serves	

EXERCISE *Return to one set of five topics you selected for the earlier exercise. Freewrite or brainstorm for five minutes on each one. Then choose a topic suitable for a two- or three-page essay. State your topic, intended audience, and purpose.*

Narrowing a familiar subject may yield not only a topic but also the main divisions for the paper. Jim's freewriting session uncovered several possible tennis topics as well as a way of approaching each: for example, by focusing on lobs, drop volleys, and overheads when writing about special shots. Ordinarily, though, the main divisions emerge only after you have gathered material to develop your topic.

Identifying Your Audience and Purpose

You can identify your purpose and audience at several different stages in the writing process. Sometimes both are set by the assignment: For example, you might be asked to write to your university or college president to recommend improvements in the school's registration system. At other times, you may have to write a draft before you can determine either. Usually, though, selecting audience and purpose occurs when you determine your topic. Think of the different types of information Jim would gather if he wrote for (1) beginning players, to offer advice on improving their game; (2) tennis buffs, to point out refinements of the game; or (3) a physics professor, to show the physical forces controlling the behaviour of tennis balls in flight.

Case History

Now that you're familiar with some narrowing strategies, let's examine the first segment of a case history showing how one student handled a writing assignment. This segment illustrates the use of a narrowing strategy to find a topic. Later segments focus on the remaining stages of the writing process.

Trudy's class has been talking and reading about memories from childhood, and about how these memories change their meaning over time. Trudy's instructor assigns a three- or four-page paper describing or narrating a childhood experience that led to an insight of some kind. Trudy begins by sorting out possible experiences to write about and comes up with two major categories: memories from elementary school and memories from secondary school. Under the first category, she includes memories of teachers who made an impression on her, a soccer game in which she scored the winning goal, and an autistic boy she knew who had trouble fitting in. In the second category, she includes memories of struggling with French and her experience of losing her boyfriend. Because the secondary school experiences still seem too close to her to write about, she decides to write about one of the memories from elementary school. After weighing the possibilities, she decides that she will be able to write the most interesting narrative about the autistic boy she once knew.

This case history continues later in this chapter

GATHERING INFORMATION

Once you have a topic, you need things to say about it. This supporting material can include facts, ideas, examples, observations, sensory impressions, and memories. Without this kind of support, papers lack force, vividness, and interest, and may confuse or mislead readers. The more support you can gather, the easier it will be for you to write a draft. Time spent gathering information is never wasted.

Strategies for Gathering Information

If you are writing on a personal topic for a creative writing class, much of your supporting material may come from your own head. Brainstorming is the best way to retrieve it. However, with academic, professional, and fact-oriented topics, you have to use research for your supporting material. But whatever the topic, personal or academic, using friends, parents, and neighbours as sounding boards and talking to local experts can also produce useful ideas.

Brainstorming   Brainstorming a topic, like brainstorming a subject, yields a set of words, fragments, and occasionally sentences that furnish ideas for the paper. Assume that Jim, the student who explored the subject of tennis, wants to show

how conditioning, concentration, and consistent play can improve one's game. His brainstorming list might look like this:

keeping ball in play	courtside distractions
don't try foolish shots	temper distractions
placing ball so opponent runs	don't continually drive ball with power
staying in good condition yourself	two-on-one drill
running	lobbing ball over opponent's head
jogging	returning a down-the-line passing shot
skipping rope keeps you on your toes	don't try spectacular overheads
keeping your mind only on the game	chance for opponent to make mistake
personal distractions	game of percentages
	games are lost, not won

You can see how some thoughts have led to others. For example, the first jotting, "keeping ball in play," leads naturally to the next one, "don't try foolish shots." "Placing ball so opponent runs" leads to "staying in good condition yourself," which in turn leads to ways of staying in condition, and so forth.

Branching is a helpful and convenient extension of brainstorming that allows you to add details to any item in your list. Here's how you might use this technique to approach "courtside distractions":

Don't worry if your brainstorming notes look chaotic and if some seem irrelevant. Sometimes the most unlikely material turns out to be the freshest and most interesting. As you organize and write your paper, you'll probably combine, modify, and omit some of the notes, as well as add others.

EXERCISE *Prepare a brainstorming sheet of supporting details for one of the topics you developed for the earlier exercise.*

Reading When you have to grapple with an unfamiliar topic, look in the library for material to develop it. Before going there, however, turn to Chapter 13 to review research guidelines for using libraries and unearthing promising references to investigate. Another option is to use an internet search engine to explore the topic on World Wide Web articles and book reviews. Once you have a list of references, start searching for the books or articles. Look through each one you find and record any information that looks useful, either as direct quotations or in your own words.

Whenever you use a direct quotation or rephrased material in your paper, you must give proper credit to the source. If you don't, you are guilty of plagiarism, a serious offence that can result in a failing grade or even expulsion.

Talking with Others   You can expand the pool of ideas gained through brainstorming or reading by talking to people around you. Imagine you're writing a paper about a taxpayers' revolt in your province. After checking the leading provincial newspapers at the library, you find that most of the discontent centres on property taxes. You then decide to supplement what you've read by asking questions about the local tax situation in your town.

Your parents and neighbours tell you that property taxes have jumped 50 percent in the last two years. The local tax assessor tells you that assessed valuations have risen sharply and that the law requires property taxes to keep pace. She also notes that this situation is causing some people on fixed incomes to lose their homes. A city council member explains that part of the added revenue is being used to repair city streets, build a new library wing, and buy more fire-fighting equipment. The rest is going to the schools. School officials tell you they're using their extra funds to offer more vocational courses and to expand the program for learning-disabled students. As you can see, asking questions can broaden your perspective and provide information that helps you to write a more worthwhile paper.

Case History   (continued)

After choosing to write about a student in elementary school, Trudy brainstorms to generate ideas. The result is a fifteen-item list. After checking her items over, Trudy decides that since she is focusing on a narrative about a boy named Steven, she will eliminate items on learning disorders and treatment of autism because they are not directly relevant to her purpose. She also decides not to deal with information on Steven's family, on where Steven is now, or on other bullies today. The remaining items are as follows:

teasing of Steven	why people bully
Steven's appearance	my mother's response
Steven at lunch hour	confronting the bullies
Steven's loneliness	effects of bullying
incident in park	taking time to listen

This case history continues later in this chapter.

ORGANIZING THE INFORMATION

If you have ever listened to a rambling speaker spill out ideas in no particular order, you know how difficult it is to pay attention to such a speech, let alone make sense of it. So, too, with disorganized writing. A garbled listing of ideas serves no one, but an orderly presentation highlights your ideas and communicates them successfully.

Your topic determines what organizational approach is best. In narrating a personal experience, such as a mishap-riddled vacation, you'd probably trace the events in the order they occurred. In describing a process, say caulking a bathtub, you'd take the reader step by step through the procedure. To describe the parts of a cell, you might work from one end to the other. Or you could first create a general picture of the central features and then fan out in either direction to cover the minor features. Other topics dictate other patterns, such as comparison and contrast, cause and effect, and illustration.

You can best organize long pieces of writing, such as research papers, by following a formal outline. Formal outlines allow you to organize large amounts of information into a logical, flowing paper. Refer to this chapter before beginning a research paper. However, for shorter papers, a simple, informal system of *flexible notes* is sufficient.

The Flexible Notes System

To create a set of flexible notes, write each of your key points at the top of a separate sheet of paper. If your paper requires a thesis statement, write it on a separate introduction sheet on its own; but for now, we will just focus on the body of the essay. Next, list under each heading the supporting details that go with that heading. Drop any details that don't fit, and expand any points that need more support. When your sheets are finished, arrange them in the order you expect to follow in your essay. The notes for the body of the tennis paper might look like this:

<u>Conditioning</u>

staying in good condition   two-on-one drill
   yourself   lobbing ball over opponent's head
running   returning a down-the-line
jogging   passing shot
skipping rope keeps you on
   your toes

<u>Concentration</u>

keeping your mind only on the game
overcome distractions: personal, courtside, temper

Consistency

keeping ball in play

don't try foolish shots

placing ball so opponent runs

don't continually drive ball with power

don't try spectacular overheads

chance for opponent to make mistake

game of percentages

games are lost, not won

Since conditioning, concentration, and consistency are simultaneous concerns, this listing arranges them according to their probable importance—starting with the least important.

Now you're ready to draft a plan showing how many paragraphs you'll have in each part of the essay and what each paragraph will cover. Sometimes the number of details suggests one paragraph; other times, you need a paragraph block—two or more paragraphs—to cover the topic. Here's a plan for the body of the tennis essay:

Conditioning

staying in good condition yourself

running   Off-the-court

jogging   conditioning

skipping rope keeps you on your toes

two-on-one drill

lobbing ball over opponent's head   On-the-court

returning a down-the-line passing shot   conditioning

Concentration

keeping your mind only on the game

overcome distractions: personal, courtside,

   temper

Consistency

keeping ball in play

don't try foolish shots

placing ball so opponent runs   Placing shots

don't continually drive ball with power

don't try spectacular overheads

chance for opponent to make mistake

game of percentages   Playing percentage

games are lost, not won

These groupings suggest one introductory paragraph, two paragraphs about conditioning, one about concentration, and two about consistency.

EXERCISE *Organize into flexible notes the supporting details that you prepared for the earlier exercise. Arrange your note pages in a logical sequence and draft a plan showing the number and content of the paragraphs in each section.*

Case History (continued)

A careful look at her brainstorming list suggests how Trudy can arrange her items in a logical order. Since she is writing a narrative, she will follow a chronological order, or time sequence. She will begin with a description of Steven in the schoolyard, proceed to the story of the bullies teasing Steven in the park and then to her mother's confrontation with the bullies, and end with the insight about taking time to listen. She draws up the following plan.

Background—Steven at Lunch Time

Searching for stick

Waving his stick

Others whisper and giggle

Steven's Appearance

Faded and second-hand clothing

Strawberry stains on mouth

Incident at Park

Bullies taunt Steven

I fail to stop them

Going Home for Help

Explaining to my mother

Heading for the park

Arriving at the Park

Steven is crying

Bullies fail to see us

My Mother's Confrontation

Mother yells

Bullies leave

We Walk Steven Home

Mother asks Steven where
    home is

Mother seems angry

**Steven Questions Why People
    Are Mean**

Steven's question

No real answer

My Thoughts Today

How Steven made a difference

Listening to someone can help

This case history continues later in this chapter.

Patterns of Development

As you think about ways to organize and develop your ideas, whether for more personal or more academic essays, it may be helpful to think about how you might consciously choose to use different modes of development, such as illustration, analysis, comparison, and argument, that we explore in later chapters.

However, it's important to remember that these modes of developing ideas do not usually occur in isolation. For example, an argument may use some narrative and illustration, and an essay that is primarily a comparison might also analyze the causes or effects of something. A comparative essay is often an argument as well, suggesting that one thing is superior to another.

Since the first writing assignment in Trudy's class asked her to write about a personal experience, Trudy chose to write a narrative about something that affected her emotionally. It's possible that her concern about special needs children could lead her to respond to later writing assignments in more analytical or objective ways. For example, she could decide to write an illustrative essay that shows examples of schoolyard bullying of special needs children. She could also write a research essay comparing different kinds of autism. Or she could write an argument that blended her personal observations with some researched information about how children should be taught empathy for special needs children.

DEVELOPING A THESIS STATEMENT

A thesis statement—one or two sentences that express the main idea in your essay—can help you stay on track. If you do not have a thesis, or point you are heading toward when you write, your reader will probably feel frustrated. Whether or not it is spelled out explicitly, the thesis statement governs and unifies the entire essay. The thesis statement points you and your reader in a specific direction. In addition, it tells your reader what to expect.

Thesis statements can emerge at several points in the writing process. If an instructor assigns a controversial topic on which you hold strong views, the statement may pop into your head right away. Usually, though, it emerges gradually, after you have gathered and examined supporting information, or during the writing process itself.

Often a preliminary thesis may evolve into something more focused and interesting as you write. In these cases, return to your original thesis and reshape it. A thesis such as "Downloading music from the internet has advantages" could become more refined: "Downloading music from the internet can help musical artists as well as their audience."

As you examine your information, search for the central point and the key points that back it up; then use these to develop your thesis statement. If you convert a topic to a question, the answer to this question may be your thesis statement. For example:

Topic:	The uncertain future of robots in Canadian industry.
Question:	What are some of the drawbacks of using robots in Canadian industry?
Thesis statement:	The expense of producing robots, the lack of qualified personnel to service them, and the moral problems of replacing workers with them all cloud the future of robots in Canadian industry.

The thesis statement stems from the specifics the student unearthed while answering the question.

Requirements of a Good Thesis Statement

Unity Unless intended for a lengthy paper, a thesis statement *focuses on just one central point or issue.* Suppose you prepare the following thesis statement for a two- or three-page paper:

> Centreville College should re-examine its policies on open admissions, vocational programs, and aid to students.

This sprawling statement would commit you to grapple with three separate issues. At best, you could make only a few general remarks about each one.

To correct matters, consider each issue carefully in light of how much it interests you and how much you know about it. Then make your choice and draft a narrower statement. The following thesis statement would suit a brief paper. It shows clearly that the writer will focus on *just one issue:*

> Because of the rising demand among high school graduates for job-related training, Centreville College should expand its vocational offerings.

Tailored Scope A good thesis statement also *tailors the scope of the issue to the length of the paper.* No writer could deal adequately with "Many first-year university and college students face crucial adjustment problems" in two or three pages. The idea is too broad to yield more than a smattering of poorly supported general statements. But paring it down to "Free time is a responsibility that challenges many first-year university and college students" results in an idea that could probably be developed adequately.

Indication of Writer's Attitude An essay is not simply a statement of fact or a bland report, but a piece of writing that reflects a particular point of view. The thesis statement implies purpose by suggesting the writer's attitude toward his or her subject. A thesis statement such as "Airport security has increased since 9/11" simply states a fact, but does not indicate the writer's attitude or position. Consider instead how the following thesis statements suggest the writer's point of view: "Increased airport security since 9/11 gives the illusion of security" or "Despite the inconvenience, increased airport security is necessary for many reasons" or "Airports should tighten security measures even more than they already have."

Accurate Forecasting   A good thesis statement further provides *an accurate forecast of what's to come*. If you plan to discuss the effects of overeating, don't say, "Overeating stems from deep-seated psychological factors and the easy availability of convenience foods." Because this statement incorrectly suggests that the paper will focus on causes, not the effects, it would only mislead and confuse your reader. On the other hand, the statement "Overeating leads to obesity, which can cause or complicate several serious health problems" accurately represents what's to follow.

Preview of Organization   Finally, a good thesis statement is precise, often previewing the organization of the paper, indicating a strategy of development. Assertions built on fuzzy, biased words, such as *fascinating, bad, meaningful*, or *interesting*, or vague statements like "My paper is about . . . " tell neither writer nor reader what's going on. Examine these two examples:

> Montreal is a fascinating city.
> My paper is about health benefits in Canada.

These thesis statements raise too many questions. Why does the writer find Montreal fascinating? because of its architecture? its night life? its theatres? its restaurants? its museums? its shops? its cultural diversity? And what about health benefits? Will the writer explain how to apply for health benefits, or defend the current system of benefits, trace its history, suggest ways of improving it? Without a clear roadmap sentence suggesting the writer's direction, the readers must labour through the paper, hoping to find their way.

Now look at the rewritten versions of those vague, imprecise thesis statements:

> Montreal's ethno-cultural diversity offers visitors the chance to sample cuisine from every continent.
> Canada's national health care system should be a two-tier system that allows patients the options of receiving medical treatment from private clinics and hospitals at their own expense or from public clinics or hospitals at public expense, because such a system would reduce waiting lists and lower the costs of health care paid by the Canadian government.

These thesis statements tell the reader not only what points the writer will make but also suggest the order and strategy of development they will follow. The Montreal essay will proceed by way of illustration, offering examples of different ethno-cultural dishes that a visitor might sample. The health care thesis statement suggests that the writer will argue why a two-tier health care system would be desirable. Note that the second thesis statement could easily be broken into two sentences, with the first sentence stating the writer's position, and the second sentence providing the road map—a preview of the writer's main points.

Placement of Thesis Statement

In most academic essays, the thesis statement comes somewhere in the first paragraph. Many essays take two or three sentences to lead into the thesis, but some, such as an essay for an in-class midterm exam, may need the thesis immediately in the first sentence. Moreover, in persuasive essays, the writer may hold off stating the thesis until close to the end of the first paragraph, especially if it is controversial. Some essays, in particular, narratives and descriptions, or those by professional writers, may have only implied thesis statements. Nonetheless, a core idea underlies and controls all effective writing.

Changing Your Thesis Statement

Unlike diamonds, thesis statements aren't necessarily forever. Before your paper is in final form, you may need to change your thesis statement several times. If you draft the thesis statement during the narrowing stage, you might change it to reflect what you uncovered while gathering information. Or you might amend it after writing the first draft so that it reflects your additions and deletions.

Tentative or final, formulated early or late, the thesis statement serves as a beacon that spotlights your purpose.

Case History   (continued)

Her essay plan completed, Trudy now drafts a thesis statement—the larger point that her entire essay will make:

> We should listen to other people, even if they seem different from us.

This case history continues on pages 51–53.

EXERCISE

1. Write a thesis statement for the flexible notes that you developed for the earlier exercise.

2. Using "Requirements of a Good Thesis Statement," explain why each of the following does or does not qualify as an effective thesis statement for a two- or three-page essay.

   a. My paper discusses the problem of employee absenteeism in Canadian industry.

   b. I really like astronomy.

   c. Although I don't know much about running a business, I know that PDT Accounting Inc. is not run well.

   d. Higher education has many problems.

   e. It is not entirely fair for teens that getting a Canadian driver's licence is more difficult than it was a few years ago.

WRITING THE FIRST DRAFT

Of course, sometimes when you sit down to write a first draft or even notes for a draft, the words won't come. All you can do is doodle or stare at the blank page. Perhaps the introduction is the problem. Many writers are terrified by the thought of the opening paragraph. They want to get off to a good start but can't figure out how to begin. If this happens to you, additional brainstorming or freewriting can make you more comfortable and may suggest an opening. Keep in mind that any lead-in you write now can be changed later. If these suggestions don't solve your problem, skip the introduction for now. Once you have drafted the body of the paper, an effective opening should come more easily.

Here are some general suggestions for writing a first draft:

1. Stack your thesis statement, flexible notes, and written plan in front of you. They will help you start thinking.
2. As you are typing, save each version as a different draft so that you can go back later to retrieve material. If you prefer to write by hand, skip every other line (double-space) and leave wide margins so that you'll have room to revise later.
3. Type or write quickly; capture the drift of your thoughts. Concentrate on content and organization. Get your main points and supporting details on paper in the right sequence. Don't spend time correcting grammatical or punctuation errors, improving your language, or making the writing flow smoothly. You might lose your train of thought.
4. Take breaks only at logical dividing points: for example, when you have finished discussing a key point. Before you start to write again, scan what you've written to refresh your memory.

These more specific suggestions can help you deal with writer's block:

1. Enter your thesis statement at the top of your first page to break the ice and build momentum.
2. Type your first paragraph, introducing your essay and stating your thesis. If you get stuck, leave it, and move on to the body of the paper.
3. Follow your plan or outline as you write. Begin with your first main point and work on each section in turn. Remember that you can change the order of main points later if a different arrangement of ideas seems more effective.
4. Look over the supporting details listed under the first heading in your flexible notes. Write a topic sentence stating the central idea of the paragraph before you start entering your supporting facts.
5. Turn the details into sentences. Use one or more sentences to explain each detail. Add other related details, facts, or examples that you could use as concluding statements.
6. When you move from one paragraph to the next, try to provide a transitional word (*However, But, In addition, Moreover*, etc.) or sentence to connect the two.

7. Write your last paragraph, ending your essay in an appropriate fashion. If you get stuck, set your conclusion aside and return to it later.

Of course, writing a draft isn't always so systematic, especially in personal writing. If you are inspired, you may want to abandon your plans and simply use your first draft to explore ideas. You can always revise later, so don't be overly concerned if you get off track. Because writing is an act of discovery, sometimes the best ideas come when you think you are digressing or coming to the end of a preliminary draft.

EXERCISE *Using the plan you prepared for the earlier exercise, write the first draft of an essay.*

Case History *(continued)*

Trudy now uses her thesis statement and essay plan to write the following draft. Notice that she chooses to write her thesis statement at the end rather than at the beginning of the essay, a common technique in the writing of narratives. Certainly this draft will need revision. We'll return to it in Chapter 5 to discuss the necessary changes.

A Memory

1   When I remember back to elementary school, I remember an autistic boy named Steven Villman. Autism is a withdrawal from reality. It's really hard to understand, and takes lots of patience. I didn't understand Steven. I used to watch him in awe during lunch times as he ran about on his tiptoes with a stick waving about in his hand like a magic wand. His sticks were his trademark. Every lunch hour, rain or shine, he would dart outside and begin his search through the woods behind the school, in search of the best stick. Steven could always be found darting in and out of the trees, gleefully shaking his stick.

2   His high-pitched screeches and nonsense babbling would never fail to catch the attention of children deep in their play. Children always found enough time to stop and stare but never to talk.

3   Steven always seemed to have a dirty film covering his clothing, which was rumoured to be bought at second-hand shops. He was a large boy with dark, messy hair who appeared to have been born with strawberry stains around his mouth.

4   Some kids would actually follow him around during lunch time, watching in awe at the odd tasks he'd perform, whispering and giggling about how weird he was.

5   One afternoon I was playing in a park located close to my house. Suddenly loud screeches alerted me as a large boy came running toward the park. Two smaller boys were trailing behind him, creeping up behind him and screeching in his ear to watch Steven's terrified reaction for their own amusement.

6   I immediately recognized the terrified boy as Steven Villman. I stood up on top of the slide and stared with wide eyes and mouth open. Murmuring and tightly holding onto his stick, Steven would bolt about like a wild animal full of fear.

7   "Hey, leave him alone, you bullies," I yelled, but the bullies paid no attention. Steven looked up to where I stood, but then quickly turned back to the bullies. I pushed myself down the slide quickly and made my way home to get some help.

8   Inside my home I stood huffing and puffing and babbling out the situation I had witnessed to my mom. I went on to explain how different Steven was from other kids. My mother took a deep breath. We headed back to the park immediately.

9   By the time we arrived at the park, Steven was now blubbering uncontrollably and hollering at the boys. Still fascinated as ever and untouched by Steven's distress, the bullies failed to see my mom and me hustling over to where they stood.

10   "You two should be ashamed of yourselves!" my mother lectured with both hands on her hips. The boys whipped their heads around to be greeted by my furious mother as I watched with a small smirk.

11   The bullies looked at one another and then walked away, without even attempting to explain their behaviour.

12   Steven watched them go with a look of relief. "Where do you live, Steven?" my mom asked.

13   "That way." Steven pointed with a long dirty finger decorated with an uncut nail. He was looking toward the ground as he swayed from side to side, as if he were rocking himself to sleep. He was wearing faded blue shorts that were a couple of sizes too small. He was without shoes or socks on his feet and was covered from head to toe in

dirt. "C'mon, Steven, we'll walk you home," my mother stated dryly, as if she were angry. We walked down the road at a slow pace listening to Steven's bare feet slap the hot concrete with each step he made. "Those bullies tricked me," Steven whined. Steven went on talking to himself rather than us, and it's a good thing he was, because it was clear that my mom had no answers to why the bullies were so mean.

14   As my mom and I walked back home, we walked in silence.

15   I still think about Steven Villman. I wonder if he realizes what a difference he can make in the lives of others. When I walked Steven home that day, I learned that we all need to listen to people who are different than we are.

This essay will be revised later in the book.

CHAPTER 4

Strategies for Developing Paragraphs

Imagine the difficulty of reading a magazine article or book if you were faced with one solid block of text. How could you sort its ideas or know the best places to pause for thought? Paragraphs help guide readers through longer pieces of writing. Some break lengthy discussions of one idea into segments of different emphasis, thus providing rest stops for readers. Others consolidate several briefly developed ideas. Yet others begin or end pieces of writing or link major segments together. Most paragraphs, though, include a number of sentences that develop and clarify one idea. Throughout a piece of writing, paragraphs relate to one another and reflect a controlling purpose. To make paragraphs fit together smoothly, you can't just sit down and dash them off. Instead, you first need to reflect on the entire essay, then channel your thoughts toward its different segments. Often you'll have to revise your paragraphs after you've written a draft.

CHARACTERISTICS OF EFFECTIVE PARAGRAPHS

Unity

A paragraph with unity develops one—and only one—key controlling idea. To ensure unity, edit out any stray ideas that don't belong and fight the urge to take interesting but irrelevant side trips; they only create confusion about your destination. The following paragraph *lacks unity:*

> Psychiatric nurses deal with dangerous mental patients, pathological personalities who may explode into violence at any moment. Sigmund Freud was one of the first doctors to study mental disorders. Today psychotherapy is a well-established medical discipline.

What exactly is this writer trying to say? We can't tell. Each sentence expresses a different, undeveloped idea:

1. Job of the psychiatric nurse
2. Freud's pioneering work in studying mental disorders
3. Present status of psychotherapy

In contrast, the following paragraph develops and clarifies only one central idea—the professional responsibilities of a psychiatric nurse:

> Psychiatric nurses deal with dangerous mental patients, pathological personalities who may explode into violence at any moment. For this reason, they must remain on guard at all times. When a patient displays anger or violence, they cannot respond in kind but must instead show tolerance and understanding. Furthermore, they must be able to recognize attempts at deception. Sometimes a mentally ill person, just prior to launching an attack, will act in a completely normal way in order to deceive the intended victim. The nurse must recognize this behaviour and be alert for any possible assault.
>
> Peggy Feltman, student

Because this paragraph focuses entirely on a discussion of responsibilities, this paragraph has unity. To check your paragraphs for unity, ask yourself what each one aims to do and whether each sentence helps that aim.

EXERCISE *Read the next two paragraphs and answer the questions.*

1   The legend—in Africa—that all elephants over a large geographical area go to a common "graveyard" when they sense death is approaching led many hunters to treat them with special cruelty. Ivory hunters, believing the myth and trying to locate such graveyards, often intentionally wounded an elephant in the

hopes of following the suffering beast as it made its way to the place where it wanted to die. The idea was to wound the elephant seriously enough so that it thought it was going to die but not so seriously that it died in a very short time. All too often, the process resulted in a single elephant being shot or speared many times and relentlessly pursued until it either fell dead or was killed when it finally turned and charged its attackers. In any case, no wounded elephant ever led its pursuers to the mythical graveyard with its hoped-for booty of ivory tusks.

Kris Hurrell, student

2   Mental health practitioners need to be sensitive to the influence of labels and diagnoses. When those in power label the "other" who makes them uncomfortable as deviant in some way, this labelling depersonalizes and objectifies the labelled person. My cousin who was bipolar found it difficult to find and keep a job because of his major mood swings. Educators can be too quick to say that a child who is restless or inattentive has attention deficit disorder, and should take Ritalin. The pharmaceutical industry has a vested interest in getting as many people as possible to take prescription drugs. In the medieval period, women were easily labelled as witches, as madwomen, or as victims of emotional instability.

1. Which of these paragraphs lacks unity? Refer to content in the paragraphs when answering.
2. How would you improve the paragraph that lacks unity?

The Topic Sentence

The topic sentence states the main idea of the paragraph. Think of the topic sentence as a rallying point, with all supporting sentences developing the idea it expresses. A good topic sentence helps you gauge what information belongs in a paragraph, thus ensuring unity. At the same time, it informs your reader about the point you're making.

Placement of the topic sentence varies from paragraph to paragraph, as the following examples show. As you read each, note how supporting information develops the topic sentence, which is italicized.

Topic Sentence Stated First   Many paragraphs open with the topic sentence. The writer reveals the central idea immediately, then builds from a solid base.

Starting about one million years ago, the fossil record shows an accelerating growth of the human brain. It expanded at first at the rate of one cubic inch of additional gray matter every hundred thousand years; then the growth rate doubled; it doubled again; and finally it doubled once more. Five hundred thousand years ago the rate of growth hit its peak. At that time, the brain was expanding at the phenomenal rate of ten cubic inches every hundred thousand years. No other organ in the history of life is known to have grown as fast as this.

Robert Jastrow, *Until the Sun Dies*

Topic Sentence Stated Last In order to emphasize the support and build gradually to a conclusion, a topic sentence can end the paragraph. Since this position creates suspense for the reader who anticipates the climactic or summarizing point, it can be particularly useful in personal or narrative writing.

An experience of my own comes handily to mind. Some years ago, when the Restaurant de la Pyramide in Vienne was without question one of the best half-dozen restaurants in the world, I visited it for the first time. After I had ordered my meal, the sommelier [wine steward] appeared to set before me a wine list of surpassing amplitude and excellence. But as I cast my eyes down this unbelievable offering of the world's most tantalizing wines, the sommelier bent over me and pointed out a wine of which I had never heard, ticketed at a price one-fifth that of its illustrious neighbors. "Monsieur," said the sommelier, "I would suggest this one. It is a local wine, a very good wine. It is not a great wine, but after all, monsieur, you are likely to pass this way only once. The great wines you will find everywhere; this wine you will find only in Vienne. I would like you to try it, while you have the opportunity." *This, to my mind, was true sophistication—on the part of M. Point for having the wine and on the part of the waiter for offering it.*

Stephen White, "The New Sophistication: Defining the Terms"

Topic Sentence Stated First and Last Some paragraphs lead with the main idea and then restate it, usually in different words, at the end. This technique allows the writer to repeat an especially important idea.

Everything is changing. . . . This is a prediction I can make with absolute certainty. As human beings, we are constantly in a state of change. Our bodies change every day. Our attitudes are constantly evolving. Something that we swore by five years ago is now almost impossible for us to imagine ourselves believing. The clothes we wore a few years ago now look strange to us in old photographs. The things we take for granted as absolutes, impervious to change, are, in fact, constantly doing just that. Granite boulders become sand in time. Beaches erode and shape new shorelines. Our buildings become outdated and are replaced with modern structures that also will be torn down. Even those things which last thousands of years, such as the Pyramids and the Acropolis, also are changing. This simple insight is very important to grasp if you want to be a no-limit person, and are desirous of raising no-limit children. *Everything you feel, think, see, and touch is constantly changing.*

Wayne Dyer, *What Do You Really Want for Your Children?*

Topic Sentence Stated in the Middle Occasionally, the topic sentence falls between background information and sentences that develop the central idea. This midpoint positioning of the topic sentence allows the writer to shift the emphasis and at the same time continue to build on the original idea. It can be particularly useful in longer, complex paragraphs.

> Over the centuries, China has often been the subject of Western fantasy. In their own way, a number of scholars, journalists, and other travelers have perpetuated this tradition in recent years, rushing to rediscover the country after its long period of isolation. Some of these visitors, justifiably impressed by the Communists' achievements in eliminating the exploitative aspects of pre-1949 mandarin society, propagated the view that the revolution, after its initial successes, had continued to "serve the people," and that China was "the wave of the future"—a compelling alternative to the disorder and materialism of contemporary Western society. Human rights were not at issue, they argued, because such Western concepts were inapplicable to China. *In the past year, however, the Chinese have begun to speak for themselves, and they are conveying quite a different picture.* In the view of many of its own people, China is a backward and repressive nation. "China is Asia's Gulag Archipelago," an elderly Chinese scholar said to me shortly after I had arrived in China last spring. "I was in Germany right after the Second World War, and I saw the horrors of Buchenwald and other concentration camps. In a way—in its destruction of the human spirit these past two decades—China has been even worse."

> David Finkelstein, "When the Snow Thaws"

Topic Sentence Implied   Some paragraphs, particularly in narrative and descriptive writing, have no topic sentence. Rather, all sentences point toward a main idea that readers must infer for themselves.

> [Captain Robert Barclay] once went out at 5 in the morning to do a little grouse shooting. He walked at least 30 miles while he potted away, and then after dinner set out on a walk of 60 miles that he accomplished in 11 hours without a halt. Barclay did not sleep after this but went through the following day as if nothing had happened until the afternoon, when he walked 16 miles to a ball. He danced all night, and then in early morning walked home and spent a day partridge shooting. Finally he did get to bed—but only after a period of two nights and nearly three days had elapsed and he had walked 130 miles.

> John Lovesey, "A Myth Is as Good as a Mile"

The details in this paragraph collectively suggest a clear central idea: that Barclay had incredible physical endurance. In most academic writing, however, clearly formulated topic sentences will help focus and unify your paragraphs.

EXERCISE   *Identify the topic sentences in each of the following paragraphs and explain how you arrived at your decisions. If the topic sentence is implied, state the central idea in your own words.*

1. Unlike governments, corporations are not democratic and not charged with advancing the public good. Instead, they exist to maximize profit for shareholders—sometimes at the cost of honesty. Just last week, the giant company Worldcom imploded under allegations of a $4 billion accounting scam. Far from being a rare occurrence, such scandals are becoming commonplace. From Enron to Dynegy to Adelphia, corporations are proving that they shouldn't be trusted, and indeed

some are downright rotten to the core. Where were the government regulators and the auditors in these scandals? These were public companies and in some cases people's pensions depended on them. Yet the size and scope of the scandals indicates that regulators turned a blind eye to the problems or were prevented from taking action.

David Suzuki, "Protesters' Message Lost on the Media"

2. What my mother never told me was how fast time passes in adult life. I remember, when I was little, thinking I would live to be at least as old as my grandmother, who was dynamic even at ninety-two, the age at which she died. Now I see those ninety-two years hurtling by me. And my mother never told me how much fun sex could be, or what a discovery it is. Of course, I'm of an age when mothers really didn't tell you much about anything. My mother never told me the facts of life.

Joyce Susskind, "Surprises in a Woman's Life"

3. It was funny how everyone in the second half of the twentieth century suddenly started buying these large, lumpy, sculptured, multicolored shoes. It was as though people discovered overnight that their footwear didn't have to be black or brown, and didn't need to conform to what was streamlined and quietly tasteful. The traditional shoe was challenged, and it collapsed at the first skirmish. Shoes could trumpet their engineered presence, their tread, their aggressive padding; they could make all manner of wild claims, converting whole populations to athletic splendor and prodigious fitness. Larry's running shoes are red and white, with little yellow insignias located near the toe. Each of the heels has a transparent built-in bubble for additional comfort and buoyancy when running on hard pavement.

Carol Shields, *Larry's Party*

4. That empty building on the left was once a school. Here in Cutback World we have discovered that the educational system operates far more efficiently if schools are not open. You should not conclude from this that we have closed all our schools. That would be foolish. There is a school downtown somewhere. Every city of at least 100 000 people in Cutback World is entitled to have a school. Ours has 15 000 students in it, which enables it to offer a full range of courses. When we pass it, you might notice some students hanging out the open windows. We regard this as a sign that classroom space is being fully utilized.

Charles Gordon "A Guided Tour of the Bottom Line"

EXERCISE

1. **Develop one of the ideas below into a topic sentence. Then write a unified paragraph that is built around it.**

    a. The career (or job or profession) I want is _____.

    b. The one quality most necessary in my chosen field is _____.

    c. The most difficult aspect of my chosen field is _____.

    d. One good example of the Canadian tendency to waste is _____.

    e. The best (or worst) thing about fast-food restaurants is _____.

2. **Write a topic sentence that would control a paragraph on each of the following:**

   a. Preparations for travelling away from home

   b. Advantages of having your own room

   c. Some landmark of the community in which you live

   e. The price of long-distance telephone calls

   e. Registering for university or college courses

Adequate Development

Students often ask for guidelines on paragraph length: "Should I aim for fifty to sixty words? seven to ten sentences? about one-quarter of a page?" The questions are natural, but the approach is wrong. Instead of targeting a particular length, ask yourself what the reader needs to know. Then supply enough information to make your point clearly. Skimpy, undeveloped paragraphs frustrate readers by forcing them to fill in the gaps for themselves, On the other hand, a rambling paragraph stuffed with useless padding dilutes the main idea and often loses the audience. The extent of paragraph length and development is influenced by the reader's expectations, as well as the writing genre or publication medium. A newspaper article might feature short paragraphs including only key facts, whereas a scientific journal might have lengthy paragraphs that offer detailed development of facts. Personal narrative writing is more likely to use short paragraphs to control dramatic pacing, while formal academic writing usually contains well-developed paragraphs of several sentences.

The details you supply can include facts, figures, thoughts, observations, steps, lists, examples, and sometimes personal experiences. Individually, these bits of information may mean little, but combined, they clearly illustrate your point. Keep in mind, however, that development isn't an end in itself, but instead advances the purpose of the entire essay.

Here are two versions of a paragraph, the first inadequately developed:

Underdeveloped Paragraph

Many sports have peculiar injuries associated with them. Repetitive use of certain body parts can cause chronic injuries in athletes who play baseball, football, or basketball. All of these common sports injuries are a result of the overuse of specific body parts. However, these injuries can be greatly reduced if athletes train properly, rest fully, and respect their bodies.

Adequately Developed Paragraph

Many sports have peculiar injuries associated with them. Repetitive use of certain body parts can cause chronic injuries in athletes who play baseball, football, or basketball. *Baseball pitchers can throw up to one hundred and fifty pitches per game. This repetitive throwing action can cause pitchers' elbows to swell. Over time, tendonitis often develops. Similarly, football linemen also suffer chronic injuries related to their sport. The constant jarring pressure during physical contact can cause severe back pain. Many linemen struggle with spinal disc injuries throughout their lives. In addition, basketball players often suffer from shin splints because of the repetitive pounding on their legs when running and jumping on a hard surface.* All of these common sports injuries are a result of the overuse of specific body parts. However, these injuries can be greatly reduced if athletes train properly, rest fully, and respect their bodies.

The first paragraph lacks examples of particular sports injuries, whereas the second one provides the needed information.

Readability also helps set paragraph length. Within a paper, paragraphs signal natural dividing places, allowing the reader to pause and absorb the material presented up to that point. Too little paragraphing overwhelms the reader with long blocks of material. Too much creates a choppy Dick-and-Jane effect that may come across as simplistic or even irritating. To counter these problems, writers sometimes use several paragraphs for an idea that needs extended development, or they combine several short paragraphs into one.

EXERCISE

1. **Indicate where the ideas in this long block of material divide logically; explain your choices.**

   During the summer following graduation from high school, I could hardly wait to get to university and be on my own. In my first weeks at university, however, I found that independence can be tough and painful. I had expected raucous good times and a carefree collegiate life, the sort depicted in old beach movies and suggested by the selective memories of sentimental alumni. Instead, all I felt at first was the burden of increasing responsibilities and loneliness. I discovered that being independent of parents who kept at me to do my homework and expected me to accomplish certain household chores did not mean I was free to do as I pleased. On the contrary, living on my own meant that I had to perform for myself all the tasks that the family used to share. Studying became a full-time occupation rather than a nightly duty to be accomplished in an hour or two, and my instructors made it clear that they would have little sympathy for negligence or even for my inability to do an assignment. However, what was more troubling about my early university life than having to do laundry, prepare meals, and complete stacks of homework was the terrifying sense of being entirely alone. Although I was independent, no longer a part of the world that had seemed to confine me, I soon realized that confinement had also meant security. I never liked the feeling that people were watching over me, but I knew that my family and friends were also watching out for me—and that's a good feeling to have. At the university, no one seemed particularly to be watching, though professors constantly evaluated the quality of my work. I felt estranged from people in those first weeks, desperately needing a confidant but fearful that the new and tenuous friendships I had made would be damaged if I were to confess my fears and problems. It was simply too early for me to feel a part of the university. So there I was, independent in the fullest sense, but feeling like a person without a country.

2. **The following short, choppy units are inadequately developed. List some details you could use to expand one of them into a good paragraph.**

Teachers should have strong interpersonal skills. When teachers fail, they usually fail in relationships.

The commercialism of Canadian society affects children from an early age. When they watch television, they are bombarded with commercials that reinforce the message that happiness comes from buying things.

3. **Scan the papers you have written in other classes for paragraphs that are over- or underdeveloped. Revise any you find.**

Organization

An effective paragraph unfolds in a clear pattern of organization so that the reader can easily follow the flow of ideas. Usually when you write your first draft, your organization reflects the flow of your thoughts. Sometimes this logic of association makes sense, but when you revise, you will often see how you can organize paragraphs more effectively. Writers do not ordinarily stop to decide on a strategy for each paragraph, but when you revise or are stuck, it's useful to understand the available choices. Here are some options:

1. The strategies discussed in Chapters 6–12, including narration, description, illustration, process analysis, cause and effect, definition, comparison, classification, and argument and persuasion
2. Commonly used sequencing patterns, including time sequence and space sequence
3. Order of climax

Four example paragraphs follow. The first, organized by *time sequence,* traces the final years of the Model T Ford, concluding with a topic sentence that sums up its impact.

In 1917, the Model T lost much of its attraction when its exterior appearance was drastically altered. The famous flat-sided brass radiator disappeared and the new style featured (in the words of the catalogue) "the stream-lined hood, large radiator and enclosed fan, crown fenders, black finish and nickel trimmings" ("crown fenders" would be described in England as domed mud-guards). Electric lighting and starting followed in 1919, and the model then continued with little alteration until 1927, when it was finally withdrawn. After a considerable pause, it was replaced by the Model A, a very conventional machine with wire wheels, three-speed gearbox and four-wheel brakes (the "T" had never made this concession to progress and continued to the last with two minute brake drums on the back wheels only). While it was in preparation, others had taken the lead, and the "A" never replaced the immortal "T" in the public fancy. Indeed, the "Tin Lizzy" or "Flivver" had become almost a national characteristic, and at the end of its eighteen years in production, the total number sold was fifteen million.

Cecil Clutton and John Stanford, The Vintage Motor-Car

Other common spatial arrangements include top to bottom, left to right, right to left, nearby to far away, far away to nearby, clockwise, and counterclockwise. Consider how the following descriptive paragraph moves from outside to inside.

Next to the laundry, across the alley, which ran like a sparkling river of broken glass and urine produced by the hordes of feral cats, giant rats and stumbling drunks who waded therein, was the Jewish Tailor. His narrow house, barely a door and a window wide, extended backwards from his work room and housed his wife and daughter, a sewing machine and a steam iron. An air of sadness, like the tape measure he wore around his neck, enveloped the place.

Moses Milstein, "Memories of Montreal—and Richness"

The next paragraph, written by a student, illustrates development by *comparison and contrast.* As in many descriptive or narrative paragraphs, the topic sentence is implied.

I have pictures of the three girls in our peach colored skirts that Mom had made for us, our moving away skirts. My sisters' skirts had sewn pleats that looked sleek and sophisticated; my skirt had box pleats that were sewn to the waist, and opened up like a Scottish kilt, and that made me feel chunky. We all had decorative dolls, but there was a difference. Their dolls looked glamorous; my doll looked dumpy. My sisters' dolls had skirts made of flexible foam that swirled and swirled. My doll's skirt looked hard, and was shaped like a bell. Their dolls' skirts were turquoise and mauve; my doll's skirt was reddish pink, the color of not quite cooked meat. It wasn't a real pink, or even red, but something in between.

Order of Climax Climactic order, often used in personal writing, creates a crescendo pattern starting with the least emphatic detail and progressing to the most emphatic. The topic sentence can begin or end the paragraph, or it can remain implied. This pattern holds the reader's interest by building suspense. Occasionally, writers reverse the order, landing the heaviest punch first; but such paragraphs can trail off, leaving the reader dissatisfied. Here is a paragraph illustrating climactic order:

The speaking errors I hear affect me to different degrees. I'm so conditioned to hearing "It don't make any difference" and "There's three ways to solve the problem" that I've almost accepted such usage. However, errors such as "Just between you and I, Arnold loves Edna" and "I'm going back to my room to lay down" still offend my sensibility. When hearing them, I usually just chuckle to myself and walk away. The "Twin I's"—irrevelant and irregardless—are another matter. More than any other errors, they really grate on my ear. Whenever I hear "that may be true, but it's irrevelant" or "Irregardless of how much I study, I still get C's," I have the urge to correct the speaker. It's really surprising that more people don't clean up their language act.

Valerie Sonntag, student

EXERCISE *From a magazine or newspaper article, select four paragraphs that illustrate different patterns of organization. Identify the topic sentence in each case; or if it is implied, state it in your own words. Point out the organization of each paragraph.*

Coherence

Coherent writing flows smoothly and easily from one sentence and paragraph to another, clarifying the relationships among ideas and thus allowing the reader to grasp connections. In contrast, incoherent writing, which fails to make connections clear, can confuse and even irritate readers. Consider how the following paragraph jumps around confusingly.

At certain times counselling can be extremely beneficial. People should be committed to becoming healthy. They should never be forced to go to counselling. Sometimes people do need to be told in a gentle way that maybe they should consider seeking counselling. A person who decides to try counselling should do some research. They have to find a counsellor who is suited to their specific needs. Sometimes it is hard for people to reach out and admit they need help. Mental health is as important as physical health. Finding a counsellor with whom a person feels safe and comfortable is important. Now that you have found a good counsellor, therapy can begin and your mental health is on its way to recovery.

This paragraph has some degree of unity, because most of its sentences relate to the writer's interest in the benefits of counselling. Unfortunately, though, its many gaps in logic create rather than answer questions, and in very bumpy prose. How does the third sentence relate to the fourth? And what do the seventh and eighth sentences have to do with the writer's main purpose: to explain how people can benefit from counselling at certain critical moments?

Now read this rewritten version. Note what has been deleted, and what has been added to improve coherence. Transitions and content additions are italicized:

> People who *are in emotional crisis or who have experienced trauma* can benefit from counselling. They should not be forced to go into counselling, *because forced treatment is not likely to be effective. Although* it can be hard at times for people to reach out and admit that they need help, counselling is most effective *when people come to it on their own and feel committed to the process. After* they decide to seek counselling, they should do some research in order to find a counsellor who is suited to their specific needs, and with whom they feel safe.

As this example shows, changing the order of sentences, and inserting connecting words or phrases can make paragraphs smoother and more coherent.

EXERCISE *Rewrite the following student paragraph to improve coherence. You may rearrange sentence order, combine and condense sentences, or add any connecting words that seem appropriate.*

> Many elderly people, as well as people that can no longer care for themselves, are placed in long-term care facilities. These surroundings can be unpleasant for many, and can cause residents to become very depressed. Within the last few years, animal therapy has become recognized as a way to improve health. Many care facilities arrange weekly visits from a local handler and their best friend, which is usually a well-trained dog. These visits provide patients with something to look forward to. The presence of a loving animal companion can comfort lonely people. Visiting with animals helps to lower blood pressure. It also can reduce stress. In turn, many patients generally become more responsive to their treatment. Residents seem happier overall and feel better when animals are allowed to visit their facility.

Coherence derives from a sufficient supply of supporting details and from your firm sense of the way your ideas go together.

As you write, and especially when you revise, signal connections to the reader by using *transitions*—devices that link sentences to one another. These common transitions are grouped according to function:

1. Connecting words and phrases
2. Repeated key words

3. Pronouns
4. Parallelism

You can use them to furnish links both within and between paragraphs.

Connecting Words and Phrases These connectors clarify relationships between sentences. The following list groups them according to function:

Showing similarity: in like manner, likewise, just as, similarly
Showing contrast: at the same time, but, even so, however, in contrast, instead, nevertheless, still, on the contrary, on the other hand, otherwise, yet
Showing results or effects: accordingly, as a result, because, consequently, hence, since, therefore, thus
Adding ideas: also, besides, first (second, third . . .), furthermore, in addition, in the first place, moreover, too
Drawing conclusions: as a result, finally, in brief, in conclusion, in short, therefore
Pointing out examples: for example, for instance, to illustrate
Showing emphasis and clarity: above all, after all, again, as a matter of fact, besides, in fact, in other words, indeed, nonetheless, that is
Indicating time: at times, after, afterward, from then on, immediately, later, meanwhile, next, now, once, previously, subsequently, then, until, while
Conceding a point: granted that, of course, to be sure, admittedly, certainly

Don't overload your paper with connectors. In well-planned prose, your message flows clearly with only occasional assistance from them.

In the following excerpt, which clarifies the difference between workers and workaholics, the connectors are italicized:

> My efforts to define workaholism and to distinguish workaholics from other hard workers proved difficult. *While* workaholics do work hard, not all hard workers are workaholics. Moonlighters, *for example,* may work 16 hours a day to make ends meet, but most of them will stop working when their financial circumstances permit. Accountants, *too,* seem to work non-stop, but many slow down after the April 30 tax deadline. Workaholics, *on the other hand,* always devote more time and thought to their work than their situation demands. Even in the absence of deadlines to meet, mortgages to pay, promotions to earn, or bosses to please, workaholics still work hard. What sets them apart is their attitude toward work, not the number of hours they work.

> Marilyn Machlowitz, "Workaholism:
> What's Wrong with Being Married to Your Work?"

DISCUSSION QUESTIONS

1. What ideas do each of the italicized words and phrases above connect?
2. What relationship does each show?

Repeated Key Words   Repeating key words, especially those that help convey a paragraph's central idea, can smooth the reader's path. The words may appear in different forms, but their presence keeps the main issues before the reader. In the following paragraph, coherence is achieved through repetition of simple phrases ("it adds," "it is") along with the word "blandness."

What is the point of the battered fry? *It adds* crunch. *It adds* weight. *It adds* calories. *What it* does not *add* is flavour. *What it* removes *is* potato-ness. *It is* a blandi-fier. And *it is* its very *blandness* that makes it popular. *Blandness* is more tenacious than any virus: *It* will always conquer a host population, wherever *it is* introduced.

Russell Smith, "Battered by Blandness"

EXERCISE   *Write a paragraph using one of the following sentences as your topic sentence. Insert the missing key word and then repeat it in your paragraph to help link your sentences together.*

1. _____ is my favourite relative.
2. I wish I had (a, an, some, more) _____.
3. _____ changed my life.
4. _____ is more trouble than it's worth.
5. A visit to _____ always depresses me.

Pronouns   Pronouns stand in for nouns that appear earlier in the sentence or in previous sentences. Mixing pronouns and their nouns throughout the paragraph prevents monotony and promotes clarity. We have italicized pronouns that aid coherence in the following excerpt from an address about Canadian literature by Robertson Davies.

In psychological terms, Canada is very much an introverted country, and *it* lives cheek by jowl with the most extroverted country known to history. Let me explain the terms. In personal psychology, the extrovert is *one* who derives *his* energy from *his* contacts with the external world; for *him*, everything lies outside and *he* moves outward toward *it*, often without much sensitivity to the response of that toward which *he* moves. The introvert, on the other hand, finds *his* energy within *himself*, and *his* concern with the outside world is a matter of what approach the outside world makes to *him*. It is absurd to say that one psychological orientation is superior to the other. Both have *their* values, but difficulties arise when *they* fail to understand one another.

Robertson Davies, "Living in a Country without a Mythology"

Some words such as *this, that, those,* and *these* also may contribute to coherence, or flow, by referring to something that has come just before. Sometimes they function as pronouns; at other times, they function as demonstrative adjectives.

Experience with diversity shows that inequities must be acknowledged and addressed for a diverse people to move forward together. *This* is a slow and sometimes painful process, but it is essential if all Canadians are to enjoy the same sense of belonging and attachment to their country. It also serves to familiarize Canadians with the history they share and the obligations that their history confers. *These* obligations include honouring the proclamations and negotiated arrangements made with First Nations peoples.

"Canadian Multiculturalism: An Inclusive Citizenship"

EXERCISE *In a magazine, newspaper, textbook, or some other written source, find two paragraphs that use pronouns or demonstrative adjectives to increase coherence. Copy the paragraphs, underline the pronouns, and explain what each refers to.*

Parallelism   Parallelism uses repetition of grammatical form to express a series of equivalent ideas. Besides giving continuity, the repetition adds rhythm and balance to the writing. Note how the following italicized constructions tie together the unfolding definition of poverty:

Poverty is staying up all night on cold nights to watch the fire, knowing one spark on the newspaper covering the walls means your sleeping children die in flames. In summer *poverty is watching* gnats and flies devour your baby's tears when he cries. The screens are torn and you pay so little rent you know they will never be fixed. *Poverty means* insects in your food, in your nose, in your eyes, and crawling over you when you sleep. *Poverty is hoping* it never rains because diapers won't dry when it rains and soon you are using newspapers. *Poverty is seeing* your children forever with runny noses. Paper handkerchiefs cost money and all your rags you need for other things. Even more costly are antihistamines. *Poverty is cooking* without food and cleaning without soap.

Jo Goodwin Parker, "What Is Poverty?"

PARAGRAPHS WITH SPECIAL FUNCTIONS

Special-function paragraphs include introductions, transitional paragraphs, and conclusions. Although introductions and conclusions may be more than one paragraph, generally one-paragraph introductions and conclusions appear in shorter essays. Transitional paragraphs may function like hinges, helping the writer swing into a different section of the paper—perhaps a different timeframe in a narrative essay, or a different argument in a more formal essay.

Introductions

A good introduction acquaints and coaxes. It announces the essay's topic and may directly state the thesis. In addition, it sets the tone for what will follow—a sombre, lighthearted, or angry introduction for personal writing, or an authoritative, confident, or persuasive introduction for an academic paper. The tone

of the introduction should fit the purpose of the paper. Thus, an amusing anecdote would not be an appropriate opening for a paper about political torture.

With essays, as with people, first impressions are important. If your opening
rouses interest, it will draw the readers into the essay and pave the way for their
acceptance of your ideas. If your beginning is mechanical, plodding, and dull,
you will likely turn readers away. Consider these weak openings:

In this paper I intend to . . .
Wars have always afflicted humankind.
As you may know, having too little time is a problem for many of us.
In the modern world of today . . .

Are you yawning yet? Ask yourself that same question about every opening
you write.

A Directly Stated Thesis   This is a common type of opening, orienting the
reader to what will follow. After providing some general background, the writer
of our example narrows her scope to a thesis that previews the upcoming sections of her essay.

> An increasing number of midlife women are reentering the workforce, pur-
> suing degrees, and getting more involved in the public arena. Several labels
> besides "midlife" have been attached to this type of person: the mature
> woman, the older woman, and, more recently, the re-entry woman. By defini-
> tion, she is between thirty-five and fifty-five years old and has been away from
> the business or academic scene anywhere from fifteen to thirty years. The aca-
> demic community, the media, marketing people, and employers are giving her
> close scrutiny, and it is apparent that she is having a greater impact on our
> society than she realizes.
>
> Jo Ann Harris, student

A Definition   This kind of introduction works particularly well in a paper that
acquaints the reader with an unfamiliar topic.

> You are completely alone in a large open space and are struck by a terrifying,
> unreasoning fear. You sweat, your heart beats, you cannot breathe. You fear you
> may die of a heart attack, although you do not have heart disease. Suppose you
> decide you will never get yourself in this helpless situation again. You go home and
> refuse to leave its secure confines. Your family has to support you. You have agora-
> phobia—a disabling terror of open spaces.
>
> "Controlling Phobias through Behaviour Modification"

A Quotation   A beginning quotation, particularly from an authority in the
field for formal papers, can be an effective springboard for the ideas that follow.
Make sure any quotation you use relates clearly to your topic.

> "Girl Power!" "Girls Rule!" These slogans now appear weekly as educators, the entertainment industry and the media celebrate spunky young women's rising successes.
>
> Douglas Todd, "In a Girl's World, It Can Be Tough Being a Boy"

An Anecdote or Personal Experience   A well-told personal anecdote or experience can draw readers in. Like other introductions, this kind should bear on what comes afterward. In the following example, an essay that decries the plight of foreign domestic workers in Canada begins with an anecdote about one typical morning for a struggling domestic worker.

> When Joyelle arrives at work, it is 7:45 on Monday morning and the bags of garbage from the weekend are stacked in the hallway of the Pintos' well-appointed condominium. The half-empty wineglasses are strewn around her employers' living room, and the faint odour of stale beer is in the air. Lugging the plastic bags down the hallway to the garbage chute and clearing up the dishes from the previous night's party have become rituals for Joyelle (all names have been changed to protect privacy).
>
> Marina Jiménez, "Domestic Crisis"

An Arresting Statement   Sometimes you can jolt the reader to attention by using surprising or even shocking content, language, or both, particularly if your essay develops an unusual or extreme position. An essay about bulimia uses shock to draw readers in:

> I no longer remember the first time I forced myself to throw up. What I do remember is how inexpert I was and how long it took before I succeeded in actually vomiting instead of just gagging and retching. I began by sticking my finger down my throat and wiggling it around, but this produced few results; it wasn't until articles about bulimia appeared in women's magazines that I finally thought to use the handle of a toothbrush instead of my forefinger. It became easy after that.
>
> Evelyn Lau, "An Insatiable Emptiness"

Intriguing Claim   An essay about anger makes an initial claim that may puzzle and intrigue readers.

> We carry around a lot of free-floating anger. What we do with it is what fascinates me.
>
> Dan Greenburg, "Sound and Fury"

Unusual Slant on a Familiar Theme   It can be difficult to find a fresh approach to the familiar subject of success and failure, but this writer cites paradoxical examples of "failure" to intrigue readers by causing them to examine their assumptions.

> John Milton was a failure. In writing "Paradise Lost," his stated aim was to "justify the ways of God to man." Inevitably, he fell short of accomplishing that and

only wrote a monumental poem. Beethoven, whose music was conceived to transcend Fate, was a failure, as was Socrates, whose ambition was to make people happy by making them reasonable and just. The inescapable conclusion seems to be that the surest, noblest way to fail is to set one's own standards titanically high.

Laurence Shames, "The Sweet Smell of Success Isn't All That Sweet"

Interesting Details   These details pique curiosity and draw readers in.

You were once a single cell. Every one of the 100 trillion cells in your body today is a direct descendent of that zygote, the primordial cell formed by the union of mother's egg and father's sperm. Each one is genetically identical (allowing for copying errors and environmental damage along the way) to that cell. Therefore, if we scraped a cell from, say, the inner lining of your cheek, its DNA would be the same DNA that, years ago in the original zygote, contained the entire plan for creating you and every part of you.

Charles Krauthammer, "Crossing Lines"

A Question or Problem   A provocative question or problem can entice the reader into the essay to find the answer.

When you leave your apartment or house, do you begin to feel better? If you leave for a week-long trip, do you find your head clears, your migraine disappears, dizziness stops, your aches and pains subside, depression fades away, and your entire attitude is better? If so, chemical pollution of the atmosphere in your home may be making you ill.

Marshall Mandell, "Are You Allergic to Your House?"

In the following introduction, the writer describes an inner conflict she experiences about the fascination with the Barbie doll that she observes in her daughter and other young girls.

I've always known there was something wrong with Barbie. She looks nice enough. And she has her own Corvette, her own band, and her own dream house. Still, I just didn't want my daughter playing with her. But how can we snub Barbie? Little girls all over Charlottesville, all over Virginia, and, yes, all over the world, seem to be spending hour after hour with her.

Mariflo Stephens, "Barbie Doesn't Live Here Anymore"

Blended Strategies   Many effective introductions contain more than one way to draw the reader in and frame their topic or argument. The following example blends a definition with a quotation and a direct statement of the thesis.

Loyal: 1. Steadfast in support and devotion to and never betraying the interests of one's homeland, government, or sovereign. 2. Faithful to a person, ideal or custom; constantly supporting or following. (French, from Old French loyal, loial, leial, fait)

—*Reader's Digest Illustrated Encyclopedic Dictionary*

The Roman senator, Seneca, called it "the holiest virtue in the human head." For most of the 2000 years since, few would have disagreed with his call for loyalty to the gods, to the state, to family and to duty. But loyalty, that once-essential virtue, is fading fast, and our sense of community and identity is disappearing with it.

Bob Harvey, "Loyalty: A Last Virtue; Me-First Attitude
Is Stripping away Our Sense of Community"

Note that the title as well as the introduction announces the direction of the essay.

EXERCISE

1. Explain why each of the preceding introductions interests or does not interest you. Does your response stem from the topic or the way the author introduces it?
2. Find magazine articles with effective introductory paragraphs illustrating at least three different techniques. Write a paragraph explaining why each impresses you.

Transitional Paragraphs

In the midst of a lengthy essay, you may need a short paragraph that announces a shift from one group of ideas to another. Transitional paragraphs summarize previously explained ideas, repeat the thesis, or point to ideas that follow. In our example, Bruno Bettelheim has been discussing a young boy named Joey, who has turned into a kind of human machine. After describing Joey's assorted delusions, Bettelheim signals his shift of emphasis from the delusions to the fears that caused them.

What deep-seated fears and needs underlay Joey's delusional system? We were long in finding out, for Joey's preventions effectively concealed the secret of his autistic behavior. In the meantime we dealt with his peripheral problems one by one.

Bruno Bettelheim, "Joey: 'A Mechanical Boy'"

The following transitional paragraph looks back as well as ahead:

Certainly these three factors—exercise, economy, convenience of short-cuts—help explain the popularity of bicycling today. But a fourth attraction sometimes overrides the others: the lure of the open road.

Mike Bernstein, student

Conclusions

A conclusion rounds out a paper and signals that the discussion has been completed. But not all papers require a separate conclusion. For example, narratives and descriptions generally end when the writer finishes the story or completes the details. Although some papers, especially personal narratives, do not always require a separate conclusion, most essays benefit from at least one concluding paragraph that drives the point home. To be effective, a conclusion must mesh logically and stylistically with what comes earlier. A long, complex paper often ends with a summary of the main points, but other options may be used for shorter papers with easy-to-grasp ideas. Most short essays have single-paragraph conclusions, while longer papers may require two or three paragraphs.

Here are some suggestions for writing solid conclusions:

1. Don't introduce new material. Draw together, round out, but don't take off in a new direction.
2. Don't tack on a trite ending in desperation when the hour is late and the paper is due tomorrow—the so-called midnight special. Your reader deserves better than "All in all, skiing is a great sport" or "Thus we can see that motorcycle racing isn't for everyone."
3. Don't apologize. Saying that you could have done a better job makes a reader wonder why you didn't.
4. Don't moralize. A preachy conclusion can undermine the position you have established in the rest of your composition.

The following examples illustrate several common types of conclusions.

Restatement of the Thesis The following conclusion reasserts the writer's thesis that "the term *youth* has been co-opted by government and corporate interests."

> By replacing the term *adult* with *youth,* governments, corporations, and the media can offer the majority of the electorate and the majority of society (baby boomers, if you will) an easy explanation for why those aged 18–35 are not receiving what they as adults need—namely employment, a living wage, and a minimal level of independence. At the same time, those with a vested interest in the status quo are creating a diversion from a multitude of other issues that will inevitably have to be addressed. All of this with one word.
>
> Andrew Beyak, "The Sweet Bird of Youth Is Showing Signs of Age"

A Summary A summary draws together and reinforces the main points.

> In conclusion, using nuclear-transfer cloning to allow people to have a child introduces a different way of reproduction for our species. Once we breach this barrier, it leaves us with no place to stop. Given all the problems outlined, the reasons for permitting cloning to produce a person are insufficiently compelling. Even in the few circumstances where the case for human cloning seems justified, there are alternative solutions. We are at an appropriate stopping place on a slippery slope. Not all reasons why a person might wish to copy his or her cells are unethical, but given there are other options open to people wishing to form a family, concerns about individual and social harms from cloning are strong enough that it is not justified to permit it. These issues affecting the creation of the next generation are important for the future of our species; we must deal with them wisely. I hope we can.
>
> Patricia Baird, "Should Human Cloning Be Permitted?"

A Question   A final question often prompts the reader to think further on the topic. If your essay is meant to be persuasive, be sure to phrase a concluding question so that the way a reasonable person would answer emphasizes your point of view. The paragraph below concludes an argument that running should not be elevated to a religion, that its other benefits are sufficient.

> Aren't those gifts enough? Why ask running for benefits that are plainly beyond its capacity to bestow?
>
> James Fixx, "What Running Can't Do for You"

A Quotation   A quotation can capture the essence of your thought and end the essay with authority.

> "We had no idea of the emotional involvement and the commitment of these women," Richard says. "Suddenly a constituency arose. Suddenly there are thousands and thousands of women who don't care about your moral position or mine—they want a baby."
>
> David Zimmerman, "Are Test-Tube Babies the Answer for the Childless?"

Ironic Twist or Surprising Observation   These approaches prompt the reader to think further about a paper's topic. The following paragraph highlights the irony of the writer's regret after he has fulfilled a seemingly desirable dream. Although living now in a premium Vancouver locale, the author regrets that his son is missing out on the cultural and economic diversity of his own youth in Montreal.

> When I grew up I bought a house in the gentle forests of the Pacific and my son walks to school among the cherry blossoms. And sometimes I am sad for him.
>
> Moses Milstein, "Memories of Montreal—and Richness"

In the following conclusion, the writer makes a surprising admission that leaves us thinking.

> I'm glad I'm greedy. I would hate to be envious.
>
> Marilyn Baker, "Greed Works"

Clever or Lighthearted Ending   In humorous or otherwise light essays, clever twists of wording can make effect endings. In this example, capitalizing on the essay's topic (clichés), the writer ends by exaggerating the fault being criticized.

> Because using clichés is as easy as falling off a log, it goes without saying that it would be duck soup to continue in this vein till hell freezes over. However, since that would be carrying coals to Newcastle, let's ring down the curtain and bid adieu to the fair topic of the cliché. (No use beating a dead horse.)

Personal Challenge   A challenge often prompts the reader to take some action.

> And therein lies the challenge. You can't merely puff hard for a few days
> and then revert to the La-Z-Boy recliner, smugly thinking that you're "in shape."
> You must sweat and strain and puff regularly, week in and week out. They're
> your muscles, your lungs, your heart. The only caretaker they have is you.
>
> Monica Duvall, student

Recommendation or Hope   Both a recommendation and a hope may restate
points already made in the essay or suggest actions to take in order to arrive at
a solution. Tomkins's conclusion conveys not only a recommendation, but also
a sense of urgency about the consequences of failing to heed his advice.

> It is not more time we need: it is fewer desires. We need to switch off the cell-
> phone and leave the children to play by themselves. We need to buy less, read less
> and travel less. We need to set boundaries for ourselves, or be doomed to mount-
> ing despair.
>
> Richard Tomkins, "Old Father Time Becomes a Terror"

EXERCISE

1. **Explain which of the above conclusions appeals to you. Does your response
   stem from the topic or from the author's handling of it?**
2. **Collect effective concluding paragraphs from magazine articles, illustrating at
   least three different techniques. Then write a paragraph explaining why each
   impresses you.**

CHAPTER 5

Strategies for Revising and Editing Your Writing

All of us at one time or another have said something careless to a friend, date, or partner and then spent the rest of the night regretting our words. When we speak, we cannot cut and paste, add and delete. When we write, however, we can use revision skills to work toward getting the wording right, so that it says exactly what we mean. Good writers don't express themselves perfectly on the first try, but they can relax, knowing that writing is a process.

Just what is revision? Don't confuse it with proofreading, the final stage of the writing process, where you carefully inspect your word choice, spelling, grammar, and punctuation. The word revision means *re-seeing*. Revision is much more drastic than proofreading, often involving an upheaval of content and organization as you become more certain about what you want to say. The writer E. M. Forster once asked, "How can I know what I think until I see what I say?" Thus, revising helps people sharpen their own ideas.

Most of what you read, including this book, has been considerably altered and improved as the writers progressed through early drafts. This fact shouldn't surprise you. After all, a rough draft is merely a first attempt to jot down some ideas in essay form. No matter how well you gather and organize your material, your ideas evolve only as you write. Sometimes the best ideas come toward the end of your first or second draft, and you might end up sacrificing entire chunks of your first draft. Moreover, often the first draft is incomplete, unclear in places, and possibly disorganized. You might even discover an entirely different approach buried within it. During revision, you keep changing things—your focus, approach to the topic, supporting material, and thesis statement—until the results satisfy you.

Inexperienced writers often mistakenly view initial drafts as nearly finished products rather than as experiments to alter, or even scrap, if need be. As a result, they often approach revision with a defensive attitude. To revise successfully, you need to control your ego and fear and become your own first critical reader. Set aside natural feelings of accomplishment ("After all, I've put a great deal of thought into this") and dread ("Actually, I'm afraid of what I'll find if I look too closely"). Instead, recognize that revision offers an opportunity to communicate more effectively with your audience.

PREPARING TO REVISE

To distance yourself from your writing and sharpen your critical eye, set your first draft aside for at least half a day, or longer if time permits. When you return to it, gear up for revision by jotting down your intended purpose and audience before you read your paper. These notations will help keep your changes on track. In addition, note any further ideas that have occurred to you.

The right attitude is vital to effective revision. Far too many students hastily skim their essays to reassure themselves that "Everything sounds O.K." Avoid such a quick-fix approach. If your draft appears fine on first reading, read it again with a more critical eye. You can also read your writing aloud so that two senses—hearing and seeing—can be involved during revision. Reading aloud can also help you gain distance on your writing, so that you can respond more as a reader than as a writer who already knows what is on the page. Look at the paper globally, checking for overall focus, before you begin checking sentences and words. Can you sum up your main idea in a sentence (or two), and is that sentence interesting and clear? Try putting yourself in your reader's place. Will your instructions for a new accounting method be clear to someone who has never done it? Will your recommendation of a new policy to address homelessness convince a cash-strapped community council? Remember: If you aren't critical now, anticipating confusion and objections, your reader certainly will be later.

Read your essay at least three times, once for each of these reasons:

To improve the focus and development of the essay as a whole
To strengthen paragraph structure and development
To sharpen sentences and words (explored more in the next chapter)

Finally, use the Personal Revision Checklist on the inside back cover of this book to note your own special areas to work on, such as insufficient specific support and evidence.

GLOBAL REVISIONS

If you inspect your draft only sentence by sentence, you can easily overlook how its parts work together. As you begin to revise, step back and view the overall essay rather than its separate parts. Consider big picture elements, such as the essay's focus and direction, audience, organization, and development. Ask questions such as "Does the beginning mesh with the end?" "Does the essay wander?" "Has anything been left out?" In this way, you can gauge how part relates to part and to the whole. Use the acronym *FACT* to guide this stage of your revision.

F Ask yourself first whether the whole essay **FITS** together, presenting a central point for a specific audience. Have you delivered what the thesis statement promises? First drafts often include paragraphs or even large sections that have little to do with the main point. Some drafts even contain ideas for different possible essays, threads that pull in different directions. Furthermore, one section of a draft might be geared to one audience (parents, for example), and another section to an entirely different audience (students, perhaps). As you read each part, verify its connection to your purpose and audience. Don't hesitate to chop out sections that don't fit, redo stray parts so they accord with your central idea, or alter your thesis statement to reflect better your supporting material. Occasionally, you might even expand one small, fertile section of your draft into an entirely new essay.

A Whenever we write first drafts, we unwittingly leave out essential material. As we revise, we need to identify and fill these gaps. Ask yourself: "Where will the reader need more information or examples to understand my message?" Then **ADD** the appropriate sentences, paragraphs, or even pages.

C First drafts often contain material that fits the thesis but doesn't contribute to the essay. Writing quickly, we tend to repeat ourselves, include uninteresting or uninformative examples, and crank out whole paragraphs when one clear sentence would suffice. As you revise, **CUT** away this clutter with a free hand. Such paring can be painful, especially if you're left with a skimpy text, but your final message will emerge with much greater clarity. As you've probably guessed, revising a draft often requires both adding and cutting.

T Carefully **TEST** the organization of your essay. The text should flow smoothly from point to point with clear transitions between the various ideas. Test the organization by outlining your major and minor points, and then check the results for logic and completeness. Alternatively, read the draft and note the progression of its paragraphs and points. Look for places where you can clarify connections between ideas and thus help your readers understand.

Chapters 6–12 explain nine different writing strategies and conclude with revision questions geared specifically to that strategy. Use these questions, together with the *FACT* of revision, to help you revise more effectively.

Case History *(continued)*

Now let's apply the *FACT* approach to Trudy's essay on Steven Villman, which you read. Like most early drafts, this draft needs work.

FIT. The thesis doesn't fit the rest of the essay very well, since the narrative doesn't really demonstrate the importance of listening. Trudy can rewrite her essay to bring out the importance of listening, or she can rewrite her thesis and conclusion so that they fit her essay better.

ADD. Trudy needs to expand her essay in a couple of places, because the reader cannot understand why the bullies tricked Steven, or whether or not the mother really is angry. Trudy also needs to supply a transition between paragraphs 3 and 4, since the reader may be confused by the jump in time and locale. She also needs to work on the conclusion, which seems rushed.

CUT. Since Trudy's purpose is more to promote compassion than to inform readers about autism, she can condense her introduction, zeroing in more immediately on her story. She can also cut some sentences that tell the reader what she has already demonstrated.

TEST. The first five paragraphs can be rearranged, combined, and condensed, since they seem rather choppy. Describing Steven's appearance before giving the description of his activities at lunchtime would be more logical. The essay does flow well for the most part, although the paragraphs seem to be broken up arbitrarily in a few places, creating choppiness.

This case history continues later in this chapter.

As you read your own essay, note on a separate sheet of paper problems to solve, ideas to add, and changes to try. If you are composing new material on the computer, you can use the cut, paste, and delete features to help you change and move text. If you are revising a hard copy of the complete essay, make your job easier by using these simple techniques:

1. To mark a deletion, cross it out lightly; you may decide to resurrect the deleted material later.
2. To add a section of text, place a letter *(A, B, C, D)* at the appropriate spot; then create the new material in a new file or at the bottom of your draft file, clearly marked with the letter. Make smaller changes within sections by crossing out on the hard copy what you don't want and writing the replacement above it or nearby. Leave inputting changes and moving blocks of new text into place until you have finished reviewing the entire draft—you may end up changing your mind.
3. To rearrange the organization, draw arrows showing where you want things to go, or cut up your draft and rearrange the sections by taping them on new sheets of paper.
4. When you are satisfied with your changes, enter them in a *new copy* of your draft file. Always keep separate files for draft versions in case you need to go back to them.

Then, when you have a new version of your draft, you might want to team up with one or more classmates and read one another's work critically. The fresh eye you bring to the task can uncover shortcomings that would otherwise go unnoticed.

REVISING ON THE COMPUTER

Computer programs allow you to write over unwanted sections of your draft, add new information, cut useless material, track changes, and move parts of the text around—all without going to hard copy. Learn all the commands of your particular software and experiment to see exactly what your options are before trying to revise on-screen. The following tips will improve your efficiency:

1. Always keep backup copies of drafts, using the *Save As* function and renaming each revision. Selected parts of older versions may prove useful later, and new essays sometimes sprout from ideas in old drafts. In addition, accidentally erasing a file or losing work due to an electrical power surge is not uncommon. Save often, and set up the automatic save function to five-minute intervals.

2. Jot down helpful ideas or comments in your text as you revise. Enclose them with a special symbol, such as < >. Delete them later if they serve no purpose.

3. If you struggle with a section of the text, create two or three versions and then pick your favourite. You might even open a new file, experiment freely, and then use the best version in your draft.

4. Don't allow the program to control how you revise. Easy-to-use, gentle-touch keyboards can lull you into a lapse of judgment and cause you to forget whether your words are worth writing. Pages of worthless material could pile up. Furthermore, don't be tempted to do what the commands make easiest—fiddling and moving. Your job in revising is to develop the essay as a whole, not to tweak sentences or move blocks of text around indiscriminately.

5. If you have to do a major revision, consider doing it on a hard copy. Hard copy revisions allow you to see the "big picture" of your essay and to compare and work with several pages at once.

6. When you finish revising, check the coherence of your draft. The writing must flow smoothly at the points where you have added, deleted, or moved sections of text. Rewrite sentences so that they are clear and logical in their new positions.

7. Relying on spell-checking tools to proofread your paper can create problems. For example, a spell-checker can't judge whether you used the wrong word (*form* instead of *from*) or confused identical sounding but differently spelled words (*their, there, they're*). *You* are still the ultimate proofreader.

EXERCISE *Use the FACT acronym to revise the draft you prepared for the earlier exercise.*

Case History   (continued)

After setting her draft aside for a couple of days, Trudy revises it carefully. Compare the original draft with the revised version below. What changes has Trudy made?

A Memory

1   I remember watching Steven Villman in horrified awe during lunch times at my elementary school. Steven always seemed to have a dirty film covering his faded clothing, which was rumoured to have been bought at second-hand stores. He was a large boy with dark hair, who appeared to be born with strawberry jam stains around his mouth.

2   Sticks were his trademark. Every lunch hour Steven would rush outside to begin his search through the woods behind the school, in search of the best stick. Darting around the trees, he would run on his tiptoes, with a stick grasped tightly in his hand, waving about like a magic wand.

3   His high-pitched screeches and nonsense babbling would never fail to catch the attention of children deep in their play. Sometimes a couple of children would follow him, giggling about how weird he was.

4   One summer afternoon I was playing alone in a park in my neighbourhood. Suddenly, loud screeches alerted me as a large boy came running toward the park like a drunken ballerina. Two smaller boys trailed him with a look of mischief sparkling in their eyes. For their own amusement the boys were sneaking up behind Steven and screeching in his ear, just to watch Steven's terrified reaction. I stared with wide eyes and mouth open. Steven's stick shook uncontrollably as he bolted like a wild animal, trying to escape the bullies. I quickly pushed myself down the slide and made my way home to get some help.

5   Inside my home, I stood huffing and puffing as I informed my mother about what I had witnessed. I went on to explain how Steven was different from other kids. When I finished my story my mother took a deep breath. We headed back to the park immediately.

6   When we arrived at the park Steven was blubbering like a baby and hollering at the boys. Still fascinated as ever and untouched by Steven's

distress, the bullies failed to see my mother and me hustling over to where they stood, poking and laughing at Steven. With both hands on her hips my mother lectured, "You two should be ashamed of yourselves." Shocked, the bullies looked at one another and then just walked away, without even attempting to explain their behaviour. Steven watched them with a look of relief as they walked out of sight. "Where do you live, Steven?" Steven pointed. "That way." He looked toward the ground as he swayed from side to side, as if he were rocking himself to sleep. Without shoes or socks on his feet, he was covered from head to toe in dirt.

7   "C'mon Steven, we'll walk you home," my mother said dryly, as if she were angry. Now I know differently.

8   We walked down the road at a slow pace, listening to Steven's bare feet slap against the hot concrete with every step he took.

9   "Those bullies tricked me," Steven whined. "Why would they want my shoes anyway?" He concentrated on his feet as he walked. "Why do kids like them always bug me . . . and what's my mom gonna say?" Steven went on talking to himself rather than to my mother and me, and it's a good thing that he was, because it was obvious my mother had no explanations as to why people could be so mean.

10   After my mother and I brought Steven home, we walked back in silence. It seemed so unfair that Steven had to deal not only with his disability, but also with the stupidity of those who didn't understand. By walking Steven Villman home that day, I learned that we all need to take the time to understand people who are different from us.

Although this draft is not perfect, Trudy's revisions have considerably improved the paper. As Trudy continues polishing her essay, she can look for ways to cut unnecessary words. By finding more accurate word choice, she can make her essay even stronger. Never stop revising your essay until you are completely satisfied with the result.

This case history continues later in this chapter.

STRENGTHENING PARAGRAPH STRUCTURE AND DEVELOPMENT

Once you finish considering the essay as a whole, examine your paragraphs one by one, applying the *FACT* approach that you used for the whole paper. Make sure each paragraph *FITS* the paper's major focus and develops a single central idea. If a paragraph needs more support or examples, *ADD* whatever is necessary. If a paragraph contains ineffective or unhelpful material, *CUT* it. *TEST* the flow of ideas from paragraph to paragraph and clarify connections, both between and within paragraphs, as necessary. Ask the basic questions in the checklist that follows about each paragraph, and make any needed revisions.

REVISION CHECKLIST FOR PARAGRAPHS

- Does the paragraph have one, and only one, central idea?
- Does the central idea help to develop the thesis statement?
- Does each statement within the paragraph help to develop the central idea?
- Does the paragraph need additional explanations, examples, or supporting details?
- Would cutting some material make the paragraph stronger?
- Would reorganization make the ideas easier to follow?
- Can the connections between successive sentences be improved?
- Is each paragraph clearly and smoothly related to those that precede and follow it?

Don't expect to escape making any changes; some readjustments will undoubtedly be needed. Certain paragraphs may be stripped down or deleted entirely, others beefed up, and still others reorganized or repositioned. Chapter 4 contains more information on writing effective paragraphs.

EXERCISE *Here are two sample student paragraphs. Evaluate each according to the Revision Checklist for Paragraphs and suggest any necessary changes.*

1. For hours we had been waiting under the overhang of an abandoned hut. None of us had thought to bring ponchos on our short hike through the woods. Soon it would be dark. Earlier in the day it had been a perfectly clear day. We all agreed that we didn't want to stand here all night in the dark, so we decided to make a dash for it.

2. Canadians are beginning to become more and more conscious about the ingredients and production that goes in the food that they are ingesting. There are many reasons that Canadians are choosing to buy organic food whenever possible. With free-range chicken products, customers know exactly where their food is coming from. Free-range chickens are not raised in factories. They can run around. Vegetables that are grown organically in a garden taste better. People who want to have optimal health should also avoid unnecessary exposure to air-borne chemicals, and should get plenty of exercise.

WRITING THE INTRODUCTION AND CONCLUSION

If you've put off writing your introduction, do it now. (See Chapter 4 for suggestions and examples.) Generally, short papers begin with a single paragraph that includes the previously drafted thesis statement, which sometimes needs to be rephrased so that it meshes smoothly with the rest of the paragraph. The introduction acquaints the reader with your topic; it should clearly signal your intention as well as spark the reader's interest. The conclusion should follow the rest of your essay and should fit your purpose, as well as the type of writing you are doing. If you are writing to inform someone about a business plan, sometimes a summary is the best type of conclusion. For an illustration or persuasive piece of writing, you might want to extend the implications of what you have been writing about, leaving the reader with a question to ponder.

Even when you do not have time to revise extensively, you can almost always improve your writing by going back to the introduction and sharpening your focus. After you have finished a draft or two, you are usually much more clear about what you want to say than when you first sat down to write. Sometimes students actually benefit by starting a whole new draft, using what they thought to be a conclusion as a new starting point,

SELECTING A TITLE

All essays require titles. Unless a good title unexpectedly surfaces while you are writing, wait until you finish the paper before choosing one. Since the reader must see the connection between what the title promises and what the essay delivers, a good title must be both accurate and specific. A specific title suggests the essay's focus rather than just its topic. For example, "A Cruel Joke" is clearer and more precise than "A Memory."

Case History   (continued)

After carefully proofreading and fine-tuning her essay, Trudy prepares the final version, which follows. Margin notes highlight key changes. Compare the revised and final version for how these changes have improved the essay.

A Cruel Joke

I remember watching Steven Villman in horrified awe during lunch times at my elementary school. Steven always seemed to have a dirty film covering his faded clothing, rumoured to have been bought at second-hand stores. He was a large boy with dark hair, rough and choppy across his forehead, who appeared to have been born with strawberry jam stains around his mouth.

General title made more specific

Second sentence slightly condensed. Third sentence made more vivid, with more appropriate verb tense "to have been born."

Sticks were his trademark. Every lunch hour Steven would rush outside to begin his search through the woods behind the school, in search of the best stick. Darting around the trees, he would run on his tiptoes, with a stick grasped tightly in his hand, waving it about like a magic wand. His high-pitched screeches and nonsense babbling would never fail to catch the attention of children deep in their play. Sometimes a couple of children would follow him, giggling, as he performed his usual ritual. Children always found enough time to stop and stare, but never dared to invite him to join them in their play.

> Second and third paragraphs combined to improve coherence. Last sentence made more precise.

I remember one summer afternoon as I played alone in a park in my neighbourhood. Loud screeches alerted me as a large boy, whom I immediately recognized as Steven Villman, came running toward the park like a drunken ballerina. Two smaller boys trailed him with a look of mischief sparkling in their eyes. For their own amusement, the boys were sneaking up behind Steven and screeching in his ear, just to watch Steven's terrified reaction. I stared with wide eyes and mouth open. Steven's stick shook uncontrollably as he bolted like a startled deer, trying to escape the bullies. I quickly pushed myself down the slide and made my way home to get some help.

> Transition improved in the first sentence by the cue "I remember one summer afternoon" and the mention of Steven's name right away. "Wild animal" replaced with a more vivid image of "startled deer."

Inside my home, I stood huffing and puffing as I informed my mother about what I had witnessed. When I finished my story, my mother put down the dishes she was washing and took a deep breath as she dried her hands on a towel. We headed back to the park immediately.

> Unnecessary sentence deleted

> More explanation of what mother was doing

When we arrived at the park Steven was crying wildly and hollering at the boys. Still fascinated as ever and untouched by Steven's distress, the bullies failed to see my mother and me hustling over to where they stood, poking and laughing at Steven. With both hands on her hips my mother scolded, "You two should be ashamed of yourselves." Shocked, the bullies looked at one another and then just walked away, without even attempting to explain their behaviour. Steven watched them with a look of relief as they walked out of sight.

> Tone improved by replacing "blubbering" with "crying," the word "lectured" with "scolded"

"Where do you live, Steven?" my mother asked. "That way." Steven pointed. He looked toward the ground as he swayed from side to side, as if he were rocking himself to sleep. Without shoes or socks on his feet, he was covered from head to toe in dirt.

> New speaker identified with new paragraph

"C'mon Steven, we'll walk you home," my mother said dryly. At the time I thought she was angry with Steven for the trouble he brought to our

> Better development as possibilities for mother's anger are suggested

neighbourhood, or maybe at me for interrupting her dishwashing, but now I know she was angry about the cruelty of the bullies.

We walked down the road at a slow pace listening to Steven's bare feet slap against the hot concrete with every step he took.

"Those bullies tricked me," Steven whined. "Why would they want my shoes anyway?" He concentrated on his feet as he walked. "Why do kids like them always bug me? And what's my mom gonna say?" Steven went on talking to himself rather than to my mother and me, and it's a good thing he did, because it was obvious my mother had no explanation for why people could be so mean.

After my mother and I brought Steven home we walked back in silence. Steven's words burned in our minds. Why was it that Steven had to deal not only with his disability, but also with the stupidity of those who didn't understand? By walking Steven Villman home that day, I learned that sometimes the kindest thing is just to take the time to understand.

> Point of essay made clearer. Question is left in reader's mind as well as the writer's.

THE FINAL STAGE: PROOFREADING YOUR DRAFT

Proofreading is the final stage of writing. Check carefully for errors in grammar, punctuation, and spelling. Since we often overlook our own errors simply because we know what we mean, proofreading can be difficult. Some writers find that they catch problems when they read their own writing out loud. Others inch through the draft deliberately, moving a finger along slowly under every word. You can repeat this procedure several times, looking first for errors in grammar, then for sentence errors and problems in punctuation and mechanics, and finally for mistakes in spelling. Be especially alert for problems that have plagued your writing in the past.

Effective proofreading calls for you to assume a detective role and probe for errors that weaken your writing. If you accept the challenge, you will certainly improve the quality of your finished work.

PEER EVALUATION OF DRAFTS

At various points in the writing process, your instructor may ask you and your classmates to read and respond to one another's papers. Peer response often proves useful because even the best writers cannot always predict how their readers will react to their writing. For example, magazine articles designed to reduce the fear of AIDS have in some cases increased anxiety about the disease.

Furthermore, writers often have difficulty seeing the problems with their own drafts because so much hard work has gone into them. What seems clear and effective to you can be confusing or boring to your reader. Comments from peers can help you see your writing from a reader's point of view.

Just as the responses of others help you, so too will your responses help them. With another person's essay, you don't have the close, involved relationship that you have with your own. Therefore, you can assess other people's drafts objectively. Moreover, experience with the practice of doing peer reviews will eventually increase your awareness of your own writing strengths and weaknesses. Knowing how to read your own work critically is one of the most important writing skills you can develop.

Responding to Peer Drafts

Responding to someone else's writing is easier than you might imagine. It's not your job to spell out how to make the draft more effective, how to organize it, what to include, and what language to use. The writer must make these decisions. Your job is not to *solve* problems, but to *identify* them. You can do that best by responding honestly to the draft.

Some responses are more helpful than others. For example, saying that the draft "looks fine" does not help the writer. Such a response doesn't point to problem areas; rather it suggests that you didn't put much effort into reading the paper carefully and critically. If a friend were wondering whether to buy clothes that look terrible, would you not tell that person *in what way* the outfit was all wrong? It can take courage as well as attention to give specific, constructive feedback, but it is far more helpful in the long run than polite, generic praise. In addition, critical but vague comments, such as "The introduction is uninteresting," are not helpful either. Point out *why* it is uninteresting. For instance, you might note: "The introduction doesn't interest me because it is very technical, and I get lost. I ask myself why I should read on." Below is another example of an ineffective response and a more effective counterpart.

Ineffective:

The paper was confusing

Effective:

Paragraphs 2, 3, and 4 confused me.
You jumped around too much. First you
wrote about your experience on the first
day of college, then you went on to how
much you enjoyed junior high school, and
finally you wrote about what you want to do
for a career. I don't see how these ideas
relate or why they are in the order that they are.

Here are some steps to follow when responding to someone else's draft.

1. Read the essay from beginning to end without interruption.
2. On a separate sheet of paper, indicate what you consider to be the main idea. The writer can then see whether the intended message has come through.
3. Identify the greatest strength and the greatest problem/weakness of the paper. Writers need both positive and negative comments.
4. Reread the paper and write either specific responses to each paragraph or your responses to general questions such as the ones that follow. In either case, don't comment on spelling or grammar unless it really inhibits your reading.

PEER RESPONSE CHECKLIST

- What is the main point of this essay?
- What is the greatest strength? What is the greatest problem?
- What material doesn't seem to fit the main point or the audience?
- What questions has the author not answered?
- Where should more details or examples be added? Why?
- At what point does the paper fail to hold my interest? Why?
- Where is the organization confusing?
- Where is the writing unclear or vague?

As you learn more strategies for successful writing, you will be able to recognize more weaknesses and strengths in peer papers. In addition, the revision questions at the end of Chapters 6–12 can guide more in-depth peer review.

An Example of Peer Response

The following is the first draft of a student essay and a partial peer response to it. The response features three of the nine peer review questions listed above and also comments on one paragraph. Before you read the response, try evaluating this essay yourself, and then compare your reactions to those of the other student.

Captive Breeding in Zoos

1   This paper is about captive breeding. Today, humans hinder nature's species' right to survive. We are making it hard for over one hundred species of animals to continue to exist. But captive breeding in the world's zoos may be just what the doctor ordered. This rescue attempt is a complex and difficult undertaking. Captive breeding of endangered species is complicated by the special social and physical requirements of individual species.

2   There are many social problems that have to be solved for the successful reproduction of endangered species in zoos. Mating is one of the most important of these problems. One propagation "must" for many felines, pandas, and pygmy hippopotamuses is the complete separation of sexes until they're "ready." Leland Stowe says that cheetahs almost never get together unless they can't see or smell each other ahead of time. When females exhibit a certain behaviour, they bring on the male.

3   Male-female compatibility is a social problem. Great apes seem to be as particular as people in choosing mates. Stowe tells about an orangutan that turned a cold shoulder on the females in the U.S. National Zoo located in Washington, D.C. Then they shipped him to the zoo in Toronto. There, he took up with one of the females. The curator of the zoo, William Zanten, says he's "been siring offspring ever since."

4   Social factors hurt care of infant primates. Sheldon Campbell talks about this in Smithsonian magazine. He writes about the problems of breeding golden marmosets. These are monkeys that live in Brazil. The scientists found that captive-born parents neglected their young. Sometimes they even killed them. The problem was due to the fact that the marmosets had no experience living in a family situation. They didn't know what to do. Emily Hahn writes about gorillas in The New Yorker. She says that those raised by humans make poor mothers. Those raised by dutiful mothers make good parents.

5   The second important stumbling block to successful captive breeding is physical problems. Ignorance of dietary needs can be bad. Stowe talks about the captive breeding of gorillas and says that when this breeding was first getting started, infants exhibited a very high mortality rate. Then the babies were given iron and meat protein, the latter rich in vitamin B-12. They were sprinkled on bananas, and the bananas were fed to the babies. The survival rate markedly improved.

6   Animals can be bred more easily if they are in an environment that duplicates that animal's natural habitat. Hooved and horned animals are an easy job because of the similarity in terrain and climate of their natural habitats to zoo habitats. Polar bears are a lot tougher. Mothers want to be left alone until their cubs are up and about. Because of this fact, the bears often kill their babies. Stowe says they solved this problem by building replicas of arctic ice caves. The mothers and cubs are left alone until they emerge from the cave. John Perry, Director of the U.S. National Zoo, said this:

The world is our zoo—a zoo that must be well managed, its resources carefully husbanded, for these are the only resources it can ever have. We have appointed ourselves the keepers of this zoo, but we cannot live outside its gates. We are of it. Our lives are inextricably intertwined with the lives of all that live within. Their fate will be ours.

7   Our endangered species can survive only by nature's implacable test—sustained births by second and third generations. It will take decades to reach such a verdict of success. Thus we can see that captive breeding is beset by many problems

What is the main point of this essay?

I think this paper is saying that the only chance for endangered species is that they reproduce in zoos but that it is hard to get them to breed in captivity.

What is the greatest strength?

I hadn't thought much about this question, so it was something new for me. I liked the examples about specific animals and the problems that they have in captivity. I especially liked the fact that the writer gave me several problems that occur when animals are bred in captivity. The writer didn't oversimplify.

What is the greatest problem/weakness?

I can't see how the paragraphs connect to the main part of the paper or to each other. They seem disconnected. What does Male-female compatibility is a social problem have to do with the problem of reproduction or with the previous paragraph on mating? Also, there are a number of very unclear statements that leave me with many questions. How are we making it hard for over a hundred species to exist? What do you mean when you say Almost never get together, bring on the male, took up with, and an easy job?

Response to paragraph 4

Do social factors always hurt the care of infant primates? Your statement seems too general. Shouldn't

you combine some of your sentences? The first six
sentences seem to abruptly jump from one point
to the next; the writing is not smooth. How did
you get from marmosets to gorillas? The jump
confuses me. Also, were the dutiful mothers
humans or gorillas?

ACTING UPON YOUR PEERS' RESPONSES

Sometimes you need strong nerves to act upon a peer response. You can easily
become defensive or discount your reader's comments as foolish. Remember,
however, that as a writer you are trying to communicate with your readers, and
that means taking seriously the problems your readers identify. Of course, you
decide which responses are appropriate; but even an inappropriate criticism
sometimes sets off a train of thought that leads to good ideas for revision.

Examine the revised version of the captive breeding essay that follows and
note how the writer has taken some of the peer responses into account. Clear
transition sentences link paragraphs to the thesis statement and to each other.
Vague statements identified in the earlier draft have been clarified. In paragraph 4, the writer connects the discussion of the marmosets to that of the
gorillas by changing the order of the sentences and combining them, thereby
identifying poor parenting as the key problem with both kinds of primates.
Finally, she indicates what she means by "dutiful mother."

As you read this version, carefully examine the margin notes, which highlight key features of the revision.

Captive Breeding: Difficult but Necessary

| | | Title: specific and accurate |

1   Today, as in the past, humans encroach upon the basic right of nature's
species to survive. Through ignorance, oversight, and technological developments, we are threatening the survival of over one hundred animal species.
Until their environments can be safeguarded against harmful human intrusion,
the last chance for the threatened species may be captive breeding in zoos.
But this rescue attempt is a complex and difficult undertaking. In particular,
each species presents social and physical problems that must be solved if
breeding is to succeed.

Introduction: arresting statement

Thesis statement and statement of organization

2   Among the social problems that complicate successful reproduction, mating problems loom especially large. For instance, the male and female of many
feline species must be kept completely separated until both animals are ready
to mate. Leland Stowe, writing in *National Wildlife* magazine, notes that cheetahs almost never mate unless kept where the one cannot see or smell the
other. Once the female shows signs of receptivity, a male is placed in her cage,

Topic sentence with link to thesis statement

Specific details: problems with cheetahs

and mating then occurs. Pandas and pygmy hippopotamuses show the same behaviour.

3   A related social problem with certain species is male-female compatibility. Great apes, for instance, seem to be as particular as human beings in choosing mates. Stowe relates an amusing case of a male orangutan that totally spurned the females in the Washington, D.C., National Zoo. Shipped to a zoo in Toronto, he succumbed to the charms of a new face and has, according to curator William Zanten, "been siring offspring ever since."

4   Social factors can also imperil proper care of infant primates. In a *Smithsonian* magazine article, Sheldon Campbell talks about the problems scientists encountered in trying to breed golden marmosets, a species of Brazilian monkey. Early attempts failed because the captive-born parents neglected and sometimes accidentally killed their babies. Observation showed that the problem occurred because the marmosets had no experience living in a family situation—they simply didn't know how to handle their offspring. Gorillas reared by humans may also make poor mothers, reports Emily Hahn in *The New Yorker*. On the other hand, those reared by dutiful mothers, whether human or gorilla, are usually good parents themselves.

5   Physical problems rival social problems as stumbling blocks to successful captive breeding. Ignorance of a species' dietary needs, for instance, can have disastrous consequences. Early in the captive breeding of gorillas, infants exhibited a very high mortality rate, Stowe notes. Then meat protein and iron, the former rich in vitamin B-12, were sprinkled on bananas and fed to the babies. As a result, the survival rate markedly improved.

6   An environment that duplicates a species' natural habitat favours easy propagation. Hooved and horned animals present few breeding problems because the zoo habitats are similar in terrain and climate to their natural habitats. Polar bears, on the other hand, present difficult problems. Unless the mothers have complete privacy until the cubs can get around, they often kill the babies. To prevent this from happening, Stowe says, zoos now construct replicas of arctic ice caves and leave mothers and cubs completely alone until the new family emerges from the cave.

7   In his book *The World's a Zoo*, John Perry, director of the U.S. National Zoo, has spoken of the need to save our endangered species:

> The world is our zoo—a zoo that must be well managed, its resources carefully husbanded, for these are the only resources it can ever have. We have appointed ourselves the keepers of this zoo, but we cannot live outside its gates. We are of it.

Our lives are inextricably intertwined with the lives of all that live within. Their
fate will be ours.

The difficulty, unfortunately, is as great as the urgency of this problem. Only
sustained births by second- and third-generation captive animals can ensure
the survival of our endangered species. And it will take decades to achieve the
necessary success.

COLLABORATIVE WRITING

In many professions, workers have to cooperate as a group to produce documents. Recognizing this fact, many instructors assign collaborative writing
projects. Writing as part of a group offers some advantages but poses some interesting challenges. A group can draw on many different perspectives and areas of
expertise, split up the work, and enjoy the feedback of a built-in peer group. On
the other hand, the group must also coordinate several efforts, resolve conflicts
over the direction of the project, deal with people who may not do their fair
share, and integrate different styles of writing.

Moreover, even though you write as part of a group, the final product
should read as though it were written by one person. Therefore, take great pains
to ensure that the paper doesn't resemble a patchwork quilt. You can help
achieve this goal by following the principles of good writing discussed throughout this book. Here are some suggestions for successful collaborative work:

1. Select a leader with strong organizational skills.
2. Make sure each person has every other group member's phone number
   and email address.
3. Analyze the project and develop a work plan with clearly stated deadlines
   for each step of the project.
4. Assign tasks on the basis of people's interests and expertise.
5. Schedule regular meetings to gauge each person's progress.
6. Encourage ideas and feedback from all members at each meeting.
7. If each member is working on a different portion of the paper, submit
   each contribution to other members of the group for peer evaluation.
8. To ensure that the finished product is written in one style and fits together
   as a whole, assign one person to compile the submissions and write the
   complete draft.
9. Allow plenty of time to review the complete draft so necessary changes
   can be made.

Collaborative writing provides an opportunity to learn a great deal from
other students. However, problems arise if one or more group members don't
do their work or skip meetings entirely. This irresponsibility compromises everyone's grade. The group should insist that all members participate, and the
leader should immediately contact anyone who misses a meeting. If a serious
problem develops despite these efforts, contact your instructor. But keep in

mind that working out the groupwork challenges is part of the assignment, and some instructors expect groups to solve these problems on their own.

COLLABORATION USING EMAIL

Increasing numbers of college students are using email to collaborate on writing projects. Email allows you to exchange material and comment at every stage of the writing process. For example, you can share

> Brainstorming ideas developed during the search for a writing topic
> Brainstorming ideas developed during the search for supporting information
> Tentative thesis statements or any general statements that will shape the document
> Individual sections of the writing project
> Copies of the entire original draft

Whenever you use email for collaborative writing, it's a good idea to designate a project leader to ensure that all members participate and to receive and distribute all materials. Your instructor may request copies of the email exchanges in order to follow your work.

MAINTAINING AND REVIEWING A PORTFOLIO

A portfolio is an organized collection of your writing, usually kept in a binder or folder. It's a good idea to retain all your work for each assignment, including the instruction sheet, your prewriting notes, and all your drafts, in case the instructor asks to see them. Organize this material either in the order of completion or by type of assignment.

Why keep a portfolio? Not only can a portfolio be a source of ideas for future writing, but it also allows you to review the progress of your current papers. In addition, should any confusion arise about a grade or an assignment, the contents of your portfolio can quickly clarify matters.

Moreover, some instructors may require you to maintain a portfolio. They will probably specify both what is to be included and how it is to be organized. Many instructors believe that portfolios help students track their progress. Furthermore, portfolios give your instructor a complete picture of all your work.

You can review your own portfolio to gain a better understanding of your writing capabilities. Answer these questions as you look over your materials:

1. With what assignments or topics was I most successful? Why?
2. What assignments or topics gave me the most problems? Why?
3. How has my planning changed? How can I make it more effective?
4. What makes my best writing good? How does this writing differ from my other work?
5. What are the problem areas in my weakest writing? How does this writing differ from my other work?

6. Did I make significant changes in response to my own critical review, a peer evaluation, or my instructor's comments? If not, why not? What kinds of changes did I make? What changes would improve the quality of my work?

7. What organizational patterns have I used? (See Chapters 6–11.) Which ones have been effective? Why? Which ones have given me trouble? Why?

8. What kinds of introductions have I used? What other options do I have for effective introductions?

9. What kinds of conclusions have I used? What other options do I have for effective conclusions?

10. What kinds of grammar or spelling errors mar my writing? Focus on these errors in future proofreading.

CHAPTER 6

Strategies for Personal Writing: Narration and Description

DRAWING FROM EXPERIENCE: NARRATIVE

Clicking off the evening news and padding toward bed, Heloise suddenly glimpsed, out of the corner of her eye, a shadow stretching across the living room floor from under the drawn curtains.

"Wh—who's there?"

No response.

Edging backward toward the phone, her eyes riveted on the shadow, she stammered, "I—I don't have any money."

Still no answer.

Reaching the phone, she gripped the receiver and started to lift it from its cradle. Just then . . .

Just now you've glimpsed the start of a *narrative*. A narrative relates a series of events. The events may be real—as in histories, biographies, or news stories—or imaginary, as in short stories and novels. The narrative urge stirs in all of us, and like everyone else, you have responded almost from the time you began to talk. As a child, you probably traded many stories with your friends, recounting an exciting visit to a circus or amusement park or an unusually funny experience with your pet. Today you may tell a friend about the odd happening in your biology laboratory or on the job.

Many classroom and on-the-job writing occasions call for narratives. Your English instructor might want you to trace the development of some literary character. Your history instructor might have you recap the events leading to a major war, or your sociology instructor could have you relate your unfolding relations with a stepparent or someone else. At work, a police officer may record the events leading to an arrest, a scientist recount the development of a research project, and a department manager prepare a brief history of an employee's work problems.

PURPOSE

A narrative, like any other kind of writing, makes a point or has a purpose. The point can either be stated or left unstated, but it always shapes the writing. Although some narratives simply tell what happened or establish an interesting or useful fact, most narratives go beyond merely reciting events. Narratives of history and biography delve into the motives underlying the events and lives they portray, while narratives of personal experience offer lessons and insights. In the following conclusion to a narrative about an encounter with a would-be mugger, the writer offers an observation on self-respect.

> I kept my self-respect, even at the cost of dirtying my fists with violence, and I feel that I understand the Irish and the Cypriots, the Israelis and the Palestinians, all those who seem to us to fight senseless wars for senseless reasons, better than before. For what respect does one keep for oneself if one isn't in the last resort ready to fight and say, "You punk!"?
>
> Harry Fairlie, "A Victim Fights Back"

ACTION

Action plays a central role in any narrative. Other writing often only suggests action, leaving readers to imagine it for themselves:

> A hundred thousand people were killed by the atomic bomb, and these six were among the survivors. They still wonder why they lived when so many others died. Each of them counts many small items of chance or volition—a step taken in time, a decision to go indoors, catching one streetcar instead of the next—that spared him. And now each knows that in the act of survival he lived a dozen lives and saw more death than he ever thought he would see. At the time, none of them knew anything.
>
> John Hersey, *Hiroshima*

This passage suggests a great deal of action—the flash of an exploding bomb, the collapse of buildings, screaming people fleeing the scorching devastation—but *it does not present the action.* Narration, however, recreates action:

> When I pulled the trigger I did not hear the bang or feel the kick—one never does when a shot goes home—but I heard the devilish roar of glee that went up

from the crowd. In that instant, in too short a time, one would have thought, even for the bullet to get there, a mysterious, terrible change had come over the elephant. He neither stirred nor fell, but every line of his body had altered. He looked suddenly stricken, shrunken, immensely old, as though the frightful impact of the bullet had paralyzed him without knocking him down. At last, after what seemed a long time—it might have been five seconds, I dare say—he sagged flabbily to his knees. His mouth slobbered. An enormous senility seemed to have settled upon him. One could have imagined him thousands of years old. I fired again into the same spot. At the second shot he did not collapse but climbed with desperate slowness to his feet and stood weakly upright, with legs sagging and head drooping. I fired a third time. That was the shot that did it for him. You could see the agony of it jolt his whole body and knock the last remnant of strength from his legs. But in falling he seemed for a moment to rise, for as his hind legs collapsed beneath him he seemed to tower upward like a huge rock toppling, his trunk reaching skywards like a tree. He trumpeted, for the first and only time. And then down he came, his belly towards me, with a crash that seemed to shake the ground even where I lay.

George Orwell, "Shooting an Elephant"

Orwell's account offers a stark, vivid replay of the shooting, leaving nothing significant for the reader to infer.

A few words of caution are in order here. Action entails not only exotic events, such as the theft of mass-destruction weapons, then the ransom demand, then the recovery of the weapons and the pursuit of the villains; but a wide variety of more normal events also qualify as action, such as a long, patient wait that comes to nothing, an unexpected kiss after some friendly assistance, a disappointing gift that signals a failed relationship. Furthermore, the narrative action must all relate to the main point—not merely chronicle a series of events.

CONFLICT

The events in our lives and our world are often shaped by conflicts that need to be resolved. In narrative writing, conflict and its resolution, if any, usually motivate and often structure the action. Some conflicts pit one individual against another or against a group, such as a union, company, or religious body. In other cases, the conflict may be between a person and nature. Often the conflict is an inner one that involves clashing impulses inside one person's head. In the following student paragraph, note how common sense and fear struggle within the writer, who has experienced a sharp, stabbing pain in his side:

Common sense and fear waged war in my mind. The first argued that a pain so intense was nothing to fool with, that it might indicate a serious or even life-threatening condition. Dr. Montz would be able to identify the problem and deal with it before it worsened. But what if it was already serious? What if I needed emergency surgery? I didn't want anyone cutting into me. "Now wait a minute," I said. "It's probably nothing serious. Most aches and pains aren't. I'll see the doctor, maybe get some pills, and the problem will clear up overnight. But what if he finds something major, and I have to spend the night in the hospital getting ready for surgery or recovering from it? I think I'll just ignore the pain."

Luis Rodriguez, student

POINT OF VIEW

Narrative writers may adopt either a first-person or third-person point of view. In first-person narratives, one of the participants tells what happened, whereas a third-person narrator tells the story from an outside perspective. Narratives you write about yourself use the first person, as do autobiographies. Biographies and histories use the third person, and fiction employs both points of view.

In first-person narration, pronouns such as *I, me, mine, we,* and *ours* identify the storyteller. With the third person, the narrator remains unmentioned, and the characters are identified by nouns and such pronouns as *he, she, him,* and *her.* These two paragraphs illustrate the difference:

First-Person Narration

After that I took the beer to the front verandah, and some bread and cheese for our supper to have with it, and I sat out there with Nancy and Jamie Walsh while the sun declined, and it became too dark to sew. It was a lovely and windless evening, and the birds were twittering, and the trees in the orchard near the road were golden in the late sunlight, and the purple milkweed flowers that grew beside the drive smelled very sweetly; and also the last few peonies beside the verandah, and the climbing roses; and the coolness came down out of the air, while Jamie sat and played on his flute, so plaintively it did your heart good. After a while McDermott came skulking around the side of the house like a tamed wolf, and leant against the side of the house, and listened also. And there we were, in a kind of harmony; and the evening was so beautiful, that it made a pain in my heart, as when you cannot tell whether you are happy or sad; and I thought that if I could have a wish, it would be that nothing would ever change, and we could stay that way forever.

Margaret Atwood, *Alias Grace*

As this example shows, first-person narrators may refer to other characters in the narrative by using nouns and third-person pronouns.

Third-Person Narration

People driving by don't notice Spit Delaney. His old gas station is nearly hidden now behind the firs he's let grow up along the road, and he doesn't bother to whitewash the scalloped row of half-tires someone planted once instead of fence. And rushing by on the Island highway today, heading north or south, there's little chance that anyone will notice Spit Delaney seated on the big rock at the side of his road-end, scratching at his narrow chest, or hear him muttering to the flat grey highway and to the scrubby firs and to the useless old ears of his neighbour's dog that he'll be damned if he can figure out what it is that is happening to him.

Jack Hodgins, "Separating"

KEY EVENTS

Any narrative includes many separate events, enough to swamp your narrative boat if you try to pack them all in. Suppose you wish to write about your recent attack of appendicitis in order to make a point about heeding early warnings of an oncoming illness. Your list of events might look like this:

Awakened	Greeted fellow	Ate lunch
Showered	employees	Returned to work
Experienced acute	Began morning's	Began afternoon's
but passing pain	work	work
in abdomen	Felt nauseated	Collapsed at work
Dressed	Met with boss	station
Ate breakfast	Took coffee break	Was rushed to
Opened garage door	Visited bathroom	hospital
Started car	Experienced more	Underwent
Drove to work	prolonged pain in	diagnostic tests
Parked in employee	abdomen	Had emergency
lot	Walked to cafeteria	operation
Entered building		

A narrative that included all, or even most, of these events would be bloated and ineffective. Thus you need to be selective, building your narrative around key events that bear directly on your purpose. Include just enough incidental details or events to keep the narrative flowing smoothly, but treat them in sketchy fashion. The pain and nausea certainly qualify as key events. Here's how you might present the first attack of pain:

My first sign of trouble came shortly after I stepped out of the shower. I had just finished towelling when a sharp pain in my lower right side sent me staggering into the bedroom, where I collapsed onto an easy chair in the corner. Biting my lip to hide my groans, I sat twisting in agony as the pain gradually ebbed, leaving me grey-faced, sweat-drenched, and shaken. What, I asked myself, had been the trouble? Was it ulcers? Was it a gallbladder attack? Did I have stomach cancer?

This passage does not simply summarize or tell that an event happened, but actively shows that an attack has occurred. Its details vividly convey the nature of the attack as well as the reactions of the victim. As in any good narrative, the writer communicates an experience to the reader.

DIALOGUE

Dialogue, or conversation, animates many narratives, enlivening the action and helping draw the reader into the story. Written conversation, however, does not duplicate real talk. When speaking with friends, we repeat ourselves, throw in irrelevant comments, use slang, lose our train of thought, and overuse expressions like *you know, uh,* and *well.* Dialogue that reproduced actual conversation would weaken any narrative.

Good dialogue resembles real conversation without copying it. It is selective, featuring economical sentences while avoiding the over-repetition of phrases such as *she said* and *he replied.* If the conversation unfolds smoothly, the speaker's identity is clear. To heighten the sense of reality, the writer may use an occasional sentence fragment, slang expression, or pause, as in this passage:

> Mom was waiting for me when I entered the house.
>
> "Your friends. They've been talking to you again. Trying to persuade you to change your mind about not going into baseball. Honey, I wish you'd listen to them. You're a terrific ballplayer. Just look at all the trophies and awards you've . . . " She paused. "Joe's mother called me this morning and asked if you were playing in the game on Saturday. Davey, I wish you would. You haven't played for two weeks. Please. I want you to. For me. It would be so good for you to go and—and do what you've always . . . "
>
> "O.K., Mom, I'll play," I said. "But remember, it's just for you."
>
> Diane Pickett, student

Note the mother's use of the slang expression "terrific" and of sentence fragments like "your friends" and "for me," as well as the shift in her train of thought and the repetition of "and." These strategies lend an air of realism to the mother's words.

Besides making your dialogue realistic, be sure that you also punctuate it correctly. Here are some key guidelines: Each shift from one speaker to another requires a new paragraph. When an expression like *he said* interrupts a single quoted sentence, set it off with commas. When such an expression comes between two complete quoted sentences, put a period after the expression and capitalize the first word of the second sentence. Commas and periods that come at the end of direct quotations are placed inside the quotation marks. Our example illustrates most of these guidelines.

WRITING A NARRATIVE
Planning and Drafting the Narrative

Most of the narratives you write for a composition class will relate a personal experience and therefore use the first person. On occasion, though, you may write about someone else and therefore use the third person. In either case, make sure the experience you choose illustrates some point. A paper that indicates only how you violated a friend's confidence may meander along to little purpose. But if that paper is shaped by some point you wish to make—for instance, that you gained insight into the obligations of friendship—the topic can be worthwhile. To get started, do some guided brainstorming, asking yourself these questions:

What experience in my life or that of someone I know would be worth narrating?

What point does this experience illustrate? (Try to state the point in one or two sentences.)

What people were involved and what parts did they play?

When you have pinpointed a topic, use further brainstorming to garner supporting material. Here are some helpful questions:

What background information is needed to understand the events?

What action should I include?

What is the nature of the conflict? Was it resolved? If so, how?

Which events play key roles, which are secondary, and which should go unmentioned?

Is any dialogue necessary?

Before you start to write, you might develop a plot outline showing the significant events in your narrative. For each one, jot down what you saw, heard, or did, and what you thought or felt.

Use the opening of your paper to set the stage for what follows. You might tell when and where the action occurred, provide helpful background information, note the incident that activated the chain of events, or identify the problem from which the action grew. If you state your main point directly, do it here or in the conclusion.

The body of the narrative should move the action forward until a turning point is about to be reached. Build the body around your key events. To prevent your reader from feeling stranded, use time signals whenever the development of the action might be unclear. Words, phrases, and clauses like *now, next, finally, after an hour,* and *when I returned* help the reader understand the sequence of events. Don't get carried away, though; a paper loaded with time signals makes the sequence seem more important than the events themselves. Finally, think about how you can best use conflict and dialogue to heighten narrative interest.

The conclusion should tie up any loose ends, settle any unresolved conflicts, and lend an air of completion to the narrative. Effective strategies to think about include introducing a surprise twist, offering a reflective summary, noting your reaction to the story's events, or discussing the aftermath.

Revising the Narrative

As you revise, follow the guidelines in Chapter 5, and in addition ask yourself these questions:

Have I made the point, stated or unstated, that I intended?

Does all of the action relate to the main point?

Is the conflict handled appropriately?

Have I included all of the key events that relate to my purpose? given each the right emphasis? used time indicators where needed?

Is my point of view appropriate?

Does my dialogue ring true?

EXAMPLE OF A STUDENT ESSAY OF NARRATION

Christmas Surprise

Rita White

1   A week before this last Christmas, the nurses who were due to work in our unit on Christmas Day planned to have a potluck as our Christmas lunch. My husband was visiting his relatives in Ontario, and I had time—too much time—to think about what to make. My favourite colleagues, Janet, Aurora, Sally, and Brenda, were working that day, and I wanted to impress them.

2   I decided I would make wonton soup.

3   At home, I searched through my collection of recipes, which were piled up in the corner of my living room. This corner is always messy. All my course books, cookbooks, and my husband's joke books are jumbled together. I promised myself many times to keep that corner better organized, but then I forget all my promises and get busy with something else—in this case, working on my recipe. I was pleasantly surprised to find it waiting for me right on top of the pile.

4   Even though I was alone on Christmas Eve, I was surprised I did not feel lonely at all. I guess it was because I was busy with all my shopping and preparation for the wonton. I chose to wrap the wonton in the Chinese imperial style which makes each wonton look like a flower. I wanted the soup to be outstanding.

5   On Christmas Day, early in the morning, I grabbed everything I needed—my rice cooker, a big bowl, and of course, the wontons, and drove to work feeling both happy and a bit nervous. At the hospital parking lot, I met Brenda who carried a big box of food. I was anxious to know what kind of food she was going to make because she was famous for her desserts, especially her Dutch apple pie and angel food cake. I must admit that I was worried about how my wonton would compare.

6   The morning seemed to drag along. Dr. Glazos, as usual, made his ward round slowly. By the time the ward round team was at my patient's bedside, it was already eleven o'clock. I was a bit worried that I might not have enough time to prepare my soup. I presented my case as quickly as possible and hoped that the round would be uncomplicated. Surprisingly, it took only ten minutes to finish the presentation. Suddenly Dr. Glazos stretched out his hand and shook hands with me. He wished me Merry Christmas and gave me a complimentary card for a Latte at the Second Cup coffee shop. I was happily surprised, particularly as Dr. Glazos, who is always serious at work and never smiles when he is working, actually smiled. I was tempted to invite him to try my wonton soup but I was afraid the other nurses would be annoyed.

7   I suddenly realized it was already fifteen minutes past eleven. I had only fifteen minutes to get my soup ready. I asked Aurora, who was in my cubicle, to keep an eye on my patient while I sneaked out to the pantry to start cooking. The water in the rice cooker always takes a long time to boil but it seemed to take even longer this time. At half past eleven, all these hungry nurses started coming in to the nurses' lounge, hoping to taste someone else's food. Finally at twenty to twelve my soup was ready to serve. It was really very presentable with white wonton floating in the hot chicken broth which was decorated with green onions and cherry blossom shaped carrots. As I looked at it, I was reminded of water lilies floating on a pond in the early morning mist. The comforting aroma wafted through the lounge. I compared my soup to the other dishes on the table, and felt proud.

8   Suddenly I started to worry again. The first round nurses were not too enthusiastic about my soup. Sally ate only two wontons instead of the three that

everybody usually takes. Brenda and the two other nurses did not even touch the soup because they did not eat pork, which was the main ingredient of the wonton. Disappointed, I worried that the whole bowl of wonton would be wasted. I decided the only way to hide this embarassment was to eat more myself so that there would not be too much left behind. I was so full afterwards that I did not have enough room to sample the dishes the other nurses brought in. When the first group of nurses finished their lunches, the second group had their turn. I went back to the unit and waited anxiously for their response. I felt like I was waiting for the results of an examination.

9   To my surprise again, this group of nurses nearly cleaned out the wonton soup. They complimented me on how delicious it was, saying that they had never tasted such good wonton before. Thrilled, I promised to copy down my recipe for them. My recipe became a hot topic around the unit.

10   I was surprised that making a bowl of soup kept me from being lonely when my husband was away and helped to me to socialize with my co-workers. In fact the whole experience was full of surprises. I think next year I will put a sprig of holly in the soup and call it Christmas Surprise.

DISCUSSION QUESTIONS

1. Identify the point of view of the narrative.
2. List the words, phrases, and clauses that serve as time signals. What has the writer accomplished by using them?
3. This narrative spans about a week. At what points has the writer omitted events? Why?
4. What larger point does the narrative make? Is it stated or implied?

SUGGESTIONS FOR WRITING

1. **Write a personal narrative about an experience that**
   a. altered either your opinion of a friend or acquaintance or your views about some important matter;
   b. taught you a lesson or something about human nature;
   c. caused you great sorrow or joy; or
   d. exposed you to the danger of serious injury or death.
   Keep in mind all the key narrative elements: purpose, action, conflict, point of view, key events, and dialogue.
2. **A maxim is a concise statement of a generally recognized truth. Noting the key elements above, write a personal narrative that illustrates one of the following maxims or another that your instructor approves:**

a. A little learning is a dangerous thing.

b. The more things change, the more they stay the same.

c. You'll catch more flies with honey than with vinegar.

d. Don't judge a book by its cover.

DESCRIPTION: DRAWING FROM OBSERVATION

A narrative often blends in description of details and impressions and events to advance the storyline. Occasionally description stands alone as, for example, in a description of lab report procedures. Usually, however, description is a part of other kinds of writing such as histories, biographies, fiction and poetry, journalism and advertising. Some descriptions create images and mood, such as when a writer paints a word picture of a boggy, fog-shrouded moor. Description can also stimulate understanding or lead to action. A historian may juxtapose the splendour of French court life with the wretchedness of a Paris slum to help explain the French Revolution. Vivid, telling descriptions of objects, persons, scenes, and events that appeal to the reader's senses can enrich your writing. For example, if you were writing a description of food cooking in a county fair, you might choose details that would appeal not only to the reader's sense of sight, but also to the reader's sense of hearing, taste, and smell, as well as touch. Consider the use of sensory impressions in the following description a student wrote about food at a county fair.

> The sound of hot dogs sizzling on a grease-spattered grill gave way to the whirling buzz of a cotton-candy machine. Fascinated, we watched as the white cardboard cone was slowly transformed into a pink, fluffy cloud. Despite their fibreglass appearance, the sticky puffs dissolved on my tongue into a sugar-like sweetness. Soon our faces and hands were gummed with a sticky mess.

A description in a report often strives for objectivity; but a description in other kinds of writing highlights and evokes impressions and emotional responses. The human mind is not merely a logical thinking machine. Because of our emotional makeup, we react with shock to a photo of a battered victim of child abuse. We feel stirrings of nostalgia upon hearing a song from our past. We smile with satisfaction when quenching our summer thirst with tart sips from a tall, frosted drink. Responses like these, as much as rational responses, are the goal of descriptive writing.

Many occasions call for description. Your chemistry instructor might ask you to characterize the appearance and odour of a series of substances prepared in the laboratory; your art instructor might want you to describe a painting; your hospitality management instructor might have you portray an appealing banquet room. On the job, a realtor might write a glowing advertisement to sell a house; a nurse might describe the postoperative status of a surgical incision; and a journalist might describe the eruption of a volcano. All are attempts to capture the world through description.

SENSORY IMPRESSIONS

Precise sensory impressions begin with close physical or mental observation. If you can re-examine your subject, do it. If not, recall it to mind; then capture its features with appropriate words. When you can't find the right words, try a comparison. Ask yourself what your subject (or part of it) might be likened to. Does it smell like a rotten egg? A ripe cantaloupe? Burning rubber? Does it sound like a high sigh? A soft rustle? To come across, the comparison must be accurate and familiar. If the reader has never smelled a rotten egg, the point is lost.

Most descriptions blend several sense impressions rather than focus on just one. In the following excerpt, Mark Twain, reminiscing about his uncle's farm, includes all five. As you read it, note which impressions are most effective.

> As I have said, I spent some part of every year at the farm until I was twelve or thirteen years old. The life which I led there with my cousins was full of charm, and so is the memory of it yet. I can call back the solemn twilight and mystery of the deep woods, the earthy smells, the faint odors of the wild flowers, the sheen of rain-washed foliage, the rattling clatter of drops when the wind shook the trees, the far-off hammering of woodpeckers and the muffled drumming of wood pheasants in the remoteness of the forest, the snapshot glimpses of disturbed wild creatures scurrying through the grass—I can call it all back and make it as real as it ever was, and as blessed. I can call back the prairie, and its loneliness and peace, and a vast hawk hanging motionless in the sky, with his wings spread wide and the blue of the vault showing through the fringe of their end feathers. I can see the woods in their autumn dress, the oaks purple, the hickories washed with gold, the maples and the sumacs luminous with crimson fires, and I can hear the rustle made by the fallen leaves as we plowed through them. I can see the blue clusters of wild grapes hanging among the foliage of the saplings, and I remember the taste of them and the smell. I know how the wild blackberries looked, and how they tasted, and the same with the pawpaws, the hazelnuts, and the persimmons; and I can feel the thumping rain, upon my head, of hickory nuts and walnuts when we were out in the frosty dawn to scramble for them with the pigs, and the gusts of wind loosed them and sent them down. I know the stain of blackberries, and how pretty it is, and I know the stain of walnut hulls, and how little it minds soap and water, also what grudged experience it had of either of them. I know the taste of maple sap, and when to gather it, and how to arrange the troughs and the delivery tubes, and how to boil down the juice, and how to hook the sugar after it is made, also how much better hooked sugar tastes than any that is honestly come by, let bigots say what they will.
>
> Mark Twain, *Autobiography*

EXERCISE *Spend some time in an environment such as a cafeteria or a city intersection. Concentrate on one sense at a time. Begin by observing what you see; then jot down the precise impressions you receive. Now do the same for impressions of touch, taste, smell, and sound.*

DOMINANT IMPRESSION

Skilful writers select and express sensory perceptions in order to create a *dominant impression*—an overall mood or feeling such as joy, anger, terror, or distaste. This impression may be identified or left for the reader to discover. Whatever the choice, a verbal picture of a storm about to strike, for example, might be crafted to evoke feelings of fear by describing sinister masses of slaty clouds, cannon salvos of thunder, blinding lightning flashes, and viciously swirling wind-caught dust.

The following paragraph establishes a sense of security as the dominant impression:

> A marvelous stillness pervaded the world, and the stars together with the serenity of their rays seemed to shed upon the earth the assurance of everlasting security. The young moon recurved, and shining low in the west, was like a slender shaving thrown up from a bar of gold, and the Arabian Sea, smooth and cool to the eye like a sheet of ice, extended its perfect level to the perfect circle of a dark horizon. The propeller turned without a check, as though its beat had been part of the scheme of a safe universe; and on each side of the *Patna* two folds of water, permanent and sombre on the unwrinkled shimmer, enclosed within their straight and diverging ridges a few white swirls of foam bursting in a low hiss, a few wavelets, a few ripples, a few undulations that, left behind, agitated the surface of the sea for an instant after the passage of the ship, subsided splashing gently, calmed down at last into the circular stillness of water and sky with the black speck of the moving hull remaining everlastingly in its centre.
>
> Joseph Conrad, *Lord Jim*

The first sentence directly identifies the impression, "security," to which the "stillness" and the "serenity" contribute. Other details also do their part: the "smooth" sea, the "perfect circle" of the horizon, the "safe universe," the quick calming of the water, and the moving hull "everlastingly" in the centre of water and sky.

EXERCISE *Go to a favourite gathering place on your campus or in your community and write a paragraph that evokes a particular dominant impression. Omit any details that run counter to your aim.*

VANTAGE POINT

Sometimes you need to write a description from either a fixed or a moving vantage point. A fixed observer remains in one place and reports only what can be perceived from there. Here is how Emily Carr describes a Native carving she encounters in a remote coastal village.

> Her head and trunk were carved out of, or rather into, the bole of a great red cedar. She seemed to be part of the tree itself, as if she had grown there at its

heart, and the carver had only chipped away the outer wood so that you could see her. Her arms were spliced and socketed to the trunk, and were flung wide in a circling, compelling movement. Her breasts were two eagleheads, fiercely carved. That much, and the column of her great neck, and her strong chin, I had seen when I slithered to the ground beneath her. Now I saw her face.

The eyes were two rounds of black, set in wider rounds of white, and placed in deep sockets under wide, black eyebrows. Their fixed stare bored into me as if the very life of the old cedar looked out, and it seemed that the voice of the tree itself might have burst from that great round cavity, with projecting lips, that was her mouth. Her ears were round, and stuck out to catch all sounds. The salt air had not dimmed the heavy red of her trunk and arms and thighs. Her hands were black, with blunt fingertips painted a dazzling white. I stood looking at her for a long, long time.

Emily Carr, "D'Sonoqua"

A moving observer views things from a number of positions, signalling changes in location with phrases such as "moving through the turnstile" and "as I walked around the corner." Below, Michael Ondaatje takes us along with a young boy as he goes out of his home in winter.

One winter night when he was eleven years old, Patrick walked out from the long kitchen. A blue moth had pulsed on the screen, bathed briefly in light, and then disappeared into darkness. He did not think it would go far. He picked up the kerosene lamp and went out. A rare winter moth. It was scuffing along the snow as if injured and he could follow it easily. In the back garden he lost it, the turquoise moth arcing up into the sky beyond the radius of the kerosene light. What was a moth doing at this time of year? He hadn't seen any for months. It may have been bred in the chicken coop. He put the hurricane lamp onto a rock and looked over the fields. Among the trees in the distance he saw what looked like more bugs. Lightning bugs within the trees by the river. But this was winter! He moved forward with the lamp.

The distance was further than he thought. Snow above the ankles of his untied boots. One hand in a pocket, the other holding a lamp. And a moon lost in the thickness of clouds so it did not shine a path for him towards the trees. All that gave direction was a blink of amber. Already he knew it could not be lightning bugs.

Michael Ondaatje, *In the Skin of a Lion*

The phrase "walked out" tells the reader that Patrick is a moving observer. The lamp which Patrick carries reveals a progressively widening picture—first the moth, then the fields and trees, and then what look like lightning bugs. The reader, like Patrick, has no idea what the lightning bugs are until later, when Patrick gets to the bank of the frozen river, and sees skaters on the river holding flaming cattails.

Whatever your vantage point, fixed or moving, report only what would be apparent to someone on the scene. If you describe how a distant mountain looks from the perspective of a balcony, don't suddenly leap to a description of a mountain flower; you couldn't see it from your vantage point.

SELECTION OF DETAILS

Effective description depends as much on exclusion as on inclusion. Don't try to pack every possible detail into your paper by providing an inventory of, for example, a room's contents or a natural setting's elements. Instead, select details that bring out the mood or feeling you intend to create. Read the following student description:

> At night, a restful stillness falls over the suburbs. . . . Everyone has vanished inside the carefully maintained homes that line the winding streets. The children have gone to bed, leaving the occasional motionless wagon or tricycle in the driveway. A light gleams in some bedroom windows. TV sets silently flicker a tranquil blue in a few living rooms. The street lamps curve protectively over the empty streets and sidewalks. The stillness is only disturbed by the brief, familiar bark of a neighbour's dog, quickly hushed, intensifying in its wake the silence that holds sway with the dark.
>
> Kim Granger, student

This writer evokes a sense of stillness by noting "the occasional motionless wagon or tricycle," that "TV sets silently flicker a tranquil blue," that "The street lamps curve protectively," that the dog is "quickly hushed." She ignores the car that cruises homeward, stereo booming; the husband and wife screaming at each other; the caterwauling catfight. Mentioning these things would detract from the desired mood.

ARRANGEMENT OF DETAILS

Description, like any other writing, must have a clear pattern of organization to guide the reader and help you fulfill your purpose. Often a spatial arrangement works well. For example, you might move systematically from top to bottom, left to right, front to back, nearby to far away, or the reverse of these patterns. To describe Saturday night at the hockey game, you might start with the crowded parking lot, move into the bustling arena, and finally zoom in on the sights and sounds of the rink. Or if you wanted to highlight the surroundings rather than the central event, the order could be reversed. Going another route, you might start with some striking central feature and then branch out to the things around it. To capture the centre of a mall, you might first describe its ornate fountain illuminated with flashing, multicoloured lights, shift to the reflection of the lights on the skylight above, and end by portraying the surrounding store fronts.

Sometimes a description follows a time sequence. For example, a writer might portray the changes in a woodland setting as winter gives way to spring and as spring, in turn, yields to summer.

ETHICAL ISSUES IN DESCRIPTION AND NARRATION

Think how you'd react to a workplace supervisor who wrote a narrative about the development of a new product that exaggerated his role and minimized your crucial contribution to the result. Imagine a police description of an auto accident that misstated the length of a car's skid marks or failed to note the icy patches of road at the scene. It might cost a blameless driver a heavy fine and a steep increase in auto insurance premiums. Imagine your irritation if a going-out-of-business sale described as "fabulous" turned out to offer only 10-percent price reductions. Clearly inaccurate and misleading narratives or descriptions create undesirable consequences. Ask yourself these questions about your narratives and descriptions:

> Have I provided a truthful account that participants will recognize and accept? Deliberate falsification of someone's behaviour that tarnishes that person's reputation is libel and could result in legal action.
> Would the writing expose any participants to possible danger if it became public? Do I need to change any names in order to protect people from potential harm?
> Does the narrative or description encourage unethical behaviour? For example, extolling the delights of using the drug ecstasy for a teenage audience is clearly unethical.
> Would readers find my writing credible if they were at the scene?
> Have I given readers adequate clues so they will recognize deliberate exaggeration?

You have an ethical obligation to present a reasonably honest, fair, and accurate portrayal of your topic.

WRITING A DESCRIPTION
Planning and Drafting a Description

If you're choosing your own topic, always select one that is familiar. Don't describe a ski run at Jasper National Park or the bridge from Prince Edward Island if you've never seen either one. Instead, opt for a place where you've worked or a locale you've visited. If you keep a journal, thumb through it for possible leads.

For each potential topic that surfaces, ask yourself the following questions. They will direct your attention to matters you'll need to address.

> What do I want to accomplish by writing this description? create one or more impressions? help the reader understand something? persuade the reader to act?
> Who is my audience, and why would this topic interest them?
> What dominant impression will I develop?

To help gather and organize support for your topic, ask yourself these additional questions:

> What details should I include?
> What sensory impressions are associated with each detail? (Jot down any words that you feel best convey the impressions.)
> How does each detail contribute to the dominant impression?
> What sequence should I follow in presenting my impressions? (Map out the sequence, setting up a 1-2-3 listing or possibly a paragraph-by-paragraph plan.)

After brainstorming a list of potential details, you might use branching to help you start accumulating sensory impressions. Here's how Kim Swiger, who wrote the passage below, used this technique:

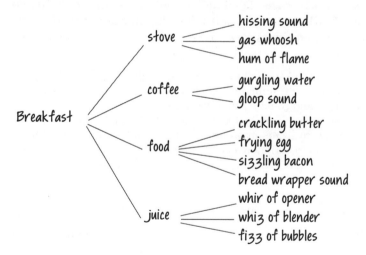

Begin your paper with an introduction that eases the reader into your topic. For example, you might provide a historical overview, ask a provocative question, or snare the reader's attention with an arresting statement.

Develop each major feature in one or more paragraphs. Present each feature in the order you've mapped out. To ensure that the reader follows your thoughts, clearly signal any shifts in vantage point or time. As you write, aim for vivid, original language. We've all encountered writers who tell us that raindrops "pitter-patter," clouds are "fleecy white," and the sun is "a ball of fire." Such stale, worn-out language does nothing to sharpen our vision of the rain, the clouds, or the sun. In contrast, read how one student uses fresh language to describe the sounds in her kitchen at breakfast time:

> Sure signs of a new day are the sounds in the kitchen as breakfast is prepared. The high sigh of the gas just before it whooshes into flame and settles into a whispering hum blends with the gurgling of the water for the morning coffee. Soon the gloop, gloop, gloop of the coffee sets up a perky beat. Then in mingles the crackle of creamy butter on a hot skillet and the shush of an egg added to the pan. Ribbons of bacon start to sizzle in the spitting grease. The soft rustle of plastic as bread is removed from its wrapper contributes to the medley. The can opener whirs, and the orange juice concentrate drops with a splat into the blender, which whizzes together the orange cylinder and splashed-in water. For minutes after the blender stops, bubbles of various sizes fizz.
>
> Kim Burson Swiger, student

A word of caution about going overboard—stringing together a chain of adjectives without considering the effect on a reader. Think how you'd react if told that

> A dented, cylindrical, silver-grey, foul-smelling, overloaded garbage can sat in the alley.

As you can see, more than the garbage can is overloaded here! Resist the temptation to burden sentences with too much description. Carefully examine your adjectives and eliminate those that don't advance your purpose.

End your paper by pulling your material together in some way. If you've created an impression or mood, you might offer your reaction to it. If you want to ensure that your reader understands the central message, you might spell it out. If you wish to persuade, you might urge some action.

Revising a Description

As you revise, apply the guidelines in Chapter 5 and ask the following questions:

- Have I written with a clear sense of purpose and audience in mind?
- Have I conveyed sights, sounds, touching, tastes, or smells? Would comparisons or more precise descriptive terms help convey my perceptions?
- Have I evoked one dominant impression? Can I strengthen this impression by adding certain selected details? by eliminating details that detract from the impression?
- Have I used an appropriate vantage point? If the observer is moving, have I signalled changes in location? Have I included only details that would be visible to the observer?
- Have I arranged my details in an order appropriate to the topic?

EXAMPLE OF A STUDENT NARRATIVE THAT INCORPORATES DESCRIPTION

Beth's Finest Hour

Elizabeth Ferguson

1   Eating out is always funny for me; I never feel quite like myself. It might be because I drink so much water (they just keep refilling it) or maybe it is because there is always too much stuff (forks, menus, glasses, etc.) on the table. Often the chairs aren't that comfortable, the atmosphere is too noisy, and the temperature is rarely right. Sometimes it is because of who I'm with. As a result of my relative disorientation and discomfort, I never expect to say or do anything extraordinary while eating out, especially with strangers. I'm usually too preoccupied with clearing my space of all crumbs. I never would have expected that what I call my "finest moment" would occur while eating out.

2   It was the summer of 2002, and I was at my very first rehearsal dinner as my father, brother and I were playing the recessional song at my P.E. teacher's, Mr. Weins's, wedding. The dinner was at a nice restaurant in North Vancouver, and we were all seated at a long white table. I was sitting between Len (my brother) and my dad, but surrounded by strangers. Being a shy 15-year-old, I was feeling particularly self-conscious. I probably went to the bathroom three or four times during the meal just to escape, and also because I was drinking so much water.

3   During one of the moments that I was actually at the table the evening reached its pinnacle. I reached out for my wineglass full of water; however, I wasn't looking when I reached, and didn't reach far enough. My hand collided with the glass and it started to tip toward the girls across from me. They saw and gasped in horror, the groomsmen saw and their eyes widened, my brother saw and felt sorry for me. I saw my life flash before my eyes . . .

> *After spilling water all over the Maid of Honour and the other girl, I run out in shame, followed by my father and brother—so ashamed of my unfortunate display that none of us can play at the wedding the next day. In his anger that they didn't have any music for the recessional, Mr. Weins punishes me by making me do squat thrusts and overhand serving drills in P.E. class for the rest of the year.*

4   With the image of eternal squat thrusts and utter humiliation before me, the only way to save myself from said fate was quick action. As the falling glass reached a 65-degree angle and the water was about to overflow, I jetted my hand out at lightning speed, grabbed the wineglass by the neck and restored it to its proper position.

5   Silence reigned over the entire table.

6   And then . . . "Whoa! How did you do that? That was crazy! Did you teach her that?" (That last question was addressed to my P.E. teacher)

7   I sat in shock as all the groomsmen looked at me in awe and commented on my savagely fast reflexes. I saw a new future . . .

LIGHTNING BETH FERGUSON, STAR GOALIE FOR TEAM CANADA, MAKES WICKED SAVES WITH HER SAVAGELY FAST REFLEXES

The next morning, when they interviewed me on Canada AM, *they asked to hear the tale, and then gave me that same strange look of awe after I told it.*

"But how did you do it?"

"I really don't know. It was an out-of-body experience."

Word got around, and before I knew it, my save was a hot topic in every newspaper and a picture of the moment was on every bus stop and bill-board. Everyone wanted an interview with that crazy girl who changed an irrevocable fate in one magnificent swoop.

8   Maybe it was only that huge in my mind. My life didn't really change after that moment, but I still remember it vividly with great joy and pride, a moment that could have ruined my appreciation of eating out forever. Now whenever I'm sitting at a cluttered table, and I reach out for my glass of water, I remember the time the Lightning Beth Ferguson took over my body and those good-looking groomsmen looked at me in awe and amazement. Sometimes, I mention it to my brother, and he gives me that same look and says: "That was crazy." I smile, because I'm reliving the moment.

DISCUSSION QUESTIONS

1. Identify descriptions in this essay from fixed and moving vantage points. How is movement indicated?

2. Point out details that appeal to the physical senses and explain how they contribute to the atmosphere in the narrative.

3. How does the essay blend description and narration together? What larger purpose seems to guide the writer in the selection of details?

SUGGESTIONS FOR WRITING *Choose one of the following topics or another that your instructor approves for an essay of description. Create a dominant impression by using carefully chosen, well-organized details observed from an appropriate vantage point. Try to write so that the reader actually experiences your description.*

1. A walk in a forest
2. Your closet
3. An exercise class
4. A classroom when the bell rings
5. A shopping centre
6. A pet store or zoo
7. A busy city intersection
8. The view from your bedroom window
9. Getting caught in a storm
10. Your house after a party

The Critical Edge

Sometimes writers weave together information from different sources. When describing a childhood experience, you might supplement your own recollections by asking relatives and friends to supply details that you've forgotten or clear up points that have become hazy. A police officer investigating an accident questions witnesses and examines physical evidence, and then uses the findings to draft an accurate report.

Integrating material from several sources into a coherent piece of writing is called *synthesis.* When you synthesize, you reflect on ideas you have found in various sources, establish on your own the connections among those ideas, and then determine how the ideas and connections can advance the purpose of your writing. Thus, synthesis features independent thinking in which *you* evaluate, select, and use the material of others—which, of course, must be properly documented—to further your own purpose.

Although synthesis can be challenging and does call for judgment on your part, following an effective procedure can help ensure success. Start by jotting down the main points of information from your sources and identifying where those points agree. A friend's memory of your childhood experience may differ markedly from your own. A police officer may find that two witnesses disagree about how an accident happened. Because different people are likely to see and describe the same event, object, or place differently, you'll need to look for contradictions and weigh each perspective in order to assess credibility. Ask yourself what might have been left out in each account.

In any kind of descriptive narrative, you choose what to emphasize from a myriad of possibilities. Consider, for example, how in "Lend Me Your Light,"

Rohinton Mistry creates the impression of the repugnant smell of his school lunchroom through carefully selected details:

> The drillhall would be filled with a smell that is hard to forget, thick as swill, while the aromas of four hundred steaming lunches started to mingle. The smell must have soaked into the very walls and ceiling, there to age and rancify. No matter what the hour of the day, that hot and dank grotto of a drillhall smelled stale and sickly, the way a vomit-splashed room does even after it is cleaned up.

If Mistry had found the smell appealing, he might have chosen to describe the fragrant smell of steaming rice or the refreshing sweetness of *chai* at the end of morning studies. Clearly, writers need to choose details that relate to the overall impression they want to convey and speak to the purpose of their writing.[*]

SUGGESTIONS FOR WRITING

1. Read "Lend Me Your Light" and "I Have a Dream," and then write a descriptive narrative that relates an experience of a particular ethnic group and incorporates material from either of the two essays.
2. Take notes from several different newspaper accounts of an important or controversial event and write an account of the event that includes your notes.

THE PERSONAL ESSAY: PROFESSIONAL MODELS

NARRATION AND DESCRIPTION READING STRATEGIES

1. Read the essay quickly to get a feel for the story and its main point.
2. Identify the main conflict that moves the story forward. Identify the major characters and what they may represent.
3. Don't get lost in the details. Note (possibly write in the margins) the overall impression or mood the description is evoking.
4. Identify a thesis statement (possibly first or last paragraph) and/or a statement of purpose. Read the essay with an anticipation of what the description is intended to accomplish.
5. Read the narrative more slowly with the main point in mind. Keep an eye on how the narrative supports the main point.

---

[*]Because synthesis involves using several sources, including information from published ones, it is important to read the sections on research in Chapters 13 and 14 and those on handling quotations and avoiding plagiarism in Chapter 15. As always, follow your instructor's guidelines for documenting sources.

READING CRITICALLY

1. Consider if the narrative would seem different if told from another person's point of view. Consider how a scene or event that is described might look very different from a different vantage point.
2. Examine what principle seems to have guided the selection of details. Has the writer created a certain mood or dominant impression by selecting certain kinds of details?
3. Ask whether the narrative really supports the author's main point. Consider what other possible perspectives or narratives could be included but are not. Would these contradict the writer's claims?

READING AS A WRITER

1. Identify the organizational pattern and decide whether it is the most effective arrangement for this piece of writing.
2. Determine the setting, conflict, characters, and development of the narrative. Note whether the writer gives enough information, or too much in places.
3. Notice any particularly effective movements in the plot. If you find a useful strategy, jot it down.
4. Observe how the writer uses dialogue. Make a note of any especially effective techniques.
5. Examine the essay for particularly effective examples of word choice.

Dan Greenburg

Sound and Fury

This familiar expression is the title of a famous novel by William Faulkner, and is originally taken from Shakespeare's Macbeth: "[Life] is a tale/Told by an idiot, full of sound and fury,/Signifying nothing." The reader may be intrigued: What does the title signify here?

Dan Greenburg is a native of Chicago who holds a bachelor of fine arts from the University of Illinois and a master of fine arts from UCLA. A prolific writer, he has authored more than forty books, including such best-sellers as How to Be a Jewish Mother, How to Make Yourself Miserable, How to Avoid Love and Marriage, *and a series of more than twenty-four children's books,* The Zack Files. *His articles have appeared in a wide and diverse range of popular magazines and been reprinted in many anthologies of humour and satire. He has been a guest on* The Today Show, Larry King Live, Late Night with David Letterman, *and other major TV talk shows.*

The brief opening paragraph suggests a larger purpose and point for the story that is about to unfold. Paragraph 2 identifies who, when, where, and why. Paragraphs 2 and 3 set up tension, conflict, even suspense. (paras.1–3)

Sound impression

1 We carry around a lot of free-floating anger. What we do with it is what fascinates me.

2 My friend Lee Frank is a stand-up comedian who works regularly in New York comedy clubs. Not long ago I accompanied him to one of these places, where he was to be the late-night emcee and where I myself had once done a stand-up act in a gentler era.

3 The crowd that night was a typical weekend bunch—enthusiastic, hostile and drunk. A large contingent of inebriated young men from Long Island had decided that a comedian named Rusty who was currently on stage was the greatest thing since pop-top cans and began chanting his name after almost everything he said: "Rus-TEE! Rus-TEE!"

4   My friend Lee knew he had a tough act to follow.

5   Indeed, the moment Lee walked on stage, the inebriated young men from Long Island began chanting "Rus-TEE! Rus-TEE!" and didn't give him a chance. Poor Lee, the flop sweat running into his eyes, tried every trick he knew to win them over, and finally gave up.

6   When he left the stage I joined him at the bar in the back of the club to commiserate.

7   "You did the best you could," I told him.

8   "I don't know," he said, "I could have handled it better."

9   "How?"

10   "I don't know," he said.

11   As we spoke, the young men who'd given him such a tough time trickled into the bar area. One of them spotted Lee and observed to a companion that Lee might want to do something about their heckling.

12   Lee thought he heard the companion reply, "I'm down," a casual acknowledgment that he was willing to have a fistfight. Lee repeated their remarks to me and indicated that he, too, was "down."

13   Though slight of frame, Lee is a black belt in Tae Kwon Do, has had skirmishes with three-card monte con men in Times Square, and once even captured a robber-rapist. I am also slight of frame but have had no training in martial arts. I did have one fistfight in my adult life (with a movie producer), but as Lee's best friend, I assumed that I was "down" as well.

14   Considering that there were more than a dozen of them and only two of us, the period of time that might elapse between our being "down" and our being down seemed exceedingly brief.

15   The young man who'd made the remark drifted toward Lee.

16   The eyes of everyone in the bar shifted slightly and locked onto the two men like heat-seeking missiles. Fight-or-flight adrenaline and testosterone spurted into dozens of male cardiovascular systems. Safeties snapped off figurative weapons. Red warning lights lit up dozens of DEFCON systems; warheads were armed and aimed. In a moment this bar area might very well resemble a saloon in a B grade western.

17   "How ya doing?" said Lee, his voice flat as unleavened bread, trying to make up his mind whether to be friendly or hostile.

18   "Okay," said the guy, a pleasant-looking, clean-cut kid in his mid-20s.

19   I was fascinated by what was going on between the two of them, each feeling the other out in a neutral, unemotional, slightly bemused manner. I saw no hostility here, no xenophobic loathing, just two young males jockeying for position, going through the motions, doing the dance, willing to engage at the slightest provocation. I had seen my cat do this many times when a stranger strayed onto his turf.

20   And then I had a sudden flash of clarity: These guys could either rip each other's heads off now or they could share a beer, and both options would be equally acceptable to them.

21   I'd felt close to critical mass on many occasions myself. But here, feeling outside the action, I could see clearly that it had to do with the enormous reservoir of rage that we men carry around with us, rage that seethes just under the surface and is ready to be tapped in an instant, with or without just provocation.

22   "What're you in town for?" asked Lee casually.

23   The guy was watching Lee carefully, making minuscule adjustments on his sensing and triggering equipment.

Touch impression

Time signal

Dialogue: The off-stage exchange between the writer and his comedian friend helps draw readers into the story.

Conflict arises in key event

Sight impression

His stance as a first-person observer allows the writer close positioning to the drama, as well as the distance to reflect on it from a somewhat detached point of view

Larger point of narrative: The reader draws a larger significance about men's "reservoir of rage" from this incident, thus reminding us of his larger point.

24   "It's my birthday," said the guy.

25   Lee mulled over this information for a moment, still considering all his options. Then he made his decision.

26   "Happy birthday," said Lee finally, sticking out his hand.

27   The guy studied Lee's hand a moment. Then, deciding the gesture was sincere, he took the hand and shook it.

28   "Thanks," he said, and walked back to his buddies.

29   All over the room you could hear safeties snapping on, warheads being unarmed. The incident was over, and in a moment it was as if it had never happened.

30   I felt I had just witnessed in microcosm the mechanism that triggers most acts of aggression, from gang fights to international conflagrations. It was so simple: a minor act of provocation. A decision on how to interpret it. Whether or not to escalate. And, in this particular case, a peaceful outcome. What struck me was how absolutely arbitrarily it had all been decided.

> Turning point: Lee takes a risk by saying "happy birthday" since the words could be taken as provocative, but instead the potential confrontation is defused in this instant.

> The writer returns to the larger purpose of the essay—to get us to think about how we have choices in how we deal with conflict. The last sentence leaves readers thinking, perhaps wondering whether they might choose to de-escalate conflict when a potential crisis arises.

DISCUSSION QUESTIONS

1. Discuss the appropriateness of Greenburg's title.

2. Does this essay have a stated or an unstated point? If it is stated, indicate where. If it is unstated, express it in your own words.

3. The expression "our being down" occurs twice in paragraph 14. Explain what it means in each instance.

4. Discuss the effectiveness of the figurative language in paragraph 16.

5. In paragraph 21 Greenburg credits "feeling outside the action" for helping him understand the rage involved in this situation as well as in others. Explain what he means.

6. How often do you think that the "equally acceptable" options mentioned in paragraph 20 occur in confrontations?

TOWARD KEY INSIGHTS

What reasons can you give for the "free-floating anger" that Greenburg mentions at the outset of the essay?

How frequently and in what ways is this anger manifested?

What are some effective strategies for coping with this anger?

SUGGESTION FOR WRITING *Write a narrative about a small incident that turned into a serious confrontation. Possible incidents might include an improper or reckless action of another driver, a minor disagreement with a friend or spouse, or retaliation for an action at a sporting event. The outcome can be peaceful or otherwise. Make sure your essay makes a larger point that could be stated or implied throughout the essay.*

Moses Milstein

Memories of Montreal—and Richness

Moses Milstein was born in 1947 in Austria and grew up in Montreal. He received degrees from McGill University, Université de Montréal, and Guelph University. He now makes his living in British Columbia as a veterinarian and is a regular contributor to the North and West Voice. *In this essay, originally published in* The Globe and Mail, *Milstein recounts memories of growing up in Montreal. He reflects with subtle nostalgia on how his experience of urban, economic, and cultural diversity growing up in Montreal will not be duplicated for his son, who is growing up in a more homogeneous, upper-middle class area of Vancouver. The essay may prompt discussion of generational, class, or ethnic differences, or of gains that may entail losses.*

1   In the April of his youth, my son walks to school in a gentle shower of cherry blossoms. Down the slopes of West Vancouver's Hollyburn Mountain he can see the houses nestled among tall cedars. Bursts of rhododendrons guard the yards and over their tops he can see the sun glinting on the placid waters of Howe Sound. He walks through this serene neighbourhood unmolested, the quiet punctuated by the thwonk of tennis balls coming from cozy courts nearby.

2   And I blame myself.

3   In the April of my childhood in the Montreal of the fifties, the way to school was still studded with chunks of sandy moraine from winter's retreating ice. With the threat of blizzards gone, I could shed my heavy winter boots, and feel the sidewalk strangely close beneath the thin soles of my shoes.

4   The corners of our street, like every street then, were held by the four corner stores. The one we used, the "Jewish" store, could be counted on for an emergency box of matzohs, or kosher Coca Cola during Passover. Although Mr. Auerbach practically lived in his store, he did, in fact, go home at night. His French competitors across the street, though, lived amidst their crowded displays of potato chips, soft drinks and fly-paper rolls—cooking, sleeping, arguing, watching TV, just behind the curtain in the back of the store.

5   You could buy a tiny bag of potato chips for a penny. My mother insisted that it was filled with sweepings.

6   Around the corner was Wing Ling, the Chinese laundry, like all Chinese laundries painted green on the outside. Within, great vats seethed with steam where Mr. Lee and his family washed and ironed our sheets, which he would then hand to me in a package wrapped in brown paper and string.

7   Next to the laundry, across the alley, which ran like a sparkling river of broken glass and urine produced by the hordes of feral cats, giant rats and stumbling drunks who waded therein, was the Jewish Tailor. His narrow house, barely a door and a window wide, extended backwards from his work room and housed his wife and daughter, a sewing machine and a steam iron. An air of sadness, like the tape measure he wore around his neck, enveloped the place.

8   His old, thick-legged wife shared his melancholic mien. Their daughter was my age and wore braces on her legs. I often wondered whether they were her parents or her grandparents, so great was the difference in their ages. According to rumour, they were, like our family, survivors of the "Krieg," the Holocaust. The tailor and his wife had each had families of their own, children and spouses. They perished somehow, I don't remember the details. Every family I knew then had a story of death and they were all mixed up in my mind. In

a DP camp after the war, the tailor met and married this woman and she was able to give birth to one more child, with crippled legs, and then no more.

9   I would rush by their sad house, and in one block was on St. Lawrence Street, noisy and bursting with commerce. Two long blocks before I reached my school.

10   My father worked on St. Lawrence Street at the Junior Trend Factory, which he pronounced "Jooniohtren." One April, when school was closed for Passover, I brought him his lunch. The elevator in his building passed floor after floor of angrily buzzing sewing machines. On some floors anonymous contractors were making clothes under other manufacturer's labels; on others I could see fancy offices where men with cigars, manicured fingers and pomaded hair struggled for ascendancy in the *shmatte* business.

11   My father worked among his friends from back home. They would usually greet me with jokes, smiles and much cheek-pinching. But when I saw them at their sewing machines their faces were closed and dark and they worked feverishly at piecework, sewing linings, sleeves, buttonholes under the critical eyes of the foreman. I left quickly.

12   Between these rows of tall, brown brick buildings, I would pass the restaurants that fed the workers. Delicatessens beckoned, their windows steamed from the smoked meat briskets waiting within, festooned with hanging salamis, rows of jars of pickled tomatoes and long banana peppers, green and red. Inside, the esteemed smoked-meat cutter stood resplendent on his pedestal, dispensing thick, greasy, spicy slices of meat onto golden rounds of rye bread. A good cutter was rumoured to be worth his substantial weight in gold and was held in reverential awe by my friends and me. Unhappily, the price of 25 cents, an hour's wages for my father, was beyond our reach.

13   The smells of the delicatessen mixed with the forest of urban smells welling out of each block—fruit stores, bakeries, taverns (for men only), poultry and egg stores, fish stores, bagel bakeries, steak houses, all of which would have me slavering until I reached that pinnacle of sensual delights, the Rachel Market. Here, the smells and sights merged as the French farmers, some able to speak Yiddish, backed their trucks up to the wide sidewalks where they set up their tables and displayed their produce. Beneath the market, down a spiral of stone steps slicked with blood, was a subterranean chamber of death. If you stood halfway down the stairs, you could see the hell waiting for the birds below. An open fire to singe their pin feathers burned in an alcove. Hooks covered the walls from which the chickens were suspended by their feet while men in bloodied aprons cut their throats, drained their blood and plucked their feathers which floated in the air until they settled among the clots of gray droppings on the floor and walls.

14   Across the street, the large bakery, Richstones, held a secret known only to the few. On Fridays, if you went to the door at the top of the loading bays, you could ask for the seconds, the crumbled cakes, broken doughnuts, smeary cupcakes. Sometimes they would give you some and sometimes they would chase you away angrily. Another example of the incomprehensible capriciousness of adults.

15   As if to remind me of my destination, I would ultimately come to the offices of Der Kanader Adler, one of three local Yiddish papers. Occasionally, one of my teachers would publish a poem there, truly the last song of the Last of the Mohicans. The Jewish Peretz School was just around the corner on Duluth Street. We were educated in Yiddish, spoke to each other in English and lived in a French neighbourhood.

16   I can recall every building and business along the two blocks to school. Many of the proprietors knew me and my family. I felt as safe and happy on the streets as in my own home and would often linger until dusk on the return home.

17   When I grew up I bought a house in the gentle forests of the Pacific and my son walks to school among the cherry blossoms. And sometimes I am sad for him.

DISCUSSION QUESTIONS

1. What contrast does the writer introduce in the first three paragraphs? What details are especially effective in highlighting the contrast? Why do you suppose that the second paragraph is only one sentence long?

2. Point out sensory details that reflect sight, sound, taste, smell, touch. Comment on the effect of these sensory impressions.

3. Why does Moses Milstein spend so much time describing the Jewish Tailor (paragraphs 7–9), whose place was enveloped by "an air of sadness"? What is the possible significance of the reference to the Holocaust?

4. How does the writer reveal a kind of double perspective, as a child and an adult? Consider the fragment that ends paragraph 14: "Another example of the capriciousness of adults." Is this the child or the adult speaking? What does the writer mean here?

5. In the last paragraph, the father states that he is sad for his son sometimes, even though his son "walks to school among the cherry blossoms." What is the paradox here? Do you think the boy would understand if his father tried to explain to him that he was missing something?

6. Does this essay have a stated or an unstated point? If it is stated, indicate where. If it is unstated, express it in your own words.

TOWARD KEY INSIGHTS

What are the advantages of living in a place of cultural and economic diversity? Are there any disadvantages?

What are the possible losses and/or gains associated with moving away from the place where you grew up?

What does Moses Milstein reveal about the nature of parent/child relationships?

Whose childhood would you prefer—the father's or the son's? Explain.

SUGGESTION FOR WRITING *Create a sense of paradox by recounting a memory of a time or place that at first glance seemed far from perfect, but which has given you riches that you have come to appreciate.*

Rohinton Mistry

Lend Me Your Light

Born in Bombay in 1952, Rohinton Mistry came to Canada in 1975 and has lived since then near Toronto. He has written three internationally acclaimed novels: Such a Long Journey *(1991),* A Fine Balance *(1995), and* Family Matters *(2002). He has won many prestigious international awards, such as the Giller Prize, the Commonwealth Writers Prize for Best Book, the Governor General's Award, and the Los Angeles Times Book Prize for fiction.*

> . . . your lights are all lit—then where do you go with your lamp? My house is all dark and lonesome—lend me your light.
>
> *Rabindranath Tagore Gitanjali*

1   We both left Bombay the same year. Jamshed first, for New York, then I, for Toronto. As immigrants in North America, sharing this common experience should have salvaged something from our acquaintanceship. It went back such a long way, to our school days at St Xavier's.

2   To sustain an acquaintance does not take very much. A friendship, that's another thing. Strange, then, that it has ended so completely, that he has erased himself out of our lives, mine and Percy's; now I cannot imagine him even as a mere bit player who fills out the action or swells a procession.

3   Jamshed was my brother's friend. The three of us went to the same school. Jamshed and my brother, Percy, both four years older than I, were in the same class, and spent their time together. They had to part company during lunch, though, because Jamshed did not eat where Percy and I did, in the school's drillhall-cum-lunchroom.

4   The tiffin carriers would stagger into the school compound with their long, narrow rickety crates on their heads, each with fifty tiffin boxes, delivering lunches from homes in all corners of the city. When the boxes were unpacked, the drillhall would be filled with a smell that is hard to forget, thick as swill, while the aromas of four hundred steaming lunches started to mingle. The smell must have soaked into the very walls and ceiling, there to age and rancify. No matter what the hour of the day, that hot and dank grotto of a drillhall smelled stale and sickly, the way a vomit-splashed room does even after it is cleaned up.

5   Jamshed did not eat in this crammed and cavernous interior. Not for him the air redolent of nauseous odours. His food arrived precisely at one o'clock in the chauffeur-driven, air-conditioned family car, and was eaten in the leather-upholstered luxury of the back seat, amidst his collection of hyphenated lavishness.

6   In the snug dining-room where chauffeur doubled as waiter, Jamshed lunched through his school-days, safe from the vicissitudes of climate. The monsoon might drench the tiffin carriers to the bone and turn cold the boxes of four hundred waiting schoolboys, but it could not touch Jamshed or his lunch. The tiffin carriers might arrive glistening and stinking of sweat in the hot season, with scorching hot tiffin boxes, hotter than they'd left the kitchens of Bombay, but Jamshed's lunch remained unaffected.

7   During the years of high school, my brother, Percy, began spending many weekend afternoons at his friend's house at Malabar Hill. Formerly, these were

the afternoons when we used to join Pesi *paadmaroo* and the others for our most riotous times in the compound, the afternoons that the adults of Firozsha Baag would await with dread, not knowing what new terrors Pesi had devised to unleash upon the innocent and the unsuspecting.

8   But Percy dropped all this for Jamshed's company. And when he returned from his visits, Mummy would commence the questioning: What did he eat? Was Jamshed's mother home? What did the two do all afternoon? Did they go out anywhere? And so on.

9   Percy did not confide in me very much in those days. Our lives intersected during the lunch routine only, which counted for very little. For a short while we had played cricket together with the boys of Firozsha Baag. Then he lost interest in that too. He refused to come when Daddy would take the whole gang to the Marine Dri *maidaan* on Sunday morning. And soon, like all younger brothers, I was seen mainly as a nuisance.

10   But my curiosity about Percy and Jamshed was satisfied by Mummy's interrogations. I knew that the afternoons were usually spent making model airplanes and listening to music. The airplanes were simple gliders in the early years; the records, mostly Mantovani and from Broadway shows. Later came more complex models with gasoline engines and remote control, and classical music from Bach and Poulenc.

11   The model-airplane kits were gifts from Jamshed's itinerant aunties and uncles, purchased during business trips to England or the U.S. Everyone except my brother and I seemed to have uncles and aunties smitten by wanderlust, and Jamshed's supply line from the western world guaranteed for him a steady diet of foreign clothes, shoes, and records.

12   One Saturday, Percy reported during question period that Jamshed had received the original soundtrack of *My Fair Lady*. This was sensational news. The LP was not available in Bombay, and a few privately imported or "smuggled" copies, brought in by people like Jamshed's relatives, were selling in the black market for two hundred rupees. I had seen the records displayed side by side with foreign perfumes, chocolates, and cheeses at the pavement stalls of smugglers along Flora Fountain.

13   Sometimes, these stalls were smashed up during police raids. I liked to imagine that one day a raid would occur as I was passing, and in the mêlée and chaos of the clash, *My Fair Lady* would fly through the air and land at my feet, unnoticed by anyone. Of course, there wasn't much I could have done with it following the miracle, because our old gramophone played only 78 rpms.

14   After strenuous negotiations in which Mummy, Percy, and I exhausted ourselves, Percy agreed to ask his friend if I could listen to the album. Arrangements were made. And the following Saturday we set off for Jamshed's house. From Firozsha Baag, the direction of Malabar Hill was opposite to the one we took to go to school every morning, and I was not familiar with the roads the bus travelled. The building had a marble lobby, and the lift zoomed us up smoothly to the tenth floor before I had time to draw breath. I was about to tell Percy that we needed one like this in Firozsha Baag, but the door opened. Jamshed welcomed us graciously, then wasted no time in putting the record on the turntable. After all, that was what I had come for.

15   The afternoon dragged by after the soundtrack was finished. Bored, I watched them work on an airplane. The box said it was a Sopwith Camel. The name was familiar from the Biggles books Percy used to bring home. I picked up the lid and read dully that the aircraft had been designed by the British industrialist and

aeronautical engineer, Thomas Octave Murdoch Sopwith, born 1888, and had been used during the First World War. Then followed a list of parts.

16   Later, we had lunch, and they talked. I was merely the kid brother, and nobody expected me to do much else but listen. They talked of school and the school library, of all the books that the library badly needed; and of the *ghatis* who were flooding the school of late.

17   In the particular version of reality we inherited, *ghatis* were always flooding places, they never just went there. *Ghatis* were flooding the banks, desecrating the sanctity of institutions, and taking up all the coveted jobs. *Ghatis* were even flooding the colleges and universities, a thing unheard of. Wherever you turned, the bloody *ghatis* were flooding the place.

18   With much shame I remember this word *ghati*. A suppurating sore of a word, oozing the stench of bigotry. It consigned a whole race to the mute roles of coolies and menials, forever unredeemable.

19   During one of our rare vacations to Matheran, as a child, I watched with detachment while a straining coolie loaded the family's baggage on his person. The big metal trunk was placed flat on his head, with the leather suitcase over it. The enormous hold-all was slung on his left arm, which he raised to steady the load on his head, and the remaining suitcase went in the right hand. It was all accomplished with much the same approach and consideration used in loading a cart or barrow—the main thing was balance, to avoid tipping over. This skeletal man then tottered off towards the train that would transport us to the little hill station. There, similar skeletal beings would be waiting with rickshaws. Automobiles were prohibited in Matheran, to preserve the pastoral purity of the place and the livelihood of the rickshawallas.

20   Many years later I found myself at the same hill station, a member of my college hikers' club, labouring up its slopes with a knapsack. Automobiles were still not permitted in Matheran, and every time a rickshaw sped by in a flurry of legs and wheels, we'd yell at the occupant ensconced within: "Capitalist pig! You bastard! Stop riding on your brother's back!" The bewildered passenger would lean forward for a moment, not quite understanding, then fall back into the cushioned comfort of the rickshaw.

21   But this type of smug socialism did not come till much later. First we had to reckon with school, school uniforms, brown paper covers for textbooks and exercise books, and the mad morning rush for the school bus. I remember how Percy used to rage and shout at our scrawny *ghaton* if the pathetic creature ever got in his way as she swept and mopped the floors. Mummy would proudly observe; "He has a temper just like Grandpa's." She would also discreetly admonish Percy, since this was in the days when it was becoming quite difficult to find a new *ghaton*, especially if the first one quit due to abuse from the scion of the family and established her reasons for quitting among her colleagues.

22   I was never sure why some people called them *ghatons* and others, *gungas*. I suppose the latter was intended to placate—the collective conferment of the name of India's sacred river balanced the occasions of harshness and ill treatment. But the good old days, when you could scream at a *ghaton*, kick her and hurl her down the steps, and expect her to show up for work next morning, had definitely passed.

23   After high school, Percy and Jamshed went to different colleges. If they met at all, it would be at concerts of the Bombay Chamber Orchestra. Along with a college friend, Navjeet, and some others, my brother organized a charitable agency that collected and distributed funds to destitute farmers in a small

Maharashtrian village. The idea was to get as many of these wretched souls as possible out of the clutches of the village money-lenders.

24   Jamshed showed a very superficial interest in what little he knew about Percy's activities. Each time they met, he would start with how he was trying his best to get out of the country. "Absolutely no future in this stupid place," he said. "Bloody corruption everywhere. And you can't buy any of the things you want, don't even get to see a decent English movie. First chance I get, I'm going abroad. Preferably the U.S."

25   After a while, Percy stopped talking about his small village, and they only discussed the concert program or the soloist's performance that evening. Then their meetings at concerts ceased altogether because Percy now spent very little time in Bombay.

26   Jamshed did manage to leave. One day, he came to say goodbye. But Percy was away working in the small village: his charitable agency had taken on the task full time. Jamshed spoke to those of us who were home, and we all agreed that he was doing the right thing. There just weren't any prospects in this country; nothing could stop its downhill race towards despair and ruin.

27   My parents announced that I, too, was trying to emigrate, but to Canada, not the U.S. "We will miss him if he gets to go," they told Jamshed, "but for the sake of his own future, he must. There is a lot of opportunity in Toronto. We've seen advertisements in newspapers from England, where Canadian Immigration is encouraging people to go to Canada. Of course, they won't advertise in a country like India—who would want these bloody *ghatis* to come charging into their fine land?—but the office in New Delhi is holding interviews and soliciting highly qualified applicants." In the clichés of our speech was reflected the cliché which the idea of emigration had turned into for so many. According to my parents, I would have no difficulty being approved, what with my education, and my westernized background, and my fluency in the English language.

28   And they were right. A few months later things were ready for my departure to Toronto.

DISCUSSION QUESTIONS

1. Consider the descriptions of the school lunch in the drillhall and Jamshed's lunch in the "air-conditioned family car" (paragraphs 4–6). What impressions do the sensory details create? What is the effect of the contrast between the two kinds of lunches?

2. Why are the narrator and his mother so curious about Jamshed's daily life (paragraphs 8–10)?

3. What does the original soundtrack of *My Fair Lady* seem to symbolize (paragraphs 12–14)?

4. When the narrator hears his brother talk with Jamshed about the ways that "*ghatis* were always flooding places," he remembers the word *ghati* "with much shame" (paragraphs 16–18). Why does the word *ghati* bring a sense of shame to the narrator? How do we infer that his attitude toward the *ghati* has changed since he was a child (paragraphs 18–21)?

5. How does this essay move in time and space? Find examples of places where the narrator provides time signals to orient the reader. Examine especially the

movements forward in time in paragraphs 20–21. What is the effect on you of these different time frames?

6. Explain how Jamshed's criticism of India (paragraph 24) relates to our impression of Jamshed, or to the larger point of this essay.

7. What criticisms and ironies does the conclusion suggest (paragraphs 27–28)?

TOWARD KEY INSIGHTS

What possible reasons are suggested for the narrator's own callousness toward the *ghati* in the past, or for his brother's rage toward the "scrawny *ghaton*" getting in his way (paragraph 21)? Can you remember examples from your childhood of your own insensitivity, or even cruelty toward those who were in a different social grouping? How was your attitude similar to or different from the narrator's?

What does the West represent to the narrator when he is in India? How do we infer that his attitude toward the West changed since he began living in Canada?

Drawing from Mistry's essay, comment on the challenges of adaptation facing those who immigrate to Canada from post-colonial countries such as India.

SUGGESTION FOR WRITING *Describe a relationship with a friend or acquaintance from a different socioeconomic level or culture. Use details that highlight the contrast.*

CHAPTER 7

Strategies for Analytical Writing: Process Analysis

EXPLAINING HOW

"Hey Bill, I'd like you to take a look at Mr. Gorgerise's car. He's really fuming. Says the engine's burning too much oil, running rough, and getting poor gas consumption. Check it out and see what you can find."

Bill begins by removing the spark plugs, hooking a remote-control starter to the starter in the car, and grounding the ignition to prevent the car's starting accidentally. Next, he fits a compression pressure gauge into the spark plug hole by cylinder number one, starts the engine, and reads and records the pressure; then he does the same for each of the other cylinders. Finally, he compares the readings with one another and the automaker's engine specs. The verdict? An excessively worn engine that needs rebuilding. Bill has carried out a *process*, just one among many that fill his workdays.

As we pursue our affairs, we perform processes almost constantly, ranging from such daily rituals as brewing a pot of coffee to taking a picture, preparing for a date, or replacing a light switch. Often we share our special technique for doing something—for example, making chicken cacciatore—by passing it on to a friend.

Many popular publications feature process analyses that help readers sew zippers in garments, build canoes, live within their means, and improve their wok technique. Process analysis also frequently helps you meet the writing demands of your courses. A political science instructor may ask you to explain how the current premier won the last election. Another instructor may call for directions relating to some process in your field—for example, analyzing a chemical compound, taking fingerprints, or obtaining a blood sample. On the job, a greenhouse crew leader may provide summer employees with directions for planting various kinds of shrubs and flowers. A sanitation department technician may write a brochure telling city residents how to get paper, glass, and metal garbage ready for recycling.

As these examples show, a process can be nontechnical, historical, scientific, natural, or technical.

KINDS OF PROCESS ANALYSIS PAPERS

Process papers fall into two categories: those intended for readers who will perform the process, and those intended to explain the process for nonperformers. Papers in either category can range from highly technical and sophisticated to nonspecialized and simple.

Processes for Readers Who Will Perform Them   The audience for these papers may be technical and professional personnel who need the information to carry out a work-related task, or individuals who want to perform the process for themselves.

A how-to-do-it paper must include everything the reader needs to know in order to ensure a successful outcome. Its directions take the form of polite commands, often addressing readers directly as "you." This approach helps involve readers in the explanation and emphasizes that the directions must, not merely should, be followed. Here is an illustration:

> To prepare a bacterial smear for staining, first use an inoculating loop to place a drop of distilled water on a clean glass microscope slide. Next, pass the loop and the opening of the tube containing the bacterial culture to be examined through a Bunsen burner flame to sterilize them. From the tube, remove a small bit of culture with the loop, and rub the loop in the drop of water on the slide until the water covers an area one and one-half inches long and approximately the width of the slide. Next, reflame the opening of the culture tube to prevent contamination of the culture, and then plug it shut. Allow the smear to air dry, and then pass the slide, smear side up, through the flame of the burner until it is warm to the touch. The dried smear should have a cloudy, milky-white appearance.
>
> Darryl Williams, student

Processes for Readers Who Won't Perform Them   These kinds of papers may tell how some process is or was performed or how it occurs or occurred. A paper might, for instance, detail the stages of grief, the procedure involved in an operation, the role of speech in the development of children's thinking, or the sequence involved in shutting down a nuclear reactor. These papers serve many purposes—for example, to satisfy popular curiosity; to point out the importance, difficulty, or danger of a process; or to cast a process in a favourable or unfavourable light. Even though the writers of such papers often explain their topic in considerable detail, they do not intend to provide enough information for readers to carry out the process.

Papers of this sort present the needed information without using polite commands. Sometimes a noun, a pronoun like *I, we, he, she,* or *it,* or a noun–pronoun combination identifies the performer(s). At other times, the performer remains unidentified. Three examples follow.

Pronouns Identify Performer

Thus, when I now approach a stack of three two-inch cinder blocks to attempt a breaking feat, I do not set myself to "try hard," or to summon up all my strength. Instead I relax, sinking my awareness into my belly and legs, feeling my connection with the ground. I breathe deeply, mentally directing the breath through my torso, legs, and arms. I imagine a line of force coming up from the ground through my legs, down one arm, and out through the stone slabs, and down again into the ground, penetrating to the center of the earth. I do not focus any attention on the objects to be broken. Although when I am lifting or holding them in a normal state of consciousness, the blocks seem tremendously dense, heavy, and hard, in the course of my one- or two-minute preparation, their reality seems to change, as indeed the reality of the whole situation changes. . . . When I make my final approach to the bricks, if I regard them at all, they seem light, airy, and friendly; they do not have the insistent inner drive in them that I do.

Don Ethan Miller, "A State of Grace: Understanding the Martial Arts"

Noun–Pronoun Combination Identifies Performers

Termites are even more extraordinary in the way they seem to accumulate intelligence as they gather together. Two or three termites in a chamber will begin to pick up pellets and move them from place to place, but nothing comes of it; nothing is built. As more join in, they seem to reach a critical mass, a quorum, and the thinking begins. They place pellets atop pellets, then throw up columns and beautiful, curving, symmetrical arches, and the crystalline architecture of vaulted chambers is created. It is not known how they communicate with each other, how the chains of termites building one column know when to turn toward the crew on the adjacent column, or how, when the time comes, they manage the flawless joining of the arches. The stimuli that set them off at the outset, building collectively instead of shifting things about, may be pheromones released when they reach committee size. They react as if alarmed. They become agitated, excited, and then they begin working, like artists.

Lewis Thomas, "Societies as Organisms"

Performer Unidentified

The analyzer was adjusted so the scale read zero and was connected to the short sampling tube, which had previously been inserted into the smokestack. The sample was taken by depressing the bulb the requisite number of times, and the results were then read and recorded. The procedure was repeated, this time using the long sampling tube and sampling through the fire door.

Charles Finnie, student

EXERCISE *Examine your favourite newspaper or magazine for examples of process analysis. Bring them to class for group discussion of which kind each represents and the writer's purpose.*

ETHICAL ISSUES

Unclear, misleading, incomplete, or erroneous instructions written for someone to follow can spawn a wide range of unwanted consequences. Often frustration and lost time are the only results. Sometimes, though, the fallout is more serious, as in the case of a lab explosion. And in extreme cases, the outcome can be potentially catastrophic, as when an accident occurs in a nuclear power plant. As writers, we have an ethical obligation to write clear and complete instructions. To help you do this, ask yourself the following questions when you're writing a process that the reader will perform.

- Have I used clear and unambiguous language so the reader will not encounter unnecessary frustration and inconvenience?
- Have I clearly indicated all requirements, such as time needed or additional supplies that have to be purchased?
- Have I clearly warned readers about any possible harm they could face?

WRITING A PROCESS ANALYSIS

Planning and Drafting the Process Analysis

As always, when the choice is yours, select a familiar topic. If you're not the outdoor type and prefer a Holiday Inn to the north woods, don't try to explain how to plan a camp-out. Muddled, inaccurate, and inadequate information will result. On the other hand, if you've pitched many a tent, you might want to share your technique with your readers.

Finding a suitable topic should be easy. Answer the following questions for each potential choice:

Will the reader find the process important, interesting, or useful?

Should I provide directions for the reader to follow, explain how the process takes place, or explain how others perform it?

Can I explain the process adequately within any assigned length?

Processes for Readers Who Will Perform Them   If you are writing a process for readers to follow, use this second set of questions to help you gather the details you need:

What separate actions make up the process? (Be especially careful not to omit any action that is obvious to you but wouldn't be to your reader. Such an oversight can ruin your reader's chances of success.)

What is the reason for each action?

What warnings does the reader need in order to perform the process properly and safely?

When you have your answers, record them in a chart similar to this one:

Action	**Reason for Action**	**Warning**
First action	First reason	First warning
Second action	Second reason	Second warning

Sometimes a reason is so obvious that no mention is necessary, and many actions don't require warnings. When you've completed the chart, review it carefully and supply any missing information. If necessary, make a revised chart.

Once you've listed the actions, group related ones together to form steps, the major subdivisions of the procedure. The following actions constitute the first step—lighting the gas barbecue—of a paper explaining how to grill hamburgers:

lift lid	spray non-stick spray on the rack
turn on main gas supply	turn on first gas burner
twist automatic starter until burner ignites	turn on second burner
close lid	let barbecue heat for 10 minutes

EXERCISE

1. **Develop a complete list of the actions involved in one of the following processes, then arrange them in an appropriate order.**

   a. Baking bread

   b. Assembling or repairing some common household device

   c. Carrying out a process related to sports

   d. Breaking a bad habit

2. **Examine your favourite newspaper or magazine for examples of process analysis. Bring them to class to discuss how they illustrate step-by-step directions.**

Start your paper by identifying the process and arousing your reader's interest. For example, you might note the importance of the process, its usefulness, or the ease of carrying it out. Include a list of the items needed to do the work, and note any special conditions required for a successful outcome. The paper explaining how to grill hamburgers might begin as follows:

> Grilling hamburgers on an outdoor grill is a simple process that almost anyone can master. Before starting, you will need a clean grill, some hamburger meat, a plate, a spatula, and some water to put out any flames caused by fat drippings. The sizzling, tasty patties you will have when you finish are a treat that almost everyone will enjoy.

DISCUSSION QUESTION *How does the writer try to induce the reader to perform the process?*

Use the body of the paper to describe the process in detail, presenting each step in one or more paragraphs so that each is distinct and easy to understand. If you've ever muttered under your breath as you struggled to assemble something that came with vague or inadequate directions, you know the importance of presenting steps clearly, accurately, and fully. Therefore, think carefully and include everything the reader needs to know. Provide the reason for each action unless the reason is obvious. Flag any difficult or dangerous step with a cautionary warning. If two steps must be performed simultaneously, tell the reader at the start of the first one. In some places, you may want to tell readers what to expect if they have completed the instructions properly. Feedback lets readers know that they are on track or that they need to redo something.

Let's see how the first step of the hamburger-grilling paper might unfold:

> The first step is to light the barbecue. Lift the lid and lightly spray the rack with a nonstick spray for gas barbecues. This will make clean-up easier later on. Next, make sure that the gas supply valve on the tank is open. Then turn the burner closest to the automatic starter to high. Immediately twist the automatic starter until the gas lights. You may have to twist it more than once. Note that, on very windy days, the automatic starter may not work effectively. Once the main burner is lit, turn the other gas burner to high until it lights as well. Do not squirt on lighter fluid, because a flame could quickly follow the stream back into the can, causing an explosion. Close the lid and let the barbecue heat up. The result will be a hot, even fire, the type that makes grilling a success.

DISCUSSION QUESTIONS

1. At what points has the writer provided reasons for doing things?
2. Where has the writer included a warning?

Some processes can unfold in *only one order.* When you shoot a free throw in basketball, for example, you step up to the line and receive the ball before lining up the shot, and you line up the shot before releasing the ball. Other processes can be carried out in an *order of choice.* When you grill hamburgers, you can make the patties either before or after you light the barbecue. If you have an option, use the order that has worked best for you.

End your paper with a few brief remarks that provide some perspective on the process. A summary of the steps often works best for longer, multistep processes. Other popular choices include evaluating the results of the process or discussing its importance. The paper on hamburger grilling notes the results.

> Once the patties are cooked through, remove them from the grill and place them on buns. Now you are ready to enjoy a mouthwatering treat that you will long remember.

Processes for Readers Who Won't Perform Them Like how-to-do-it processes, process descriptions intended for non-doers require you to determine the steps, or for natural processes, the stages, and their functions before you start to write. In addition, since this type of essay does not enable readers to perform the process, think carefully about why you're presenting the information, and let that purpose guide your writing. For instance, if you're trying to persuade readers that the use of rabbits in cosmetics testing should be discontinued, the choices you make in developing your steps should reflect that purpose.

To arouse your reader's interest, you might begin with a historical overview or a brief summary of the whole process, or you could note its importance, among other possible options. The following introduction to an essay on the aging of stars provides a brief historical perspective:

> Peering through their still-crude telescopes, eighteenth-century astronomers discovered a new kind of object in the night sky that appeared neither as the pinprick of light from a distant star nor as the clearly defined disk of a planet but rather as a mottled, cloudy disk. They christened these objects planetary nebulas, or planetary clouds. . . . Modern astronomers recognize planetary nebulas as the fossil wreckage of dying stars ripped apart by powerful winds.

Because the reader will not perform the process, supply only enough details in the body of the paper to provide an intelligent idea of what the procedure entails. Make sure the reader knows the function of each step or stage and its place in the overall process. Present each in one or more paragraphs with clear transitions between the steps or stages. The following excerpt points out the changes that occur as a young star, a red giant, begins the aging process:

As the bloated star ages, this extended outer atmosphere cools and contracts, then soaks up more energy from the star and again puffs out: with each successive cycle of expansion and contraction, the atmosphere puffs out a little farther. Like a massive piston, these pulsations drive the red giant's atmosphere into space in a dense wind that blows with speeds up to 15 miles per second. In as little as 10 000 years, some red giants lose an entire sun's worth of matter this way. Eventually this slow wind strips the star down close to its fusion core.

As with processes aimed at performers, end your paper with a few remarks that offer some perspective. You might, for example, evaluate the results of the process, assess its importance, or point out future consequences. The ending of the essay on star aging illustrates the last option:

The cloud of unanswered questions surrounding planetaries should not obscure the real insight astronomers have recently gained into the extraordinary death of ordinary stars. In a particularly happy marriage of theory and observation, astronomers have discovered our own sun's fate. With the interacting stellar winds model, they can confidently predict the weather about 5 billion years from now; very hot, with *really* strong gusts from the east.

Adam Frank, "Winds of Change"

Revising the Process Analysis

To revise, follow the guidelines in Chapter 5, and ask yourself these questions:

Have I written consistently for someone who will perform the process or someone who will merely follow it?

If my paper is intended for performers, have I included every necessary action? Have I explained any purpose that is unclear? Have I warned about any steps that are dangerous or might be performed improperly?

Are my steps presented in an appropriate order? Developed in sufficient detail? Have I considered appropriate ethical issues?

EXAMPLE OF A STUDENT ESSAY OF PROCESS ANALYSIS

The ABCs of CPR

Kathy Petroski

1   A heart attack, choking, or an electric shock—any of these can stop a person's breathing. The victim, however, need not always die. Many lives that would otherwise be lost can be saved simply by applying the ABCs of CPR—cardio-pulmonary resuscitation. Although presence of mind is essential, CPR requires no special equipment. Here's how it is performed. When you are certain that the victim's breathing and pulse have stopped, start CPR immediately. If breathing

and circulation aren't restored within five minutes, irreversible brain damage occurs.

2   A stands for opening the airway. Lay the victim in a supine (face up) position on a firm surface. Then tilt the head as far back as possible by gently lifting the chin with one hand. In an unconscious person, the tongue falls to the back of the throat and blocks the air passages. Hyperextending the head in this fashion pulls the tongue from that position, thus allowing air to pass. At the same time tilt the forehead back with the other hand until the chin points straight upward. The relaxed jaw muscles will then tighten, opening the air passage to the lungs. Remove your hand from the forehead and, using your first two fingers, check the mouth for food, dentures, vomitus, or a foreign object. Remove any obstruction with a sweeping motion. These measures may cause the patient to start breathing spontaneously. If they do not, mouth-to-mouth resuscitation must be started.

3   B stands for breathing. Position one hand on the forehead and pinch the victim's nostrils shut with the index finger and thumb of your other hand. Open your mouth, and place it over the victim's mouth so that a tight seal is formed. Such contact allows air to reach and expand the lungs. If the seal is incomplete, you will hear your own breath escaping. Deliver two quick, full breaths without allowing the victim's lungs to deflate completely between breaths; then remove your mouth and allow him or her to exhale passively. At this point, check the carotid pulse to determine whether the heart is beating. To do so, place the tips of your index and middle fingers laterally into the groove between the trachea (windpipe) and the muscles at the side of the neck. If no pulse is evident, artificial circulation must be started.

4   C means circulation. Locate the lower end of the sternum (breastbone), and move upward approximately the width of two fingers. At this point, firmly apply the heel of one hand, positioning the fingers at right angles to the length of the body and keeping them slanted upward. If the hand is positioned any higher or lower on the sternum, serious internal injuries in the abdomen or chest are possible. Now place the heel of your second hand on top of your first. The fingers may be interlaced or interlocked, but they must not touch the chest, or the force of your compressions may fracture ribs.

5   Keeping your elbows straight and pushing down from the shoulders, apply firm, heavy pressure until the sternum is depressed approximately one and one-half to two inches. Rock forward and backward in a rhythmic fashion, exerting pressure with the weight of your body. This action squeezes the heart

against the immobile spine with enough pressure to pump blood from the left ventricle of the heart into general circulation. Compress the chest, and then immediately release the pressure, fifteen times. Do not, at any point in the cycle, remove your hands from the chest wall. Counting the compressions aloud will help develop a systematic cycle, which is essential for success. When the fifteen have been completed, pinch the nose as described above, seal the victim's mouth with your own, and deliver two quick breaths of air. Then compress the chest an additional fifteen times. Alternate respiration and compression steps, timing yourself so as to deliver approximately eighty compressions per minute.

6   At various intervals, quickly check the effectiveness of your CPR technique. Lift the eyelids and notice if the pupils are constricted—a key sign that the brain is receiving enough oxygen. In addition, if the bluish colour of the victim is decreasing and spontaneous breathing and movement are increasing, the victim has responded favourably.

7   To maximize the chances for survival, do not interrupt this technique for more than five or ten seconds. Continue the ABCs of CPR until competent medical help or life-support equipment arrives.

DISCUSSION QUESTIONS

1. How does the writer use the letters *A, B,* and *C* from the CPR technique in this paper?
2. How does the opening paragraph prepare the reader for what follows?
3. Where does the essay indicate the purposes of actions?
4. What order has the writer used? Explain why this order is a good choice.
5. Is the writer merely explaining how the process is carried out, or does she intend for the reader to follow the directions? Defend your answer.

SUGGESTIONS FOR WRITING *Write a process analysis on one of the topics below or one approved by your instructor. The paper may provide instructions for the reader to follow, tell how a process is performed, or describe how a process develops. Prepare a complete list of steps, arrange them in an appropriate order, and follow them as you write the body of your essay.*

1. A natural process, such as erosion, that you observe or research
2. Breaking a bad habit
3. The stages in a technical process such as paper production
4. The stages in a student's adjustment to college
5. Placing an order over the internet

6. Training a dog or other pet
7. Using a particular computer program
8. The stages in the development of an argument
9. Carrying out a process related to your hobby
10. Preparing your favourite meal

The Critical Edge

Is there only one way to study effectively, develop a marketing campaign, or cope with a demanding supervisor? No, of course not. As you've already learned, not all processes unfold in a single, predetermined order. For this reason, there are many different approaches to writing about processes.

Imagine you are writing a process paper about the writing process itself. The steps in the process would be determined by the nature of the writing situation, the purpose and audience for the writing. Informal writing to a friend would require fewer steps than formal, academic writing. For example, when you write an email to a good friend, you probably just start typing without any preliminaries and press "send" as soon as you are finished. However, in formal writing such as job applications or academic research essays, the writing process involves careful planning, drafting, revising, and editing.

Sometimes the same writing occasion may allow for differing procedures. If you're writing an essay for your English class, you might brainstorm for ideas, develop a detailed outline, rough out a bare-bones draft, and add details as you revise. In talking to other students with the same assignment, you might find that they prefer to write a much longer draft and then whittle it down. Others might do very little brainstorming or outlining but a great deal of revising, often making major changes in several drafts. Even in the more complex challenge of writing research essays, variations are possible: One student might prepare the list of works cited before writing the final draft, while another might perform this task last.

But the fact that processes can differ does not mean that all processes are equal—or even correct. Sometimes important and even popular processes have been disputed in print. If you want to assess a process description, you need to do some of your own investigations or research. Informed disagreements exist about the order of processes, such as how language developed, or how children mature emotionally or cognitively. Police officers debate the best way to handle drunks, and management experts argue about how best to motivate employees. When you investigate such controversies, determine which view is supported by the best evidence and seems most reasonable. Then, as a writer, you can present the accounts in an appropriate order, comparing one to the other and perhaps indicating which one you think merits acceptance.*

*If you rely on information obtained through interviews, read Chapter 14. If you rely on published sources, read the sections on library and internet research in Chapter 13 and those on handling quotations and avoiding plagiarism in Chapter 15. As always, follow your instructor's guidelines for documenting sources.

SUGGESTIONS FOR WRITING

1. Interview several students about the stages they experienced in a developing friendship, and write a paper that discusses these stages. Note any discrepancies in the accounts provided by different students.

2. Research a controversial process, such as the extinction of the dinosaurs. After presenting different theories about the process, explain which one seems most plausible and why.

PROCESS ANALYSIS ESSAYS: PROFESSIONAL MODELS

READING STRATEGIES

1. Determine the reason you are reading the process essay. If it is to follow instructions, you need to read in one way; if it is to understand a process, you need to read differently.

2. If you are going to follow the instructions, read over the process first to get an understanding of the whole. Look for specific warnings or feedback you should consider. Get an idea of what the end result should look like. Gather any equipment you need. Then follow the process step by step, checking after each step to make certain the results you are obtaining match those described in the process.

3. If you want to understand the process thoroughly, first read it quickly to get an overview. As you read through again more slowly, take notes outlining the major steps of the process.

READING CRITICALLY

1. Check to see if the process could be completed differently or more effectively. Are there any cautions or warnings not included in the essay that should have been there?

2. If the writer is explaining a process, is there evidence that his or her account is correct? Verify that there is good reason to believe the given account. If you believe there might be competing accounts of the process, test your suspicion by doing some research.

READING AS A WRITER

1. Observe how the writer uses verbs to indicate actions.

2. Notice how the writer gets from step to step in the process. If there is a strategy you could use, make note of it.

Rod McQueen

Millionaire Questionnaire

Born in Guelph, Ontario, in 1944, Rod McQueen has worked as a reporter, editor, director of public affairs at the Bank of Nova Scotia, and managing business editor at Maclean's. *He has won many awards for his writing, including the National Business Book Award for* Who Killed Confederation Life? The Inside Story. *He has authored six other books, including* The Last Best Hope—How to Start and Grow Your Own Business. *He is now a Toronto-based senior writer at* The Financial Post. *Rod McQueen's clear, tightly structured essay "Millionaire Questionnaire" might also have been called "Steps to Starting a Small Business" or "Setting a Goal and Succeeding."*

1   Lottery tickets are a waste of money. Everybody knows the improbable odds—one in 13 million.

2   There's a better way to become a millionaire. You've already got everything you need—right inside.

3   Here's the four-word secret: Start your own business.

4   Have you got what it takes?

5   After five years of interviewing the presidents of Canada's 50 Best Managed Private Companies, I've identified the top 10 steps to success.

6   **1. Find a need and fill it.** Have a plan and follow it. Newfoundland's Lorraine Lush concluded that her neighbours needed work skills. For 14 years she'd been a secretary, so she taught the first 65 students what she knew best: secretarial skills.

7   Today, The Career Academy has 22 programs, 3000 students and 15 campuses.

8   **2. Believe in yourself.** If you don't, who will? When free trade arrived in 1989, observers predicted the demise of Morrison Lamothe Inc., an Ottawa bakery begun in the 1930s. Third-generation president John Morrison didn't heed the so-called experts.

9   The firm focused on private-label frozen dinners. Almost half of the product line is new in the last four years, and the firm is tackling the U.S.

10   **3. Exude optimism.** Nobody wants to deal with a dud. Geoff Chutter runs Whitewater West Industries Ltd., of Richmond, B.C., making waterslides and wave pools.

11   Talking to this man is like taking a tonic. Despite having the best job in the world, Chutter has twice run for Parliament because he believes he can make a public policy difference.

12   **4. Be flexible.** Bend the rules. Take chances. Mining exploration fell two-thirds from 1987 to 1992, and with it went the drilling tool business of Fordia, in St. Laurent, Que.

13   Fordia's Alain Paquet took a chance and chased customers in South America. "Your life is at risk when traveling in those areas," he says after being robbed in Venezuela. "You can get killed for nothing if you're not careful." He and the company both survived. Fordia now sells in 28 countries.

14   **5. Exercise vision.** This is the capacity to see the invisible. In September, 1996, a stranger arrived at Crila Plastic Industries Ltd., in Mississauga, Ont., promoting an unlikely product, a plastic that looked and acted like wood.

Sidebar annotations:

Title implies a process: questions and answers on how to become a millionaire

Several introductory strategies are employed to engage the audience: arresting statement (para. 1), personal challenge (paras. 2 and 3), and rhetorical question (para. 4)

Thesis: clearly asserts the essay's focus on the top ten steps to success as identified by the presidents of Canada's 50 Best Managed Private Companies (para. 5)

Each of the ten steps to success is expressed as a direct assertion to the audience, giving the essay a consistent format and focusing the audience on the process (paras. 5–24)

The use of specific personal examples demonstrates and explains each of the 10 steps to success while engaging the audience with "real" anecdotes that are likely to be relatable to our own experiences.

15   Intrigued, Crila president Peter Clark flew to Britain, obtained North American rights, and now sells two million board feet of Extrudawood per month in an industry where a million board feet of anything in a year is a good sale.

16   **6. Accept help and advice.** Honour what people have to offer. Edmonton-based Fountain Tire doesn't just wait to hear ideas, it goes looking.

17   Says CEO Brian Hesje: "It's more productive to be humbled by those that succeed rather than have the false sense of security that comes from visiting the less successful."

18   **7. Tap the passion within.** Be resourceful. Trust your instincts. "I believe entrepreneurs are being visited by divine inspiration," says clothing designer Linda Lundström. "I also believe an entrepreneur can visualize something and make it happen."

19   How else to explain the moment when a bird-dropping spattered her car windshield while Lundström drove on an expressway. She combined that unhappy impact with a message she read on a passing truck and concluded that her La Parka line would do well. Her instincts were accurate.

20   **8. Fulfill customers' needs and exceed their expectations.** Glegg Water Conditioning, of Guelph, Ont., shipped a key component to a U.S. client, but customs problems meant a 24-hour delay.

21   A Lear jet was chartered to deliver the item that very day. "We'll do whatever it takes to look after our clients," says president and CEO Robert Glegg.

22   **9. Never give up.** True character means never accepting defeat. Robert Mills and his son, Ray, of Calgary, spent nine months in 1989 making 1000 sales calls. They sold only two of their pumps.

23   In the tenth month, Ray sold 15 pumps to one company. Today, Kudu Industries Inc., employs 100 and has annual sales of $35 million.

24   **10. Dream it and do it.** Olympic cyclist Louis Garneau's racing gear and helmet business, based in St.-Augustin, Quebec, began with one sewing machine in his father's garage. Montreal's Karel Velan filled his order book using a four-page leaflet before he'd manufactured his first valve.

25   Not every start-up succeeds; annual failure rates run to 20 percent.

26   But what that also means is that out of 100 new businesses launched tomorrow, 30 will still be alive in five years.

27   Of those, 20 percent will be scraping by, 60 percent will be doing middling well, but 20 percent will be spectacularly successful.

28   Each of those six firms will have anywhere from 30 to 100 employees plus annual sales as high as $50 million.

29   And each of those individual founders will be millionaires.

30   Six millionaires for every 100 entrants.

31   I like those odds. Don't you?

32   You have the power to make of tomorrow exactly what you want.

> The inspirational tone throughout the essay is reasserted at the end with the personal challenge to become successful by applying the process steps explained in the essay (paras. 31 and 32).

DISCUSSION QUESTIONS

1. Why do you suppose the writer uses examples to illustrate each step? What examples do you find especially vivid?

2. Consider the brevity of the paragraphs in this article, especially the introductory and concluding paragraphs. Why do you think the writer has written such short paragraphs?

3. Find examples of the writer's use of numbers and statistics, quotations, and rhetorical questions. Comment on their effect.

4. Do you trust the writer's advice in this essay? Why or why not?

TOWARD KEY INSIGHTS

What reasons besides financial ones might people have for starting a small business? If you were to "find a need and fill it," what business would you start?

If you were to start a business or become a partner in an existing business immediately after leaving school, would you prefer to start your own small business or or join a corporation? Explain.

Some people believe that superstores, large chains, and shopping malls make it difficult for small businesses to compete successfully. What is your view? Where do you prefer to take your business?

SUGGESTION FOR WRITING *Think of an endeavour outside the business realm where it is important to "believe in yourself," and write an essay explaining how to be successful in this activity.*

Beth Wald

Let's Get Vertical!

Beth Wald (born 1960) first felt the attraction of the mountains when, at age sixteen, she took a backpacking trip to Canada. A native of Minnesota, she studied botany and Russian at the University of Minnesota and then, in the mid-1980s, began a dual career as a freelance writer and photographer. Her career and her love of climbing have taken her around the world. Her articles have appeared in a variety of climbing and outdoor magazines, as have her photographs, which include environmental and cultural subjects as well as sports and travel. From 1988 to 1992, she was a contributing editor for Climbing Magazine. *In our selection, Wald acquaints potential recruits with the sport of rock climbing.*

1   Here I am, 400 feet up on the steep west face of Devil's Tower,* a tiny figure in a sea of petrified rock. I can't find enough footholds and handholds to keep climbing. My climbing partner anxiously looks up at me from his narrow ledge. I can see the silver sparkle of the climbing devices I've jammed into the crack every eight feet or so.

2   I study the last device I've placed, a half-inch aluminum wedge 12 feet below me. If I slip, it'll catch me, but only after a 24-foot fall, a real "screamer." It's too difficult to go back; I have to find a way up before my fingers get too tired. I must act quickly.

3   Finding a tiny opening in the crack, I jam two fingertips in, crimp them, pull hard, and kick my right foot onto a sloping knob, hoping it won't skid off. At

---

*A large, flat-topped formation, 876 feet high, in northeastern Wyoming.

the same time, I slap my right hand up to what looks like a good hold. To my horror, it's round and slippery.

4   My fingers start to slide. Panic rivets me for a second, but then a surge of adrenalin snaps me back into action. I scramble my feet higher, lunge with my left hand, and catch a wider crack. I manage to get a better grip just as my right hand pops off its slick hold. My feet find edges, and I regain my balance. Whipping a chock (wedge) off my harness, I slip it into the crack and clip my rope through a carabiner (oblong metal snaplink). After catching my breath, I start moving again, and the rest of the climb flows upward like a vertical dance.

5   **The Challenges and Rewards** I've tried many sports, but I haven't found any to match the excitement of rock climbing. It's a unique world, with its own language, communities, controversies, heroes, villains, and devoted followers. I've lived in vans, tepees, tents, and caves; worked three jobs to save money for expenses; driven 24 hours to spend a weekend at a good rock; and lived on beans and rice for months at a time—all of this to be able to climb. What is it about scrambling up rocks that inspires such a passion? The answer is, no other sport offers so many challenges and so many rewards.

6   The physical challenges are obvious. You need flexibility, balance, and strength. But climbing is also a psychological game of defeating your fear, and it demands creative thinking. It's a bit like improvising a gymnastic routine 200 feet in the air while playing a game of chess.

7   Climbers visit some of the most spectacular places on earth and see them from a unique perspective—the top! Because the sport is so intense, friendships between climbers tend to be strong and enduring.

8   **Anyone Can Climb** Kids playing in trees or on monkey bars know that climbing is a natural activity, but older people often have to relearn to trust their instincts. This isn't too hard, though. The ability to maintain self-control in difficult situations is the most important trait for a beginning climber to have. Panic is almost automatic when you run out of handholds 100 feet off the ground. The typical reaction is to freeze solid until you fall off. But with a little discipline, rational thinking, and/or distraction tactics such as babbling to yourself, humming, or even screaming, fear can change to elation as you climb out of a tough spot.

9   Contrary to popular belief, you don't have to be superhumanly strong to climb. Self-confidence, agility, a good sense of balance, and determination will get you farther up the rock than bulging biceps. Once you've learned the basics, climbing itself will gradually make you stronger, though many dedicated climbers speed up the process by training at home or in the gym.

10   Nonclimbers often ask, "How do the ropes get up there?" It's quite simple; the climbers bring them up as they climb. Most rock climbers today are "free climbers." In free climbing, the rope is used only for safety in case of a fall, *not* to help pull you up. (Climbing without a rope, called "free soloing," is a *very* dangerous activity practiced only by extremely experienced—and crazy—climbers.)

11   First, two climbers tie into opposite ends of a 150-foot-long nylon rope. Then one of them, the belayer, anchors himself or herself to a rock or tree. The other, the leader, starts to climb, occasionally stopping to jam a variety of aluminum wedges or other special gadgets, generically referred to as protection, into cracks in the rock. To each of these, he or she attaches a snaplink, called a carabiner, and clips the rope through. As the leader climbs, the belayer feeds out the rope, and it runs through the carabiners. If the leader falls, the belayer holds

the rope, and the highest piece of protection catches the leader. The belayer uses special techniques and equipment to make it easy to stop falls.

12   When the leader reaches the end of a section of rock—called the pitch—and sets an anchor, he or she becomes the belayer. This person pulls up the slack of the rope as the other partner climbs and removes the protection. Once together again, they can either continue in the same manner or switch leaders. These worldwide techniques work on rock formations, cliffs, peaks, even buildings.

13   **Rocks, Rocks Everywhere** Some of the best climbing cliffs in the country are in the Shawangunk Mountains, only two hours from New York City. Seneca Rocks in West Virginia draws climbers from Washington, D.C., and Pittsburgh, Pennsylvania. Chattanooga, Tennessee, has a fine cliff within the city limits. Most states in the U.S. and provinces in Canada offer at least one or two good climbing opportunities.

14   Even if there are no large cliffs or rock formations nearby, you can climb smaller rocks to practice techniques and get stronger. This is called bouldering. Many climbers who live in cities and towns have created climbing areas out of old stone walls and buildings. Ask someone at your local outdoor shop where you can go to start climbing.

15   **Get a Helping Hand** There's no substitute for an expert teacher when it comes to learning basic techniques and safety procedures. One of the best (and least expensive) ways to learn climbing is to convince a veteran climber in your area to teach you. You can usually meet these types at the local crag or climbing shop.

16   As another option, many universities and colleges, some high schools, and some YMCAs have climbing clubs. Their main purpose is to introduce people to climbing and to teach the basics. Other clubs, such as the Appalachian Mountain Club in the eastern U.S. and the Mountaineers on the West Coast, also provide instruction. Ask at your outdoor shop for the names of clubs in your area.

17   If you live in a place completely lacking rocks and climbers, you can attend one of the fine climbing schools at the major climbing area closest to you. Magazines like *Climbing*, *Rock & Ice*, and *Outside* publish lists of these schools. Once you learn the basics, you're ready to get vertical.

18   In rock climbing, you can both lose yourself and find yourself. Life and all its troubles are reduced to figuring out the puzzle of the next section of cliff or forgotten in the challenge and delight of moving through vertical space. And learning how to control anxiety, how to piece together a difficult sequence of moves, and how to communicate with a partner are all skills that prove incredibly useful back on the ground!

DISCUSSION QUESTIONS

1. Discuss the effectiveness of Wald's title.

2. At the beginning of the essay, Wald notes that she is 400 feet up one side of Devil's Tower and positioned above her climbing partner. What do you think these statements accomplish?

3. In which paragraphs does Wald detail the actual process of climbing? What do the remaining paragraphs in the body of the essay accomplish?

4. Point out two places in the first four paragraphs where Wald cites reasons for her actions.

5. What attributes does Wald believe a rock climber must have? Refer to the essay when answering.

6. After reading this essay, are you ready to begin rock climbing? Does your answer stem from Wald's content, the manner of presentation, or both? Discuss.

TOWARD KEY INSIGHTS

What challenging activities appeal to you?

What level of risk are you willing to accept in an activity?

How do you account for your attitude about taking risks?

SUGGESTION FOR WRITING *Write a process paper in which you explain the attributes required and the steps involved in one of your recreational activities.*

CHAPTER 8

Strategies for Analytical Writing: Cause and Effect

EXPLAINING WHY

Like the two sides of a coin, cause and effect are inseparably linked. Together they make up *causation*. Cause probes the reasons why actions, events, attitudes, and conditions exist. Effect examines their consequences. Causation is important because it can explain historical events, natural happenings, and the actions and attitudes of individuals and groups. It can help us anticipate the consequences of personal actions, natural phenomena, or government policies.

Everyone uses questions of causation in daily life. For example, Scott wonders why Sue *really* broke off their relationship, and Jennifer speculates on the consequences of changing her major. People wonder why child abuse and homelessness are on the rise, and millions worry about the effects of corporate cost-cutting and rising crime rates.

Inevitably, you will have to write papers and reports that employ causation. Your instructors might ask you to write on topics such as the causes of the Quebec separatist movement, the psychological consequences of workplace violence, the reasons behind high divorce rates, or the effects of fertilizers on plant growth. In the workplace, you may need to write a report explaining why a certain product malfunctions, a proposal detailing what might happen if a community redesigns its traffic pattern, or a study explaining how increased security costs might affect business.

PATTERNS IN CAUSAL ANALYSIS

Several organizational patterns are used in a causal analysis. Sometimes, a single cause produces several effects. For instance, poor language skills prevent students from keeping up with required reading, taking adequate notes, and writing competent papers and essay exams. Below, the outline on the left shows a pattern for a paper that traces a single cause with multiple effects; on the right, we're shown how this pattern could be used for a paper analyzing the effects of having poor language skills in school.

I. Introduction: identifies cause	I. Poor language skills
II. Body	II. Body
A. Effect number 1	A. Can't keep up with required reading
B. Effect number 2	B. Can't take adequate notes
C. Effect number 3	C. Can't write competent papers or exams
III. Conclusion	III. Conclusion

Alternatively, you might discuss the cause after the effects are presented.

On the other hand, several causes may join forces to produce one effect. For example, lumber production in British Columbia has decreased over the last few years because stumpage fees are higher, international demand is lower, and foreign competition is stronger. Note how the outline below on the left shows a pattern for an analysis of how multiple causes may contribute to a single effect; on the right, you'll see how this pattern could be used for an outline on the reasons for a decrease in B.C. lumber production.

I. Introduction: identifies effect	I. Decrease in B.C. lumber production
II. Body	II. Body
A. Cause number 1	A. Higher stumpage fees
B. Cause number 2	B. Lower international demand
C. Cause number 3	C. Stronger foreign competition
III. Conclusion	III. Conclusion

As an alternative, you can also discuss the effects following the presentation of causes.

At times, a set of events forms a causal chain, with each event the effect of the preceding one and the cause of the following one. For example, a student sleeps late and so misses breakfast and ends up hungry and distracted, which in turn results in a poor performance on an exam. Interrupting the chain at any point halts the sequence. Such chains can be likened to a row of falling dominoes. The U.S. entry into the Vietnam War illustrates a causal chain: One major cause of the war was a widespread belief in the domino theory, which held that, if one nation in Southeast Asia fell to the communists, all would fall, one after the other. Causal chains can also help explain how devices function and social changes proceed. The next two outlines show the pattern for a paper that explains a causal chain. The outline on the right gives an example of how one cause (sleeping late) leads to an effect (missing breakfast) that in turn becomes another cause (becoming hungry and distracted) that leads to yet another effect.

I.	Introduction	I.	Introduction
II.	Body	II.	Body
	A. Cause		A. Sleep late
	B. Effect		B. Miss breakfast
	C. Cause		C. Become hungry and distracted
	D. Effect		D. Perform poorly on exam
III.	Conclusion	III.	Conclusion

In many situations, the sequence of causes and effects is too complex to fit the image of a chain. Suppose you are driving to a movie on a rainy night. You approach an intersection screened by bushes, and, because you have the right-of-way, you start to drive across. Suddenly, a car with unlit headlights looms directly in your path. You hit the brakes but skid on the slippery pavement and crash into the other car, crumpling its left fender and damaging your own bumper. Later, as you think through the episode, you become aware of its complexities.

Obviously, the *immediate cause* of the accident was the other driver's failure to heed the stop sign. But other causes also played roles: the bushes and unlit headlights that kept you from seeing the other car sooner; the starts and stops, speedups and slowdowns that brought the two cars to the intersection at the same time; the wet pavement that made you more likely to skid; and the movie that brought you out in the first place.

You also realize that the effects of the accident go beyond the fender and bumper damage. After the accident, a police officer ticketed the other driver. As a result of the delay, you missed the movie. Further, the accident unnerved you so badly that you couldn't attend classes the next day and therefore missed an important writing assignment. Because of a bad driving record, the other driver lost his licence for sixty days. Clearly, the effects of this accident rival the causes in complexity.

Here's how you might organize a multiple cause–multiple effect essay:

I.	Introduction	I.	The accident
II.	Body	II.	Body
	A. Cause number 1		A. Driver ran stop sign
	B. Cause number 2		B. Bushes and unlit headlights impaired
	C. Cause number 3		C. Wet pavement caused skidding
	D. Effect number 1		D. Missed the movie
	E. Effect number 2		E. Unnerved so missed classes next day
	F. Effect number 3		F. Other driver lost licence
III.	Conclusion	III.	Conclusion

In some situations, you might first present the effects, then turn to the causes.

EXERCISE

1. **Read the following paragraph on political change in Ireland, and then arrange the events in a causal chain:**

   At a key moment, labour, business, and government leaders abandoned ideological differences and constructed a shared socio-economic strategy. These factors, in concert with strategic investment in education and a focused effort to attract new foreign direct investment, produced over 500 000 new jobs in the 1990s. Ireland's recent economic success has been achieved, in part, through a social or strategic partnership. Armed with a consensus on the problem, they took a long-term, strategic approach to economic and social change. The steps they took established a positive labour relations climate and stabilized the macro-economic and fiscal situation in Ireland.

   "Strategic Partnership," The Strategic Partnership Study Group, Province of Newfoundland and Labrador, June 2002

2. **Trace the possible effects of the following occurrences:**

   a. You pick out a salad at the cafeteria and sit down to eat. Suddenly, you notice a large green worm on one of the lettuce leaves.

   b. As you leave your lab, you trip and break your arm.

REASONING ERRORS IN CAUSAL ANALYSIS

Ignoring Multiple Causes

An effect rarely stems from a single cause. The person who believes that permissive parents have caused the present upsurge of sexually transmitted diseases or the one who blames television violence for the climbing numbers of emotionally disturbed children oversimplifies the situation. Permissiveness and violence perhaps did contribute to these conditions. However, numerous other factors have also undoubtedly played important parts.

Mistaking Chronology for Causation

Don't assume that, just because one event follows another, the first necessarily causes the second. Therese breaks a mirror just before Wade breaks their engagement; then she blames the cracked mirror. Youth crime rates may have declined since the Youth Criminal Justice Act was introduced, but does this mean that the introduction of the Youth Criminal Justice Act has necessarily caused the decline in youth crime rates? Don't misunderstand: One event *may* cause the next event, but before you go on record with your conclusion, make sure that you're not dealing with mere chronology.

Confusing Causes with Effects

Young children sometimes declare that the moving trees make the wind blow. Similarly, you may assume that Tara's relationship breakdown caused her depression, whereas perhaps, her undiagnosed depression caused her relationship breakdown. Scan your evidence carefully in order to avoid such faulty assertions.

EXERCISE *Which of the following statements point toward papers that focus on causes? Which point toward papers focusing on effects? Explain your answers.*

1. There are many reasons why more male students than female students drop out of school.

2. While offshore oil exploration will produce new jobs, it may also damage the marine environment in a number of ways.

3. Children who live in poverty are twice as likely as other children to have poor health, low scores on school readiness exams, and high remediation needs.

ETHICAL ISSUES

Causation is not immune from abuse, either accidental or deliberate. Imagine the consequences of an article that touts a new herbal remedy but fails to mention several serious side effects that could harm many users. Think about the possible strain on your relationship with a friend if she unjustly suspects you of starting a vicious rumour about her. Writing cause-and-effect papers creates an ethical responsibility. Asking and answering the following questions can help you meet that obligation.

- Have I tried to uncover all of the causes that might result in a particular outcome? A report blaming poor instruction alone for a high failure rate in a town's public schools almost certainly overlooks such factors as oversized classes, inadequate facilities, and economic deprivation.

- Have I carefully weighed the importance of the causes I've uncovered? If only two or three of the classes in the school system are oversized, then the report should not dwell on the significance of class size.

- Have I tried to uncover and discuss every important effect, even one that might damage a case I'm trying to make? A report emphasizing the beneficial effects of jogging would be negligent if it failed to note the potential for injury.

- What would be the consequences if people acted on my advice?

Careful evaluation of causes and effects fulfills not only your writing obligation but also your ethical one.

WRITING A CAUSAL ANALYSIS
Planning and Drafting the Causal Analysis

Because you have probably speculated about the causes and effects of several campus, local, provincial, or national problems, writing this type of paper should pose no great difficulty. Depending on the assignment, perhaps your personal experience will suggest something promising. Topics such as "Why I Dislike (or Like) Sports Cars" and "How My Father's (or Someone Else's) Death Has Changed My Life" might work well. Nonpersonal topics also offer writing possibilities. For instance, "What's Behind Teenage Suicides?" and "The Impact of Global Markets on Canadian Corporations" would prompt you to draw on library resources.

The strategies previously mentioned can also help you find several topics. Answer these questions about each potential candidate:

What purpose guides this writing?

Who is my audience? Will the topic interest them? Why or why not?

Shall I focus on causes, effects, or both?

Brainstorming your topic for supporting details should be straightforward. If you're dealing with causes, pose these questions about each one:

How significant is this cause?

Could it have brought about the effect by itself?

Does it form part of a chain?

Precisely how does it contribute to the effect?

For papers dealing with effects, use these questions:

How important is this effect?

What evidence will establish its importance?

Charting your results can help you prepare for writing the paper. To tabulate causes, use an arrangement like this one:

Cause	Contribution to Effect
First cause	Specific contribution
Second cause	Specific contribution

For effects, use this chart:

Effect	Importance
First effect	Why important
Second effect	Why important

Once your items are tabulated, carefully examine them for completeness. Perhaps you've overlooked a cause or effect or have slighted the significance of one you've already mentioned. Think about the order in which you'd like to discuss your items and prepare a revised chart that reflects your decision.

Use the opening of your paper to identify your topic and indicate whether you plan to discuss causes, effects, or both. You can signal your intention in a number of ways. To prepare for a focus on causes, you might use the words *cause, reason,* or *stem from,* or you might ask why something has occurred. To signal a paper on effects, you might use *effect, fallout,* or *result,* or you might ask what has happened since something took place. Read these examples:

Signals causes: Sudbury's recent decrease in street crime stems primarily from its expanded educational program, growing job opportunities for young people, and falling rate of drug addiction.

Signals effects: Canadian travel in the U.S. has been affected in several ways since September 2001.

At times, you may choose a dramatic attention-getter. For a paper on the effects of radon, a toxic radioactive gas present in many homes, you might note, "Although almost everyone now knows about the hazards associated with smoking, eating high-cholesterol foods, and drinking excessively, few people are aware that just going home could be hazardous to one's health." However, if you use an arresting statement, be sure the content of your paper warrants it.

How you organize the body of the paper depends on your topic. Close scrutiny may reveal that one cause was indispensable; the rest merely played supporting roles. If so, discuss the main cause first. For example, when analyzing your car accident, start with the failure of the other driver to yield the right-of-way; then fan out to any other causes that merit mentioning. Sometimes you'll find that no single cause was at fault but that all of them helped matters along. Combinations of this kind lie at the heart of many social and economic concerns, such as depression and urban crime rates. Weigh each cause carefully and rank the causes in importance. If your topic and purpose would profit from building suspense, work from the least important cause to the most important. For analyzing causal chains, chronological order works most effectively.

If space won't permit you to deal adequately with every cause, pick out the two or three you consider most important and limit your discussion to them. To avoid giving your reader an oversimplified impression, acknowledge that other causes exist. However, ensure that you stay on topic. Even with no length limitation, don't attempt to trace every cause to more remote causes and then to still more remote ones. Instead, determine a sensible cutoff point that accords with your purpose, and don't go beyond it.

Treat effects as carefully as you treat causes. Keep in mind that effects often travel in packs, and try to arrange them in some logical order. If they occur together, consider order of climax. If one follows the other in a chainlike sequence, present them in that fashion. If you are close to the maximum length permitted, limit your discussion to the most interesting or significant effects.

Whatever order you choose for your paper, don't jump helter-skelter from cause to effect to cause in a way that leaves your reader bewildered.

Moreover, as you write, don't restrict yourself to a bare-bones discussion of causes and effects. For instance, if you're exploring the student parking problem on campus, you might describe the jammed lots or point out that students often miss class because they have to drive around looking for available spots. Similarly, don't simply assert that the administration's insensitivity contributes to the problem. Instead, cite examples of their refusal to answer letters about the situation or to discuss it. To provide statistical evidence of the problem's seriousness, you might note the small number of lots, the limited spaces in each, and the approximate number of student cars on campus.

It's important to remember, however, that you're not just listing causes and effects; you're showing the reader their connection in order to serve a larger purpose. Let's see how one student handled this connection. After you've read "Why Students Drop Out of University," the student essay in this chapter, carefully re-examine paragraph 3. Note how the sentence beginning "In many schools" and the two following it show precisely how poor study habits develop. Note further how the sentence beginning "This laxity produces" and the three following it show precisely how such poor habits result in "a flood of low grades and failure." University students who read this causal analysis are better armed to avoid poor study habits and their consequences.

Causal analyses can end in several ways. A paper discussing the effects of acid rain on Canada's lakes and streams might specify the grave consequences of failing to deal with the problem or express the hope that something will be done. Frequently, writers use their conclusions to emphasize the relative importance of the causes or effects.

Revising the Causal Analysis

Follow the guidelines in Chapter 5 and answer these questions as you revise your causal analysis:

Have I made the right decision in electing to focus on causes, effects, or both?
Have I determined all important causes and effects? Have I avoided mistakenly labelling something as an effect merely because it follows something else? Have I avoided confusing causes with effects?
Am I dealing with a causal chain? An immediate cause and several supporting causes? Or multiple causes and effects?
Have I presented my causes and effects in an appropriate order?
Have I supported my discussion with sufficient details?

EXAMPLE OF A STUDENT ESSAY OF CAUSE AND EFFECT

Why Students Drop Out of University

Diann Fisher

1   Each fall, a new crop of first-year university students, wavering between high hopes for the future and intense anxiety about their new status, scan campus maps searching for their classrooms. They have been told repeatedly that university is the key to a well-paying job, and they certainly don't want to support themselves by flipping hamburgers or working at some other dead-end job. So, notebooks at the ready, they await what university has in store. Unfortunately many of them—indeed, over 30 percent—will not return after the first year. Why do so many students leave? There are several reasons. Some find the academic program too hard, some lack the proper study habits or motivation, others fall victim to the temptations of the environment, and a large group leave for personal reasons.

2   Not surprisingly, the academic shortcomings of university students have strong links to high school. In the past, a high school student who lacked the ability or desire to get postsecondary education or training could still find a job with decent pay, perhaps in the resource sector. Now that possibility scarcely exists, so many poorly prepared students feel compelled to try college or university. Getting accepted by some schools isn't difficult. Once in, though, the student who has taken nothing beyond general mathematics, English, and science faces serious trouble when confronted with advanced algebra, first-year English, and biological or physical science. Most universities do offer remedial courses and other assistance that may help some weaker students to survive. In spite of everything, however, many others find themselves facing ever-worsening grades and either fail or just give up.

3   Like academic shortcomings, poor study habits have their roots in high school, where even average students can often breeze through with a minimum of effort. In many schools, outside assignments are rare and so easy that they require little time or thought to complete. To accommodate slower students, teachers frequently repeat material so many times that slightly better students can grasp it without opening their books. And when papers are late, teachers

often don't mark them down. This laxity produces students who can't or don't want to study, students totally unprepared for the rigorous demands of university. There, courses may require several hours of study each week in order to be passed with even a C. In many programs, outside assignments are commonplace and demanding. Instructors expect students to grasp material after one explanation, and many won't accept late papers at all. Students who don't quickly develop disciplined study habits may face low grades and failure.

4   Poor student motivation aggravates faulty study habits. Students who thought high school was boring find even less allure in the more challenging university offerings. Lacking any commitment to do well, they shrug off assigned papers, skip classes, and avoid doing required reading. Over time, classes gradually shrink as more and more students stay away. With final exams upon them, some return in a last-ditch effort to salvage a passing grade, but by then it is too late. Eventually, repetition of this scenario forces the students out.

5   In addition, the wide range of freedoms offered by the university environment can overwhelm even well-prepared newcomers. While students are in high school, parents are on hand to make them study, push them off to class, and send them to bed at a reasonable hour. Once away from home and parents, however, far too many students become caught up in a constant round of parties, dates, and other distractions that seem more fascinating than school work. Again, if such behaviour persists, poor grades and failure result.

6   Personal reasons also take a heavy toll on students who might otherwise complete their programs successfully. Often, money problems are at fault. For example, a student may lose a scholarship or grant, fail to obtain needed work, or find that the family can no longer afford to help out. Some students succumb to homesickness; some are forced out by an illness, injury, or death in the family; and yet others become ill or injured themselves and leave to recuperate. Finally, a considerable number become disillusioned with their programs or the size, location, or atmosphere of their schools and decide not to return.

7   What happens to the students who drop out? Some re-enroll later, often in less demanding schools that offer a better chance of academic success. Of the remainder, the great majority find jobs. Most, whatever their choice, go on to lead productive, useful lives. In the meantime, campus newcomers need to know about the dangers that tripped up so many of their predecessors and make every effort to avoid them.

DISCUSSION QUESTIONS

1. Identify the thesis statement in this essay. Who is the audience and what is the larger purpose for this essay?
2. Trace the causal chain that makes up paragraph 2.
3. In which paragraphs does the writer discuss causes? effects?

SUGGESTIONS FOR WRITING *Use one of the topics below, or another that your instructor approves, to develop a causal analysis. Determine which causes and/or effects to consider. Scrutinize your analysis for errors in reasoning, settle on an organization, and write the essay.*

1. Effects of the internet or email on family life, social life, or work life
2. Causes and/or effects of a particular kind of stress
3. Causes and/or effects of bullying in public schools or elsewhere
4. Effects of an unwise choice that you have made
5. Reasons for the popularity of a particular trend among teenagers (street racing, iPods®, text-messaging, gang culture) or another group of people
6. Effects of a recent change in policy regarding health care, education, law, or other public policy
7. Effects of media coverage of a recent incident of violence that has occurred in Canada or elsewhere
8. Effects (or mixture of causes and effects) of a particular obsession or minor addiction (worry, gossip, video games, cell phones, etc.)
9. Reasons for (or effects of) your choice to go to college or university
10. Benefits of participating in a particular healthful practice or sport

The Critical Edge

Although nearly everyone recognizes the role of causation in human affairs, people's opinions differ about the causes and effects of important matters. What lies behind the widespread incivility in society today? Why are women more likely than men to leave management jobs? How do video games affect children? What impact does electronic fraud have on society? Obviously such questions lack simple answers; as a result, even when investigators agree on the causes and effects involved, they often debate their relative importance.

Suppose your women's studies instructor has asked you to investigate the departure of women from managerial positions. Library and internet searches reveal several articles on this topic that identify a number of causes. Some women leave because they find it harder to advance than men do, and as a result they seldom attain senior positions. Others leave because they receive lower salaries than their male counterparts. Still others leave because of the stifling effects of corporate rigidity, unrealistic expectations, the demands of raising a family, or possibly diminished chances of marriage. Although most articles cite these causes, the relative importance of each cause is debatable. For example, one researcher emphasizes family concerns by discussing them last and at greatest length. Another puts the chief blame on obstacles to upward mobility—the "glass ceiling" that blocks women from upper-level positions along with an "old-boys network" of entrenched executives that parcels out jobs among its members.

Once you've finished your research, your job is to sift through all these causes and synthesize the views of your sources with your own views. Before you start to write, though, take some time to consider carefully each cause and effect you've uncovered. Obviously you should ground your paper on well-supported and widely acknowledged causes and effects, but you might also include more speculative ones as long as you clearly indicate their hypothetical nature. For example, one researcher mentions corporate rigidity as a reason that women leave management jobs, but she also clearly labels this explanation as a theory and backs it with only a single example. As you examine your research, ask yourself these critical questions as well as any others that occur to you: Does any researcher exhibit obvious bias? Do the studies cited include a sufficient number of examples to be meaningful? Do the statistics appear reliable, or are some out of date, irrelevant, or skimpy? Have the researchers avoided reasoning errors? Whenever you find a flaw, note where the problem lies so that you can discuss it in your writing if you choose. Such discussions often clear up common misconceptions.

There are various possibilities for organizing your paper. If your sources substantially agree on the most important cause, you might begin with that cause and then take up the others. A second possibility, the order-of-climax arrangement, reverses the procedure by starting with secondary causes and ending with the most significant one. You can use the same options for organizing effects. When no clear consensus exists about the relative importance of the different causes and effects, organize the material in a way that is easy to understand and interesting to read.*

SUGGESTIONS FOR WRITING

1. Read three articles on the causes of a major social controversy, such as one related to First Nations land claims, immigration policies, or drug policies, and incorporate those causes and your own views in a paper.

2. Write an essay that corrects a common misconception about the causes or effects of a matter about which you feel strongly. Possibilities might include the

---

*Because this type of paper draws on published information, it is important to read the sections on research in Chapters 13 and 14 and those on handling quotations and avoiding plagiarism in Chapter 15 before you start to write. As always, follow your instructor's guidelines for documenting sources.

causes of homelessness in your region or the effects of various kinds of sentencing on young offenders.

CAUSE AND EFFECT ESSAYS: PROFESSIONAL MODELS

READING STRATEGIES

1. Identify the central event of the essay from which the causes and effects stem.
2. Determine whether the writer is identifying a chain of causes that yield a single result or multiple causes for the same event.
3. Read carefully before determining the writer's main point. In more sophisticated academic writing, writers often first present several causes or effects, both worthy and unworthy. Only after ruling some out with key explanations do they reveal which ones they think are most plausible.
4. It can be helpful to make a diagram showing the connection between the causes and the effects.

READING CRITICALLY

1. Evaluate the evidence the writer gives for the relationship between cause and effect. How does he or she prove that the causes link to the effects as described?
2. Determine whether there could be other causes or effects that the writer hasn't mentioned.
3. Writers often confuse "correlation" for causation. Just because something happens before or around another event doesn't mean that it is the cause of the event. Does the writer confuse correlation and causation?

READING AS A WRITER

1. Note how the writer organizes the causes and effects to keep them clear and distinct.
2. Observe what devices the writer uses to demonstrate the connection between the causes and the effects.
3. Examine how the writer pulls his or her ideas together in the conclusion.

Richard Tomkins

Old Father Time Becomes a Terror

Richard Tomkins is consumer industries editor of the Financial Times, *where he has been a member of the editorial staff since 1983. He is currently based at the company's London head-quarters, where he leads a team of journalists covering the consumer goods sector and writes about consumer trends. Previously, he was the FT's marketing correspondent; and from 1993 to 1999, he was a correspondent in the newspaper's New York bureau, where he covered the consumer goods sector. Earlier positions in London included writing about the transport sector and corporate news. Tomkins was born in Walsall, England, in 1952. His formal education ended at the age of seventeen. Before becoming a journalist, he was a casual labourer, a factory worker, a truck driver, a restaurant cashier, a civil servant, and an assistant private secretary to a government minister. He left government service in 1978 to hitchhike around the world and, on returning to the U.K. in 1979, joined a local newspaper as a trainee reporter. He joined the FT as a subeditor four years later. In this selection, Tomkins discusses the time squeeze that many people are experiencing and offers a way to combat the problem.*

> Introduction contrasts the leisurely 1960s (paragraphs 1–5) with the time-stressed present.

1   It's barely 6:30 a.m. and already your stress levels are rising. You're late for a breakfast meeting. Your cell-phone is ringing and your pager is beeping. You have 35 messages in your email, 10 calls on your voicemail, and one question on your mind.

2   Why was it never like this for Dick Van Dyke?

3   Somehow, life seemed much simpler in the 1960s. In *The Dick Van Dyke Show*, the classic American sitcom of the era, Rob Petrie's job as a television script-writer was strictly nine-to-five. It was light when he left for work and light when he got home. There was no teleconferencing during his journey from the Westchester suburbs to the TV studio in Manhattan.

4   At work, deadlines loomed, but there was plenty of time for banter around the office typewriter. There was no Internet, no voicemail, no fax machine, no CNN. The nearest Petrie came to information overload was listening to a stream of wisecracks from his colleague Buddy Sorrell about Mel, the bald producer.

5   Meanwhile, at home, Rob's wife Laura—Mary Tyler Moore—led a life of leisure. After packing little Richie off to school, she had little to do but gossip with Millie, the next-door neighbour, and prepare the evening meal. When Rob came home, the family sat down to dinner: then it was television, and off to bed.

6   Today, this kind of life seems almost unimaginable. The demands on our time seem to grow ever heavier. Technology has made work portable, allowing it to merge with our personal lives. The nine-to-five job is extinct: in the U.S. people now talk about the 24-7 job, meaning one that requires your commitment 24 hours a day, seven days a week.

7   Home life has changed, too. Laura and Millie no longer have time for a gossip: they are vice-presidents at a bank. Richie's after-school hours are spent at karate classes and Chinese lessons. The only person at home any more is Buddy, who went freelance six months ago after being de-layered by Mel.

8   New phrases have entered the language to express the sense that we are losing control of our lives. "Time famine" describes the mismatch between things to do and hours to do them in, and "multi-tasking" the attempt to reconcile the two. If multi-tasking works, we achieve "time deepening," making better use of

the time available: but usually it proves inadequate, resulting in "hurry sickness" and an increasingly desperate search for "life balance" as the sufferer moves closer to break-down.

9   It was not supposed to be this way. Technology, we thought, would make our lives easier. Machines were expected to do our work for us, leaving us with ever-increasing quantities of time to fritter away on idleness and pleasure.

10   But instead of liberating us, technology has enslaved us. Innovations are occurring at a bewildering rate: as many now arrive in a year as once arrived in a millennium. And as each invention arrives, it eats further into our time.

| Body: main points presented in paragraphs 10–31 |

| Gives cause and effects of time stress and technology (paragraphs 10–14) |

11   The motor car, for example, promised unimaginable levels of personal mobility. But now, traffic in cities moves more slowly than it did in the days of the horse-drawn carriage, and we waste our lives immobilized by congestion.

12   The aircraft promised new horizons, too. The trouble is, it delivered them. Its very existence created a demand for time-consuming journeys that we would never previously have dreamed of undertaking—the transatlantic shopping expedition, for example, or the trip to a convention on the other side of the world.

13   In most cases, technology has not saved time, but enabled us to do more things. In the home, washing machines promised to free women from the drudgery of the laundry. In reality, they encouraged us to change our clothes daily instead of weekly, creating seven times as much washing and ironing. Similarly, the weekly bath has been replaced by the daily shower, multiplying the hours spent on personal grooming.

14   Meanwhile, technology has not only allowed work to spread into our leisure time—the laptop-on-the-beach syndrome—but added the new burden of dealing with faxes, emails and voicemails. It has also provided us with the opportunity to spend hours fixing software glitches on our personal computers or filling our heads with useless information from the Internet.

15   Technology apart, the Internet points the way to a second reason why we feel so time-pressed: the information explosion.

| Gives cause and specific effects of the information explosion |

16   A couple of centuries ago, nearly all the world's accumulated learning could be contained in the heads of a few philosophers. Today, those heads could not hope to accommodate more than a tiny fraction of the information generated in a single day.

17   News, facts, and opinions pour in from every corner of the world. The television set offers 150 channels. There are millions of Internet sites. Magazines, books and CD-ROMs proliferate.

18   "In the whole world of scholarship, there were only a handful of scientific journals in the 18th century, and the publication of a book was an event," says Edward Wilson, honorary curator in entymology at Harvard University's museum of comparative zoology. "Now, I find myself subscribing to 60 or 70 journals or magazines just to keep me up with what amounts to a minute proportion of the expanding frontiers of scholarship."

19   There is another reason for our increased stress levels, too: rising prosperity. As ever-larger quantities of goods and services are produced, they have to be consumed. Driven on by advertising, we do our best to oblige: we buy more, travel more, and play more, but we struggle to keep up. So we suffer from what Wilson calls discontent with super abundance—the confusion of endless choice.

| Gives cause and effects of rising prosperity |

| Discusses distribution of time stress to balance his arguments (paragraphs 20–26) |

20   Of course, not everyone is overstressed. "It's a convenient shorthand to say we're all time-starved, but we have to remember that it only applies to, say, half

the population," says Michael Willmott, director of the Future Foundation, a London research company.

21   "You've got people retiring early, you've got the unemployed, you've got other people maybe only peripherally involved in the economy who don't have this situation at all. If you're unemployed, your problem is that you've got too much time, not too little."

22   Paul Edwards, chairman of the London-based Henley Centre forecasting group, points out that the feeling of pressures can also be exaggerated, or self-imposed. "Everyone talks about it so much that about 50 percent of unemployed or retired people will tell you they never have enough time to get things done," he says. "It's almost got to the point where there's stress envy. If you're not stressed, you're not succeeding. Everyone wants to have a little bit of this stress to show they're an important person."

23   There is another aspect to all of this too. Hour-by-hour logs kept by thousands of volunteers over the decades have shown that, in the U.K., working hours have risen only slightly in the last 10 years, and in the U.S., they have actually fallen—even for those in professional and executive jobs, where the perceptions of stress are highest.

24   In the U.S., John Robinson, professor of sociology at the University of Maryland, and Geoffrey Godbey, professor of leisure studies at Penn State University, both time-use experts, found that, since the mid-1960s, the average American had gained five hours a week in free time—that is, time left after working, sleeping, commuting, caring for children and doing the chores.

25   The gains, however, were unevenly distributed. The people who benefited the most were singles and empty-nesters. Those who gained the least—less than an hour—were working couples with pre-school children, perhaps reflecting the trend for parents to spend more time nurturing their offspring.

26   There is, of course, a gender issue here, too. Advances in household appliances may have encouraged women to take paying jobs: but as we have already noted, technology did not end household chores. As a result, we see appalling inequalities in the distribution of free time between the sexes. According to the Henley Centre, working fathers in the U.K. average 48 hours of free time a week. Working mothers get 14.

Discusses first general effect of time stress: maximizing pleasure in minimum time

27   Inequalities apart, the perception of the time famine is widespread and has provoked a variety of reactions. One is an attempt to gain the largest possible amount of satisfaction from the smallest possible investment of time. People today want fast food, sound bytes and instant gratification. And they become upset when time is wasted.

28   "People talk about quality time. They want perfect moments," says the Henley Centre's Edwards. "If you take your kids to a movie and McDonald's and it's not perfect, you've wasted an afternoon, and it's a sense that you've lost something precious. If you lose some money you can earn some more, but if you waste time you can never get it back."

Discusses second general effect: buying time

29   People are also trying to buy time. Anything that helps streamline our lives is a growth market. One example is what Americans call concierge services—domestic help, child care, gardening and decorating. And on-line retailers are seeing big increases in sales—though not, as yet, profits.

30   A third reaction to time famine has been the growth of the work-life debate. You hear more about people taking early retirement or giving up high-pressure jobs in favour of occupations with shorter working hours. And bodies such as Britain's National Work-Life Forum have sprung up, urging employers to end the long-hours culture among managers—"presenteeism"—and to adopt family-friendly working policies.

31   The trouble with all these reactions is that liberating time—whether by making better use of it, buying it from others or reducing the amount spent at work—is futile if the hours gained are immediately diverted to other purposes.

> Discusses third general effect: re-evaluating jobs, long work hours

32   As Godbey points out, the stress we feel arises not from a shortage of time, but from the surfeit of things we try to cram into it. "It's the kid in the candy store," he says. "There's just so many good things to do. The array of choices is stunning. Our free time is increasing, but not as fast as our sense of the necessary."

33   A more successful remedy may lie in understanding the problem rather than evading it.

> Conclusion: summarizes sources of time stress and offers solutions (paragraphs 33–36)

34   Before the industrial revolution, people lived in small communities with limited communications. Within the confines of their village, they could reasonably expect to know everything that was to be known, see everything that was to be seen, and do everything that was to be done.

35   Today, being curious by nature, we are still trying to do the same. But the global village is a world of limitless possibilities, and we can never achieve our aim.

36   It is not more time we need: it is fewer desires. We need to switch off the cellphone and leave the children to play by themselves. We need to buy less, read less and travel less. We need to set boundaries for ourselves, or be doomed to mounting despair.

DISCUSSION QUESTIONS

1. Identify the thesis statement of this essay and suggest why it is located at this spot.

2. The following sentence appears in paragraph 4: "There is no Internet, no voicemail, no fax machine, no CNN." What does the structure of this sentence accomplish?

3. Reread paragraph 14 and then suggest Tomkins's intention in using the word "opportunity."

4. Explain the meaning of "the confusion of endless choice" at the end of paragraph 19. Then suggest examples that illustrate this idea.

5. Why do you think Tomkins calls attention to groups that are unstressed (paragraph 21) and to studies showing the time gains for some groups?

TOWARD KEY INSIGHTS

Regarding the essay's final sentence, what type of boundaries do you think time-stressed individuals should set?

How can people establish these boundaries without sacrificing quality of life?

Do you think that Canadians are generally as time-stressed as Americans? Why or why not?

SUGGESTION FOR WRITING *Write an essay discussing the causes and/or effects of some type of stress other than time stress. Possibilities might include academic or financial stress or the stress associated with personal relationships. Develop your paper with appropriate examples.*

Kristine Nyhout

Send in the Clowns

Kristine Nyhout is a freelance writer living in London, Ontario. She frequently writes on family issues, particularly the joys and challenges of raising a special needs child. "Send in the Clowns" traces the physical and emotional benefits of laughter.

1   You exercise, eat the right foods and take vitamins. If you really want to stay healthy, try laughing more each day. It may sound silly, but health professionals are taking laughter seriously and using it to help people heal. Twenty years ago, the best-seller *Anatomy of an Illness* inspired the first research. When author Norman Cousins was diagnosed with a rare arthritis-like disease, he refused to accept pain as a fact of life. With his physician's approval, he checked in to a hotel and watched funny movies. He timed the effects: a belly laugh kept pain at bay for two hours. Now mainstream scientists are investigating humour's effects on health: it's no joke because jocularity has real psychological and physiological effects—from reducing stress to affecting production of hormones.

2   So the next time you visit a hospital, you may well see a red-nosed therapeutic clown or humour specialist—health professionals trained to get laughs—among white-coated doctors. Comedy carts filled with doses of satirical verse or slapstick films roll down the corridors. Consultants even bring the comedy preventive to workplace wellness seminars—apparently laughter also boosts creativity and productivity. Regina therapist Catherine Ripplinger Fenwick recognized the importance of humour when she battled breast cancer eight years ago. "I didn't laugh enough." She outfitted herself with a laughter first aid kit, took up clowning during her chemotherapy, and noticed the "wows" of life. Now she lectures government employees and others in the benefits of mirth.

3   Bringing humour into hospital helps defuse patient anxiety and change attitudes. One of the new healing clowns, registered nurse Dee Preikschas of

Kitchener, Ont., tuned in to humour's healing power when her husband became ill. Now she's one of a number of therapeutic clowns in Canada who often work with children. Once Preikschas was dispatched to the bedside of a 10-year-old boy recovering from an appendectomy—he hated his IV and wasn't eating. By giving the kid a "magic" hammer that made a smashing noise at the offending IV, the clown got the boy to laugh—and cooperate. Clowns also bring comfort. Joy Van Herwaarde, who calls herself Joybells when she's clowning, says, "Humour can make someone less aware of the pain and can make them feel less lonely." Indeed, when a 101-year-old woman at Good Samaritan Hospital in Edmonton neared death, she asked for Joybells's brand of comfort. In Hamilton, Ont., nurse Sharon Orovan is using and studying humour to fend off panic attacks.

4   Humour also packs a physical punch. A sort of pharmacist of silliness, humour specialist Barbara Wetmore-Patel of London, Ont., dispenses videos and joke books from her comedy cart. How does it work? The laughing response can lower both heart rate and blood pressure, increase T-cell activity to fend off illness, and may improve digestion. Wetmore-Patel has seen how humour helps seniors in retirement homes and palliative care hospitals feel better physically. Laughing may release endorphins—chemicals in the brain responsible for the feeling of well-being known as runner's high—into the bloodstream, taking the edge off pain.

5   What's more, laughter may actually help keep you from getting sick. When you laugh, an antibody called immunoglobulin A travels from the bloodstream to the salivary glands where it blocks viruses from their usual port of entry, explains Herb Lefcourt, a psychology professor at the University of Waterloo. Lefcourt's research found that people who used humour more in their daily lives had higher levels of immunoglobulin A in their saliva. And when your body is under stress (as in a fight-or-flight confrontation), your immune system is suppressed. Lefcourt found humour defuses that state of arousal, allowing the immune system to continue doing its job.

6   Laughter can also lead to deeper breathing and relaxed muscles, according to physiologist David Garlick at the University of New South Wales in Sydney, Australia. Tense muscles can mean increased heart rate and blood pressure. Adrenaline levels and mental stress may also go up, Garlick adds. You may not be able to meditate during a meeting, but as Garlick points out, "Laughter is the usual way of helping to relieve muscle tension."

7   You don't have to be a stand-up comic to reap the health benefits of a chuckle—just look on the light side of life.

DISCUSSION QUESTIONS

1. Study the introductory paragraph and the concluding paragraph. What is the relationship between these two paragraphs? Identify the thesis statement. Where do you find out that the essay will focus on effects?

2. Identify five or six positive effects of laughter that are discussed in paragraphs 2–6.

3. How are paragraphs 4, 5, and 6 related? On what basis did the writer make the decision to separate these paragraphs?

4. What examples, or brief anecdotes, does the writer use to illustrate the benefits of laughter?

5. While this essay focuses on the effects of laughter, it also has a persuasive, or argumentative, slant. What strategies does the writer use to persuade you that laughter is beneficial for health? Why do you suppose the writer does not cite statistics to strengthen her argument?

TOWARD KEY INSIGHTS

To what extent do you agree with Kristine Nyhout that physical health and emotional health may be related?

Can a person decide to seek out opportunities for laughter? Why or why not?

How can humour help with other stressful situations besides physical illness?

Are there ever times when humour could strike the wrong note?

SUGGESTION FOR WRITING *Interview three or four people who are knowledgeable about some aspect of health, and write an essay persuading your reader of the positive effects of a specific healthful practice, such as weight lifting, vegetarianism, or meditation. Explain the benefits with short anecdotes, examples, and quotations from your interviewees.*

CHAPTER 9

Strategies for Analytical Writing: Definition

ESTABLISHING BOUNDARIES

The holiday movies were coated with schmaltziness.
Once the bandage is off the wound, swab the proud flesh with disinfectant.
That hockey player is a goon.

Do you have questions? You're not alone. Many people would question the sentences above: "What does *schmaltziness* mean?" "How can flesh be *proud?*" "What is a *goon* in hockey?" To avoid puzzling and provoking your own readers, you'll often need to explain the meaning of some term. The term may be unfamiliar (*schmaltziness*), used in an unfamiliar sense (*proud flesh*), or mean different things to different people (*goon*). Whenever you clarify the meaning of some term, you are *defining*.

Humans are instinctively curious. We start asking about meanings as soon as we can talk, and we continue to seek and supply definitions all through life. In school, instructors expect us to explain literary, historical, scientific, technical, and social terms. On the job, a member of a company's human resources department might prepare a brochure that explains the meaning of such terms as *corporate responsibility* and *product stewardship* for new employees. An accountant might define *statistical sampling inventory* in a report calling for a change in the inventory system. A special education teacher might write a memo explaining *learning disabled* to the rest of the staff.

When you define, you identify the features that distinguish a term, thereby establishing its boundaries and separating it from all others. Knowing these features enables both you and your reader to use the term appropriately.

Sometimes a single word, phrase, or sentence can settle a definition question. To clear up the mystery of "proud flesh," all you'd need to do is insert the parenthetical phrase (excessively swollen and grainy) after the word *proud.* But when you're dealing with new terms—such as *chronic fatigue* and *virtual reality*—brief definitions won't provide the reader with enough information for proper understanding.

Abstract terms—those standing for things we can't see, touch, or otherwise detect with our five senses—often require extended definitions, too. It's impossible to capture the essence of *democracy, hatred,* or *bravery* in a single sentence: The terms are too complex, and people have too many differing ideas about what they mean. The same holds true for some concrete terms—those standing for actions and things we can perceive with our five senses. For example, some people limit the term *drug pusher* to full-time sellers of hard drugs such as cocaine and heroin. Others extend the term to full- and part-time sellers of any illegal substance. Thus, writing an argument recommending life sentences for convicted drug pushers would require you to tell just what you mean by the term so that the reader would have solid grounds for judging your position.

TYPES OF DEFINITIONS

Three types of definitions—synonyms, essential definitions, and extended definitions—serve writers' needs. Although the first two seldom require more than a word or a sentence, an extended definition can run to several pages. However, the three types are related. Synonyms and essential definitions share space between the covers of dictionaries, and are starting points for extended definitions.

Synonyms

Synonyms are words with very nearly the same meanings. *Lissome* is synonymous with *lithe* or *nimble,* and *condign* is a synonym of *worthy* and *suitable.* Synonyms let writers clarify meanings of unfamiliar words without using cumbersome explanations. To clarify the term *expostulation* in a quoted passage, all you'd have to do is add the word *objection* after it in brackets. However, since synonyms are not identical twins, using them as definitions puts a slightly different shade of meaning on a message. For example, to "protest" and to "object" have similar meanings, but saying that we "object" to the establishment of a toxic waste site in our area sounds much weaker than saying we "protest" against such a site. Still, synonyms may provide convenient shorthand definitions, if used judiciously.

Essential Definitions

An essential definition does three things: (1) names the item being defined, (2) places it in a broad category, and (3) distinguishes it from other items in that category. Here are three examples:

Item Being Defined	Broad Category	Distinguishing Features
A howdah	is a covered seat	for riding on the back of an elephant or camel.
A voiceprint	is a graphical record	of a person's voice characteristics.
To parboil	is to boil meat, vegetables, or fruits	until they are partially cooked.

Writing a good essential definition requires careful thought. Suppose your instructor has asked you to write an essential definition of one of the terms listed in an exercise, and you choose *vacuum cleaner*. Coming up with a broad category presents no problem: A vacuum cleaner is a household appliance. The hard part is pinpointing the distinguishing features. The purpose of a vacuum cleaner is to clean floors, carpets, and upholstery. You soon realize, however, that these features alone do not separate vacuum cleaners from other appliances. After all, carpet sweepers also clean floors, and whiskbrooms clean upholstery. What feature then does distinguish vacuum cleaners? After a little thought, you realize that, unlike the other items, a vacuum cleaner works by suction. You then write the following definition:

> A vacuum cleaner is a household appliance that uses suction to clean floors, carpets, and upholstery.

The same careful attention is necessary to establish the distinguishing features of any essential definition.

Limitations of Essential Definitions   Essential definitions have certain built-in limitations. Because of their brevity, they often can't do full justice to abstract terms such as *cowardice, love, jealousy, power*. Problems also arise with terms that have several settled meanings. The word *jam* when used as a noun would require at least three essential definitions: (1) a closely packed crowd, (2) a fruit preserve, and (3) a difficult situation. But despite these limitations, an essential definition can be useful by itself or as part of a longer definition. Writers often build an extended definition around an essential definition.

Pitfalls in Preparing Essential Definitions   When you prepare an essential definition, guard against these flaws:

> *Circular definition*. Don't define a term by repeating it or changing its form slightly. A definition of a psychiatrist as "a physician who practises psychiatry" will only frustrate someone who's never heard of psychiatry. Avoid circularity and choose terms the reader can understand, for example, "A psychiatrist is a physician who diagnoses and treats mental disorders."

Overly broad definition. Shy away from loose definitions that cover too much territory. If you define a skunk as "an animal that has a bushy tail and black fur with white markings," your definition is not precise. Many cats and dogs also fit this description. But if you add "and that ejects a foul-smelling secretion when threatened," you will clear the air—of any misconceptions at least.

Overly narrow definition. Don't hem in your definition too closely, either. The definition of a kitchen blender as "a bladed electrical appliance used to chop foods" is too restricted. Blenders perform other operations, too. To correct the error, add the missing information: "A kitchen blender is a bladed electrical appliance used to chop, mix, whip, liquefy, or otherwise process foods."

Omission of main category. Avoid using "is where" or "is when" instead of naming the main category. Here are examples of this error: "A bistro is where food and wine are served" and "An ordination is when a person is formally recognized as a minister, priest, or rabbi." The reader will not know exactly what sort of thing (a bar? a party?) a *bistro* is and may think that *ordination* means a time. Note the improvement when the broad categories are named: "A bistro is a small restaurant where both food and wine are served" and "An ordination is a ceremony at which a person is formally recognized as a minister, priest, or rabbi."

EXERCISE

1. **Identify the broad category and the distinguishing traits in each of these essential definitions:**
   a. Gangue is useless rock accompanying valuable minerals in a deposit.
   b. A catbird is a small songbird with a slate-coloured body, a black cap, and a catlike cry.
   c. A soldier is a man or woman serving in an army.
   d. A magnum is a wine bottle that holds about one-and-a-half litres.

2. **Indicate which of the following statements are acceptable essential definitions. Explain what is wrong with those that are not. Correct them.**
   a. A scalpel is a small knife that has a sharp blade used for surgery and anatomical dissections.
   b. A puritan is a person with puritanical beliefs.
   c. A kraal is where South African tribes keep large domestic animals.
   d. A rifle is a firearm that has a grooved barrel and is used for hunting large game.

3. **Write an essential definition for each of the following terms:**
   a. spam   c. hit man
   b. mad cow disease   d. jock

Extended Definitions

Sometimes it's necessary to go beyond an essential definition and write a paragraph or whole paper explaining a term. Terms with differing meanings also frequently require extended definitions. New technical, social, and economic terms often require extended definitions. For example, a computer scientist might need to define *data integrity* so that computer operators understand the importance of maintaining it. Furthermore, extended definition is crucial to interpretation of the law, as we see when courts clarify the meaning of concepts such as obscenity.

Extended definitions are not merely academic exercises; they are fundamental to your career and your life. A police officer needs to have a clear understanding of what counts as *reasonable grounds for search and seizure;* an engineer must comprehend the meaning of *stress;* a nuclear medical technologist had better have a solid grasp of *radiation*. And all of us are concerned with the definition of our basic rights as citizens.

Extended definitions are montages of other methods of development—narration, description, process analysis, illustration, classification, comparison, and cause and effect. Often, they also often define by negation—explaining what a term *does not* mean. The following paragraphs show how one writer handles an extended definition of *sudden infant death syndrome*. The student begins by presenting a case history (illustration), which also incorporates an essential definition and two synonyms.

> Jane and Dick Smith were proud new parents of an eight-pound, ten-ounce baby girl named Jenny. One summer night, Jane put Jenny to bed at 8:00. When she went to check on her at 3:00 A.M., Jane found Jenny dead. The baby had given no cry of pain, shown no sign of trouble. Even the doctor did not know why she had died, for she was healthy and strong. The autopsy report confirmed the doctor's suspicion—the infant was a victim of the "sudden infant death syndrome," also known as SIDS or crib death. SIDS is the sudden and unexplainable death of an apparently healthy, sleeping infant. It is the number-one cause of death in infants after the first week of life and as a result has been the subject of numerous research studies.

DISCUSSION QUESTIONS

1. What synonyms does the writer use?
2. Which sentence presents an essential definition?

In the next paragraph, the writer turns to negation, pointing out some of the things that researchers have ruled out about SIDS.

> Although researchers do not know what SIDS is, they do know what it is not. They know it cannot be predicted; it strikes like a thief in the night. Crib deaths occur in seconds, with no sound of pain, and they always happen when the child is sleeping. Suffocation is not the cause, nor is aspiration or

regurgitation. Researchers have found no correlation between the incidence of SIDS and the mother's use of birth control pills or the presence of fluoride in water. Since it is not hereditary or contagious, only a slim chance exists that SIDS will strike twice in the same family.

Finally, the student explores several proposed causes of SIDS as well as how parents may react to the loss of their child.

As might be expected, researchers have offered many theories concerning the cause of crib death. Dr. R. C. Reisinger, a National Cancer Institute scientist, has linked crib deaths to the growth of a common bacterium, *E. coli*, in the intestines of newborn babies. The organisms multiply in the intestines, manufacturing a toxin that is absorbed by the intestinal wall and passes into the bloodstream. Breast milk stops the growth of the organism, whereas cows' milk permits it. Therefore, Dr. Reisinger believes, bottle-fed babies run a higher risk of crib death than other babies. . . .

The loss of a child through crib death is an especially traumatic experience for the family. Parents often develop feelings of guilt and depression, thinking they somehow caused the child's death. To alleviate such feelings, organizations have been established to help parents accept the fact that they did not cause the death.

Trudy Stelter, student

ETHICAL ISSUES

How we define a term can have profound consequences. For centuries, the practice of defining Africans as "subhuman" helped justify slavery. During the 1930s and early 1940s, labelling Jews as "vermin" was used to fuel the attempt to exterminate them in both Nazi Germany and much of the rest of Western Europe. Even in the absence of malice, definitions can have far-reaching effects, both good and bad. Definitions of certain learning disabilities affect whether or not a student in the public school system is eligible for extra assistance. Recently, the definition of "terrorist," which has political, legal, and military implications, has come under intense scrutiny. Answering the following questions will help you think about possible ethical implications of your definitions.

- Have I carefully evaluated all the features of my definition? For example, a definition of "excessive force" by the police would be unfair if it included actions that constitute reasonable means necessary to subdue highly dangerous suspects.
- Have I slanted my definition to reflect a prejudice? Let's say a writer opposed to casino gambling is defining "gambling addicts." The paper should focus on those who spend an excessive amount of time in casinos, bet and often lose large sums of money, and in so doing neglect family,

financial, and personal obligations. It would be unfair to include those who visit casinos occasionally and strictly limit their losses.

■ Have I avoided unnecessary connotations that might be harmful? A definition of teenagers that overemphasizes their swift changes in mood might be unfair, perhaps even harmful, since it may influence the reactions of readers.

WRITING AN EXTENDED DEFINITION

Planning and Drafting the Extended Definition

As in any type of writing, purpose will guide your choice of topic in writing definitions. Generally you don't want to spend time telling readers something they already know. For instance, why define *table* when the discussion would likely put your reader to sleep?

If you are writing an extended definition, choose an abstract term or one that is concrete but unfamiliar to your reader. An extended definition of a specialized term that the reader may not understand such as *computer virus* might well prove interesting and informative for a reader. Use one of the strategies on pages 33–39 to unearth promising topics. Then answer these questions about them:

Which topic holds the most promise? Why?

What purpose will guide my writing?
    To clarify a technical or specialized concept
    To show how I am using the term
    To persuade the reader to adopt my attitude toward it
    To discuss some neglected facet of the term

For what audience am I writing?

Here's a helpful process to follow as you think your definition through. Imagine that you are defining an abstract term such as *democracy*. First, select a clear example that illustrates what you wish to define, and brainstorm to uncover major identifying characteristics. If you are brainstorming about the United States as an example for *democracy*, your list might include majority rule, free elections, a separately elected chief executive, a constitution, and basic human rights. Next, test these characteristics against other legitimate examples and retain only the characteristics that apply. Although Canada is clearly a democracy, it doesn't have a separately elected chief executive. Moreover, Canada was a democracy for more than a century before getting its own constitution. Finally, the People's Republic of China—which is not a democracy—has elections. What, then, truly constitutes a democracy? Finally, test your unfolding definition against a clear counter-example such as Myanmar (military dictatorship) or Saudi Arabia (kingdom). If your definition fits these examples, you will need to change it.

Now evaluate what methods you might use to develop your definition. Each method has its own set of special strengths, as the following list shows:

Narration.	Tracing the history of a new development or the changing meaning of a term
Description.	Pointing out interesting or important features of a device, event, or individual
Process.	Explaining what a device does or how it is used, how a procedure is carried out, or how a natural event takes place
Illustration.	Tracing changes in meaning and defining abstract terms
Classification.	Pointing out the different categories into which an item or an event can be grouped
Comparison.	Distinguishing between an unfamiliar and a familiar item
Cause and effect.	Explaining the origins and consequences of events, conditions, problems, and attitudes
Negation.	Placing limitations on conditions and events and correcting popular misconceptions

Examine your topic in light of this list and select the methods of development that seem most promising. Don't hesitate to use a method because the purpose was not mentioned here. If you think that a comparison will help your reader understand some abstract term, use it.

Chart the methods of development you plan to use, and then brainstorm each method in turn to gather the details that will inform the reader. When you've finished, look everything over, rearrange the details as necessary, add any new ones you think of, and prepare a revised chart. The example that follows is for a paper using four methods of development.

Narration	Classification	Process	Negation
First supporting detail	First supporting detail	First supporting detail	First supporting detail
Second supporting detail	Second supporting detail	Second supporting detail	Second supporting detail

Definition papers can begin in various ways. If you're defining a term with no agreed-upon meaning (for example, *conservatism*), you might note some differing views of it and then state your own. If the term reflects some new social, political, economic, or technological development (such as the *wireless internet*), you might mention the events that brought it into being. A colloquial or slang term often yields an attention-getting opener. A paper defining *chutzpah* might begin by illustrating the brash behaviour of someone with this trait. Occasionally, an introduction includes a short definition, perhaps taken from a dictionary. If you do include a dictionary definition, use the full name of the dictionary (*The Canadian Oxford Dictionary* says . . .), but usually it is best to come up with your own definition rather than relying on a dictionary definition.

In writing the body of the paper, present the methods of development in whatever order seems most appropriate. A paper defining *drag racing* might first describe the hectic scene as the cars line up for a race, then classify the different categories of vehicles, and finally explain the steps in a race. One defining *intellectual* might start by showing the differences between intellectuals and scholars, then name several prominent intellectuals and note how their insights have altered our thinking, and conclude by trying to explain why some people distrust intellectuals.

Definition papers can end in a number of ways. If you're defining some undesirable condition or event (such as the *sudden infant death syndrome*), you might refer to new research initiatives that may yield solutions. If you're reporting on some new development (such as *nanotechnology*), you might include predictions about its economic or social impact. Choose whichever type of ending best supports your main idea.

Revising the Extended Definition

Use the general guidelines in Chapter 5 and these specific questions as you revise your extended definition:

Are my purpose and audience clear and appropriate?
If I've used an essential definition, does it do what it should, and does it avoid the common pitfalls?
Are the methods of development suitable for the topic?
Is the paper organized effectively?
Are there other factors or examples I need to consider?
Have I considered appropriate ethical issues?

EXAMPLE OF A STUDENT ESSAY OF DEFINITION

The Food Chain

Michael Galayda

1   It is a truism that we must eat to stay alive and that all the plants and animals we dine on must do the same. How many of us, though, ever stop to consider whether or not any pattern underlies all the cross-dining that goes on? There is a pattern, and to understand it we must first familiarize ourselves with the concept of a food chain. Such a chain can be defined as a hierarchy of organisms in a biological community, or ecosystem, with each member of the chain feeding on the one below it and in turn being fed upon by the one above it. To put the matter more simply, a food chain starts with a great quantity of plant stuffs which are eaten by a large number of very hungry diners. These diners are then eaten by a lesser number of other animals, which in turn fall prey to an even smaller number of creatures. With the passage of time, the uneaten organisms die and become part of the soil for the plant to grow in.

2   To illustrate, let's look for a moment at one particular biological community, a marshy ecosystem, and a few events that might take place there. First, there are the marsh grasses, with millions of grasshoppers busily feeding upon them. When one grasshopper isn't looking, a shrew sneaks up and eats it. This process is repeated many times as the day wears on. Later, toward sunset, as the stuffed and inattentive shrew is crossing an open stretch of ground, a hawk swoops out of the sky and eats the rodent. The food chain is completed when the marsh hawk dies and its corpse fertilizes the marsh grasses.

3   This illustration is not meant to suggest that hawks eat only shrews or shrews eat only grasshoppers; the cycle is much more complicated than that, involving what biologists call trophic levels—the different feeding groups in an ecosystem. For example, some creatures eat green plants and some eat meat. There are five major trophic levels. The beginning point for any food chain is green plants, known as producers, which absorb sunlight and through the process of photosynthesis turn carbon dioxide, water, and soil nutrients into food, especially carbohydrates, that animals can assimilate.

4   All of the other life forms subsist either directly or indirectly on the producers. Animals that feed directly on green plants are the herbivores, called primary consumers. This group includes, among other creatures, most insects, rodents, and hooved animals. The secondary consumers are the carnivores and omnivores. The term carnivore, meaning an animal that eats only flesh, is more familiar than the term omnivore, which designates an animal that eats both green plants and flesh. Carnivores include such animals as lions, leopards, eagles, and hawks; whereas omnivores are represented by foxes, bears, humans, and so on.

5   The last feeding group in the food chain consists of the decomposers: bacteria and fungi. These microorganisms recycle the waste products of living animals and the remains of all dead things—plants, herbivores, omnivores, and carnivores alike—into fertilizers that plants, the producers, can use.

6   Obviously each trophic level must produce more energy than it transfers to the next higher level. With animals, a considerable part of this energy is lost through body heat. The muscles that pump the lungs, continually pushing air out of the body and sucking it back in, consume energy. The muscles in the arms and legs sweat out energy. All of the life-supporting systems of the organism use energy to keep it going. Everything from worms to people lives in accordance with this law of energy loss. As long as life's fires burn, energy is lost, never to be regained.

7   Throughout history we humans have tried to manipulate the food chain so as to provide ever-greater outputs of energy. On the one hand, we have tried, by whatever means we could employ, to rid our fields of harmful birds, insects, and rodents, and our animals of diseases and parasites. On the other, we have constantly striven to produce healthier and more productive strains of plants and animals. Often these attempts have been spectacularly successful. Sometimes, though, the results have proved disastrous, as with the insecticide DDT.

8   Farmers first began using DDT on a large scale in 1946, right after it had proved its effectiveness in tropical military operations in World War II. As expected, the product proved equally effective as an agricultural pesticide, but there were some unexpected and disastrous side effects. The difficulties were caused by excessive DDT washing off crops, entering irrigation canals, and from there flowing to streams, rivers, and lakes. All living creatures in the path of the chemical were contaminated—worms, fish, ducks, indeed all forms of aquatic life. Contaminated worms poisoned songbirds, causing massive die-offs of birds, and many humans developed serious health problems from eating contaminated aquatic animals. Although the government has severely restricted the use of DDT in this country, the whole episode stands as a warning of what can happen when humans manipulate the food chain.

9   As time continues and the population grows, efforts will be made to further increase the food supply. Let us hope that in doing so we won't act in haste and create catastrophes of even greater magnitude.

DISCUSSION QUESTIONS

1. Identify the essay's essential definition and explain how it functions.
2. What is accomplished by the last three sentences in paragraph 1?
3. What method of development does the writer use in paragraph 2?
4. What methods of development are combined in paragraphs 3–5?
5. Cite three places in the essay where the writer uses brief definitions.

SUGGESTIONS FOR WRITING *Write an extended definition using one of the following suggestions or one approved by your instructor. The term you define may be new, misused, or misunderstood, or may have a disputed meaning. Develop the essay by any combination of writing strategies.*

1. Literacy
2. Storm chaser
3. Multiculturalism
4. Stress
5. Cybervandals

6. Emotional intelligence
7. Computer virus
8. Biodiversity
9. Pandemic
10. Rap music

The Critical Edge

Definitions are always social creations. The meaning of a word depends on a shared understanding of how to use the word among people in communities. As a result, writers who use abstract words such as *justice, love,* or *charisma* to convey a message may need to consult a number of sources to determine how others have used the words. With their findings of this research in mind, the writers can stake out their own meanings of those words.

If you were writing an extended definition of the word *dance* for a humanities class, you would probably discover that people have used the word in different ways. As you read *The Dance as an Artwork*, you might at first like Frank Thiess's definition of dance as the use of the body for expressive gesture; but as you mull over that definition, you realize that it is both too broad and too narrow. While some forms of dance, such as ballet, feature expressive gesture, so does pantomime or even a shaken fist; and neither of these qualifies as dance. A square dance clearly qualifies, but does it represent expressive gesture? Then you turn to *Philosophy in a New Key*, in which Susanne Langer defines dance as "a play of Powers made visible," and stresses that dancers seem to be moved by forces beyond themselves. You recognize that this definition may apply to religious dance forms, that dancers sometimes appear swept away by the music, and that you yourself have experienced a feeling of power when dancing. Nevertheless, upon reflection you decide that people watch dancers for less mystical reasons, and that it's usually the dancer's skill and artistry that attracts viewers. Finally, you discover that Francis Sparshott, in *The Theory of the Arts*, defines dance as a rhythmical, patterned motion that transforms people's sense of their own existence according to the dance they do. As you evaluate Sparshott's contention, you decide that it has considerable merit, although you aren't convinced that every dance transforms our sense of existence. When you think about the kinds of dance you know and the various definitions you have uncovered, you conclude that these writers, like the blind men who felt different parts of an elephant and tried to describe it, are each only partly correct. For your humanities paper, you decide to synthesize the different definitions. You might explain that all dance involves a rhythmical, patterned movement of the body for its own sake. Sometimes such movement can transform our sense of existence, as in trance dances or even waltzes. Other dances, such as story ballets, use rhythmical movements as expressive gestures that tell stories or convey emotions. Still other dances may suggest the manifestation of powers beyond the dances themselves. You proceed to explain each of these features with details drawn both from your sources and from personal experience.

Writing this kind of paper requires you to look critically at the definitions of others. Do they accurately reflect the examples you know about? Do they describe examples that do not fit the definition? Are any parts of the definition questionable? Once you've answered these questions, you can then draw on the appropriate elements of the definitions to formulate your own. You might organize such a paper by developing each definition in a separate section, first presenting it in detail and then pointing out its strengths and weaknesses. In the final section, you could offer your own definition and support it with your reasoning and suitable examples.*

SUGGESTIONS FOR WRITING

1. Read "The Sweet Smell of Success . . . " and "The Company Man." Then write your own definition of success, taking into account the views expressed in these essays.

2. Do some reading about an abstract term, such as *pornography, democracy, marriage,* or *terrorism,* in at least three sources. Use the sources to develop your own definition of the term.

3. If you are familiar with a particular type of jargon from an area you know well (sports, computers, music, etc.), define this language for a reader uninitiated to this specialized language. This essay might blend different strategies of development such as illustration, for you need to provide examples and definitions along the way. Alternatively, you might choose to organize your essay mainly around one extended definition of a significant word or phrase.

DEFINITION ESSAYS: PROFESSIONAL MODELS

READING STRATEGIES

1. Clearly identify the term being defined, and the broad category to which it belongs.
2. As you read, note distinguishing characteristics of the concept.
3. If there is definition by negation, identify what the term is not to be confused with.

---

*Because you need to draw on published sources, it is important to read the sections on research in Chapters 13 and 14 and those on handling quotations and avoiding plagiarism in Chapter 15 before you start to write. As always, follow your instructor's guidelines for documenting sources.

4. Observe any analogies, similes, or metaphors that can help readers understand the concept by seeing what it resembles.
5. Consider whether you have unanswered questions or points of confusion.

READING CRITICALLY

1. Ask yourself whether the definition makes sense to you.
2. Test the definition to see if it is too narrow. If a person defines literature as works of fiction, the definition could leave out poetry.
3. Test the definition to see if it is too broad. If a person defines literature as works of writing, the definition would include phone books—a clearly unintended consequence of the definition.
4. Note whether the definition has a simple explanatory purpose, or a persuasive angle.

READING AS A WRITER

1. Notice how the writer uses the introduction to explain the importance of the concept and the definition.
2. Identify the key strategies the writer uses to construct a definition—stating the broad category and distinguishing characteristics; providing examples; saying what the term is not to be confused with; drawing comparisons.
3. Observe how the writer limits the definition so that it is not too general.
4. Note whether the writer illumines a specialized concept, redefines a term in a new way, clarifies the meaning of the term for a particular context, or calls attention to an overlooked facet of the term.

Laurence Shames

The Sweet Smell of Success Isn't All That Sweet

Laurence Shames (born 1951) is a native of Newark, New Jersey, and a graduate of New York University. After completing his education, he began a career as a nonfiction writer, contributing to such publications as Playboy, McCall's, Esquire, Vanity Fair, *and the* New York Times. *His 1986 book,* The Big Time: The Harvard Business School's Most Successful Class and How It Shaped America, *explores the contributions of the 1949 graduating class to the worlds of business and public service. A later work,* The Hunger for More *(1991), focuses on the search for values in a world of greed. This concern for values is also apparent in the following selection, which attacks contemporary attitudes about success.*

1   John Milton was a failure. In writing "Paradise Lost," his stated aim was to "justify the ways of God to men." Inevitably, he fell short of accomplishing that and only wrote a monumental poem. Beethoven, whose music was conceived to transcend Fate, was a failure, as was Socrates, whose ambition was to make people happy by making them reasonable and just. The inescapable conclusion seems to be that the surest, noblest way to fail is to set one's own standards titanically high.

2   The flip-side of that proposition also seems true, and it provides the safe but dreary logic by which most of us live: The surest way to succeed is to keep one's strivings low—or at least to direct them along already charted paths. Don't set yourself the probably thankless task of making the legal system better; just shoot at becoming a partner in the firm. Don't agonize over questions about where your talents and proclivities might most fulfillingly lead you; just do a heads-up job of determining where the educational or business opportunities seem most secure.

3   After all, if "success" itself—rather than the substance of the achievements that make for success—is the criterion by which we measure ourselves and from which we derive our self-esteem, why make things more difficult by reaching for the stars?

4   What is this contemporary version of success really all about?

5   According to certain beer commercials, it consists in moving up to a premium brand that costs a dime or so more per bottle. Credit-card companies would have you believe success inheres in owning their particular piece of plastic.

6   If these examples sound petty, they are. But take those petty privileges, weave them into a fabric that passes for a value system, and what you've got is a national mood that has vast motivating power that can shape at least the near future of the entire country.

7   Under the flag of success, modern-style, liberal arts colleges are withering while business schools are burgeoning—and yet even business schools are having an increasingly hard time finding faculty members, because teaching isn't considered "successful" enough. Amid a broad consensus that there is a glut of lawyers and an epidemic of strangling litigation, record numbers of young people continue to flock to law school because, for the individual practitioner, a law degree is still considered a safe ticket.

8   The most sobering thought of all is that today's M.B.A.'s and lawyers are tomorrow's M.B.A.'s and lawyers: Having invested so much time and money in their training, only a tiny percentage of them will ever opt out of their early chosen fields. Decisions made in accordance with today's hothouse notions of ambition are locking people into careers that will define and also limit their activities and yearnings for virtually the rest of their lives.

9   Many, by external standards, will be "successes." They will own homes, eat in better restaurants, dress well and, in some instances, perform socially useful work. Yet there is a deadening and dangerous flaw in their philosophy: It has little room, little sympathy and less respect for the noble failure, for the person who ventures past the limits, who aims gloriously high and falls unashamedly short.

10   That sort of ambition doesn't have much place in a world where success is proved by worldly reward rather than by accomplishment itself. That sort of ambition is increasingly thought of as the domain of irredeemable eccentrics, of people who haven't quite caught on—and there is great social pressure not to be one of them.

11   The result is that fewer people are drawn to the cutting edge of noncommercial scientific research. Fewer are taking on the sublime, unwinnable challenges of the arts. Fewer are asking questions that matter—the ones that

Introduction: paragraphs 1–4; captures attention by ironically attacking high success standards, defending low standards

Body: paragraphs 5–12

Development by examples and brief definitions

Development by effect

Development by comparison, examples, and causes

Development by effects

Development by effects and argument

Development by effects

Development by effects

can't be answered. Fewer are putting themselves on the line, making as much of their minds and talents as they might.

Development by effect, cause, and comparison

12   The irony is that today's success-chasers seem obsessed with the idea of *not settling*. They take advanced degrees in business because they won't settle for just a so-so job. They compete for slots at law firms and investment houses because they won't settle for any but the fastest track. They seem to regard it as axiomatic that "success" and "settling" are opposites.

Conclusion: argues against contemporary notions of success

13   Yet in doggedly pursuing the rather brittle species of success now in fashion, they are restricting themselves to a chokingly narrow swath of turf along the entire range of human possibilities. Does it ever occur to them that, frequently, success is what people settle for when they can't think of something noble enough to be worth failing at?

DISCUSSION QUESTIONS

1. Shames notes in paragraph 3 that "'success' itself—rather than the substance of the achievements that make for success—" seems to be the touchstone by which we measure our worth. What do you think he means? Why is the distinction positioned at this point?

2. Why do you think Shames ends his essay with a rhetorical question, that is, one for which no answer is expected?

3. To what extent do you agree with Shames's idea of success? Discuss.

TOWARD KEY INSIGHTS

What evidence do you find that not all people are consumed by the desire for money?

What qualities do you consider crucial to living a "good" life and to happiness?

SUGGESTION FOR WRITING *Write a definition essay explaining how the popular view of responsibility, greed, marriage, single life, friendship, or some other concept needs redefining. Use whatever writing strategies advance your purpose.*

Stephen L. Carter

The Insufficiency of Honesty

Stephen L. Carter (born 1954) earned a B.A. degree from Stanford University in 1976 and a law degree from Yale University in 1979. Between 1979 and 1982, he worked as a law clerk, first for the U.S. Court of Appeals, District of Columbia circuit, and then for Justice Thurgood Marshall of the U.S. Supreme Court. Since 1982, he has served on the faculty of the Yale Law School. Carter has authored three books: Reflections of an Affirmative Action Baby (1991),

The Culture of Disbelief (1993), and Integrity (1996), from which our selection is adapted. In our selection, Carter defines integrity by distinguishing it from honesty.

1   A couple of years ago I began a university commencement address by telling the audience that I was going to talk about integrity. The crowd broke into applause. Applause! Just because they had heard the word "integrity": that's how starved for it they were. They had no idea how I was using the word, or what I was going to say about integrity, or, indeed, whether I was for it or against it. But they knew they liked the idea of talking about it.

2   Very well, let us consider this word "integrity." Integrity is like the weather: everybody talks about it but nobody knows what to do about it. Integrity is that stuff that we always want more of. Some say that we need to return to the good old days when we had a lot more of it. Others say that we as a nation have never really had enough of it. Hardly anybody stops to explain exactly what we mean by it, or how we know it is a good thing, or why everybody needs to have the same amount of it. Indeed, the only trouble with integrity is that everybody who uses the word seems to mean something slightly different.

3   For instance, when I refer to integrity, do I mean simply "honesty"? The answer is no; although honesty is a virtue of importance, it is a different virtue from integrity. Let us, for simplicity, think of honesty as not lying; and let us further accept Sissela Bok's definition of a lie: "any intentionally deceptive message which is *stated*." Plainly, one cannot have integrity without being honest (although, as we shall see, the matter gets complicated), but one can certainly be honest and yet have little integrity.

4   When I refer to integrity, I have something very specific in mind. Integrity, as I will use the term, requires three steps: discerning what is right and what is wrong; acting on what you have discerned, even at personal cost; and saying openly that you are acting on your understanding of right and wrong. The first criterion captures the idea that integrity requires a degree of moral reflectiveness. The second brings in the ideal of a person of integrity as steadfast, a quality that includes keeping one's commitments. The third reminds us that a person of integrity can be trusted.

5   The first point to understand about the difference between honesty and integrity is that a person may be entirely honest without ever engaging in the hard work of discernment that integrity requires: she may tell us quite truthfully what she believes without ever taking the time to figure out whether what she believes is good and right and true. The problem may be as simple as someone's foolishly saying something that hurts a friend's feelings; a few moments of thought would have revealed the likelihood of the hurt and the lack of necessity for the comment. Or the problem may be more complex, as when a man who was raised from birth in a society that preaches racism states his belief in one race's inferiority as a fact, without ever really considering that perhaps this deeply held view is wrong. Certainly the racist is being honest—he is telling us what he actually thinks—but his honesty does not add up to integrity.

Telling Everything You Know

6   A wonderful epigram sometimes attributed to the filmmaker Sam Goldwyn goes like this: "The most important thing in acting is honesty; once you learn to fake that, you're in." The point is that honesty can be something one *seems* to have. Without integrity, what passes for honesty often is nothing of the kind; it is fake honesty—or it is honest but irrelevant and perhaps even immoral.

7   Consider an example. A man who has been married for fifty years confesses
to his wife on his deathbed that he was unfaithful thirty-five years earlier. The
dishonesty was killing his spirit, he says. Now he has cleared his conscience and
is able to die in peace.

8   The husband has been honest—sort of. He has certainly unburdened himself. And he has probably made his wife (soon to be his widow) quite miserable
in the process, because even if she forgives him, she will not be able to remember him with quite the vivid image of love and loyalty that she had hoped for.
Arranging his own emotional affairs to ease his transition to death, he has
shifted to his wife the burden of confusion and pain, perhaps for the rest of her
life. Moreover, he has attempted his honesty at the one time in his life when it
carries no risk; acting in accordance with what you think is right and risking no
loss in the process is a rather thin and unadmirable form of honesty.

9   Besides, even though the husband has been honest in a sense, he has now
twice been unfaithful to his wife: once thirty-five years ago, when he had his
affair, and again when, nearing death, he decided that his own peace of mind
was more important than hers. In trying to be honest he has violated his marriage vow by acting toward his wife not with love but with naked and perhaps
even cruel self-interest.

10   As my mother used to say, you don't have to tell people everything you know.
Lying and nondisclosure, as the law often recognizes, are not the same thing.
Sometimes it is actually illegal to tell what you know, as, for example, in the dis-
closure of certain financial information by market insiders. Or it may be
unethical, as when a lawyer reveals a confidence entrusted to her by a client. It
may be simple bad manners, as in the case of a gratuitous comment to a colleague on his or her attire. And it may be subject to religious punishment, as
when a Roman Catholic priest breaks the seal of the confessional—an offense
that carries automatic excommunication.

11   In all the cases just mentioned, the problem with telling everything you know
is that somebody else is harmed. Harm may not be the intention, but it is certainly the effect. Honesty is most laudable when we risk harm to ourselves; it
becomes a good deal less so if we instead risk harm to others when there is no
gain to anyone other than ourselves. Integrity may counsel keeping our secrets
in order to spare the feelings of others. Sometimes, as in the example of the wayward husband, the reason we want to tell what we know is precisely to shift our
pain onto somebody else—a course of action dictated less by integrity than by
self-interest. Fortunately, integrity and self-interest often coincide, as when a
politician of integrity is rewarded with our votes. But often they do not, and it is
at those moments that our integrity is truly tested.

Error

12   Another reason that honesty alone is no substitute for integrity is that if forth-
rightness is not preceded by discernment, it may result in the expression of an
incorrect moral judgment. In other words, I may be honest about what I believe,
but if I have never tested my beliefs, I may be wrong. And here I mean "wrong"
in a particular sense: the proposition in question is wrong if I would change my
mind about it after hard moral reflection.

13   Consider this example. Having been taught all his life that women are not as
smart as men, a manager gives the women on his staff less-challenging assignments than he gives the men. He does this, he believes, for their own benefit:

he does not want them to fail, and he believes that they will if he gives them tougher assignments. Moreover, when one of the women on his staff does poor work, he does not berate her as harshly as he would a man, because he expects nothing more. And he claims to be acting with integrity because he is acting according to his own deepest beliefs.

14   The manager fails the most basic test of integrity. The question is not whether his actions are consistent with what he most deeply believes but whether he has done the hard work of discerning whether what he most deeply believes is right. The manager has not taken this harder step.

15   Moreover, even within the universe that the manager has constructed for himself, he is not acting with integrity. Although he is obviously wrong to think that the women on his staff are not as good as the men, even were he right, that would not justify applying different standards to their work. By so doing he betrays both his obligation to the institution that employs him and his duty as a manager to evaluate his employees.

16   The problem that the manager faces is an enormous one in our practical politics, where having the dialogue that makes democracy work can seem impossible because of our tendency to cling to our views even when we have not examined them. As Jean Bethke Elshtain has said, borrowing from John Courtney Murray, our politics are so fractured and contentious that we often cannot even reach *disagreement*. Our refusal to look closely at our own most cherished principles is surely a large part of the reason. Socrates thought the unexamined life not worth living. But the unhappy truth is that few of us actually have the time for constant reflection on our views—on public or private morality. Examine them we must, however, or we will never know whether we might be wrong.

17   None of this should be taken to mean that integrity as I have described it presupposes a single correct truth. If, for example, your integrity-guided search tells you that affirmative action is wrong, and my integrity-guided search tells me that affirmative action is right, we need not conclude that one of us lacks integrity. As it happens, I believe—both as a Christian and as a secular citizen who struggles toward moral understanding—that we *can* find true and sound answers to our moral questions. But I do not pretend to have found very many of them, nor is an exposition of them my purpose here.

18   It is the case not that there aren't any right answers but that, given human fallibility, we need to be careful in assuming that we have found them. However, today's political talk about how it is wrong for the government to impose one person's morality on somebody else is just mindless chatter. *Every* law imposes one person's morality on somebody else, because law has only two functions: to tell people to do what they would rather not or to forbid them to do what they would.

19   And if the surveys can be believed, there is far more moral agreement in America than we sometimes allow ourselves to think. One of the reasons that character education for young people makes so much sense to so many people is precisely that there seems to be a core set of moral understandings—we might call them the American Core—that most of us accept. Some of the virtues in this American Core are, one hopes, relatively noncontroversial. About 500 American communities have signed on to Michael Josephson's program to emphasize the "six pillars" of good character: trustworthiness, respect, responsibility, caring, fairness, and citizenship. These virtues might lead to a similarly noncontroversial set of political values: having an honest regard for ourselves and others, protecting freedom of thought and religious belief, and refusing to steal or murder.

Honesty and Competing Responsibilities

20   A further problem with too great an exaltation of honesty is that it may allow us to escape responsibilities that morality bids us bear. If honesty is substituted for integrity, one might think that if I say I am not planning to fulfill a duty, I need not fulfill it. But it would be a peculiar morality indeed that granted us the right to avoid our moral responsibilities simply by stating our intention to ignore them. Integrity does not permit such an easy escape.

21   Consider an example. Before engaging in sex with a woman, her lover tells her that if she gets pregnant, it is her problem, not his. She says that she understands. In due course she does wind up pregnant. If we believe, as I hope we do, that the man would ordinarily have a moral responsibility toward both the child he will have helped to bring into the world and the child's mother, then his honest statement of what he intends does not spare him that responsibility.

22   This vision of responsibility assumes that not all moral obligations stem from consent or from a stated intention. The linking of obligations to promises is a rather modern and perhaps uniquely Western way of looking at life, and perhaps a luxury that only the well-to-do can afford. As Fred and Shulamit Korn (a philosopher and an anthropologist) have pointed out, "If one looks at ethnographic accounts of other societies, one finds that, while obligations everywhere play a crucial role in social life, promising is not preeminent among the sources of obligation and is not even mentioned by most anthropologists." The Korns have made a study of Tonga, where promises are virtually unknown but the social order is remarkably stable. If life without any promises seems extreme, we Americans sometimes go too far the other way, parsing not only our contracts but even our marriage vows in order to discover the absolute minimum obligation that we have to others as a result of our promises.

23   That some societies in the world have worked out evidently functional structures of obligation without the need for promise or consent does not tell us what we should do. But it serves as a reminder of the basic proposition that our existence in civil society creates a set of mutual responsibilities that philosophers used to capture in the fiction of the social contract. Nowadays, here in America, people seem to spend their time thinking of even cleverer ways to avoid their obligations, instead of doing what integrity commands and fulfilling them. And all too often honesty is their excuse.

DISCUSSION QUESTIONS

1. Discuss the effectiveness of Carter's title.

2. Identify the thesis statement of this essay.

3. What writing strategies does Carter use to develop his essay? Refer to specific parts of the essay when answering.

4. In paragraph 8, Carter notes that the husband's deathbed confession "carries no risk." Explain what he means.

5. Point out the linking devices that Carter uses to connect paragraphs.

6. Identify what paragraphs constitute Carter's conclusion and explain why it is effective.

7. Discuss examples of situations you have known when people displayed honesty without integrity and also situations when people displayed honesty with integrity.

TOWARD KEY INSIGHTS

To what extent do you believe that our moral obligations extend beyond our promises and stated intentions?

Do North Americans typically try to fulfill their "absolute minimum obligation"? What evidence can you cite to support your answer?

SUGGESTION FOR WRITING *Write an essay defining loyalty. Use appropriate examples and whatever writing strategies will further your purpose.*

CHAPTER 10

Strategies for Finding Patterns: Comparison

SHOWING RELATIONSHIPS

> Which candidate for mayor should get my vote, Ken Conwell or Jerry Mander?
> What is it about online shopping that you prefer?
> Doesn't this tune remind you of a Shania Twain song?
> Is high school in Australia harder or easier than high school in Canada?

Everyone makes *comparisons,* not just once in a while, but day after day. When we compare, we examine two or more items for likenesses, differences, or both. Comparison has a purpose. Sometimes when the similarities between two things are obvious, we may choose to emphasize how two things which appear at first glance to be similar are actually quite different. On the other hand, when the differences are obvious, we may choose to demonstrate how two things which impress us with their differences actually share underlying similarities.

Putting items side by side can help us weigh the relative merits of each item and choose between alternatives. Comparison often serves an evaluative purpose, showing why one person, thing, or plan of action is superior to another. It may also help us clarify our preferences and decide on matters small and large.

At a restaurant, we may compare the appeal and value of ordering a pasta dinner with the appeal and value of ordering a sub sandwich. Comparison also influences our more important decisions. We weigh majoring in chemistry against majoring in physics, buying against renting, working for Macintosh against working for IBM. An instructor may ask us to write a paper comparing the features of two behavioural organization models. An employer may have us weigh two proposals for decreasing employee absenteeism and write a report recommending one of them.

Comparison also acquaints us with the unfamiliar. To help Canadian readers understand the English sport of rugby, a sportswriter might compare its field, team, rules, and scoring system with those for football. To teach students about France's government, a political science textbook might compare the makeup and election of its parliament to that of Canadian parliament, and the method of selecting its president and premier to the Canadian method of selecting leaders.

Both academic assignments and jobs call for comparative analysis. A music instructor may ask you to compare baroque and classical music and their contributions to later musical developments. A psychology instructor may want you to compare two different types of psychosis and assess the legal and medical ramifications of each. A biology instructor might have you consider how the features of two different kinds of body cells enable them to perform their functions. A criminology instructor might ask you how a restorative justice model compares with a model of adversarial justice in a specific context. In the workplace, comparisons are also common because they help people make decisions. An office manager may compare several telephone systems to determine which one would be most useful for the company; a nurse may assess the condition of a patient before and after a new medicine is given; an insurance agent may point out the features of two insurance policies to highlight the advantages of one.

SELECTING ITEMS FOR COMPARISON

Any items you compare must share some common ground. For example, you could compare two golfers on driving ability, putting ability, and sand play, or two cars on appearance, gas consumption, and warranty; but you can't meaningfully compare a golfer with a car, any more than you could compare guacamole with Guadalajara or chicken with charcoal. There's simply no basis for comparison.

Any valid comparison, on the other hand, presents many possibilities. Suppose you head the music department of a large store and have two excellent salespeople working for you. The manager of the store asks you to prepare a one- or two-page report that compares their qualifications for managing the music department in a new branch store. Assessing their abilities becomes the guiding purpose that motivates and controls the writing. You can immediately rule out points such as eye colour, hairstyle, and religion, which have no bearing on job performance. Instead, you must decide what managerial traits the job requires and the extent to which each candidate possesses them. Your thinking might result in a list like this.

Points of Similarity or Difference	Pat	Mike
1. Ability to deal with customers, sales skills	Excellent	Excellent
2. Effort: regular attendance, hard work on the job	Excellent	Excellent
3. Leadership qualities	Excellent	Good
4. Knowledge of ordering and accounting procedures	Good	Fair
5. Musical knowledge	Excellent	Good

This list tells you which points to emphasize and suggests Pat as the candidate to recommend. You might briefly mention similarities (points 1 and 2) in an introductory paragraph, but the report would focus on differences (points 3, 4, and 5), since you're distinguishing the relative merits of two employees.

EXERCISE   *Compare two fine dining restaurants in order to recommend one of them. List the points of similarity and difference that you might discuss. Differences should predominate because you will base your decision on them.*

DEVELOPING A COMPARISON

Successful comparisons depend on ample, well-chosen details that show just how the items under consideration are alike and different. Such support helps the reader grasp your meaning. Read the following student comparative paragraphs and note how the concrete details convey the striking differences between south and north 14th Street:

On 14th Street running south from P Street are opulent luxury stores such as Birks and Holt Renfrew, and small but expensive clothing stores with richly dressed mannequins in the windows. Modern skyscraping office buildings hold banks and travel bureaus on the ground floors and insurance companies and corporation headquarters in the upper storeys. Dotting the concretescape are high-priced movie theatres, gourmet restaurants, multilevel parking garages, bookstores, and candy- and novelty-gift shops, all catering to the prosperous population of the city. This section of 14th Street is relatively clean: The city maintenance crews must clean up after only a nine-to-five populace and the Saturday crowds of shoppers. The pervading mood of the area is one of bustling wealth during the day and, in the night, calm.

Crossing P Street toward the north, one notes a gradual but disturbing change in the scenery of 14th Street. A panhandler sits nodding on the sidewalk in front of a rundown hotel, too tired, or too drugged, to bother asking for money. A liquidation store promises bargains, but the window display shows an unattractive tangle of chains, watches, knives, and dusty tools. Outside a tavern with opaque windows, a homeless person is curled up, sleeping beneath a tattered blanket. On the opposite side of the street, a restaurant advertising curry competes for customers with the house of noodles and pizza-to-go restaurant. Sometimes, even when the air is chill, one sees young women in short skirts, low-cut tops, and high boots standing near the curb, or leaning into the windows of cars momentarily stopped, talking to the drivers.

Vivid details depict with stark clarity the economic differences between the north and south ends of the street. These differences contribute to the writer's implied thesis: *The stark contrast between wealth and poverty on opposite ends of the same street is disturbing.*

ORGANIZING A COMPARISON

Comparison papers can be organized by two basic patterns: *block pattern*, also called comparison of wholes; and *alternating pattern*, also called comparison by parts. Typically a comparison paper uses some combination of these two patterns.

The Block Pattern   The block pattern first presents all of the points of comparison for one item and then all of the points of comparison for the other. Here is the comparison of the two salespeople, Pat and Mike, outlined according to the block pattern:

    I.   Introduction: mentions similarities in sales skills and effort but recommends Pat for promotion
   II.   Specific points about Mike
        A. Leadership qualities
        B. Knowledge of ordering and accounting procedures
        C. Musical knowledge
  III.   Specific points about Pat
        A. Leadership qualities
        B. Knowledge of ordering and accounting procedures
        C. Musical knowledge
  IV.   Conclusion: reasserts that Pat should be promoted

For a shorter paper or one that includes only a few points of comparison, the block pattern can work well, since the reader can remember all the points from the first block while reading the second. Be careful, however, that you do not dwell too long on one half of the comparison without mentioning the other, or your essay might seem to break in two. Often the reader may find it easier to follow a modified block pattern, in which you refer to the first item of comparison throughout the second block.

The Alternating Pattern   The alternating pattern presents a point about one item, then follows immediately with a corresponding point about the other. Organized in this way, the Pat-and-Mike paper would look like this:

    I. Introduction: mentions similarities in sales skills and effort but recommends Pat for promotion
  II. Leadership qualities
     A. Mike's qualities
     B. Pat's qualities
 III. Knowledge of ordering and accounting procedures
     A. Mike's knowledge
     B. Pat's knowledge
 IV. Musical knowledge
     A. Mike's knowledge
     B. Pat's knowledge
  V. Conclusion: reasserts that Pat should be promoted

If there are many points of comparison, the alternating method, which deals with each point in turn, can help your reader grasp similarities and differences. Be aware, however, that moving back and forth between two different poems or two different historical periods may become rather dizzying. To ground your reader, you may need to blend the two approaches. For example, when comparing heroines from two books, you might give an overview of the two books' similarities in the block approach, and then use the alternating approach to focus on salient points of difference.

Once you select your pattern, arrange your points of comparison in an appropriate order. Take up closely related points one after the other. Depending on your purpose, you might work from similarities to differences or the reverse. Often, a good writing strategy is to move from the least significant to the most significant point so that you conclude with a punch.

EXERCISE *Using the points of comparison you selected for the earlier exercise, prepare two different outlines for a paper, one organized according to the block pattern, and one according to the alternating pattern.*

USING ANALOGY

An *analogy*, a special type of comparison, calls attention to one or more similarities underlying two different kinds of items that seem to have nothing in common. While some analogies stand alone, most clarify concepts in other kinds of writing. Whatever their role, they follow the same organizational pattern as ordinary comparisons.

An analogy often explains something unfamiliar by likening it to something familiar. Here is an example:

    The atmosphere of Earth acts like any window in serving two very important functions. It lets light in, and it permits us to look out. It also serves as a shield to keep out dangerous or uncomfortable things. A normal glazed window lets us keep our houses warm by keeping out cold air, and it prevents rain, dirt, and unwelcome insects and animals from coming in. . . . Earth's atmospheric window also helps to keep our planet at a comfortable temperature by holding back radiated heat and protecting us from dangerous levels of ultraviolet light.

Lester del Ray, The Mysterious Sky

Conversely, an analogy sometimes highlights the unfamiliar in order to help illuminate the familiar. The following paragraph discusses the qualities and obligations of an unfamiliar person, the mountain guide, to shed light on a familiar practice—teaching:

> The mountain guide, like the true teacher, has a quiet authority. He or she engenders trust and confidence so that one is willing to join the endeavor. The guide accepts his leadership role, yet recognizes that success (measured by the heights that are scaled) depends upon the close co-operation and active participation of each member of the group. He has crossed the terrain before and is familiar with the landmarks, but each trip is new and generates its own anxiety and excitement. Essential skills must be mastered; if they are lacking, disaster looms. The situation demands keen focus and rapt attention: slackness, misjudgment, or laziness can abort the venture.

Nancy K. Hill, "Scaling the Heights: The Teacher as Mountaineer"

When you develop an analogy, keep these points in mind:

1. Your readers must be well acquainted with the familiar item. If they aren't, the point is lost.
2. The items must indeed have significant similarities. You could develop a meaningful analogy between a kidney and a filter or between cancer and anarchy but not between a fiddle and a flapjack or a laser and Limburger cheese.
3. The analogy must truly illuminate. Overly obvious analogies, such as one comparing a battle to an argument, offer few or no revealing insights.
4. Overextended analogies can tax the reader's endurance. A multipage analogy between a heart and a pump would likely overwhelm the reader with all its talk of valves, hoses, pressures, and pumping.

ETHICAL ISSUES

Although an old adage declares that "comparisons are odious," most people embrace comparisons except when they are unfair. Unfortunately, unfair comparisons are often drawn. For example, advertisers commonly magnify trivial drawbacks in competitive products while exaggerating the benefits of their own merchandise. Politicians run attack ads that distort their opponents' views and demean the opponents' character. And when scientific theories clash, supporters of one view have been known to alter their findings in order to undermine the other position. Your readers expect all comparisons to meet certain ethical standards. Ask and answer these questions to help ensure that your comparisons you write are solid.

- Have I avoided skewing one or both of my items in order to ensure a particular outcome?
- Are the items I'm comparing properly matched? It would be unethical to compare a student essay to a professional one in order to demonstrate the inadequacy of the former.
- If I'm using an analogy, is it appropriate and ethically fair? Comparing immigration officials to Nazi storm troopers would trivialize the suffering and deaths of millions of Nazi victims and taint immigration officials with a terrible label.

WRITING A COMPARISON

Planning and Drafting the Comparison

Don't write merely to fulfill an assignment; if you do, your paper will likely ramble aimlessly and fail to deliver a specific message. Instead, build your paper around a clear sense of purpose. Do you want to show the superiority of one product or method over another? Do you want to show how sitcoms today differ from those twenty years ago? Purpose governs the details you choose and the organization you follow. Whether you select your own topic or write on an assigned one, answer these questions:

What purpose will my comparison serve?
Who will be my audience and why will they want to read the essay?
What points of similarity or difference will I discuss?

To develop the comparison, draw up a chart similar to this one.

Item A	Item B
First point of comparison	First point of comparison
Second point of comparison	Second point of comparison

Next, brainstorm each point in turn, recording appropriate supporting details. When you finish, stand back and ask these questions:

Do all the details relate to my purpose?
Do any new details come to mind?
In what order should I organize the details?

When you decide upon an order, copy the points of comparison and the details, arranged in the order you will follow, into a chart like the one below.

Item A	Item B
First point of comparison	First point of comparison
First detail	First detail
Second detail	Second detail
Second point of comparison	Second point of comparison

Use the introduction to identify your topic and arouse the reader's interest. If you intend to establish the superiority of one item over the other, you might call attention to your position. If you're comparing something unfamiliar with something familiar, you might explain the importance of understanding the unfamiliar item.

Organize the body of your paper according to whichever pattern—block or alternating—suits its length and the number of points you're planning to take up. If you explain something familiar by comparing it with something unfamiliar, start with the familiar item. If you try to show the superiority of one item over another, proceed from the less to the more desirable one.

Write whatever kind of conclusion will round off your discussion effectively. Many comparison papers end with a recommendation or a prediction. A paper comparing two brands of stereo receivers might recommend purchasing one of them. A paper comparing a familiar sport, such as football, with an unfamiliar one, such as rugby, might predict the future popularity of the latter. Unless you've written a lengthy paper, don't summarize the likenesses and differences you've presented. If you've done a proper writing job, your reader already has them clearly in mind.

Revising the Comparison

Revise your paper in light of the general guidelines in Chapter 5 and the questions that follow:

Have I accomplished my purpose, whether to examine the advantages and disadvantages of two alternatives or to acquaint the reader with something unfamiliar?

For something unfamiliar, have I shown clearly just how it is like and unlike the familiar item?

Have I consistently written with my audience in mind?

Have I considered all points of similarity and difference that relate to my purpose?

Have I included appropriate supporting details?

Are my comparisons arranged effectively?

EXAMPLE OF A STUDENT ESSAY OF COMPARISON

Real vs. Fake Conversation

William Nichols

1   Have you ever been engaged in a conversation where you have no interest in the subject or who you are talking to? Of course. Now ask yourself what it feels like to be in a conversation that has your full attention. You are sure to notice many differences. For simplicity, I will call these two types of conversations real and fake, the fake conversation being the one which you wish you were never part of. These fake conversations are not limited to talks with teachers, parents, law enforcement officials, but could in fact include even the closest people in your life, since it is the level of interest in the topic that determines engagement. While real and fake conversations are very different, they can be assessed by examining the degree of conversational engagement or disengagement, as the case may be.

2   In a real conversation, the listener is genuinely interested in what the speaker has to say. This is not the case in a fake conversation, where the listener is not really listening, but usually either trying to get away or thinking only about what he or she wants to say. If we examine the body language, eye contact, emotion and overall interest displayed by the participants in both real and fake conversations, we will see that the differences are reflected in the type and level of engagement.

3   For a conversation to be real, all parties involved should show interest in what the others are saying and be aware of the messages that they are conveying through body language, eye contact, and emotion. The use of body language and eye contact is integral to making good conversation. Body language is often quite subtle, as even the slightest movement such as leaning toward someone or away from someone can be quite revealing. One obvious form of body language is the use of hands. Our hands help us stay focused while conveying our message to the listener. For example, consider how you might use your hands when you are on the phone talking to someone. When you are describing something, you might not even notice how much you are using gestures. If you are trying to describe a building or a shape, you may trace this shape with your hands, even though you are talking on the phone and no one can see you. It seems ridiculous in hindsight, yet most of us use our

hands in such circumstances because we are fully engaged in conversation and genuinely interested in communicating our thoughts to others. Now imagine how you use your hands while talking person-to-person. Using your hands while talking person-to-person shows that you are thinking about what you are saying and that you are trying to get your message across by whatever means possible.

4   Another form of effective body language to use in conversation is eye contact. In a real conversation all persons involved make eye contact quite frequently, but in a fake conversation, people often look off into the distance, or down at a newspaper. Eye contact tells people we are listening intently or that we are speaking directly to them. Both eye contact and the use of hands can directly show emotion.

5   Showing emotion when speaking demonstrates that we care about what we are saying or about what is being said and that we are in fact engaged in a real conversation. The emotion found in a fake conversation is very different from that of a real one. In a real conversation, the participants look animated and attentive; they may smile, laugh, frown, or widen their eyes as they speak and listen. In a fake conversation, sometimes one person is serious about what is being discussed and the other is bored. While in a fake conversation, we may find ourselves becoming distracted by the smallest of things, such as the pattern on the other person's shirt. Obviously, when distracted, we fail to maintain eye contact and are not engaged in animated body language. Our disinterest is readily apparent to all . . . unless we are able to maintain the appearance of interest by staying in the conversation and sending enough body language cues to deceive our conversation partners. By pretending or faking interest, we make the other person feel as if we are genuinely participating. In fake conversations, we may be engaged in a game with ourselves in order to keep us from admitting to the other person that we are in fact totally bored and distracted.

6   When people are engaged in a fake conversation, they lack interest in those with whom they are conversing or the subject of the conversation. Fake conversations, which may occur with a teacher, parent, neighbour, or co-worker, are revealed not only by how we act but also by what we say. Clichéd statements about the nice weather suggest that the person would probably prefer not to be talking at all. Fake conversation is often bland and lacks in any real substance. Usually people stay in such conversations out of guilt and fear of offending. We don't want to admit to the other person—or sometimes even to ourselves—that we are completely bored by the conversation we are in.

7   Although all conversations use similar tools of communication, the body language, eye contact, and degree of emotional engagement are different in real and fake conversations. In a real conversation, participants engage physically in many ways, and there is frequent, focused eye contact, but in a fake conversation, participants are disengaged and eye contact is uncommon. While we all can probably admit to being in a fake conversation, how many of us can really admit to knowing someone was trying to maintain a fake conversation with us? By remaining attentive to the real and fake conversational dynamics described above, next time you'll know.

DISCUSSION QUESTIONS

1. Comment on the significance of the rhetorical questions in the introductory and concluding paragraphs.
2. Point out effective supporting details in the essay. What do they accomplish?
3. What pattern of organization does the writer use? Examine how the whole essay and individual paragraphs are organized.
4. What concrete details does the writer use to distinguish real conversations from fake ones?

SUGGESTIONS FOR WRITING

1. **Write a comparison essay on one of the topics below or another that your instructor approves. Determine the points you will discuss and how you will develop and arrange them. Emphasize similarities, differences, or both.**
   a. An arts education versus a technical education
   b. The physical or mental demands of two jobs
   c. Two advertisements for similar products
   d. An online course and a face-to face course
   e. Two popular trends among people your age
   f. A day-to-day relationship and a virtual one
   g. Two different forms of exercise
   h. Two cultural customs approaches toward dating
2. **Develop an analogy based on one of the following sets of items or another set that your instructor approves. Proceed as you would for any other comparison.**
   a. Ending a relationship and leaving a job
   b. Drug addiction and shopping addiction
   c. Troubleshooting a computer and writing an essay
   d. Learning to drive and learning a new language
   e. Taking an exam and going to the dentist

    f. A parent and a farmer

    g. A workaholic and an alcoholic

    h. A cluttered garage and a disorderly mind

The Critical Edge

Although you may rely on your own knowledge or findings to develop many comparisons, in some cases you may synthesize material from other sources.

Let's say that your business management instructor has asked you to prepare a report on the management styles of two high-profile chief executive officers (CEOs) at successful companies that manufacture the same kinds of products. You realize that you need to do some reading in business periodicals such as *Canadian Business, The Economist,* and *Fortune* in order to complete this assignment. Your sources reveal that the first CEO favours a highly centralized managerial structure with strict limits on what can be done by all employees except top executives. The company has pursued foreign markets by establishing factories overseas and has aggressively attempted to merge with or acquire its domestic competitors. The second CEO has established a decentralized managerial structure that allows managers at various levels of the company to make key decisions. The company has also established a strong foreign presence, but it has done so primarily by entering into joint ventures with foreign firms. Most of its domestic expansion has resulted from the construction of new plants rather than from mergers or takeovers. Both CEOs have borrowed heavily to finance their companies' expansion. These three differences and one similarity are your points of comparison, which you can organize using either the block or alternating pattern. You might conclude by indicating which of the two management styles is more effective.

After you've read the views expressed by your sources, examine them critically. Does any of the information about the two CEOs seem slanted so that it appears to misrepresent their management styles? For example, do any of the writers seem to exaggerate the positive or negative features of centralized or decentralized management? Do appropriate examples support the writers' contentions? Does any relevant information appear to be missing? Does any source contain material that isn't related to your purpose? Judging the works of others in this fashion helps you write a better report.*

---

*Because you rely on published sources for your information, it is important to read the sections on research in Chapters 13 and 14 and those on handling quotations and avoiding plagiarism in Chapter 15 before you start to write. As always, follow your instructor's guidelines for documenting sources.

SUGGESTIONS FOR WRITING

1. Read at least two essays in this book on a similar issue (for example, the articles on cloning or on multiculturalism in Chapter 11), and then compare the views of these two writers. In your comparison, make an argument for which essay or article is more persuasive.

2. After reading several reviews of the same movie, compare and contrast these reviews in order to demonstrate how film critics bring different values to their viewing.

COMPARISON ESSAYS: PROFESSIONAL MODELS

READING STRATEGIES

1. Identify your purpose for reading the comparison and the author's purpose for the comparison. Does the author compare in order to acquaint the reader with something new, or to suggest the relative merits of one thing over another?
2. Identify the items that are being compared, and identify the basis for the comparison.
3. Identify the pattern of organization (alternating point by point, block, or a blended approach) that is used in the comparison.
4. Read carefully to establish the points of similarities and differences. When the information might be necessary for future purposes, it can be helpful to create a table that matches similarities and differences.

READING CRITICALLY

1. Explore whether there are any biases underlying the comparison. Does the writer seem to give fair treatment to all items being compared? Test whether the basis for comparison is logically consistent.
2. Determine if the writer emphasizes similarities, differences, or both. Does the author go beyond ticking off similarities and differences and make a larger point in the essay? Does the writer have something fresh to say and avoid dwelling on the obvious?
3. Identify whether there are other similarities or differences or more illustrative details that could have been brought in.

READING AS A WRITER

1. Examine how the author organized the essay. Was the organization effective in guiding the reader through the essay? Note what organizational pattern was most effective.

2. Notice transitional words and phrases such as *in contrast, on the other hand, while, whereas* that indicate contrast, or words such as *just as, like, similarly, both* that help the writer draw distinctions and parallels. Note also the sentences that the writer uses for transitions.

3. Observe how much detail was used to substantiate the comparison.

Douglas Todd

In a Girl's World, It Can Be Tough Being a Boy

Title sets up differences, suggests direction

Douglas Todd writes a regular column on religion and ethics for The Vancouver Sun. *In the following essay Todd argues that boys are now on the losing end of the gender battle, particularly in education.*

1 "Girl Power!" "Girls Rule!" These slogans now appear weekly as educators, the entertainment industry, and the media celebrate spunky young women's rising successes.

Introduction: paragraphs 1–4; background and social context; significance of following contrasts

2 Girls now do better in school than boys. Many employers are patting themselves on the back for hiring more females than males. Vancouver's Sarah McLachlan, who organized a big money-making all-women concert festival called Lilith Fair, is becoming an international icon for "Girl Power."

3 Unfortunately, the cheering for girls' triumphs is drowning out the quiet worries of a bunch of others—boys. Just as girls were stereotyped as sweet low-achievers in the '50s, now boys seem to be suffering from being pigeon-holed as unruly good-for-littles.

4 The notion of gender inequity has been turned on its head. While some commentators declare it's now a good time to be a girl, they're not dropping the other shoe: it's a troublesome, even crummy, time to be a boy.

5 A recent *Globe and Mail* column is typical of the current blindness. Education writer Jennifer Lewington analysed an Ontario study that found Grade 3 girls were doing better than boys at writing, as well as being more confident than boys about writing. Grade 3 girls were also doing better than boys at math, but weren't quite as confident as boys about numbers.

Body: paragraphs 5–17; alternating pattern throughout

Differences in elementary school

6 What angle did the *Globe* column pursue? It explored ways to improve girls' confidence in math—even though they were already doing better than boys in the subject. It didn't focus on the more pressing problem: helping Grade 3 boys catch up in both math and writing.

7 Lewington's column is just one small example of an education bias that drives at least one Vancouver school teacher to distraction. The teacher says many of her colleagues, like much of the public, generally view girls as delightful, boys as trouble.

8 The teacher was at a recent conference where a female education specialist told the audience the only things boys are better at than girls is sports. As a mother of boys and a teacher, she could barely contain herself. (As a father of boys, I can also tell you this is increasingly becoming a topic among pro-feminist mothers and fathers of boys, at least those not afraid to discuss such spicy issues.)

9   It's a mug's game to try to figure out whether boys or girls are more hard-done-by today. Both are undoubtedly having a tough time, particularly because of meaner economics, higher divorce rates, and greater role confusion. But girls, at least, are winning the fight for attention.

10   We see a flood of lifestyle articles about girls who lose confidence when they become adolescents.

11   But we see little about a similarly devastating emotional slide for boys. We hear a lot about how parents and teachers with low expectations for girls will fulfill their own prophecies; we don't hear how the same attitude can doom boys to mediocrity or worse.

12   One of the few people to raise the alarm for boys is B.C. Teachers Federation professional development specialist Patrick Clarke. He believes the public hasn't noticed what's befallen boys because the switch has happened so fast—within the past 10 years.

13   Clarke's research has found almost 80 percent of B.C. honour-roll students now are girls. B.C.'s education ministry also says about 60 percent of current graduates with honours are girls (with the highest marks going to Asian girls, who, prevailing wisdom falsely argues, should be twin victims, of both their ethnicity and gender), which reverses test results of the early '80s.

14   What's more, girls dominate school clubs and student councils. "To put it bluntly, the girls are running the place," says Clarke, who, rightly or wrongly, carefully avoids blaming teachers or feminism for boys' crisis.

15   Confirming the trend, British and Australian studies show at least one out of three boys succumbing to mass images that say the only way to glory lies in professional sports, or Beavis and Butthead–style laziness and mischief.

16   In Britain, while girls 15 to 17 are becoming more optimistic, boys are becoming more pessimistic and introverted, suffering from low self-esteem and lack of ambition, which lead to poor study habits. A large minority of Britain's young men may be forming a new rogue underclass, writes Edward Balls in *Danger: Men Not at Work.*

17   As a father of girls, Clarke says part of him recognizes that every boy who drops off the career path opens up another place for his daughters in an increasingly competitive marketplace. But his sense of social justice tells him he can't give in to such self-interest.

18   And while many others declare it's about time girls ruled the world, or at least the Western world (where girls' advances are far more pronounced), they might not enjoy telling that directly to a struggling 12-year-old boy. After all, he had absolutely nothing to do with centuries-old customs that confined women to narrow roles.

19   While it's undeniable the top echelon of the business world is still dominated by men in suits, that doesn't mean much for boys (and the vast majority of men) who are just trying to get by, who weren't raised among the wealth and privilege that often opens the doors to such million-dollar positions. Young women are now doing fine in most professions.

20   Although it might seem shocking to some people stuck in outdated gender trenches, it could be time for affirmative-action education programs for boys similar to those that encouraged girls in the maths and sciences.

DISCUSSION QUESTIONS

1. Identify the thesis statement. Why do you think it is located where it is?

2. Consider colloquialisms such as the word "crummy," as Todd declares "it's a troublesome, even crummy, time to be a boy" (paragraph 4). What other examples of colloquialisms or slang can you find? Given that this article was originally written for a newspaper, comment on how Todd can use such an informal, casual writing style without losing authority.

3. How does the writer support his claim that girls are now "winning the fight for attention" (paragraph 9)?

4. How is the writer careful to qualify his argument by acknowledging the problems that females have faced? What does he mean when he refers to "outdated gender trenches" (paragraph 20)?

TOWARD KEY INSIGHTS

To what extent do you think that the problems for boys that Todd alludes to may be an inevitable result of feminist gains? What disturbing implications about gender equity are raised by this article?

Do you agree that for many boys today, "the only way to glory lies in professional sports, or Beavis-and-Butthead–style laziness and mischief" (paragraph 15)? Why or why not?

In your view, what different issues do males and females face in adolescence?

What do you think of Todd's suggestion that it could be time "for affirmative-action education programs for boys" (paragraph 20)?

SUGGESTION FOR WRITING *Drawing from your own experience, compare and contrast the treatment of males and females in a particular context, such as a specific sport, a place of employment, the news media, or Hollywood.*

Nancy Masterson Sakamoto

Conversational Ballgames

Nancy Masterson Sakamoto graduated Phi Beta Kappa from UCLA with a degree in English. Married to a Japanese artist and Buddhist priest, she lived in Japan for twenty-four years before moving with her husband and two sons to Honolulu in 1982. While in Japan, she was visiting professor at the University of Osaka. She gave in-service training to Japanese junior and senior high school English teachers and talks on intercultural topics, both in English and in Japanese, to various business, educational, and women's groups. In addition to her book, Polite Fictions: Why Japanese and Americans Seem Rude to Each Other, *still used as a textbook in Japanese universities, she coauthored a research project report sponsored by the Japanese Ministry of Education and wrote various articles for Japanese English-teaching publications. In*

Hawaii, she has been a speaker and seminar leader for many educational, business, and professional organizations. Her current position is professor of American Studies, Shitennoji Gakuen University (Hawaii branch). In this essay, she discusses the divergent conversational styles of Americans and Japanese, just one example of the many differences that distinguish different cultures.

1   After I was married and had lived in Japan for a while, my Japanese gradually improved to the point where I could take part in simple conversations with my husband and his friends and family. And I began to notice that often, when I joined in, the others would look startled, and the conversational topic would come to a halt. After this happened several times, it became clear to me that I was doing something wrong. But for a long time, I didn't know what it was.

2   Finally, after listening carefully to many Japanese conversations, I discovered what my problem was. Even though I was speaking Japanese, I was handling the conversation in a western way.

3   Japanese-style conversations develop quite differently from western-style conversations. And the difference isn't only in the languages. I realized that just as I kept trying to hold western-style conversations even when I was speaking Japanese, so my English students kept trying to hold Japanese-style conversations even when they were speaking English. We were unconsciously playing entirely different conversational ballgames.

4   A western-style conversation between two people is like a game of tennis. If I introduce a topic, a conversational ball, I expect you to hit it back. If you agree with me, I don't expect you simply to agree and do nothing more. I expect you to add something—a reason for agreeing, another example, or an elaboration to carry the idea further. But I don't expect you always to agree. I am just as happy if you question me, or challenge me, or completely disagree with me. Whether you agree or disagree, your response will return the ball to me.

5   And then it is my turn again. I don't serve a new ball from my original starting line. I hit your ball back again from where it has bounced. I carry your idea further, or answer your questions or objections, or challenge or question you. And so the ball goes back and forth, with each of us doing our best to give it a new twist, an original spin, or a powerful smash.

6   And the more vigorous the action, the more interesting and exciting the game. Of course, if one of us gets angry, it spoils the conversation, just as it spoils a tennis game. But getting excited is not always the same as getting angry. After all, we are not trying to hit each other. We are trying to hit the ball. So long as we attack only each other's opinions, and do not attack each other personally, we don't expect anyone to get hurt. A good conversation is supposed to be interesting and exciting.

7   If there are more than two people in the conversation, then it is like doubles in tennis, or like volleyball. There's no waiting in line. Whoever is nearest and quickest hits the ball, and if you step back, someone else will hit it. No one stops the game to give you a turn. You're responsible for taking your own turn.

8   But whether it's two players or a group, everyone does his best to keep the ball going, and no one person has the ball for very long.

9   A Japanese-style conversation, however, is not at all like tennis or volleyball. It's like bowling. You wait for your turn. And you always know your place in line. It depends on such things as whether you are older or younger, a close friend or a relative stranger to the previous speaker, in a senior or junior position, and so on.

10   When your turn comes, you step up to the starting line with your bowling ball, and carefully bowl it. Everyone else stands back and watches politely, murmuring encouragement. Everyone waits until the ball has reached the end of the alley, and watches to see if it knocks down all the pins, or only some of them, or none of them. There is a pause, while everyone registers your score.

11   Then, after everyone is sure that you have completely finished your turn, the next person in line steps up to the same starting line, with a different ball. He doesn't return your ball, and he does not begin from where your ball stopped. There is no back and forth at all. All the balls run parallel. And there is always a suitable pause between turns. There is no rush, no excitement, no scramble for the ball.

12   No wonder everyone looked startled when I took part in Japanese conversations. I paid no attention to whose turn it was, and kept snatching the ball halfway down the alley and throwing it back to the bowler. Of course the conversation died. I was playing the wrong game.

13   This explains why it is almost impossible to get a western-style conversation or discussion going with English students in Japan. I used to think that the problem was their lack of English language ability. But I finally came to realize that the biggest problem is that they, too, are playing the wrong game.

14   Whenever I serve a volleyball, everyone just stands back and watches it fall, with occasional murmurs of encouragement. No one hits it back. Everyone waits until I call on someone to take a turn. And when that person speaks, he doesn't hit my hall back. He serves a new ball. Again, everyone just watches it fall.

15   So I call on someone else. This person does not refer to what the previous speaker has said. He also serves a new ball. Nobody seems to have paid any attention to what anyone else has said. Everyone begins again from the same starting line, and all the balls run parallel. There is never any back and forth. Everyone is trying to bowl with a volleyball.

16   And if I try a simpler conversation, with only two of us, then the other person tries to bowl with my tennis ball. No wonder foreign English teachers in Japan get discouraged.

17   Now that you know about the difference in the conversational ballgames, you may think that all your troubles are over. But if you have been trained all your life to play one game, it is no simple matter to switch to another, even if you know the rules. Knowing the rules is not at all the same thing as playing the game.

18   Even now, during a conversation in Japanese I will notice a startled reaction, and belatedly realize that once again I have rudely interrupted by instinctively trying to hit back the other person's bowling ball. It is no easier for me to "just listen" during a conversation, than it is for my Japanese students to "just relax" when speaking with foreigners. Now I can truly sympathize with how hard they must find it to try to carry on a western-style conversation.

19   If I have not yet learned to do conversational bowling in Japanese, at least I have figured out one thing that puzzled me for a long time. After his first trip to America, my husband complained that Americans asked him so many questions and made him talk so much at the dinner table that he never had a chance to eat. When I asked him why he couldn't talk and eat at the same time, he said that Japanese do not customarily think that dinner, especially on fairly formal occasions, is a suitable time for extended conversation.

20   Since westerners think that conversation is an indispensable part of dining, and indeed would consider it impolite not to converse with one's dinner partner, I found this Japanese custom rather strange. Still, I could accept it as a

cultural difference even though I didn't really understand it. But when my husband added, in explanation, that Japanese consider it extremely rude to talk with one's mouth full, I got confused. Talking with one's month full is certainly not an American custom. We think it very rude, too. Yet we still manage to talk a lot and eat at the same time. How do we do it?

21   For a long time, I couldn't explain it, and it bothered me. But after I discovered the conversational ballgames, I finally found the answer. Of course! In a western-style conversation, you hit the ball, and while someone else is hitting it back, you take a bite, chew and swallow. Then you hit the ball again, and then eat some more. The more people there are in the conversation, the more chances you have to eat. But even with only two of you talking, you still have plenty of chances to eat.

22   Maybe that's why polite conversation at the dinner table has never been a traditional part of Japanese etiquette. Your turn to talk would last so long without interruption that you'd never get a chance to eat.

DISCUSSION QUESTIONS

1. Sakamoto notes in paragraph 1 that she "had lived in Japan for a while" and in paragraph 2 that she has listened "carefully to many Japanese conversations." Why does she note these facts at the outset of her essay?

2. What purpose is served by the first two sentences of paragraph 3?

3. Why do you think Sakamoto uses various games—tennis, volleyball, bowling—to help explain the differences between Western and Japanese conversational styles?

4. Point out specific supporting details that help make this comparison successful.

5. For what audience is Sakamoto writing? Refer to the essay when answering.

6. Sakamoto ends paragraph 17 with the assertion that "Knowing the rules is not at all the same thing as playing the game." Explain what she means.

TOWARD KEY INSIGHTS

In what ways other than conversational style might cultures exhibit pronounced differences?

What problems might these differences create, and how can we best deal with them?

SUGGESTIONS FOR WRITING

1. Write a paper that explores a misunderstanding between you and someone else that arose because of a difference in cultures, generations, or outlooks.

2. If you have come to Canada from another country or are familiar with the customs of another culture, compare and contrast two different kinds of cultural values or attitudes in a specific area: dating, gift-giving, teacher/student relationships, entertaining, etc.

CHAPTER 11

Strategies for Finding Patterns: Classification

GROUPING INTO CATEGORIES

Help Wanted, Situations Wanted, Real Estate, Personal. Do these terms look familiar? They do if you've ever scanned the classified ads of the newspaper. Ads are grouped into categories, and each category is then subdivided. The people who assemble this layout are *classifying*. Figure 11.1 shows the main divisions of a typical classified ad section and a further breakdown of one of them.

As this figure indicates, grouping allows the people who handle ads to divide entries according to a logical scheme and helps readers find what they are looking for. Imagine the difficulty of checking the real estate ads if all the entries were run in the order in which the ads were placed. Classification helps writers and readers come to grips with large or complex topics. It breaks a broad topic into categories according to some specific principle, presents the distinctive features of each category, and shows how the features vary among categories. Segmenting the topic simplifies the discussion by presenting the information in small, neatly sorted piles rather than in one jumbled and confusing heap.

Furthermore, classification helps people make choices. Identifying which groups of consumers—students, accountants, small-business owners—are most

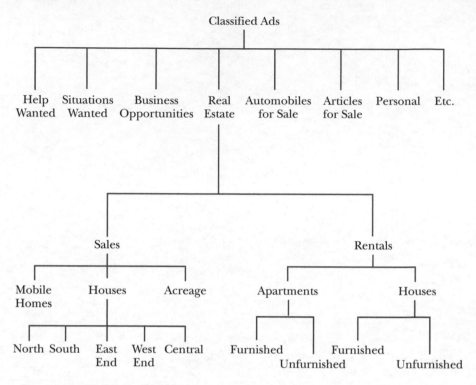

Figure 11.1 A Typical Classified Ad Section

likely to buy a new product allows the manufacturer to advertise in appropriate media. Knowing the engine size, manoeuvrability, seating capacity, and gas consumption of typical subcompact, compact, and intermediate-size cars helps customers decide which one to buy.

Because classification plays such an important part in our lives, it is a useful writing tool in many situations. Your accounting instructor may ask you to categorize accounting procedures for retail businesses. In a computer class, you may classify computer languages and then specify appropriate applications for each grouping. For an industrial hygiene class, you might categorize different types of respiratory protective equipment and indicate when each type is used.

SELECTING CATEGORIES

People classify in different ways for different purposes, which generally reflect their interests. A clothing designer might classify people according to their fashion sense, an advertising executive according to their age, and a politician according to their party affiliations.

When you write a classification paper, choose a principle of classification that suits not only your purpose but also your audience. If you're writing for students, don't classify instructors according to their manner of dress, their body build, or their car preferences. These breakdowns aren't relevant. Instead, organize by a more useful principle of classification—perhaps by teaching styles, concern for students, or grading policies.

Sometimes it's helpful or necessary to divide one or more categories into subcategories. If you do, use just one principle of classification for each level. Both levels in Figure 11.2 meet this test because each reflects a single principle: place of origin for the first, number of cylinders for the second.

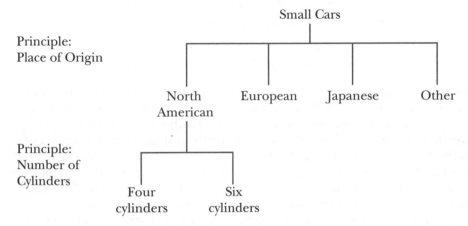

Figure 11.2   Proper Classification of Small Cars

Now examine Figure 11.3. This classification is *improper* because it groups cars in two ways—by place of origin and by kind—making it possible for one car to end up in two different categories. For example, the German Porsche is both a European car and a sports car. When categories overlap in this way, confusion reigns and nothing is clarified.

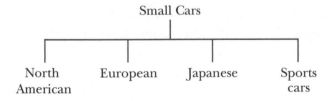

Figure 11.3   Improper Classification of Small Cars

EXERCISE

1. **How would each of the following people be most likely to classify the families living in a Canadian town?**

   a. The member of Parliament who represents the city

   b. A social worker

   c. The director of the local credit bureau

2. **The following lists contain overlapping categories. Identify the inconsistent item in each list and explain why it is faulty.**

Nurses	Pictures	Voters in Saskatoon
Surgical nurses	Oil paintings	Liberals
Psychiatric nurses	Magazine illustrations	Conservatives
Emergency room nurses	Lithographs	Saskatchewan Party
Terminal care nurses	Watercolours	New Democrats
Night nurses	Etchings	Nonvoters

NUMBER OF CATEGORIES

Some classification papers discuss every category included within the topic. Others discuss only selected categories. Circumstances and purpose dictate the scope of the discussion. Suppose you work for the finance department of your province and are asked to write a report that classifies the major nonservice industries in a certain city and assesses their strengths and weaknesses. Your investigation shows that food processing, furniture making, and the production of auto parts account for over 95 percent of all nonservice jobs. Two minor industries, printing and toy making, provide the rest of the jobs. Given these circumstances, you'd probably focus on the first three industries, mentioning the others only in passing. However, if printing and toy making were significant industries, they too would require detailed discussion.

DEVELOPING CATEGORIES

Develop every category using specific, informative details that provide a clear picture. The following excerpt from a student paper classifying public restrooms for women discusses two of the writer's three categories:

Luxurious washrooms are found in upscale department stores, chic boutiques, and the better restaurants. This aristocrat of public facilities usually disdains the term *washroom*, masquerading instead under the alias of *ladies' room*. Upon entering its plush environs, the user is captivated by its elegance. Thick carpet reaches up to cushion tired feet, wood panelled or brocade velvet walls shut the outside world away, and softly glowing wall sconces soothe the eyes. Inviting armchairs and gold-and-velvet tables add to the restful, welcoming atmosphere, and the latest issues of upscale magazines such as *Vogue* and *Elle* entice customers to sit and read. Mirrors in carved frames, designer basins with gleaming gold faucets, and creamy scented soap suggest a spa-like luxury. Soft music, piped in through invisible speakers, may take patrons back in time, as if no one is waiting for them outside the door.

The adequate washroom offers utility without the swankiness of its lavish cousin. Typically located in a large shopping mall or mass-market department store, it is a stark world of hard, unadorned surfaces—tile floors, tile walls, and harshly glaring fluorescent lights recessed in the ceiling. For those who wish to rest, there is a garishly coloured Naugahyde couch and next to it a battered metal or wood table holding a few tattered copies of *Homemakers, People, Canadian Living,* and similar publications. The mirrors have steel frames; the sinks, set in a formica counter, have plain chrome faucets; and the soap dispenser emits a thin stream of unscented liquid. There is no soothing music—just the relentless whining of someone's tired child.

The concrete details in these paragraphs effectively characterize each category and clearly distinguish between them. Imagine how vague and indistinct the categories would be without these details.

ETHICAL ISSUES

Classification can seem quite innocent, and yet it can cause great harm. In India, an entire population group numbering millions of people was once classified as "untouchables" and so was denied the jobs and rights of other citizens. In Canada during World War II, innocent people of Japanese descent were classified as a threat and were stripped of property and moved away from their homes. In many high schools, students are often lumped into categories with labels such as "preps," "geeks," "jocks," "druggies," "skids," or "goth." Clearly you have to evaluate the appropriateness and consequences of your classification scheme. To avoid problems, ask and answer these questions:

- Is my classification called for by the situation? It may be appropriate to classify students in a school environment according to their reading skills, but classifying factory workers in this fashion may be inappropriate and unfair to the people involved.
- Have I avoided the use of damaging classifications? People naturally resent stereotyping.
- Have I applied my classification without resorting to overgeneralization? In a paper classifying student drinkers, it would be a mistake, and even harmful, to imply that all college students drink excessively.
- Could my classification promote harmful behaviour? When classifying the behaviour patterns of young urban dwellers, it would be unethical to present favourably the lifestyle of a group that uses hard drugs and engages in criminal activities.

We are ethically responsible for the classification systems that we use in our writing. Always examine the one you use for suitability, fairness, and potential harm.

WRITING A CLASSIFICATION

Planning and Drafting the Classification

Many topics that interest you are potential candidates for classification. If you're selecting your own topic, you might explain the different kinds of rock music, take a humorous look at different types of teachers, or, in a more serious vein, identify different types of discrimination. As always, use one or more of the narrowing strategies to help stimulate your thinking. As possibilities come to mind, examine each one in light of these questions:

> What purpose will this classification serve?
> Who is my audience and what will interest them?
> What are the categories of this topic?
> What features distinguish my categories from one another?

Next, determine whether you'll discuss every category or only selected ones, and then set up a classification chart similar to the one following.

Category 1	**Category 2**	**Category 3**
First distinguishing feature	First distinguishing feature	First distinguishing feature
Second distinguishing feature	Second distinguishing feature	Second distinguishing feature

Such a chart helps you see the relationships among categories and provides a starting point for developing your specific details. Proceed by jotting down the details that come to mind for each distinguishing feature of every category. Then prepare a second chart with the distinguishing features and details arranged in the order in which you want to present them.

Begin your paper by identifying your topic and capturing your reader's attention in some way. A paper classifying hair dyes might point out their growing popularity among both men and women. In more personal writing, you could cite a personal experience that relates to your topic. As always, circumstances dictate your choice.

In the body, discuss your categories in whatever order best suits your purpose. Order of climax—least important, more important, most important—often works well. Or perhaps your topic suggests arranging the categories by behaviour, income, education, or physical characteristics. Whatever your arrangement, signal it clearly to your reader. Don't merely start the discussions of your categories by saying *first . . . , second . . . , another . . . , next . . . ,* or *last.* These words offer no hint of the rationale behind your order.

In addition, make sure the arrangement of material within the categories follows a consistent pattern. Recall the two categories of washrooms. In each case, after noting where the washroom can be found, the writer discusses its floor, walls, and lighting, moves to the furniture, and ends by discussing the sinks, soap, and sound.

The strategies for ending a classification paper are as varied as those for starting it. A paper on hair dyes might conclude by exploring the wider cultural implications of their popularity. In other cases, you might weigh your evidence that one item is stronger or more useful than the other for a particular purpose or function.

Revising the Classification

Revise your paper by following the guidelines in Chapter 5 as well as by asking yourself these questions:

Does my classification have a clear sense of purpose and audience?
Does my principle of classification accord with my purpose?
Do any of my categories overlap?
Have I chosen an appropriate number of categories?
Are these categories developed with sufficient details?
Are the categories and details arranged in an effective order?

EXAMPLE OF A STUDENT ESSAY OF CLASSIFICATION

Get Used to It

Luke Kingma

1   In the world of education, there are those that are meant to teach, and there are those that should stay away. The poor teachers mix with the good and form the education system that we are acquainted with today. Unfortunately, those individuals who have yet to find the right job for their talents can add to the frustrations of student life. I suppose it could be argued that students must learn to deal with all personality types and levels of competence when interacting with others throughout life. Indeed, students owe a debt of gratitude to all those teachers who can take even the most ill-shaped mind and mould it into an objective-thinking unit; however, struggling students should be aware that teachers often fall into the following categories before they sign up for a class.

The Genius

2   Viewed by average students as second only to Einstein, this mastermind is primarily a knowledge-focused individual who ignores all other aspects of life. A teacher like this is hired for credentials, not for an amazing teaching record. This teacher's intellect is on display each class in a plethora of mind-boggling

detail. Imagine someone who can explain the Standard Model of Quantum Mechanics on the blackboard in ten seconds or less. This person may be smart, but intelligence alone does not make a teacher.

3   Although naturally intelligent, this teacher does not comprehend how some students do not understand the lecture. A question directed at a genius teacher from a perplexed student will result in a confused and slightly frustrated look, followed by an explanation exactly like the one given before. This teacher puts forth no effort to make certain a student understands the material before progressing. Students who understand what is being taught are able to move on; those who do not are left grasping at straws. Lecturing is the teacher's job; students must teach themselves if they are to keep up.

The Hider

4   Hiders are excessive introverts. Why these people chose teaching as a career is beyond most students. They shy away from the limelight and avoid communication as best they can. Chameleon-like, they blend in with the chalkboard, quietly scribbling notes for the class to copy down. They avoid eye contact when students attempt to ask questions. The floor, the lecture notes, or the wall behind the students often make for a better target. An excellent tactic they use for avoiding questions is directing the struggling student back to the textbook. Unfortunately, the textbook is usually the source of the student's confusion. There is only one thing worse than a two-hour class with a hider—a three-hour one. Through these gruelling hours, students can only strive to stay awake and not miss anything for the big exam. Morning and evening classes worsen the dryness of the session. The drone of the fan, tapping on the chalkboard, and lack of enthusiasm entice students into a long nap.

The Crammer

5   These tough guys assume that students are only taking one class each semester: theirs. They often begin the semester by telling the class in an almost evangelistic way, "This will be the one, most important and interesting class in all of your schooling . . . and perhaps provide your greatest lesson in life." A summary of grades for a past class is also given, and the particular focus is on those who failed or barely passed. The audience is not given any encouragement that they will achieve their usual grade average in this class. Students are left to try their best to keep up in the class, with no time for questions—they can review at home. The pile of homework given every night assumes that every other class is unimportant, so grades in the other classes may suffer. To top it off, this

teacher often wears a slight, arrogant smirk while watching students frantically jot down notes and scramble to raise a seemingly "un-raisable" grade. Nothing is ever good enough for crammers.

The Know-It-All

6   Often spotted in universities, these instructors know everything there is to know about everything—except the subject they supposedly majored in. More often than not, these teachers establish their authority on the first day about how many and which kinds of high-profile institutions they have taught at. Of course, these biographies never include reasons why they moved from one university to another; we are left to assume that they came to their current position of their own accord.

7   Somehow, these often loud attention-seekers get away with teaching nothing of the subject, and they justify leaving half-way through a class to let students "discuss their studies and work on projects." Often, if a student manages to gather up enough nerve to ask a Know-It-All a question about the course, the Know-It-All shoots back: "It's in the textbook. READ IT!" After struggling through the course, those students who survived move on without a secure foundation, often wondering what they actually learned and floundering in subsequent classes.

The Class Master

8   This may be the first undesirable teacher a grade-school student will encounter, and perhaps is the most damaging to a young mind. These teachers love to point out the obvious faults of their students—small or large—both in schoolwork and in personality. The tough survive; the weak get pounded. Every word that comes out of Class Master's mouth is undeniable, undisputable truth—at least in this teacher's own mind. These educators are on a mission: to make clones of themselves. Really, it's a "god complex," as many students have put it. These teachers want to save the world from drowning in its own stupidity. They seem to stick with the job simply because of the power it holds: a reign of terror over quivering students. When Class Masters step outside their classroom, they're just regular "schmos" walking down the street. Of these five undesirable types, the Class Master is the one students could do without the most.

9   Students encounter these types of undesirable teachers all too often, so students and administrators should be on the alert. Sadly, it is probably a fact of life that these types will forever be in our education system, so we might as well get used to it and learn from our experiences. In fact, no matter where we

end up in life, we will have to deal with people such as these, so we might as well learn how to deal with them while we are growing up.

DISCUSSION QUESTIONS

1. What is the writer's purpose in developing this classification? Where does he state it?
2. In what order has the author arranged his categories? Refer to the essay when answering.
3. Demonstrate that the writer has avoided overlapping categories.
4. How might he have refined further the categories of undesirable teachers?

SUGGESTIONS FOR WRITING *Write a classification paper on one of the topics below or one approved by your instructor. Determine your purpose and audience, select appropriate categories, decide how many you'll discuss, develop them with specific details, and arrange them in an effective order.*

1. College pressures
2. Pet owners (or types of pets)
3. Kinds of extreme sports
4. Alternative medicines
5. Websites
6. Computer games
7. Party-goers
8. Car advertisements
9. Canadian TV shows
10. Easy to make recipes
11. Music for driving
12. Attitudes toward death
13. Lies
14. Ways to break off a relationship
15. Bores

The Critical Edge

Classification provides an effective tool for organizing material into categories. Sometimes you will be able to draw on your own knowledge or experience to determine or develop categories, but often you will supplement what you bring to a writing assignment with research.

Suppose that for an introductory business course, you're asked to prepare a paper that explores major types of investments. After consulting a number of books and magazines, you conclude that stocks, bonds, and real estate represent the three main categories of investments and that each category can be divided into several subcategories. Bonds, for example, can be grouped according to issuer: corporate, municipal, and federal.

At this point, you recognize that the strategy of classification would work well for this assignment. Reading further, you learn about the financial risks, rewards, and tax consequences associated with ownership. For example, Canada

Savings Bonds offer the greatest safety, while corporate bonds, as well as stocks and real estate, entail varying degrees of risk depending on the financial condition of the issuer and the state of the economy. Similarly, the income from the different categories and subcategories of investments is subject to different kinds and levels of taxation.

After assimilating the information you've gathered, you could synthesize the views expressed in your sources as well as your own ideas about investments. You might organize your categories and subcategories according to probable degree of risk, starting with the least risky investment and ending with the most risky. For your conclusion you might offer purchase recommendations for different groups of investors such as young workers, wealthy older investors, and retirees.

When preparing to use the material of others in your writing, be sure to examine its merits. Do some sources seem more convincing than others? Why? Do any recommendations stem from self-interest? Are any sources overloaded with material irrelevant to your purpose? Which sources offer the most detail? Asking and answering questions such as these will help you write a more informed paper.*

SUGGESTIONS FOR WRITING

1. Examine the professional essays on gender issues or cultural diversity in this textbook, and then write a paper that draws upon these sources and classifies their content.

2. Reflect on the professional essays that you've studied and then write a paper that presents an appropriate classification system for them, perhaps based on the writers' levels of diction, tone, or reliance on authorities.

CLASSIFICATION ESSAYS: PROFESSIONAL MODELS

READING STRATEGIES

1. Identify your purpose for reading the essay and the writer's purpose for the classification.

2. Identify the principle of classification that is being used, and the distinguishing features of each category. It can be useful to make a table that identifies each major classification and identifies the distinctive features of each category.

---

*Because you'll rely on published sources, it is important to read the sections on handling quotations and avoiding plagiarism in Chapter 15 before you start to write. As always, follow your instructor's guidelines for documenting sources.

READING CRITICALLY

1. Determine the purpose for the classification.
2. Try to come up with an alternative classification system.
3. Check whether the categories of the classification are clear and distinct, or whether they overlap.
4. Note whether the principle of classification is logically consistent. Note whether it is a complete system, or whether some categories are omitted.

READING AS A WRITER

1. Note whether the essay arranges categories in a logical sequence such as largest to smallest, or least desirable to most desirable.
2. Observe whether the write gives each category about the same amount of space, and gives similar kinds of information for each category.

Marion Winik

What Are Friends For?

Marion Winik (born 1958) is a graduate of Brown University and of Brooklyn College, where she earned a master of fine arts degree in creative writing. Since graduation, she has pursued a career in education, writing, and marketing. Her writings include poems, short stories, essays, and books, and the shorter pieces have appeared in a variety of major newspapers and popular magazines. Her 1998 book Lunch-Box Chronicles: Notes from the Parenting Underground *discusses her experiences of raising her sons after her husband's death. In this selection, Winik takes a humorous look at the different categories of friends and the benefits derived from each one.*

> Introduction describes the value of friends.

1   I was thinking about how everybody can't be everything to each other, but some people can be something to each other, thank God, from the ones whose shoulder you cry on to the ones whose half-slips you borrow to the nameless ones you chat with in the grocery line.

> Body begins.
> (Paragraphs 2–14)

2   Buddies, for example, are the workhorses of the friendship world, the people out there on the front lines, defending you from loneliness and boredom. They call you up, they listen to your complaints, they celebrate your successes and curse your misfortunes, and you do the same for them in return. They hold out through innumerable crises before concluding that the person you're dating is no good, and even then understand if you ignore their good counsel. They accompany you to a movie with subtitles or to see the diving pig at Aquarena Springs. They feed your cat when you are out of town and pick you up from the airport when you get back. They come over to help you decide what to wear on a date. Even if it is with that creep.

> First category: buddies

> Second category: relatives

3   What about family members? Most of them are people you just got stuck with, and though you love them, you may not have very much in common. But there is that rare exception, the Relative Friend. It is your cousin, your brother, maybe even your aunt. The two of you share the same views of the other family members.

Meg never should have divorced Martin. He was the best thing that ever happened to her. You can confirm each other's memories of things that happened a long time ago. Don't you remember when Uncle Hank and Daddy had that awful fight in the middle of Thanksgiving dinner? Grandma always hated Grandpa's stamp collection; she probably left the window open during the hurricane on purpose.

4   While so many family relationships are tinged with guilt and obligation, a relationship with a Relative Friend is relatively worry-free. You don't even have to hide your vices from this delightful person. When you slip out Aunt Joan's back door for a cigarette, she is already there.

5   Then there is that special guy at work. Like all the other people at the job site, at first he's just part of the scenery. But gradually he starts to stand out from the crowd. Your friendship is cemented by jokes about co-workers and thoughtful favors around the office. Did you see Ryan's hair? Want half my bagel? Soon you know the names of his turtles, what he did last Friday night, exactly which model CD player he wants for his birthday. His handwriting is as familiar to you as your own.

Third category: co-workers

6   Though you invite each other to parties, you somehow don't quite fit into each other's outside lives. For this reason, the friendship may not survive a job change. Company gossip, once an infallible source of entertainment, soon awkwardly accentuates the distance between you. But wait. Like School Friends, Work Friends share certain memories which acquire a nostalgic glow after about a decade.

7   A Faraway Friend is someone you grew up with or went to school with or lived in the same town as until one of you moved away. Without a Faraway Friend, you would never get any mail addressed in handwriting. A Faraway Friend calls late at night, invites you to her wedding, always says she is coming to visit but rarely shows up. An actual visit from a Faraway Friend is a cause for celebration and binges of all kinds. Cigarettes, Chips Ahoy, bottles of tequila.

Fourth category: faraway friends

8   Faraway Friends go through phases of intense communication, then may be out of touch for many months. Either way, the connection is always there. A conversation with your Faraway Friend always helps to put your life in perspective: when you feel you've hit a dead end, come to a confusing fork in the road, or gotten lost in some crackerbox subdivision of your life, the advice of the Faraway Friend—who has the big picture, who is so well acquainted with the route that brought you to this place—is indispensable.

9   Another useful function of the Faraway Friend is to help you remember things from a long time ago, like the name of your seventh grade history teacher, what was in that really good stir-fry, or exactly what happened that night on the boat with the guys from Florida.

10   Ah, the Former Friend. A sad thing. At best a wistful memory, at worst a dangerous enemy who is in possession of many of your deepest secrets. But what was it that drove you apart? A misunderstanding, a betrayed confidence, an unrepaid loan, an ill-conceived flirtation. A poor choice of spouse can do in a friendship just like that. Going into business together can be a serious mistake. Time, money, distance, cult religions: all noted friendship killers. . . .

Fifth category: former friends

11   And lest we forget, there are the Friends You Love to Hate. They call at inopportune times. They say stupid things. They butt in, they boss you around, they embarrass you in public. They invite themselves over. They take advantage. You've done the best you can, but they need professional help. On top of all this, they love you to death and are convinced they're your best friend on the planet.

Sixth category: love-to-hate friends

Seventh category:
hero friends

Eighth category:
new friends

Conclusion uses a
memorable observation that
meshes stylistically
with rest of essay.

12   So why do you continue to be involved with these people? Why do you tolerate them? On the contrary, the real question is, What would you do without them? Without Friends You Love to Hate, there would be nothing to talk about with your other friends. Their problems and their irritating stunts provide a reliable source of conversation for everyone they know. What's more, Friends You Love to Hate make you feel good about yourself, since you are in so much better shape than they are. No matter what these people do, you will never get rid of them. As much as they need you, you need them too.

13   At the other end of the spectrum are Hero Friends. These people are better than the rest of us, that's all there is to it. Their career is something you wanted to be when you grew up—painter, forest ranger, tireless doer of good. They have beautiful homes filled with special handmade things presented to them by villagers in the remote areas they have visited in their extensive travels. Yet they are modest. They never gossip. They are always helping others, especially those who have suffered a death in the family or an illness. You would think people like this would just make you sick, but somehow they don't.

14   A New Friend is a tonic unlike any other. Say you meet her at a party. In your bowling league. At a Japanese conversation class, perhaps. Wherever, whenever, there's that spark of recognition. The first time you talk, you can't believe how much you have in common. Suddenly, your life story is interesting again, your insights fresh, your opinion valued. Your various shortcomings are as yet completely invisible.

15   It's almost like falling in love.

DISCUSSION QUESTIONS

1. Comment on the effectiveness of Winik's title.
2. Characterize the level of diction that Winik uses in her essay
3. What elements of Winik's essay interest you the most? What elements interest you the least?

TOWARD KEY INSIGHTS

What traits characterize the various types of friends that you have?

In what ways are these friendships mutually beneficial?

SUGGESTION FOR WRITING *Write an essay classifying the various types of dates, employers, sales techniques, or vacations that you consider undesirable. Choose an appropriate number of categories and support them with appropriate specific details.*

Kerry Banks

As a Dad, Will I Do Right by My Daughter?

Kerry Banks is a freelance journalist. He has written six books and has won nine writing awards for his feature magazine work. He has written articles for numerous publications, including Equinox, Harrowsmith, Maclean's, *and* Chatelaine. *Since 1992, he has written a weekly sports column for the Vancouver news-and-entertainment weekly,* The Georgia Straight. *Banks's essay, "As a Dad, Will I Do Right by My Daughter?" reflects on the contemporary pitfalls of being a first-time father of a daughter. Having read a book about the different kinds of fathers who affect their daughters' self-image in different, sometimes troubling ways, Banks questions women he knows about their experiences of fathers. Banks presents the results of his research in a way that is sympathetic and engaging.*

1   My daughter's first word was "Da-Da." At least, that's how I remember it. Her mother, Anne, insists it was actually "dog." Whatever the true order, it was a thrill to hear her identify me by name. I think the bond between us grew a little closer at that moment. I know the weight of responsibility suddenly gained several pounds.

2   Riley is our first child and she is full of surprises. As she nears one year of age, we are amazed to discover how much she enjoys books, how quickly she can ransack a room and how deeply she is attached to the TV remote control. The first surprise, though, was her sex.

3   Both Anne and I come from families dominated by male progeny, and the odds seemed to suggest a son. When he turned out to be a she, it immediately struck me how little I knew about girls. With a son, I would be on familiar turf; I would instinctively know where he was heading and how he would feel when he got there. With a daughter, I would only be guessing. Each stage of her development would be a mystery to me.

4   Being a first-time parent is never easy, but I think it is especially tough for fathers these days. Our role is in flux. The "good provider" and "stern father" figures are as out of style as the hula-hoop. Modern dads are expected to be more actively involved in child rearing. We are supposed to change more diapers, spend more time at home, be more sensitive, and avoid gender stereotyping of our children at all costs.

5   Unfortunately, we have no role models on whom to base our behaviour. It is hard to feel confident when you are making things up as you go along. Pressured by society to be different from our fathers and struggling to achieve domestic equilibrium with our wives, we cannot help but feel anxious. So, as I confronted the reality of having a daughter, I could only wonder: what sort of father was I going to be?

6   As I was mulling over this conundrum, a book entitled *Women and Their Fathers: The Sexual and Romantic Impact of the First Man in Your Life* came across my desk. Contrary to popular wisdom, the author, New York journalist Victoria Secunda, contends it is the father, not the mother, who has the more profound impact in shaping a daughter's self-image. According to Secunda, the way dad and daughter get along largely determines how the daughter will see herself as an adult, and what she will expect from men.

7   Secunda classifies fathers into categories—"templates for their daughters' future attachments," she calls them. Fathers are doting, distant, demanding, absent or seductive. She classifies daughters too. A particular type of father does not necessarily produce a single type of daughter, but the way the relationship plays out produces daughters who are favoured, good, competitive, fearful or maverick. As I read the sobering litany of the ways in which each father type can damage his daughter's psyche, little Riley began to assume the fragility of a package of gelignite. Did so much of what she would become depend on me?

8   I began questioning women I knew about the impact of their fathers on their lives. Few of their relationships fit Secunda's categories precisely, but some patterns were evident. It was, for example, not difficult to find examples of the **distant father**—most of the women I spoke with had fathers who were remote in some way. But it was harder to correlate cause and effect. According to Secunda, distant fathers can produce a myriad of emotional consequences. Their daughters may or may not become sexually promiscuous, suffer from anorexia nervosa, be unable to achieve orgasm or marry men who don't notice them.

9   Sometimes, women raised by distant fathers deliberately seek out men who are diametrically different. Terrie Orr is a case in point. Orr, a soft-spoken but strong-willed 39-year-old Vancouver homemaker, says she has always been drawn to men with dynamic outgoing characters—men quite unlike her father, who is a quiet, unemotional reserved man. Orr refers to her dad as an "armchair father." His main interest, she recalls, was his job on the Canadian Pacific Railway. He occupied most of his leisure time with solitary pursuits, such as watching TV, doing carpentry and gardening. Orr says it was her effervescent mother who kept the family's five kids in line. "It was strange. Even though Dad was around a lot, you never had the feeling that he was really there."

10   Orr's most vivid memory of her father was one rare occasion when he stepped out of character. On Mother's Day, when Orr was 10, her father suggested that his wife sleep in as a treat while he took the kids out for a stroll in the woods near their home in Winnipeg. "We walked for two or three hours. I remember sunshine and open fields and laughing and skipping along. It was one of the only times he initiated something with the family."

11   Orr still finds her father an enigma, although she knows that her own reserved personality somewhat resembles his. Ironically, her relationship with her sales manager husband, Laurie Stein, is in some respects a mirror image of her own parents' merger of opposites. But, in this case, it is her husband who is the socializer.

12   Orr says that one of the things that attracted her to Laurie was his natural affinity for children: "He likes to play and fool around with our two boys and be naughty."

13   Orr's distant father does not sound much like me, but I do tend to be the introspective type. In fact, my wife does not hesitate to describe me as "moody." And truth be told, I exhibit other "distant father" danger signs—obsession with my work and a reluctance to discuss my feelings on personal subjects openly. Uptight, macho, WASP, self-obsessed: as I read Secunda's book, these psychological buzzwords began doing a noisy dance in my male psyche.

14   Maybe it's just self-justification, but I think some of the distance that exists between fathers and daughters is a product of our sexual blueprints. Men tend to deal with their emotions differently from women. It does not mean we do not have any. The challenge I will face with Riley is to make sure our differences never destroy the bonds between us.

15   At the other end of the emotional spectrum is the **doting father**—the daddy who makes everything all right. Annemarie Beard, 35, a stylish, sassy production manager with a Vancouver advertising firm, says she was "always the light in my father's eye." In sharp contrast to her two brothers, she was "spoiled and treated like a princess." Beard says her father, a chemical engineer, was always physically affectionate and ready to play. Only when she reached puberty did "the bubble burst," as her father began to pull away.

16   This is evidently a common reaction among fathers, according to Vancouver family therapist Mary Trokenberg. "As daddy's little girl grows into womanhood and becomes more sexually aware, many men don't know how to handle it. When men feel fragile and in doubt, they withdraw, and as a result, children feel abandoned."

17   Today, Annemarie Beard says the bond with her father has been restored. Yet, she admits that her early idealization of him had its consequences. "It took me a long time to grow up. I had to discover that not all men are like my father."

18   Author Secunda says many women with doting fathers are drawn to men who resemble their fathers—men who will protect them and keep them in the pampered style to which they are accustomed. Often, they tend to be older men. This is certainly true of Beard. "I had my first date at 15," she says. "He was 35." Today, she continues to feel most comfortable with older men. She likes their secure nature and the attentive manner in which they treat her. "Older men seem delighted just to have a younger woman around."

19   Doting and distant are polar opposites. Logically, therefore, I can't possibly be the doting type. So, why is it that Anne and I are already divided over the issue of protectiveness, which is one of the characteristics Secunda attributes to doting dads? I think Anne is too carefree with Riley; she feels I worry too much. And yet, how can I not worry? Our once benign household has suddenly become a nest of dangers—electrical outlets, open staircases, hot liquids, bottled poisons. So, if I am doting now, it is only for Riley's own good. This stage will surely pass. Once she is old enough to take care of herself, I will let her climb trees and play tackle football. Maybe.

20   Another of Secunda's archetypes, the **demanding father**, casts a dual-edged shadow over his daughter's life. Secunda says the best sort of demanding fathers are those who are stern but fair—they inspire confidence and ambition in their daughters. But when the sternness is not balanced by tenderness and support, daughters may be left with painful legacies.

21   Bonita Thompson, a vivacious, high-energy, 45-year-old Vancouver lawyer, traces much of what she has accomplished in life to her demanding father's influence. A chartered accountant, he was wrapped up in his career and spent little time with her three sisters and one brother. But Thompson forged a bond with him through sports. "From age 6 to 16, I was dad's caddie on the golf course. He taught me a sense of gentlemanly conduct, sportsmanship, ethics and setting high standards for yourself."

22   But some of his standards were impossibly high. "I'd bring home my report card with an average of 94 percent, and he'd say, 'Why isn't it 100 percent?' He was joking, but there was a barb underneath it."

23   As far back as she can recall, Thompson always had a strong desire to achieve. Yet, even as her law career flourished, she sensed there was something lacking. "After each of my achievements, I'd feel empty." Eventually, Thompson realized that "all I had done in life was a continuing effort to elicit my father's praise."

24   Thompson's failed first marriage was to a man very similar to her father. Her current husband is the antithesis. "He's a free spirit, a warm, outgoing humorous person. And he's a bit of a rascal and a rule breaker. He's the nurturer in our family. He stayed home and raised our child."

25   The problem of fathers who are grudging with praise often surfaced in my conversations with women. I may be in dangerous waters here too. Neither of my parents expressed support easily, and it's going to be hard for me to break the mould.

26   The discussions with my female friends did little to relieve my angst. I kept seeing bits of my character reflected in the darker side of their fathers' images. As for Secunda's book, I was left wondering whether a healthy relationship between a father and a daughter is possible at all.

27   Mary Trokenberg, the therapist, helped me put it in perspective: "Some of the ways in which daughters develop has to do with their fathers, but not all. The danger with these sorts of self-help books is that people will think one-dimensionally. When you divide people into categories, you lose the nuances and fail to see other possibilities."

28   This makes sense to me. While I will undoubtedly have a major influence on Riley, I suspect her view of men will also be shaped by what she sees in the relationship between my wife and me, and in her mother's attitudes toward men generally.

29   As for being distant, doting or demanding, I will try to keep my conflicting impulses in balance. Like any new parent, I have hopes. I want Riley to be an independent thinker, confident and creative. I want her to be a woman who is involved in the world, a woman who likes men and who can tell a joke. Most of all, I want her to be happy.

30   I don't know yet how I will deal with the familiar crises of fatherhood, such as when Riley begins dating boys with green hair and nose rings. But there is time to learn, and I will need to trust my instincts. For now, I am content simply to share the extraordinary discoveries of Riley's young life—and her awe at seeing the night stars for the first time, the giddy tingle of walking barefoot on a freshly mown lawn, the magical spell of a street musician's guitar. For now, just being Da-Da is enough.

DISCUSSION QUESTIONS

1. Why does the writer think that being a father today is more difficult for him personally than it might be for other people? (See paragraphs 2–3.) Why is being a father generally more difficult today than it might have been for fathers in the past? (See paragraphs 4–5.) How does this discussion of difficulties with the paternal role make the reader receptive to what follows?

2. What does Kerry Banks mean when he says: "As I read the sobering litany of the ways in which each father type can damage his daughter's psyche, little Riley began to assume the fragility of a package of gelignite" (paragraph 7).

3. Why does Kerry Banks follow his description of the "distant father" with the description of the "doting father" (paragraph 15)? Explain the three main categories of fathers that the writer deals with in your own words. Why do you suppose that Banks does not discuss two other categories of fathers—the absent

or seductive father—(paragraph 7) in detail? What is the principle for classification of fathers in the essay?

4. Why does Kerry Banks talk to women he knows about their relationships with their fathers (paragraph 8)? What does he find out from these women? How do these interviews influence the writer's attitude toward fathering?

5. Study the conclusion of this essay. How does Kerry Banks expand the scope of his essay outward, enlarging the context and significance of what he has been discussing? How does he also come full circle?

TOWARD KEY INSIGHTS

From your own experience, or from your observations of gender roles in other families, do you also conclude that the roles of fathers are "in flux" (paragraph 4)? Why or why not?

Kerry Banks writes that "men tend to deal with their emotions differently from women" (paragraph 14). How does he qualify this claim? To what extent do you agree with this generalization? Is it possible to make meaningful generalizations about such gender differences? Why or why not?

Kerry Banks quotes a therapist as saying, "When you divide people into categories, you lose the nuances and fail to see other possibilities" (paragraph 27). Do you also see problems with classifying people? Why or why not? What are the reasons that we put people into categories?

SUGGESTION FOR WRITING *Write an essay that classifies a certain group of people into categories according to a clear principle—kinds of university students, instructors, coaches, concert-goers, clothes shoppers. In your essay, acknowledge any potential problems with classifying in this way.*

CHAPTER 12

Strategies for Convincing Others: Argument and Persuasion

What did you think of that movie?"

"It was fun."

"Did you really think so? I thought it dragged on too long. I had a hard time believing in the story too."

"I don't know how you can say that!"

Argument or quarrel? Many people would ask, "What's the difference?" To them, the two terms both suggest angry disagreement.

However, a well-presented argument is not fiercely adversarial. Even when writers of argument have strong passions, they demonstrate respect for their audience, and for the complexities of the issue. Since an argument by definition has more than one side, a successful writer does not oversimplify or distort in order to score points or advance a claim.

You are probably most familiar with the idea of clear-cut pro and con divisions of classical arguments and debates, which aim to confirm or refute a particular position, attitude, or hypothesis. Arguments have at least two sides, and many have multiple sides. Some arguments are attempts to establish a common ground or seek consensus, such as when a family discusses where to go on a holiday, or company managers debate the best ways to boost productivity.

Sometimes people use arguments to persuade neutral or undecided others to a point of view or a new course of action, as when a salesperson tries to convince someone to try a new product or a social or political activist tries to influence people to sign a petition.

In the many communities to which you belong, there are no doubt some things you would like to be different. For example, you might like to see more healthy food choices in the university or college cafeteria, or more bicycle paths in your local community. You might want to influence young people on campus to get out and vote. In your family, you might wish to persuade other family members to have a more structured arrangement for doing household chores. The ability to argue well can help you effect positive change by influencing other people in school, work, and civic communities.

At university, you are often asked to demonstrate through argument what you have learned. A business instructor may ask you to defend a particular management style. A political science instructor may want you to support or oppose limiting the number of terms that members of Parliament can serve. A special education instructor may have you write a case for increased funding for exceptional students. If you identify a problem, such as an inefficient schedule, and propose a workable solution, you are using a common form of argument. In the workplace, a computer programmer may argue that the company should change its account-keeping program, an automotive service manager call for new diagnostic equipment, or a union president make a case that a company's employees merit raises. In many arenas, argument is used to justify or defend a previously established decision or course of action, such as when a department manager sends her boss a memo justifying some new procedure that she implemented.

Some arguments take the form of exploratory dialogues, in which people test different perspectives or possibilities. Exploratory arguments allow you to air doubts about your own position, explain why certain reasons and evidence have weight with you, and address alternative positions and arguments that attract you. They can also help you to find a position before you craft a more committed and focused argument. Using exploratory arguments can help clarify your assumptions and values as you consider other points of view and acquire new information. Engaging in exploratory argument as a kind of social conversation can be an enjoyable and enlivening experience.

When preparing to write an argument, you need to be aware that certain kinds of topics just aren't arguable. There's no point, for instance, in trying to tackle questions of personal preference or taste (Is red prettier than blue?). Such contests quickly turn into "it is," "it isn't" exchanges that establish nothing except the silliness of the contenders. Questions of simple fact (Was Pierre Trudeau prime minister in 1972?) don't qualify either, because only one side has the facts as ammunition. We turn to argument only when there is room for debate.

APPEALS IN ARGUMENT AND PERSUASION

Argument is a form of persuasion. The word *argument*, however, connotes an emphasis on logic and reason, while the word *persuasion* has a broader meaning, suggesting an emphasis on swaying the reader's attitudes by appealing to values and emotions. Effective arguments are grounded in logical, structured evidence, rational appeals known as *logos*. However, since people are not just thinking machines, most effective arguments also include appeals to people's emotions, as well as to their sense of ethical fairness. Emotional appeals in argument are classically referred to as *pathos*, and ethical appeals known as *ethos* are based on the character of the speaker/writer. Since readers often form conclusions based on their judgments of the writer's trustworthiness, effective arguers convey attitudes of authority, accuracy, and integrity.

Using Qualifiers

Sometimes the zeal to win your audience over will tempt you to make overly general, sweeping claims. For example, a student writing about drug use at raves originally claims: "Raves offer the opportunity for young people to find the respect and acceptance that is lacking in our culture." Yet after reflection, the student carefully revised her sweeping claim that respect is lacking in our culture: "Raves offer the opportunity for young people to find the respect and acceptance that often appears to be lacking in teen culture." Qualifiers such as "often appears" can help make claims more persuasive than blanket claims that the reader may question. When you are making large claims that could be disputed, consider using qualifiers such as "it seems that" or "it appears" to limit your claim. For example, if you are arguing about the importance of manners for young people, you do not want to charge all young Canadians with rudeness. Instead, you could qualify your claim by saying something such as "Some young people aren't aware of the social rules that make social interactions smooth and enjoyable."

Using Primary and Secondary Research in Argument

While it is possible to use your own experience, observations, and skills in logic to build a strong argument in a personal writing assignment, for formal writing, you are usually expected to use research to support your claims. Let's say that you're taking an education course and are asked to write a paper arguing for or against the effectiveness of computers as an educational tool in elementary schools. Obviously, this assignment would require you to synthesize the results of your outside reading as well as your own conclusions drawn from your observations of computer use in the classrooms. It would, in short, require both secondary (that is, library) research and direct observations (see Chapters 13 and 14), which is itself a form of primary research. Remember that before you use library and internet sources, you will need to read the sections on taking notes, handling quotations, and avoiding plagiarism in Chapters 13 and 15. As always, follow your instructor's guidelines for documenting sources.

RATIONAL APPEAL

Among family, friends, and your community, and certainly in professional circles, you are usually expected to reach your conclusions on the basis of sound reasons and appropriate evidence. Reasons are the key points you use to defend your conclusions. For instance, if you support safe injection sites for intravenous drug users, one reason might be the considerable reduction in AIDS-related deaths that could result. You could cite figures that project the number of deaths likely to be prevented by safe injection sites. If you oppose the program, one reason might be the drug dependency that will continue. To support this reason, you could quote a respected authority who verifies that dependency will become entrenched. Often the reasons you cite will draw on causal logic, using the word *because* to show the link between reasons and the conclusion you draw. Consider how a student writer uses the word *because* to link two reasons with the claim which follows.

> Because of the combination of continuous dancing and insufficient fluids, the drug ecstasy is especially dangerous when it is used at raves.

Even if you do not entirely convince your audience, they should at least be able to see your position as a plausible one. If you or your readers have rigid, unmovable assumptions, there can be no real argument, because you are not really listening to one another. Argument presupposes that both you and your readers are reasonable people who have a vested interest in reaching some kind of common ground. You and your audience need to have some shared principles about what counts as evidence.

The different kinds of rational evidence used in argument include established truths, personal experience, primary source information, statistical findings, and opinions of authorities.

Established Truths

These are facts that no one can seriously dispute. Here are some examples:

Historical fact: The Canadian Charter of Rights and Freedoms prohibits racial discrimination.

Scientific fact: The layer of ozone in the earth's upper atmosphere protects us from the sun's harmful ultraviolet radiation.

Geographical fact: Alberta has the largest oil reserves in Canada.

Established truths aren't arguable themselves but do provide strong backup for argumentative propositions. For example, citing the abundant oil supply in the western regions could support an argument that Canada should promote the increased use of Canadian oil to supply its energy needs.

Some established truths, the result of careful observations and thinking over many years, basically amount to enlightened common sense. The notion that everyone possesses a unique combination of interests, abilities, and personality characteristics illustrates this kind of truth. Few people would seriously question it.

Opinions of Authorities

An authority is a recognized expert in some field. Authoritative opinions—the only kind to use—play a powerful role in winning readers over to your side. The views of metropolitan police chiefs and criminologists could support your position on ways to control urban crime. Researchers who have investigated the effects of air pollution could help you argue for stricter smog-control laws. Whatever your argument, don't settle for less than heavyweight authorities, and, when possible, mention their credentials to your reader. This information makes their statements more persuasive. For example, "Ann Marie Forsythe, a certified public accountant and vice-president of North American operations for Touche Ross Accounting, believes that the finance minister's tax cut proposal will actually result in a tax increase for most Canadians." You should, of course, also cite the source of your information. Follow your instructor's guidelines.

The following paragraph from an article arguing that youth crime is becoming more violent illustrates the use of authority:

> According to Roy O'Shaughnessy, clinical director of British Columbia's Youth Court Services, Youth Forensic Psychiatric Services, the perception that a segment of young people is becoming more brutally violent is well-founded. "The type of crime we're seeing now is different from what we saw 10 years ago," says O'Shaughnessy, whose unit does psychiatric assessments of delinquents between the ages of 12 and 17. "We're seeing more use of weapons, more gang-related activity, more violent behaviour."
>
> Brian Bergman, "When Children Are Vicious"

Beware of biased opinions. The agribusiness executive who favours farm price supports or the labour leader who opposes any restrictions on picketing may be writing merely to guard old privileges or garner new ones. Unless the opinion can stand close scrutiny, don't put it in your paper; it just weakens your case. Be especially careful with internet sources. If you are using a general search engine, the first results of your key word search may be those sites that have paid for priority placement on the list. If you are writing a formal academic argument, you might want to search scholarly databases such as Academic Search Premier, Canadian NewsDisc, or Canadian Periodical Index for articles that have been juried by specialists in the field.

Because authorities don't always see eye to eye, their views lack the finality of established truths. Furthermore, their opinions sway readers only if the audience accepts the authority as authoritative. Although advertisers successfully present hockey players as authorities on shaving cream and credit cards, most people would not accept their views on the safety of nuclear energy.

Primary Source Information

You need to support most types of arguments with primary source information—documents or other materials produced by individuals directly involved with the issue or conclusions you reached by carrying out an investigation yourself. For example, to argue whether or not Newfoundland should have joined Confederation, you would want to examine the autobiographies of those involved in making the decision and perhaps even the historical documents that prompted it. To take a position on the violence in gangster rap, you would want to analyze the actual lyrics in a number of songs. To make a claim about media coverage of a terrorist act, you would want to read the newspaper and magazine accounts of correspondents who were on the scene. To convince readers to adopt your solution for the homeless problem, you might want to visit a homeless shelter or interview (in a safe place) some homeless people. This type of information can help you reach sound conclusions and build strong support for your position. Most university and college libraries contain a significant amount of primary source materials that you can draw on for an argument. Document the sources you use according to your instructor's guidelines.

Statistical Findings

Statistics—data showing how much, how many, or how often—can also buttress your argument. Most statistics come from books, magazines, newspapers, handbooks, encyclopedias, and reports, but you can use data from your own investigations as well. The Statistics Canada website is a good source of authoritative statistics on many different topics.

Because statistics are often misused, many people distrust them, so any you offer must be credible and reliable. First, make sure your sample isn't too small. Don't use a one-day traffic count to argue for a traffic light at a certain intersection. City Hall might counter by contending that the results are atypical. To make your case, you'd need to count traffic for perhaps two or three weeks. You must have a large enough representative sampling to support the kinds of conclusions you draw. In addition, do not push statistical claims too far. You may know that two-thirds of Tarrytown's factories pollute the air excessively, but don't argue that the same figures probably apply to a different town. There's simply no carryover. Also, keep alert for biased or poorly researched statistics; they can cause as serious a credibility gap as biased opinions. Generally, recent data are better than old data, but either must come from a reliable source. For example, older information from *The Globe and Mail* would probably be more accurate than current data from tabloid newspapers. Note how the following writer uses statistics to support the argument about the influence of the news media:

> And, the news media plays an important role in feeding the public view that we're in the middle of a crime wave. In 1995, the Fraser Institute studied media coverage of violent crime. In 1989, the murder rate in Canada was 2.4 per 100 000 people, and the two national networks (CBC and CTV) spent 10 percent of their airtime covering murder stories. By 1995, the murder rate had dropped to 2.04 per 100 000 people. However, national television news coverage of murder had more than doubled on both networks to fill 25 percent of airtime.
>
> Susan McClelland, "Distorted Picture"

Statistics from newspaper or journal articles, graphs, tables, and charts can help strengthen your case, but be sure to select data responsibly from credible sources, and to document them correctly.

Personal Experience

You yourself may be a credible authority on some issues. Personal experience can sometimes deliver an argumentative message more forcefully than any other kind of evidence. Suppose that two years ago a speeder ran into your car and almost killed you. Today you're arguing for stiffer laws against speeding. Chances are you'll rely mainly on expert opinions and on statistics showing the number of people killed and injured each year in speeding accidents. However, describing the crash, the slow, pain-filled weeks in the hospital, and the months spent hobbling around on crutches may well provide the persuasive nudge that wins your reader over.

Often the experiences and observations of others, gathered from books, magazines, or interviews, can support your position. If you argue against chemical waste dumps, the personal stories of people who lived near them and suffered the consequences—filthy ooze in the basement, children with birth defects, family members who developed a rare form of cancer—can help sway your reader.

Despite its usefulness, personal experience generally reinforces but does not replace other kinds of evidence. Some readers will discount personal experience as biased. Moreover, unless personal experience has other more objective support, readers may reject it as atypical or trivial.

EVALUATION OF EVIDENCE

Once you have gathered the appropriate evidence, you need to use certain standards to evaluate that evidence before you use it. That a piece of information is in some way connected to your topic does not make it good evidence or qualify it for inclusion in your paper. Readers won't be convinced that trains are dangerous merely because you were in a train wreck. You should not reach a conclusion based on such flimsy evidence either. In order to reach a reasonable conclusion and defend a position with suitable evidence, you should apply the following principles.

Evaluation Criteria	Explanations
How credible are the sources of the information? How reliable is the evidence?	Not all sources are equally reliable. For example, Statistics Canada data about population change is more credible than a local newspaper's estimate, and both are likely more valid than your own estimate.
How much confirming evidence is there?	With evidence, more is better. One scientific study on the efficacy of high-

	protein diets would be good, but several would be better. One authority who claims that global warming is a reality becomes more credible when confirmed by several other authorities.
How much contradictory evidence is there?	If several scientific studies or authorities point to the efficacy of high-protein diets while several other studies find such diets harmful, clearly you would need to weigh the evidence carefully. To present the evidence honestly, you would have to include evidence from both sides in your paper.
How well established is the evidence?	Extremely well-established evidence, such as the evidence for atoms, becomes the basis for textbooks and is assumed in most other research. This evidence is usually unquestionable (although occasionally it can be overturned). Such evidence makes a solid foundation for arguments.
How well does the evidence actually fit or support the claim?	False connections between ideas weaken arguments. For example, the fact that most Canadians are immigrants or descendents of immigrants has no bearing on whether the country is admitting too many or too few immigrants. To make a case for or against some policy on immigration, the evidence would have to focus on good or bad results, not numbers.
What does the evidence actually allow you to conclude?	Conclusions should flow from the evidence without exaggeration. For example, studies showing that TV violence causes children to play more aggressively do not warrant the conclusion that it causes children to kill others.

Sometimes unwarranted conclusions result because a writer fails to take competing claims and evidence into consideration. You need to weigh the credibility, quantity, reliability, and applicability of all the available evidence to reach and defend a conclusion.

REASONING STRATEGIES

Reasons and evidence are fitted together through three reasoning strategies: induction, deduction, and analogy.

Induction

An argument from induction occurs when a general claim is supported by specific evidence, whether direct observations, statistical data, or scientific studies. Most of our conclusions are supported inductively. When we conclude that a movie is worth watching because our friends liked it, when we decide a college program is effective because most of the graduates get jobs, or even when we support a scientific hypothesis based on formal experimentation, we are basing a conclusion on bits of evidence. We need to be thoughtful in reaching such conclusions. Are our friends like us, and are they trustworthy? Are the jobs graduates are getting good jobs? Does the experiment really prove the hypothesis? All the principles for evaluating evidence apply.

Induction makes our conclusions probable but rarely proves them. To prove something by induction, we must check every bit of evidence, and often that's just not practical or possible. However, the greater the number of observations and the larger the populations surveyed, the more strongly the conclusion is supported. If you ask ten out of fifteen thousand students whether they like the meal plan, you cannot draw a conclusion about the tastes of the entire student body.

You have several options for organizing an inductive argument. You might begin by posing a direct or indirect question in order to capture the reader's interest, or you might simply state the position you want to argue. The body of the paper then provides the supporting evidence. In the conclusion, you re-affirm your position or suggest the consequences of that position. You can also raise a general question, evaluate how your evidence answers that question, and then draw your conclusion from that answer.

The following short example illustrates inductive argument:

> Bologna is perhaps the most popular of all luncheon meats. Each day, thousands of individuals consume bologna sandwiches at noontime without ever considering the health consequences. Perhaps they should.
>
> The sodium content of bologna is excessively high. On the average, three ounces contain over 850 milligrams, three times as much as a person needs in a single day. In addition, bologna's characteristic flavour and reddish color are caused by sodium nitrite, which is used to prevent the growth of botulism-causing organisms. Unfortunately, sodium nitrite combines with amines, natural compounds already in most foods, to form nitrosamines, which have been proved to cause cancer in laboratory animals. Finally, from a nutrition standpoint, bologna is not a good food choice. The fat content is around 28 percent, the water content ranges upward from 50 percent, and the meat includes very little protein.
>
> Health-conscious people, then, will choose better fare for lunch.
>
> Alison Russell, student

When writing an induction argument, in addition to presenting the available evidence, there are two other important things you should do. First, demonstrate the credibility of your evidence. Why should the reader find the evidence credible? In the above example, the argument would have been much stronger if the writer had established the source of the evidence.

> On the average, as indicated on any store package, three ounces contain over 850 milligrams of sodium, three times as much as a person needs in a single day, according to the American Medical Association.

If possible, try to show how the evidence fits the conclusion you want to reach.

> Excess sodium and fat, low protein content, and the presence of a possible carcinogen are all considered by nutritionists to be unhealthy. Health-conscious people, then, will choose better fare for lunch.

Deduction

Deduction is the reverse of induction. Instead of formulating a conclusion after considering pieces of evidence, you start with an observation that most people accept as true and then show how certain conclusions follow from that observation. For example, to convince a friend to study harder, you begin with the assumption that a profitable career requires a good education; proceed to argue that for a good education students must study diligently; and conclude that, as a result, your friend should spend more time with the books. Politicians argue deductively when they assert that we all want to act in ways beneficial to future generations and then point out how the policies they favour will ensure that outcome.

As with induction, you have several options when organizing a deductive argument. You might begin with the position you intend to prove, with a question that will be answered by the argument, or with a synopsis of the argument. The body of the paper works out the implications of your assumption. In the conclusion, you could directly state (or restate, in different words) your position, suggest the consequences of adopting or not adopting that position, or pose a question that is easily answered after reading the argument. Here is a short example of deductive argument:

> The sex object stereotype is extremely damaging to women in particular and society as a whole. The ideal of physical beauty portrayed by the stereotype is unattainable and unrealistic. Most women do not have this idealized body shape: full breasts, tiny waist, and narrow hips. To attain these features, most women would have to resort to surgical alterations or starvation diets. Even so, all women must ultimately fail this beauty test in time, for the sex object is, above all else, young. Mere mortals cannot compare with these perpetually young, airbrushed, and anorexic visions of beauty. Given the

impossible and limiting expectations of the sex object stereotype, many women feel physically inadequate and are driven to unhealthy, and, ultimately, unsuccessful extremes in pursuit of an unnatural body image. A society that instills an impossible expectation of beauty for women is complicit in eroding the self-esteem of many women. So, in order to maintain and develop positive self-esteem in women, we as a society should resist the perpetuation of the sex object stereotype that is so prevalent in advertising and other forms of media.

When arguing from deduction, you need to make clear how your conclusions follow from the agreed-upon premises.

Reductio ad Absurdum A common and powerful form of deduction called *reductio ad absurdum* ("to reduce to absurdity") is used to attack an opponent's position by showing that its consequences are absurd if carried to their logical end. For example, to counter the position that the government should impose no restrictions on parents' rights to discipline their children, you might point out that, carried to its logical extreme, such a policy would allow individuals to beat their children. This absurd result makes it clear that certain restrictions should apply. The question then becomes where we should draw the line.

Syllogism Sometimes a deductive argument is built around a categorical syllogism, a set of three statements that follow a fixed pattern to ensure sound reasoning. The first statement, called the major premise, names a category of things and says that all or none of them share a certain characteristic. The minor premise notes that a thing or group of things belong to that category. The conclusion then states that the thing or group logically must share the characteristics of the category. Here are two examples:

Major premise:	All persons are mortal.
Minor premise:	Sue Davis is a person.
Conclusion:	Therefore, Sue Davis is mortal.
Major premise:	No dogs have feathers.
Minor premise:	Spot is a dog.
Conclusion:	Therefore, Spot does not have feathers.

Note that in each case, both major and minor premises are indisputably true, and so the conclusion follows logically. A syllogism in which one premise or both is false will not be logical. For example, if the major premise of your syllogism is that all Canadians support policies of multiculturalism, your unsound premise invalidates your conclusion.

Syllogisms frequently appear in stripped-down form, with one of the premises or the conclusion omitted. The following example omits the major premise: "Because Wilma is a civil engineer, she has a strong background in mathematics." Obviously the missing major premise is as follows: "All civil engineers have a strong background in mathematics."

Syllogistic Argument at Work   A syllogism can occur anywhere in an essay: in the introduction to set the stage for the evidence, at various places in the body, and even in the conclusion in order to pull the argument together. Here is an example that uses a syllogism in the introduction:

> In 1966, when the Astrodome was completed in Houston, Texas, the managers concluded that it would be impossible to grow grass indoors. To solve their problem, they decided to install a rug-like synthetic playing surface that was fittingly called Astroturf. In the ensuing years, many other sports facilities have installed synthetic turf. Unfortunately, this development has been accompanied by a sharp rise in the number and severity of injuries suffered by athletes—a rise clearly linked to the surface they play upon. <u>Obviously, anything that poses a threat to player safety is undesirable. Because synthetic turf does this, it is undesirable and should be replaced by grass.</u>
>
> Denny Witham, student

To support his position, the writer then notes that turf, unlike grass, often becomes excessively hot, tiring players and increasing their chances of injury; seams can open up between sections of turf and lead to falls; players can run faster on artificial turf and thus collide more violently; and the extreme hardness of turf leads to torn ligaments and tissues when players slam their toes into it.

Avoiding Misuse of Syllogisms   Two cautions are in order. *First,* make sure any syllogism you use follows the proper order. The writer of the following passage has ignored this caution:

> Furthermore, Robinson has stated openly that he supports a ban on all clearcut logging practices. For many years now, the Green Party has taken the same environmentalist stand. Robinson's position places him firmly in the Green Party camp. I strongly urge anyone supporting this man's candidacy to reconsider. . . .

Restated in syllogistic form, the writer's argument goes like this:

> Green Party members support a ban on all clearcut logging practices.
> Robinson supports a ban on all clearcut logging practices.
> Therefore, Robinson is a supporter of the Green Party.

The last two statements reverse the proper order, and as a result the syllogism proves nothing about Robinson's politics: He may or may not be "in the Green Party camp."

Second, make sure the major premise of your syllogism is in fact true. Note this example:

> All Conservatives are opposed to environmental protection.
> Mary is a Conservative.
> Therefore, Mary is opposed to environmental protection.

But is every Conservative an anti-environmentalist? In some communities, political conservatives have led fights against air and water pollution, and most conservatives agree that at least some controls are worthwhile. Mary's sympathies, then, may well lie with those who want to heal, rather than hurt, the environment.

EXERCISE *Which of these syllogisms is satisfactory, which have false major premises, and which is faulty because the last two statements reverse the proper order?*

1. All singers are happy people.
   Mary Harper is a singer.
   Therefore, Mary Harper is a happy person.

2. All cowards fear danger.
   "Chicken" Cacciatore is a coward.
   Therefore, "Chicken" Cacciatore fears danger.

3. All cats like meat.
   Towser likes meat.
   Therefore, Towser is a cat.

4. No salesperson would ever misrepresent a product to a customer.
   Sabrina is a salesperson.
   Therefore, Sabrina would never misrepresent a product to a customer.

Analogy in Argument

An analogy compares two unlike situations or things. Arguers often use analogies to contend that, because two items share one or more likenesses, they are also alike in other ways. Familiar analogies assume that humans respond to chemicals as rats do and that success in school predicts success on the job. You have used analogy if you ever pressed your parents for more adult privileges, such as a later curfew, by arguing that you were like an adult in many ways.

However, because its conclusions about one idea rest upon observations about a different idea, analogy is the weakest form of rational appeal. Analogies never prove anything. But they often help explain and show probability and therefore are quite persuasive.

For an analogy to be useful, it must feature significant similarities that bear directly on the issue. In addition, it must account for any significant differences between the two items. It is often helpful to test an analogy by listing the similarities and differences. Here's an effective analogy, used to back an argument that a liberal education is the best kind to help us cope successfully with life:

> Suppose it were perfectly certain that the life and fortune of every one of us would, one day or other, depend upon his winning or losing a game of chess.

Don't you think that we should all consider it to be a primary duty to learn at least the names and the moves of the pieces; to have a notion of a gambit, and a keen eye for all the means of giving and getting out of check? Do you not think that we should look with a disapprobation amounting to scorn, upon the father who allowed his son, or the state which allowed its members, to grow up without knowing a pawn from a knight?

Yet it is a very plain and elementary truth, that the life, the fortune, and the happiness of every one of us, and, more or less, of those who are connected with us, do depend upon our knowing something of the rules of a game infinitely more difficult and complicated than chess. It is a game which has been played for untold ages, every man and woman of us being one of the two players in a game of his or her own. The chessboard is the world, the pieces are the phenomena of the universe, the rules of the game are what we call the laws of Nature. The player on the other side is hidden from us. We know that his play is always fair, just, and patient. But also we know, to our cost, that he never overlooks a mistake, or makes the smallest allowance for ignorance. To the man who plays well, the highest stakes are paid, with that sort of overflowing generosity with which the strong shows delight in strength. And one who plays ill is checkmated—without haste, but without remorse. . . .

Well, what I mean by Education is learning the rules of this mighty game. In other words, education is the instruction of the intellect in the law of Nature, under which name I include not merely things and their forces, but men and their ways; and the fashioning of the affections and of the will into an earnest and loving desire to move in harmony with those laws. For me, education means neither more nor less than this. Anything which professes to call itself education must be tried by this standard, and if it fails to stand the test, I will not call it education, whatever may be the force of authority, or of numbers, upon the other side.

Thomas Henry Huxley, "A Liberal Education and Where to Find It"

To develop an argument by analogy, brainstorm the two items being compared for significant similarities and prepare a chart that matches them up. The greater the number and closeness of these similarities, the better the argument by analogy.

EMOTIONAL APPEAL

Although effective argument relies mainly on reason, an emotional appeal can lend powerful reinforcement. Indeed, emotion can win the hearts and the help of people who would otherwise passively accept a logical argument but take no action. Each Christmas, newspapers raise money for local charities by running stark case histories of destitute families. Organizations raise funds to fight famine by displaying brochures that feature skeletal, swollen-bellied children. Still other groups use emotion-charged stories and pictures to solicit support for environmental protection, to combat various diseases, and so on. Less benignly, advertisers use emotion to play upon our hopes, fears, and vanities in order to sell mouthwash, cars, clothes, and other products. Politicians paint themselves as fiscally responsible, trustworthy toilers for the public good while lambasting their opponents as being callous and unconcerned with social justice. In evaluating or writing an argument, ask yourself whether the facts warrant the emotion. Is the condition of the destitute family truly cause for pity? Is any politician unwaveringly good, any other irredeemably bad?

The following passage from a student argument favouring assisted suicide for the terminally ill represents an appropriate use of emotion:

> When I visited Grandpa for the last time, he seemed imprinted on the hospital bed, a motionless, skeleton-like figure tethered by an array of tubes to the droning, beeping machine at his bedside. The eyes that had once sparkled with delight as he bounced grandchildren on his knee now stared blankly at the ceiling, seemingly ready to burst from their sockets. His mouth, frozen in an open grimace, emitted raspy, irregular noises as he fought to breathe. Spittle leaked from one corner of his mouth and dribbled onto the sheet. A ripe stench from the diaper around his middle hung about the bedside, masking the medicinal sickroom smells. As I stood by the bedside, my mind flashed back to the irrepressible man I once knew, and tears flooded my eyes. Bending forward, I planted a soft kiss on his forehead, whispered "I love you, Gramps," and walked slowly away.
>
> Dylan Brandt Chafin, student

To develop an effective emotional appeal, identify the stories, scenes, or events of the topic that arouse the strongest emotional response within you. Do some thinking about the types of words that best convey the emotion you feel. Then write the section so that it builds to the kind of emotional conclusion that will help your argument.

ETHICAL APPEAL

Before logic can do its work, the audience must be willing to consider the argument. If a writer's tone offends the audience, perhaps by sounding arrogant or mean-spirited, the reasoning will fail to penetrate. But if the writer comes across as pleasant, fair-minded, and decent, gaining reader support is much easier. The image that the writer projects is called the ethical appeal.

If you write with a genuine concern for your topic, a commitment to the truth, and a sincere respect for others, you will probably come across reasonably well. When you finish writing, check whether occasional snide comments or bitter remarks slipped unnoticed onto the page. In the following excerpt from Martin Luther King's famous "I Have a Dream" speech, King does not give way to angry venting, but makes a strong ethical appeal to people's sense of justice:

> Now is the time to make real the promises of democracy; now is the time to rise from the dark and desolate valley of segregration to the sunlit path of racial justice; now is the time to lift our nation from the quicksands of racial injustice to

the solid rock of brotherhood; now is the time to make justice a reality for all of God's children.

Martin Luther King, Jr., "I Have a Dream"

FERRETING OUT FALLACIES

Fallacies are lapses in logic that weaken your argument. The fallacies described below are among the most common. Correct any you find in your own arguments, and call attention to those used by the opposition.

Hasty Generalization

Hasty generalization results when someone bases a conclusion on too little evidence. The student who tries to see an instructor during one of her office hours, finds her out, and goes away muttering, "She's never there when she should be" is guilty of hasty generalization. Perhaps the instructor was delayed by another student, attended a special department meeting, or went home ill. Even if she merely went shopping, that's not a good reason for saying she always shirks her responsibility. Several more unsuccessful office visits would be needed to make such a charge stick.

Non Sequitur

From the Latin meaning "It does not follow," this fallacy draws unwarranted conclusions from seemingly ample evidence. Consider this example: "Bill's been out almost every night for the last two weeks. Who is she?" These evening excursions, on their own, point to no particular conclusion. Bill may be studying in the library, participating in campus organizations, taking night classes, or walking. Of course, he could be with a new girlfriend, but that conclusion requires other evidence.

Stereotyping

A person who commits this fallacy attaches one or more supposed characteristics to a group or one of its members. Typical stereotypes include "Latins make better lovers," "Blondes have more fun," and "Teenagers are lousy drivers." Stereotyping racial, religious, ethnic, or national groups can destroy an argument. The images are often malicious and are always offensive to fair-minded readers.

Card Stacking

In card stacking, the writer presents only part of the available evidence on a topic, deliberately omitting essential information that would alter the picture considerably. For instance: "College students have a very easy life; they attend classes for only twelve to sixteen hours a week." This statement ignores the many hours that students must spend studying, doing homework and/or research, writing papers, and earning enough money to pay tuition.

Either/Or Fallacy

The either/or fallacy asserts that only two choices exist when in fact several options are possible. A salesperson who wants you to buy snow tires may claim, "Either buy these tires or plan on getting stuck a lot this winter." But are you really that boxed in? You might drive only on main roads that are plowed immediately after every snowstorm. You could use public transportation when it snows. You could buy radial tires for year-round use, or you could buy tires from another dealer. If very little snow falls, you might not need special tires at all.

However, not all either/or statements are fallacies. The instructor who checks a student's record and then issues a warning, "Make at least a C on your final, or you'll fail the course," is not guilty of a reasoning error. No other alternatives exist. Most situations, however, offer more than two choices.

Begging the Question

A person who begs the question asserts the truth of some unproven statement. Here is an example: "Vitamin A is harmful to your health, and all bottles should carry a warning label. If enough of us write to the Minister of Health, we can get the labelling we need." But how do we know vitamin A does harm users? No evidence is offered. People lacking principles often use this fallacy to hit opponents below the belt: "We shouldn't allow an environmental terrorist like Paul Watson to run for political office." Despite a lack of suitable evidence, voters are sometimes swayed by such faulty logic and vote for the other candidate.

Circular Argument

Circular argument, a first cousin to begging the question, supports a position merely by restating it. "Pauline is a good manager because she runs the company effectively" says, in effect, that "something is because something is." Repetition replaces evidence.

Arguing off the Point

The writer who commits this fallacy, which is sometimes called "ignoring the question" or "a red herring," sidetracks an issue by introducing irrelevant information. To illustrate: "Vancouver has a more moderate climate than Toronto. Besides, too many Torontonians are moving to Vancouver. They are creating congestion and driving up the price of real estate. Many Vancouverites are angry that the cost of buying a home is so high." The writer sets out to convince that

Vancouver offers a more enjoyable climate than Toronto but then abruptly shifts to increasing congestion and rising house prices in Vancouver—a trend that has no bearing on the argument.

The Argument *ad Hominem*

The Latin term "to the man" designates an argument that attacks an individual rather than that individual's opinions or qualifications. Note this example: "Sam Bernhard doesn't deserve promotion to personnel manager. His divorce was a disgrace, and he's always writing letters to the editor. The company should find someone more suitable." This attack completely skirts the real issue—whether Sam's job performance entitles him to the promotion. Unless his personal conduct has caused his work to suffer, it should not enter into the decision.

Appeal to the Crowd

An appeal of this sort arouses an emotional response by playing on the irrational fears and prejudices of the audience. Terms like *terrorists, fascists, bleeding hearts, right-wingers, welfare chisellers,* and *law and order* are tossed about freely to sway the audience for or against something. Consider the following excerpt from a famous speech:

> The streets of our country are in turmoil. The universities are filled with students rebelling and rioting. Communists are seeking to destroy our country. Russia is threatening us with her might, and the public is in danger. Yes, danger from within and without. We need law and order. Yes, without law and order our nation cannot survive. Elect us, and we shall by law and order be respected among the nations of the world. Without law and order our republic shall fall.

Tapping the emotions of the crowd can sway large groups and win acceptance for positions that rational thinking would reject. Think what Adolf Hitler, the author of the foregoing excerpt, brought about in Germany.

Guilt by Association

This fallacy points out some similarity or connection between one person or group and another. It tags the first with the sins, real or imagined, of the second. The following excerpt from a letter protesting a speaker at a lecture series illustrates this technique:

> The next slated speaker, Dr. Sylvester Crampton, was for years a member of the Economic Information Committee. This foundation has very strong ties with other ultraright-wing groups, some of which have been labelled fascistic. When he speaks next Thursday, whose brand of patriotism will he be selling?

Post Hoc, ergo Propter Hoc

The Latin meaning, "after this, therefore because of this," refers to the fallacy of assuming that because one event follows another, the first caused the second. Such weak thinking underlies many popular superstitions ("If a black cat crosses your path, you'll have bad luck") and many connections that cannot be substantiated ("Since video games have become so popular, childhood obesity rates have risen. Therefore, video games cause childhood obesity."). Sometimes one event does cause another: A sudden thunderclap might startle a person into dropping a dish. At other times, coincidence is the only connection. Careful research and thinking will help determine whether A caused B, or whether these two events just happened to occur at about the same time.

Faulty Analogy

This is the error of assuming that two circumstances or things are similar in all important respects, when in fact they are not. Here's an example: Sean McIntyre, midget hockey coach, tells his players, "Scotty Bowman has won the Stanley Cup seven times by insisting on excellent defensive positional play and requiring excellent physical conditioning. We're going to win the midget championship by following the same methods." McIntyre assumes that because he and Bowman are coaches, he can duplicate Bowman's achievements by using Bowman's methods. Several important differences, however, mark the two situations:

1. Bowman has had very talented players, obtained through the player draft or trades; McIntyre can choose only from the children in his community.
2. Bowman's players have been paid professionals who very likely were motivated, at least in part, by the financial rewards that come from winning the Stanley Cup; McIntyre's players are amateurs.
3. "Excellent defensive positional play" is probably easier for professional players than for midget players to attain.
4. Very few of Bowman's players could resist his insistence on "excellent physical conditioning" because they were under contract. Could McIntyre expect his players, essentially volunteers, to accept the same physical demands that Bowman has expected?

EXERCISE *Identify and explain the fallacies in the following examples. Remember that understanding the faulty reasoning is more important than merely naming the fallacy.*

1. After slicing a Golden Glow orange, Nancy discovers that it is rotten. "I'll never buy another Golden Glow product," she declares emphatically.
2. A campaigning politician states that, unless the federal government appropriates funds to help people living in poverty, they will all starve.

3. A husband and wife see an X-rated movie called *Swinging Wives*. A week later the husband discovers that his wife, while supposedly attending an evening class, has been unfaithful to him. He blames the movie for her infidelity.

4. "Look at those two motorcycle riders trying to pick a fight. All those cycle bums are troublemakers."

5. "Bill really loves to eat. Some day he'll have a serious weight problem."

6. "Because no-fault divorce is responsible for today's skyrocketing divorce rate, it should be abolished."

7. "This is the best-looking picture in the exhibit; it's so much more attractive than the others."

8. "I am against the proposed ban on smoking in public places. As long as I don't inhale and I limit my habit to ten cigarettes a day, my health won't suffer."

ETHICAL ISSUES

When writing an argument, we may wish to raise awareness, change attitudes, or spark some action. These objectives create an ethical responsibility for both the quality and the possible consequences of our arguments. Suppose a doctor writing a nationally syndicated advice column recommends an over-the-counter product that may cause a serious reaction in users who also take a certain prescription drug. Clearly this writer has acted irresponsibly and risks legal action if some readers suffer harm. Asking and answering the following questions can help you avoid any breach of ethics.

- Have I carefully considered the issue I'm arguing and the stance I'm taking? Since you're trying to get others to adopt your views, you'll need to make sure they are very credible or make clear that your position is tentative or dependent on certain conditions.

- Am I fair to other positions on the issue? Careless or deliberate distortion of opposing views is ethically dishonest and could raise doubts about your credibility.

- Are my reasons and evidence legitimate? It is unethical to present flawed reasons as if they were credible or falsify evidence.

- Do I use fallacies or other types of faulty thinking to manipulate the reader unfairly?

- What consequences could follow if readers adopt my position? Say a writer strongly opposes genetically modified foods and advocates disruption of installations that help develop them. If some who are convinced by the argument then proceed to act on the writer's advice, innocent people could be injured.

WRITING AN ARGUMENT

Planning and Drafting the Argument

When you write an argument, you don't simply sit down and dash off your views as though they came prefabricated. Instead, look at argument as an opportunity to think things through, to gradually and often tentatively come to some conclusions, and then, begin to draft your position in stages with the support you have discovered. If you are using outside sources to find support for your argument, you need to use your active reading and critical thinking skills as you sift and evaluate potential supporting materials. You need to weigh the merits of different writers' opinions, look for evidence of bias, weigh the type and amount of support backing each assertion, and select the key points to include in your paper. Try to keep an open mind as you are formulating your thesis.

Some instructors assign argument topics, and some leave the choice of topic to you. If you are choosing, many options are available. Interesting issues—some local, some of broader importance—crowd our newspapers, magazines, and TV airways, vying for attention. Because several of them have probably piqued your interest, there's a good chance you won't have to rely on the strategies on pages 33–39 to help you choose your topic.

Some students approach an argument with such strong attitudes that they ignore evidence that contradicts their thinking. Don't make this mistake. Instead, maintain an open mind as you research your issue, and then, after careful thought, choose the position you'll take. Often, several possible positions exist; and sometimes you end up changing your position after you have researched the topic.

Exploring Your Topic

You never really start an argument with a blank page. There is almost always an ongoing conversation about the issue. Before you enter this conversation, it helps to be informed by researching the topic. If your paper is based on sources, you may want to review Chapters 13 and 15 for ideas and information about proper documentation. You may want to talk to others to get their views on the matter. Or you might make your own formal or informal observations; if so, you may be helped by the additional research strategies in Chapter 14.

As you investigate possible positions, ask and answer the following questions about each:

What are the reasons for the various positions?
What values are at stake, and what conclusions do they imply?
What common ground or shared principles exist among various positions?
What kinds of evidence support the position?
How substantial is the evidence?
If the evidence includes statistics and authoritative opinions, are they reliable? Or are they flawed for some reason?

What are the objections to each position, and how can they be countered?
If the issue involves taking some action, what might be its consequences?

To help with this stage of the process, prepare a chart that summarizes your findings for each position; then examine it carefully to identify the best position to argue for. The example below illustrates a three-position issue:

Position 1	Position 2	Position 3
Evidence and evaluation	Evidence and evaluation	Evidence and evaluation
Objections and how countered	Objections and how countered	Objections and how countered
Consequences	Consequences	Consequences

One effective technique for developing an argument is to first write a dialogue between two or three people that explores the various sides of an issue without trying to arrive at any conclusion. Writing such a dialogue can help start your mental energy flowing, reveal the issue from many sides, and give you ideas about developing effective material for your paper.

Arguments for Different Purposes

When you write any kind of argument, you may find yourself drawing on all the different writing strategies you have previously learned. As you contemplate your position and evidence, consider the purpose of your argument and how the purpose will affect the strategies you choose to employ. Arguments take many different forms, depending on the purpose, audience, and genre for the argument. An argument that takes the form of a critique may include a comparative analysis that demonstrates the relative merits of one item over another. An argument that takes the form of a complaint letter may use causal analysis to outline a problem and then propose a solution. An argument in a business context may also establish that something is a problem, and then recommend a new policy. An argument that takes the form of a formal research paper in an academic discipline will make its case with the help of information from primary and secondary sources.

Some arguments try to establish that something is a fact—nursing is hard work, residences are poor study places, bologna is an unhealthy food. This type of paper usually relies on assorted evidence, perhaps some combination of statistics, authoritative opinion, and personal experience. For example, to prove that nursing is demanding, you might narrate and describe some of the strenuous activities in a typical nursing day, cite hospital nursing supervisors who verify the rigours of the job, and perhaps give statistics on nurses who quit the profession because of stress.

Argument as Problem and Solution

If you want to propose a change to an existing structure or policy, you must first prove that a problem exists before your audience will be receptive to hearing about a solution. As you investigate the extent of the problem, you may decide that it does not really need solving, or even that the real problem is different than you originally thought. As you attempt to convince your audience to accept your solution, you are likely to blend different writing strategies into your argument. You may use description and illustration to identify the problem, and cause/effect analysis as you examine causes, including hidden causes, and possible effects. Sometimes you can come up with effective solutions by addressing the causes, or you can explore new ways to improve the situation. In some cases, you may have to explain the process of implementing your solution and/or defend (argue) its feasibility by showing that it will not have unacceptable consequences.

Arguments that propose a new action or policy may identify a need or a problem, and they generally recommend the implementation of a practical project, program, or action that will meet existing needs. For example, if there is no place on campus where students can gather to meet each other informally or study, a writer might propose the construction of a study lounge for students. Arguments that defend or oppose a broader social, political, or cultural policy—for example, whether Olympic athletes should have random drug-testing, or whether Canadian ports should have stricter security measures—must demonstrate the need for a new policy, how the need can best be addressed, and the benefits that will result. Arguments that propose a new policy or recommend a new action often use verbs such as *should, need,* or *ought.*

Argument as Evaluation and Critique

Reviews and critiques are arguments that evaluate something against specific criteria. Some reviews provide a short summary of content as background information, but the overall thesis should reflect your judgment, and the rest of the review develops reasons for this judgment. If you are asked to critique a movie, you need to commit yourself to a point of view on the quality of that movie rather than simply summarizing what happened. For example, your thesis for a movie review might be something like "The latest Harry Potter movie does not live up to the hype it has generated." If you are looking at criteria such as the quality of acting, special effects, music, and pacing, use specific examples and details for each criterion you are evaluating. Remember to establish criteria for your evaluation that are in accord with what the movie, or restaurant, or writer is trying to do; you can't fault the movie for not being a book, a café for not being a five-star restaurant, or an essay for not having music. Moreover, if you are evaluating a text, you need to establish that you have not come to it with preformed judgments, but have tried to understand and appreciate it on its own terms.

If you are evaluating a text or comparing two texts, your evaluation does not have to be absolutely negative or positive, but you do have to decide whether to emphasize strengths or weaknesses. Typically the evaluation of a text, movie, or essay is mixed, something like "Although this movie has amazing chemistry between the two stars, other weaknesses seriously compromise its quality." If you want to emphasize weaknesses, subordinate the strengths and put the weaknesses afterward, since whatever you end with makes the greatest impression on the reader. If you want to emphasize positives, end on a positive note. By the way, evaluations of texts and works of art usually employ the present tense throughout, except in the beginning when you are describing your experiences of entering a movie theatre, or picking up a book. If you are asked to write a comparative evaluation, in which you assert the greater value of someone or something as compared to a similar person, thing, or work of art, you can refer to Chapter 9 on structuring comparisons.

Considering Your Audience in Argument

With an argument, as with any essay, purpose and audience are closely linked. You should always imagine that your audience is a group of readers who are neutral or opposed to your position, because there's no point in preaching to the converted. Take a little time to analyze these readers so that you can tailor your arguments appropriately. Pose these questions as you proceed:

> What are the readers' interests, expectations, and needs concerning this issue?
> What evidence is most likely to convince them?
> What objections and consequences would probably weigh most heavily with them?
> How can I win people over and deal with objections?

Building Bridges with a Rogerian Argument

As you reflect on the issues that concern you, consider who the people are who have the power to change things, why they might resist change, and how you could overcome their resistance. If your audience is likely to be resistant or even hostile, you may want to use a *Rogerian argument*. Named for psychologist Carl Rogers, this type of argument emphasizes the speaker or writer's ability to look at things from the other's point of view. You can show that you understand and respect the position of the other by summarizing and acknowledging opposing points of view in a fair and accurate way. If you seek to establish some common ground before getting into your argument, you can often reduce the antagonism that people with opposing views might feel toward your position. For example, if you are arguing about an emotionally charged issue such as assisted suicide or changes in Canada's health-care system that affect people directly, you can acknowledge in your introduction that these challenging issues have troubling ethical implications that people are right to worry about. After you build a bridge of shared values and respect with your audience, you can then present a position that addresses opposing concerns without compromising your views.

You can also reduce audience resistance if you acknowledge possible objections early on, responding to them if you can, or making concessions where necessary. For example, if you are arguing that more money needs to be targeting special educational initiatives, you can acknowledge that these initiatives are expensive, but then emphasize that the long-term benefits include a more equitable and stable society.

If your argument is highly controversial or your audience highly resistant, delay stating your thesis until you have built a case by establishing common ground, anticipating possible objections, providing necessary background, and using other strategies such as humour or an apt illustrative narrative to draw your audience to your side.

In addition, you can adapt the language of your argument to the audience's concerns and interests. To convince an audience of farmers that organic farming is viable, you might stress the added income they would gain from selective consumers willing to pay more for organic food; while for an audience of nutritionists, you might note the health benefits that would result. Even though you are unlikely to convince everyone, it is best to adopt the attitude that most readers can be convinced if your approach is appealing and your evidence is sound.

Drafting the Argument

When you have a good grasp of your position, reasons, evidence, and approach, you're ready to draft your paper. A typical introduction arouses the reader's interest and sometimes presents the proposition—a special thesis statement that names the issue and indicates which position the writer will take. It can declare that something is a fact, support a policy, call for a certain action, or assert that something has greater value than something else. Here are examples:

1. Carron College does not provide adequate recreational facilities for its students. *(Declares something is fact.)*
2. Our company's policy of randomly testing employees for drug use has proved effective and should be continued. *(Supports policy.)*
3. Because the present building is overcrowded and unsafe, the people of Midville should vote funds for a new junior high school. *(Calls for action.)*
4. The new Ford Fire-Eater is superior to the Honda Harmony in performance and economy. *(Asserts value.)*

Any of the techniques previously mentioned can launch your paper. For example, in arguing for stepped-up AIDS education, you might jolt your reader by describing a dying victim. If your issue involves unfamiliar terms, you might define them up front; and if the essay is long, you could preview its main points.

After the introduction comes the evidence, arranged in whatever order you think works best. If one of your points is likely to arouse resistance, hold it back and make points your reader can more easily accept first. Where strong resistance is not a factor, you could begin or end with your most compelling piece of evidence.

The strategies discussed in earlier chapters can help you develop an argument. Some papers incorporate one strategy, while others rely on several. Let's see how you might combine several in an argument against legalized casino gambling. You might open with a brief *description* of the frantic way a gambling addict keeps pulling the lever of a slot machine, his eyes riveted on the spinning dials, his palms sweating, as flashing lights and wailing sirens announce winners at other machines. Next, you could offer a brief *definition* of gambling fever so that the writer and reader are on common ground; and then, to show the dimensions of the problem, *classify* the groups of people who are especially addicted. Finally, after detailing the negative *effects* of the addiction, you might end by *comparing* gambling addiction with drug addiction, noting that both provide a "high" and both kinds of addicts know their habits hurt them.

Whatever strategies you use, make sure that substantiating evidence is embedded within each one. Strategies by themselves don't convince. For example, in discussing the negative effects of gambling, you might cite statistics that show the extent and nature of the problem. An expert opinion might validate your classification of addicts. Or you might use observation data to verify gambling's addictive effects.

Besides presenting evidence, use this part of your paper to refute—that is, to point out weaknesses or errors in—the opposing position. You might try the following:

■ *Point out any evidence that undermines that position.* If one viewpoint holds that drug testing violates cherished privacy rights, you might note that employers already monitor phone calls, check employees' desks, and violate privacy in other ways.

■ *Identify faulty assumptions and indicate how they are faulty: They don't lead to the implied conclusion, they lack the effectiveness of an alternative, or they are false or unsupported.* If you oppose drug testing, you could point out problems in the assumption that such tests are necessary to protect the public. Closer supervision of work performance might be a better protection; after all, fatigue, stress, negligence, and alcohol abuse can all result in serious problems, and they are not detected by drug tests.

■ *Identify problems in the logic of the argument.* Are there missing premises, faulty connections between reasons, or conclusions that don't follow from the premises? The argument against drug testing usually proceeds by asserting that privacy is a fundamental right, that drug testing violates privacy, and that therefore drug testing should not be allowed. There is a missing premise, however: that because privacy is a fundamental right it should never be violated. This premise is, in fact, at the heart of the dispute and therefore cannot be accepted as a reason to disallow drug testing.

You can place refutations throughout the body of the paper or group them together just ahead of the conclusion. Whatever you decide, don't adopt a gloating or sarcastic tone that will alienate fair-minded readers. Resist the urge to engage in straw man tactics—calling attention to imaginary or trivial weaknesses of the opposing side so that you can demolish them. Shrewd readers easily spot such ploys. Finally, don't be afraid to concede secondary or insignificant points to the opposition. Arguments always have two or more sides; you can't have all the ammunition on your side. (If you discover that you must concede major points, however, consider switching sides.) Here is a sample refutation from a student paper:

Not everyone agrees with workplace drug testing for employees in public transportation companies, electric utilities, nuclear power plants, and other industries involving public safety. Critics assert that such tests invade privacy and therefore violate one of our cherished freedoms. While the examination of one's urine does entail inspection of something private, such a test is a reasonable exception because it helps ensure public safety and calm public fears. Individuals have a right to be protected from the harm that could be caused by an employee who abuses drugs. An airline pilot's right to privacy should not supersede the security of hundreds of people who could be injured or killed in a drug-induced accident. Thus the individual's privacy should be tempered by concern for the community—a concern that benefits all of us.

Annie Louise Griffith, student

Conclude in a manner that sways the reader to your side. Depending on the argument, you might restate your position, summarize your main points, predict the consequences if your position does or doesn't prevail, or make an emotional appeal for support or action.

Revising the Argument

Review the guidelines in Chapter 5 and ask yourself these questions as you revise your argument paper:

Appropriate topic and thesis Is my topic a clearly debatable one? Have I narrowed my topic to a clearly defined thesis that runs throughout the essay? Is my proposition clearly evident and of the appropriate type—that is, one of fact, policy, action, or value?

Focus Do I have a clear purpose I want to achieve through my argument, and do I maintain this sense of purpose and direction throughout? Is my thesis clear and strategically positioned? Are my main points clearly related to my thesis?

Awareness of audience Is the paper aimed at the audience I want to reach? Have I tailored my argument to appeal to that audience? Have I kept a respectful tone throughout, even when dealing with possible objections to my argument?

Thoroughness Have I examined all of the main positions? Have I assessed the evidence supporting each one? Have I considered the objections to each position and either countered these objections or made concessions where necessary?

Rational appeal Do I have enough solid evidence to support my claims? Is my evidence sound, adequate, and appropriate to the argument? Are my authorities qualified? Have I established their expertise? Are they biased? Will my audience accept them as authorities? Do my statistics adequately support my position? Have I pushed my statistical claims too far?

Emotional appeal If I've included an emotional appeal—perhaps by including a short narrative or story that fits with my larger purpose—does it centre on those emotions most likely to sway the reader? Have I addressed possible reader resistance by adequately refuting opposing arguments? Have I avoided sentimentality and self-pity?

Ethical appeal Have I made a conscious effort to present myself as a fair and reasonable person? Have I weighed the possible consequences if my paper were to persuade someone to take action?

Logic Have I established logical links between my claims and my evidence? Have I avoided overly broad claims and sweeping generalizations, especially ones that contain words such as "all" and "never"? If the proposition takes the form of a syllogism, is it sound? If faulty, have I started with a faulty premise, or reversed the last two statements of the syllogism? If I've used analogy, are my points of comparison pertinent to the issue? Have I noted any significant differences between the items being compared? Is my argument free of fallacies?

Organization Does my argument follow an effective organizational plan, such as the order of climax? Have I developed my position with one or more writing strategies? Are transitions smooth, from one point to the next? Do I end with an effective conclusion, rather than going on too long or stopping short?

EXAMPLE OF A STUDENT ESSAY OF ARGUMENT

Teaching Boys to Be Nonviolent and Still Be Boys

Kelly Dussin

1   This week I attended a memorial service for a colleague's daughter-in-law. She was only 39 years old and the mother of two young children, and was the alleged victim of a domestic dispute. Just about every day, the news is filled with stories of violence such as murders, stabbings, domestic abuse, robberies, abductions, sports violence, and school shootings like the one by a 14-year-old in Taber, Alberta, in 1999. The news reports note the youth of those engaged in violence, but do not dwell on the fact that most of these crimes of violence are committed by males. Anti-violence educator Jackson Katz states in his video *Tough Guise* that "in the United States, 85 percent of all murders are committed by men and over 90 percent of all assault, domestic abuse, date abuse, rape, [and] child sexual abuse are committed by men." He also notes that "81 percent of boys who are abused will grow up to abuse and 76 percent of all homicides are males killing males." Of course, while many crimes of violence are committed by males, most males do not grow up to be abusers or criminals. Still, as a teacher assistant who works with adolescents, many of them male, and as mother of two boys, I am concerned about what kinds of cultural messages boys are receiving about what it means to be a man.

2   Many people might argue that boys have always engaged in acts of violence and that fighting at school or at home was just part of what being

a boy was all about. Some might say that we can't always expect boys will always want to sit quietly and talk things out, and that most young males are active, sometimes more active than teachers would like. Some schools are so alarmed about bullying that they may have a policy of zero tolerance for the roughhousing that boys are prone to. As a teaching assistant, parent and citizen, I find it difficult to know how to promote peaceful alternatives to violence while still respecting boys' needs to be active and physical. How can we teach boys to be nonviolent in a culture of masculinity that glorifies violence, while still allowing boys to be boys?

3   In North America, the culture of masculinity promotes ideals of toughness, independence, and cool. Myriam Miedzian, author of *Boys Will Be Boys,* describes the values of "the masculine mystique as toughness, dominance, repression of empathy, [and] extreme competitiveness" (Introduction). She believes these values are reflected in "criminal activity and are evidenced in the messages and policies of political leaders" (Introduction). William Pollack, Ph.D., author of *Real Boys*, believes we need to rescue our sons from the "myths of boyhood." Pollack suggests that we expect boys to grow up too fast, "with too little preparation for what lies in store, too little emotional support, not enough opportunity to express feelings and often with no option of going back or changing course" (xxiv). This emphasis on independence in turn leads to boys "feeling ashamed of their vulnerability, masking their emotions and ultimately their true selves" (xxiv). Experts such as Miedzian, Pollack, and Katz all agree that our culture teaches boys to follow an unwritten code of boyhood that encourages toughness.

4   This unwritten code of what it means to be a man contributes to male violence. When Jackson Katz interviewed teen boys for his video *Tough Guise* to find out what their definition of being a man was, teens used words such as the following: "physical, strong, intimidating, powerful, tough, independent, control." Katz theorizes that "masculinity is a guise, a front put up to gain respect by being violent." When Katz asked these same teens what happens when males do not fit the above definition, they used labels such as "wuss, wimp, sissy, fag."

5   When I asked my 19-year-old son, who viewed Katz's video with me, what he thought about Katz's claims, he agreed that boys are taught to be tough. My son went on to say that he always felt that he had to be tough at school or he would have been labelled a "wimp or a wuss." I asked him what "tough" meant, and he said, "I played rugby and hockey and I never backed down from a fight even if I knew it was wrong." I was saddened to realize that my son

knowingly admits he can distinguish right from wrong, but the fear of not meeting the expectations of what a man is could make him choose wrong over right. The scary thing is that he still feels the same way as he did in high school.

6   Even young boys' toys have evolved to reflect our fascination with male toughness. Katz shows in *Tough Guise* how toys such as GI Joe action figures (not dolls) have become more mean and menacing over the years, and their body shape has changed drastically since their introduction in 1964. GI Joe (in relation to human biceps) had a "biceps measurement of 12.2″" in 1964 and in 1998, his biceps measured 26.8″. In comparison, baseball player Mark McGuire's biceps measurement was 20″ at the height of his career." GI Joe also does something Barbie never did: he goes to war, a violent game that boys can learn from movies, television, video games and the daily news.

7   The link between masculinity and violence is perpetrated by the media— especially movies and video games. Many of the movies today are full of violence; man against man; man against woman. Slasher films are particularly disturbing in which sexualized violence is "deliberately designed to arouse" (*Tough Guise*). Some might argue that movies have always been violent, but the images have become much more disturbing over the years. Katz points out the difference between 1950's tough guy Humphrey Bogart, 1980's Sylvester Stallone in *Rambo*, and 1990's Arnold Schwarzenegger in *The Terminator*. Bogart has a little pistol while Schwarzenegger and Stallone both have huge guns. But it is not just the size of the guns that have changed. Schwarzenegger and Stallone also have very large, well-muscled bodies designed to intimidate. Boys can't help internalizing messages about the power of violence from movies such as *Terminator* or *Die Hard*. Recreation for boys is often linked with violence. Many of the video games that boys play, sometimes for hours a day, are full of graphic violence. "Young Canadians in a Wired World" reported that almost half of Canadian males aged 9–17 play video games every day, and about 60 percent prefer what are euphemistically called "action games." According to the Media Awareness Network, in September 2002, the extremely "violent <u>Grand Theft Auto 3</u> was the second most popular game in the world."

8   Violence in sports, with few exceptions (i.e., golf, bowling, swimming) seems to be increasing. Fights in hockey, football, basketball not only take place during the play, but at times even involve the fans. Players are expected to participate in fights and some are hired for that very reason. Violence in sports has always been considered to be outside of the law, and even though some violent incidents have been dealt with in the courts, the convictions have

had little effect in decreasing the violence. But it is not only violence in sports that affects our boys: it is the expectation that they will play tough under any circumstances, even when injured, and that winning is worth any cost. Miedzian gives the example of Bobby Knight, a university basketball coach who would "put a box of sanitary napkins in the locker of one of his players so that he would get the point that Knight considered him less than masculine" (198). This same coach also commented on television that "if a woman can't do anything about rape, she may as well lie back and enjoy it" (199). These are very powerful messages being sent to our boys.

9   Music with violent lyrics sends antisocial messages to boys. The Media Awareness Network reports that "'rage' music, filled with profanity and hate" has moved from the margins to the mainstream. In recent years, the music of singers such as "Eminem, Dr. Dre and Limp Bizkit—all known for their bleak anthems of violence and hatred, often aimed at women, gays and lesbians" has become hugely popular. Heavy Metal, Rap and Gangsta Rap music often contain lyrics that talk of violence, drugs, and suicide. Lyrics such as Motley Crue's "Get my ways at will / Go for the throat, / Going in for the kill" (*Boys Will Be Boys* 249) describe a fantasy about assaulting a woman. Often these kinds of music are delivered by artists in a mean and menacing manner. In *Boys Will Be Boys*, Miedzian talks about the "violence that often occurs at or after concerts" (250). Rapes, stabbings or murders are not uncommon occurrences at these concerts.

10   So what can we do to teach our boys to be nonviolent and still be boys? How can we help boys learn more positive images of masculinity?

11   I interviewed Jesse Padget, a pastor, and youth care worker, Paul McClelland, who has developed Hot Rod High, an innovative new program to teach youths about hot rods and life skills. While the program is for both males and females, the majority of the students are male. When I asked Jesse why he thought so many of our boys are struggling in school and life in general, he replied that "we are teaching boys to be good, not to be boys." He went on to say, "Over my years of ministering, I have learned that the males in my congregation were bored out of their trees during my sermons. But when the guys were doing something, like working on a car, they would talk. Guys need to be hands-on, and boys need to be taught where they fit in society. They are often disoriented and rebellious when they start school." Paul McClelland set up Hot Rod High not only for young people to build hot rods, but also to develop skills in communication, teamwork, goal-setting and safe street smarts that boys can

use throughout their lives. I can vouch for the power of this program, as my youngest son has been a student. For the last three years, things at school and in his life were in turmoil. Attending this program has given him a new sense of belonging and a new direction.

12   We need to appreciate that boys develop differently from girls, and that many boys do need outlets for their physical energy. However, we can attempt to counter the destructive messages about violence boys often receive from popular culture while still allowing them to be boys. We can encourage positive male role models and mentoring, we can teach empathy and nurturing skills, and we can enroll our boys in programs such as Hot Rod High that encourage positive, hands-on learning. Most importantly, we can, once we are aware of the factors that contribute to male violence, do what we can to eliminate the onslaught of violent messages from the media and other areas in our homes. While we cannot eliminate violence, or the cultural messages that approve it, we can teach boys critical thinking skills that will allow them to choose healthy models of what it means to be a man.

Works Cited

Dussin, Aaron. Personal interview. 24 Mar. 2005.

Hot Rod High. DVD. GS Productions, 2005.

Katz, Jackson. *Tough Guise.* Video. Media Education Foundation, 1999.

McClelland, Paul. Personal interview. 30 Mar. 2005.

Media Awareness Network. "The Business of Media Violence." 18 August 2005. http://www.media-awareness.ca/english/issues/violence/business_media_violence.cfm 2005.

Media Awareness Network. "Young Canadians in a Wired World." 2001. http://www.cfc-efc.ca/docs/mnet/00002_en.htm Retrieved August 15, 2005.

Miedzan, Myriam. *Boys Will Be Boys.* New York: Doubleday, 1991.

Padgett, Jesse. Personal interview. 30 Mar. 2005.

Pollack, William. *Real Boys: Rescuing Our Sons from the Myths of Boyhood.* New York: Henry Holt and Company, LLC, 1998.

DISCUSSION QUESTIONS

1. Identify the author's central purpose. What is her thesis, or proposition? Is it one of fact, policy, action, or value?

2. Why does the writer include a discussion of how action figures have changed over years? How does this observation relate to her argument?

3. What type of supporting evidence does the writer use in her argument? Identify examples.

4. What is the effect of the rhetorical question that is used throughout the essay?

5. What type of conclusion does the writer use?

SUGGESTIONS FOR WRITING *Write an argument on a topic you feel strongly about. Study all sides of the issue so you can argue effectively and appeal to a particular audience. Be sure to narrow and focus your argument. Support your proposition with logical evidence. Here are some possibilities to consider:*

1. Compulsory writing courses
2. Global warming
3. Saving endangered species
4. Corporate involvement in education
5. A controversial First Nations issue
6. Tuition fees for post-secondary education
7. Helmet laws
8. Export of water
9. Management of fisheries
10. Genetically modified foods

The Critical Edge

By its very nature, a successful argument requires critical thinking. This chapter has given you the tools you need to test the logic and evaluate the evidence of argumentative positions. After all, rarely are writers assigned to generate an idea on their own and then argue for it. Instead, because most important issues have already been debated in print, they enter a discussion that's already underway. Sometimes it's on a topic of national interest, such as the desirability of politically correct speech and writing or the need to limit the number of terms elected officials can serve. At other times, the topic may be more localized: Should your province outlaw teacher strikes, your company install new equipment to control air pollution, or your university or college reduce its sports programs? On any of these issues, form your view as you read and assess the arguments of other writers.

A good way to take stock of conflicting opinions is to make a chart that summarizes key reasons and evidence on each side of the argument. Here is a segment of a chart that presents opposing viewpoints on whether industrial air pollution is related to the threat of global warming:

Pro-threat side

Industrial emissions of carbon dioxide, methane, and chlorofluorocarbons let sun's rays in but keep heat from escaping.

              Andrew C. Revkin, student

Atmospheric levels of carbon dioxide are now 25 percent higher than in 1860. Computer models indicate continuing rise will cause temperature increase of 3–9°F.

              Revkin

No-threat side

Natural sources account for almost 50 percent of all carbon dioxide production.

              Dixy Lee Ray

The computer models are inaccurate, don't agree with each other, and fail to account for the warming effects of the oceans.

              H. E. Landsberg

Even though you investigate the reasons and evidence of others, deciding what position to take and how to support it—that is, establishing your place in the debate—is the real work of synthesis. Therefore, after evaluating your sources, outline the main points you want to make. You can then incorporate material that supports your argument. Let's say that you're considering the issue of global warming. After examining the differing viewpoints, you might conclude that, although those who believe that global warming is occurring sometimes overstate their case, those who disagree tend to dismiss important scientific evidence. Moreover, when comparing the credentials of the pro-threat group against the no-threat group, you discover that many of the researchers in the no-threat group are indirectly members of lobby groups and are not themselves scientists. Since you have decided that global warming is a serious threat, you decide to argue for immediate environmental action. You might begin your paper by pointing out the dire environmental consequences of global warming if it is proved beyond the shadow of a doubt, then offer evidence supporting this possibility, acknowledge and answer key opposing viewpoints, and finally offer your recommendations for averting a crisis.*

SUGGESTION FOR ORAL ARGUMENTATION

Oral argumentation through formal debate is an enjoyable and effective exercise that promotes research and argumentation skills, a commitment to honesty and truth, and an attitude of respect for others and their ideas. In preparing for a formal debate, the debaters must first conduct primary and/or secondary research on the proposition they will be addressing so that they may defend either a pro or a con position. Because the debaters are not aware of the position they will take on the proposition while conducting their research, their priority is to establish clear facts and specific arguments that could be offered as proofs for either side of the proposition. Once debaters are aware of the side of the proposition they will argue, they can draw from their research to develop a

---

*Note that papers requiring research must be documented correctly. Before starting to write this type of paper, read the sections on handling quotations and avoiding plagiarism in Chapter 15. As always, follow your instructor's guidelines for documenting sources.

clear and concise argument for or against the proposition. Since the debaters have conducted their research prior to taking a pro or con position, they should be able to advance either argument with a thorough understanding of opposing views. This knowledge encourages an atmosphere of respect and tolerance.

After the debaters have completed their research on a proposition, they divide into teams representing pro and con positions. Each team then prepares opening statements outlining its arguments and compiles a set of proofs or examples that defends its positions. The actual debate can be structured in the following way:

STRUCTURING A DEBATE (ABOUT 60 MINUTES)

- Moderator asserts resolution and invites speakers from each team to direct opening statements to audience
- Each side gives opening statements outlining argument (3–5 minutes each)
- Speakers from each team give proofs
- Short break allows students to prepare statements and questions for cross-examination
- Cross-examination: Each side presents responses and rebuttals in turn (may also include questions from audience)
- Moderator asks audience to render written decision assessing debate teams according to criteria:
  - clarity of expression
  - thoroughness of research
  - effective use of rational, emotional, and/or ethical appeals
  - poise and effectiveness of oral delivery
- Moderator announces results at end of debate

PROPOSITIONS FOR DEBATE

Propositions for debate can be found after the readings classified as "argument." Alternatively, try one of the following propositions.

- Canada's policy on refugees should be stricter (or more liberal).
- Decriminalization of marijuana is (or is not) justifiable.
- Victims of crimes should (not) be compensated by the perpetrator.
- The internet should be subject to stricter (looser) controls.
- Animal testing should (not) be banned.
- Grading for university English classes should (not) be abolished.
- Seal hunting in Canada should be illegal (legal).
- Governmental invasion of personal privacy in cyberspace is (un)justifiable.
- Exclusive corporate advertising on college campuses is (un)ethical.
- High schools should (not) put stronger emphasis on trades and apprenticeships.
- Cigarette taxes should (not) be raised.

SUGGESTIONS FOR RESEARCH-BASED ARGUMENTS

1. Use primary and secondary sources to investigate the placement of special needs students with mental and emotional disabilities in mainstream rather than special classes in your community. To gather primary information, you might interview people who work in the school system, or visit classrooms with and without students who have disabilities. To gather secondary research, you might consult educational journals. After researching this issue, write a paper addressed to the school board or other stakeholder arguing for a change in the present policy.

2. Read several sources that explore problems related to a broad topic such as free trade, or policies on drugs, health care, or the environment, and then write an argument that incorporates the views expressed in the sources and that suggests the extent of the problem. Be sure to narrow your subject and define your thesis.

3 Using outside sources, investigate a current social problem in your community, such as an increase in homelessness, drug abuse, or reckless street racing. Then write a paper addressed to a community council recommending a new course of action or policy.

4. Identify something you consider to be a problematic law or policy. Perhaps you see this law or policy as unjust, unfairly applied, outdated, or too expensive to enforce. Examine several sources that discuss this law, and then write a paper that identifies the problem and proposes a reasonable solution.

5. Analyze the rhetorical strategies in a recent influential speech by a major politician. If you prefer, you might choose to analyze an article from a website, such as the Canadian Centre for Policy Alternatives (**www.policyalternatives.ca**), The Fraser Institute (**www.fraserinstitute.ca**), or the Canadian Federation of Students (**www.cfs.ca**). Draw on your knowledge of argument and other writing strategies in order to show why you think the speech is or is not persuasive. Remember that your purpose is not simply to say whether or not you agree with the speaker or writer, but to evaluate the quality of the logic and other persuasive techniques in this speech or article.

6. If your instructor gives you free choice of topics, you could consult a Canadian website, such as one of the following that features articles on controversial issues for ideas to get you started:

   www.policyalternatives.ca (Canadian Centre for Policy Alternatives)

   www.Canadians.org (Council of Canadians—a citizens' watchdog group devoted to social and environmental concerns)

   www.rabble.ca (progressive alternative to mainstream media)

   Alternatively, you could look for topical ideas in opinion pieces, columns, or commentary available on Canadian newspaper websites. Examples:

   www.canada.com (contains daily newspapers from Canadian cities; the section called "Forums" features colloquial debate from ordinary Canadians that might trigger an idea for you if you're stuck)

   www.nationalpost.com/commentary

   www.globeandmail.com/columnists

   www.canada.com/calgary/calgaryherald/columnists

CHAPTER 13

Strategies for Researching: Using Secondary Research

Scene: A dark, sinister-looking laboratory. In the centre of the stage stands a large laboratory bench crowded with an array of mysterious chemistry apparatus. Tall, cadaverous, and foreboding, Dr. Frankenslime leers as he pours the contents of a tube through a funnel and into a bubbling flask. A short, hunched-over figure looks on with interest. Suddenly the doctor spreads his arms wide and flashes a sardonic smile.

Frankenslime: Igor! At last! At last I've got it! With this fluid, I can control . . .

Research, yes. But not all researchers are mad scientists, or even scientists—or mad, for that matter. You might not be any of these things, but no doubt you have been asked to prepare *research papers* for writing classes in the past. This type of assignment typically asks you to gather information from a variety of sources and then focus, organize, and present it in a formal paper that documents your sources. When you finish the paper, you have a solid grasp of your topic and pride in your accomplishment. Moreover, the research process familiarizes you with the correct handling of documentation. Finally, the experience helps you learn how to meet the research demands of future courses and jobs.

For many students, the thought of writing a research paper triggers feelings of anxiety and fears of drudgery. Some feel overwhelmed by the amount of material in a college or university library and the need to make a lengthy search for useful information. Others doubt that they could have anything to say about a topic that hasn't already been said: What's the point of simply rehashing what experts have already said much better? Still others are daunted by how much there might actually be to say about their topic.

But writing a research paper really isn't so formidable. You can acquaint yourself with library and electronic resources that provide easy access to the information you need. Moreover, reading what others have written on a topic gives you new ideas and opportunities to draw your own conclusions. And as a writer, you can limit your topic so that it doesn't balloon out of control.

Research writing is common to both coursework and on-the-job writing. A history professor might require a long report on the causes of the War of 1812. A business instructor might ask you to trace the history of a company, evaluate an advertising campaign, or review the Japanese style of management. A building trades instructor might call for a short report comparing the effectiveness of several new insulating materials. At work, a marketing analyst might report on the development costs, sales potential, and competition for a product the company is developing. An engineer might write a journal article that summarizes recent developments in plastic fabrication. A physical therapist might prepare a seminar paper that evaluates different exercise programs to follow arthroscopic surgery.

Whatever the writing project, let your purpose guide your research and determine the information you use. When you write, your conclusions based on your reading and your purpose—not your notes—should dictate what you say.

LEARNING ABOUT YOUR LIBRARY

Before starting a library research paper, take time to familiarize yourself with your library. Many libraries offer guided tours, and almost all of them display floor plans that show where and how the books are organized. If your library doesn't have tours, browse through it on your own and scan its contents. As you do, note the following features:

Catalogue Search Terminals: All libraries have an internal index of their books and often most of their other holdings as well. These indexes are searchable on the library's catalogue computer terminals, which are generally arranged together on the main floor of the library.

Computerized Databases: Databases provide searchable listings of articles in magazines and newspapers and often even provide the full text of the article. Most libraries purchase subscriptions to commercial databases specializing in particular subject areas.

Internet Search Terminals: Most libraries have computers reserved for internet searches, although many students use their own computers at home. The sheer size of the World Wide Web provides access to an almost endless variety of information. Internet access to library catalogues and databases is often available as well, allowing users to search and order materials from home, prior to picking them up at the library.

Stacks: These are the bookshelves that hold books and bound periodicals (magazines and newspapers). Stacks are either open or closed. Open stacks allow you to go directly to the books you want, take them off the shelf, and check them out. Closed stacks do not allow you direct access to shelved material. Instead, staff member brings you what you want.

Periodical Area: Here you find current and recent issues of magazines, journals, and newspapers. If your topic calls for articles that have appeared within the last few months, you're likely to find them in this area.

Microfilm and Microfiche Files: Microfilm is a filmstrip bearing a series of photographically reduced printed pages. Microfiche is a small card with a set of photographically reduced pages mounted on it. Often, most of a library's magazine and newspaper collection is on film. Ask a librarian how to work the viewing machines.

Reserve Area: This area contains books that instructors have had removed from general circulation so students can use them for particular courses. Ordinarily, you can keep these books for only a few hours or overnight.

Reference Area: This area houses the library's collection of specialized encyclopedias and indexes, almanacs, handbooks, dictionaries, and other reference tools. You'll also find one or more reference guides—for example, Eugene P. Sheehy's *Guide to Reference Books* (1996)—that can direct you to useful reference tools. To ensure that these books are always available, most libraries require that they be read within the building. A librarian is usually on duty in the reference area to answer questions.

CHOOSING A TOPIC

Instructors take different approaches in assigning library research papers. Some want explanatory papers, other want papers that address a two-sided question, and still others allow students a free choice. An explanatory paper takes no position but provides information that gives the reader a better grasp of the topic. For example, it may explain the key advantages of solar heating, thereby clearing up popular misconceptions. An argument paper, on the other hand, attempts to sway the reader toward one point of view—for instance, that solar heat is commercially feasible. Some instructors specify not only the type of paper but also the topic. Others restrict students to a general subject area, ask them to pick topics from lists, or give them free choice. If you have little say in the selection, take a positive view: At least you won't have to wrestle with finding a topic.

Whatever the circumstances, it's a good idea to follow a paced schedule that establishes completion dates for the various stages of your paper. A timetable encourages planning, clarifies both your progress and the work remaining, and provides an overview of the entire project. You can use the following sample schedule as a guide.

Sample schedule for a library research paper

Activity	Target Date	Completion Date
Topic Selection	_____	_____
Working Bibliography	_____	_____
Research Question and Tentative Thesis	_____	_____
Note Taking	_____	_____
Working Outline	_____	_____
First Draft	_____	_____
Second Draft	_____	_____
Revised Drafts	_____	_____
Date Due:		_____

Topics to Avoid

If you have free rein to pick your topic, how should you proceed? To begin, rule out certain types of topics.

- Those based entirely on personal experience or opinion, such as "The Thrills I Have Enjoyed Waterskiing" or "Newfoundland Has More Scenic Beauty than Ontario." Such topics can't be supported by library research. Don't hesitate, however, to include personal judgments and conclusions that emerge from your reading.

- Those fully explained in a single source. An explanation of a process, such as cardiopulmonary resuscitation, or the description of a place, such as the Gobi Desert, does not require co-ordination of materials from various sources. Although you may find several articles on such topics, they will basically repeat the same information.

- Those that are very new, such as yesterday's top news story. Often it's impossible to find sufficient source material about such topics.

- Those that are overly broad. Don't try to tackle such elephant-sized topics as "The Causes of World War II" or "Recent Medical Advances." Instead, slim them down to something like "The Advent of Jet Fighters" or "Eye Surgery with Laser Beams."

- Those that have been worked over and over, such as abortion and the decriminalization of marijuana. Why bore your reader with information and arguments that are all too familiar already?

EXERCISE *Using the advice on topics to avoid, explain why each of the following would or would not be suitable for a library research topic:*

1. genetic counselling
2. neoconservatism
3. globalism
4. how last night's riot got started

5. creating a balcony patio garden
6. a Third World hot spot as described on the evening news
7. reforming the financing of provincial election campaigns

Drawing on Your Interests

Let your interests guide your choice. A long-standing interest in hockey might suggest a paper on the pros and cons of expanding the number of teams in the National Hockey League. An instructor's lecture might spark your interest in a historical event or person, an economic crisis, a scientific development, a sociological trend, a medical milestone, a political scandal, or the influences on an author. An argument with a friend might spur you to investigate latch-key children. A television documentary might arouse your curiosity about a group of Aboriginal people. A recent article or novel might inspire you to explore the occult or some taboo.

Be practical in selecting a topic. Why not get a head start on a particular aspect of your major field by researching it now? Some management, marketing, or advertising strategy, or the beginnings of current contract law, or medical ethics—all of these topics qualify. Think about your audience, the availability of information, and the instructor's guidelines for your paper.

When you are developing the focus of your paper, it's often helpful to brainstorm your topic, skim-read internet articles, and sketch ideas using the branching or clustering techniques. For example, if you're exploring the topic of child abuse, preparing a clustering diagram like the one in Figure 13.1 can help you decide how to narrow your topic, as well as providing a rough map of areas to research. The more you brainstorm, the richer your map will be. Brainstorming often yields a set of questions, perhaps based on the writing strategies discussed earlier, that can guide your research. Often it is helpful to write down your main research question, followed by a series of related questions that elaborate on it. For example, a student wishing to explore the topic of psychological abuse might use a clustering diagram to develop the following set of questions:

What can be done to help victims of psychological abuse?
What is psychological abuse?
What long-term and short-term effects does it have on a child?
How can a child living at home be helped?
Are there services to help limit the abuse?
Is family therapy an option?
What is family therapy, and what does it do?
What psychological help is available for an adult who experienced childhood abuse?
What therapies work best?
What do they do?
How effective are they?

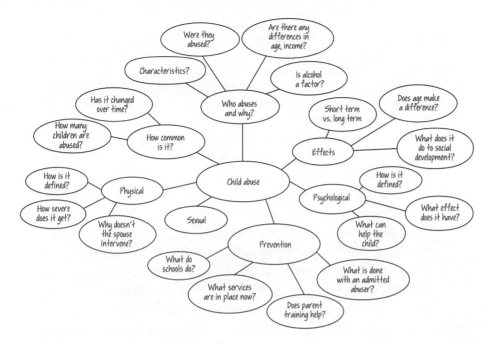

Figure 13.1 Clustering Diagram on Child Abuse

These questions make research easier. After all, the purpose of research is to answer questions. Later, as you examine source material, you will seek specific answers to specific questions, instead of randomly generating information. However, more often than not, ideas don't fall neatly into place as you probe for a topic and a focus. Don't be discouraged by false starts and blind alleys. Think of yourself as an explorer who will gradually become well versed in your chosen topic.

Case History

Keith Jacque was a first-year composition student majoring in criminal justice when he wrote the library research paper at the end of this chapter. The assignment was to write about a recent technological development or an innovative solution to a social problem. Intrigued by the possible solutions to the problem of prison overcrowding, Keith decided to explore several options: building more prisons, developing early release programs for the least dangerous criminals, setting up house-arrest programs verified by electronic monitoring systems, better utilizing halfway houses, converting empty military bases into prisons, and re-evaluating legal codes to determine which offences should require incarceration. After a little thought, Keith realized that in order to develop his paper properly he would need to concentrate on only one option. Because he had recently watched a televised report on electronic monitoring and had found it interesting, he decided to investigate this topic.

To establish a focus for his paper, Keith drafted a series of questions suggested by the writing strategies discussed in Chapters 6–12. Here are the questions he developed:

Could I *narrate* a brief history of electronic monitoring?

Could I *describe* how a monitoring system works?

Could I *classify* monitoring systems?

Could I *compare* monitoring systems to anything?

Could I explain the *process* involved in monitoring?

What *causes* led to the development of monitoring?

What kind of *effects* is monitoring likely to have?

What systems best *illustrate* the essence of monitoring?

Is there a widely accepted *definition* of electronic monitoring?

Could I *argue* for or against the expanded use of monitoring?

These writing strategies can often help you narrow a subject down to a manageable topic.

For background reading, Keith consulted two general information sources: the Corrections Canada website and the online *Encyclopaedia Britannica.* After preparing a list of possible entries ("electronic monitoring," "electronic surveillance," "electronic incarceration," "home incarceration," and "house arrest"), he began searching for those entries and found some general information. But none of it helped him to focus a thesis, a specific point of view, for his paper.

At this point, drawing on what he had learned from his criminal justice instructor and the television report, Keith brainstormed in order to determine a possible focus for his paper. He came up with the following list:

1. Brief history of electronic monitoring

2. Technical problems in developing systems

3. Types of monitoring systems

4. Benefits of monitoring

5. Problems associated with monitoring

Upon reflection, Keith eliminated the second item because it would require reading highly technical material, which he might not understand. The other items were interesting to him, and he believed that they would also interest his audience—fellow students at the professional college he attended.

Next, Keith used branching to expand his list and guide his research, concentrating on what he knew at this stage.

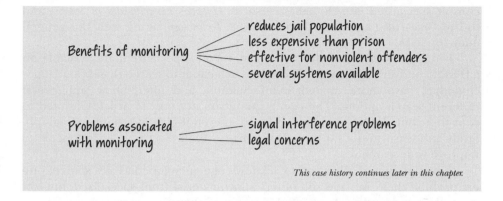

This case history continues later in this chapter.

ASSEMBLING A WORKING BIBLIOGRAPHY

Once you have a topic, you're ready to see whether the library has the resources you need to complete the project. This step includes checking additional reference tools and compiling a working bibliography—a list of promising sources of information. This section discusses these reference tools and how to use them.

Encyclopedias

What They Are   Encyclopedias fall into two categories, general and specialized. General encyclopedias, such as *The Canadian Encyclopedia* and the *Encyclopaedia Britannica*, offer articles on a wide range of subjects. Specialized encyclopedias cover one particular field, such as advertising or human behaviour. Most encyclopedias, like the *Britannica*, are available online or in electronic versions. Electronic versions are superior to the older bound versions because they are frequently updated. Here's a sampling of specialized encyclopedias:

> *Encyclopedia of Advertising*
>
> *Encyclopedia of Education*
>
> *Encyclopedia of Environmental Science*
>
> *Encyclopedia of Human Behavior: Psychology, Psychiatry, and Mental Health*
>
> *Encyclopedia of Social Work*
>
> *Encyclopedia of World Art*
>
> *Harper's Encyclopedia of Science*
>
> *International Encyclopedia of the Social Sciences*
>
> *McGraw-Hill Encyclopedia of Science and Technology*

How to Use Them   Traditional bound encyclopedias are sometimes a convenient launching pad for certain broad fields of study, such as history or literature. For a nonspecialized topic, such as the impact of commercial television during the 1950s, check articles on *television* in one or more general encyclopedias. For a specialized aspect of television, such as the development of the picture tube, consult specialized encyclopedias, such as *Harper's Encyclopedia of Science* and the *McGraw-Hill Encyclopedia of Science and Technology,* along with the general encyclopedias.

Today, most encyclopedias, both general and specialized, are available on CD-ROM or over the internet. They are much easier to search than bound encyclopedias, have more up-to-date information, and often allow you several different search options. The results guide you not only to articles devoted to your topic but also to others that refer to it, even if only in a single paragraph. Study and learn to use the search options for each electronic encyclopedia to improve your searches.

Some instructors allow you to acknowledge encyclopedias as a source; others prohibit their use; and still others allow material from specialized, but not general, encyclopedias. As always, follow your instructor's requirements. If you are using bound encyclopedia sources, record the following information for each note you take:

    Title of article

    Author(s) of article (Not always available. Sometimes only initials at the end of an article identify an author. In that case, check the list of contributors at the front of the first volume for the full name.)

    Name of encyclopedia

    Year of publication

    For specialized encyclopedias, also include the number of volumes in the set, the encyclopedia editor, and the place of publication.

Most important, check for bibliographies at the ends of articles and copy down any reference that looks promising.

Electronic Encyclopedias   If you use an electronic encyclopedia, record the publication medium, the name of the vendor (for example, Microsoft for a Microsoft product), and the name and date of the electronic publication, as well as the article title and author.

When you've finished your exploratory reading in encyclopedias, turn to the library's online catalogue and periodical indexes—the prime sources of information for library research papers.

Computerized Library Catalogue

What It Is   Library computer catalogues list all the books in the library, along with other holdings, such as journals, newspapers, government documents, CD-ROMs, videos, and electronic recordings. It often also provides additional information, such as whether a book has been checked out and, if so, the return date. Some catalogues include links to the catalogues of other libraries. Books are usually catalogued using Library of Congress call numbers, although some libraries use the Dewey decimal system.

Despite the number of catalogue systems available, all use search terminals that consist of a computer screen and keyboard on which to enter requests for information. Some terminals also have printers for copying material shown on the screen. To use the unit properly, read the instructions at the terminal or ask a librarian. Remember, if you misspell a word, the catalogue will not find any matches.

Search systems allow you to restrict your searches by material type and location, as in Figure 13.2. These systems also let you conduct searches by author, title, subject, key term (those appearing in book titles and descriptions), or Boolean terms (key terms using AND, OR, NEAR, and NOT). Typically, you begin a search by selecting a category—such as Author, Title, Subject, or Key Words—and then entering your specific search request. Figure 13.3 illustrates a subject search of the library catalogues of all the campuses of Kwantlen University College. (The drop-down menus also allow you to restrict your search to individual campus catalogues and to search by author, title, subject or material type.) Figure 13.4 shows the initial section of the list of works discovered by the search, including the call number, date of publication or production, location and availability of the work. Figure 13.5 illustrates the specific detail that is offered about a single selected work, including a brief description of the contents and a list of categories that could be used in additional searches. The search system also provides links to additional searches for works by the same author and for works on similar topics. Most libraries have handouts and seminars that explain the different procedures and options of their specific system.

Often, a key term search can be the most useful way to approach a topic. In this type of search, the computer checks the titles and descriptions of books for the key terms you enter and lists any that it finds. Different key terms produce varying strings of articles, so it is a good idea to try different words or phrases for the same topic. For example, if you're searching for material on "electric cars," you might also try "electronic cars," "alternative fuels," and so on. Because these searches are very rapid, you can experiment with different combinations of terms to focus your search. For instance, if you're asked to write a paper on some aspect of Japanese culture, you might investigate such combinations as "Japanese business," "Japan AND education," and "Japanese feminists." Because key term searches allow you to use Boolean logic terms like *and, or, near, but,* and *not,* they are especially useful for narrowing a broad focus.

Obtaining the Books Successful subject and key term searches often turn up more book titles than a single screen can accommodate. When this happens (see Figures 13.4 and 13.5), you will need to scroll down or click on the Next Page option to view the rest of the list. But with especially long lists (e.g., 1000 results), you may need to narrow your focus and start a new search. For example, "Japan AND education" might be narrowed to "Japan AND primary education."

Subject searches are more focused than key word searches. But when searching with subjects, rather than key words, you may be surprised that the subject you entered yielded nothing.

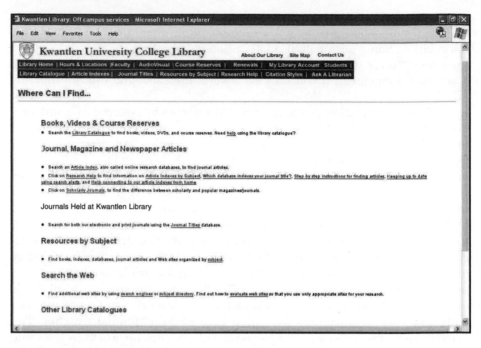

Figure 13.2 Kwantlen University College Library's opening screen allows you to select the specific type of resources and locations for your search.

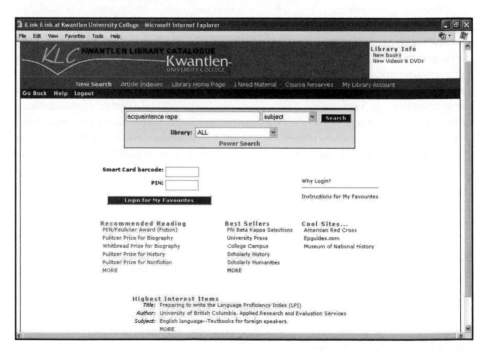

Figure 13.3 The online library catalogue screen allows you to perform searches by author, title, subject, and key terms for resources at any or all of its four campus libraries.

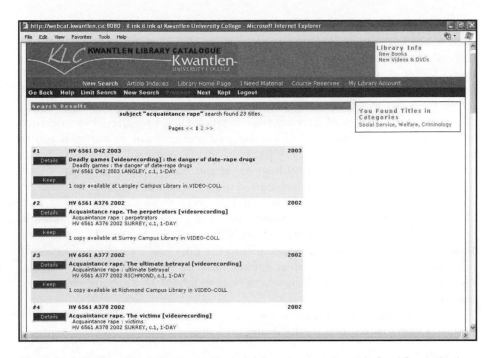

Figure 13.4 The Search Results Screen provides basic information about the works found. By selecting the "Details" command next to any of the works listed, you can get further information about that selected work.

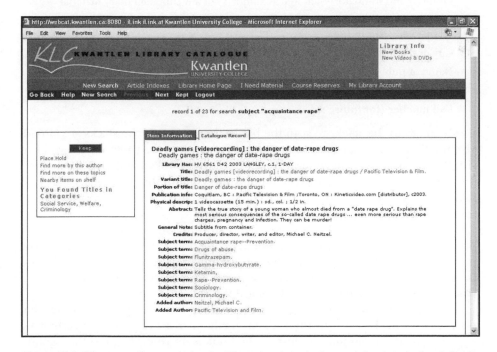

Figure 13.5 This screen offers comprehensive information about the first work listed on the Search Results Screen above.

Consider for a moment the vast number of possible wordings that exist for each subject. For example, the subject *multiculturalism* could be worded as *cultural pluralism* or *cultural integration.* No library system could sort all their books under so many headings. So the subject you enter must exactly match the subject headings that the library system uses. To find the right headings, locate the *Library of Congress Subject Headings,* a large book usually located near the search terminals, and look up your subject. (If it uses the Dewey decimal system, then consult the *Sears List of Subject Headings.*) For example, if you're researching *multiculturalism* (a Canadian term), you will not find books catalogued under that heading. Instead, as the *Subject Headings* guide shows, books on multiculturalism are catalogued under "Pluralism (social studies)." So you would use that subject for the search, instead of *multiculturalism.*

When you have found a promising title, click on the appropriate command to call up the relevant information. This is illustrated in Figures 13.4 and 13.5. By selecting the "Details" command next to the title, you are able to get specific information about the work. Most systems indicate whether the book is in the library or checked out and allow you to reserve a book by entering the request into the computer.

If your terminal has a printer, use it to make a copy of each promising reference. Otherwise, record the following information:

Author(s)

Title

Editor(s) and translator(s), as well as author(s) of any supplementary material

Total number of volumes (if more than one) and the number of the specific volume that you want to use

City of publication

Name of publisher

Date of publication

Call number (for future reference)

Next, go to the stacks to scan the books themselves. If the stacks are closed, give the librarian a list of your call numbers and ask to see the books. If you can visit the stacks, locate the general areas where your books are shelved. Once you find your book, spend a few extra minutes browsing in the general area around it. Since all books on a topic are shelved together, you may discover other useful sources.

Skim each book's table of contents and any introductory material, such as a preface or introduction, to determine its scope and approach. Also check the index and note the pages with discussions that relate to your topic. Finally, thumb through any portions that look promising. If the book isn't relevant, place it in the reshelving area and discard the reference information.

Note that if a book is missing from the shelf and the computer indicates that nobody has checked it out, then it's probably on reserve or in the reshelving area. Check at the circulation desk; if the book is on reserve, go to that section and examine it there. If someone has checked the book out and the due date is some time away, perhaps a library nearby will have a copy. For a book in reshelving, you may need to return the next day to see if it shows up.

EXERCISE

1. Select five of the following topics. Go to the online catalogue and find one book about each. List each book's call number, author, title, publisher, and date of publication. Because subject headings may vary, use more than one subject search. For example, if you find nothing under "mountaineering," check "mountain climbing" or "backpacking."

    a. Adolescent emotional development   h. Mountaineering
    b. Albania   i. Aboriginal water craft
    c. Canadian youth violence   j. CUSO opportunities
    d. Terry Fox   k. Professional hockey wages
    e. Multiple intelligences   l. Fly fishing
    f. Music piracy on the internet   m. Telecommunications
    g. Shania Twain   n. Zen Buddhism

2. Provide your instructor with a list of the books you found that appear useful for developing your paper's topic. For each book, furnish the information specified in Exercise 1 above, along with a brief note indicating why you think the book will be useful.

Periodical and Database Indexes

What They Are Periodical indexes catalogue articles in magazines and newspapers. Older indexes may be in book form; but current indexes are on microfilm, microfiche, or CD-ROMs, or subscription *databases*. The most current computerized databases are available to libraries only through subscription. This means that, although they are available on the internet, you would not be able to access them from home unless you log in to the library system first. Some databases are available as CD-ROMs as well, although this format is less popular.

Updated frequently, sometimes every week, periodical indexes provide access to information that hasn't yet found its way into books and perhaps never will. Their listings allow you to examine new topics, follow developments in older ones, and explore your topic in greater depth than you could by using books alone.

Most library database terminals are intended for student operation, but some are restricted to library personnel. For specialized database services, you may have to pay a service fee, but it's likely to be small.

The *Readers' Guide to Periodical Literature*, available since 1900 in printed form, is now available online in many subscription services and on CD-ROMs. The *Guide* indexes the material in over 200 widely circulated magazines—articles by subject and author, and other categories by title and author. The *Guide* is especially useful for finding material on historical events and on social, political, and economic developments. The *Guide* also includes scientific, technical, and even literary articles intended for a general audience rather than specialists, but such articles do not include all the available research.

Figure 13.6 shows the arrangement of the index and the "see also" cross-references that direct you to related subject headings.

The *Magazine Index,* available on microfilm or online, indexes some 400 popular publications by author, title, and subject. Updated monthly, it covers a five-year period and includes references to articles no more than two weeks old. The viewing machines for units using microfilm resemble small television sets and have motorized controls that allow swift movement through the filmstrip. Accompanying the viewer are coded reels of microfilm containing the indexed articles, together with a reader/printer that allows you to read articles and obtain printed copies. Your librarian will demonstrate how these machines work. The producers of the index also publish a listing of recent articles on twenty to thirty current topics.

Two helpful periodical indexes that refer exclusively to Canadian sources are the *Canadian News Disc* and the *Canadian Business and Current Affairs Index.* The *Canadian News Disc* compiles articles from eleven major Canadian daily newspapers, including *The Globe and Mail,* the *Toronto Star,* and the *Vancouver Sun.* The *Canadian Business and Current Affairs Index* covers most major

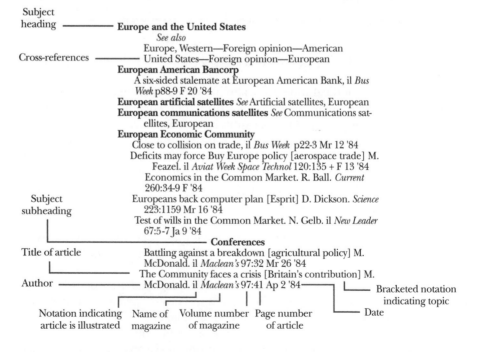

Figure 13.6 Arrangement of the Index

From *Readers' Guide to Periodical Literature,* May, 1984. Copyright ©1984 by the H. W. Wilson Company. Reproduced by permission.

Canadian magazines and periodicals. Both of these indexes, and others like them, are accessible online at most university, college, and municipal libraries.

In addition, the *National Newspaper Index* covers five national newspapers in the U.S.: the *Christian Science Monitor,* the *Los Angeles Times,* the *New York Times,* the *Wall Street Journal,* and the *Washington Post.* But *NewsBank* may be your best bet for a topic of regional interest. This CD-ROM database covers more than 500 newspapers in the United States and Canada, indexing articles on politics, economics, business, the environment, and the entertainment world. All these periodical indexes are often available through one subscription service at your library.

General-Purpose and Professional Database Indexes

Periodical databases are efficient because they allow you to search quickly in a wide range of journals, magazines, and newspapers. Some databases, such as *ERIC* (Educational Resources Information Center) or *Medline* (National Library of Medicine), provide access to articles appearing in professional journals. These articles, however, are usually aimed at a specialized audience and may be difficult to comprehend. Perhaps the best place to start a search is with a general periodical database, such as *First Search* or *InfoTrac.* These databases provide access to listings of articles, arranged and subdivided by subject, that have appeared in over a thousand magazines and newspapers, including the entries in various

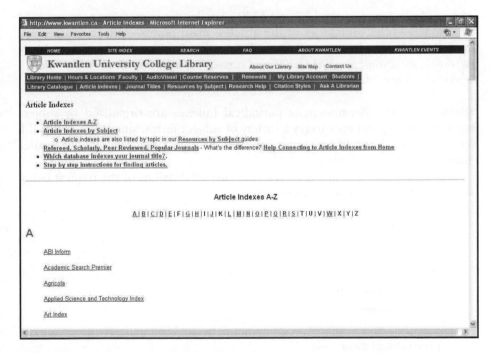

Figure 13.7 Kwantlen University College Library's opening screen for online Article Indexes and Databases allows you to begin your search by subject or individual indexes, which are listed alphabetically.

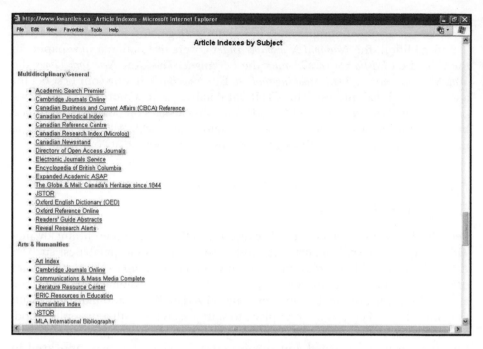

Figure 13.8   Article indexes can be found within general subject groupings.

other indexes (see Figures 13.7 and 13.8). Articles are sometimes accompanied by abstracts—brief summaries of the articles' main points—and in some cases, the full articles can be accessed. *A word of caution: Don't mistake an abstract for the full article; an abstract is a 200- to 300-word summary of a journal article and should not be used as a source. Always locate and read the full article before taking notes.*

Subject Search   Because most periodical indexes are organized by subject headings, it's a good idea to try a variety of subject terms, since each yields different articles. If what you enter matches a subject heading, the computer directs you to a list of articles.

Along the way, one of the screens may list subdivisions of the request being searched, as in the following example:

> **Acquaintance rape, subdivisions of**
>
> —analysis
>
> —cases
>
> —investigation
>
> —laws, regulations, etc.
>
> —media coverage
>
> —moral and ethical aspects
>
> —personal narratives
>
> —prevention

—psychological aspects

—research

—social aspects

—statistics

—studying and teaching

—usage

Such a listing can uncover facets of your topic that you hadn't considered and that might enrich your final paper. For example, the subdivision "personal narratives" might contain an experience that would provide a powerful opening for the paper. Similarly, articles catalogued under "statistics" could provide information on the scope of the acquaintance rape problem. Often these subdivisions or alternate subject headings are active links; so you can click on them to be directed to more specific information.

Key Word Search If your entries don't match a subject heading, the computer may automatically switch to a key word search and display a list of articles anyway. If your subject yields only a few articles, you can initiate a key word search that may uncover more. Just follow the instructions for beginning the search and then enter your key words (see example in Figure 13.9). For example, if your topic is "teenage suicide," you could enter two key words with AND—"teenagers AND suicide." The computer will check titles and abstracts for the key terms and provide a list of the corresponding articles (see example in

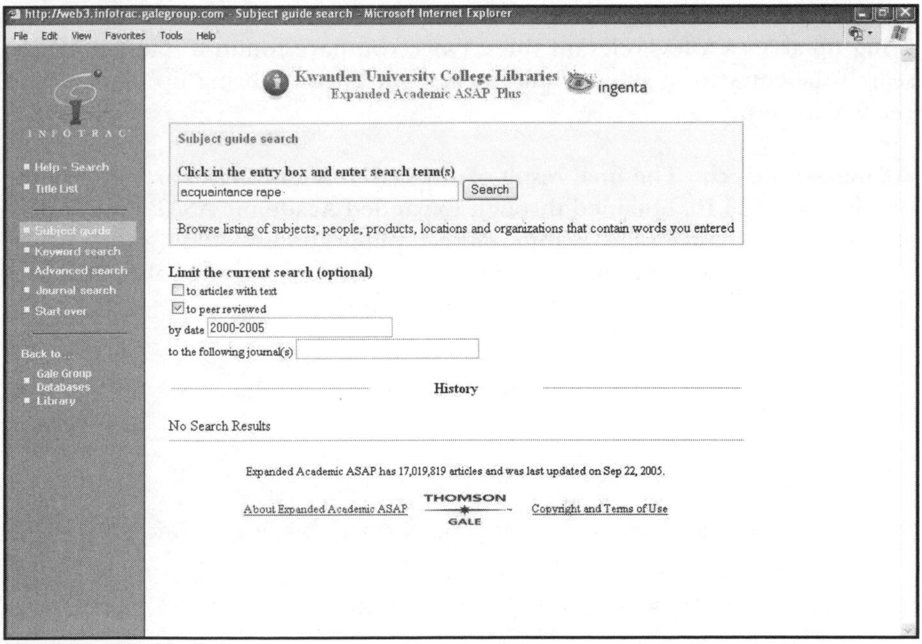

Figure 13.9 Search Screen for Expanded Academic ASAP

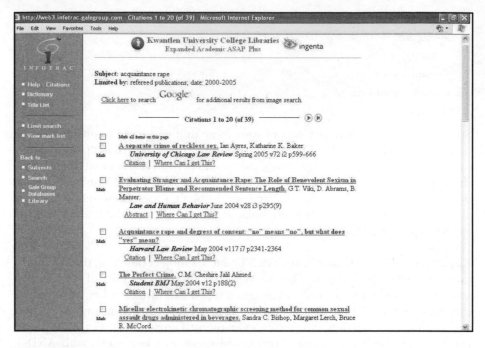

Figure 13.10 List of Results
Click on the underscored "Text" to see the complete article.

Figure 13.10). This search may not be as specific as a subject search, but it will bring up at least a few relevant titles. Once you have found a relevant article, search the entry for a subject link to click on. This will bring up more closely related articles.

Advanced Search The final result of any search is a listing of articles like the one in Figure 13.10, obtained through Expanded Academic ASAP Plus, for the subject "acquaintance rape" within refereed publications:

Sometimes the result of a search may be formatted like the following list of magazine articles from an older version of *Infotrac:*

An open letter to a rape victim. Gail Elizabeth Wyatt. *Essence,*
April 1992 v22 n12 p80(3). Mag. Coll.: 64B0749.
—Abstract Available—
Holdings: AS Magazine Collection

Between seduction and rape. (date rape) Kathy Dobie. *Vogue,* Dec 1991 v181
n12 p154(4). Mag. Coll.: 62G6035.
—Abstract Available—
Holdings: AS Magazine Collection

Rape on campus: is your daughter in danger? Kate Fillion. *Chatelaine*, August 1991 v64 n8 p33(5). Mag. Coll.: 61A5794.

Holdings: AS Magazine Collection

This listing shows that all three magazines are available in the library and that two articles are abstracted in the computer. (If the database provides the full text of an article, the notation "full text available" appears after the citation.) The coded notation "Mag. Coll." indicates that the magazine is available on microfilm ("magazine collection"). The first two numbers and the letter in the code identify the number of the microfilm cassette. The remaining numbers indicate the microfilm page on which the article starts. The exact listings of your system may be somewhat different from what's shown here; however, the same kind of information should be available. Besides the previously mentioned specialized indexes, many others are available that you could use to supplement your search of general indexes. Here is a brief sampling of some of them:

Applied Science and Technology Index, 1958–present (indexed by subject)

Education Index, 1929–present (indexed by subject and author)

Humanities Index, 1974–present (indexed by subject and author)

International Index to Periodicals, 1907–1964 (indexed by subject and author; entitled *Social Sciences and Humanities Index*, 1965–1974, and then separated into the *Humanities Index* and the *Social Sciences Index*)

Social Sciences and Humanities Index, 1965–1974 (indexed by subject and author)

Social Sciences Index, 1975–present (indexed by subject and author)

All are available on compact discs and online.

With periodical indexes and databases, as with the library computerized catalogue, don't give up if a subject heading yields few or no entries. Instead, explore related headings. For example, if your topic is teenage marriages, look also under "adolescence," "divorce," and "teen pregnancies." Browse through the system and try a variety of options. Use this search as an opportunity to gain different perspectives on your research project.

Obtaining the Articles If the index provides hard copies, print a copy of each promising reference you find, or email copies of the article or listing to your home email. Otherwise, record the following information.

Author(s), if identified

Title of article

Name of periodical

Volume or issue number (for professional and scholarly journals only)

Date of periodical

For newspapers, the edition name (city, metro) if more than one published, and section letter

The page range of the entire article

Obtain hard copies of any articles you might use for your paper, and check the topic sentences of paragraphs for essential points. Also, scan any accompanying abstracts or summaries. If an article appears useful, check its bibliography, which might include additional useful sources. Keep the records for articles that seem promising and useful, and discard the others.

Check the remaining references, including the ones from encyclopedia bibliographies, against the library's periodical catalogue to see which periodicals are available and where they are located. Libraries frequently keep current issues in a periodical room or some other special section. Back issues of magazines are often kept on microfilm or bound into hardcover volumes and shelved. Most newspapers are on microfilm or in online databases. Check the articles for which you don't have hard copies in the same manner that you checked the others.

EXERCISE *Select five of the following topics and find one magazine or journal article about each. Use at least three different periodical indexes or databases to locate the articles. List the author, if given; the title of the article; the name of the magazine; its date; the page range; and the name of the index/database used.*

1.	Acting schools	**11.**	Louis St. Laurent
2.	Aeronautical research	**12.**	Nuclear fusion
3.	Black holes	**13.**	Oral history
4.	Campaign funds	**14.**	Roots Canada Co.
5.	Collective bargaining	**15.**	Television industry
6.	Fibre optics	**16.**	Unemployment
7.	Fundamentalism	**17.**	Vegetarianism
8.	Holography	**18.**	Wayne Gretzky
9.	Investment trusts	**19.**	X-ray astronomy
10.	Leveraged buyouts	**20.**	York University

The Internet

What It Is The internet is a worldwide network that links the computer systems of educational institutions, government agencies, businesses, professional organizations, and individuals. The internet offers a number of services, including the World Wide Web, electronic mail (email), newsgroups, and listservs. It allows you to check the holdings of college, university and public city libraries; obtain information from online books, magazines, and newspapers; access research and government documents; gather viewpoints and information from numerous organizations and individuals; and communicate with people around the world or at the next computer station. This abundance of information and perspectives, sometimes not more than a day old, can greatly enhance your research. But remember that you'll still need to consult traditional sources in addition to using the internet.

If you don't already know how to access the internet and World Wide Web, you can easily learn. Your college or university may offer training seminars. In addition, a number of excellent, easy-to-follow books are available, and many internet search engines are extremely user-friendly.

World Wide Web During the 1990s, the World Wide Web exploded into international prominence. It gained quick popularity because it is easy to use and offers visuals (including many sites dedicated to art) and hypertext—that is, text with links to other related sites. Webpages include text, graphics, sound, video clips, entire computer programs, files that can be downloaded, and even animated images.

To use the World Wide Web, you need access to a computer with a web browser, such as *Netscape Navigator* or *Microsoft Internet Explorer,* and you need an internet service provider to connect you to the Web. Universities and colleges offer internet services to all enrolled students. To access the university's internet services, you first need to obtain a login name, a password, and an email address. If you encounter problems, personnel in the computer labs can probably answer many of your questions.

Each webpage has an address called a URL (uniform resource locator), which allows the browser to locate that page (e.g., **www.kwantlen.ca**).

How to Use It The irony of internet searches is that because the internet includes millions of computers and offers a stupendous amount of information, finding just the material you want can be quite difficult. To solve this problem, several indexes, or *search engines,* have been developed to connect any search term or terms with potentially millions of sites that include the key words. The easiest way to connect with these search engines is to simply select the search command or its nearest equivalent on your browser or Internet service. You can also enter the direct address (URL) of the search engine in the address window. Figure 13.11 provides the URLs of several popular search engines. Because the various search engines often select differently and produce different results, it's a good idea to use several engines or a metasearch engine (e.g., **www .ixquick.com**) while conducting your search.

Search Engine	Address
Google	www.google.ca
Alta Vista	www.altavista.digital.com
Lycos	www.lycos.com
Excite	www.excite.com
WebCrawler	webcrawler.com
Yahoo	www.yahoo.com

Figure 13.11 Popular Search Engines

While each search engine works in a slightly different manner, they all provide similar sorts of information. When prompted by the key words or phrases you enter, the engine searches and returns lists of links to information containing these words. Such engines reduce to a much more manageable size the job of finding what you want on the internet. Still, expect the job to require patience, since search engines often provide information that isn't useful. For that reason, you'll often want to narrow your search when you begin. Single terms such as "health," "cancer," or "crime" could list a million possible sites; instead, you may want to search for "ovarian cancer" or even "ovarian cancer cures." Most search engines allow you to search with multiple key words to further narrow the search.

You can scroll through the list of sites the engine has found. The sites are usually accompanied by a short description that may help you decide whether they are useful. If you click on the link, the search engine will connect you to the webpage.

Figures 13.12, 13.13, and 13.14 show the results of searching the subject "robotic advances." Figure 13.12 shows a search engine screen with the search subject entered, Figure 13.13 shows some of the websites found during the search, and Figure 13.14 shows a webpage with potentially useful information.

When viewing a webpage, you may notice menus, highlighted words, or specially marked graphics. These features, called *hyperlinks,* are active links that can take you to a different location: another section within the original page, a different page within the same website, or a different website. Following these hyperlinks allows you to explore related information from a variety of sources. As you move from webpage to webpage, browsers provide an easy way to navigate. Most have "back" and "forward" buttons that allow you to move to other sites. If you move back far enough, you eventually return to your main search site or even your homepage.

When you find an interesting site, you can print it, or you can "bookmark" it, allowing you easy future reference to the page. You'll need to keep track of any site addresses that you use, since you must include them in your bibliography.

Figure 13.12 Screen Showing Search Entry
Google, Inc. used by permission.

Web   Images   Groups   News   Local^New!   more »

robotic advances   [Search]   Advanced Search
                                          Preferences
Search: ● the web ○ pages from Canada

Web   Results 1 - 10 of about 1,610,000 for robotic advances. (0.29 seconds)

Recent Exciting **Advances** in **Robotics**
How new technologies are modifying our way of life.
www.primidi.com/2004/12/21.html - 29k - Cached - Similar pages

Welcome To **Robotics** World
Complete Advance Robotic System for Advance Users and R&D People ... Advance Robotics
System Pioneer 3-DX / PeopleBot Docking Station ...
www.roboworld.com.sg/roboshop/product_ list.aspX?Category=Advance+Robotics+System - 84k - Cached - Similar pages

Smart Mobs: Recent Exciting **Advances** in **Robotics**
Recent Exciting Advances in Robotics. The Era of Sentient Things. Posted by Roland
at 12:20 AM. Robotics news are dominated these days by the $100 ...
www.smartmobs.com/archive/ 2004/12/22/recent_exciting.html - 30k - Cached - Similar pages

Robotic heart surgery - a status report
It is expected that as experience and technology advance, robotic procedures will
be applied to most other forms of heart surgery. ...
heartdisease.about.com/library/weekly/aa060401a.htm - 33k - Cached - Similar pages

WEL Networks -> Relocating -> New in the Waikato
Robotic Advances at National Milk Testing Centre. The new robot installed at
Testlink Milk Analysis is the first of its type in the Milk analysis has gone ...
www.wel.co.nz/rel_story_sept02.html - 17k - Cached - Similar pages

NASA Internet **Robotics** Resources
Autonomous Mobile Robot Lab · Intelligent Servosystems Laboratory - advance design
and real-time control of sophisticated servosystems such as robotic hands ...
www.androidworld.com/prod34.htm - 39k - Cached - Similar pages

Symposium on **Advances** in **Robot** Dynamics and Control
Vibration Suppression in Robotic Systems;. Advances in Control of Industrial...
The Advances in Robot Dynamics and Control Symposium is part of the 2003 ...
cronos.rutgers.edu/~mavro/ardc.htm - 23k - Cached - Similar pages

Sebastian Thrun's Homepage
Recent Advances in Robot Learning contains seven papers on robot learning written
by leading researchers in the field. As the selection of papers ...
robots.stanford.edu/papers/franklin.book.html - 12k - Cached - Similar pages

3Com | **Advance** the Network
Manufacturer of hubs, modems, NICs, routers, and switches.
www.3com.com/ - 27k - 26 Nov 2005 - Cached - Similar pages

Technological **advances** in **robotics** and the history and modern ...
Technological applications of robots and industrial robotics.
www.wordquests.info/robotics.html - 14k - Cached - Similar pages

Try searching for **robotic advances** on Google Book Search

Goooooooooogle ▶

Result Page: 1 2 3 4 5 6 7 8 9 10   **Next**

robotic advances   [Search]

Search within results | Language Tools | Search Tips | Dissatisfied? Help us improve

Figure 13.13 Screen Showing Results of Search
Google, Inc. used by permission.

subscribe online for **free**

click here SPONSORS

FEATURES - NEWS - SUBSCRIBE NOW! - FREE PRODUCT INFO - PRODUCTS - HOME

APPLIANCE MANUFACTURER

Thursday, Dec 18

SEARCH AM!

Design and Engineering Solutions for the Global Appliance Industry

 Want to use this article? CLICK HERE for options!

Software Breakthrough Advances Robotic Painting
Complex breakthrough makes automation simpler.

Albert L. Harlow, Jr.

Posted on: 06/01/2000

Listing of controllable spray painting or coating variables

Whether wet or powder, variables in spray painting that influence painting results, such as color and thickness, include many things. A list of the controllable or measurable variables in an ARTomation system is given below:

- Temperature:
  a. Coating / viscosity.
  b. Atmosphere.

- Humidity.

- Speed at which nozzle passes over the part's surface.

- Angle of inference relative to a surface, or part's position relative to the gun.

- Spray gun nozzle and cap.

- Fluid or powder's delivery rate.

- Spray gun settings:
  Wet: Atomization and Fan Air.
  Powder: Conveying Air and Fluidizing Air

Inside AM Online

About AM
Advertiser Index
Article Archives
Association Listings
Books
Breaking News
NEW! Bulletin Board
Buyers Guide
Calendar of Events
Classifieds
Contact Us
Editorial Guidelines
Excellence in Design
Feature Articles
FREE Product Info
Industry Research
Let Us Know
List Rental
Media Kit
New Products
NEW! Online
Showrooms
Product Innovations
Reprints
Shipments/Forecasts
Subscribe
Home

Figure 13.14   Online Article

Evaluating Internet Material   Because anyone can post anything on the internet, it is crucial that you check the accuracy and validity of any information you obtain from it. A source that sounds like a research centre—for example, the Institute for Social Justice—could be a political or even a cult organization giving out one-sided or false information for its own purposes. While articles in professional journals (both paper and online) are reviewed by experts to ensure that the information is reliable, no such safeguard exists for general information on the internet. Carelessly researched or ethically questionable material is commonplace. Here are some guidelines for checking the validity of an internet source:

1. Is the source a reputable professional organization (for example, the Canadian Medical Association, McGill University, or *Maclean's* magazine)? Keep in mind that anyone can make up a professional-sounding name, so be alert. If in doubt, do a search on that organization's name to see what other websites have to say about it.

2. Is there an identified author whose credentials can be checked? If there is no email contact listed or if you can't find another way to verify the contents of the website, don't use it. You can also do a search using the author's name to see what other websites have to say about him or her.

3. Is the tone of the site professional?

4. Is the information consistent with the other material you have found?

5. Does the site explain how the data were obtained?

6. Does the site appear to misuse any data? For instance, is the sample too small? Are the claims pushed too far? Are the statistics biased? Does it use data from nonexistent studies or falsely quote other researchers?

Examine the webpage shown in Figure 13.14. This article gives an author's name, *Albert L. Harlow, Jr.*, which increases the credibility of the report. However, a search of this name shows that the author is founder and vice president of a robotics technology company, which demonstrates expertise but suggests a bias in favour of such technologies. A check of the homepage shows that Appliance Manufacturer is an established organization promoting applied technologies. Thus, you can conclude that this group would have the professional expertise to make certain the article is credible. However, they might also have a bias. As a result, they might stress the effectiveness of such technologies rather than dwell on the negatives. So this website is definitely usable for listing the positive aspects of robotic painting; but you would need other sources to provide the negative aspects.

Sometimes, of course, you may want to check out webpages that present the views of individuals or organizations with strong but slanted positions to gain a better understanding of their perspective. But don't consider such pages to be reliable sources. When using the internet, "Reader beware" is a prudent attitude.

Email   You probably have your own email address. You may also have an email address provided to you by your university or college. In some cases, your professor may be using a web-based instructional program that includes email specific to your class. It is a good idea to jot down the email addresses of other students in your class, making certain it is the one they use most often, so that you can exchange ideas. Your professor, however, may prefer that you use the school email.

You can also use email as a research tool to contact knowledgeable people about your research topic and get swift answers to your questions. Use this approach, however, as a last resort, since busy people have limited time. If you must contact experts, don't bother them with questions that you could easily answer by reading background material. Reserve email for specific queries that defy answer after extensive research.

Most search engines have clearly identified directories that allow you to look up an email address if you know a person's name. Sometimes you can find the name of an expert through the webpages of major universities. If you do get a response to your query, evaluate it carefully; an overburdened expert may dash off a quick response with little thought while doing something else.

Newsgroups A newsgroup is a group of people who discuss a common interest by posting their responses to a common address for everyone to read. These discussions can be informal and often are not monitored; as a result, they leave something to be desired as a source for research. Still, your university system will likely give you access to newsgroups, so ask your computer centre for an instruction sheet. A word of caution: Many newsgroups are intolerant of uninformed people intruding upon their conversation. Common *netiquette* (the etiquette of the internet) calls for you to read what has already been written, learn the rules of the list, and think before you write.

Listservs A listserv consists of numerous email addresses that make up a mailing list of people interested in a particular topic. Once you sign up, everything posted to that listserv is sent to your email address. People who subscribe to three or four listservs may receive thirty or forty email messages every day. If you post a question on a listserv, you may get dozens of responses from professionals interested in the topic; and sorting out the validity of the different responses can be difficult. As with newsgroups, netiquette calls for you to acquire an understanding of your subject and follow the discussions on the listserv for some time before you post a question or a response. Your university computer professionals can probably supply you with instructions on how to find and sign up for a listserv. You can access a subject index of listservs at **www.liszt.com**.

FAQs Whenever you find a promising website, newsgroup, or listserv, you will often see a link for FAQs (frequently asked questions). It's a good idea to read the FAQs first, since they may well answer your questions.

EXERCISE

1. Using an appropriate search engine, find information on each of the following topics:
   a. the United Nations
   b. current crime statistics
   c. sexual harassment
   d. current government immigration policy

2. Enter the name of a major university into a search engine. You should find that university's homepage. Try to access the university's library to find what books are available on a topic of your choice. You might try Simon Fraser University, Queen's University, or the University of New Brunswick.

Adjusting Your Topic

After finishing your search for sources, you may need to adjust the scope and emphasis of your topic. If you start with "Early Nuclear-Powered Submarines" but fail to turn up enough sources, you might expand your emphasis to "Early Nuclear-Powered Warships." On the other hand, if you're working with "Early Nuclear-Powered Warships" and find yourself floundering in an ocean of sources, you might zero in on one type of vessel. Gathering evidence helps develop your judgment about how many sources you need to do the job.

Case History (continued)

Once Keith Jacque had selected a focus for his paper on electronic monitoring, he began compiling his working bibliography. First, he turned to the library's computer catalogue and began his search for books and government documents by entering the subject "house arrest." But he found nothing. Next he tried "electronic monitoring of prisoners." This entry yielded a cross-reference directing him to the entries "punishment—North America" and "criminal statistics—analysis." These two entries yielded a list of seven books and eleven government documents. Further examination revealed that three of the books and four of the documents appeared promising.

Keith's search for periodical articles took him to the college's *Infotrac* database. Through trial and error, he found three useful subject headings: "home detention," "electronic monitoring of prisoners," and "criminal statistics—analysis." A search of these subjects turned up twenty-four journal articles, all of which were available in the library. Eight looked as if they would be useful. Three newspaper articles seemed suitable, and a search of *NewsBank* revealed another promising newspaper article.

Keith also searched the World Wide Web. He used Google and entered complete phrases in quotation marks, such as "electronic incarceration," "home detention," "electronic monitoring," and "incarceration, electronic." Many of the websites he found were not relevant to his topic, but he persisted and finally found three that seemed promising. One, from an organization concerned with public policy, discussed the indirect costs of incarceration. The other two, from Corrections Canada and from the Probation Division of Georgia's Department of Corrections, discussed alternatives to jail sentences.

Keith realized that many of his sources were either very general or exclusively U.S.–based, and he wanted to know more about how electronic monitoring is perceived in Canada. He sought and obtained his instructor's permission to conduct primary research on electronic monitoring in Canada. His instructor suggested he interview a criminology professor who could tell him about a 1989 pilot project on monitoring in British Columbia, the first of its kind in Canada. Keith was able to obtain a telephone interview, which he carefully recorded with permission. The interview provided information not only on the B.C. pilot study results, but also on advantages and disadvantages of monitoring.

Satisfied that ample information was available, Keith carefully evaluated the content of the articles and of pertinent sections of the books and government documents he had located. His instructor had suggested that one good way to approach a topic is to pose a question about it and then draft a *tentative* answer. Here's how Keith proceeded:

Q. What benefits does electronic monitoring offer jurisdictions that adopt it?

A. Electronic monitoring is less expensive than incarceration, presents no serious problems, and offers a choice among several systems.

This answer provided a *tentative thesis,* an informed opinion that guided Keith's later note taking, giving him a sense of direction and indicating what information would probably prove useful and what was likely to be useless. Tentative theses can be altered or changed if necessary. If later reading indicated that electronic monitoring can sometimes be more expensive than incarceration, Keith could alter his thesis accordingly.

This case history continues later in this chapter.

TAKING NOTES

To take notes, read your references carefully and record significant information. You might review or even expand your original research questions so that you can read with a better sense of purpose. Notes are the raw materials for your finished product, so develop them accurately.

Evaluating Your Sources

Evaluate your sources by considering these factors.

The Expertise of the Author Judge an author's expertise by examining his or her professional status. Let's say you're searching for information on a new cancer treatment drug. An article by the director of a national cancer research centre would be a better source than one by a staff writer for a popular magazine. Similarly, a historian's account of a national figure will probably have more balance and depth than a novelist's popularized account of that person's life. Gauging a writer's credentials is not difficult. Articles in periodicals often note authors' job titles along with their names. Some even supply thumbnail biographies. For a book, check its title page, preface, or introduction, and—if it's been left on—the dust jacket. Finally, notice whether the writer has other publications on this general subject. If your sources include two or more items by one person, or if that person's name keeps cropping up as you take notes, you're probably dealing with an expert.

The Credibility of the Publication A book's credibility hinges on its approach and its reception by reviewers. Cast a cautious eye on books that take a popular rather than a scholarly approach. For research papers, scholarly treatments are more reliable. In addition, examine what reviewers said when a book first appeared. There are two publications that excerpt selected reviews of new books and provide references to others. The *Book Review Digest* (1905 to present) deals mainly with nontechnical works, while the *Technical Book Review Index* (1935 to present) covers technical and scientific books. Turn first to the volume for the year the book came out. If you don't find any reviews, scan the next year's index. Often books published in the fall are not reviewed until the following year.

Like books, periodical articles can take either a scholarly or a popular tack. Editors of specialized journals and of some wide-circulation magazines—for example, *Equinox* and *The Atlantic Monthly*—publish only in-depth, accurate articles. Most newsstand publications, however, popularize news to some extent, and some deliberately strive for sensationalism. Popularizing may result in broad, general statements, skimpy details, and a sensational tone.

Don't automatically reject a source because the writer lacks expertise or offers a popularized treatment. Often, especially when writing about a current topic, you need to use material that falls short in some way. Remember, though, that you undertake research to become more knowledgeable about a topic than general readers. When you have to use information from popular periodicals in your paper, acknowledge the shortcomings to your readers.

Mechanics of Note Taking

Traditionally, the most effective approach to note taking was to use note cards. Some students still take notes this way, although computers and portable computer devices have largely replaced cards. But even when recording notes electronically, you can improve your organization by following a modified version of the card method. Remember to save after every entry if you are recording electronically.

If you are using cards, note each important point on a large index card to avoid confusion with the smaller bibliography cards. Record only one note per card, even when you take several notes from a single page of a book, because you may use the notes at different points in your paper. If you can't fit a note on a single card, continue the note on a second card and paperclip or staple the two together. Cards allow you to test different arrangements of notes and use the best one to write the paper.

If you are using a computer for note taking, create a new file called "Notes" in your new essay's main folder. Keep it distinct from your bibliography file. Record each piece of information in its own paragraph or point-form paragraph, skipping a line in between. Separating paragraphs allows you to move information around later to find the best arrangement.

Before you take a note, indicate its source at the bottom of the card or at the beginning (or end) of each computer paragraph. You will then have all the details necessary for documenting the information if you use it in your paper. Usually, the author's last name and the page number suffice, since the bibliography card or file contains all other details. To distinguish between two authors with the same last name or between two works by the same author, add initials or partial titles. *Don't forget to include the page number or numbers for each note.* Otherwise, you'll have to waste time looking them up when you cite your sources in the paper.

Summarize briefly the contents of the note at the top of the card. If using a computer, use the highlighter function to highlight the key phrases. Later, when you construct an outline, these notations will help you sort your points into categories and subcategories.

Responding to Notes

As you take notes, reflect on your topic and try to come up with new ideas, see connections to other notes, and anticipate future research. Think of yourself as having a conversation with your sources, and record your responses on the backs of your note cards or in a separate "New ideas" file. Ask yourself these questions: Does this information agree with what I have learned so far? Does it suggest any new avenues to explore? Does it leave me with questions about what's been said? Although it may take a few minutes to record your responses to a note, this type of analysis helps you write a paper that reflects *your* judgments, decisions, and evaluations, not one that smacks of notes merely patched together from different sources.

Types of Notes

A note can be a summary, paraphrase, or quotation. Whenever you use any kind of note in your paper, give proper credit to your source. Failure to do so results in plagiarism—that is, literary theft—a serious offence even when committed unintentionally.

Summary A summary condenses original material, presenting its core ideas *in your own words*. In order to write an effective summary, you must have a good grasp of the information, and this comprehension ensures that you are ready to use the material in your paper. You may include brief quotations if you enclose them in quotation marks. A properly written summary presents the main points in their original order without distorting their emphasis or meaning, and it omits supporting details and repetition. Summaries, then, gather and focus the main points.

Begin the summarizing process by asking yourself, "What points does the author make that have an important bearing on my topic and purpose?" To answer, note especially the topic sentences in the original document, which often provide essential information. Copy the points in order; then condense and rewrite them in your own words. Figure 13.15 summarizes the Bertrand Russell passage that follows. We have underscored key points in the original.

> Under the influence of the romantic movement, a process began about a hundred and fifty years ago, which has continued ever since—a process of revaluing the traditional virtues, placing some higher on the scale than before, and others lower. The tendency has been to exalt impulse at the expense of deliberation. The virtues that spring from the heart have come to be thought superior to those that are based upon reflection: a generous man is preferred to a man who is punctual in paying his debts. *Per contra*, deliberate sins are thought worse than impulsive sins: a hypocrite is more harshly condemned than a murderer. The upshot is that we tend to estimate virtues, not by their capacity for providing human happiness, but by their power of inspiring a personal liking for the possessors, and we are not apt to include among the qualities for which we like people, a habit of reflecting before making an important decision.
>
> The men who started this movement were, in the main, gentle sentimentalists who imagined that, when the fetters of custom and law were removed, the heart would be free to display its natural goodness. Human nature, they thought, is good, but institutions have corrupted it; remove the institutions and we shall all become angels. Unfortunately, the matter is not so simple as they thought. Men who follow their impulses establish governments based on pogroms, clamour for war with foreign countries, and murder pacifists and Negroes. Human nature unrestrained by law is violent and cruel. In the London Zoo, the male baboons fought over the females until all the females were torn to pieces; human beings, left to the ungoverned impulse, would be no better. In ages that have had recent experience of anarchy, this has been obvious. All the great writers of the Middle Ages were passionate in their admiration of the law; it was the Thirty Years' War that led Grotius to become the first advocate of international law. Law, respected and enforced, is in the long run the only alternative to violent and predatory anarchy; and it is just as necessary to realize this now as it was in the time of Dante and Grotius.
>
> What is the essence of law? On the one hand, it takes away from private citizens the right of revenge, which it confers upon the government. If a man steals your money, you must not steal it back, or thrash him, or shoot him; you must establish the facts before a neutral tribunal, which inflicts upon him such punish-

ment as has seemed just to the disinterested legislators. On the other hand, <u>when two men have a dispute, the law provides a machinery for settling it</u>, again on principles laid down in advance by neutrals. The advantages of law are many. It diminishes the amount of private violence, and settles disagreements in a manner more nearly just than that which would result if the disputants fought it out by private war. <u>It makes it possible for men to work without being perpetually on the watch against bandits. When a crime has been committed it provides a skilled machine for discovering the criminal.</u>

<u>Without law, the existence of civilized communities is impossible.</u> In international law, there is as yet no effective law, for lack of an international police force capable of overpowering national armies, and it is daily becoming more evident that this defect must be remedied if civilization is to survive. Within single nations there is a dangerous tendency to think that moral indignation excuses the extra-legal punishment of criminals. In Germany an era of private murder (on the loftiest grounds) preceded and followed the victory of the Nazis. In fact, nine-tenths of what appeared as just indignation was sheer lust for cruelty; and this is equally true in other countries where mobs rob the law of its functions. In any civilized community, toleration of mob rule is the first step towards barbarism.

Bertrand Russell, "Respect for Law," *San Francisco Review,* Winter 1958, 63–65.

Necessity for law

About a century and a half ago, there began a still-existing preference for impulsive actions over deliberate ones. Those responsible for this development believed that people are naturally good but institutions have perverted them. Actually, unfettered human nature breeds violence and brutality, and law is our only protection against anarchy. The law assumes the responsibility for revenge and settles disputes equitably. It frees people from the fear of being victimized by criminals and provides a means of catching them. Without it, civilization could not endure.

Russell, pp. 63-65

Figure 13.15 Summary

EXERCISE

1. Select two passages that your instructor approves from an essay in the Reader, and prepare summary note cards or computer notes for them.

2. Submit summaries of three pieces of information that you plan to use in writing your paper, along with complete versions of the original.

Paraphrase To paraphrase is to restate material *in your own words* without attempting to condense it. Unlike a summary, a paraphrase allows you to present an essentially complete version of the original material. A note of caution, however: don't copy the original source nearly verbatim, changing only a word here and there. To do so is to plagiarize. To avoid this offence, follow a read, think, and write-without-looking-at-the-original strategy when you take notes so that you concentrate on recording the information in your own words. Then verify the accuracy of your notes by checking them against the original source. Here is a sample passage; Figure 13.16 is its paraphrase.

> Over time, more and more of life has become subject to the controls of knowledge. However, this is never a one-way process. Scientific investigation is continually increasing our knowledge. But if we are to make good use of this knowledge, we must not only rid our minds of old, superseded beliefs and fragments of magic, but also recognize new superstitions for what they are. Both are generated by our wishes, our fears, and our feelings of helplessness in difficult situations.
>
> Margaret Mead, "New Superstitions for Old,"
> *A Way of Seeing,* New York: McCall, 1970, 266.

Combatting Superstitions

As time has passed, knowledge has asserted its sway over larger and larger segments of human life. But the process cuts two ways. Science is forever adding to the storehouse of human knowledge. Before we can take proper advantage of its gifts, however, we must purge our minds of old and outmoded convictions, while recognizing the true nature of modern superstitions. Both stem from our desires, our apprehensions, and our sense of impotence under difficult circumstances.

Mead, p. 266

Figure 13.16 Paraphrase

EXERCISE *Paraphrase a short passage from one of your textbooks. Submit a complete version of the passage with the assignment.*

Quotation A quotation is a copy of original material. Since your paper should demonstrate that you've mastered your sources, don't rely extensively on quotations. You need practice in expressing yourself. As a general rule, avoid quotations except when

- the original displays special elegance or force
- you really need support from an authority
- you need to back up your interpretation of a passage from a literary work

Paraphrasing a passage as well written as the one below would rob it of much of its force.

> Man is himself, like the universe he inhabits, like the demoniacal stirring of the ooze from which he sprang, a tale of desolation. He walks in his mind from birth to death the long resounding shores of endless disillusionment. Finally, the commitment to life departs or turns to bitterness. But out of such desolation emerges the awful freedom to choose beyond the narrowly circumscribed circle that delimits the rational being.
>
> Loren Eiseley, *The Unexpected Universe*

Special rules govern the use of quotations. If, for clarity, you need to add an explanation or substitute a proper name for a personal pronoun, enclose the addition in *brackets*.

> The American Declaration of Independence asserts that "the history of the present King of Great Britain [George III] is a history of repeated injuries and usurpations. . . ."

Reproduce any grammatical or spelling errors in a source exactly as they appear in the original. To let your reader know that the original author, not you, made the mistake, insert the Latin word *sic* (meaning "thus") within brackets immediately after the error.

> As Wabash notes, "The threat to our enviroment [*sic*] comes from many directions."

If you exclude an unneeded part of a quotation, show the omission with an ellipsis—three spaced periods (. . .). Indicate omissions *within sentences* in the following way:

> Writing in *Step by Step*, 1936–1939, Winston Churchill observed, "To France and Belgium the avalanche of fire and steel which fell upon them twenty years ago . . . [was] an overpowering memory and obsession."

When an omission comes *at the end of a sentence* and what is actually quoted can also stand as a complete sentence, use an unspaced period followed by an ellipsis.

> In his second inaugural address, American President Lincoln voiced his hopes for his nation: "With malice toward none, with charity for all, with firmness in the right as God gives us to see the right, let us strive on to finish the work we are in. . . ."

Do the same when you drop *a whole sentence* within a quoted passage.

> According to newspaper columnist Grace Dunn, "Williamson's campaign will undoubtedly focus primarily on the legalized gambling issue because he hopes to capitalize on the strong opposition to it in his district. [. . .] Nonetheless, commentators all agree he faces an uphill fight in his attempt to unseat the incumbent."

Don't change or distort when you delete. Tampering like the following violates ethical standards:

Original passage: This film is poorly directed, and the acting uninspired; only the cameo appearance by Laurence Olivier makes it truly worth seeing.

Distorted version: This film is . . . truly worth seeing.

You can summarize or paraphrase original material but retain a few words or phrases to add vividness or keep a precise shade of meaning. Simply use quotation marks but no ellipsis.

> Government spokesperson Paula Plimption notes that, because of the "passionate advocacy" of its supporters, the push to roll back property taxes has been gaining momentum across the country.

When you copy a quotation onto a note card or into your Notes file, place quotation marks at the beginning and the end so you won't mistake it for a paraphrase or a summary when you write the paper. If the quoted material starts on one page of the book and ends on the next, use a slash mark (/) to show exactly where the page shift comes. Then if you use only part of the quotation in your paper, you'll know whether to use one page number or two.

Don't expect to find a bonanza on every page you read. Sometimes one page yields several notes, another page nothing. If you can't immediately gauge the value of some material, take it down. Useless information can be discarded later. Save your Notes file often, and keep backup copies as you add to it, in case you somehow corrupt the file. If you are using cards, place an elastic band around your growing stack. Store them in a large envelope closed with a snap or string and label the bundle with your name and address. Submit them with your completed paper if your instructor requests.

Case History (continued)

Working bibliography in hand, Keith Jacque prepared his Notes file. Most of his notes were summaries of the source material, but in a few cases he chose quotations because of the importance of the source or the significance of the material. For example, one quotation cited a former Canadian Attorney General who pointed out the disproportionate number of crimes committed by habitual violent offenders. Another quotation cited a key reason for the growing use of electronic monitoring: the high cost of prisons. Still another detailed various difficulties encountered in transmitting signals.

As Keith took notes, a plan for his paper began to emerge. The introduction would explain the reasons behind the growing use of electronic monitoring. The body would present a brief history of monitoring and then detail the different kinds of systems available, examine the problems, and point out their effectiveness.

This case history continues later in this chapter.

Organizing and Outlining

Next comes your formal outline, the blueprint that shows the divisions and sub-divisions of your paper, the order of your ideas, and the relationships between ideas and supporting details. An outline is a tool that benefits both writer and reader.

A formal outline follows the pattern shown below:

    I.

      A.

      B.

         1.

         2.

            a.

            b.

    II.

You can see the significance of an item by its numeral, letter, or number designation and by its distance from the left-hand margin; the farther it's indented, the less important it is. All items with the same designation have roughly the same importance.

Developing Your Outline

Developing an outline is no easy job. It involves arranging material from various sources in an appropriate manner. Sorting and re-sorting your notes is a good way to proceed. First, determine the main divisions of your paper, and then sort the notes by division. Next, review each grouping carefully to determine further subdivisions and sort it into smaller groupings. Finally, use the groupings to prepare your outline.

There are two types of formal outlines: *topic* and *sentence.* A topic outline presents all entries as words, short phrases, or short clauses. A sentence outline presents them as complete sentences. To emphasize the relationships among elements, items of equal importance have parallel phrasing. Although neither form is better than the other, a sentence outline includes more details and also your perspective on each idea. Many students first develop a topic outline, do additional research, and then polish and expand this version into a sentence outline. While it's easy to be sloppy in a topic outline, forming a sentence outline requires you to reach the kinds of conclusions that will become the backbone of your paper. The following segments of a topic and a sentence outline for a paper on tranquilizer dependence illustrate the difference between the two:

Topic Outline

II. The tranquilizer abuse problem

    A. Reasons for the problem

        1. Over-promotion

        2. Over-prescription

        3. Patient's misuse

            a. Dosage

            b. Length of usage

    B. Growth of the problem

Sentence Outline

II. Tranquilizers are widely abused.

    A. Several factors account for the abuse of tranquilizers.

        1. Drug companies over-promote their product.

        2. Doctors often unnecessarily prescribe tranquilizers.

        3. Patients often do not follow their doctors' instructions.

            a. Some patients take more than prescribed doses

            b. Some continue to use tranquilizers beyond the prescribed time.

    B. The problem of tranquilizer abuse appears to be growing.

Note that the items in the sentence outline are followed by periods, but those in the topic outline are not.

Keying Your Notes to Your Outline

When your outline is finished, key your notes to it by writing or entering the letter and number combination—such as IIA or IIIB2—at the top of each card or at the beginning of each computer note. Now arrange the notes in the order shown in the outline. (On the computer, you can often use the automatic alphabetization sort function.) Finally, starting with the first note, number them all consecutively. That way, if they later get out of order, you can easily reorganize them. You might have a few stragglers left over when you complete this keying. Some of these may be worked into your paper as you write or revise it.

Case History   (continued)

Sorting and re-sorting was challenging and at times frustrating for Keith. Since some of his material could be arranged in different ways, he found himself experimenting, evaluating, and rearranging as he tried various options. After much thought and some trial and error, the following *initial draft* of his outline emerged:

I.   Reasons why monitoring used

    A. Serious crime problem and number of people in prisons

    B. High cost of prisons

II.   Brief history of electronic monitoring

III. Types of monitoring systems

    A. Programmed-contact systems

    B. Continuous-contact systems

    C. Hybrid systems

IV.   Problems with these systems

    A. Practical problems

        1. Offenders' problems

        2. Transmission difficulties

    B. Legal problems

        1. Do the systems violate constitutional rights?

        2. "Net-widening" effect

V.   Effectiveness of electronic monitoring

    A. Effectiveness with low-risk offenders

    B. Cost effectiveness

VI.   Expanded use of monitoring likely

This version is marked by nonparallel structure and inadequate attention to some points. But despite these weaknesses, it provided an adequate blueprint for the first draft of Keith's paper.

This case history concludes later in this chapter.

ETHICAL ISSUES

When you present information you've gathered from a variety of sources, you want to proceed in an ethically responsible way. Asking and answering the following questions can help you to do just that.

Have I carefully researched my topic, making sure that my conclusions are well founded? Imagine the consequences if slipshod testing by an auto company led to the erroneous conclusion that the steering mechanism on one of its models had met current safety standards.

Have I adequately acknowledged any evidence that runs counter to the conclusions I draw? A paper that stresses the advantages of private schools but deliberately avoids mentioning their disadvantages could be a form of deception.

Have I properly documented my sources? Using someone else's words or ideas without giving proper credit is a form of academic dishonesty.

Have I honestly represented the authority of my sources? If you read an article touting almond extract as a cure for cancer that was written by a practising foot doctor, it would be dishonest to suggest that the article was written by a "prominent research scientist." Refer to someone as an expert only when that person's credentials warrant the label.

Could my information have an undesirable effect on the readers? If so, how can I address their concerns? A report describing a new antibiotic-resistant strain of tuberculosis might alarm some readers, and therefore the writer should provide appropriate reassurances of the limited risk to most people.

WRITING YOUR RESEARCH PAPER

Some students think of a library research paper as a series of quotations, paraphrases, and summaries, one following the other throughout the paper. Not so. Certainly, you use the material of others; but *you* select and organize it according to *your purpose. You* develop insights, and *you* draw conclusions about what you've read. You can best express your conclusions by setting your notes aside, stepping back to gain some perspective, and then expressing your sense of what you've learned. Many students find it helpful to write two or three pages that summarize what they want to say as well as whom they want to reach with their message and why. Like all forms of writing, research papers are written for some purpose and aimed at some audience.

Writing the First Draft

Your final research results are expressed in a thesis. You've already drafted a tentative thesis, and now you need to refine or revise it to accommodate any changes in your perspective on the topic. Position the thesis in the introductory part of your paper unless you're analyzing a problem or recommending a solution; then you might hold back the thesis until later in the essay. If you do hold it back, state the problem clearly at the outset. Because of the paper's length, it's a good idea to reveal your organizational plan in your introductory section.

Write the paper section by section, following the divisions of your outline. But keep in mind that you're not locked into its pattern. If you see an opportunity to develop an important idea that you omitted from your outline, try it. If you discover that it might be better to introduce an item earlier than you intended, go ahead. Just be sure to check your organization later. As you write, think of yourself as supporting the conclusions you have reached with the appropriate material from your notes, not just as stringing these items together. Then incorporate the material from your notes with your own assessments and with transitional elements that clarify your information and orient the reader. As you proceed, use the writing strategies presented earlier in the book.

Because of the paper's length, you probably need to connect its major sections with transitional paragraphs to pull together the material already covered and prepare the reader for what follows. Don't fret if the style bumps along or connections aren't always clear. These problems can be smoothed out when you revise. You do, however, need to know how to document your sources properly, handle quotations, and avoid plagiarism. Chapter 15 presents guidelines on these important subjects.

On occasion, you may want to include supplementary information that would interrupt the flow of thought if you placed it in the paper. When this happens, use an *explanatory note* using the footnote function.[1] A typical explanatory note might clarify or elaborate upon a point, discuss some side issue, or define a term used in a specialized way.

When you finish writing, let this version sit for a day or two. Then revise it, just as you would with a shorter essay. Keep track of all your sources so that preparing the bibliography goes smoothly.

Preparing Your Finished Copy

Follow the revision guidelines in Chapter 5. In addition, verify that you have

- included all key information
- clearly organized your material
- not overloaded your paper with quotations
- worked in your own observations
- put in-text documentation and source information in proper form

Prepare your final draft on a word-processor. Double-space throughout, including indented block quotations and the list of works you used to prepare the paper.

Two systems for formatting and documenting library research papers are in common use: the Modern Language Association (MLA) system, favoured by many English and humanities instructors, and the American Psychological Association (APA) system, used by many social science and psychology instructors.

MLA System for Preparing Papers

- Number each page in the upper right-hand corner, 1 centimetre (approximately $1/2$ inch) from the top. Precede each number with your last name.
- Starting 2.5 centimetres (1 inch) from the top of the first page, type your full name, the instructor's name, the course designation, and the date, all flush with the left-hand margin.
- Double-space below the date, and centre the title; then double-space before starting the first paragraph.

---

[1]This is an explanatory note. Position it at the bottom of the page, spaced four lines away from the main text. If more than one note occurs on a page, double-space between them. If the note carries over to the next page, separate it from your text with a solid, full-length line. Put two spaces above the line and two spaces below it. Most word-processor programs create footnotes automatically.

- Leave 2.5-centimetre (1-inch) margins on all four sides except at the top of the first page. Set the indents for the first line of each paragraph to five spaces.

- The MLA system does not require a title page. If your instructor wants one, however, centre the following on the page: (1) the title of the paper about 5 centimetres (2 inches) below the top of the sheet, (2) your name in the middle of the sheet, and (3) the instructor's name, course designation, and date about 5 centimetres (2 inches) from the bottom. Do not use all uppercase letters. Repeat the title on the first text page, centred about 5 centimetres (2 inches) from the top.

- Begin the bibliography on a new page that follows the text of the paper, and give it the heading *Works Cited*. Centre the heading on the page.

- List each bibliography entry alphabetically according to the author's last name, or, if no author is given, by the first significant word in the title. For a work with more than one author, alphabetize by the name that comes first. If there's more than one entry for an author, use three unspaced hyphens in place of the author's name, followed by a period and a double space, in the second and subsequent entries.

- Begin the first line of each entry at the left-hand margin and indent any subsequent lines five spaces.

APA System for Preparing Papers

- The APA system requires a title page. Centre the following on the page: (1) the title of the paper about 10 centimetres (4 inches) from the top and (2) your name, two lines below the title. About three-quarters of the way from the top, provide the course designation, the name of your instructor, and the date, double-spaced and flush with the right-hand margin. At 5 centimetres (2 inches) from the top of the page, type the words *RUNNING HEAD*, flush with the left-hand margin; then enter a colon and a word or phrase that identifies the paper's topic. Type the running head in capital letters; enter everything else in capital and lowercase letters.

- Repeat the title of the paper on the first text page, centred about 3.75 centimetres ($1^1/_2$ inches) from the top and typed in capital and lowercase letters.

- Number every page of the text in the upper right-hand corner, starting with the title page. Position the first two or three words of the title five spaces to the left of the page number.

- Leave 5-centimetre (1-inch) margins at the bottom and at both sides of each page. Indent the first line of each paragraph five spaces.

- Begin the bibliography on a new page that follows the text of the paper, and give it the heading *References*. Centre this heading on the page. Follow the alphabetizing and positioning guidelines for the MLA system, except that, if the listing includes more than one entry for an author, repeat the author's name.

■ Indent the first line of each entry five spaces and begin any subsequent lines at the left-hand margin.

Case History   *(continued)*

Using his outline and thesis statement as a guide, Keith prepared a first draft of his paper, following the MLA format required by his instructor. It didn't happen easily. In order to ensure an effective presentation, he checked his notes carefully to determine which material would provide the strongest support for his conclusions. He was careful to use his own words except when he was quoting. To achieve smoothness, he tried to connect his major sections with transitions, aware that he could polish these connections when he revised the paper.

When he had completed the first draft, Keith set it aside for two days in order to distance himself from his writing. Then he returned to it and revised it carefully. Reading the paper from the perspective of a slightly skeptical critic, he looked for unsupported claims, questions that readers might have, sections that might be confusing or poorly organized, and weak transitions. Like most writers, Keith found sections that could be improved. Next, he revised his initial topic outline and followed it when drafting the sentence outline. Keith then prepared the final draft of the paper itself. Direct your attention to its noteworthy features, which include italicized notations indicating where Keith used the writing strategies discussed earlier in the text (Chapters 6–12).

EXAMPLE OF A STUDENT RESEARCH PAPER

Sentence Outline

Thesis statement: House arrest offers a choice of several monitoring systems, presents no insurmountable problems, proves effective in controlling low-risk offenders, and costs less than incarceration.

I. The use of house arrest stems from serious crime problems in both Canada and the United States.

    A. Extensive use of prisons in Canada and the U.S. has led to economic and social problems.

    B. Violent crimes committed by chronic offenders have led to tougher crime-control legislation.

    C. This legislation has increased the country's prison population and the cost of incarceration.

    D. As a result, many jurisdictions have adopted house-arrest programs for low-risk offenders.

II. Electronic monitoring has a short history.

    A. The idea first appeared in the comic *Spiderman*.

    B. A New Mexico judge asked computer companies to develop an electronic bracelet.

    C. Monitoring was first used in 1984 to control offenders, and the concept quickly spread across the country.

III. Electronic monitoring devices fall into three categories.

    A. A programmed-contact system calls the offender's home during curfew periods and reports absences.

        1. A computer may simply record the offender's voice.

        2. A computer may compare the voice heard over the phone to a recording of the offender's voice.

        3. The offender may wear an encoded bracelet and insert it into a special telephone transmitter.

> Sentence outline: Note use of complete sentences throughout, the periods following section and subsection markers, and the indentation arrangement.

        4.   A camera may transmit photos of the offender over telephone lines.

   B.   A continuous-signal system requires the offender to wear a transmitter that sends uninterrupted electronic signals.

   C.   A hybrid system combines programmed-contact and continuous-signal techniques.

        1.   The programmed-contact component usually includes voice- and photo-transmission units.

        2.   Jurisdictions can tailor systems to their needs.

IV.   Electronic systems have created practical and legal problems.

   A.   Practical problems include both difficulties experienced by offenders and transmission difficulties.

        1.   Encoded bracelets can cause offenders discomfort and embarrassment.

        2.   Telephone lines and objects in the offender's home can interfere with signal pickup.

   B.   Legal problems include possible infringement of rights and the net-widening effect.

        1.   Charging surveillance fees and limiting surveillance to the least dangerous persons may infringe on offenders' equal-protection rights.

        2.   Monitoring may violate the right to privacy of others in offenders' homes.

        3.   Net-widening can result in an excessive number of individuals under house arrest.

V.   Electronic monitoring has proved effective with low-risk offenders.

   A.   Offenders successfully completed monitoring programs in B.C.

   B.   Monitoring costs less than incarceration.

VI.   The advantages of house arrest over prison sentences should increase the use of this humane alternative in Canada.

2.5 cm

1 cm

Jacque 1

Keith Jacque

Professor Reinking

English 250

May 8, 1999   **double-space throughout**

House Arrest: An Attractive Alternative to Incarceration

In Canada, as in the United States, crime is a serious economic and social problem that has led to expanded prison use in both countries. The cost of running the justice system alone in Canada is about $7.3 billion, while the criminal justice system in the United States costs about $26.7 billion to run (Johnson). It is expensive to put people in prisons: It costs about $200 000 to build a Canadian prison cell, and $70 000 annually to keep an offender in prison. Canada also has many of the same problems with overcrowding in prisons as does the United States. Prison cells, like hospital beds, seem to get filled as fast as they are provided. Prisons have also been criticized for failing to rehabilitate; they have even been called "universities of crime." Criminology Professor Hollis Johnson says that there is fairly good evidence "that sending people to prison amplifies their deviance" as offenders are socialized into the prison subculture. Yet Canada, which is second only to the United States worldwide in its use of prisons, continues to expand its prison use.

2.5 cm

Although violent crimes have hardened society's attitudes toward criminals and brought about demands for "get tough" policies in dealing with all kinds of offences, most violent crimes are committed by "a tiny fraction of the population" who are often chronic offenders (Barr). In the United States, tough federal legislation such as the Crime Control Act of 1984 and the Anti-Drug Abuse Act of 1986 has led to mandatory incarceration for certain habitual offenders and for persons convicted of specified drug offences, respectively (United States, *Prison Projections* 12).

The introduction of mandatory sentencing guidelines, now common on the state as well as the federal level, provides

2.5 cm

Paper is double-spaced throughout.

Title reflects main thrust of paper.

Opening paragraph cites negative effects of extensive prison use.

Effect of nonviolent and violent crimes

Causal chain

Jacque 2

Causal chain

consistent punishment for similar crimes. It has led, however, to
an explosion in the number of prison inmates, which by mid-1996
totalled over 1.1 million, according to the Justice Department's
Bureau of Justice Statistics ("BJS Reports" 1). Between 1980 and
1995, the U.S. prison population increased by 242 percent
("Inmate Populations" 10). Many of these inmates are guilty of
nonviolent offences. In 1997, three-quarters of all prisoners fell
into the nonviolent category (Richey 3).

Statistics, forecasts of
prisoner increases, costs
provide interest, depth

In the United States the prison population is expected to keep
growing. The National Council on Crime and Delinquency has
estimated that the total number of prisoners might reach 1.4 million by the year 2000, a jump of 24 percent over the 1995 level
("Inmate Populations" 10). The Bureau of Prisons has projected
construction costs of some four billion dollars for new federal
prisons scheduled to open in the 1996–2006 decade and
between ten billion and fourteen billion dollars for the new state
prisons required to house the anticipated increase in prisoners
("Inmate Populations" 10).

Author's name introduces
short run-in quote within
quotation marks; page
number follows name.

Even these figures don't tell the whole story. Director of the
Federal Bureau of Prisons J. Michael Quinlan (114) comments that,
over the lifetime of a prison, "construction costs are only 5–7 percent of the total expense. This means that from 15 to 20 times the
construction costs will have to be budgeted over the life of each
prison now being built." Underestimating operating costs can

Effect of underestimating
costs

result in unused facilities as in Florida where, in 1992, two newly
constructed 900-person prisons and a 336-person death-row
facility remained empty because the state lacked the money to
operate them (Katel 63).

Overcrowding and the high costs of prisons have seriously
undermined state spending on public services and created a
number of hidden expenses. In Michigan, for example, corrections spending increased over 300 percent between 1979 and

Jacque 3

1989, as compared to a 98 percent increase in social services spending and a 40 percent increase in education spending (Baird 122). And these figures do not include hidden costs such as welfare payments to the families of imprisoned offenders and the loss of tax revenues from prisoners removed from the job market (Lynch).

Faced with the social and educational consequences of current policy, many state legislators have recommended using prison space only for violent offenders and developing, for non-violent ones, low-cost alternatives that provide adequate public protection. At times, results have been mixed. In the early 1980s, for example, the state of Georgia attempted to relieve severe prison overcrowding by greatly expanding the use of closely supervised probation. While significant cost savings were realized, tremendous work overloads on the probation staff resulted (Probation Division).

Another alternative to prison sentences besides probation is a form of house arrest that "confines an offender to a specific site . . . during specific hours" and supervises the offender by means of an electronic monitoring system, sometimes referred to as EMS (BC *EMS Discussion Paper* 2–3). While this technology has been used in the United States since approximately 1984, it was introduced to Canada by some provinces in the late 1980s. Perhaps it is time for us to consider whether electronic monitoring should be promoted more widely in Canada, perhaps even on the federal level. It offers a choice of several monitoring systems, presents no insurmountable problems, is effective in controlling low-risk offenders, and costs less than incarceration.

Electronic monitoring[1] has curious roots—the comic *Spiderman*. The idea first occurred in 1979 to New Mexico Judge

---

[1]This alternative is sometimes called electronic tethering, electronic surveillance, electronic house arrest, or electronic incarceration.

Margin annotations:

Comparison of spending figures

Definition of term

Omission within sentence, ellipsis

Rationale for essay's focus

Thesis statement reflects paper's content, previews organization.

Explanatory note

Jacque 4

Narrative relates brief history
of monitoring.

Double citations show two
sources with essentially
identical information;
shortened titles distinguish
between separate articles
by same author.

Classification of monitoring
systems

Definition of system

Comparison of systems

Jack Love, who observed that Kingpin, Spiderman's nemesis, used
an electronic bracelet to control his crime-fighter enemy. Love
asked computer companies to develop a similar device
(Scaglione, "Jails" 32; Sullivan 51). The first house-arrest program
using electronic monitoring was implemented in 1984, and five
years later programs had been established in over a hundred
jurisdictions across more than thirty states (Peck 26; Scaglione,
"Under Arrest" 26). By 1993, the number of offenders being electronically monitored throughout the United States totalled 65 650
(Carey and McLean 1).

The U.S. Department of Justice classifies electronic monitoring systems according to their signalling characteristics (United
States, *Electronic Monitoring* 1). Types include programmed contact, continuous signal, and hybrid systems—a combination of the
first two.

With a programmed-contact system, a computer calls an offender's residence on a random basis during established curfew
periods and reports any unauthorized absence to correctional
authorities. Various levels of sophistication are possible depending upon how much certainty is desired. In the simplest system,
the computer merely records the offender's voice. Correctional
authorities then review the taped responses the next day to
determine any curfew violations. A variant approach uses a pre-
recording of the offender's voice, which the computer compares
to the voice heard during random calls. If the two do not match,
the computer can immediately notify authorities of a violation.
Voice systems are comparatively inexpensive as no special
equipment needs to be installed in the offender's home or worn
by the individual (Hofer and Meierhoefer 36–37).

A more sophisticated means of checking on offenders makes
use of an encoded bracelet worn by the offender. Again, a computer calls randomly during curfew. Instead of answering in the
usual manner, however, the offender responds by inserting the

Jacque 5

bracelet into a special transmitter attached to the telephone. The bracelets can be made in such a way that unauthorized attempts to remove them will damage their transmitting ability (Hofer and Meierhoefer 36–37).

Visual verification probably offers the best assurance against curfew violation. A special camera that can transmit photographs over telephone lines is installed in the offender's home. During calls, the computer can request the monitored individual to provide a variety of poses to the camera. These photographs can then be stored in the computer for later review or compared immediately to a reference key for the individual (Hofer and Meierhoefer 37).

Continuous-signal systems, unlike programmed-contact systems, require the offender to wear a transmitter that sends a continuous sequence of electronic signals, often several times a minute, to his or her home telephone. If a break in transmission occurs during a detention period, the monitoring computer notifies authorities. The transmitters are relatively small and generally worn on a tamper-resistant strap around the ankle. Attempts to remove the strap could cause the unit to stop sending signals or could be detected during periodic inspections. These systems provide a greater degree of supervision than programmed-contact systems, which check on offenders only intermittently (Hofer and Meierhoefer 38–39).

Hybrid systems combine programmed-contact and continuous-signal techniques in order to realize the advantages of each (United States, *Electronic Monitoring* 1). Typically, the programmed-contact component includes both voice and video units. This component can function as a backup for continuous-signal monitoring or as a supplement to it. In the first case, the computer is programmed to call for voice-video identification whenever the offender's transmitter fails to send a continuous signal. In the second case, the computer randomly calls for voice-video

| *Process* explained |

| *Comparison* of systems; *definition* of system |

| *Comparison* of systems |

Jacque 6

verification as well as receives transmitter signals (Scaglione, "Jails" 36).

Jurisdictions can develop hybrid systems tailored to their individual needs. For example, a house-arrest program for drunk drivers could employ a continuous-signal transmitter supplemented by random telephone verification. Home monitoring equipment could even include a Breathalyzer to determine and transmit to the computer the offender's blood-alcohol level during telephone verification calls (Scaglione, "Jails" 36). A variation of this type of system is used in Annapolis, Maryland, where video cameras have been installed in the homes of some convicted drunk drivers. The offenders are called periodically and required to give themselves a blood-alcohol test in front of the camera (Peck 28).

Not surprisingly, electronic monitoring has resulted in some practical problems and legal concerns. Most problems arise with those who wear encoded verification bracelets or transmitters. These offenders complain that the devices cause physical discomfort or embarrassment. Correction officials can adjust the fit of the device or suggest that offenders wear a cut-off tube sock, tennis-type wrist band, or other type of padding under the strap. Wearers, however, must find their own ways of coping with embarrassment. In studying the electronic monitoring of federal parolees, Beck, Klein-Saffran, and Wooten found that offenders could be quite innovative in explaining why they were wearing units. When questioned by strangers, "the majority told the truth, while other parolees stated that [the unit] was a heart monitor, pager, battery charger for a video camera, or a fish caller" (29).

Transmitting difficulties have created other practical problems. In some areas, existing telephone lines may be inadequate or incompatible with the transmitting characteristics of certain monitoring systems. In other cases, the offender's home may cause difficulties. Ford and Schmidt, who conducted research for the U.S. National Institute of Justice, point out that

Cites article with three authors; page number follows quotation

Brackets enclose explanatory words inserted into quotation.

Examples of problems

Jacque 7

The typical room has dead space in which the receiver cannot
pick up the transmitter's signal. In particular, metal tends to limit
the range of the transmitter; kitchens are therefore an especially
difficult environment. Transmission breaks have also been attributed to metal furniture, faulty wiring, other electronic devices,
bathroom fixtures, waterbeds, and even certain sleeping positions. Mobile homes constitute a problem for offenders trying
to do yard chores: the range outside the building is as little as
ten feet, as compared to as much as 200 feet from a mainframe
building. (3)

Other researchers have noted similar interference problems.
In one situation, authorities suspected noncompliance when they
discovered breaks in an offender's continuous signal transmis-
sions. These breaks always occurred during the same time
period and only on Sundays. Investigation revealed that a large
rock and metal coffee table was blocking the signal from the
transmitter on the offender's ankle while he was watching football
on television (Beck, Klein-Saffran, and Wooten 27).

Most practical problems associated with electronic monitoring pose no serious challenge. Troublesome bracelets and
transmitters can be adjusted or padded. Offenders often develop
ingenious explanations for the units they wear. Difficulties in signal
transmission can often be overcome by having trained technicians
install equipment or by having offenders slightly modify their
routine. Legal problems, on the other hand, pose a greater
challenge.

Electronic surveillance programs necessarily involve some
type of entry into offenders' homes. Therefore, they need careful
examination to ensure that they don't violate the equal protection
and right to privacy provisions of the U.S. Constitution. The
American Civil Liberties Union is concerned that two common
practices—charging a fee to cover surveillance costs and

Extended quotation
indented ten spaces,
without quotation marks,
double-spaced

Period precedes citation.

Transition paragraph
summarizes solutions to
practical problems, looks
ahead to legal problems.

Jacque 8

restricting surveillance to classes of offenders least likely to violate house arrest—may infringe on the equal protection clause of
the U.S. Constitution. The first practice, the ACLU notes, can dis-
criminate against young and indigent offenders by imprisoning
them because they cannot pay their fees. The second, by singling
out persons guilty only of property crimes and without serious
criminal records or histories of drug abuse, may target dispropor-
tionately high numbers of white-collar offenders (Petersilia 3).

Because electronic monitoring programs are always voluntary, participants essentially waive their right to privacy. By
agreeing to a program in lieu of prison, they have indicated their
willingness to undergo surveillance. Still, as the Bureau of Justice
Assistance notes, court rulings may uphold a convicted person's
right to privacy if electronic surveillance "cannot be justified in
terms of an articulated security interest, ability to deter future
criminal conduct or ability to reduce the risk of flight" (United
States, *Electronic Monitoring* 5). Furthermore, electronic monitoring can invade the privacy of others in the offender's home.
Family members who have not committed an offence and have
not waived their right to privacy can accidentally be photographed or recorded. To prevent such intrusions, Kentucky,
Nevada, and West Virginia have banned the use of equipment that
might accidentally record extraneous sights and sounds. And
because North Carolina prohibits photographing juveniles, visual
verification cannot be used in that state (Scaglione, "Jails" 34).

Besides protecting an offender's constitutional rights, correction officials must try to avoid a "net-widening" effect when
electronic monitoring is used. This effect occurs when a judge
approves surveillance for offenders who would formerly have
received probation but denies it to anyone who would formerly
have gone to prison. The result is a "widening of the net of social
control" to encompass more individuals. When such abuses take
place, the system does not provide an option for those who would

---

Quotation indicates precise
conditions that justify
monitoring.

Definition of term

Jacque 9

otherwise have gone to prison, and it serves as a new form of punishment for those who would otherwise have been placed on probation. Prison overcrowding is not reduced, and the costs of punishment actually rise because of the excess number of individuals under surveillance (Morris and Tonry 225). The net-widening effect has been avoided in some jurisdictions by establishing strict rules for the selection of participants. New Jersey, for instance, restricts alternative punishment programs to offenders who have already been sentenced to prison (Hofer and Meierhoefer 22).

A pilot project on electronic monitoring introduced in British Columbia in 1987 has provided convincing evidence that electronic monitoring works well in supervising low-risk prisoners. Candidates for this study were carefully screened, and those with a history of violence or those facing a charge of a violent nature were ineligible (BC *EMS Pilot Project Evaluation* 11). The 92 offenders assessed suitable and taken through the entire project all completed their sentences successfully (BC *Pilot Project* 16). In its report afterward, the chair of the Canadian Bar Association (C.B.A.) John Conroy recommended going "on record supporting, in principle, the use of electronic monitoring as an alternative to imprisonment where imprisonment is not considered necessary in the public interest" (20). Conroy also called for legislative changes to the "bail and probation provisions in the *Criminal Code of Canada*" to encourage the use of electronic monitoring, though only as an alternative to imprisonment so that judges are not tempted to widen the net (21).

The British Columbia program was also a success on the level of public acceptance. In a personal interview, criminologist Hollis Johnson said that groups such as Mothers Against Drunk Drivers (M.A.D.D.) who were at first opposed to the program later became its greatest proponents. "Once they got involved in the development of the program, they began to see that these people

Argument in favour of monitoring	
Qualification of thesis where necessary	
Argument in favour of monitoring	

Jacque 10

Interview supplements
library research.

would be placed under greater control than their counterparts who would be sent to prisons on weekends." While the public may see electronic monitoring as overly lenient at first, in fact it can provide an effective, round-the-clock supervision of offenders who would otherwise be contributing to the problem of prison overcrowding.

Although electronic monitoring can reduce prison over-crowding, it is not, of course, a cure-all for the problems associated with our criminal justice system. It is also true that we need to guard against the potential for widening the net "so that increasing numbers of people are placed under . . . surveillance" (Johnson). It is important that we do not violate our Charter of Rights and Freedoms in the implementation of this technology. Still, electronic monitoring may help with economic and human waste of our punitive prison system. While the start-up costs associated with electronic monitoring may seem high, these decrease later once the system is in longer use. With prison sentencing, as Hollis Johnson pointed out, there are hidden costs as well as the obvious ones. Prisoners don't earn a wage, don't contribute to their families or society, and leave prison with a stigma that makes it difficult for them to get hired later. Electronic monitoring offers advantages over prison sentences for nonviolent offenders. Several systems are available; no insurmountable problems are evident; low-risk offenders are effectively controlled; and the costs are less than for incarceration. As we begin the twenty-first century in Canada, we can look to electronic monitoring as a humane, practical alternative to prison sentencing.

Independent conclusion
acknowledges and answers
possible objections.

Independent conclusion
draws together and
reinforces main points
of paper; predicts future
of house-arrest programs
in Canada.

Jacque 11

Works Cited

Baird, Christopher. "Building More Prisons Will Not Solve Prison Overcrowding." *America's Prisons: Opposing Viewpoints.* Ed. David Bender, Bruno Leone, and Stacey Tipp. San Diego: Greenhaven, 1991. 118–24.

Barr, William. "Corraling the Hard-Core Criminal." *Detroit News and Free Press* 18 Oct. 1992, state ed.: B3.

Beck, James L., Jody Klein-Saffran, and Harold B. Wooten. "Home Confinement and the Use of Electronic Monitoring with Federal Parolees." *Federal Probation* Dec. 1990: 22–31.

"BJS Reports: Nation's Jail and Prison Incarceration Rate Almost Doubled During Last Decade." *Corrections Digest* 24 Jan. 1997: 1–2.

British Columbia. Ministry of Attorney General. Corrections Branch. *Electronic Monitoring System for Offender Supervision.* Discussion Paper. 2nd edition. British Columbia: GPO, 1987.

--- Ministry of Solicitor General. Corrections Branch. *Electronic Monitoring for Offender Supervision: Pilot Project Evaluation* by Linda Neville, et al. British Columbia: GPO, 1989.

Carey, Anne R., and Elys A. McLean. "Electronic Prison Bars." *USA Today* 30 Sept. 1993: A1.

Conroy, John. *Electronic Monitoring: Report of the Special Committee on Imprisonment and Release.* Canadian Bar Association. Ottawa: GPO, 1988.

Entry for collection containing several authors' contributions compiled by three editors

Entry for newspaper article

Entry for occupational journal article, with three authors

Entry for occupational journal article, no author given

Entry for government discussion paper, no author given

Entry for government document with more than one author

Entry for newspaper item with two authors

Entry for legal report with one author

Jacque 12

Ford, Daniel, and Annesley K. Schmidt. *Electronically Monitored Home Confinement*. United States. National Institute of Justice, Department of Justice. Washington: GPO, 1989.

Georgia. Probation Division of the Georgia Department of Corrections. *Alternatives to Incarceration* 1 July 1997. 3 Feb. 1998 <http://www.harvard.edu/~innovat/aiga87.html>.

Hofer, Paul J., and Barbara S. Meierhoefer. *Home Confinement: An Evolving Sanction in the Federal Criminal Justice System*. Washington: Federal Judicial Center, 1987.

"Inmate Populations, Costs and Projection Models." *Corrections Compendium* Jan. 1997: 10–11.

Johnson, Hollis. Personal interview. 16 Feb. 1999.

Katel, Peter. "New Walls, No Inmates." *Newsweek* 18 May 1992: 63.

Lynch, Allen. *Cost Effectiveness of Incarceration*. Leroy Collins Institute for Public Policy. 1 July 1997 <http://www.dos.state.fl.us/fgils/agencies/fcc/reports/crime.html>.

Morris, Norval, and Michael Tonry. *Between Prison and Probation: Intermediate Punishments in a Rational Sentencing System*. New York: Oxford UP, 1990.

Peck, Keenan. "High-Tech House Arrest." *Progressive* July 1988: 26–28.

Petersilia, Joan. *House Arrest*. United States. National Institute of Justice, Department of Justice. Washington: GPO, 1988.

Entry for government document, two authors given

Entry for internet report, no author given

Entry for book with two authors

Entry for personal interview

Entry for popular magazine article with one author

Entry for internet report, one author given

Entry for government document, one author given

Jacque 13

Quinlan, J. Michael. "Building More Prisons Will Solve Prison Overcrowding." *America's Prisons: Opposing Viewpoints.* Ed. David Bender, Bruno Leone, and Stacey Tipp. San Diego: Greenhaven, 1991. 112–16.

Richey, Warren. "Bulging Cells Renew Debate over Prisons As Tools to Fight Crime." *Christian Science Monitor* 22 Jan. 1997: 3.

Scaglione, Fred. "Jails without Walls." *American City & County* Jan. 1989: 32–40.

---. "You're Under Arrest—At Home." *USA Today* Nov. 1988; 26–28.[1]

Sullivan, Robert E. "Reach Out and Guard Someone: Using Phones and Bracelets to Reduce Prison Overcrowding." *Rolling Stone* 29 Nov. 1990: 51.

United States. Department of Justice. Bureau of Justice Assistance, Office of Justice Programs. *Electronic Monitoring in Intensive Probation and Parole Programs.* Washington: GPO, 1989.

---. Senate. Subcommittee on Federal Spending, Budget, and Accounting, Committee on Governmental Affairs. *Prison Projections: Can the United States Keep Pace?* 100th Cong., 1st. sess. Washington: GPO, 1987.

Entry for occupational journal article with one author

Second entry for author; three unspaced hyphens substitute for author's name

Second entry for government document, no author given

[1]The magazine *USA Today*, not the newspaper of that name.

CHAPTER 14

Strategies for Researching: Using Primary Sources

The library isn't the only source of information for research writing. Investigators also gather information through *primary research,* which includes such activities as consulting public records in local, provincial, and federal archives, performing experiments, conducting interviews, sending out questionnaires, and making direct observations of various kinds.

This chapter focuses on the latter three types, the most common primary research strategies.

THE VALUE OF PRIMARY RESEARCH

What makes primary research so valuable? First, it allows individuals and organizations to collect recent information, often unavailable elsewhere, that precisely suits their needs. A company that has developed a new product can't turn to published data to estimate its sales prospects; such information simply doesn't exist. But polling test users with a well-crafted questionnaire could suggest some answers and perhaps also some tips for improving the product. Similarly, someone wanting to gauge the success of an ongoing clothing drive by a local charitable organization might interview its director.

Even when published material exists, it may not contain desired information. Although numerous articles discuss student attitudes about required courses, you probably wouldn't find a report that explores student reaction to a new general-education requirement at your college or university. You could, however, assemble this information by distributing a questionnaire. The findings might even contradict and therefore cause you to question the conclusions of others.

Primary research can also yield unexpected and significant material. Suppose you're investigating adult illiteracy, and you interview a professor with a specialty in this area of study. She explains the reasons why people who can't read resist help and supplies several relevant examples. Such information might not appear anywhere in print. Certainly the resulting report would carry more weight and elicit more interest than one without such insights.

You can integrate primary research into a report that consists largely of *secondary research,* the kind that depends on library materials. The student who wrote the research paper on electronic monitoring incorporated the results of a personal interview with a criminology professor knowledgeable about a pilot program in British Columbia. This interview provided information on the scope, operation, success rate, and cost advantage of the program. Often, however, writers detail the findings of primary research in separate reports. This would be the case if, for example, your employer asked you to interview users of a new computer system in order to determine their degree of satisfaction with it.

GENERAL PRINCIPLES FOR PRIMARY RESEARCH

Like all research, primary research requires well-formulated questions. Such questions must be specifically focused, contain clearly defined terms, and be answerable by the actual research. A vague, general question such as "What attitudes do Canadians have about their government?" lacks the necessary precision and therefore can't be resolved. What kinds of attitudes? What level or branch of government? Which Canadians? How would you gather their opinions? A more realistic question might be "According to the Kwantlen University College faculty, how adequate is the new government proposal for funding of academic research in this country?" You could easily develop and distribute to faculty members a questionnaire addressing the different provisions of the proposal. But keep in mind that you can't resolve ethical or philosophical questions through primary research. While you could use a questionnaire to determine student attitudes about the police using sobriety spot checks, such information won't decide the ethical issue of whether the police should use such spot checks.

For valid results, conduct your primary research in an impartial manner. Always aim to determine facts rather than to justify some belief you hold. This means, first of all, that you must develop questions that have no built-in bias. If you poll other students and ask them to tell you "how teachers on this campus marked their papers unreasonably hard," those responding might falsify their answers to give you what you want. Instead, use neutral phrasing such as "Do you believe teachers on this campus marked your papers fairly or unfairly? Explain." Second, don't rely on atypical sources and situations for your data. If you investigate the adequacy of parking space on campus, don't deliberately observe the parking lots on a day when some special event has flooded the campus with visitors. Careful readers will see what you have done and reject your findings.

Just as you avoid bias when gathering information, so also should you report your results fairly. For example, don't use inaccurate interpretations of your findings to make them agree with the conclusions you're after. If you believe peer editing produces questionable results, don't claim that the students in a class you observed spent their time sneering at one another's work when in fact they were offering constructive criticism. Similarly, don't report conclusions that are unsupported by your actual research. If you observe a large number of violent acts while watching Saturday cartoons, don't leap to the conclusion that the violence in the cartoons causes violent behaviour in children. You simply don't have the evidence needed to support that assertion. Finally, don't cover up results that you don't like. If your survey of teachers' marking practices shows that most of your respondents believe instructors mark fairly, don't hide the fact because it doesn't match what you expected to discover. Instead, report your findings accurately and rethink your original position. The following section further explores ethical matters.

ETHICAL ISSUES

Today, most people chuckle at an advertising ploy for a product recommended by "nine out of ten doctors." We recognize that the doctors were handpicked and don't represent an objective sample of adequate size. As a result, little harm occurs. With primary research, however, distorted investigating and reporting are sometimes hard to detect and can have significant consequences.

Let's say the officials of Hafford, Saskatchewan, alarmed at a sharp rise in car accidents caused by distracted drivers, schedule a meeting attempting to ban cell phone use by those driving within city limits. It would be unethical for a reporter opposed to the ban to write a supposedly objective feature article on the issue but include interviews only with people who share his views. Now suppose a presumably neutral group in the city of Winnipeg, Manitoba, distributes a questionnaire to residents to gauge their reaction to a proposed gambling casino. It would be unethical to include a biased question such as "Should the city deprive its residents of the revenue that a casino can provide?" Finally, imagine that a city manager, concerned by reports of motorists running a red light at a major intersection, asks the Department of Motor Vehicles to investigate. A department employee conducts a twenty-minute observation and then writes a report indicating that surveillance cameras are not needed there. Clearly, the employee has acted unethically in drawing a conclusion after such a limited observation. To help ensure that your primary research reports are ethically responsible, ask and answer the following questions:

Have I attempted to avoid bias in gathering and evaluating information?

Are my data based on an adequate sample size? If not, have the limitations of the sample been indicated clearly?

Is my information printed objectively and completely without any intentional effort to omit findings that run counter to my position?

Whether I'm preparing an interview, questionnaire, or direct observation report, are the people involved aware that they are part of a study and how the information will be used? Are they protected from harm that might result from their inclusion?

Do I have permission to name in my report persons interviewed or observed?

In an interview report, would the interviewee recognize and accept statements attributed to him or her?

Have I noted any apparent bias in the interviewee?

In a questionnaire report, have I avoided any biased questions?

INTERVIEWS

During an interview, questions are asked and answered. Some interviews amount to little more than brief, informal chats. Others, like those discussed here, may feature extended conversations, involve a series of questions, and require careful preparation. Interviewing an informed person provides you with first-hand answers to your queries, lets you ask follow-up questions, and gives you access to the most up-to-date thinking.

If you major in a business program, an instructor may require you to question a personnel manager about the company's employee relations program. If your field is social work, you might have to interview a case worker as part of your study of some kind of family problem. On the job, you might have to talk with prospective employees and then assess their suitability for a position in the company. Police officers routinely interview witnesses to accidents and crimes, and journalists do the same in pursuit of stories.

Choosing the Interviewee

Professional and technical personnel are a rich source of interview candidates. The faculty of any university can provide insights into a wide range of subjects. Doctors, pharmacists, and other health professionals can draw on their expertise to help you, as can lawyers, engineers, researchers, corporation managers, and government employees.

Whom you interview depends, of course, on what you wish to know. For information on the safe disposal of high-level nuclear waste, you might consult a physics professor. If you want an expert view on the causes of homelessness, contact an authority such as a sociologist, who could provide objective information. If, however, you want to gain a sense of what it's like to be homeless, you might interview the manager of a shelter or (in a safe place) one or more homeless people.

Preparing for the Interview

If you don't relish the thought of phoning to request an interview, keep in mind that most interviewees are eager to discuss their areas of expertise and are often flattered by the opportunity. The worst that can happen is that you get turned down; and in that event, you can always find someone else in the same field.

Before you phone, review your own upcoming commitments and try to determine which ones you could reschedule if necessary. You may need to make an adjustment to accommodate the schedule of a busy person. When you call, indicate who you are, why you are calling, what you wish to interview about, and how much time you'd like.

If the person agrees to meet with you, then ask when would be convenient. Carefully record the time, day, and place of the interview; and if for any reason you need to cancel, be sure to call well in advance.

Before the interview, do as much background reading as possible. This reading will help you develop a list of key questions and avoid those with obvious and readily available answers. Write out your questions to help ensure that the interview will proceed smoothly.

Good questions permit elaboration and don't call for simple "yes" or "no" answers. To illustrate:

Poor: Is it difficult to work with adult illiterates? (The obvious answer is "yes.")

Better: What have you found most challenging about working with adult illiterates?

On the other hand, don't ask overly broad questions that can't be answered in a relatively brief interview.

Poor: What's wrong with primary-school education?

Better: Why do you think so many children have trouble learning to read?

Avoid questions that are biased and may insult the interviewee.

Poor: Why do you bother to work with adult illiterates?

Better: Why did you decide to work with adult illiterates?

Likewise, avoid questions that restrict the interviewee's options for answering.

Poor: What do you think accounts for the poor academic performance of so many Canadian secondary-school students—too much TV watching or overly large classes?

Better: People often blame the poor academic performance of so many Canadian students on too much TV watching or overly large classes. What importance do you attach to these factors? Do you think other factors contribute to the problem?

The number of questions you prepare depends on the length of the interview. It's a good idea to draft more questions than you think you'll have time to ask, then arrange them in order of importance. If the interviewee keeps to the schedule, you'll obtain your desired information. If the interviewee grants you extra time, you will be ready to get more information.

Conducting the Interview

Naturally you'll want to arrive on time and to bring a notepad and a pen. Sometimes you can make an audio-recording of an interview but only if you ask permission first. Because most people warm up slowly, you might start with one or two brief, general questions that provide you with useful background. Possibilities include "What is the nature of your specialty?" and "How long have you been working in this field?"

Proceed by asking your most important questions first. If you believe that a question hasn't been answered or that an answer is incomplete, don't hesitate to ask follow-up questions.

As the interview unfolds, take notes but don't attempt to copy everything that's said. Instead, jot down key phrases and ideas that will serve as memory prompts. If you want to capture an essential explanation or some other important material in the interviewee's own words, ask the person to speak slowly while you copy them down. When the interview is over, thank the person for talking to you. You may also offer to supply a copy of the finished report. With the answers to your questions fresh in your mind, expand on your notes by filling in details, supplying necessary connections between points that were made, and noting your reactions.

Writing about the Interview

The project you're working on determines how to handle your interview information. If you're preparing a research paper, identify and blend the relevant interview material into your other research and document it properly.

Often, however, you are asked to prepare a separate report of the interview. Then, as with any other report, you need to organize and present the material in an effective order, not merely in the order it occurred. Your topic, purpose, and audience determine the arrangement you select. In any event, remember to establish the context for the report, identify the interviewee and his or her position, and present the information accurately.

EXAMPLE OF A STUDENT INTERVIEW REPORT

Budget Cuts Affect Police:

An Interview Report with Officer Robert Timmons

Holly Swain

Confronted with a billion-dollar budget deficit, the provincial government has been forced to make sharp budget cuts. One of these cuts is the allocation to the police. This decision has threatened the loss of some police jobs and

> Paragraph 1: establishes context for interview

aroused considerable controversy. How, many ask, will the police, who were already on a tight budget, be able to provide the public with adequate protection when they have even less money and fewer personnel?

Sentence 1, paragraph 2:
identifies interviewee and
his position

Remainder of report:
presents information
provided by interviewee

When Officer Robert Timmons first heard that the premier might call for police cutbacks, he didn't believe they would become a reality. Timmons thought the premier was just making "political noise." Actually, the chief of police did at first propose cutting 350 jobs, Timmons' among them, to help meet a $19 million cutback. This proposal was rejected in favour of one that combined demotions, pay cuts, and the elimination of special programs. In addition, the amounts allotted for other purposes were also cut.

All of these actions, Timmons says, have had an unfortunate effect on the operations of the police. As an example, he mentions a sergeant who was demoted to "accident reconstructionist," a job requiring him to review severe accidents and reconstruct what happened for the court. This demotion, Timmons says, has taken an excellent police officer out of the field, where he's most needed, and put him behind a desk.

Timmons notes several bad effects of cuts in the allocation for gasoline. Because of these cuts, police officers are expected to drive just one hundred and fifty kilometres a night. Timmons thinks this limitation has a "direct effect on the public." A motorist stranded on a highway might not be spotted and aided by an officer who is unable to make another run through that territory. Late-night accidents might go undiscovered, with serious or fatal consequences for those involved. Many more speeders and drunk drivers will escape being caught.

As of now, Timmons says, there are only 3000 provincial police, about 400 fewer than needed. Each year, 100 to 200 officers retire. These vacancies need to be filled; however, according to Timmons, the police academy has been closed for over a year. The personnel shortages that already exist and the cutbacks resulting from the budget troubles are making it harder and harder for the police to do an adequate job of protecting the public.

Officer Timmons understands that the government needs to control its spending. However, he believes that the present budget cutbacks for a department that is already understaffed are very unwise. "I feel the premier should have given the matter more thought," he says.

QUESTIONNAIRES

A questionnaire consists essentially of a series of statements or questions to which recipients are asked to respond. Questionnaires help individuals and organizations determine what select groups of people think about particular products, services, issues, and personal matters. You have probably completed a variety of questionnaires yourself, including teacher evaluations and market surveys.

Questionnaires are used extensively both on campus and in the workplace. A social science instructor might ask you to prepare a survey that explores community reaction to a recently implemented penalty for graffiti artists. A business instructor might want you to survey a test-market group to determine its response to some new product. In fact, some marketing classes focus on survey techniques. But even if marketing isn't your specialty, learning how to construct questionnaires can serve you well in your career. If you work in the hotel, restaurant, or other service field, you could use a questionnaire to gauge customer satisfaction. The same holds true if you manage or own a small repair service. As a landscape specialist, you might survey the people in your community to learn what planting and maintenance services they desire.

Developing the Questionnaire

When you develop a questionnaire, you need to target precisely what you want to know and what group you intend to survey. You could survey restaurant customers to determine their attitudes about the service and the quality of the food or to assess the types of food they prefer. Zero in on only one area of interest, and then explore it with appropriate questions.

Begin the questionnaire with a clear explanation of what you intend to accomplish, and supply brief but clear instructions on how to respond to each part. Keep the questionnaire as short as possible, preferably no longer than a page or two. The longer the survey is, the less likely people are to answer all the questions.

As you draw up your questions, take care to avoid these common errors:

1. Don't ask two questions in the same sentence. Their answers may be different.

   Unacceptable: Do you find that this year's Ford Taurus has better acceleration and fuel economy than last year's model?

To correct this fault, use separate sentences.

   Better: Do you find that this year's Ford Taurus has better acceleration than last year's model?

   Better: Do you find that this year's Ford Taurus has better fuel economy than last year's model?

2. Don't include vague or ambiguous questions. Since people won't understand your intent, their answers may not reflect their beliefs.

> *Unacceptable:*   Is assisted suicide a good idea?
>
> *Better:*   Should assisted suicide be permitted for terminally ill patients?

3. Avoid biased questions. They might antagonize those who don't share your views and cause them not to complete the questionnaire.

> *Unacceptable:*   Should taxpayers continue to waste money on renovating the North Park Bridge?
>
> *Better:*   Should taxpayers spend an additional $100 000 to complete the North Park Bridge renovation?

Most questionnaire items fall into the categories that follow. The information you want determines which you choose. Often you need to include several or all of the categories in your questionnaire.

Two-Choice Items   Some items have two possible responses: yes/no, true/false, male/female.

> *Example:*   Do you plan to repaint your house during the summer months?
>
> ☐   yes
>
> ☐   no

Multiple-Choice Items   Often there are several possible responses to a questionnaire item. When you prepare this type of item, make sure that you include all significant choices and that the choices share some common ground. Don't ask if someone's primary vehicle is subcompact, compact, full-size, automatic, or manual, because size and type of transmission are unrelated. To determine whether the vehicle is automatic or manual, use a separate item.

> *Example:*   Check the income group that describes your combined family income.
>
> ☐   less than $10 000 a year
>
> ☐ $10 000–$20 000 a year
>
> ☐ $20 000–$30 000 a year
>
> ☐ $30 000–$40 000 a year
>
> ☐ $40 000–$50 000 a year
>
> ☐   over $50 000 a year

Checklists   Checklists allow respondents to mark more than one option. They can help you determine the range of factors that led to a decision.

> *Example:*   Please check any of the following factors that help explain why you decided not to re-enroll your child in Good Growth Private School:

☐   can no longer afford tuition

☐   moved

☐   dissatisfaction with child's progress

☐   disagree with school's educational approach

☐   conflict with teacher

☐   conflict with other staff

☐   child unhappy with school

☐   child had conflict with other children

Ranking Lists   Sometimes you may need to ask people to rank their preferences. This information allows them to select the most suitable option from
among several possibilities.

> *Example:*   Designating your first choice as "1," please rank your
> preferences in music from 1 through 5.
>
> ☐   classical
>
> ☐   country and western
>
> ☐   jazz
>
> ☐   rock and roll
>
> ☐   rap

Using the responses to this item, the manager of a local radio station could
broadcast the type of music that listeners clearly prefer.

Scale Items   When you are trying to determine the extent to which members
of a group support or oppose some issue, using a scale can be helpful. Be sure
to have people respond to a statement, *not* a question.

> *Example:*   Please circle the response that best reflects your feel-
> ings about the statement below.
>
> SA = strongly agree, A = agree, N = no opinion,
>
> D = disagree, SD = strongly disagree
>
> Women should be allowed to fly combat aircraft in
> time of war.
>
> SA   A   N   D   SD

Open-Ended Items   When you want to gather ideas from other people, you
might turn to open-ended items—those that don't limit the reader's response.
If you do, keep such items narrow enough to be manageable. You should know,
however, that readers are less likely to complete open-ended items and that they
are difficult to sort and tally.

Example: Please list the three improvements that you would most like to see in Lowden's high school curriculum.

_____

_____

_____

_____

_____

EXAMPLE OF A STUDENT QUESTIONNAIRE

Survey on Public Smoking

Kelly Reetz

Please take a few minutes to fill out this questionnaire. My purpose is to determine the smoking habits and attitudes toward public smoking of Bartram College male smokers.

Two-choice item

1. Do you smoke cigarettes? (check one)

    ____   yes

    ____   no

Multiple-choice item

2. If you smoke, indicate how many cigarettes each day. (check one)

    ____   less than half a pack

    ____   between a half and a whole pack

    ____   between one and two packs

    ____   more than two packs

Multiple-choice item

3. If you smoke, what are you likely to do upon entering a public place with no posted smoking restrictions? (check one)

    ____   smoke freely

    ____   check to see whether your smoking is bothering others

    ____   ask others whether they would be bothered if you smoke

    ____   not smoke

Checklist

4. Check the statements you believe are true.

    ____   My health is at risk only if I am a smoker.

    ____   Secondhand smoke contains the same ingredients as directly inhaled smoke.

    ____   Secondhand smoke poses no health risk to nonsmokers.

    ____   Secondhand smoke poses a health risk to nonsmokers.

_____ Secondhand smoke poses less of a health risk than directly inhaled smoke.

5. Please rate each of the statements below, using the following scale: SA = strongly agree, A = agree, N = no opinion, D = disagree, SD = strongly disagree

Scale items

_____ There should be no restrictions on public smoking.

_____ Smoking should be prohibited in stores, banks, offices, and workshops.

_____ Smoking and nonsmoking sections in restaurants should be separated by a barrier that smoke cannot penetrate.

_____ Smokers and nonsmokers should have separate workplace lounges.

_____ All public smoking should be prohibited.

6. Please add one or two comments you might have regarding public smoking. _____

Open-ended item

_____

Testing and Administering the Questionnaire

When you have finished making up the questionnaire, ask several people to respond to the items to test their effectiveness. Are any items vague, ambiguous, biased, or otherwise faulty? If so, rewrite and retest them.

To ensure that you obtain an accurate assessment, make certain that you select an appropriate cross-section of recipients. For example, assume that you and many of your campus friends dislike early morning classes. You decide to draw up a questionnaire to sample the attitudes of other students. You suspect that many students share your dislike, and you plan to submit your findings to the college president for possible action. To obtain meaningful results, you would have to sample a sizeable group of students. Furthermore, this group would need to include representative numbers of first-year and upper-year students, since these classes may not share a uniform view. Failure to sample properly can call your results into question and cause the administration to disregard them. Proper sampling, on the other hand, pinpoints where dissatisfaction is greatest and suggests a possible response. Thus, if first-year students register the most objections, the administration might decide to reduce the number of first-year classes meeting at 8 A.M.

Totalling the Responses

When the recipients have finished marking the questionnaire, you need to total the responses. Even without computer scoring, this job is easier than you might think. Simply prepare a table that lists the questionnaire items and the possible responses to each; then go through the questionnaire and add up the number of times each response is marked.

When you finish, turn your numbers into percentages, which provide an easier-to-understand comparison of the responses. Simply divide the number of times each possible response is checked by the total number of questionnaires, and then multiply the result by 100.

Writing the Questionnaire Report

When you write your report, don't merely fill it with numbers and responses to the questionnaire items. Instead, look for patterns in the responses and try to draw conclusions from them. Follow the order of the questionnaire items in presenting your findings.

Typically, a report consists of two or three sections. The first, "Purpose and Scope," explains why the survey was performed, how many questionnaires were distributed and returned, and how the recipients were contacted. The second section, "Results," reports the conclusions that you have drawn. Finally, if appropriate, a "Recommendations" section offers responses that seem warranted based on the survey findings.

EXAMPLE OF A STUDENT QUESTIONNAIRE REPORT

Findings from a Smoking Questionnaire
Distributed to Bartram College Students

Kelly Reetz

Purpose and Scope of Survey

| Provides background details on project, profile of respondents |

This survey was carried out to determine the smoking habits and attitudes toward public smoking of Bartram College's male students. The assignment was one of my requirements for completing Public Health 201. Each of the 240 male students in Crandall Hall received a copy of the questionnaire in his mailbox, and 72 completed questionnaires were returned. This latter number represents 10 percent of the college's male student population and therefore can be considered a representative sample. Of those responding, 37 (or 51 percent) were cigarette smokers, and 35 (or 49 percent) were nonsmokers. Of the smokers, all but 11 percent smoked more than a pack of cigarettes a day.

Results of Survey

Smokers seemed fairly considerate of nonsmokers in public places. Only 16 percent said they would smoke freely. In fact, 51 percent said they wouldn't smoke at all. The remaining 33 percent indicated they would either look around to see whether they were bothering others or ask others whether they objected to cigarette smoke.

> Discusses responses to questionnaire item 3

In general, respondents seemed aware that secondhand smoke poses a health risk. Seventy-six percent believe that such smoke contains the same ingredients as directly inhaled smoke, and an amazing 96 percent believe that anyone exposed to secondhand smoke may be at risk. Only 3 percent think no health risk is involved.

> Discusses responses to questionnaire item 4

Opinions were strongly divided on the matter of banning all public smoking, with 79 percent strongly opposed and 21 percent strongly in favour. As might be expected, all of the smokers fell into the first group, but a surprising 51 percent of the nonsmokers did too. A sharp division was equally apparent between supporters and opponents of restaurant barriers, with 81 percent for or strongly for them and 19 percent against or strongly against them. In contrast to the findings on a smoking ban, all of the smokers favoured barriers. Respondents overwhelmingly (90 percent to 10 percent) endorsed prohibiting smoking in stores and banks and providing separate workplace lounges. Nobody registered a "no opinion" vote on any of the statements under item 5.

> Discusses responses to questionnaire item 5

Responses to items 3–5 reveal an awareness among smokers of the dangers posed by secondhand cigarette smoke, a concern for the well-being of nonsmokers, and a willingness to accept restrictions, though not an outright ban, on public smoking. This attitude was consistent for both light and heavy smokers. For their part, about half the nonsmokers showed a tolerant attitude by supporting smoking restrictions but rejecting an outright ban.

> Discusses patterns in responses to items 3–5

No smokers, but 71 percent of the nonsmokers, responded to the request to provide one or two additional comments. All of these comments dealt with how the respondents would act if bothered by someone else's smoke. Two-thirds said they would move to another place, half of the remainder said they would ask the smoker to stop, and the other half said they would remain silent rather than risk an argument.

> Discusses responses to item 6

Recommendations

As noted previously, this survey included only male students. To determine how its results compare with those for females, the same questionnaire should be administered to a similar group of female students.

DIRECT OBSERVATIONS

Often direct observation is the most effective means of answering research questions. If you want to know the extent and nature of violence in children's TV cartoons, watching a number of shows tells you. Similarly, a researcher who seeks information about living conditions in a poor area of some city can obtain it by visiting that locale. Such observations furnish firsthand answers to our questions.

At school and on the job, you may need to report your own observations. If you're majoring in business, an instructor might require a report on the work habits of employees at a small local company. If your field is biology, you might need to assess and report on the environmental health of a marsh, riverbank, or other ecological area. On the job, a factory superintendent might observe and then discuss in writing the particulars of some problem-plagued operation. Police officers routinely investigate and report on accidents, and waste-management specialists inspect and report on potential disposal sites.

The following suggestions can help you make your observations, record them, and then write your report.

Preparing to Make the Observations

First, determine the purpose of your observations and keep the purpose firmly in mind as you proceed. Otherwise, you'll overlook important details and record less-than-helpful information. Obviously, observing a classroom to assess the interaction of students calls for a different set of notes than if you were observing the teacher's instructional style or the students' note-taking habits.

Next, establish the site or sites that can best supply you with the information you need. If you're trying to determine how students interact in the classroom, then the time of day, kind of class, and types of students all make a difference. You might have to visit more than one class in order to observe the different types of behaviour.

If your observations take place on private property or involve an organized group such as a legislative body, you need to obtain permission and make an appointment. Also, you might want to supplement your observations with an interview. Ordinarily, the interview takes place after you have made your observations so that you can ask about what you've seen. If technical information is needed in advance, the interview should precede the observations. However, you should have done research first so that you do not waste the expert's time and goodwill by asking about information that is reasonably available.

Because you'll probably be making a great many individual observations, try to develop a chart and a code for recording them. Suppose you're comparing the extent to which students interact with one another and with the instructor in first-year and third-year writing courses. After much thought, you might develop a chart like the one following:

Class Designation: English 1100				
Minutes into observation when inter-action occurred	Classroom location of interacting students	Number and sex of students	Subject of interaction	Length of interaction

In developing your code, you would undoubtedly use M = male and F = female to distinguish the sexes. To show the location of the interacting students, FC = front of class, MC = middle of class, and BC = back of class would probably work quite well. Coding the kinds of interactions presents a more difficult task. Here, after considering several possibilities, you might decide upon these symbols: CR = class related, SR = school related, SP = sports, D = dating, O = other matters. To save writing time, you'd probably want to use "min." for "minutes" and "sec." for "seconds" when recording the lengths of the interactions.

Making the Observations

If your visit involves a scheduled appointment, be sure to arrive on time and be ready to take notes. Select a location where you can observe without interfering. If you are observing people or animals, remember that they need to adjust to you before they behave naturally.

Before you begin taking notes, record any pertinent general information. If you're observing a class, you might note the time it is meeting, its size, the name of the instructor, and whether he or she is present when you arrive. If you're observing an apartment, record the location and condition of the building, the time of the visit, and the general nature of the environment. Note also whether the landlord as well as the tenant knew you were coming: It is amazing how much cleanup landlords can carry out when they know an observer is arriving soon.

Don't feel as though you must take extensive notes. However, do record enough details to ensure that you won't forget any important events, activities, or features. If you have a chart and coding system, rely on it as much as possible when recording information. Refer to the chart on page 316 for how the coded notes for part of a classroom visit might look.

If you haven't developed a chart, take enough notes so that you can produce a thorough report. Try to follow some note-taking pattern. When observing the condition of an apartment, you could proceed from room to room, jotting down observations such as "Front hallway, entranceway: paint peeling in large strips from wall, paint chips on floor. Hallway dark, bulb burned out. Linoleum curling up along sides. Cockroaches running along lower moulding." Remain as objective as possible as you take notes. Record what you see, hear, and smell, and avoid judgmental language. If you must record a subjective impression, identify it as such.

Class Designation: English 1100				
Minutes into observation when inter-action occurred	Classroom location of interacting students	Number and sex of students	Subject of interaction	Length of interaction
0 3 Instructor arrived 5 20	FC MC FC, MC, BC FC, MC	M-M F-F M-M-M-F-F M-F-M	SP D CR CR	1 min. 30 sec. 3 min. 45 sec. 1 min.

Ask questions if necessary, but rely primarily on what you observe, not what you're told. If the landlord of a rundown apartment you're visiting tells you that he's repainting the building but you see no signs that this is happening, ignore what he says or report it along with an appropriate cautionary comment. When you finish, thank the person(s) who made your observations possible or helped you in other ways.

When you leave the observation site, expand your notes by adding more details. Supply any needed connections and record your overall impressions. For example, suppose you are expanding your notes on student interactions in an English class. You might note that the greatest number of interactions occurred before and immediately after the instructor arrived, that all student–student interactions involved individuals seated together, that student–instructor interactions included students in all parts of the room, and that all the latter interactions were about subject-related matters. This information might stimulate interesting speculation concerning the student–student and student–teacher relationships in the class, causing you to conclude that the students were hesitant about having exchanges with the instructor. As you proceed, record only what you actually observed, not what you wanted or expected to observe.

If upon reviewing your notes you find that you require more information, you may need to arrange a second or even a third visit to the observation site.

Writing the Report

Once your notes are in final form, you can start writing your report. On the job, your employer may specify a certain form to follow. As a general rule, all such reports reflect their purposes, focus on relevant information, and remain objective.

Usually you begin by explaining the reason for the investigation, noting any preliminary arrangements that were made, and if appropriate, providing an overview of the observation site. Depending upon the nature of the report, the primary means of organization may be as follows:

Narration. A report on the changing conduct of a child over a three-hour period in a daycare centre would probably be organized by narration.

Description. A report assessing the storm damage in a large urban area could present its details in spatial order.

Classification. A visit to a toxic-waste dump suspected of violating government regulations might produce a report classifying the types of wastes improperly stored there.

Point-by-point comparison. If you're comparing two possible sites for a baseball stadium, shopping mall, or other structure, a point-by-point comparison probably best suits your purpose.

Cause and effect. This pattern works well for reporting events whose effects are of special concern, such as the testing of a new siren intended to scare birds from an airport runway.

Process. This arrangement is indicated when readers want to know step-by-step how a process is carried out: for example, a new test for determining the mineral content of water.

Conclude the report by discussing the significance of the findings and making any other comments that seem justified.

EXAMPLE OF A STUDENT OBSERVATION REPORT

Observations of a Rundown Apartment Building

Caleb Thomas

To fulfill part of the requirements for Social Service 321, I observed the housing conditions in a poor residential area in our city. The building I selected is located at the corner of Division Avenue and Hall Street, an area where most of the residents hold minimum-wage jobs or receive some form of public assistance.

| Gives reason for visit, location of site |

I met the building supervisor, who had agreed to this visit, at 9:30 A.M. on Friday, April 15, 2006. The brick sides of the three-storey apartment building appeared to be in good repair, but one second-storey window was broken out and boarded up. Most windows had standard window shades, but a few were blocked with sheets or black plastic bags. Two had no coverings of any kind. Overall, the building's appearance was similar to that of several nearby apartment buildings.

| Notes preliminary arrangements, provides overview of site location |

Heavy traffic clogged Division Avenue at the time of my visit. Next to the apartment building stood three single-storey wooden buildings housing an adult video store, a bar, and a novelty shop, all with boarded windows and

| Continues overview of site location |

peeling paint. Across the street, a single-storey Salvation Army Store occupied the entire block. In front of it, three women in short skirts walked slowly back and forth, eyeing the cars that passed. Two men sat on crates, their backs to the building, drinking something out of paper bags.

The supervisor opened the unlocked metal door of the apartment building, and we went in. The hallway was lighted by a single dim bulb located on the wall toward the rear. Other bulbs along the wall and in two light fixtures hanging from the ceiling appeared burned out. Scraps of newspaper and chips of paint that had peeled from the ceiling and walls littered the floor. A strong urine-like smell pervaded the air.

Stating that he couldn't show me an occupied apartment because he "respected the privacy of the tenants," the supervisor took me to an unoccupied apartment on the first floor. He had trouble unlocking the wooden door; the key appeared to stick in the lock. The inside of the door had two bolt locks, one just above the door handle and the other one near the floor. The door opened into a short hall with rooms off either side. Here, as in the building entrance, paint chips from the peeling walls and ceiling littered the floor. A battered socket on the wall held a single bulb, but when I flicked its switch, the bulb did not light. On the hall floor, linoleum curled at the edges. When I bent down to examine it more closely, several cockroaches scurried under the curl.

The first door on the right-hand side of the hall led into a 3-by-4–metre room that the supervisor identified as the living room. Here the walls had been recently painted—by a former tenant, the supervisor said—and a strong paint smell was still apparent. However, nothing else had been done to the rest of the room. The radiator was unshielded, several nail heads protruded from the stained and uncovered wooden floor, and the sagging ceiling had several long cracks. Plaster chips dotted the floor.

A small kitchen was situated behind the living room. Again, linoleum floor covering curled from the baseboard, and cockroaches scurried for cover. The kitchen was furnished with a battered-looking gas stove, but there was no refrigerator (the supervisor said one was on order). The surface of the sink was chipped and had many brownish stains. When I turned on the faucet, a rusty brown stream of water spurted out. I asked for a sample to be tested for lead content, but the supervisor refused.

The bathroom, located at the end of the hall, had no radiator. Its floor tiles, broken in a number of places, exposed a long section of rotted wood. The toilet, with seat missing, would not flush when I tried it but simply made a hissing

---

Describes building's hallway

Describes apartment hallway

Describes apartment living room

Describes apartment kitchen

Describes apartment bathroom

noise. A brown stain spread over the bottom of the bathtub and a large portion of its sides. The wall tiles around the tub bulged outward and appeared ready to collapse into the tub. The supervisor offered the observation that there had been "some trouble with the plumbing."

Two small bedrooms opened off the left side of the hall. Like the living room both had unprotected radiators, uncovered wooden floors, and cracked ceilings. Walls were papered rather than painted, but long strips of the wall-paper were missing. In one bedroom a piece of plasterboard hung on the wall as if covering a hole. The windows in both bedrooms were covered with sheets tacked to the wall.

> Describes apartment bedrooms

When I had finished looking at the bedrooms, the supervisor quickly escorted me from the apartment and the building, declaring that he was too busy to show me any other vacant apartments. He also said he had no time to answer any questions.

Clearly the building I visited fails to meet the city housing code: The living conditions are not what most people would consider acceptable. A careful investigation, including a test of the water and of the paint for lead content, seems called for to determine whether this apartment constitutes a health risk.

> Discusses significance of findings

CHAPTER 15

Strategies for Documentation

In order to acknowledge and handle sources, you must know how to (1) prepare proper bibliographical references, (2) document sources within your text, (3) handle quotations, and (4) avoid plagiarism.

The kind of information included in bibliographical references depends on the type of source and the documentation system. Two systems are in common use: the Modern Language Association (MLA) system and the American Psychological Association (APA) system. The entries that follow illustrate basic MLA and APA conventions. For more information, consult the *MLA Handbook for Writers of Research Papers*, 6th ed., 2003, and the *Publication Manual of the American Psychological Association*, 5th ed., 2001. When documenting online sources, consult the website noted to supplement the information in the *Manual*.

PREPARING MLA AND APA BIBLIOGRAPHIC REFERENCES

Books

The basic bibliographic reference for a book includes the name of the author, the title of the book, the place of publication, the name of the publisher, and the date of publication. Other information is added as necessary. The order of presentation depends upon which system of listing sources, the MLA or APA, is used. Note that the APA system uses initials rather than first and middle names for authors, editors, and translators.

■ A Book with One Author

Ondaatje, Michael. <u>The English Patient</u>. Toronto: Vintage Books, 1993.   MLA

Ondaatje, M. (1993). *The English patient.* Toronto: Vintage Books   APA

■ A Book with Two Authors

Finnbogason, Jack, and Al Valleau. <u>A Canadian Writer's Guide</u>. Toronto: Nelson, 1997.   MLA

Finnbogason, J., & Valleau, A. (1997). *A Canadian writer's guide.* Toronto: Nelson.   APA

Note that the APA system reverses the name of the second author and uses "&" instead of "and" between the names. In titles and subtitles, only the first word and proper nouns and adjectives are capitalized. Both the MLA and APA systems use the hanging indent for entries in the reference list. Start the first line of each entry flush to the left margin and indent all subsequent lines five spaces (hanging indent). Most software has automatic functions for creating hanging indents.

■ A Book with More Than Three Authors

Alder, Roger William, et al. <u>Mechanisms in Organic Chemistry</u>. New York: Wiley, 1971.   MLA

Alder, R. W., Finn, T., Bradley, M. A., & Li, A. W. (1971). *Mechanisms in organic chemistry.* New York: John Wiley.   APA

The MLA system permits the use of "et al." for four or more authors or editors (listing all authors is also permitted); the APA system gives up to and including six author or editor names in the reference list. Substitute "et al." for the seventh or more.

■ A Book with a Title That Includes Another Title

The MLA offers two options: You may omit underlining the embedded title, or you may set it off with quotation marks.

Tanner, John. <u>Anxiety in Eden: A Kierkegaardian Reading of</u> Paradise Lost. Oxford:
Oxford UP, 1992.

MLA

Tanner, John. <u>Anxiety in Eden: A Kierkegaardian Reading of "Paradise Lost."</u>
Oxford: Oxford UP, 1992.

MLA

The APA offers no guidelines for this situation. However, the general guidelines
for italics apply if you use the first option.

Tanner, J. (1992). *Anxiety in Eden: A Kierkegaardian Reading of* Paradise Lost.
Oxford: Oxford University Press.

APA

■ A Book with Corporate or Association Authorship

United Nations, Public Administration Division. <u>Local Government Training</u>. New
York: UN, 1968.

MLA

United Nations, Public Administration Division. (1968). *Local government training*.
New York: Author.

APA

When the author of the work is also the publisher, the APA system uses the word
"Author" following the place of publication. If the work is published by another
organization, its name replaces "Author."

■ An Edition Other Than the First

Waldman, Neil, and Sarah Norton. <u>Canadian Content</u>. 3rd ed. Toronto: Harcourt
Brace, 1996.

MLA

Waldman, N., & Norton, S. (1996). *Canadian content* (3rd ed.). Toronto: Harcourt
Brace.

APA

■ A Book in Two or More Volumes

Bartram, Henry C. <u>The Cavalcade of America</u>. 2 vols. New York: Knopf, 1959.

MLA

Bartram, H. C. (1959). *The cavalcade of America* (Vols. 1–2). New York: Alfred Knopf.

APA

■ A Reprint of an Older Work

Matthiessen, F. O. <u>American Renaissance: Art and Expression in the Age of
Emerson and Whitman</u>. 1941. New York: Oxford UP, 1970.

MLA

Matthiessen, F. O. (1970). *American renaissance: Art and expression in the age of
Emerson and Whitman*. New York: Oxford University Press. (Original work
published 1941)

APA

■ **A Book with an Editor Rather Than an Author**

Toye, William, ed. <u>The Oxford Companion to Canadian Literature</u>. Toronto: Oxford,
    1983.   `MLA`

Toye, W. (Ed.). (1983). *The Oxford companion to Canadian literature*. Toronto: `APA`
    Oxford.

■ **A Book with Both an Author and an Editor**

Conrad, Joseph. <u>Heart of Darkness</u>. Ed. Robert Hampson. London: Penguin, 1995.   `MLA`

Conrad, J. (1995). *Heart of darkness*. (R. Hampson, Ed.). London: Penguin. (Original   `APA`
    work published 1902)

■ **A Translation**

Beauvoir, Simone de. <u>All Said and Done</u>. Trans. Patrick O'Brian. New York: Putnam,   `MLA`
    1974.

Beauvoir, S. de. (1974). *All said and done* (P. O'Brian, Trans.). New York: G. P. Putnam.   `APA`
    (Original work published 1972)

■ **An Essay or Chapter in a Collection of Works by One Author**

Woolf, Virginia. "The Lives of the Obscure." <u>The Common Reader</u>, First Series. New   `MLA`
    York: Harcourt, 1925. 111–18.

Woolf, V. (1925). The lives of the obscure. In V. Woolf, *The common reader*, first   `APA`
    series (pp. 111–118). New York: Harcourt Brace.

■ **An Essay or Chapter in an Anthology**

Blaise, Clark. "A Class of New Canadians." <u>Pens of Many Colours: A Canadian</u>   `MLA`
    <u>Reader</u>. Ed. Eva C. Karpinski and Ian Lea. Toronto: Harcourt Brace Jovanovich,
    1993: 218–26.

Blaise, C. (1993). A class of new Canadians. In E. C. Karpinski and I. Lea (Eds.),   `APA`
    Pens of many colours: a Canadian reader (pp. 218–226). Toronto: Harcourt
    Brace Jovanovich.

Periodicals

Periodicals include newspapers, popular magazines, and specialized occupational and scholarly journals. The basic information for a periodical article
includes the name of the article's author, the name of the periodical, the title of
the article, the date of publication, the page range of the entire article, and, for
scholarly journals, the volume number of the periodical. Again, the order of

presentation depends on the documentation system used. The MLA and APA systems capitalize periodical titles identically; however, the MLA style omits an introductory *the* from these titles. As illustrated by our example for a signed article in a daily newspaper, the two systems follow different formats for showing when an article does not appear on consecutive pages. Note also that the systems capitalize the titles of articles differently and that the APA system precedes page numbers for newspaper articles with "p." or "pp."

■ An Article in a Scholarly Journal Consecutively Paged through the Entire Volume

MLA   Pfennig, David. "Kinship and Cannibalism." Bioscience 47 (1997): 667–75.

APA   Pfennig, D. (1997). Kinship and cannibalism. *Bioscience, 47,* 667–675.

■ An Article in a Scholarly Journal That Pages Each Issue Separately

MLA   Block, Joel W. "Sodom and Gomorrah: A Volcanic Disaster." Journal of Geological Education 23.5 (1976): 74–77.

APA   Block, J. W. (1976). Sodom and Gomorrah: A volcanic disaster. *Journal of Geological Education, 23*(5), 74–77.

■ An Unsigned Article in a Scholarly Journal

MLA   "Baby, It's Cold Inside." Science 276 (1997): 537–38.

APA   Baby, it's cold inside. (1997). *Science, 276,* 537–538.

■ A Signed Article in an Occupational or a Popular Magazine

MLA   Gopnik, Adam. "The Good Soldier." New Yorker 24 Nov. 1997: 106–14.

APA   Gopnik, A. (1997, November 24). The good soldier. *The New Yorker, 73,* 106–114.

■ An Unsigned Article in an Occupational or a Popular Magazine

MLA   "Robot Productivity." Production Engineering May 1982: 52–55.

APA   Robot productivity. (1982, May). *Production Engineering, 29,* 52–55.

■ A Signed Article in a Daily Newspaper

MLA   Aird, Elizabeth. "Take Men as Sexual Victims, Please." Vancouver Sun 14 February 1998:A5.

APA   Aird, E. (1998, February 14). Take men as sexual victims, please. *Vancouver Sun,* p. A5.

■ An Unsigned Article in a Daily Newspaper

"The Arithmetic of Terrorism." <u>Washington Post</u> 14 Nov. 1997:A26.

MLA

The arithmetic of terrorism. (1997, November 14). *Washington Post*, p. A26.

APA

Encyclopedia Articles

When documenting familiar works, such as *The Canadian Encyclopedia,* the basic information for the MLA system includes the name of the article's author if known, the title of the article, the name of the encyclopedia, and the date of the edition.

Sobieszek, Robert A. "Photography." <u>World Book Encyclopedia</u>. 1991 ed.

MLA

The APA system requires additional information for all encyclopedia citations, as does the MLA system when less familiar publications are documented. Again, the order of presentation differs for the two systems.

Fears, J. Rufus. "Emperor's Cult." <u>Encyclopedia of Religion</u>. Ed. Mircea Eliade. 16 vols. New York: Macmillan, 1987.

MLA

Fears, J. R. (1987). Emperor's cult. In *The encyclopedia of religion* (Vol. 5, pp. 101–102). New York: Macmillan.

APA

For an anonymous article, references for both the MLA and APA systems begin with the article's title. With the APA system, position the publication date, within parentheses, after this title. The remaining format is identical to the citations with an author.

Government Documents

The basic information for a federal, provincial, or foreign government publication that is documented using the MLA system includes the name of the author, the title of the publication, the name of the government and the agency issuing the publication, the place of publication, the name of the printing group, if known, and the date. If no author is named, begin by identifying the government and then cite the government agency as the author. The APA system presents similar information but omits the government name, adds a cataloguing code where one exists, and follows a different order of presentation.

Helix, Jefferson. <u>Environmental Impact of Fish Farming in British Columbia</u>. British Columbia Ministry of Environment. A Discussion Paper: Queen's Printer for British Columbia, 1997.

MLA

Helix, J. (1997). *Environmental Impact of Fish Farming in British Columbia.* British Columbia, Ministry of Environment. Victoria: Queen's Printer for British Columbia.

APA

MLA   Canada. Department of Finance. <u>Annual Report 1991–1992</u>. Ottawa: Queen's
      Printer, 1994.

APA   Canadian Department of Finance. (1993). *Annual Report 1991–1992*. Ottawa:
      Queen's Printer.

MLA   United States. Cong. Office of Technology Assessment. <u>The Biology of Mental
      Disorders</u>. 102nd Cong., 2nd sess. Washington: GPO, 1992.

APA   U.S. Congress, Office of Technology Assessment. (1992). *The biology of mental
      disorders* (SUDOCS No. Y3.T22/2:2/B57/10). Washington, DC: U.S. Government
      Printing Office.

Other Sources

The information presented and the order of presentation depend on the type
of source and the documentation system.

■ Book Reviews

MLA   Koenig, Rhoda. "Billy the Kid." Rev. of <u>Billy Bathgate</u>, by E. L. Doctorow. <u>New York</u>
      20 Feb. 1989: 20–21.

APA   Koenig, R. (1989, February 20). Billy the Kid [Review of the book *Billy Bathgate*].
      New York, 21, 20–21.

If the review is untitled, follow the above formats but omit the missing
element.

■ Published Interviews

MLA   Noriega, Manuel. "A Talk with Manuel Noriega." By Felipe Hernandez. <u>News Report</u>
      20 Mar. 1997: 28–30.

The APA system does not include a documentation format for published interviews. If you are using the APA format and your paper includes material from a
published interview, we suggest that you document as follows:

APA   Hernandez, F. (1997, Mar. 20). A talk with Manuel Noriega. [Interview with Manuel
      Noriega]. *News Report*, 15, 28–30.

If the interview is untitled, then in place of a title, use the word "Interview,"
without quotation marks or underlining, for the MLA system. For the APA system, follow the example above, omitting any mention of a title.

■ **Personal Interviews**

If you conducted the interview yourself and are using the MLA system, start with the name of the person interviewed and follow it with the kind of interview and the date conducted.

Newman, Paul. Personal interview. 19 May 2005. | MLA |

For the APA system, a personal interview is considered personal correspondence and is not included in the References list. Instead, use an in-text parenthetical citation. Include the name of the person interviewed, the notation "personal communication," and the date: (P. Newman, personal communication, May 19, 1997).

■ **Audiovisual Media**

Frankenstein. Dir. James Whale. Perf. Boris Karloff, John Boles, Colin Clive, and Mae | MLA |
    Clarke. Universal, 1931.

If you are interested in the contribution of a particular person, start with that person's name. Use the term *film* in MLA format, and use the same model for videocassette and DVD recordings.

Whale, James, dir. Frankenstein. Perf. Boris Karloff, John Boles, Colin Clive, and Mae | MLA |
    Clarke. Universal, 1931.

In the APA format, the citation begins with an individual's name and his or her contribution to the *motion picture* (use this term, not *film*). The country of origin (where it was made and released) is now required.

Whale, J. (Director). (1931). *Frankenstein* [Motion picture].United States: Universal. | APA |

■ **Television and Radio Programs**

Basic citations follow the formats below:

The Independent Eye. Prod. M. Paris and J. Robertson. Knowledge Network. Know, | MLA |
    Burnaby. 13 Feb. 1999.

Paris, M., & Robertson, J. (Producers). (1999, February 13). *The independent eye.* | APA |
    Burnaby, B.C.: Knowledge Network.

Use these formats when additional information is pertinent:

Peril at End House. By Agatha Christie. Dir. Renny Rye. Prod. Brian Eastman. Perf. | MLA |
    David Suchet and Hugh Fraser. Mystery. Introd. Diana Rigg. PBS. WKAR, East
    Lansing. 12 Aug. 1993.

Exton, C. (Script Writer), & Rye, R. (Director). (1993). *Peril at End House* [Television | APA |
    series episode]. In B. Eastman (Producer), *Mystery*. Washington, DC: Public
    Broadcasting Service.

With the APA system, the scriptwriter's and the director's names appear in the author's position. In-text references begin with the first name in the bibliographical reference (for example, Exton, 1993).

■ Sound Recordings

MLA Smith, Bessie. <u>The World's Greatest Blues Singer</u>. LP. Columbia, 1948.

In MLA style, list the medium (Audiocassette, LP, etc.) only when the recording is not a CD. If you mention the name of a particular item on the sound recording, set it off with quotation marks, as shown below. If the recording date is important, place it before the medium.

MLA Smith, Bessie. "Downhearted Blues." By Alberta Watson. <u>The World's Greatest Blues Singer</u>. LP. Columbia, 1948.

The APA format requires identification of all formats, including a CD.

APA Smith, B. (1948). *The Essential Bessie Smith*. [CD]. New York: Columbia Records.

Recording dates, if different from the copyright year, follow the entry, enclosed in parentheses, with no final period.

APA Hunter, A. (1921). Downhearted blues [Recorded by B. Smith]. *On the world's greatest blues singer* [LP]. New York: Columbia Records.

■ Computer Software

MLA <u>Data Desk</u>. Computer software. Vers. 6.0. Data Description, 1997.

APA *Data Desk* (Version 6.0) (1977). [Computer software]. Ithaca, NY: Data Description, Inc.

In the APA system, only specialized software or computer programs are listed in the References. Standard commercial software and languages should be cited by their proper name and version in the text itself.

■ CD-ROMs and Other Databases

MLA Norman, J. L. "Barcelona." <u>Software Toolworks Multimedia Encyclopedia</u>. CD-ROM. Disc 1. Danbury, CT: Grolier, 1996.

APA Norman, J. L. (1992). Barcelona. *Software Toolworks Multimedia Encyclopedia* [CD-ROM]. Boston: Grolier.

The APA Manual (5th ed.) takes the view that all aggregated databases are the same type of source, regardless of the format or manner of access (CD-ROM, library or university server, or online Web supplier). Follow the model above when you need to cite an entire CD-ROM (not a document from it). In a reference to information taken from a database (even a CD-ROM), give a "retrieval statement" containing the date you retrieved the document, article, piece of data, as well as the full correct name of the database. When you retrieve information from an online database, end the entry with a correct and complete URL for the specific document or version. In this case, the name of the database is omitted, unless this information will help in the retrieval from a large or complex website. (See online models in the next section.)

Online Sources

The most recent edition of the *Publication Manual of the American Psychological Association* provides the APA's newest guidelines for documenting online sources. You can consult the association's website for up-to-date information about citing electronic sources:

www.apastyle.org/elecref.html

The examples here follow the latest guidelines for the MLA (2003) and APA (2001). Be sure to ask your instructor which format to follow, and then use that format consistently. Often source data from a website are incomplete, perhaps lacking an author, a title or any recognizable page or paragraph number. Include all the available information. The recommendation from APA is that you cite document locations rather than homepages and that the referenced address (URL) actually works for that file. Remember: Your goal is to enable your reader to find the source. When the actual address (URL) is extremely long or unusable, the MLA allows you to use the homepage for your source.

■ Books on the World Wide Web

The basic information for an electronic book documented by the MLA system includes the name(s) of the author(s), if known; the title of the book; the place and date of original publication, if applicable; the electronic site, if named; the date of electronic publication if the online version has never been published in print, or if it is part of a scholarly project; the sponsor of the site; the date the material was retrieved; and the online address.

Locke, John. An Essay Concerning Human Understanding. London, 1690. Institute | MLA

of Learning Technologies. 1995. Columbia U. 24 June 2000 <http://

www.ilt.columbia.edu/projects/digitexts/locke/understanding/title.html>.

The APA *Publication Manual* does not show a model for documenting online books; however, the *Manual* treats all nonperiodical internet documents in one category, including multipage or multipart documents, such as books or reports. Follow the general guidelines for a printed book and conclude with appropriate electronic source information, as modelled here.

Locke, John. (1995). *An essay concerning human understanding.* New York: | APA

Columbia University. (Original work published 1690). Retrieved June 24, 2000,

from http://www.ilt.columbia.edu/projects/digitexts/locke/understanding/

title.html

When some of the basic information is not provided, use whatever is available.

MLA   Chaney, Walter J., William J. Diehm, and Frank Seeley. <u>The Second 50 Years: A</u>
<u>Reference Manual for Senior Citizens</u>. Weed, CA: London Circle, 1999.
8 August 2000 <http://londoncircle.com/2d50.html>.

APA   Chaney, W. J., Diehm, W. J., & Seeley, F. (1999). *The second 50 years: A reference*
manual for senior citizens. Weed, CA: London Circle. Retrieved August 8, 2000,
from http://londoncircle.com/2d50.html

To cite part of an electronic book, place the part's title after the name(s) of the author(s) or, in APA format, after the date of publication. APA also cites a chapter or section identifier following the title of the complete document.

MLA   Dawson, Marie. Introduction. <u>Methods of Sociological Investigation</u>. New York:
Harmon, 1997. 6 Sept. 2000 <http://www.harmon.edu/edu-books.html>.

APA   Trochim, W. M. K. (2002). Language of research. In *The research methods know-*
ledge base (Foundations sec.). Cincinnati, OH: Atomic Dog. Retrieved
September 6, 2003, from http://www.trochim.human.cornell.edu/kb/language.htm

■ Periodicals on the World Wide Web

Periodicals online include specialized occupational and scholarly journals, popular magazines, newspapers, and newsletters. The basic information for a periodical includes the author's name, if known; the title of the article; the title of the periodical; the volume number; the date the article was published; the number of paragraphs in the article or its page numbers; the date the material was retrieved; and the online address.

The APA recommends using the models for print periodicals when documenting online articles that do not vary from their printed versions. In such cases, add [Electronic version] after the title and before the period to complete the citation. When the electronic format alters the printed version (e.g., no pagination, added data or links), then cite as an online document, using a retrieval statement and the name of the database and/or the URL. APA guidelines ask for the identification of the server or the website in a retrieval statement only when it would be helpful for finding the source; for example, it is not necessary to state "Retrieved from the World Wide Web" since it is the most common access point to the internet.

MLA   Cervetti, Nancy. "In the Breeches, Petticoats, and Pleasures of Orlando." <u>Journal of</u>
<u>Modern Literature</u> 20.2 (1996): 32 pars. 8 Jan. 1998 <http://www.indiana.edu/
~iupress/journals/mod-art2.html>.

APA   Cervetti, N. (1996). In the breeches, petticoats, and pleasures of Orlando. *Journal*
of Modern Literature, 20(2). Retrieved January 8, 1998 from http://
www.indiana.edu/~iupress/journals/mod-art2.html

Navarro, Mireya. "Women in Sports Cultivating New Playing Fields." New York Times on the Web 13 Feb. 2001. 22 Feb. 2001 <http://www.nytimes.com>.

MLA

Navarro, M. (2001, February 13). Women in sports cultivating new playing fields. *New York Times on the Web*. Retrieved February 22, 2001, from http://www.nytimes.com/2001/02/13/sports/13WOME.html

APA

"No Link Found in Violence, Videos." Boston Globe Online 8 Aug. 2000. 27 Aug. 2000 <http://www.boston.com>.

MLA

No link found in violence, videos. (2000, August 8). *Boston Globe Online*, p. A14. Retrieved August 27, 2000, from http://www.boston.comdailyglobe2/...nk_found_in_violence_videos+.shtml

APA

Oakes, Jeannie. "Promotion or Retention: Which One Is Social?" Harvard Education Letter. Jan.–Feb. 1999. 7 pars. 8 Aug. 2000 <http://www.edletter.org>.

MLA

Oakes, J. (1999, January–February). Promotion or retention: Which one is social? *Harvard Education Letter*. Retrieved August 8, 2000, from http://www.edletter.org/past/issues/1999-jf/promotion.shtml

APA

■ Periodicals Accessed through an Online Library Service or Large Network Provider

Increasingly, full-text articles are available online at libraries or at home through services provided by private institutions such as LexisNexis, ProQuest Direct, or public institutions like governments, that maintain extensive databases. These services may or may not provide an online address for accessed material. If you know the service's homepage, and you're documenting by the MLA system, cite the author's name, if known; the title of the article; the title of the periodical; the date the article was published; the page numbers for the article; the name of the database; the name of the library service; the name of the library; the date the material was accessed; and the online address of the service's homepage.

Clemetson, Lynette. "A Ticket to Private School." Newsweek 27 Mar. 2000. LexisNexis. Ferris State University Library Web Database Access. 5 May 2000 <http://library.ferris.edu/databaseframes.html>.

MLA

The APA documentation system provides the same information but omits any online addresses except World Wide Web addresses.

Clemetson, L. (2000, March 27). A ticket to private school. *Newsweek*. Retrieved May 5, 2000, from Ferris State University Library Web Database Access (LexisNexis).

APA

For MLA style, when no online address is provided, it is necessary to identify the keyword(s) you used to find the material.

MLA   Wilson-Smith, Anthony. "Hockey Night in Reality." <u>Maclean's</u> 14 Oct. 2002:4. <u>EBSCO</u>
        <u>Host Research Databases</u>. Kwantlen University College Online Article Index. 18
        Oct. 2002. Key words: Hockey; Canada.

APA   Wilson-Smith, A. (2002, October 14). Hockey night in reality. *Maclean's*. Retrieved
        October 18, 2002, from Kwantlen University College Online Article Index
        (EBSCO Host Research Databases). Key words: Hockey; Canada.

■ **Encyclopedia Articles**

The basic information for an encyclopedia article accessed through the World
Wide Web includes the author's name, if known; the title of the article; the
name of the encyclopedia; and the date of the edition, and the online address.
MLA style also names the vendor. For encyclopedia articles accessed through a
CD-ROM, name this media after the title of the database for MLA format. The
format is not required information in APA style, unless this information is
needed for retrieval.

MLA   Daniel, Ralph Thomas. "The History of Western Music." <u>Britannica Online:</u>
        <u>Macropaedia</u>. 1995. Encyclopaedia Britannica. 14 June 1995
        <http://www.eb.com:180/cgi-bin/g:DocF=macro/5004/45/0.html>.

APA   Daniel, R. T. (1995). The history of western music. In *Britannica Online*:
        Macropaedia. Retrieved June 14,1995, from http://www.eb.com:180/
        cgi-bin/g:DocF=macro/5004/45/0.html

■ **Government Documents**

The basic information for a government document includes the name of the
author, if known; the title; the name of the government and agency issuing the
document; the place of publication and printing group, if known; the date of
publication; the date the material was retrieved; and the online address. If no
author is given, begin by identifying the government and then give the government agency as the author. For the APA system, omit the government name, and
add a cataloguing code if one is available.

MLA   Georgia State. Probation Division of the Georgia Department of Corrections.
        <u>Alternatives to Incarceration</u>. 1 July 1997. 3 Feb. 1998 <http://www.harvard.edu/
        ~innovat/aiga87.html>.

APA   Probation Division of the Georgia Department of Corrections. (1997, July 1).
        Alternatives to Incarceration (CSP No. 239875). Retrieved February 3, 1998
        from http://www.harvard.edu/~innovat/aiga87.html

■ **Personal Home Page**

The basic information for a personal homepage documented according to the
MLA style system includes the name of its originator, if known; the title of the

site, if any (use *Home page* or other such description if no title is given); the date the material was retrieved from the site; and the online address (URL).

Lanthrop, Olin. Home page. 24 June 2000 <http://www.cognivis.com/olin/photos.htm>.   MLA

The APA *Manual* offers no specific guidelines for personal homepages. We suggest that you follow the pattern below, which conforms to general APA practice. Note that the APA system, unlike the MLA, includes the date of the latest webpage revision, if known, in parentheses.

Lanthrop, O. (2000, May 28). Homepage. Retrieved June 24, 2000, from http://   APA
cognivis.com/olin/photos.htm

■ Newsgroups, Electronic Mailing Lists, and Email

MLA gives guidelines for including newsgroups, electronic mailing lists (sometimes called listservs), and email within the Works Cited list. APA format treats email as personal communications, which are cited in parentheses in the text only. Newsgroups, online forums, discussion groups, and electronic mailing lists that maintain archives can be cited in the References, but the APA cautions that there must be a scholarly purpose. When in doubt, treat these sources as a personal communication.

Corelli, Aldo. "Colleges and Diversity." Online posting. 20 Apr. 1993. <learning-   MLA
house.michigan.edu>.

Nicholson, Brad. "Casino Gambling." Email to author. 2 Feb. 2001. . . . as reported in   MLA
his study (B. Nicholson, personal communication, February 2, 2001).

Trehub, A. (2002, January 28). The conscious access hypothesis [Msg. 18].   APA
Message posted to University of Houston Psyche Discussion Forum:
http://listserv.uh.edu/cgi-bin/wa?A2=ind0201&L=psyche-b&
F=&S=&P=2334

EXERCISE

1. **Using the MLA system, write a proper reference for each of the following sets of information:**

   a. A book entitled Gas Conditioning Fact Book. The book was published in 1962 by Dow Chemical Company in Midland, Michigan. No author is named.

   b. An unsigned article entitled Booze Plays a Big Role in Car Crashes. The article was published in the November 28, 1997, state edition of the Detroit News. It appears on page 2 of section C.

   c. An essay written by C. Wright Mills and entitled The Competitive Personality. The essay appeared in a collection of Mills's writings entitled Power, Politics, and People. The collection was published in 1963 by Ballantine Books in New York. The book is edited and introduced by Irving Louis Horowitz. The essay appears on pages 263 through 273.

d. An unsigned article entitled Global Warming Fears on Rise. The article was published in the October 25, 1997, issue of Newswatch magazine. It appears on pages 29 to 31.

e. A book written by Guy Vanderhaeghe and entitled The Englishman's Boy. The book was published in 1996 by McClelland & Stewart Inc. in Toronto.

f. A book written by Kate Chopin and entitled The Awakening. The book, edited by Margaret Culley, was published in 1976 by W. W. Norton and Company in New York.

g. An article written by James E. Cooke and entitled Alexander Hamilton. The article appears on pages 31 and 32 of the World Book Encyclopedia, Volume 9, published in 1996.

h. An article written by Sarah McBride and entitled Young Deadbeats Pose Problems for Credit-Card Issuers. The article was published in the November 28, 1997, Toronto edition of The Globe and Mail. It appears on pages 1 and 6 of section B.

i. A book written by Magdalena Dabrowski and Rudolph Leopold and entitled Egon Schiele. The book was published in 1997 by the Yale University Press in New Haven, Connecticut.

j. A book written by Jean Descola and entitled A History of Spain. The book, translated by Elaine P. Halperin, was published in 1962 by Alfred A. Knopf in New York.

k. An article written by John T. Flanagan and Raymond L. Grimer and entitled Mexico in American Fiction to 1850. The article was published in 1940 in a journal called Hispania. It appears on pages 307 through 318. The volume number is 23.

l. A Canadian government document entitled Marine Fisheries Review. It was published by the Federal Department of Fisheries in 1993. No author is given.

m. A book written by David Kahn and entitled The Codebreakers. The second edition of the book was published in 1996 by Scribner's in New York.

n. A book written by Joseph Blotner and entitled Faulkner: A Biography. The book was published in two volumes in 1974 by Random House in New York.

o. An article written by Calvin Tompkins and entitled The Importance of Being Elitist. The article was published in the November 24, 1997, issue of The New Yorker. It appears on pages 58 through 69.

p. A book written by Thomas Beer and entitled Stephen Crane: A Study in American Letters. The book was published in 1923 and reprinted in 1972 by Octagon Books in New York.

q. A review of a book written by Jacques Barzun and entitled The Culture We Deserve. The review, by Beth Winona, appeared in the March 1989 issue of American Issues magazine and was titled Barzun and Culture. It appeared on pages 46 through 50.

r. An interview of playwright Neil Simon. The interview was entitled Neil Simon on the New York Theater and appeared in the September 3, 1997, issue of the Long Island News, on pages C4–5. The interviewer was Pearl Barnes.

s. A film entitled Casablanca. The film was directed by Michael Curtiz and starred Humphrey Bogart, Ingrid Bergman, Claude Rains, and Paul Henreid. It was released in 1942 by Warner Brothers.

t. A television program entitled Grizzly. It appeared on CBUT, Vancouver, on February 3, 1997. The station is part of the CBC.

2. **Prepare a proper MLA entry for each of the works you plan to use in writing your paper.**

HANDLING IN-TEXT CITATIONS

Both the MLA and APA systems use notations that appear within the text and are set off by parentheses. The systems are illustrated by the following examples.

Basic Citation Form

For the MLA system, the citation consists of the last name of the author and the page numbers of the publication in which the material originally appeared. The APA system adds the year to the citation. At the writer's option, the items may be grouped together or separated, as shown in the following examples. The bibliographic references preceding the passages follow the MLA format.

- **Bibliographic Reference**

Rothenberg, Randall. "Life in Cyburbia." <u>Esquire</u> Feb. 1996: 56–63.

- **Passage and Citation**

A mania for the Internet has invaded many important aspects of our culture. Newspapers run stories on it, businesses have rushed to set up websites, and the Speaker of the House of Representatives has stated that even our poorest children have a stake in the Internet (Rothenberg 59).

> MLA

Rothenberg states that a mania for the Internet has invaded many important aspects of our culture. Newspapers run stories on it, businesses have rushed to set up websites, and the Speaker of the House of Representatives has stated that even our poorest children have a stake in the Internet (59).

> MLA

. . . our poorest children have a stake in the Internet (Rothenberg, 1996, p. 59).

> APA

Rothenberg (1996) states . . . have a stake in the Internet (p. 59).

> APA

- **Bibliographic Reference**

Weider, Benjamin, and David Hapgood. <u>The Murder of Napoleon</u>. New York: Congdon, 1982.

> MLA

■ **Passage and Citation**

MLA

Four different autopsy reports were filed. All the reports agreed that there was a cancerous ulcer in Napoleon's stomach, but none of them declared that the cancer was the cause of death. Nevertheless, cancer has become accepted as the cause (Weider and Hapgood 72).

APA

. . . Nevertheless, cancer has become accepted as the cause (Weider & Hapgood, 1982, p. 72).

If a source has more than three authors (more than five for the APA), use "et al.," meaning "and others," for all but the first-named one.

■ **Bibliographic Reference**

Baugh, Albert C., et al. <u>A Literary History of England</u>. New York: Appleton, 1948.

■ **Passage and Citation**

MLA

Although no one knows for certain just when Francis Beaumont and John Fletcher started collaborating, by 1610 they were writing plays together (Baugh et al. 573).

APA

. . . writing plays together (Baugh et al., 1948, p. 573).

Authors with the Same Last Name

If your citations include authors with the same last name, use the initials of their first names to distinguish them.

■ **Bibliographic References**

Adler, Jerry. "Search for an Orange Thread." <u>Newsweek</u> 16 June 1980: 32–34.

Adler, William L. "The Agent Orange Controversy." <u>Detroit Free Press</u> 18 Dec. 1979, state ed.: B2.

■ **Passage and Citation**

MLA

As early as 1966, government studies showed that dioxin-contaminated 2,4,5-T caused birth defects in laboratory animals. Later studies also found that this herbicide was to blame for miscarriages, liver abscesses, and nerve damage (J. Adler 32).

APA

. . . miscarriages, liver abscesses, and nerve damage (J. Adler, 1980, p. 32).

Separate Works by the Same Author

If your references include two or more works by the same author, add shortened forms of the titles to your in-text citation if you follow the MLA system. Underline shortened book titles and use quotation marks around article and essay titles. For the APA system, use the conventional name-date-page number entry.

■ Bibliographic References

Mullin, Dennis. "After U.S. Troops Pull Out of Grenada." <u>U.S. News & World Report</u> 14 Nov. 1983: 22–25.

---. "Why the Surprise Move in Grenada—and What Next." <u>U.S. News & World Report</u> 7 Nov. 1983: 31–34.

■ Passage and Citation

As the rangers evacuated students, the marines launched another offensive at Grand Mal Bay, then moved south to seize the capital and free the governor (Mullin, "Why the Surprise" 33).

> MLA

. . . and free the governor (Mullin, 1983b, p. 33).

> APA

As the APA example illustrates, if the two works appeared in the same year, put an "a" or a "b," without quotes, after the date to identify whether you are referring to the first or second entry for that author in the bibliography.

Two Separate Sources for the Same Citation

If two sources provide essentially the same information and you wish to mention both in one parenthetical citation, alphabetize them according to their authors' last names, group them together with a semicolon between them, and position the citation as you would any other citation.

■ Bibliographic References

Bryce, Bonnie. "The Controversy over Funding Community Colleges." <u>Detroit Free Press</u> 13 Nov. 1988, state ed.: A4.

Warshow, Harry. "Community College Funding Hits a Snag." Grand Rapids Press 15 Nov. 1988, city ed.: A2.

■ Passage and Citation

In contending that a 3 percent reduction in state funding for community colleges would not significantly hamper their operations, the governor overlooked the fact that community college enrollment was expected to jump by 15 percent during the next year (Bryce A4; Warshow A2).

> MLA

APA

. . . enrollment was expected to jump by 15 percent during the next year (Bryce, 1988, p. A4; Warshow, 1988, p. A2).

Unsigned References

When you use a source for which no author is given, the in-text citation consists of all or part of the title, the appropriate page numbers, and, for the APA system, the date.

■ **Bibliographic Reference**

"Money and Classes." Progressive Oct. 1997: 10.

■ **Passage and Citation**

MLA

According to the General Accounting Office, repairing the country's dilapidated school buildings would carry a price tag of over 110 billion dollars. Furthermore, constructing the 6000 buildings needed to end classroom overcrowding would cost many billions more ("Money and Classes" 10).

APA

. . . many billions more ("Money and Classes," 1997, p. 10).

Citing Quotations

When the quotation is run into the text, position the citation as shown below.

■ **Bibliographic Reference**

Schapiro, Mark. "Children of a Lesser God." Harper's Bazaar Apr. 1996: 205–6+.

■ **Passage and Citation**

MLA

U.N. investigators who have studied the extent of child labour in Third World countries estimate that "as many as 200 million children go to work rather than to school . . . making everything from clothing and shoes to handbags and carpets" (Schapiro 205).

APA

". . . handbags and carpets" (Schapiro, 1996, p. 205).

With longer, indented quotations, skip two horizontal spaces after the end punctuation and type the reference in parentheses.

■ **Bibliographic Reference**

Klymlicka, Will. "Immigrants, Multiculturalism and Citizenship." Strategies for Successful Writing. 2nd Canadian Edition. Ed. James A. Reinking, et al. Toronto: Pearson, 2006: 46–63.

■ **Passage and Citation**

One commentator offers this assessment of the focus of Canada's multiculturalism policy, which is often misunderstood by its critics:

> In reality, most of the focus of multiculturalism policy (and most of its fund-
> ing) has been directed to promoting civic participation in the larger
> society and to increasing mutual understanding and co-operation between
> the members of different ethnic groups. More generally, the multicultural-
> ism policy has never stated or implied that people are under any duty or
> obligation to retain their ethnic identity/practices "freeze-dried," or indeed
> to retain them at all. On the contrary, the principle that individuals should
> be free to choose whether to maintain their ethnic identity has been one of
> the cornerstones of the policy since 1971 and continues to guide existing
> multiculturalism programs. Multiculturalism is intended to make it possible
> for people to retain and express their identity with pride if they so choose,
> by reducing the legal, institutional, economic or societal obstacles to this
> expression. It does not penalize or disapprove of people who choose not
> to identify with their ethnic group, or describe them as poor citizens or as
> lesser Canadians. (Klymlicka 46)

> . . . describe them as poor citizens or as lesser Canadians. (Klymlicka,
> 2006, p. 46)

APA

Indirect Citations

If you use a quotation from person A that you obtained from a book or article
written by person B, or you paraphrase such a quotation, put "qtd. in" before the
name of the publication's author in the parenthetical reference.

■ **Bibliographic Reference**

Klein, Joe. "Ready for Rudy." New York 6 Mar. 1989: 30–37.

■ **Passage and Citation**

Rudolph Giuliani favors the death penalty for "the murder of a law-enforcement
officer, mass murder, a particularly heinous killing" but would impose it only
"when there is certainty of guilt well beyond a reasonable doubt" (qtd. in
Klein 37).

MLA

". . . there is certainty of guilt well beyond a reasonable doubt" (qtd. in Klein,
1989, p. 37).

APA

Authors Identified in Text

Sometimes you need to introduce a paraphrase, summary, or quotation with the name of its author. In this case, the page number may be positioned immediately after the name or follow the material cited.

■ Bibliographic Reference

Jacoby, Susan. "Waiting for the End: On Nursing Homes." <u>New York Times Magazine</u>
     31 Mar. 1974, city ed.: 80.

■ Passage and Citation

MLA	Susan Jacoby (80) sums up the grim outlook of patients in bad nursing homes by noting that they are merely waiting to die.
MLA	Susan Jacoby sums up the grim outlook of patients in bad nursing homes by noting that they are merely waiting to die (80).
APA	Susan Jacoby (1974, p. 80) sums up . . .
APA	Susan Jacoby (1974) sums up . . . waiting to die (p. 80).

EXERCISE *Using the MLA system, write a proper in-text citation for each of the bibliographic references you prepared for part 2. Assume that you have not used the author's name to introduce the material you cite.*

HANDLING QUOTATIONS

Set off quotations fewer than five lines long (fewer than forty words long for the APA system) with quotation marks and run them into the text of the paper. For longer quotations, omit the quotation marks and indent the material from the left-hand margin (five spaces for the APA system). Double-space the text. If you quote part or all of one paragraph, don't further indent the first line. If you quote two or more consecutive paragraphs, indent each one's first line three additional spaces (five for the APA system). Use single quotation marks for a quotation within a shorter quotation and double marks for a quotation within a longer, indented quotation. The following examples illustrate the handling of quotations. The documentation and indentation follow the MLA guidelines.

■ Short Quotation

     Ellen Goodman offers this further observation about writers who peddle formulas for achieving success through selfishness: "They are all Doctor Feelgoods, offering placebo prescriptions instead of strong medicine. They give us a way to live with ourselves, perhaps, but not a way to live with each other" (16).

■ Quotation within Short Quotation

The report further stated, "All great writing styles have their wellsprings in the personality of the writer. As Buffon said, 'The style is the man'" (Duncan 49).

■ Quotation within Longer, Indented Quotation

Barbara Tuchman's The Proud Tower presents a somewhat different view of the new conservative leaders:

> Besides riches, rank, broad acres, and ancient lineage, the new government also possessed, to the regret of the liberal opposition, and in the words of one of them, "an almost embarrassing wealth of talent and capacity." Secure in authority, resting comfortably on their electoral majority in the House of Commons and on a permanent majority in the House of Lords, of whom four-fifths were conservatives, they were in a position, admitted the same opponent, "of unassailable strength." (4)

Always provide some context for material that you quote. Various options exist. When you quote from a source for the first time, you might provide the author's full name and the source of the quotation, perhaps indicating the author's expertise as well. The passage just above omits the author's expertise; the passage below includes it.

> Writing in Newsweek magazine, Riena Gross, chief psychiatric social worker at Illinois Medical Center in Chicago, said, "Kids have no real sense that they belong anywhere or to anyone as they did ten or fifteen years ago. Parents have loosened the reins, and kids are kind of floundering" (74).

Or you might note the event prompting the quotation and then the author's name.

> Addressing a seminar at the University of Toronto, Dr. Joseph Pomeranz speculated that "acupuncture may work by activating a neural pain suppression mechanism in the brain" (324).

On other occasions you might note only the author's full name and expertise.

> Economist Richard M. Cybert, president of Carnegie-Mellon University, offers the following sad prediction about the steel industry's future: "It will never be as large an industry as it has been. There are a lot of plants that will never come back and many laborers that will never be rehired" (43).

When quoting from a source with no author given, introduce the quotation with the name of the source.

Commenting upon the problems that law enforcement personnel have in coping with computer crime, <u>Credit and Financial Management</u> magazine pointed out, "A computer crime can be committed in three hundredths of a second, and the criminal can be thousands of miles from the 'scene,' using a telephone" ("Computer Crime" 43).

After first citing an author's full name, use only the last name for subsequent references.

In answering the objections of government agencies to the Freedom of Information Act, Wellford commented, "Increased citizen access should help citizens learn of governmental activities that weaken our First Amendment freedoms. Some administrative inconvenience isn't too large a price to pay for that" (137).

Page numbers are not helpful when you cite passages from plays and poems since these literary forms are available in many editions. When you quote from a play, identify the act, scene, and line numbers. Use Arabic numbers separated by periods. Here's how to cite Act 2, Scene 1, lines 295–300 of Shakespeare's *Othello:*

> That Cassio loves her, I do well believe it;
> That she loves him, 'tis apt, and of great credit:
> The Moor, how be it that I endure him not,
> Is of a constant, loving, noble nature;
> And I dare think he'll prove to Desdemona
> A most dear husband. (<u>Othello</u> 2.1. 295–300)

When quoting from a short poem, use "line" or "lines" and the line number(s).

In "Dover Beach," Matthew Arnold offers this melancholy assessment of the state of religion:

> The Sea of Faith
> Was once, too, at the full, and round earth's shore
> Lay like the folds of a bright girdle furl'd.
> But now I only hear
> Its melancholy, long, withdrawing roar. (lines 21–25)

In quoting poetry that has been run into the text, use a slash (/) to indicate the shift from one line to the next in the original:

In his ode "To Autumn," Keats says that autumn is the "Season of mists and mellow fruitfulness, / Close bosom-friend of the maturing sun" (lines 1–2).

AVOIDING PLAGIARISM

While documenting your sources properly strengthens the authority of your writing, failing to document properly weakens your personal and academic or professional credibility. This failure to document, whether intentional or not, may be regarded as plagiarism.

Plagiarism is a form of academic dishonesty. It occurs when a writer uses another person's material without properly acknowledging the debt. Almost all students know that the most obvious forms of plagiarism—such as buying a paper from a paper mill—are unethical. Often, however, plagiarism happens because students are careless in their note taking, or because they simply don't understand what must be acknowledged and documented. In our computerized world, where we have become used to downloading music and sharing software, it might be tempting to rationalize that material from the internet is free for the taking. Some students might imagine that they can escape the obligation to cite sources by changing a word here or there, or cutting and pasting information from different sources. However, unless the material is clearly common knowledge that will not ever be questioned or challenged, any material from external sources, including the internet, must be cited. Both intentional and unintentional plagiarism are unacceptable.

Plagiarism is a serious ethical breach. It degrades the quality of education for students and for institutions. It is unfair to the majority of students who are struggling to learn the challenging task of incorporating relevant research into their own writing in a responsible way. Students who plagiarize cheat themselves of genuine learning; they are also robbing the original writer of due recognition.

The consequences of plagiarism are often severe. Depending on the school policy, students caught plagiarizing risk getting a zero for that assignment, failing the course, or even being suspended or expelled. In 2002, 44 business and economics students at a major B.C. university were suspended for plagiarizing a tutor's work; the suspensions were noted on the students' transcripts. Large groups of students at other Canadian universities have been suspended for academic dishonesty. Instructors who are used to reading student essays can usually notice when the voice of the writer changes, or when the quality of the writing is inconsistent. In addition, many schools have plagiarism detection software that helps instructors track plagiarism, even if it is just a few sentences that have been raided from a source. It's easy for professors to use search engines to check whether particular phrases, sentences, or paragraphs have been copied from websites—and many do.

Any summary, paraphrase, quotation, statistics, or graphics you include in your paper must be documented. The only types of information escaping this requirement are those listed below:

1. *Common knowledge.* Common knowledge is information that most educated people would know. For instance, there's no need to document a statement that the Pacific National Exhibition attracts thousands of visitors each year. However, if you include precise daily, monthly, or yearly figures, then documentation is necessary.

2. *Your own conclusions.* As you write your paper, you incorporate your own conclusions at various points. Such comments require no documentation. The same holds true for your own research. If you polled students on a campus issue, simply present the findings as your own.

3. *Facts found in many sources.* Facts such as the year of Shakespeare's death, the size of the national debt, and the location of the Taj Mahal need not be documented.

4. *Standard terms.* Terms widely used in a particular field require no documentation. Examples include such computer terms as *mouse, phishing,* and *download.*

Any piece of information not set off with quotation marks must be in your own words. Otherwise, even though you name your source, you are plagiarizing by presenting the original phrasing as your own.

The following passages illustrate the improper and proper use of source material in conveying James L. Buckley's thoughts on the potential environmental impact of development in the United States.

Original Passage

One might contend, of course, that our country's biological diversity is so great and the land is so developed—so criss-crossed with the works of man—that it will soon be hard to build a dam anywhere without endangering some species. But as we develop a national inventory of endangered species, we certainly can plan our necessary development so as to exterminate the smallest number possible . . .

James L. Buckley, "Three Cheers for the Snail Darter," *National Review,* September 14, 1979: 1144–45.

■ Plagiarism

Our country's biological diversity is so great and the land is so developed that it will soon be hard to build a dam anywhere without endangering some species. But as we develop a national inventory of endangered species, we certainly can plan our necessary development so as to exterminate the smallest number possible.

This writer has clearly plagiarized. The absence of Buckley's name and the failure to enclose his words in quotation marks create the impression that this passage is the student's own work.

■ Plagiarism

Our country's biological diversity is so great and the land so developed that in the near future we may pose a threat to some creature whenever we construct a dam. By developing a national inventory of endangered species, however, we can plan necessary development so as to preserve as many species as possible (Buckley 1144).

This version credits the ideas to Buckley, but the student has plagiarized by failing to put quotation marks around the phrasing (underlined above) that was copied from the original. As a result, readers will think that the passage represents the student's own wording.

■ **Proper Use of Original**

The United States has so many kinds of plants and animals, and it is so built up, that in the near future we may pose a threat to some living thing just by damming some waterway. If, however, Americans knew which of their nation's plants and animals were threatened, they could use this information to preserve as many species as they can (Buckley 1144).

This student has identified the author and used her own words. As a result, she has not plagiarized.

Students who are uncertain about what constitutes plagiarism are responsible to educate themselves. They may consult online sources such as:

■ "How Not to Plagiarize" (from the University of Toronto)
■ "Avoiding Plagiarism: Mastering the Art of Scholarship" (from the University of California at Davis) available at **www.plagiarism.org**

Whenever you are unsure whether material requires documentation, supply a reference. And always handle direct quotations by following the guidelines.

READER

Neil Bissoondath

No Place Like Home

Neil Bissoondath has written several critically acclaimed books of fiction and nonfiction that explore themes of migration, alienation, and identity. His works of fiction include A Casual Brutality, The Worlds Within Her, *and* The Unyielding Clamour of the Night. *Neil Bissoondath's provocative discussion of identity politics and multiculturalism,* The Cult of Multi-Culturalism in Canada *(1994), provides a broader and more in-depth discussion of the ideas and concerns raised in his essay "No Place Like Home,"* which is reproduced below.*

1   Three or four years into the new millennium, Toronto, Canada's largest city, will mark an unusual milestone. In a city of three million, the words "minorities" and "majority" will be turned on their heads and the former will become the latter.

2   Reputed to be the most ethnically diverse city in the world, Toronto has been utterly remade by immigration, just as Canada has been remade by a quarter century of multiculturalism.

3   It is a policy which has been quietly disastrous for the country and for immigrants themselves.

4   The stated purpose of Canada's *Multiculturalism Act* (1971) is to recognize "the existence of communities whose members share a common origin and their historic contribution to Canadian society". It promises to "enhance their development" and to "promote the understanding and creativity that arise from the interaction between individuals and communities of different origins." The bicultural (English and French) nature of the country is to be wilfully refashioned into a multicultural "mosaic."

5   The architects of the policy—the Government of then–Prime Minister Pierre Elliot Trudeau—were blind to the fact that their exercise in social engineering was based on two essentially false premises. First, it assumed that "culture" in the large sense could be transplanted. Second, that those who voluntarily sought a new life in a new country would *wish* to transport their cultures of origin.

6   But "culture" is a most complex creature; in its essence, it represents the very breath of a people. For the purposes of multiculturalism, the concept has been reduced to the simplest theatre. Canadians, neatly divided into "ethnic" and otherwise, encounter each other's mosaic tiles mainly at festivals. There's traditional music, traditional dancing, traditional food at distinctly untraditional prices, all of which is diverting as far as it goes—but such encounters remain at the level of a folkloric Disneyland.

7   We take a great deal of self-satisfaction from such festivals; they are seen as proof of our open-mindedness, of our welcoming of difference. Yet how easily we forget that none of our ethnic cultures seems to have produced poetry or literature or philosophy worthy of our consideration. How seductive it is, how reassuring, that Greeks are always Zorbas, Ukrainians always Cossacks: we come away with stereotypes reinforced.

**New Internationalist*, September 1998, Issue 305, p. 20+.

8   Not only are differences highlighted, but individuals are defined by those differences. There are those who find pleasure in playing to the theme, those whose ethnicity ripens with the years. Yet to play the ethnic, deracinated and costumed, is to play the stereotype. It is to abdicate one's full humanity in favour of one of its exotic features. To accept the role of ethnic is also to accept a gentle marginalization. It is to accept that one will never be just a part of the landscape but always a little apart from it, not quite belonging.

9   In exoticizing and trivializing cultures, often thousands of years old, by sanctifying the mentality of the mosaic-tile, we have succeeded in creating mental ghettos for the various communities. One's sense of belonging to the larger Canadian landscape is tempered by loyalty to a different cultural or racial heritage.

10   When, for instance, war broke out between Croatia and Serbia, a member of the Ontario legislature, who was of Croatian descent, felt justified in declaring: "I don't think I'd be able to live next door to a Serb." That he was speaking of a fellow Canadian was irrelevant. *Over there* mattered more than *over here*—and the cultural group dictated the loyalty. Ironic for a country that boasted about its leading role in the fight against apartheid.

11   Often between groups one looks in vain for the quality that Canadians seem to value above all—tolerance. We pride ourselves on being a tolerant country, unlike the United States, which seems to demand of its immigrants a kind of submission to American mythology. But not only have we surrendered a great deal of ourselves in pursuit of the ideal—Christmas pageants have been replaced by "Winterfests"; the antiracist Writers Union of Canada sanctioned a 1994 conference which excluded whites—but tolerance itself may be an overrated quality, a flawed ideal.

12   The late novelist Robertson Davies pointed out that *tolerance* is but a weak sister to *acceptance.* To tolerate someone is to put up with them; it is to adopt a pose of indifference. Acceptance is far more difficult, for it implies engagement, understanding, an appreciation of the human similarities beneath the obvious differences. Tolerance then is superficial—and perhaps the highest goal one can expect of Canadian multiculturalism.

13   Another insidious effect of this approach is a kind of provisional citizenship. When 100-metre sprinter Ben Johnson won a gold medal at the Seoul Olympics, he was hailed in the media as the great Canadian star. Days later, when the medal was rescinded because of a positive drug test, Johnson became the Jamaican immigrant—Canadian when convenient, a foreigner when not. Tolerated, never truly accepted, his exoticism always part of his finery, he quickly went from being one of *us* to being one of *them.*

14   This makes for an uneasy social fabric. In replacing the old Canada, based on British and French tradition, with a mosaic (individual tiles separated by cement), we have shaken our sense of identity. In a country over 130 years old, we are still uncertain who we are.

15   A major 1993 study found that 72 per cent of the population wants, as one newspaper put it, "the mosaic to melt." Canadians were found to be "increasingly intolerant" of demands for special treatment made by ethnic groups—a Chinese group who wanted a publicly funded separate school where their children would be taught in Chinese by Chinese teachers; a Muslim group who claimed the right to opt out of the Canadian judicial system in favour of Islamic law. Canadians wanted immigrants to adopt Canada's values and way of life.

16   Many immigrants agree. They recognize that multiculturalism has not served their interests. It has exoticized, and so marginalized, them, making the realization

of their dreams that much harder. The former rector of the Université du Québec à Montréal, Claude Corbo, himself the grandson of Italian immigrants, has pointed out that multiculturalism has kept many immigrants "from integrating naturally into the fabric of Canadian and Quebec society. . . . We tell people to preserve their original patrimony to conserve their values, even if these values are incompatible with those of our society."

17   Which leads to the other false premise on which multiculturalism is based. It assumes that people who choose to emigrate not only can but also *wish to* remain what they once were.

18   The act of emigration leaves no-one unscathed. From the moment you board a plane bound for a new land with a one-way ticket, a psychological metamorphosis begins—and the change occurs more quickly, more deeply and more imperceptibly than one imagines.

19   I arrived alone in Toronto from Trinidad in 1973, an 18-year-old with dreams but no experience of the world. A year later, I returned to Trinidad to visit my parents. Within days I realized the extent of the change that had come not only to me, but to all I had left behind. Even after so short a time, old friends had become new strangers, and old places remained only old places. Already Trinidad—its ways, its views, its very essences—was receding, becoming merely a memory of place and childhood experience. *Feeling* had already been wholly transferred to the new land, to this other country which had quickly become my home. Certainly, for others the process is slower and often less evident—but it is inexorable. The human personality is not immutable.

20   Multiculturalism, which asked that I bring to Canada the life I had in Trinidad, was a shock to me. I was seeking a new start in a land that afforded me that possibility. I was *not* seeking to live in Toronto as if I were still in Trinidad— for what would have been the point of emigration? I am far from alone in this. As the political scientist Professor Rias Khan of the University of Winnipeg put it: "People, regardless of their origin, do not emigrate to preserve their culture and nurture their ethnic distinctiveness. . . . Immigrants come here to become Canadians; to be productive and contributing members of their chosen society. . . . Whether or not I preserve my cultural background is my personal choice; whether or not an ethnic group preserves its cultural background is the group's choice. The state has no business in either."

21   The immigrant dream—of financial and social success; of carving out a place within the larger society—is grand in its simplicity. Requiring great courage, it is self-limiting on no level. All one asks is the freedom and fairness—through anti-discrimination legislation, if necessary—to fulfill one's potential. A vital part of that freedom is the latitude to recognize and welcome inevitable change in society and the migrant. One may treasure a private, personal identity built from family lore and experience, all the while pursuing the public integration vital to wider success. To be put in the position of either obliterating the past or worshipping it is, for the individual, an unnecessary burden that leads to a false and limiting theatre of the self.

22   Not long ago, my daughter's teacher wanted to know what kind of family the children in her first-grade class came from. For most of the children, born in Quebec City into francophone families that have been here for over 200 years, the answer was straightforward.

23   Then it was my daughter's turn. Her father, she explained, was born in Trinidad into an East Indian family; having lived in Canada for a long, long

time, he was Canadian. Her mother was born in Quebec City, a francophone. She herself was born in Montreal.

24   "Ahh!" the teacher exclaimed brightly, "So you're from a West Indian family!"

25   My daughter returned home deeply puzzled. At six years of age she had been, with the best of intentions, handed an identity crisis.

26   In some ways she was lucky. We were able to sort out her confusions. In other parts of the country—in Toronto or Vancouver—where ethnic identity has become a kind of fetish, my daughter would have had to deal with a far more complex proposal. To be true to her inherited ethnicities, she would be: Franco-Quebecoise-First Nations-Indian-Canadian. Indeed, for her to describe herself as simply "Canadian" with no qualifying hyphen would be almost antagonistic.

27   The weight of this hyphen was signalled as far back as 20 years ago by the feminist writer Laura Sabia when she said: "I was born and bred in this amazing land. I've always considered myself a Canadian, nothing more, nothing less, even though my parents were immigrants from Italy. How come we have all acquired a hyphen? We have allowed ourselves to become divided along the line of ethnic origins, under the pretext of the 'Great Mosaic.' A dastardly deed has been perpetuated upon Canadians by politicians whose motto is 'divide and rule. . . . I am a Canadian first and foremost. Don't hyphenate me."

28   Or, one might add, future generations.

29   Canadian multiculturalism has emphasized difference. In so doing, it has retarded the integration of immigrants into the Canadian mainstream while damaging Canada's national sense of self. Canada has an enviable record in dealing with racism; our society, while hardly perfect (we too have our racists of all colours), remains largely free of racial conflict. And yet we do ourselves a disservice in pursuing the divisive potential in multiculturalism. With an ongoing battle against separatism in Quebec, with east-west tensions, we are already a country uncomfortably riven. Our "mosaic" does not help us.

30   In recognition of its growing unpopularity, official multiculturalism has had its status downgraded from a ministry, to a directorate, to a department. Canada, for the foreseeable future, will continue to be a nation open to immigrants—and one committed to combating racism, sexism and the various other forms of discrimination we share with other societies. Beyond this, because of the damage already inflicted by multiculturalism, we need to focus on programs that seek out and emphasize the experiences, values and dreams we all share as Canadians, whatever our colour, language, religion, ethnicity or historical grievance. And pursue *acceptance* of others—not mere *tolerance* of them.

31   Whatever policy follows multiculturalism, it should support a new vision of Canadianness. A Canada where no one is alienated with hyphenation. A nation of cultural hybrids, where every individual is unique and every individual is a Canadian, undiluted and undivided. A nation where the following conversation, so familiar and so enervating to many of us, will no longer take place:

32   "What nationality are you?"

33   "Canadian."

34   "No, I mean, what nationality are you *really*?"

35   The ultimate goal must be a cohesive, effective society enlivened by cultural variety; able to define its place in the world. Only in this way might that member of the Ontario legislature and his neighbour no longer see each other as Serb and Croat but as Canadians with a great deal more in common than their politically sanctioned blindness allows them to perceive.

36　　In the end, immigration is a personal adventure. The process of integration that follows it is a personal struggle within a social context that may make the task either more or less difficult. Multiculturalism in Canada has the latter effect but it may matter very little, because integration—the remaking of the self within a new society with one's personal heritage as invaluable texture—is finally achieved in the depths of one's soul. Many Canadians, like me, have simply ignored multiculturalism, by living our lives as fully engaged with our new society as possible, secure in the knowledge of the rich family past that has brought us here.

37　　I will never forget the bright summer evening many years ago when, fresh off the plane from a trip to Europe, I stood on my apartment balcony gazing out at the Toronto skyline, at the crystal light emanating off Lake Ontario and beyond. I took a deep breath of the cooling evening air and knew, deep within my bones, that it was good to be home.

Lorna Crozier

Almost Human

In the following reading, Lorna Crozier provides graphic details that shock the reader into recognizing the plight of lab animals like chimpanzees.

Crozier is an award-winning Canadian poet. On the site www.randomhouse.ca/features/ droppedthreads/crozier.html, Crozier talks about herself and her work: "I was born in Saskatchewan and now live on Vancouver Island, where I teach at the University of Victoria. My books have won numerous awards, including the Governor General's Award for Poetry and two Pat Lowther Awards for the best book of poetry by a Canadian woman. I have sworn to remain a poet and never write fiction, but have discovered a growing attraction to the personal essay, which I think is an extended lyric poem with a few more rooms to wander in, a few more windows to let in the light."

The following selection is a heartfelt cry for humanity to consider how it treats its fellow creatures in the name of scientific investigation.

1　　The necropsy reports for Pablo and Annie cover two 8 1/2 by 11-inch pages in small print in the newsletter I receive in the mail. The footnotes explaining medical terms such as fibrosis, glomerulopathy and peritonitis take up two more. You realize the brutal significance of the length of these reports when you notice they are void of explanation. They merely state what the autopsies found.

2　　A brief translation of the medical language would simply say that Pablo died at age 31, and Annie a few months later at 43, because their systems shut down. What it wouldn't say is that they died because of the abuse they suffered in the past. It turned their livers to leather. It infected the lining of their lungs and abdomens. It created adhesions from scarring that limited blood flow, twisting Annie's intestine and causing gangrene, atrophying one of Pablo's testicles until it rotted inside him. Though the perpetrators' names are known, the evidence accumulated, no one will be called to account for this; no one will be charged with a crime. Perhaps this absence of justice is, ironically, a kind of warped justice, for surely it is not a few individuals but our whole species that should be put on trial.

3   Chimpanzees, like Annie and Pablo, are our closest relatives. They share almost 99 percent of our DNA. You get a sense of this affinity when you look at a chimpanzee staring back at the photographer who snapped its picture in the wild. You've seen this look before—in a person you know—your brother maybe, your friend, a child. You sense our kinship when you see a photo of a lean and smiling, grey-haired woman sitting under the trees with a group of playful chimpanzees, like a clutch of giggling children, some exposing their bellies to be tickled. The caption tells you this picture was taken in Tanzania's Gombe National Park, and the woman is the revered Jane Goodall, who has been studying chimpanzees in the wild for over 40 years and who has documented, among other things, that they, like humans, use tools.

4   A second set of pictures gives us a different sense of what it means to be almost human: a surrogate astronaut chimp helmeted and harnessed into a NASA space capsule, his eyes wide with what we'd call shock or terror; another in a Shriner-like fez riding a unicycle maniacally around a circus ring. The laughing crowd doesn't know she's been trained by beatings and electric shocks, nor that her teeth have been knocked out with a crowbar so she can't bite. Here's a second carnival chimp, now retired, with a lit cigarette in his pursed mouth, smoke curling from his small cage that sits outside a bar in Maineville, Ohio. And from a family photo album, here's a baby chimp dressed in a blue jumpsuit and rocked in the arms of his human mother, a bottle in the woman's hand. The name "Boom-Boom" and the date "June, 1963" are neatly printed below in white ink.

5   Five years later, we can see this same chimpanzee when he's too big and strong for his foster family to control. Photos from the archives of a research lab show us him and others like him strapped to steel tables for one of the several hundred biopsies they will endure before they are isolated in cement basement cages, their bodies used up.

6   There's blood in these pictures, white-suited men and scalpels. And when it's possible to see the chimpanzees' faces, heads lolling back or to the side, you don't want to look in their eyes. Their similarities to us, their 99 percent DNA match, has brought them here—far from the forests of their ancestors, far from rain and sun on their upturned faces, the trees' green canopies, the morning calls of birds, the communal hunts and sharing of food, the learning of tools, the gestures of grief, the chase games, the tickling, the familial love.

7   Pablo and Annie were stolen from their mothers in Africa, Annie around 1960 and Pablo 10 years later, and shipped to the United States where they became circus performers. Annie charmed children dressed like a little girl— except for the collar and chain around her neck. Pablo's incisors were pulled and his canine teeth filed to the gum to protect his trainer from skin-puncturing bites. After they became too big and strong to handle, as all chimps do become, including those we watch in movies and on TV, the circuses sold them to a facility in New York where they became lab animals. The Laboratory for Experimental Medicine and Surgery in Primates (LEMSIP) made good use of these two individuals. In his 10 years there, Pablo, who wouldn't offer his arm for the needle and flailed about his narrow cage to avoid it, was knocked down 220 times by sedating darts. Frequently they quilled his lip and forehead, piercing him with infections that eventually turned his dark face pale and freckled. He went through over 30 punch-liver, bone marrow and lymph node biopsies. The stress eventually led him to chew off one of his fingers. In 1992 he was injected with 10,000 times the standard infectious dose of HIV.

8   Annie became part of the breeding program at LEMSIP and was the first of her species to be successfully artificially inseminated. Chimpanzees and humans share a deep mother love for their children. Annie's were taken from her, sold to different labs, and she didn't see them again. However, she never lost her maternal compassion for younger chimpanzees. Like Pablo, Annie was also used in invasive biomedical research but less often than he, perhaps because she became anorexic and had to be treated repeatedly for wounds that occurred while she was being drugged.

9   Both Pablo and Annie would have died in the lab in solitary cages isolated from others of their kind. After decades of torture, they would have died alone. They would have died unmourned. But in 1997, LEMSIP closed. Most of the animals were sold to another research facility, but not Annie and Pablo. Their combined 38 years as test subjects came to an end.

10   Early one September morning, Annie, in her cage, was loaded into a horse-like trailer with six other chimpanzees, and pulled behind a blue and white pickup. After travelling hundreds of kilometres north, the truck stopped at the American/Canadian border. Tense exchanges of words and documents flew back and forth before the driver could pull out of customs and into Quebec on the final 40 minutes of the journey that would end at a farm south of Montreal. In a few months, Pablo would make the same 12-hour trip from New York with four others who, like him, had been infected with the HIV virus and used in AIDS research. In the pickup was the veterinarian Richard Allen. Before this final drive, he and his wife, Gloria Grow, the force behind the chimpanzees' release, had visited the lab to get to know the individuals who would be coming to their newly constructed sanctuary in Canada. It was Gloria's determination that freed the primates from their lives of isolation, terror and pain. In spite of protests from neighbours terrified of AIDS, road-blocks of municipal and federal regulations, and the huge responsibility of caring for such creatures, she rallied Richard, her two sisters and their husbands, the farm's hired man, and a group of volunteers to help her build, concrete block by concrete block, the facility they call the Fauna Foundation. When the truck and trailer pulled down the driveway to the farm, a new home was waiting for the chimpanzees.

11   Never again would the animals be darted, sliced open, infected. Never again would they find themselves in 5 by 5 by 7-foot cages. Immediately upon their arrival, they were moved from the trailer to a huge house built with chimpanzees in mind. It has capacious, high-ceilinged rooms large enough to run, jump, climb and swing in; rooms with windows full of rain or sun, breezes blowing through the screens. There are elevated platforms, sliding doors to isolate the chimpanzees or bring them together, open courts where they can play on high bars and ropes, private nooks where they can build sleep nests, and a barred outdoor verandah with picnic tables, hanging tires and tunnels. The facility is a place where chimpanzees can learn to be chimpanzees again. A place where Gloria, her family, staff and volunteers work day and night to bring them out of the pain-filled darkness that has been their experience with human beings.

12   It was there, three years ago, that I met the chimpanzees in the nearly tropical heat of a southern Quebec summer. The sanctuary at that time had 15 of them, including Pablo and Annie, who'd been in residence for two years. I'd gone there with my friend Anny Scoones, who owns a Vancouver Island farm not that different from Fauna before the chimps arrived. The Scoones property is

populated with naked-neck chickens, ducks, dogs, cats, goats, horses and calves—many of them strays or wounded creatures no one else wants. One of them, an old race horse named Kyle, had worn down his teeth from chewing at the wooden fence of his too-small enclosure after his days at the race track had ended. He had a good two years at the Scooneses' farm, wandering down the ditch along the driveway, knee-high in delicious grasses, his arthritis somehow less painful when he was in the wind and sun. Like those who work at Fauna, my friend spends much of her day taking care of the injured and unwanted. The sanctuary had invited her to visit, and she asked me to come along.

13   I had agreed with some reluctance. I am the kind of person who cries at dog food commercials, who insists my husband take the cats to the vet for their shots, and who turns off a nature program on TV before the final five minutes when the narrator informs us of the habitat destruction or poaching or simple human stupidity that is destroying another creature who is of commercial use or who is getting in our way. To put it simply, what we are doing to them makes me physically ill; some mornings it keeps me in bed. This is not something I am proud of. Closing my eyes to what is going on is cowardly, to say the least, and it makes me helpless. I send money, I give benefit readings, I write poems, but until this point I had avoided going to the front line. I didn't know if I could take it; I didn't know if I could make myself face a group of creatures we had grievously harmed. How could I look them in the eye?

14   My friend and I went to Fauna sentimental and ignorant about chimpanzees. We later admitted to each other that we had expected to bond with at least one chimp, to become its buddy. We thought we'd get to sit beside it, stroke it as we would a dog, hold its hand, get a kiss. We'd conveniently forgotten the repercussions of abuse, the bigness of these animals, their unpredictability, anger and fear. For months after their arrival, one of the younger females was terrified of floors and wouldn't put her feet on any kind of solid surface. She'd spent her whole life in a lab cage with bars all around, including the top and bottom. This kind of cage, barely bigger than a telephone booth, was suspended on chains so food and waste would fall through, and it and the occupant could be hosed down with the utmost efficiency. Chimps like her, test subjects since the day they were born, had never felt the earth beneath their feet.

15   Another chimpanzee, an older female named Rachel, who clearly displayed symptoms of a tortured past, stomped her feet and shook her head as if there were something in her memory she wanted to get rid of. She bit her hand repeatedly. Perhaps because of its remarkable resemblance to a human's, she saw it as the thing that had harmed her over and over again in the lab. Yet day by day she and the other maltreated animals show signs of progress. Gloria and her staff note each small change, like the evening Pablo set aside his distrust and fear and offered his feet to be tickled. We saw Rachel's macabre dance of self-abuse, but our second morning there, we watched her reach through the bars of the outside compound and groom Gloria's red-glossed toenails with long, dark fingers.

16   For our own safety and for theirs, we watched the chimpanzees a few feet away from the barred walls of their indoor living quarters. If they were excited or upset, we were asked to stay outside where we waited well back from the fence to see if any would venture into the outdoor enclosure. From our brief and distant encounter, what do my friend and I remember about Pablo and Annie? She was the matriarch, we were told, as we watched her wait for the other chimps to

be fed before she'd eat on her own. And she liked to walk around with a plastic purse full of raisins. This charming character quirk, which may have originated in her circus days, made her easy to pick out. She was also the only chimpanzee in her group who did not climb. Darts shot into her feet had paralyzed her toes, and they'd lost their ability to grip and flex. Because of the paleness of Pablo's face and jaw, we could easily identify him as well. And it didn't take us long to recognize the gruff cough that was his way of laughing, breaking through the normal noises of yelling, screaming, bar ringing and smacking.

17   The individuality of each chimpanzee announces itself, even to strangers, but three years after our Fauna visit, Annie and Pablo stand out for me because of their deaths. Their four-year respite had been far too short. They had adjusted to their new home where everyone expected them to live until their 70s, the average life expectancy of a chimpanzee. In spite of knowing their history, no one had guessed how sick they were inside. What the autopsies revealed makes each day the caretakers spend with the other chimpanzees more precarious and precious. And this new information, along with the details of Annie and Pablo's pasts, forces anyone who knows their stories to face what these stories mean. What do their deaths say about us? Where along the way did our species lose its awe for other living beings and come to regard them as toys rejigged to perform silly tasks or as living test tubes used to battle human diseases and crank up our longevity? We look into the mirror of another face and see the sameness that is there not with a sense of wonder but with a terrible pragmatism: how can we put this commonality to profitable use?

18   To be "almost human" is dangerous. Whenever you hear that phrase, translate it as meaning *less* than us. Even well-meaning researchers claim that "trainable" creatures like African Grey Parrots and chimps have the intelligence of a human four-year-old, rather than the intelligence of a 10- or 20-year-old bird or primate. It's as if the only brightness in the world is our own. What gets ignored in the comparison between chimpanzees and us is their ability to navigate the rain forest, flying through and above the dense green canopy and moving with graceful ease across the unmapped forest floor; their preternatural sense of smell and sight that alerts them to prey or danger invisible to us; and their use of tools—a stick poked into a termite nest to serve as a bridge for the insects to climb from the nest to a chimpanzee's waiting fingers, or a stone to break open rinds of fruit. Drop us into their back yard with only our wits and instincts to guide us and how would we score on a <u>primate's intelligence scale</u>? How long could we survive?

19   Declaring a creature *love* better than all these? What does that combination of sounds even mean? My guess is that my two cats growling at one another are not debating the difference between sign and signifier, between the abstract and concrete, the clichéd and the fresh. The passive cat backs up, the other one begins to groom himself, purring in contentment over the proof of his dominance, at least as I see and hear it. We need words because we don't know the lexicon of peacock cries, the dialects of whales, the 80 different sounds a dog can make. Yes, we can speak, but we can't buzz and dance a nectar map in the sky.

20   In Fauna's newsletter, Gloria describes Annie and Pablo's response to their human companions at the end of their lives. On his last day, Pablo, in a display of trust, overcame his fear of needles and reached out his arm for an injection. A few months later in her final hours, Annie, obviously in pain and separated by choice from the other chimpanzees, stuck out her toes and fingers for Gloria to

touch and leaned her head toward Gloria for a kiss. The two females both about the same age—one dark, the other fair; one chimpanzee, the other human—clearly understood each other's feelings.

21   In a perfect world Annie and Pablo would have died in the wild among their own kind, touching at the end another chimpanzee, perhaps a member of their family. But animals like them, torn from their kin at an early age or born in captivity, don't fit in.

22   They wouldn't have survived if they'd been set free in the forests of Africa. The last four years of their lives at the sanctuary were as good as they could get. Fauna offered them refuge and though they were caged, it offered them release. They became part of a family of chimpanzees; they ate good food, played games of chess, celebrated birthday parties with balloons that rained Smarties when they popped, built giant sleeping nests and napped in the afternoon sun. Their caretakers became friends. Pablo and Annie ended up with the best of what it means to be human, people who deny any superiority and who believe that chimpanzees are complex, loveable, aggressive, loud, brave, dangerous and holy. There's nothing *almost human* allows us to sentimentalize, to dress it up in doll's clothing and train it to dance on its hind legs, to replace its family with ourselves, to cage it in an ersatz Africa and charge tourists to snap photographs, to send it up in space, to hurl it into a wall to test the efficacy of seat belts, to biopsy its liver until there is no unscarred section big enough to punch through. And how, we have to ask, do we give ourselves permission to do these things? What is the one percent difference in our DNA that makes chimpanzees and other creatures expendable while we are not?

23   For centuries, vivisectionists have insisted that the major difference between us and them is that we feel and they don't. In his journals, Charles Darwin noted the common practice of severing the vocal chords of a cat so that it couldn't scream while the scientists were conducting their experiments. They created silence, not because the sound of the cat's pain upset them and caused them guilt—animals feel no pain, they insisted—but because they found the noise distracting. Yet any of us who have lived with cats, dogs and other domestic companions know they suffer. We've seen it in their eyes; we've heard it in the intonation of their calls. We know they exhibit a range of emotions—love, jealousy, anger, fear, even empathy and grief.

24   Shortly after Pablo's death, he was laid on a blanket, and the doors of the other cages were slid open. Annie was one of the first to arrive. She touched his face and chest and smelled his body. She then turned to the human caretakers outside the room, squealed and offered her fingers through the bars. All the chimpanzees sat with Pablo for a while. One poured water in his face and in his ear; another opened his eyelids and looked into his eyes. Then they each took turns grooming him. Could grief and love be more clearly enacted, at least to human eyes?

25   No words were exchanged. None were needed. Yet so much of human superiority rests on the assertion that we can talk and they can't. Perhaps this claim is the height of our arrogance, for it assumes that human language is the only—or the most superior—form of communication. We most revere the intelligence of creatures whom we can train to sound, or gesture, like us. Split the tongue of a crow and it can speak; work with a gorilla and it may sign. We seem to forget that none of us with our huge brains has learned to "speak" whale-talk, tree-talk or dog-talk, barking in local dialects our pooch can understand. Although training

animals to "speak" may lead us to a new understanding of their psychology, as some researchers claim, aren't we going about this search for a common language the wrong way? Aren't we missing something?

26   The honeybee's dance, the ruffed grouse's drumming, the 200 raven calls discernable to our instruments of measure, the gopher's whistles, the dolphin's clicks, the wolf's howls, the skylark's rising, the chimpanzee's pantings, grunts and screams? Why are the three simple phonemes of the word *almost* about them.

Source: Lorna Crozier, "Almost Human," Border Crossings. A Magazine of the Arts Issue No. 93, <http://www.bordercrossings.com>. Reprinted with permission.

READING COMPREHENSION QUESTIONS

1. *Literal:* What kind of candy was popular at the chimpanzees' birthday parties?

2. *Vocabulary in Context:* Without using a dictionary and using context clues, what does the underlined term "primate's intelligence scale" mean in the selection?

3. *Restructuring:* How was Rachel's grooming Gloria's red-glossed toenails significant?

4. *Inference:* Why are chimpanzees used as substitutes for human subjects in biomedical research sometimes?

5. *Prediction:* How can the use of animal subjects in scientific research be reduced?

6. *Evaluation:* Evaluate evidence supporting Crozier's suggestion that all members of our human species should be put on trial for the suffering of Annie and Pablo.

7. *Personal Response:* Would you like to adopt an adult chimpanzee as a pet?

Gail Deagle

Euthanasia Reconsidered

At the time she wrote this paper, Gail Deagle was a part-time nursing student living in Grande Prairie, Alberta. Her paper illustrates the use of research as well as argumentation.

1   Discussions on controversial topics such as euthanasia, physician-assisted suicide, and the withdrawal or withholding of medical treatment are commonly held within our homes, workplaces, and governments. The last several decades have seen an increase in right-to-die activist movement groups across the nation. This is in part a result of many people being afraid that the tremendous advances in medical therapy available may expose them to unnecessary and extraordinary treatment, which would serve only to prolong their suffering in the face of death. Society's beliefs about end-of-life care and the right to make personal choices are changing. At one time, it was considered immoral and unethical to assist or aid a person to escape from pain and suffering of a terminal illness by means of murder or suicide. Many people now feel they have the right to choose voluntary death in the terminal stages of their illnesses when they are no longer able to cope. Our

nation is under great pressure by citizens and activist groups to legalize euthanasia. I believe that the legalization of euthanasia would lead to abuse of that legislation.

2   Once legalized, euthanasia would become a commonplace method of dealing with serious and terminal illnesses. One of the reasons for this is that medical and technical advances in palliative care and pain control would be threatened with the sanctioning of euthanasia as a method for relieving pain and suffering. We would see an eventual decline in available funds and resources for palliative care. In the state of Oregon, where euthanasia has been legalized, there has been a reduction of funds allocated to those essential services required for the care of the terminally ill. The same has been found in the Netherlands, where euthanasia is also a legal option. Post-implementation studies have shown that terminally ill patients are presented with fewer options for community-based, end-of-life care. Because supportive services in the Netherlands have been reduced, people tend to seek out end-of-life options. An important point to consider is that when given options, most people will not exercise their option of euthanasia when they have adequate pain control and end-of-life care.

3   Another point to consider is that it is entirely feasible that our government may choose the least expensive route of care in dealing with the terminally ill. Members of the International Anti-Euthanasia Task Force have addressed their fears that legalized euthanasia might be abused: "The cost effectiveness of hastened death is undeniable. The earlier a patient dies, the less costly is his or her care" (Tort, 2000, p. 115). It has been shown that in the Netherlands, medical treatment options are frequently withheld from those who require palliative treatment. They are left to seek out the services of physicians who will assist them in succumbing to an early death. In Oregon, health management organizations (HMOs) are planning to cover the cost of assisted suicide and, as stated earlier, have reduced funding available for palliative care.

4   Not only do our governments hold a significant amount of authority in determining how our health-care needs are met, but physicians possess incredible power as well. Barney Sneiderman, a professor in the Faculty of Law at the University of Manitoba, is concerned that physicians have the potential to abuse guidelines when they take on the role of judge and jury (1994, p. 102). Legalization would enhance the power of control for doctors, not the patients where the control is intended. Where there is legislation approving euthanasia, there are no guarantees to safeguard against possible abuse. The Netherlands model of euthanasia is one we should be watching closely when determining possibilities of abuse after legalization. Explicit guidelines were set up in that model, but those guidelines are not being followed in the fashion intended. There is nothing in place to protect citizens from abuse. That country has found that there has been a progression from the people for whom euthanasia was initially intended to those who are receiving it now. Initially, the terminally ill were the only recipients of physician-assisted suicide or euthanasia. There has been a rapid progression to include those who are chronically ill, those with psychological afflictions, and finally those who are unable to make or communicate decisions for themselves. There are on average 130 000 deaths per year in the Netherlands, 1000 of which a doctor actively caused or hastened without the patients' request.

5   Rather than requests for euthanasia being initiated by the patient, as the guidelines require, requests in the Netherlands most commonly come from family members of patients. Families become exhausted with caregiving, as

there are few resources available for assistance. Given the option, many people choose to have their loved ones put to death instead of continuing the burden of caregiving. If euthanasia is legalized in Canada, the requests for assistance in dying should come voluntarily from individuals when they feel they can no longer cope with the burdens of the dying process. As seen in the Netherlands model, however, many will request assistance when they see themselves as burdens or nuisances. The next step is that requests for euthanasia will come from family or friends, as the patient is increasingly perceived as a burden on them. The reduced value placed on a life in our society and reduced available resources would play a role in this progression. In 1997, the Hemlock Society issued a press release "which asked that family members and other *agents* be able to procure court orders to kill *a demented parent, a suffering severely disable* [sic] *spouse, or a child* if their lives are *too burdensome to continue*" (italics in original) (Tort, 2000, p. 137).

6   Our society has a declining value for human life. Our abortion policy proves that we are a society that already accepts ridding ourselves of unwanted lives. Our society is one of convenience. Mothers who are inconvenienced by the prospect of giving birth to a child have an abortion. Family members inconvenienced by the duty of caring for one of their own who is terminally ill could seek euthanasia with or without the patient's knowledge or consent.

7   The disabled are wary and fearful that our country will legalize euthanasia. The apparent devaluation of human life brings fear to disabled persons that they will be killed against their will. Adolf Hitler set a mandate to "grant those who are by all human standards incurably ill a merciful death" (Tort, 2000, p. 118). The need for hospital beds during the war spurred Hitler to secretly euthanize the incurably insane and those with advanced senility or other conditions that caused the individual to be a burden on society. Diane Coleman, founder and president of Not Dead Yet, claims that our society demonstrates significant prejudice against disabled persons, that society views the disabled as better off dead. She feels Dr. Jack Kevorkian is seen as a hero, which is the reason he has not been convicted of his crimes (Tort, p. 134). The majority of people Kevorkian has performed euthanasia on are those with disabilities, not with terminal illnesses. Coleman goes on to say:

> According to Stephen Drake, Not Dead Yet's leading expert on Kevorkian, *The press have ignored his primary agenda to push for a class of human beings on which doctors can do live experimentation and organ harvesting. In his book,* Prescription Medicide, *he writes that assisted suicide is just a first step to achieving public acceptance of this agenda.* In written testimony that Kevorkian submitted in his first trial, he said, *The voluntary self-elimination of individual and mortally diseased or crippled lives taken collectively can only enhance the preservation of public health and welfare. . . .* (italics in original).

8   Given the trends seen in the Netherlands and hearing testimony from those advocating legalization of euthanasia, the disabled population has just cause to feel threatened.

9   The value we place on human life, particularly that of the disabled, was evidenced when Mike Wallace of the television program *60 Minutes* interviewed a disabled woman on television. During the interview, he questioned her about whether she felt she was a burden to society and openly discussed the costs of her health care. Similar comments to any other minority groups would never have been tolerated.

10   Depression is a common reason for requesting assisted suicide in the Netherlands. In 1982, the Law Reform Commission in Canada defined the word "euthanasia" as "the act of ending the life of a person, from compassionate motives, when he is already terminally ill or when his suffering has become unbearable" (p. 17). My concern is with the terminology "unbearable suffering." It is not specified that the person must be terminally ill *and* be suffering unbearably. Will someone challenge the legal system with charges of discrimination because euthanasia is reserved only for those people with terminal illnesses? Euthanasia is provided in the Netherlands, ambiguously enough, for people suffering mental anguish. An example is a woman distraught over the loss of her 20-year-old son four months earlier. Dutch courts ruled that mental suffering is grounds for euthanasia. It is suggested that a more appropriate treatment for depression is counselling and/or medication (Robinson, 2001, p. 4). Diagnosis of depression can be difficult, but the condition is very treatable.

11   The process of legalization of euthanasia most certainly raises moral and ethical questions and concerns for all citizens in Canada. It is important that we look at the models already in place to evaluate their effectiveness and drawbacks. There is strong evidence to suggest that the same abuse of euthanasia as occurs in the Netherlands model would inevitably occur in Canada. Intentions behind strict guidelines have not been sufficient in enforcing the Netherlands' program. Involuntary euthanasia and the killing of people with afflictions other than terminal illnesses are occurring despite guidelines to the contrary. It is irresponsible to think that Canada would not see the same issues arise. There is a natural progression from euthanasia for those who are terminally ill and make a request for assistance to the eradication of a life that does not fall within those parameters.

References

Law Reform Commission of Canada. (1983). *Report on euthanasia, aiding suicide and cessation of treatment.* Ottawa: Supply and Services Canada.

Robinson, B.A. (2001). Euthanasia and physician assisted suicide: All sides of the issues. *About Alternative Religions.* Retrieved April 25, 2001 from **wysiwyg://16/http://www.religioustolerance.org/euthanas.htm.**

Sneiderman, B., & Kaufert, J.M., (Eds.). *Euthanasia in the Netherlands: A model for Canada?* Brandon, MB: University of Manitoba. Legal Research Institute.

Torr, J.D. (Ed.) (2000). *Euthanasia opposing viewpoints.* San Diego: Greenhaven.

Brad Evenson

Native Postmodern

Brad Evenson has worked in journalism for 13 years and is currently the medical writer for the National Post *newspaper. He won the National Newspaper Award for investigative reporting in 1997 and was a National Magazine Award nominee in 1998 for an article about Prime Minister Jean Chretien's speech disorder. Based in Ottawa, he studied theology before becoming a journalist. Evenson's essay entitled "Native Postmodern" raises questions about the ways in which the modern, government-supported powwow has created a "homogeneous culture" far removed from authentic aboriginal traditions. While acknowledging that powwows can foster a sense of identity and even self-esteem among some natives, the essay uses irony to highlight problems with commercialization and stereotyping.*

1   A feather is down. The aboriginal dancers freeze on the grass. The aboriginal Vietnam War veterans in camouflage pants freeze, too, in the shade of a vinyl tent. The woman selling aboriginal Arizona silver jewellery and aboriginal Harley-Davidson T-shirts falls silent. The aboriginal kid wearing L.A.-style baggy pants and a black Raiders cap stares in the sweltering Sunday heat. On the grill, a traditional buffalo burger sizzles untended. "All dancers, we have an eagle feather down," cries a man on the loudspeaker. "Everybody stop."

2   It is the National Aboriginal Day powwow in Ottawa and a feather is down, but nobody knows what to do about it. The aboriginal dancers, about two dozen of them, most in street clothes, crane their necks to spot it. The white spectators in the bleachers look on, concern etched on their sunburned foreheads. The loudspeaker guy says, we have to ask an elder. A conference. Muted voices emerge from a spruce-bough shelter where powwow officials are clustered. Long moments pass. After all, an eagle feather is some kind of sacred aboriginal symbol, isn't it?

3   "It's okay," he says finally. "It's not an eagle feather. . . ."

4   Thirty years ago, most North American natives had only heard of powwows from old stories or the movies, wistful memories of great gatherings in the prideful time before Canadian Christian residential schools and the U.S. cavalry wiped out their traditional way of life. Powwows all but disappeared for a century. But in the past few decades, resurgent interest in native culture has resurrected them on an extraordinary scale.

5   Powwow culture is burning brightly across North America, with powwows held every weekend, some attended by as many as 60,000 people. Casinos put up millions in prize money for dance competitions, powwow videos are sold over the Internet at twenty-five dollars a pop, colleges offer courses in drumming and beadwork, traditional foods and herbal remedies are in unprecedented demand. The modern powwow is a mix of country fair and spiritual revival, at a cost of up to twenty dollars a person. The annual Grand River powwow at Ontario's Six Nations Reserve is one of Canada's biggest, pulling in a quarter million dollars at the gate—before the government subsidy.

6   There is little argument powwows foster a sense of identity. They draw natives together and break down the isolation they can feel in a largely white culture. But the modern powwow has also created a homogeneous culture, a blend of the kitschy and the outright phoney that is no more authentic than a plastic tomahawk in a Tokyo duty-free shop. Powwow culture is a stew of dozens of native cultures, a sort of Disney version of the ultimate tribe that some traditional native leaders, academics, and artists find distressing.

7   Then add to that mix a New Age brand of native spiritualism so overwrought it elevates a feather from a token of respect to the status of consecrated icon. If a feather falls in the forest, does anyone hear it? And if so, should he stop dancing?

8   The term powwow originated in the U.S. with the Chickasaw people, and means, literally, the burning of tobacco, a communal ceremony practised when bands came together. Similar gatherings took place across much of North America for centuries for a variety of reasons: for trade, to speak about the dead,

to discuss the needs of the community, or even to discuss war. During the 1960s, many natives realized powwows were also a terrific way to earn money from tourists, and soon the mass production of medicine wheels, pipes, and skin drums began. "We were making tomahawks, all kinds of things," recalls Michael Doxtater, a Mohawk now teaching Indian studies at Cornell University in Ithaca, New York. "We put ourselves through school with the medicine-wheel craze."

9   The problem was tourists weren't the only ones buying. Natives scooped up the Indian kitsch in equal numbers, but instead of hanging the stuff over their basement minibars, many took it seriously. Many still do. And that rankles a number of native leaders who fear the hucksterism common at powwows is eroding their ancient traditions. "There are too many phoney elders, too many phoney spiritual people, medicine people," says Rene Tenasco, grand chief of the Algonquin Anishinabeg Nation. Today, many self-described medicine people charge a hefty fee to pass on their wisdom. "It's a money-making thing at all levels," says Tenasco.

10   Tenasco still winces at the memory of a powwow he attended two years ago. With storm clouds threatening, a group of "elders" offered to ward off the rain with chants and prayers. "What is that all about?" he groans. "You have fakes that come along and exploit the goodwill of young people or people in general who are searching. And once these people find out the truth, they generally walk away."

11   For now, however, few are walking away. Powwow culture holds natives in a seductive embrace best described by what it is not. It's not traditional Indian culture. It's not unique to individual tribes or nations, although it has regional nuances. It's neither urban nor reservation-based. "It's our version of fast-food culture, I guess," says Doxtater.

12   No modern powwow is complete without shawl-making contests, sweat-lodge ceremonies (with entry fees), clothing and jewellery bazaars, story-telling sessions, and crafts festooned with enough coloured feathers to fill a tropical aviary. In powwow culture, looking native is the crucial first step. But what's native? A headband? A cowboy hat? Braids? "You look at some of the outfits and you know that it comes from watching Indian movies," sighs Shelley Niro, an Ontario Mohawk filmmaker who recently completed a film which features a powwow, *Honey Moccasin*. "For years everybody was wearing headdresses, but not every tribe wore headdresses."

13   Natives mix and match and embellish the art, dances, songs, and spiritual beliefs of different bands. Mohawks do Sioux sun dances, Micmacs paint Blackfoot images on paddles, Crees make and sell Navajo blankets, Algonquins fry buffalo burgers. It is virtually impossible to attend a powwow anywhere in Canada without smelling burning sweet grass, seeing Hopi-style beadwork, Haida-style salmon and raven motifs, grass dancing, and hearing the tattoo of an enormous skin drum. Then there is the dream catcher, the most ubiquitous powwow prop of all.

14   A willow hoop woven with string, a dream catcher is a good-luck charm of the Lakota people, a Plains tribe. According to the traditional story, Iktomi, the trickster and teacher of wisdom, appeared before an old Lakota spiritual leader in the form of a spider. While he wove a perfect web, Iktomi explained, "If you believe in the great spirit, the web will catch your good ideas and the bad ones will go through the hole in the middle." The Lakota would hang dream catchers above their beds to sift their dreams.

15   Dream catchers have become as common as Amway products across North America—a kind of universal symbol of native spirituality. There are dream catcher Web pages, earrings, and air fresheners. New Age magazines advertise dream-catcher kits and audio tapes narrating the dream catcher legend. In Regina, natives hang them from their rear-view mirrors so their cars won't be stolen by the Oldsmobile Gang, a notorious group of native car thieves operating in the area. "It's better than the Club," laughs Tom Doré, referring to the widely used anti-theft device. Doré, a Mohawk who teaches introductory Indian studies at Saskatchewan Indian Federated College in Regina, says people actually believe that dream catchers show native solidarity. "If I put a dream catcher on my mirror the kids who steal cars won't steal mine because it's one of the brother's."

16   During the Christian residential-school era, which reached its peak in the late-1800s, native culture was all but extinguished. "For nearly a century, parents and grandparents in reserve communities were legally compelled to turn their children over to the custody of residential school authorities," notes the *Report of the Royal Commission on Aboriginal Peoples*. "Children were beaten for speaking their own language, and Aboriginal beliefs were labelled 'pagan.'" When the schools began to close in the 1950s, many natives from smaller, isolated, "fly-in" communities were drawn towards the larger tribes that seemed to hold onto their language and customs, such as the Lakota, the Blackfoot, and the Plains Cree. Young Sioux men travelled the country teaching the sun dance and drumming. This explains the prevalence of the dream catcher, the grass dance, the big drum, and the medicine wheel—all Plains Indian traditions—and goes a long way towards explaining the curious sameness of powwow culture. "A lot of Indian people were seeking a sense of Indianness," says Stephen Augustine, a Canadian Museum of Civilization ethnologist and hereditary Micmac chief.

17   Even larger nations have been drawn to the extravagant practices of the Plains tribes. "In a lot of tribes on the East coast, the chief, when he gets elected to office, will opt to be crowned with a Plains Cree headdress, which is totally out of whack with our culture," says Augustine.

18   Many natives believe governments have for decades promoted a kind of pan-Indian nation, with a common spiritual belief system, cultural hallmarks, and aspirations. After all, it is easier to deal with a homogeneous group than with a fractious collection of tribes with different political goals. For example, last year the federal government declared June 21 to be National Aboriginal Day. This irks many natives who value the uniqueness of their cultures. "The idea of pan-Indianism is seen in a negative light because it's like pan-Europeanism," says Augustine. "I mean, do you speak European or what language do you speak? Do you speak white? There's fifty-two different indigenous languages in Canada and each of us have different spiritual belief systems that are not congruent with each other."

19   Governments have regarded powwows as at worst benign, and possibly even useful—for example, as a panacea after the tensions of Oka and Douglas Lake. They spend millions each year on cultural grants to fund what are essentially profitable events. Art King, a Heritage Canada official in charge of native issues, says he sees a new grant request to fund a powwow once a week. In 1979, Mike Doxtater joined the organizing committee of the Grand River powwow at Ontario's Six Nations Reserve. He quit not long after, annoyed that the committee went looking for a provincial grant. "Powwows have been, right from the

start, supported by government as what they perceive to be the approved cultures for Indians," says Doxtater. "The question among people is, well, if that's the case, is it really an Indian thing?"

20   This issue of authenticity is central to the bitter controversy surrounding B.C. Bishop Hubert O'Connor. The now seventy-one-year-old O'Connor was the highest-ranking Roman Catholic official in Canada ever convicted of a sex crime. In 1996 he was found guilty of rape and indecent assault for offences taking place while he was the principal of a residential school in Williams Lake, B.C., in the mid-sixties, but after serving six months, filed an appeal. The appeal court set aside his conviction, ordering an acquittal on the charge of indecent assault and a new trial on the charge of rape. Last June, that charge was stayed in return for O'Connor's apology at a native healing ceremony in Alkali Lake, not far from where the offences occurred. While his victim, Marilyn Belleau, was satisfied by O'Connor's participation, many natives were outraged both at the leniency shown and at the inappropriateness of the ritual. Viola Thomas, of the United Native Nations of British Columbia, said the healing circle is not even part of B.C. native culture, but was copied from Manitoba natives.

21   The development of a pan-Indian nation also troubles Tom Doré because it creates a stereotype that many natives feel they must live up to. "Like every Indian has a medicine pouch, every Indian likes powwow music, every Indian burns sweet grass," he says sarcastically. "When I smell burning sweet grass, it gives me a headache. Does that mean I can't be an Indian?" Powwow culture sometimes merely replaces one stereotype with another.

22   In downtown Regina, says Doré, the way to look like a real Indian is to wear a baseball cap backwards, a black leather or jean jacket, Nike T-shirt, and "homeboy" pants with baggy crotch. They call each other "Bro," like American blacks. "They're so unsure of their own culture," he says, "they have to latch on to what somebody else has done."

23   Criticizing powwows is easier, of course, for people like Doré who are secure with their own identity. For those natives whose addictions and poverty are rooted in their lack of identity and low self-esteem, the powwow is strong medicine. "A lot of it is tacky and cliché-ridden and it gets a bit much after a while, but I just think that it allows you to contribute or participate," says filmmaker Shelley Niro. "My dad came from an age where you had to be really ashamed of being an Indian. He didn't speak his language, he went through that experience where [an Indian] couldn't go to a wine store and buy a bottle of wine, and you were sort of treated like servants. And then, when the powwow scene started, he was always invited to carry the flag as a war veteran, and doing that, even though he was paid for doing it, I think it really meant a lot to him."

24   Something that troubles Niro, as well as other native critics, is that powwow culture isn't just for natives any more. Many New Age whites are showing up, and the sight of beaded moccasins on plump, alabaster legs with blue veins annoys many natives. "If you look in any of the New Age sections of bookstores, half of them are all native spirituality books, and it's kind of gross," she says, adding that the New Age invasion diminishes her art by making it seem trendy and flaky instead of rooted in something authentic. "You know, it's like I'm doing this airhead art." Doxtater calls it "shake-and-bake shamanism."

25   Augustine, who's an ethnologist, says centuries of Christian influence and education have led to natives trying to become priest-like figures themselves, which runs counter to native traditions. "What our teachings tell us usually is

that we are simple, we are common people. There's no mysticism, there's no magic in our spirituality; it's everyday, it's down-to-earth, and all it does is talk about truth, and honesty, and respect and those things. So people who go around charging [money] and saying I'm going to get you in a sweat-lodge ceremony and you'll see all these visions, and lights . . . I mean, that's hinging on evangelism in a native context."

26   So what about when an eagle feather falls? Stop dancing?

27   "Actually, the reverence for the eagle feather is part of Indian teachings, but it's not presented that way by the powwow practitioners," says Doxtater, who hosts annual spiritual gatherings near Oka, Quebec.

28   "[There's] a teaching that asks young people to be very careful and look after eagle feathers," Doxtater explains. "What they're saying, really, is this: if you can honour the feather from a dead bird, if you can respect these inanimate objects, you may do all right with your neighbours."

29   Most tribes give different symbolic meaning to the eagle feather. Some regard it as a fallen warrior; others as a token of respect; a few tribes don't consider it anything special at all. Perhaps the only appropriate postmodern response may be what merchant Billy Desjarlais did after the Ottawa powwow when he dropped a box of eagle feathers in a shallow puddle in the parking lot. "You've gotta dry-clean them," he said wearily. "If they're stained, they're not worth nearly as much."

Martin Luther King, Jr.

I Have a Dream

Martin Luther King, Jr. (1929–1968) has earned lasting fame for his part in the civil rights struggles of the 1950s and 1960s. Born in Atlanta, Georgia, he was ordained a Baptist minister in his father's church in 1947. A year later, he graduated from Morehouse College, then went on to take a Bachelor of Divinity degree at Crozier Theological Seminary (1951) and a Ph.D. in Philosophy at Boston University (1954), after which he accepted a pastorate in Montgomery, Alabama. King's involvement with civil rights grew when he organized and led a boycott that succeeded in desegregating Montgomery's bus system. In 1957, he founded and became the first president of the Southern Christian Leadership Conference and assumed a leading role in the civil rights movement. King advocated a policy of nonviolent protest based on the beliefs of Thoreau and Gandhi and never veered from it despite many acts of violence directed at him. The success of King's crusade helped bring about the passage of the Civil Rights Act of 1964 and the Voting Rights Act of 1965 and won him the Nobel Peace Prize in 1964. King was assassinated on April 4, 1968, in Memphis, Tennessee. The speech "I Have a Dream" was delivered August 28, 1963, at the Lincoln Memorial in Washington, D.C., before a crowd of 200 000 people who had gathered to commemorate the centennial of the Emancipation Proclamation and to demonstrate for pending civil rights legislation. It stands as one of the most eloquent pleas ever made for racial justice.

1   I am happy to join with you today in what will go down in history as the greatest demonstration for freedom in the history of our nation.

2   Five score years ago, a great American, in whose symbolic shadow we stand today, signed the Emancipation Proclamation. This momentous decree came as

a great beacon light of hope to millions of Negro slaves who had been seared in the flames of withering injustice. It came as a joyous daybreak to end the long night of their captivity.

3   But one hundred years later, the Negro still is not free; one hundred years later, the life of the Negro is still sadly crippled by the manacles of segregation and the chains of discrimination; one hundred years later, the Negro lives on a lonely island of poverty in the midst of a vast ocean of material prosperity; one hundred years later, the Negro is still languishing in the corners of American society and finds himself in exile in his own land.

Description

4   So we've come here today to dramatize a shameful condition. In a sense we've come to our nation's capital to cash a check. When the architects of our republic wrote the magnificent words of the Constitution and the Declaration of Independence, they were signing a promissory note to which every American was to fall heir. This note was the promise that all men, yes, black men as well as white men, would be guaranteed the unalienable rights of life, liberty, and the pursuit of happiness.

5   It is obvious today that America has defaulted on this promissory note in so far as her citizens of color are concerned. Instead of honoring this sacred obligation, America has given the Negro people a bad check; a check which has *metaphor* come back marked "insufficient funds." But we refuse to believe that the bank of justice is bankrupt. We refuse to believe that there are insufficient funds in the great vaults of opportunity of this nation. And so we've come to cash this check, a check that will give us upon demand the riches of freedom and the security of justice.

Imagery   Chains
racism = sinking,
dark, valleys, flame
Hope = light, joy,
sunlit path, solid rock

6   We have also come to this hallowed spot to remind America of the fierce urgency of now. This is no time to engage in the luxury of cooling off or to take the tranquilizing drug of gradualism. Now is the time to make real the promises of democracy; now is the time to rise from the dark and desolate valley of segregation to the sunlit path of racial justice; now is the time to lift our nation from the quicksands of racial injustice to the solid rock of brotherhood; now is the time to make justice a reality for all of God's children. It would be fatal for the nation to overlook the urgency of the moment. This sweltering summer of the Negro's legitimate discontent will not pass until there is an invigorating autumn of freedom and equality.

personification
alliteration

7   Nineteen sixty-three is not an end, but a beginning. And those who hope that the Negro needed to blow off steam and will now be content will have a rude awakening if the nation returns to business as usual. There will be neither rest nor tranquility in America until the Negro is granted his citizenship rights. The whirlwinds of revolt will continue to shake the foundations of our nation until the bright day of justice emerges.

8   But there is something that I must say to my people, who stand on the worn threshold which leads into the palace of justice. In the process of gaining our rightful place, we must not be guilty of wrongful deeds. Let us not seek to satisfy our thirst for freedom by drinking from the cup of bitterness and hatred. We must forever conduct our struggle on the high plain of dignity and discipline. We must not allow our creative protests to degenerate into physical violence. Again and again we must rise to the majestic heights of meeting physical force with soul force. The marvelous new militancy, which has engulfed the Negro community, must not lead us to a distrust of all white people. For many of our white brothers, as evidenced by their presence here today, have come to realize

that their destiny is tied up with our destiny. And they have come to realize that their freedom is inextricably bound to our freedom. We cannot walk alone. And as we walk, we must make the pledge that we shall always march ahead. We cannot turn back.

9   There are those who are asking the devotees of Civil Rights, "When will you be satisfied?" We can never be satisfied as long as the Negro is the victim of the unspeakable horrors of police brutality; we can never be satisfied as long as our bodies, heavy with the fatigue of travel, cannot gain lodging in the motels of the highways and the hotels of the cities; we cannot be satisfied as long as the Negro's basic mobility is from a smaller ghetto to a larger one; we can never be satisfied as long as our children are stripped of their selfhood and robbed of their dignity by signs stating "For Whites Only"; we cannot be satisfied as long as the Negro in Mississippi cannot vote and a Negro in New York believes he has nothing for which to vote. No! No, we are not satisfied, and we will not be satisfied until "justice rolls down like waters and righteousness like a mighty stream."

Positive images

10   I am not unmindful that some of you have come here out of great trials and tribulations. Some of you have come fresh from narrow jail cells. Some of you have come from areas where your quest for freedom left you battered by the storms of persecution and staggered by the winds of police brutality. You have been the veterans of creative suffering. Continue to work with the faith that unearned suffering is redemptive. Go back to Mississippi. Go back to Alabama. Go back to South Carolina. Go back to Georgia. Go back to Louisiana. Go back to the slums and ghettos of our Northern cities, knowing that somehow this situation can and will be changed. Let us not wallow in the valley of despair.

Emotional Appeal (Hope) → Ethical Appeal

11   I say to you today, my friends, that even though we face the difficulties of today and tomorrow, I still have a dream. It is a dream deeply rooted in the American dream. I have a dream that one day this nation will rise up and live out the true meaning of its creed, "We hold these truths to be self-evident, that all men are created equal." I have a dream that one day on the red hills of Georgia, sons of former slaves and the sons of former slave owners will be able to sit down together at the table of brotherhood. I have a dream that one day even the state of Mississippi, a state sweltering with the heat of injustice, sweltering with the heat of oppression, will be transformed into an oasis of freedom and justice. I have a dream that my four little children will one day live in a nation where they will not be judged by the color of their skin, but by the content of their character.

12   I HAVE A DREAM TODAY!

13   I have a dream that one day down in Alabama—with its vicious racists, with its Governor having his lips dripping with the words of interposition and nullification—one day right there in Alabama, little black boys and black girls will be able to join hands with little white boys and white girls as sisters and brothers.

14   I HAVE A DREAM TODAY!

15   I have a dream that one day every valley shall be exalted, every hill and mountain shall be made low. The rough places will be plain and the crooked places will be made straight, "and the glory of the Lord shall be revealed, and all flesh shall see it together."

16   This is our hope. This is the faith that I go back to the South with. With this faith we will be able to hew out of the mountain of despair, a stone of hope. With this faith we will be able to transform the jangling discords of our nation into a beautiful symphony of brotherhood. With this faith we will be able to work

repetition

together, to pray together, to struggle together, to go to jail together, to stand up for freedom together, knowing that we will be free one day. And this will be the day. This will be the day when all of God's children will be able to sing with new meaning, "My country 'tis of thee, sweet land of liberty, of thee I sing. Land where my fathers died, land of the pilgrim's pride, from every mountain side, let freedom ring." And if America is to be a great nation, this must become true. *—Quotes*

17   So let freedom ring from the prodigious hilltops of New Hampshire; let freedom ring from the mighty mountains of New York; let freedom ring from the heightening Alleghenies of Pennsylvania; let freedom ring from the snow-capped Rockies of Colorado; let freedom ring from the curvaceous slopes of California. But not only that. Let freedom ring from Stone Mountain of Georgia; let freedom ring from Lookout Mountain of Tennessee; let freedom ring from every hill and molehill of Mississippi. "From every mountainside, let freedom ring."

18   And when this happens, and when we allow freedom to ring, when we let it ring from every village and every hamlet, from every state and every city, we will be able to speed up that day when all of God's children, black men and white men, Jews and Gentiles, Protestants and Catholics, will be able to join hands and sing in the words of the old Negro spiritual: "Free at last. Free at last. Thank God Almighty, we are free at last."

- Builds to end of speech (suspense)
- 1st person
- Racism is lg. problem → wrong + does not see person on inside
- injustice to a section of people

Chris MacDonald

Yes, Human Cloning Should Be Permitted

Dr. Chris MacDonald is a Canadian philosopher whose research interests include business ethics, health care ethics, professional ethics, and ethical theory. Some of his most recent publications have been related to ethical issues in the biotechnology industry. As you read the article, "Yes, Human Cloning Should Be Permitted,"* note how he responds to specific points in Patricia Baird's argument calling for a ban on human cloning.

1   Patricia Baird's discussion of human cloning (*Annals RCPSC*, June 2000) challenges the prospect of nuclear-transfer cloning for the purposes of human reproduction. Baird reviews a long list of familiar worries about human cloning, but the most striking feature of her discussion is its frankness in placing the onus of justification on the shoulders of those who would permit human cloning. The reasons for permitting cloning, she argues, are "insufficiently compelling," so cloning should be prohibited. The implication is that any new technology should be forbidden unless and until enough justification can be found for allowing its use.

2   Baird is to be commended for her frankness. But the onus is misplaced, or at least too severe. One need not be a single-minded defender of liberty to think that, contrary to Baird's implication, we need good reasons to limit the actions of others, particularly when those actions do no clear and specific harm. The fact that a portion of society—even a majority—finds an activity distasteful is insufficient grounds for passing a law forbidding it. For example, it is presumably

*©The Royal College of Physicians and Surgeons of Canada.

true that at one point, roughly 90 percent of the public (the same proportion that Baird says is against human cloning) was opposed to homosexuality. Does (or did) this justify action on the part of government to ban homosexual lifestyles? Surely not.

3   There may be a flaw in my analogy. Human cloning, according to critics, has harmful effects (or at least risks). Indeed, Baird suggests that the arguments regarding potential physical and psychological harm to clones have been "well delineated." In fact, a convincing case has yet to be made for the claim that the physical and psychological risks to clones are more severe than, or different in kind from, those faced by children produced in more traditional ways. Identical twins live with the psychological "burden" of not being genetically unique. Children born to women over 35 are at an increased risk of genetic illness. Children resulting from in-vitro fertilization or other reproductive technologies live with the knowledge that their origins were unusual. They may even live with the knowledge that their genetic profile has been manipulated (for example, through pre-implantation selection of embryos). Human cloning for reproductive purposes is another novel—and as yet untested—medical technology. As such, it should be approached with caution. Thorough animal trials should be completed before attempts on humans are contemplated. But this is true of any new medical technology.

4   Baird worries about the shift that human cloning might provoke in the way that we view children. This in turn would change the type of community that we are. The central worry is that human cloning "commodifies" children (i.e., that cloning may make us think of children as a commodity or product to be bought and sold). Why would cloning have this effect? Is it simply because it is likely to be expensive, so that it costs money to have children? Surely this is insufficient to worry us. Raising children already costs money—the statistics show us how many hundreds of thousands of dollars it costs to raise a child through to adulthood. Yet no one has suggested that we see our children as products, or love them any less. (In the mid-1940s—before publicly funded health care—my grandparents sold their car to pay the hospital bill related to my father's birth, so "purchasing" the birth of a child is nothing new!)

5   Baird argues that an "important part of human identity is the sense of arising from a maternal and a paternal line while at the same time being a unique individual." Yet without supporting evidence, this sounds like pop psychology. And we can reply in kind: most people I know do not identify with both their maternal and paternal lineages. One of my friends, who was raised by a single mother, identifies with her maternal eastern European heritage, and not with the French paternal heritage implied by her surname. Another friend identifies with his father's black heritage, rather than with his maternal Chinese lineage, despite his Asian physical features. Such patterns are not unusual. Dual heritage may be normal, but it hardly seems central to our conception of ourselves as humans. And identical twins seem none the worse for the knowledge that they are not genetically unique individuals. Claims about challenges to what makes us "human" may be powerful rhetorical devices, but they must be substantiated if they are to be convincing.

6   Baird is correct to exhort us to look beyond harms to identifiable individuals to the social implications that human cloning might have. As a comparison, think of fetal sex selection. Most of us think that sex selection is a bad thing— not because of any purported harm to the child, but because we worry about the

social implications of valuing children of one sex over those of another. So Baird rightly reminds us that focusing on potential harms to individuals constitutes a "dangerously incomplete framing" of the problem. Furthermore, cloning (and genetic technology in general) is sufficiently new—and its implications sufficiently poorly understood—to warrant a healthy respect, and even the allowance of a margin of safety. But this does not suggest the need for the ban that Baird (with others) proposes. What these worries suggest is a need for caution, for discussion, and for regulation. For instance, laws limiting the number of clones that might be created from one individual, restricting the combination of cloning with genetic modification, and defining lines of parental obligation, would alleviate many of the concerns associated with human cloning. (Françoise Baylis argues that cloning is so likely to be used in combination with gene transfer that we should think of cloning as an enhancement technology rather than as a reproductive technology, in her article "Human cloning: three mistakes and a solution," which has been accepted for publication in the *Journal of Medicine and Philosophy*.)

7   What I have said here should not be taken as an absolute defence of human cloning in all circumstances. (Indeed, there may be only a few circumstances in which cloning is appropriate.) Nor have I suggested that public monies should be spent on cloning research. All I have suggested is that a ban on research leading toward human cloning is unwarranted by the arguments raised thus far. Caution and discretion are warranted; a ban is not.

8   Finally, I worry that Baird's point of view exemplifies the way in which human reproductive cloning is being singled out, among cloning-related techniques, as a bogeyman. Almost in chorus, scientists are pleading with regulators not to place restrictions on cloning experimentation per se. At the same time, most scientists seem to be more than willing to swear off reproductive cloning, and indeed to wring their hands over the moral implications of its use. Yet this has the air of a too-hasty concession. The scientific community seems to be too willing to condemn one unpopular application of cloning technology, on the basis of too little convincing argumentation, to appease those who oppose cloning technology in general. But human cloning for reproductive purposes has legitimate, morally acceptable applications—for example, for infertile couples, and for gay couples. And none of the criticisms have been convincingly made. We should not let reproductive human cloning be abandoned as the moral sacrificial lamb of the cloning debate.

Carol Geddes

Growing Up Native

Born in the Yukon, Carol Geddes is a member of the Tlingit Nation. After graduating from Carleton University, she earned a graduate degree in communications from Concordia University. She currently serves on the Teslin Tlingit Council as a representative for her First Nation, and is the representative for the Dekl'weidi clan for her government. A film writer and producer, Geddes named her production company "The Thing with Feathers Productions" after the eagle, the symbol of her clan. Among her 25 documentary films are Doctor, Lawyer, Indian Chief *(1986),* Half a World Apart . . . And a Lifetime Away *(1996), and* Picturing a People: George Johnston, Tlingit Photographer *(1997). She is also the producer of* Creation *(2001), an animated version of the Tlingit creation myth and currently working on* Two Winters: Tales from Above the Earth. Maclean's *magazine selected Geddes as one of "100 Canadians to watch" in the 1990s. In the following selection, Geddes chronicles the years of discrimination that native peoples have endured at the hands of whites and calls for a revival of native cultures.*

1   I remember it was cold. We were walking through a swamp near our home in the Yukon bush. Maybe it was fall and moose-hunting season. I don't know. I think I was about four years old at the time. The muskeg was too springy to walk on, so people were taking turns carrying me—passing me from one set of arms to another. The details about where we were are vague, but the memory of those arms and the feeling of acceptance I had is one of the most vivid memories of my childhood. It didn't matter who was carrying me—there was security in every pair of arms. That response to children is typical of the native community. It's the first thing I think of when I cast my mind back to the Yukon bush, where I was born and lived with my family.

2   I was six years old when we moved out of the bush, first to Teslin, where I had a hint of the problems native people face, then to Whitehorse, where there was unimaginable racism. Eventually I moved to Ottawa and Montreal, where I further discovered that to grow up native in Canada is to feel the sting of humiliation and the boot of discrimination. But it is also to experience the enviable security of an extended family and to learn to appreciate the richness of the heritage and traditions of a culture most North Americans have never been lucky enough to know. As a film-maker, I have tried to explore these contradictions, and our triumph over them, for the half-million aboriginals who are part of the tide of swelling independence of the First Nations today.

3   But I'm getting ahead of myself. If I'm to tell the story of what it's like to grow up native in northern Canada, I have to go back to the bush where I was born, because there's more to my story than the hurtful stereotyping that depicts Indian people as drunken welfare cases. Our area was known as 12-mile (it was 12 miles from another tiny village). There were about 40 people living there—including 25 kids, eight of them my brothers and sisters—in a sort of family

compound. Each family had its own timber plank house for sleeping, and there was one large common kitchen area with gravel on the ground and a tent frame over it. Everybody would go there and cook meals together. In summer, my grandmother always had a smudge fire going to smoke fish and tan moose hides. I can remember the cosy warmth of the fire, the smell of good food, and always having someone to talk to. We kids had built-in playmates and would spend hours running in the bush, picking berries, building rafts on the lake and playing in abandoned mink cages.

4   One of the people in my village tells a story about the day the old lifestyle began to change. He had been away hunting in the bush for about a month. On his way back, he heard a strange sound coming from far away. He ran up the crest of a hill, looked over the top of it and saw a bulldozer. He had never seen or heard of such a thing before and he couldn't imagine what it was. We didn't have magazines or newspapers in our village, and the people didn't know that the Alaska Highway was being built as a defence against a presumed Japanese invasion during the Second World War. That was the beginning of the end of the Teslin Tlingit people's way of life. From that moment on, nothing turned back to the way it was. Although there were employment opportunities for my father and uncles, who were young men at the time, the speed and force with which the Alaska Highway was rammed through the wilderness caused tremendous upheaval for Yukon native people.

5   It wasn't as though we'd never experienced change before. The Tlingit Nation, which I belong to, arrived in the Yukon from the Alaskan coast around the turn of the century. They were the middlemen and women between the Russian traders and the Yukon inland Indians. The Tlingit gained power and prestige by trading European products such as metal goods and cloth for the rich and varied furs so much in fashion in Europe. The Tlingit controlled Yukon trading because they controlled the trading routes through the high mountain passes. When trading ceased to be an effective means of survival, my grandparents began raising wild mink in cages. Mink prices were really high before and during the war, but afterwards the prices went plunging down. So, although the mink pens were still there when I was a little girl, my father mainly worked on highway construction and hunted in the bush. The Yukon was then, and still is in some ways, in a transitional period—from living off the land to getting into a European wage-based economy.

6   As a young child, I didn't see the full extent of the upheaval. I remember a lot of togetherness, a lot of happiness while we lived in the bush. There's a very strong sense of family in the native community, and a fondness for children, especially young children. Even today, it's like a special form of entertainment if someone brings a baby to visit. That sense of family is the one thing that has survived all the incredible difficulties native people have had. Throughout a time of tremendous problems, the extended family system has somehow lasted, providing a strong circle for people to survive in. When parents were struggling with alcoholism or had to go away to find work, when one of the many epidemics swept through the community, or when a marriage broke up and one parent left, aunts, uncles, and grandparents would try to fill those roles. It's been very important to me in terms of emotional support to be able to rely on my extended family. There are still times when such support keeps me going.

7   Life was much simpler when we lived in the bush. Although we were poor and wore the same clothes all year, we were warm enough and had plenty to eat. But even as a youngster, I began to be aware of some of the problems we would

face later on. Travelling missionaries would come and impose themselves on us, for example. They'd sit at our campfire and read the bible to us and lecture us about how we had to live a Christian life. I remember being very frightened by stories we heard about parents sending their kids away to live with white people who didn't have any children. We thought those people were mean and that if we were bad, we'd be sent away, too. Of course, that was when social workers were scooping up native children and adopting them out to white families in the south. The consequences were usually disastrous for the children who were taken away—alienation, alcoholism and suicide, among other things. I knew some of those kids. The survivors are still struggling to recover.

8   The residential schools were another source of misery for the kids. Although I didn't have to go, my brothers and sisters were there. They told stories about having their hair cut off in case they were carrying head lice, and of being forced to do hard chores without enough food to eat. They were told that the Indian culture was evil, that Indian people were bad, that their only hope was to be Christian. They had to stand up and say things like "I've found the Lord," when a teacher told them to speak. Sexual abuse was rampant in the residential school system.

9   By the time we moved to Whitehorse, I was excited about the idea of living in what I thought of as a big town. I'd had a taste of the outside world from books at school in Teslin (a town of 250 people), and I was tremendously curious about what life was like. I was hungry for experiences such as going to the circus. In fact, for a while, I was obsessed with stories and pictures about the circus, but then when I was 12 and saw my first one, I was put off by the condition and treatment of the animals.

10   Going to school in Whitehorse was a shock. The clash of native and white values was confusing and frightening. Let me tell you a story. The older boys in our community were already accomplished hunters and fishermen, but since they had to trap beaver in the spring and hunt moose in the fall, and go out trapping in the winter as well, they missed a lot of school. We were all in one classroom and some of my very large teenage cousins had to sit squeezed into little desks. These guys couldn't read very well. We girls had been in school all along, so, of course, we were better readers. One day the teacher was trying to get one of the older boys to read. She was typical of the teachers at that time, insensitive and ignorant of cultural complexities. In an increasingly loud voice, she kept commanding him to "Read it, read it." He couldn't. He sat there completely still, but I could see that he was breaking into a sweat. The teacher then said, "Look, she can read it," and she pointed to me, indicating that I should stand up and read. For a young child to try to show up an older boy is wrong and totally contrary to native cultural values, so I refused. She told me to stand up and I did. My hands were trembling as I held my reader. She yelled at me to read and when I didn't she smashed her pointing stick on the desk to frighten me. In terror, I wet my pants. As I stood there fighting my tears of shame, she said I was disgusting and sent me home. I remember feeling this tremendous confusion, on top of my humiliation. We were always told the white teachers knew best, and so we had to do whatever they said at school. And yet I had a really strong sense of receiving mixed messages about what I was supposed to do in the community and what I was supposed to do at school.

11   Pretty soon I hated school. Moving to a predominantly white high school was even worse. We weren't allowed to join anything the white kids started. We were the butt of jokes because of our secondhand clothes and moose meat sandwiches.

We were constantly being rejected. The prevailing attitude was that Indians were stupid. When it was time to make course choices in class—between typing and science, for example—they didn't even ask the native kids, they just put us all in typing. You get a really bad image of yourself in a situation like that. I bought into it. I thought we were awful. The whole experience was terribly undermining. Once, my grandmother gave me a pretty little pencil box. I walked into the classroom one day to find the word "squaw" carved on it. That night I burned it in the wood stove. I joined the tough crowd and by the time I was 15 years old, I was more likely to be leaning against the school smoking a cigarette than trying to join in. I was burned out from trying to join the system. The principal told my father there was no point in sending me back to school so, with a Grade 9 education, I started to work at a series of menial jobs.

12   Seven years later something happened to me that would change my life forever. I had moved to Ottawa with a man and was working as a waitress in a restaurant. One day, a friend invited me to her place for coffee. While I was there, she told me she was going to university in the fall and showed me her reading list. I'll never forget the minutes that followed. I was feeling vaguely envious of her and once again, inferior. I remember taking the paper in my hand, seeing the books on it and realizing, Oh, my God, I've read these books! It hit me like a thunderclap. I was stunned that books I had read were being read in university. University was for white kids, not native kids. We were too stupid, we didn't have the kind of mind it took to do those things. My eyes moved down the list, and my heart started beating faster and faster as I suddenly realized I could go to university, too!

13   My partner at the time was a loving supportive man who helped me in every way. I applied to the university immediately as a mature student but when I had to write Grade 9 on the application, I was sure they'd turn me down. They didn't. I graduated five years later, earning a bachelor of arts in English and philosophy (with distinction). . . .

14   Today, there's a glimmer of hope that more of us native people will overcome the obstacles that have tripped us up ever since we began sharing this land. Some say our cultures are going through a renaissance. Maybe that's true. Certainly there's a renewed interest in native dancing, acting and singing, and in other cultural traditions. Even indigenous forms of government are becoming strong again. But we can't forget that the majority of native people live in urban areas and continue to suffer from alcohol and drug abuse and the plagues of a people who have lost their culture and have become lost themselves. And the welfare system is the insidious glue that holds together the machine of oppression of native people.

15   Too many non-native people have refused to try to understand the issues behind our land claims. They make complacent pronouncements such as "Go back to your bows and arrows and fish with spears if you want aboriginal rights. If not, give it up and assimilate into white Canadian culture." I don't agree with that. We need our culture, but there's no reason why we can't preserve it and have an automatic washing machine and a holiday in Mexico, as well.

16   The time has come for native people to make our own decisions. We need to have self-government. I have no illusions that it will be smooth sailing—there will be trial and error and further struggle. And if that means crawling before we can stand up and walk, so be it. We'll have to learn through experience.

17   While we're learning, we have a lot to teach and give to the world—a holistic philosophy, a way of living with the earth, not disposing of it. It is critical that we

all learn from the elders that an individual is not more important than a forest; we know that we're here to live on and with the earth, not to subdue it.

18   The wheels are in motion for a revival, for change in the way native people are taking their place in Canada. I can see that we're equipped, we have the tools to do the work. We have an enormous number of smart, talented, moral Indian people. It's thrilling to be a part of this movement.

19   Someday, when I'm an elder, I'll tell the children the stories: about the bush, about the hard times, about the renaissance, and especially about the importance of knowing your place in your nation.

Karen S. Peterson

Cohabiting Is *Not* the Same as Commitment

Are couples who live together less likely to marry? Some experts believe that rather than serving as a test run for marriage, cohabitation deters many men from tying the knot. This article, by reporter Karen S. Peterson, appeared in the July 8, 2002, edition of USA Today.

1   Women living unmarried with guys and expecting a lasting, committed marriage down the line had better review their options [says] researcher Scott Stanley. His research finds that men who cohabit with the women they eventually marry are less committed to the union than men who never lived with their spouses ahead of time. Stanley presented his findings at a 2002 conference sponsored by the Coalition for Marriage, Family and Couples Education in Washington, D.C.

2   But rather than settle anything for the more than 5 million unmarried American couples who live together, the research will likely spark the ongoing dispute over living together vs. marriage, and true commitment vs. a spirit of "maybe I do," in Stanley's words. And it will also raise fresh questions about who's more of a slacker in the commitment department: men or women.

3   Stanley, co-director of the Center for Marital and Family Studies at the University of Denver, says the evidence from his research is so strong that cohabiting women "should be very careful about how aligned they are with a particular man if he does not show any strong sense of marriage and a future together."

4   Men who either drift into marriage "through inertia" following a cohabiting arrangement or who are "dragged down the aisle" by women who finally put their feet down are not good marriage risks, he says.

5   Many researchers agree with Stanley: It is young men, not women, who move toward marriage with the speed of a wounded sloth. Their findings will reinforce stereotypes and infuriate many of both sexes who want to look before they leap. But still it is men, these researchers say, who drag their feet—big time.

Testing the Relationship

6   Stanley says his results do not mean there are not "a lot of super men out there," who have cohabited and are dedicated to their women both before and after heading down the aisle. But his findings do hold up on average, he says, and are reinforced by another of his current research projects.

7   The cohabiting women in Stanley's small but pioneering study did not show differences in commitment to their unions before or after marriage. He speculates that men who want "to test marriage out first" are less committed to the institution in general and their partners specifically than men who move directly to marriage without cohabiting. And he speculates that women are still socialized to put relationships first and tend to be as committed to both the union and the partner, after marriage as they were before it.

8   His findings will interest those who monitor marriage trends. Setting up shop together—before marriage or without any plans to marry—has become commonplace. Between 50% and 60% of new marriages now involve couples who have lived together first.

9   Many who live together feel it is a vaccination against divorce. "I've been dating the same girl for three years, and it just seemed the natural progression for our relationship, the next step to take," says Scott Tolchinsky, 23, of Bethesda, Md., who has just set up housekeeping with his girlfriend. "You see so many get divorced that you want to try things out."

10   Divorce is "just a huge issue for my generation," says Rosanne Garfield, 28, of Arlington, Va. "My family has not had good success with marriage. I was living with my boyfriend for the last year. I told him to make a decision (about marriage), and that ended it. But it would never cross my mind not to live together with someone before marrying him." Ironically, the divorce rate among those who once lived together is higher than among those who have not. Experts say that is often because those who choose to cohabit are not great believers in marriage in the first place.

11   Stanley sees other factors at play. In his study on live-ins who married, less religious men were particularly apt to be less committed. It may be that higher divorce rates among onetime cohabitors are a result of "the presence of males who are less dedicated, less religious and more negative" than males who didn't cohabit, he says.

12   The co-author of *Fighting for Your Marriage*, Stanley helped develop a communication skills course for couples based on 20 years of the center's research. Much of its work is funded by the National Institute of Mental Health. His current study is based on a sub-sample of 207 men and women married 10 years or less and culled from ongoing marital research on 950 adults nationwide. Standard assessments of commitment were employed during telephone interviews.

13   Stanley says his results dovetail with those from a controversial Rutgers University study released June 25. That research by sociologist David Popenoe has become a hot topic. Popenoe will elaborate further on his findings at the "Smart Marriages" conference.

14   The Rutgers study found that young men are reluctant to marry because just living with a woman is easier. They fear the cost of a divorce. They are not excited about sharing the everyday chores of parenting with their future wives. And they'd like to be financially stable first.

15   Both he and Popenoe agree, Stanley says, that "it is a bigger switch for men than women to go from being non-married to married. And men are more reluctant to throw that switch."

16   Women, Stanley says, are more willing to sacrifice for others, more willing to undergo the burdens that babies bring. And women's fertile years are limited. They hear their biological clocks ticking while men hear only the sounds of silence.

Seekers of Commitment

17   Many experts agree men are the foot-draggers. Atlanta psychiatrist Frank Pittman, author of *Grow Up!*, says men still have not been raised to be good candidates for today's egalitarian marriages. "Marriages is by its nature, total, permanent and equal. In that way it is different from any other relationship or activity." Men are still reluctant to move toward such a binding relationship, he says.

18   But the Rutgers study is causing a fuss elsewhere. The Alternatives to Marriage Project (AtMP) debunks the concept that men would rather have a live-in lover than a wife. Marshall Miller and Dorian Solot, live-ins themselves and co-founders of the non-profit group supporting non-marrieds, say that "men actually tend to be more interested in marriage than women." Among the polls and surveys they cite:

- A 1996 Gallup poll found 39% of unmarried men would prefer to be married; 29% of unmarried women would.
- A government-funded survey of high-schoolers, from 1996–2000, found 38% of senior boys believe marriage leads to a fuller and happier life: 29% of senior girls said so.
- A 1994 government-funded survey found 59% of unmarried men ages 18–35 want to get married; 48% of women agreed.

19   Men are committed to women, Miller says. "Their only hesitation is whether to commit to the institution of marriage."

20   Steve Penner of Brighton, Mass., called *USA Today* to object to the Rutgers survey. Over the last 20 years, he says, he has talked to more than 21,000 single as head of LunchDates, an upscale dating service in the Boston area. Both the men and women of today seek commitment, he says. "I really think we are picking on men. Men and women are equally looking for relationships."

21   Whether or not anyone wants to commit depends on age, financial situation and life experiences, not gender, many other say. "People are always saying all men are dogs," Tolchinsky says. "But there are lots of nice men out there who are looking to settle down. Maybe women are looking in the wrong places."

Days of Delayed Unions

22   Both sexes are delaying marriage today for financial reasons, Penner says. "They both want to buy a house first. They both want to pursue a career. These are the children of the baby boom generation, and the men and women are very similar." Indeed, both sexes are tending to marry later. The median age for first marriage for men is now about 27; for women, it is 25.

23   Her generation is waiting, says Garfield. "We have had experiences with functional and dysfunctional families all around us." A lasting commitment really depends on "trial and error," she says. And living together first is a good option.

24   Maybe, says researcher Scott Stanley. But still, there are his findings on men who cohabit first vs. those who don't, the men who live with a woman but 10 years after marriage don't feel a solid commitment to them. He says to women: "If you want someone to marry, choose someone who won't live with you."

Laura Robinson

Starving for the Gold

A former member of Canada's national cycling and nordic skiing teams, Laura Robinson (1958–) is known for her articles on sports and recreation, and particularly women athletes. Her commentaries have appeared in the Toronto Star, *the* Globe and Mail, Canadian Living, Toronto Life, Saturday Night, NOW Magazine, *and* Up Here. *She has also published* She Shoots, She Scores: Canadian Perspectives on Women in Sport *(1997) and* Crossing the Line: Sexual Assault in Canada's National Sport *(1998), a book that details the abuse in the world of minor league hockey; she is currently working on* Clearing Hurdles: The Business and Politics of Women in Sport. *Robinson no longer participates in sports competitively. Instead, she enjoys recreational ski racing, cycling, and running. In this article Robinson portrays a frightening picture of the way young female athletes are treated by their male coaches.*

Preparing to Read

As you prepare to read think about competitive sports and athletes. What does it take for someone to become a top athlete? How does pursuing this level of achievement influence the lives of those athletes? What is the appeal of competitive sports, both to the participants as well as to the observers? What benefits does one enjoy as a top athlete? What disadvantages or drawbacks might there be? In international competitions, such as the Olympic Games, why are some countries consistently winners in particular sports? Think specifically of sports such as gymnastics and figure skating, where many young women compete. As either a participant or a spectator, what role do you see coaches playing in competitive sports?

1   Imagine for a moment you are an Olympic athlete. If you pictured a male athlete, try again. Actually, you are a woman, engaged in rigorous year-round training. Now, imagine that your body-fat percentage is less than half the average for a reasonably active woman your age. As a result, your menstrual cycle has stopped; you no longer have a period. You are a textbook case of anorexia nervosa, obsessed with weight and body shape. Perhaps you are bulimic, and resort to compulsive binge eating, followed by violent purging—vomiting, fasting or the taking of laxatives and diuretics. If you are a junior athlete, in your early teens, you are effectively delaying the onset of puberty and stunting normal growth.

2   A rational observer would conclude that you are seriously ill. A rational observer would not suspect that you had been driven to these life-threatening disorders by your coach.

3   According to five women, former members of Canada's national sports teams, their coaches' insistence on excessive thinness threatened their physical health. The athletes' identities have been disguised for reasons that will presently be made clear.

4   The first woman, while still a junior, was told by her coach that she should "think about" losing weight. "I was 5-foot-5 and weighed 135, but he said, 'Look, all the top women, all the senior women are thin.' So I thought, 'Maybe I am a little chubby.' I started to train for the Calgary Olympics. By late 1987, I weighed less than 110. I was constantly hungry, but I told myself, 'This is a good feeling.' I lost another five pounds the week before our qualifying competition, but I felt

extremely weak and didn't make the team." Her standing began to suffer, and two years later she retired from active competition.

5   Says another woman, "Looking back, I can see how stupid it was. The coaches were saying, 'Hey, we've got the thinnest team around, the girls are looking great.' We didn't have great results, but that didn't seem to matter. I was just a teenager, and a coach's attitude means everything when you're young. Now, I'm angry. They screwed up my mind, and I'll never be able to look at food again the way I did before."

6   A third athlete, now attending university, wrote in a study of athletic amenorrhea (cessation of the menstrual period): "Pressure was always felt to be lean, and considerable emphasis was placed on being beneath 12 per-cent body fat. It seemed that the primary goal was to maintain a low body-fat composition. Often, it was felt this was more important than actual performance."

7   This pressure was applied in unmistakable ways. One coach held contests to see who could leave the most food uneaten on her plate at training camp. Yet another athlete experienced anxiety attacks over the caliper tests and pool dunking (total submersion in order to accurately gauge a subject's body fat). "After the tests, we'd compare results," she says. "Our coach would announce at dinner who had the lowest fat percentage, and the roller-coaster eating would start all over again."

8   One's first reaction to these charges is a measure of disbelief. We hesitate to think that coaches would do such things—but not so long ago, our athletes were supplied with anabolic steroids because it was "necessary" in order to win, because "everyone else did it." A conspiracy of silence surrounded these activities. Ben Johnson's and Angella Issajenko's physiques were obviously artificial: the changes in their bodies couldn't be attributed to natural causes. Every athlete, every sports journalist and sports official had ample cause for suspicion. No one spoke up.

9   Next, one might ask: Where are the women coaches, who presumably wouldn't participate in this nonsense? An answer is suggested by the dismissal in February of Ken Porter, Athletics Canada's former director of track and field technical programs. Mr. Porter claimed that he was fired in part because he wished to promote black and women coaches, and deplored the relegation of women to "a ghetto-type position as team chaperone."

10   Third, why hasn't coaching malfeasance come to light? Well, it has. The Dubin Report, commissioned after Ben Johnson tested positive for anabolic steroids at the 1988 Seoul Olympics, concluded that coaches must assume responsibility for the "health, welfare, moral education and preparation for life of the athlete." Since then, another report, prepared for the federal Minister of Fitness and Amateur Sport, found that athletes feel they are coerced into "harmful practices . . . and believe their concerns on the subject of personal harm are ignored." A third report, undertaken on behalf of the same ministry, is due within the next month. It is said to address the issue of physical and sexual abuse.

11   The reports stack up, the problems are studied to death, and the bad-apple coaches are seldom weeded out.

12   According to Marion Lay, manager of the Women's Program at Sport Canada (the funding agent for our national teams), "Coaches who manipulate through food and body image are robbing women of their self-esteem and self-respect. But what safe place is there for an athlete who feels abused?"

13   The women who confided in me asked for anonymity because some of them intend to work within the system; but even those who maintain only a casual interest fear that if they speak out they will be perceived as "traitors" to sport.

Ms. Lay's reaction says it all: "Of course, they can't reveal their identities. There's no mechanism to protect them."

14   Why this particular form of abuse? Helen Lenskyj, a sports sociologist at the Ontario Institute for Studies in Education, cites the emergence during the 1970s of a prepubescent body type—the very young, very thin gymnast, minus hips and breasts, whose appearance continues to influence judges when it comes to awarding points for artistic merit in the so-called esthetic sports. As a result, coaches everywhere decided that their athletes should look like Soviet gymnast Olga Korbut. In fact, leanness is a factor in both esthetic and endurance sports—to a point. Athletes shouldn't carry extra pounds. The trouble is that not everyone is prepubescent and can't possibly look that way, no matter what she does.

15   Another factor, according to Marion Lay, is simply resistance to change. The last two decades have seen a dramatic increase in the number of female competitors. Ms. Lay feels that often coaches haven't come to terms with this fact: "There's an attitude of, 'Yes, we'll let you in, but you have to play the game our way, look the way we want you to look.' Women have to give things up in order to enter sports." In other words, the predominant view (because men control sports) is that sports are male. If a woman is going to take part, she'd better resemble a man. If she's got womanly hips, she can't really be an athlete, because real athletes aren't women—and so on, all round the vicious circle.

16   Little wonder that even so cautious an organization as the Coaching Association of Canada (CAC) raises the shocking notion that nearly one-third of all women athletes have some sort of eating disorder. This figure, culled from unspecified studies, appears in the National Coaching Certification Program's Level III Course—mandatory at a national-team level. The course describes the symptoms of anorexia and bulimia, and provides checklists for their detection, but assumes that the person studying the materials isn't the source of the difficulty. According to Tom Kinsman, the CAC's executive director, "These are problems that weren't talked about before, so we didn't write about them. I hope a new awareness will go a long way in helping people raise the issues with dignity and security. But I can tell you the process won't be nice, clean and clear-cut."

17   Apparently not. In fact, these issues were under discussion when I began competing over 20 years ago. One of the problems has always been, as Mr. Kinsman admits, if a coach acts improperly, it's up to the sport's governing body, not the CAC, to discipline him—an unlikely scenario if athletes are too intimidated to lodge complaints, and "believe their concerns are ignored" when and if they do so.

18   It is important not to trivialize the issue here. Demeaning comments and sexist behaviour aren't confined to the world of sports. Yes, it's crude and counterproductive to criticize an athlete in front of her peers. If a coach's first reaction to every woman who passes by is "What a lardass," the message sinks in. These things are wounding, but women everywhere face similar indignities daily. Nor do I suggest that every coach is like Charlie Francis, Ben Johnson's steroid supplier.

19   A skeptic would argue that plenty of non-athletic teenagers are anorectic, that countless women punish their bodies for doubtful ends (silicone implants and face-lifts spring to mind), that a certain number of women athletes would succumb to eating disorders even with the most supportive and caring coach. As well, an athlete places such extraordinary demands on her body that it's hard to pinpoint cause and effect.

20   All this may be so. But it can't be denied that Canada's most senior coaches are exacerbating—if not creating—a problem of terrible magnitude.

21   With devastating results. First, long-term amenorrheics are susceptible to a loss in bone density or osteoporosis (abnormally porous or weakened bones). If these conditions persist, one in three such athletes will suffer a fracture. A 1985 study found that even athletes with irregular (as opposed to nonexistent) periods were nearly four times more prone to stress fractures than those whose periods were uninterrupted.

22   Next, and more serious, is the fact that athletes engage in regular aerobic activity, which reduces low-density lipoprotein-cholestrol. So far, so good—LDL-C is a contributing factor in coronary ailments. But because an amenorrheic woman's estrogen secretions are low, this positive effect is reversed. Up go the LDL-C levels; up goes the risk of heart disease.

23   Lastly, it's been predicted that almost 15 per cent of anorectics and bulimics will die over the course of 30 years as a direct result of their disorders. There hasn't been a verifiable instance yet among Canadian athletes—but these are early days.

24   So the question remains. Why would a coach encourage such dangerous behaviour? Anorectic athletes are too unhealthy to do well over the long haul; you can't compete at the international level if you're starving yourself. Many athletes eventually break down and disappear from view. Unless they're household names, no one notices. They're interchangeable, there are plenty more where they came from.

25   One answer has been suggested by Ms. Lenskyj, the OISE sports psychologist: it's imitative crime. In addition to underage gymnasts like Olga Korbut, a fair number of older European athletes are much too thin. I could name an entire cycling team whose members are plainly anorectic. They're fast on the road, but they're burning out even faster. Watch for them at the Barcelona Olympics, because they won't be competing in a couple of years.

26   But Marion Lay's comments earlier about forced make-overs may be closer to the mark. Notes Karin Jasper, a Toronto psychotherapist, "The athletic look is lean with narrow hips, and we have learned that women dislike the size of their hips, stomachs and thighs, those areas most connected with pregnancy." Constant harping on these areas—the first ones to catch a male coach's eye—is enough to stir up instant insecurity. "The ideal male athlete has narrow hips, but that's not normal for women," says Ms. Lenskyj. "Dieting can't change skeletal structure. Only a few girls have bodies that correspond to a male's in terms of leanness. If coaches use weight and fat percentages as a tool to manipulate athletes, it is a form of sexual abuse."

27   The inescapable conclusion is that the coach, unused to women in sport, wants them to look like boys. Or, failing that, like little girls. This syndrome assumes even more ominous overtones when you consider the inordinate number of women athletes and coaches who wind up as romantic items. I remember a Canadian national team where every member was living with or married to her coach or technical adviser. One hesitates to speculate on these unions. According to Karin Jasper, an unfortunate side-effect of self-starvation is often a loss of sexual drive. The coach gets less than he bargained for in that department. The other possibility is that his fondest wish has come true—he has found someone who's lost all outward signs of womanhood—no breasts, no hips, no period. It makes you wonder whether he might not be happier coaching little boys.

28   The real imperative here is obviously control over someone less powerful, someone malleable and eager to please. Given that girls begin their athletic careers very young, they don't get a chance to develop into well-rounded human beings in any sense. I personally believe that many male coaches don't like, and are ill-equipped to deal with, grown women. There's no other explanation for the ceaseless humiliation and ridicule—the construction of a closed system where trauma becomes a tool to produce great-looking girls, the thinnest team around.

29   Is change possible in the world of organized sports? Let's give coaches the benefit of the doubt. Maybe they think that all these things will actually help us bring home lots of medals. Remember the outcry when Canada's skaters "failed" to win Gold and had to "settle for" Bronze. Third-best in the world translated as "not good enough." (The logical extension of this sort of thinking is that, whatever an athlete's body is like, it's never right. It's too fat, too thin, too this or too that.)

30   When our athletes, being human, made mistakes, they were savagely criticized by the media. As a result, every athlete, man or woman, becomes a performance machine. Karin Jasper is not surprised: "We talk to girls and women about overcoming perfectionism, about not basing their evaluation of themselves on all-or-nothing standards. But athletes are taught to see themselves this way. Either they win, or they don't. When their entire value is based on performance, they won't be viewed as a whole person, they're one-dimensional."

31   Under these conditions, even an influx of women coaches would do little good. Until the system asks what's best for a given person, not an athlete, it's stuck in the all-or-nothing groove. For male coaches to change, they'd have to re-examine their priorities, their own sexuality, their entire basis for coaching. That's not going to happen.

32   The real tragedy is that sports can feel so good, so refreshing and exciting and freeing. I entered organized sports when I was 14. I was lucky. I had people who made sure I got to the races on time, but also gave me plenty of books to read. Still, I couldn't help but be affected to some degree. I was obsessed with exercise; I overtrained. That was my response to the pressure, and it wasn't healthy. Even now, I tend to avoid scales. I have to think twice if someone asks me if I consider myself thin. I escaped the worst of it, but my attitudes remain.

33   One of the women whose own sad story I recounted earlier has started to coach girls between the ages of 12 and 16. "They ask me if they're overweight," she says, "and I tell them, 'If you think you can work with your weight, then you're fine. This is the body God has given you, so enjoy it.' " That's encouraging, as far as it goes—although the fact that 12-year-old athletes anguish about their weight is food for thought. But, because of her experiences, this woman is incapable of saying, "This is the body God has given me, so I'll enjoy it." That has been taken from her and nothing can compensate her for such a loss.

Russell Baker

[handwritten: P.O.V. on issue]

School vs. Education

Russell Baker (1925–) was born in a rural town in Virginia and grew up in New Jersey and Maryland. He received his B.A. in English from Johns Hopkins University in 1947 and worked as a reporter for the Baltimore Sun and then the New York Times. In 1962 he began writing his "Observer" column for the Times, which was syndicated in over 400 newspaper for more than two decades. His topics range from the mundane everyday annoyances to serious social problems, and his style is generally casual but thoughtful. In 1979 he received the Pulitzer Prize for distinguished commentary; he received the Prize again for his autobiography Growing Up *(1982). His collections of columns and essays include* All Things Considered *(1965),* Poor Russell's Almanac *(1972),* So This Is Depravity *(1980)* The Rescue of Miss Yaskell and Other Pipe Dreams *(1983), and* There's a Country in My Cellar *(1990). The following piece, first published in his* New York Times *column in 1975, interwines serious commentary on American education and values with a spoof on what our schools teach. As you read it, think about the serious message Baker wants to communicate to us.*

1   By the age of six the average child will have completed the basic American education and be ready to enter school. If the child has been attentive in these preschool years, he or she will already have mastered many skills.

2   From television, the child will have learned how to pick a lock, commit a fairly elaborate bank holdup, prevent wetness all day long, get the laundry twice as white, and kill people with a variety of sophisticated armaments.

3   From watching his parents, the child, in many cases, will already know how to smoke, how much soda to mix with whiskey, what kind of language to use when angry, and how to violate the speed laws without being caught.

4   At this point, the child is ready for the second stage of education, which occurs in school. There, a variety of lessons may be learned in the very first days.

5   The teacher may illustrate the economic importance of belonging to a strong union by closing down the school before the child arrives. Fathers and mothers may demonstrate to the child the social cohesion that can be built on shared hatred by demonstrating their dislike for children whose pigmentation displeases them. In the latter event, the child may receive visual instruction in techniques of stoning buses, cracking skulls with a nightstick, and subduing mobs with tear gas. Formal education has begun.

6   During formal education, the child learns that life is for testing. This stage lasts twelve years, a period during which the child learns that success comes from telling testers what they want to hear.

7   Early in this stage, the child learns that he is either dumb or smart. If the teacher puts intelligent demands upon the child, the child learns he is dumb and soon quits bothering to tell the testers what they want to hear.

[handwritten margin notes: "Good verbs used to describe learning", "stages repeated", "Repetition of 'formal' leading to ethical appeal of real education"]

8   At this point, education becomes more subtle. The child taught by school that he is dumb observes that neither he, she, nor any of the many children who are even dumber, ever fails to be promoted to the next grade. From this, the child learns that while everybody talks a lot about the virtue of being smart, there is very little incentive to stop being dumb.

9   What is the point of school, besides attendance? the child wonders. As the end of the first formal stage of education approaches, school answers this question. The point is to equip the child to enter college.

10   Children who have been taught they are smart have no difficulty. They have been happily telling testers what they want to hear for twelve years. Being artists at telling testers what they want to hear, they are admitted to college joyously, where they promptly learn that they are the hope of America.

metaphor

11   Children whose education has been limited to adjusting themselves to their schools' low estimates of them are admitted to less joyous colleges which, in some cases, may teach them to read.

12   At this stage of education, a fresh question arises for everyone. If the point of lower education was to get into college, what is the point of college? The answer is soon learned. The point of college is to prepare the student—no longer a child now—to get into graduate school. In college the student learns that it is no longer enough simply to tell the testers what they want to hear. Many are tested for graduate school; few are admitted.

professional, important — 1st person jobs

13   Those excluded may be denied valuable certificates to prosper in medicine, at the bar, in the corporate boardroom. The student learns that the race is to the cunning and often, alas, to the unprincipled.

14   Thus, the student learns the importance of destroying competitors and emerges richly prepared to play his role in the great simmering melodrama of American life.

imagery of rich

15   Afterward, the former student's destiny fulfilled, his life rich with Oriental carpets, rare porcelain, and full bank accounts, he may one day find himself with the leisure and the inclination to open a book with a curious mind, and start to become educated.

"real" → irony

Suspense
- Builds up point in stages

- message about how authoritarian and structured school can be
- Sometimes no creativity, all about testing + getting good marks
- Ignores other talents children have — no real life lessons no choice in material
"formal" education

Jamie O'Meara

Guns, Sex, and Education

Guns and schools—put these two nouns together and immediately you conjure up tragedies such as Columbine High School in the U.S. or Myers High School in Taber, Alberta. Naturally, most people would concur that firearms have no place in our schools. But in this article from Saturday Night, Jamie O'Meara argues that in order to counter children's natural curiosity, gun education should, in fact, be part of our schools' curricula. Gun education, he argues, including handling and even firing guns, is the only way to remove the mystique of firearms and the only way to get kids to think about guns in a responsible manner.

Jamie O'Meara is the editor-in-chief of Hour, an alternative weekly newspaper in Montreal. This article first appeared in Saturday Night on May 20, 2000.

CRITICAL THINKING *Do you feel that guns have a place in our schools under controlled circumstances? What might be the benefits of introducing firearms into the current curricula of our high schools?*

1   The first thing I noticed was its weight. It wasn't just cold, it was heavy, like the rock you pick up when you're six years old, with visions of windowpanes dancing in your head. By itself, it's just a rock. In your hand, it has power. That's how the gun felt.

2   It was a 9-mm military-issue Browning semi-automatic, I think, obtained from a friend who had joined the army cadets. Because of its weight, I had a hard time levelling it at the car battery we'd put halfway up the slope of the abandoned gravel pit at the back of our rural Ontario farm. This was where my brother and I spent a good part of our summers, with our .22-calibre rifles and .177 pellet guns, keeping the pop-bottle population under control. This gun, though, felt different than the ones we'd been shooting since we were kids. Fascinatingly so.

3   Borrowing my stance from every cop show ever made, I lined up my plastic prey and squeezed the trigger five times in quick succession. The first shot hit the battery and the next four thumped into the earth about twenty feet in front of me. A box of fifty rounds later, I was no closer to hitting my target with any regularity and, frankly, my hand was beginning to hurt. I packed the gun away and returned it to my buddy. (He, after exhausting its cachet among our friends, tossed it in a local river.)

4   All in all: boring.

5   And that may be a hard concept to grasp if, like most North Americans, you were raised on a steady diet of *Rambo, The Terminator,* and *Mad Max*: they showed that guns are fun, the implements of adventure. If you're holding one, people do what you want them to do. All of that's pretty attractive to young people, for whom power and control often seem in scarce supply. So why would a kid voluntarily give up the chance to play with a handgun?

6   Certainly not because of parental warnings. Lock the booze cabinet with double-plated armour and that's not going to save your Smirnoff. Threaten blindness and the wrath of all saints and that's not going to stop adolescents from masturbating. And tell children that guns are dangerous and that's not going to stop them from wanting to use one if it's accessible—in the gun cabinet, from a store, or in the schoolyard. All you can hope to do is teach them to act responsibly if the occasion arises.

7   Which is why guns belong in our schools.

8   Any parent knows that the best way to defuse the curiosity of a child is to address it head on, to transform the mysterious into the mundane. If memory serves, there is no place more mundane than school. Adding a firearm component to the current curricula in regions where guns are prevalent would achieve two things: it would satisfy the inherent inquisitiveness that children have about guns; and it would allow educators to monitor the reactions children have to the weapons—something that might have been of inestimable value to the faculty at Columbine High School in Colorado.

9   In Canada, it may be argued that guns aren't prevalent enough—in homes or on the streets—to warrant a proactive approach to gun education. Tragedies such

as the one last year in Taber, Alberta, and the recent spate of youth shootings in Toronto indicate otherwise.

10   Put a kid on a firing range under strict controls, oblige him to fire hundreds of rounds at a circular target over lengthy periods of time, and what happens? Dirty Harry becomes a junior biathlete, without the skis. The kids who maintain an interest can be funnelled into gun clubs, where they can work through their attraction under the watchful eyes of trainers adept at spotting potential problems.

11   As long as guns have a mystique, they'll seem powerful. As long as kids feel there's power in guns, they'll be tempted to get their hands on them. And sooner or later someone who possesses a gun is going to want to use it. The solution is to address this desire early on and supply children with the rules of conduct. It's the same principle that lies behind sex education.

12   Think about it: sex education is taught so that kids will have a better understanding of how their bodies work, why they feel sexual desires, and how to act (or not) on those desires. Basically, we equip our kids with sexual knowledge so that they'll have the confidence to act responsibly. The same argument holds true for gun education: that, armed with knowledge and familiarity, kids will be better equipped to think about guns in a responsible manner. (In fact, the classic argument against sex education—that by providing kids with dangerous information they can't handle, we're encouraging them to run out and recklessly try it for themselves—is exactly the objection you're likely to hear raised against gun instruction.)

13   We accept the natural sexual curiosity of children and teenagers, and have legislated protection for them in the form of education, rather than pretending that the curiosity doesn't exist. Children are also curious about guns. We should give them the same protection. We don't want our kids shooting first and asking questions later.

Catherine Pigott

Chicken-Hips*

Catherine Pigott, producer for the Canadian Broadcasting Corporation's This Morning, *became aware of women's issues when she taught English in Gambia in the early 1980s. Since then she has continued to champion women's concerns, recently serving on the Advisory Committee to the Afghan Women's Organization and producing the 1998 Canadian project and report "Muslim Women in the Media." The idea for* Chicken Hips *occurred to Pigott after she watched Katherine Gilday's documentary on eating disorders entitled* The Famine Within. *Soon after an interview with Gilday, Pigott was moved to pen the following essay.*

1   The women of the household clucked disapprovingly when they saw me. It was the first time I had worn African clothes since my arrival in tiny, dusty Gambia,

and evidently they were not impressed. They adjusted my head-tie and pulled my *lappa,* the ankle-length fabric I had wrapped around myself, even tighter. "You're too thin," one of them pronounced. "It's no good." They nicknamed me "Chicken-hips."

2   I marvelled at this accolade, for I had never been called thin in my life. It was something I longed for. I would have been flattered if those ample-bosomed women hadn't looked so distressed. It was obvious I fell far short of their ideal of beauty.

3   I had dressed up for a very special occasion—the baptism of a son. The women heaped rice into tin basins the size of laundry tubs, shaping it into mounds with their hands. Five of us sat around one basin, thrusting our fingers into the scalding food. These women ate with such relish, such joy. They pressed the rice into balls in their fists, squeezing until the bright-red palm oil ran down their forearms and dripped off their elbows.

4   I tried desperately, but I could not eat enough to please them. It was hard for me to explain that I come from a culture in which it is almost unseemly for a woman to eat too heartily. It's considered unattractive. It was even harder to explain that to me thin is beautiful, and in my country we deny ourselves food in our pursuit of perfect slenderness.

5   That night, everyone danced to welcome the baby. Women swivelled their broad hips and used their hands to emphasize the roundness of their bodies. One needed to be round and wide to make the dance beautiful. There was no place for thinness here. It made people sad. It reminded them of things they wanted to forget, such as poverty, drought and starvation. You never knew when the rice was going to run out.

6   I began to believe that Africa's image of the perfect female body was far more realistic than the long-legged leanness I had been conditioned to admire. There, it is beautiful—not shameful—to carry weight on the hips and thighs, to have a round stomach and heavy, swinging breasts. Women do not battle the bulge, they celebrate it. A body is not something to be tamed and moulded.

7   The friends who had christened me Chicken-hips made it their mission to fatten me up. It wasn't long before a diet of rice and rich, oily stew twice a day began to change me. Every month, the women would take a stick and measure my backside, noting with pleasure its gradual expansion. "Oh Catherine, your buttocks are getting nice now!" They would say.

8   What was extraordinary was that I, too, believed I was becoming more beautiful. There was no sense of panic, no shame, no guilt-ridden resolves to go on the miracle grape-and-water diet. One day, I tied my *lappa* tight across my hips and went to the market to buy beer for a wedding. I carried the crate of bottles home on my head, swinging my hips slowly as I walked. I felt transformed.

9   In Gambia, people don't use words such as "cheating," "naughty," or "guilty" when they talk about eating. The language of sin is not applied to food. Fat is desirable. It holds beneficial meanings of abundance, fertility and health.

10   My perception of beauty altered as my body did. The European tourists on the beach began to look strange and skeletal rather than "slim." They had no hips. They seemed devoid of shape and substance. Women I once would have envied appeared fragile and even ugly. The ideal they represented no longer made sense.

11   After a year, I came home. I preached my new way of seeing to anyone who would listen. I wanted to cling to the liberating belief that losing weight had nothing to do with self-love.

12   Family members kindly suggested that I might look and feel better if I slimmed down a little. They encouraged me to join an exercise club. I wandered around the malls in a dislocated daze. I felt uncomfortable trying on clothes that hung so elegantly on the mannequins. I began hearing old voices inside my head: "Plaid makes you look fat. . . . You're too short for that style. . . . Vertical stripes are more slimming. . . . Wear black."

13   I joined the club. Just a few weeks after I had worn a *lappa* and scooped up rice with my hands, I was climbing into pink leotards and aerobics shoes. The instructor told me that I had to set fitness goals and "weigh in" after my workouts. There were mirrors on the walls and I could see women watching themselves. I sensed that even the loveliest among them felt they were somehow flawed. As the aerobics instructor barked out commands for arm lifts and leg lifts, I pictured Gambian women pounding millet and dancing in a circle with their arms raised high. I do not mean to romanticize their rock-hard lives, but we were hardly to be envied as we ran like fools between two walls to the tiresome beat of synthesized music.

14   We were a roomful of women striving to reshape ourselves into some kind of pubertal ideal. I reverted to my natural state: one of yearning to be slimmer and more fit than I was. My freedom had been temporary. I was home, where fat is feared and despised. It was time to exert control over my body and my life. I dreaded the thought of people saying, "She's let herself go."

15   If I return to Africa I am sure the women will shake their heads in bewildered dismay. Even now, I sometimes catch my reflection in a window and their voices come back to me. "Yo! Chicken-hips!"

Anjula Razdan

What's Love Got to Do with It?

For thousands of years, marriage was traditionally an arrangement based on economic and social considerations. It is only over the last century or so that marriage was the capstone of a loving relationship. But with over half of all marriages ending in divorce, are we going about this the wrong way? Many countries still view marriage as a political, social, and economic arrangement. The Western view of marriage is considered odd by many cultures that consider arranged marriages far more fruitful and intelligent than ones based on something as fickle as love. Are arranged marriages healthier than romantic attraction?

Anjula Razdan is associate editor of Utne *magazine, in which this article was first published in the May/June 2003 issue.*

CRITICAL THINKING *Is love the most important element in a marriage? What other factors are important for a successful marriage?*

1   One of the greatest pleasures of my teen years was sitting down with a bag of cinnamon Red Hots and a new LaVyrle Spencer romance, immersing myself in another tale of star-crossed lovers drawn together by the heart's mysterious

alchemy. My mother didn't get it. "Why are you reading that?" she would ask, her voice tinged with both amusement and horror. Everything in her background told her that romance was a waste of time.

2   Born and raised in Illinois by parents who emigrated from India 35 years ago, I am the product of an arranged marriage, and yet I grew up under the spell of Western romantic love—first comes love, then comes marriage—which both puzzled and dismayed my parents. Their relationship was set up over tea and samosas by their grandfathers, and they were already engaged when they went on their first date, a chaperoned trip to the movies. My mom and dad still barely knew each other on their wedding day—and they certainly hadn't fallen in love. Yet both were confident that their shared values, beliefs, and family background would form a strong bond that, over time, would develop into love.

3   "But, what could they possibly know of real love?" I would ask myself petulantly after each standoff with my parents over whether or not I could date in high school (I couldn't) and whether I would allow them to arrange my marriage (I wouldn't). The very idea of an arranged marriage offended my ideas of both love and liberty—to me, the act of choosing whom to love represented the very essence of freedom. To take away that choice seemed like an attack not just on my autonomy as a person, but on democracy itself.

4   And, yet, even in the supposedly liberated West, the notion of choosing your mate is a relatively recent one. Until the 19th century, writes historian E.J. Graff in *What Is Marriage For?: The Strange Social History of Our Most Intimate Institution*, arranged marriages were quite common in Europe as a way of forging alliances, ensuring inheritances, and stitching together the social, political, and religious needs of a community. Love had nothing to do with it.

5   Fast forward a couple hundred years to 21st-century America, and you see a modern, progressive society where people are free to choose their mates, for the most part, based on love instead of social or economic gain. But for many people, a quiet voice from within wonders: Are we really better off? Who hasn't at some point in their life—at the end of an ill-fated relationship or midway through dinner with the third "date-from-hell" this month—longed for a matchmaker to find the right partner? No hassles. No effort. No personal ads or blind dates.

6   The point of the Western romantic ideal is to live "happily ever after," yet nearly half of all marriages in this country end in divorce, and the number of never-married adults grows each year. Boundless choice notwithstanding, what does it mean when the marital success rate is the statistical equivalent of a coin toss?

7   "People don't really know how to choose a long-term partner," offers Dr. Alvin Cooper, the director of the San Jose Marital Services and Sexuality Centre and a staff psychologist at Standford University. "The major reasons that people find and get involved with somebody else are proximity and physical attraction. And both of these factors are terrible predictors of long-term happiness in a relationship."

8   At the moment we pick a mate, Cooper says, we are often blinded by passion and therefore virtually incapable of making a sound decision.

9   *Psychology Today* editor Robert Epstein agrees. "[It's] like getting drunk and marrying someone in Las Vegas," he quips. A former director of the Cambridge Center for Behavioral Studies, Epstein holds a decidedly unromantic view of courtship and love. Indeed, he argues it is our myths of "love at first sight" and

"a knight in a shining Porsche" that get so many of us into trouble. When the heat of passion wears off—and it always does, he says—can be left with virtually nothing "except lawyer's bills."

10   Epstein points out that many arranged marriages result in an enduring love because they promote compatibility and rational deliberation ahead of passionate impulse. Epstein himself is undertaking a bold step to prove his theory that love can be learned. He wrote an editorial in *Psychology Today* last year seeking women to participate in the experiment with him. He proposed to choose one of the "applicants," and together they would attempt to fall in love—consciously and deliberately. After receiving more than 1,000 responses, none of which seemed right, Epstein yielded just a little to impulse, asking Gabriela, an intriguing Venezuelan woman he met on a plane, to join him in the project. After an understandable bout of cold feet, she eventually agreed.

11   In a "love contract" the two signed on Valentine's Day this year to seal the deal, Epstein stipulates that he and Gabriela must undergo intensive counseling to learn how to communicate effectively and participate in a variety of exercises designed to foster mutual love. To help oversee and guide the project, Epstein has even formed an advisory board made up of high-profile relationship experts, most notably Dr. John Gray, who wrote the best-selling *Men Are From Mars, Women Are From Venus*. If the experiment pans out, the two will have learned to love each other within a year's time.

12   It may strike some as anathema to be so premeditated about the process of falling in love, but to hear Epstein tell it, most unions fail exactly because they aren't intentional enough; they're based on a roll of the dice and a determination to stake everything on love. What this means, Epstein says, is that most people lack basic relationship skills, and, as a result, most relationships lack emotional and psychological intimacy.

13   A divorced father of four, Epstein himself married for passion—"just like I was told to do by the fairy tales and by the movies"—but eventually came to regret it. "I had the experience that so many people have now," he says, "which is basically looking at your partner and going, 'Who are you?'" Although Epstein acknowledges the non-Western tradition of arranged marriage is a complex, somewhat flawed institution, he thinks we can "distill key elements of [it] to help us learn how to create a new, more stable institution in the West."

14   Judging from the phenomenon of reality-TV shows like *Married by America* and *Meet My Folks* and the recent increase in the number of professional matchmakers, the idea of arranging marriages (even if in nontraditional ways) seems to be taking hold in this country—perhaps nowhere more powerfully than in cyberspace. Online dating services attracted some 20 million people last year (roughly one-fifth of all singles—and growing), who used sites like Match.com and Yahoo Personals to hook up with potentially compatible partners. Web sites' search engines play the role of patriarchal grandfathers, searching for good matches based on any number of criteria that you select.

15   Cooper, the Stanford psychologist and author of *Sex and the Internet: A Guidebook for Clinicians,* and an expert in the field of online sexuality, says that because online interaction tends to downplay proximity, physical attraction, and face-to-face interaction, people are more likely to take risks and disclose significant things about themselves. The result is that they attain a higher level of psychological and emotional intimacy than if they dated right away or hopped in the sack. Indeed, online dating represents a return to what University of Chicago Humanities Professor Amy Kass calls the "distanced nearness" of

old-style courtship, an intimate and protected (cyber)space that encourages self-revelation while maintaining personal boundaries.

16   And whether looking for a fellow scientist, someone else who's HIV-positive, or a B-movie film buff, an online dater has a much higher likelihood of finding "the one" due to the computer's capacity to sort through thousands of potential mates. "That's what computers are all about—efficiency and sorting," says Cooper, who believes that online dating has the potential to lower the nation's 50 percent divorce rate. There is no magic or "chemistry" involved in love, Cooper insists. "It's specific, operationalizable factors."

17   Love's mystery solved by "operationalizable factors"! Why does that sound a little less than inspiring? Sure, for many people the Internet can efficiently facilitate love and help to nudge fate along. But, for the diehard romantic who trusts in surprise, coincidence, and fate, the cyber-solution to love lacks heart. "To the romantic," observes English writer Blake Morrison in *The Guardian,* "every marriage is an arranged marriage—arranged by fate, that is, which gives us no choice."

18   More than a century ago, Emily Dickinson mocked those who would dissect birds to find the mechanics of song:

> Split the Lark—and you'll find the Music—
> Bulb after Bulb, in Silver rolled—
> Scantily dealt to the Summer Morning
> Saved for your Ear when Lutes be old.
>
> Loose the Flood—you shall find it patent—
> Gush after Gush, reserved for you—
> Scarlet Experiment! Skeptic Thomas!
> Now, do you doubt that your Bird was true?

19   In other words, writes Deborah Blum in her book, *Sex on the Brain,* "kill the bird and [you] silence the melody." For some, nurturing the ideal of romantic love may be more important than the goal of love itself. Making a more conscious choice in mating may help partners handle the complex personal ties and obligations of marriage; but romantic love, infused as it is with myth and projection and doomed passion, is a way to live outside of life's obligations, outside of time itself—if only for a brief, bright moment. Choosing love by rational means might not be worth it for those souls who'd rather roll the dice and risk the possibility of ending up with nothing but tragic nobility and the bittersweet tang of regret.

20   In the end, who really wants to examine love too closely? I'd rather curl up with a LaVyrle Spencer novel or dream up the French movie version of my life than live in a world where the mechanics of love—and its giddy, mysterious buzz—are laid bare. After all, to actually unravel love's mystery is, perhaps, to miss the point of it all.

Wayson Choy

I'm a Banana and Proud of It

Now a teacher of English at Toronto's Humber College and a faculty member at the Humber School for Writers, Wayson Choy (1939–) was born and raised in British Columbia, where he was the first Chinese Canadian to enroll in the University of British Columbia's creative writing program. Since that time, Choy has won the 1996 Trillium Award and the 1996 Vancouver City Book Award for his first novel, The Jade Peony, *which is about Vancouver's Chinatown during the Depression and World War II. Choy followed* The Jade Peony *with the critically acclaimed* Paper Shadows: A Chinatown Childhood, *a memoir about his own experiences growing up in Vancouver's Chinatown and the discovery of hidden truths about his childhood. Choy describes his childhood as being "like a Chinese box that opens in a variety of different ways, revealing dif-ferent levels, each sliding compartment a secret"; in* Paper Shadows, *he explores the challenges of growing up with his Chinese heritage often in conflict with the influences of the North American culture in which he was living.*

Choy is currently working on a new novel, a sequel to The Jade Peony *called* The Ten Thousand Things.

Preparing to Read

In this essay, which first appeared in the Globe and Mail's *Facts and Arguments column, Wayson Choy proudly defines himself as a "banana," an affectionate nickname for integrated North American children of Chinese parents. Before reading this essay think about nicknames and the role that they play in our lives. Who assigns nicknames? Who uses them? What makes some nicknames stick and others fade? Are nicknames positive or negative? Do you have a nickname? Do you like it? Does it appropriately reflect who you are?*

1   Because both my parents came from China, I took Chinese. But I cannot read or write Chinese and barely speak it. I love my North American citizenship. I don't mind being called a "banana," yellow on the outside and white inside. I'm proud I'm a banana.

2   After all, in Canada and the United States, native Indians are "apples" (red out-side, white inside); blacks are "Oreo cookies" (black and white); and Chinese are "bananas." These metaphors assume, both rightly and wrongly, that the culture here has been primarily anglo-white. Cultural history made me a banana.

3   History: My father and mother arrived separately to the B.C. coast in the early part of the century. They came as unwanted "aliens." Better to be an alien here than to be dead of starvation in China. But after the Chinese Exclusion laws were passed in North America (late 1800s, early 1900s), no Chinese immi-grants were granted citizenship in either Canada or the United States.

4   Like those Old China village men from *Toi San* who, in the 1850s, laid down cliff-edge train tracks through the Rockies and the Sierras, or like those first women who came as mail-order wives or concubines and who as bond-slaves were turned into cheaper labourers or even prostitutes—like many of those men and

women, my father and mother survived ugly, unjust times. In 1917, two hours after he got off the boat from Hong Kong, my father was called "chink" and told to go back to China. "Chink" is a hateful racist term, stereotyping the shape of Asian eyes: "a chink in the armour," an undesirable slit. For the Elders, the past was humiliating. Eventually, the Second World War changed hostile attitudes toward the Chinese.

5   During the war, Chinese men volunteered and lost their lives as members of the American and Canadian military. When hostilities ended, many more were proudly in uniform waiting to go overseas. Record Chinatown dollars were raised to buy War Bonds. After 1945, challenged by such money and ultimate sacrifices, the Exclusion laws in both Canada and the United States were revoked. Chinatown residents claimed their citizenship and sent for their families.

6   By 1949, after the Communist took over China, those of us who arrived here as young children, or were born here, stayed. No longer "aliens," we became legal citizens of North America. Many of us also became "bananas."

7   Historically, "banana" is not a racist term. Although it clumsily stereotypes many of the children and grandchildren of the Old Chinatowns, the term actually follows the old Chinese tendency to assign endearing nicknames to replace formal names, semicomic names to keep one humble. Thus, "banana" describes the generations who assimilated so well into North American life.

8   In fact, our families encouraged members of my generation in the 1950s and sixties to "get ahead," to get an English education, to get a job with good pay and prestige. "Don't work like me," Chinatown parents said. "Work in an office!" The *lao wah-kiu* (the Chinatown old-timers) also warned, "Never forget—you still be Chinese!"

9   None of us ever forgot. The mirror never lied.

10   Many Chinatown teen-agers felt we didn't quite belong in any one world. We looked Chinese, but thought and behaved North American. Impatient Chinatown parents wanted the best of both worlds for us, but they bluntly labelled their children and grandchildren *"juk-sing"* or even *"mo no."* Not that we were totally "shallow bamboo butt-ends" or entirely "no brain," but we had less and less understanding of Old China traditions, and less and less interest in their village histories. Father used to say we lacked Taoist ritual, Taoist manners. We were, he said, *"mo li."*

11   This was true. Chinatown's younger brains, like everyone else's of whatever race, were being colonized by "white bread" U.S. family television programs. We began to feel Chinese home life was inferior. We co-operated with English-language magazines that showed us how to act and what to buy. Seductive Hollywood movies made some of us secretly weep that we did not have moviestar faces. American music made Chinese music sound like noise.

12   By the 1970s and eighties, many of us had consciously or unconsciously distanced ourselves from our Chinatown histories. We became bananas.

13   Finally, for me, in my 40s or 50s, with the death first of my mother, then my father, I realized I did not belong anywhere unless I could understand the past. I needed to find the foundation of my Chinese-ness. I needed roots.

14   I spent my college holidays researching the past. I read Chinatown oral histories, located documents, searched out early articles. Those early citizens came back to life for me. Their long toil and blood sacrifices, the proud record of their patient, legal challenges, gave us all our present rights as citizens. Canadian and

American Chinatowns set aside their family tongue differences and encouraged each other to fight injustice. There were no borders. "After all," they affirmed, *"Daaih ga tohng yahn . . .* We are all Chinese!"

15   In my book, *The Jade Peony,* I tried to recreate this past, to explore the beginnings of the conflicts trapped within myself, the struggle between being Chinese and being North American. I discovered a truth: these "between world" struggles are universal.

16   In every human being, there is "the Other"—something that makes each of us feel how different we are to everyone else, even to family members. Yet, ironically, we are all the same, wanting the same security and happiness. I know this now.

17   I think the early Chinese pioneers actually started "going bananas" from the moment they first settled upon the West Coast. They had no choice. They adapted. They initiated assimilation. If they had not, they and their family would have starved to death. I might even suggest that all surviving Chinatown citizens eventually became bananas. Only some, of course, were more ripe than others.

18   That's why I'm proudly a banana: I accept the paradox of being both Chinese and not Chinese.

19   Now at last, whenever I look in the mirror or hear ghost voices shouting, "You still Chinese!", I smile.

20   I know another truth: In immigrant North America, we are all Chinese.

William Lutz

With These Words, I Can Sell You Anything

1   One problem advertisers have when they try to convince you that the product they are pushing is really different from other, similar products is that their claims are subject to some laws. Not a lot of laws, but there are some designed to prevent fraudulent or untruthful claims in advertising. Even during the happy years of nonregulation under President Ronald Reagan, the FTC did crack down on the more blatant abuses in advertising claims. Generally speaking, advertisers have to be careful in what they say in their ads, in the claims they make for the products they advertise. Parity claims are safe because they are legal and supported by a number of court decisions. But beyond parity claims there are weasel words.

2   Advertisers use weasel words to appear to be making a claim for a product when in fact they are making no claim at all. Weasel words get their name from the way weasels eat the eggs they find in the nests of other animals. A weasel will make a small hole in the egg, suck out the insides, then place the egg back in the nest. Only when the egg is examined closely is it found to be hollow. That's the way it is with weasel words in advertising: Examine weasel words closely and you'll find that they're as hollow as any egg sucked by a weasel. Weasel words appear to say one thing when in fact they say the opposite, or nothing at all.

"Help"—The Number One Weasel Word

3   The biggest weasel word used in advertising doublespeak is "help." Now "help" only means to aid or assist, nothing more. It does not mean to conquer, stop, eliminate, end, solve, heal, cure, or anything else. But once the ad says "help," it can say just about anything after that because "help" qualifies everything coming after it. The trick is that the claim that comes after the weasel word is usually so strong and so dramatic that you forget the word "help" and concentrate only on the dramatic claim. You read into the ad a message that the ad does not contain. More importantly, the advertiser is not responsible for the claim that you read into the ad, even though the advertiser wrote the ad so you would read that claim into it.

4   The next time you see an ad for a cold medicine that promises that it "helps relieve cold symptoms fast," don't rush out to buy it. Ask yourself what this claim is really saying. Remember, "helps" means only that the medicine will aid or assist. What will it aid or assist in doing? Why, "relieve" your cold "symptoms." "Relieve" only means to ease, alleviate, or mitigate, not to stop, end, or cure. Nor does the claim say how much relieving this medicine will do. Nowhere does this ad claim it will cure anything. In fact, the ad doesn't even claim it will *do* anything at all. The ad only claims that it will aid in relieving (not curing) your cold symptoms, which are probably a runny nose, watery eyes, and a headache. In other words, this medicine probably contains a standard decongestant and some aspirin. By the way, what does "fast" mean? Ten minutes, one hour, one day? What is fast to one person can be very slow to another. Fast is another weasel word.

5   Ad claims using "help" are among the most popular ads. One says, "Helps keep you young looking," but then a lot of things will help keep you young looking, including exercise, rest, good nutrition, and a facelift. More importantly, this ad doesn't say the product will keep you young, only "young *looking*." Someone may look young to one person and old to another.

6   A toothpaste ad says, "Helps prevent cavities," but it doesn't say it will actually prevent cavities. Brushing your teeth regularly, avoiding sugars in foods, and flossing daily will also help prevent cavities. A liquid cleaner ad says, "Helps keep your home germ free," but it doesn't say it actually kills germs, nor does it even specify which germs it might kill.

7   "Help" is such a useful weasel word that it is often combined with other action-verb weasel words such as "fight" and "control." Consider the claim, "Helps control dandruff symptoms with regular use." What does it really say? It will assist in controlling (not eliminating, stopping, ending, or curing) the *symptoms* of dandruff, not the cause of dandruff nor the dandruff itself. What are the symptoms of dandruff? The ad deliberately leaves that undefined, but assume that the symptoms referred to in the ad are the flaking and itching commonly associated with dandruff. But just shampooing with *any* shampoo will temporarily eliminate these symptoms, so this shampoo isn't any different from any other. Finally, in order to benefit from this product, you must use it regularly. What is "regular use"—daily, weekly, hourly? Using another shampoo "regularly" will have the same effect. Nowhere does this advertising claim say this particular shampoo stops, eliminates, or cures dandruff. In fact, this claim says nothing at all, thanks to all the weasel words.

8   Look at ads in magazines and newspapers, listen to ads on radio and television, and you'll find the word "help" in ads for all kinds of products. How often do you read or hear such phrases as "helps stop . . . ," "helps overcome . . . ,"

"helps eliminate . . . ," "helps you feel . . . ," or "helps you look . . ."? If you start looking for this weasel word in advertising, you'll be amazed at how often it occurs. Analyze the claims in the ads using "help," and you will discover that these ads are really saying nothing.

9   There are plenty of other weasel words used in advertising. In fact, there are so many that to list them all would fill the rest of this book. But, in order to identify the doublespeak of advertising and understand the real meaning of an ad, you have to be aware of the most popular weasel words in advertising today.

Virtually Spotless

10   One of the most powerful weasel words is "virtually," a word so innocent that most people don't pay any attention to it when it is used in an advertising claim. But watch out. "Virtually" is used in advertising claims that appear to make specific, definite promises when there is no promise. After all, what does "virtually" mean? It means "in essence of effect, although not in fact." Look at that definition again. "Virtually" means *not in fact*. It does *not* mean "almost" or "just about the same as," or anything else. And before you dismiss all this concern over such a small word, remember that small words can have big consequences.

11   In 1971 a federal court rendered its decision on a case brought by a woman who became pregnant while taking birth control pills. She sued the manufacturer, Eli Lilly and Company, for breach of warranty. The woman lost her case. Basing its ruling on a statement in the pamphlet accompanying the pills, which stated that, "When taken as directed, the tablets offer virtually 100% protection," the court ruled that there was no warranty, expressed or implied, that the pills were absolutely effective. In its ruling, the court pointed out that, according to *Webster's Third New International Dictionary,* "virtually" means "almost entirely" and clearly does not mean "absolute" *(Whittington* v. *Eli Lilly and Company,* 333 F. Supp. 98). In other words, the Eli Lilly company was really saying that its birth control pill, even when taken as directed, *did not in fact* provide 100 percent protection against pregnancy. But Eli Lilly didn't want to put it that way because then many women might not have bought Lilly's birth control pills.

12   The next time you see the ad that says that this dishwasher detergent "leaves dishes virtually spotless," just remember how advertisers twist the meaning of the weasel word "virtually." You can have lots of spots on your dishes after using this detergent and the ad claim will still be true, because what this claims really means is that this detergent does not *in fact* leave your dishes spotless. Whenever you see or hear an ad claim that uses the word "virtually," just translate that claim into its real meaning. So the television set that is "virtually trouble free" becomes the television set that is not in fact trouble free, the "virtually foolproof operation" of any appliance becomes an operation that is in fact not foolproof, and the product that "virtually never needs service" becomes the product that is not in fact service free.

New and Improved

13   If "new" is the most frequently used word on a product package, "improved" is the second most frequent. In fact, the two words are almost always used together. It seems just about everything sold these days is "new and improved." The next time you're in the supermarket, try counting the number of times you see these words on products. But you'd better do it while you're walking down just one aisle, otherwise you'll need a calculator to keep track of your counting.

14   Just what do these words mean? The use of the word "new" is restricted by regulations, so an advertiser can't just use the word on a product or in an ad without meeting certain requirements. For example, a product is considered new for about six months during a national advertising campaign. If the product is being advertised only in a limited test market area, the word can be used longer, and in some instances has been used for as long as two years.

15   What makes a product "new"? Some products have been around for a long time, yet every once in a while you discover that they are being advertised as "new." Well, an advertiser can call a product new if there has been "a material functional change" in the product. What is "a material functional change," you ask? Good question. In fact it's such a good question it's being asked all the time. It's up to the manufacturer to prove that the product has undergone such a change. And if the manufacturer isn't challenged on the claim, then there's no one to stop it. Moreover, the change does not have to be an improvement in the product. One manufacturer added an artificial lemon scent to a cleaning product and called it "new and improved," even though the product did not clean any better than without the lemon scent. The manufacturer defended the use of the word "new" on the grounds that the artificial scent changed the chemical formula of the product and therefore constituted "a material functional change."

16   Which brings up the word "improved." When used in advertising, "improved" does not mean "made better." It only means "changed" or "different from before." So, if the detergent maker puts a plastic pour spout on the box of detergent, the product has been "improved," and away we go with a whole new advertising campaign. Or, if the cereal maker adds more fruit or a different kind of fruit to the cereal, there's an improved product. Now you know why manufacturers are constantly making little changes in their products. Whole new advertising campaigns, designed to convince you that the product has been changed for the better, are based on small changes in superficial aspects of a product. The next time you see an ad for an "improved" product, ask yourself what was wrong with the old one. Ask yourself just how "improved" the product is. Finally, you might check to see whether the "improved" version costs more than the unimproved one. After all, someone has to pay for the millions of dollars spent advertising the improved product.

17   Of course, advertisers really like to run ads that claim a product is "new and improved." While what constitutes a "new" product may be subject to some regulation, "improved" is a subjective judgment. A manufacturer changes the shape of its stick deodorant, but the shape doesn't improve the function of the deodorant. That is, changing the shape doesn't affect the deodorizing ability of the deodorant, so the manufacturer calls it "improved." Another manufacturer adds ammonia to its liquid cleaner and calls it "new and improved." Since adding ammonia does affect the cleaning ability of the product, there has been a "material functional change" in the product, and the manufacturer can now call its cleaner "new," and "improved" as well. Now the weasel words "new and improved" are plastered all over the package and are the basis for a multimillion-dollar ad campaign. But after six months the word "new" will have to go, until someone can dream up another change in the product. Perhaps it will be adding color to the liquid, or changing the shape of the package, or maybe adding a new dripless pour spout, or perhaps a _____. The "improvements" are endless, and so are the new advertising claims and campaigns.

18   "New" is just too useful and powerful a word in advertising for advertisers to pass it up easily. So they use weasel words that say "new" without really saying it. One of their favorites is "introducing," as in, "Introducing improved Tide," or "Introducing the stain remover." The first is simply saying, here's our improved soap; the second, here's our new advertising campaign for our detergent. Another favorite is "now," as in, "Now there's Sinex," which simply means that Sinex is available. Then there are phrases like "Today's Chevrolet," "Presenting Dristan," and "A fresh way to start the day." The list is really endless because advertisers are always finding new ways to say "new" without really saying it. If there is a second edition of this book, I'll just call it the "new and improved" edition. Wouldn't you really rather have a "new and improved" edition of this book rather than a "second" edition?

Acts Fast

19   "Acts" and "works" are two popular weasel words in advertising because they bring action to the product and to the advertising claim. When you see the ad for the cough syrup that "Acts on the cough control center," ask yourself what this cough syrup is claiming to do. Well, it's just claiming to "act," to do something, to perform an action. What is it that the cough syrup does? The ad doesn't say. It only claims to perform an action or do something on your "cough control center." By the way, what and where is your "cough control center"? I don't remember learning about that part of the body in human biology class.

20   Ads that use such phrases as "acts fast," "acts against," "acts to prevent," and the like, are saying essentially nothing, because "act" is a word empty of any specific meaning. The ads are always careful not to specify exactly what "act" the product performs. Just because a brand of aspirin claims to "act fast" for headache relief doesn't mean this aspirin is any better than any other aspirin. What is the "act" that this aspirin performs? You're never told. Maybe it just dissolves quickly. Since aspirin is a parity product, all aspirin is the same and therefore functions the same.

Works Like Anything Else

21   If you don't find the word "acts" in an ad, you will probably find the weasel word "works." In fact, the two words are almost interchangeable in advertising. Watch out for ads that say a product "works against," "works like," "works for," or "works longer." As with "acts," "works" is the same meaningless verb used to make you think that this product really does something, and maybe even something special or unique. But "works," like "acts," is basically a word empty of any specific meaning.

Like Magic

22   Whenever advertisers want you to stop thinking about the product and to start thinking about something bigger, better, or more attractive than the product, they use that very popular weasel word, "like." The word "like" is the advertiser's equivalent of a magician's use of misdirection. "Like" gets you to ignore the product and concentrate on the claim the advertiser is making about it. "For skin like peaches and cream" claims the ad for a skin cream. What is this ad really claiming? It doesn't say this cream will give you peaches-and-cream skin. There is no verb in this claim, so it doesn't even mention using the product. How is skin ever like "peaches and cream"? Remember, ads must be read literally and exactly,

according to the dictionary definition of words. (Remember "virtually" in the Eli Lilly case.) The ad is making absolutely no promise or claim whatsoever for this skin cream. If you think this cream will give you soft, smooth, youthful-looking skin, you are the one who has read that meaning into the ad.

23   The wine that claims "It's like taking a trip to France" wants you to think about a romantic evening in Paris as you walk along the boulevard after a wonderful meal in an intimate little bistro. Of course, you don't really believe that a wine can take you to France, but the goal of the ad is to get you to think pleasant, romantic thoughts about France and not about how the wine tastes or how expensive it may be. That little word "like" has taken you away from crushed grapes into a world of your own imaginative making. Who knows, maybe the next time you buy wine, you'll think those pleasant thoughts when you see this brand of wine, and you'll buy it. Or, maybe you weren't even thinking about buying wine at all, but now you just might pick up a bottle the next time you're shopping. Ah, the power of "like" in advertising.

24   How about the most famous "like" claim of all, "Winston tastes good like a cigarette should"? Ignoring the grammatical error here, you might want to know what this claim is saying. Whether a cigarette tastes good or bad is a subjective judgment because what tastes good to one person may well taste horrible to another. Not everyone likes fried snails, even if they are called escargot. (*De gustibus non est disputandum,* which was probably the Roman rule for advertising as well as for defending the games in the Colosseum.) There are many people who say all cigarettes taste terrible, other people who say only some cigarettes taste all right, and still others who say all cigarettes taste good. Who's right? Everyone, because taste is a matter of personal judgment.

25   Moreover, note the use of the conditional, "should." The complete claim is, "Winston tastes good like a cigarette should taste." But should cigarettes taste good? Again, this is a matter of personal judgment and probably depends most on one's experiences with smoking. So, the Winston ad is simply saying that Winston cigarettes are just like any other cigarette: Some people like them and some people don't. On that statement, R. J. Reynolds conducted a very successful multimillion-dollar advertising campaign that helped keep Winston the number-two-selling cigarette in the United States, close behind number one, Marlboro.

Can't It Be Up to the Claim?

26   Analyzing ads for doublespeak requires that you pay attention to every word in the ad and determine what each word really means. Advertisers try to wrap their claims in language that sounds concrete, specific, and objective, when in fact the language of advertising is anything but. Your job is to read carefully and listen critically so that when the announcer says that "Crest can be of significant value . . ." you know immediately that this claim says absolutely nothing. Where is the doublespeak in this ad? Start with the second word.

27   Once again, you have to look at what words really mean, not what you think they mean or what the advertiser wants you to think they mean. The ad for Crest only says that using Crest "can be" of "significant value." What really throws you off in this ad is the brilliant use of "significant." It draws your attention to the word "value" and makes you forget that the ad only claims that Crest "can be." The ad doesn't say that Crest *is* of value, only that it is "able" or "possible" to be of value, because that's all that "can" means.

28   It's so easy to miss the importance of those little words, "can be." Almost as easy as missing the importance of the words "up to" in an ad. These words are very popular in sale ads. You know, the ones that say, "Up to 50 percent Off!" Now, what does that claim mean? Not much, because the store or manufacturer has to reduce the price of only a few items by 50 percent. Everything else can be reduced a lot less, or not even reduced. Moreover, don't you want to know 50 percent off of what? Is it 50 percent off the "manufacturer's suggested list price," which is the highest possible price? Was the price artificially inflated and then reduced? In other ads, "up to" expresses an ideal situation. The medicine that works "up to ten times faster," the battery that lasts "up to twice as long," and the soap that gets you "up to twice as clean"—all are based on ideal situations for using those products, situations in which you can be sure you will never find yourself.

Unfinished Words

29   Unfinished words are a kind of "up to" claim in advertising. The claim that a battery lasts "up to twice as long" usually doesn't finish the comparison—twice as long as what? A birthday candle? A tank of gas? A cheap battery made in a country not noted for its technological achievements? The implication is that the battery lasts twice as long as batteries made by other battery makers, or twice as long as earlier model batteries made by the advertiser, but the ad doesn't really make these claims. You read these claims into the ad, aided by the visual images the advertiser so carefully provides.

30   Unfinished words depend on you to finish them, to provide the words the advertisers so thoughtfully left out of the ad. Pall Mall cigarettes were once advertised as "A longer finer and milder smoke." The question is, longer, finer, and milder than what? The aspirin that claims it contains "Twice as much of the pain reliever doctors recommend most" doesn't tell you what pain reliever it contains twice as much of. (By the way, it's aspirin. That's right; it just contains twice the amount of aspirin. And how much is twice the amount? Twice of what amount?) Panadol boasts that "nobody reduces fever faster," but, since Panadol is a parity product, this claim simply means that Panadol isn't any better than any other product in its parity class. "You can be sure if it's Westinghouse," you're told, but just exactly what it is you can be sure of is never mentioned. "Magnavox gives you more" doesn't tell you what you get more of. More value? More television? More than they gave you before? It sounds nice, but it means nothing, until you fill in the claim with your own words, the words the advertisers didn't use. Since each of us fills in the claim differently, the ad and the product can become all things to all people, and not promise a single thing.

31   Unfinished words abound in advertising because they appear to promise so much. More importantly, they can be joined with powerful visual images on television to appear to be making significant promises about a product's effectiveness without really making any promises. In a television ad, the aspirin product that claims fast relief can show a person with a headache taking the product and then, in what appears to be a matter of minutes, claiming complete relief. This visual image is far more powerful than any claim made in unfinished words. Indeed, the visual image completes the unfinished words for you, filling in with pictures what the words leave out. And you thought that ads didn't affect you. What brand of aspirin do you use?

32   Some years ago, Ford's advertisements proclaimed "Ford LTD—700 percent quieter." Now, what do you think Ford was claiming with these unfinished words? What was the Ford LTD quieter than? A Cadillac? A Mercedes Benz? A BMW? Well, when the FTC asked Ford to substantiate this unfinished claim, Ford replied that it meant that the inside of the LTD was 700 percent quieter than the outside. How did you finish those unfinished words when you first read them? Did you even come close to Ford's meaning?

Combining Weasel Words

33   A lot of ads don't fall neatly into one category or another because they use a variety of different devices and words. Different weasel words are often combined to make an ad claim. The claim, "Coffee-Mate gives coffee more body, more flavor," uses Unfinished Words ("more" than what?) and also uses words that have no specific meaning ("body" and "flavor"). Along with "taste" (remember the Winston ad and its claim to taste good), "body" and "flavor" mean nothing because their meaning is entirely subjective. To you, "body" in coffee might mean thick, black, almost bitter coffee, while I might take it to mean a light brown, delicate coffee. Now, if you think you understood that last sentence, read it again, because it said nothing of objective value; it was filled with weasel words of no specific meaning: "thick," "black," "bitter," "light brown," and "delicate." Each of those words has no specific, objective meaning, because each of us can interpret them differently.

34   Try this slogan: "Looks, smells, tastes like ground-roast coffee." So, are you now going to buy Taster's Choice instant coffee because of this ad? "Looks," "smells," and "tastes" are all words with no specific meaning and depend on your interpretation of them for any meaning. Then there's that great weasel word "like," which simply suggests a comparison but does not make the actual connection between the product and the quality. Besides, do you know what "ground-roast" coffee is? I don't, but it sure sounds good. So, out of seven words in this ad, four are definite weasel words, two are quite meaningless, and only one has any clear meaning.

35   Remember the Anacin ad—"Twice as much of the pain reliever doctors recommend most"? There's a whole lot of weaseling going on in this ad. First, what's the pain reliever they're talking about in this ad? Aspirin, of course. In fact, any time you see or hear an ad using those words "pain reliever," you can automatically substitute the word "aspirin" for them. (Makers of acetaminophen and ibuprofen pain relievers are careful in their advertising to identify their products as nonaspirin products.) So, now we know that Anacin has aspirin in it. Moreover, we know that Anacin has twice as much aspirin in it, but we don't know twice as much as what. Does it have twice as much aspirin as an ordinary aspirin tablet? If so, what is an ordinary aspirin tablet, and how much aspirin does it contain? Twice as much as Excedrin or Bufferin? Twice as much as a chocolate chip cookie? Remember those Unfinished Words and how they lead you on without saying anything.

36   Finally, what about those doctors who are doing all that recommending? Who are they? How many of them are there? What kind of doctors are they? What are their qualifications? Who asked them about recommending pain relievers? What other pain relievers did they recommend? And there are a whole lot more questions about this "poll" of doctors to which I'd like to know the answers, but you get the point. Sometimes, when I call my doctor, she tells me to take two aspirin and call her office in the morning. Is that where Anacin got this ad?

Read the Label, or the Brochure

37   Weasel words aren't just found on television, on the radio, or in newspaper and magazine ads. Just about any language associated with a product will contain the doublespeak of advertising. Remember the Eli Lilly case and the doublespeak on the information sheet that came with the birth control pills. Here's another example.

38   In 1983, the Estée Lauder cosmetics company announced a new product called "Night Repair." A small brochure distributed with the product stated that "Night Repair was scientifically formulated in Estée Lauder's U.S. laboratories as part of the Swiss Age-Controlling Skincare Program. Although only nature controls the aging process, this program helps control the signs of aging and encourages skin to look and feel younger." You might want to read these two sentences again, because they sound great but say nothing.

39   First, note that the product was "scientifically formulated" in the company's laboratories. What does that mean? What constitutes a scientific formulation? You wouldn't expect the company to say that the product was casually, mechanically, or carelessly formulated, or just thrown together one day when the people in the white coats didn't have anything better to do. But the word "scientifically" lends an air of precision and promise that just isn't there.

40   It is the second sentence, however, that's really weasely, both syntactically and semantically. The only factual part of this sentence is the introductory dependent clause—"only nature controls the aging process." Thus, the only fact in the ad is relegated to a dependent clause, a clause dependent on the main clause, which contains no factual or definite information at all and indeed purports to contradict the independent clause. The new "skincare program" (notice it's not a skin cream but a "program") does not claim to stop or even retard the aging process. What, then, does Night Repair, at a price of over $35 (in 1983 dollars) for a .87-ounce bottle do? According to this brochure, nothing. It only "helps," and the brochure does not say how much it helps. Moreover, it only "helps control," and then it only helps control the "*signs* of aging," not the aging itself. Also, it "encourages" skin not to *be* younger but only to "look and feel" younger. The brochure does not say younger than what. Of the sixteen words in the main clause of this second sentence, nine are weasel words. So, before you spend all that money for Night Repair, or any other cosmetic product, read the words carefully, and then decide if you're getting what you think you're paying for.

Other Tricks of the Trade

41   Advertisers' use of doublespeak is endless. The best way advertisers can make something out of nothing is through words. Although there are a lot of visual images used on television and in magazines and newspapers, every advertiser wants to create that memorable line that will stick in the public consciousness. I am sure pure joy reigned in one advertising agency when a study found that children who were asked to spell the word "relief" promptly and proudly responded "r-o-l-a-i-d-s."

42   The variations, combinations, and permutations of doublespeak used in advertising go on and on, running from the use of rhetorical questions ("Wouldn't you really rather have a Buick?" "If you can't trust Prestone, who can you trust?") to flattering you with compliments ("The lady has taste." "We think

a cigar smoker is someone special." "You've come a long way baby."). You know, of course, how you're *supposed* to answer those questions, and you know that those compliments are just leading up to the sales pitches for the products. Before you dismiss such tricks of the trade as obvious, however, just remember that all of these statements and questions were part of very successful advertising campaigns.

43   A more subtle approach is the ad that proclaims a supposedly unique quality for a product, a quality that really isn't unique. "If it doesn't say Goodyear, it can't be polyglas." Sounds good, doesn't it? Polyglass is available only from Goodyear because Goodyear copyrighted that trade name. Any other tire manufacturer could make exactly the same tire but could not call it "polyglas," because that would be copyright infringement. "Polyglas" is simply Goodyear's name for its fiberglass-reinforced tire.

44   Since we like to think of ourselves as living in a technologically advanced country, science and technology have a great appeal in selling products. Advertisers are quick to use scientific doublespeak to push their products. There are all kinds of elixirs, additives, scientific potions, and mysterious mixtures added to all kinds of products. Gasoline contains "HTA," "F-130," "Platformate," and other chemical-sounding additives, but nowhere does an advertisement give any real information about the additive.

45   Shampoo, deodorant, mouthwash, cold medicine, sleeping pills, and any number of other products all seem to contain some special chemical ingredient that allows them to work wonders. "Certs contains a sparkling drop of Retsyn." So what? What's "Retsyn"? What's it do? What's so special about it? When they don't have a secret ingredient in their product, advertisers still find a way to claim scientific validity. There's "Sinarest. Created by a research scientist who actually gets sinus headaches." Sounds nice, but what kind of research does this scientist do? How do you know if she is any kind of expert on sinus medicine? Besides, this ad doesn't tell you a thing about the medicine itself and what it does.

Advertising Doublespeak Quick Quiz

46   Now it's time to test your awareness of advertising doublespeak. (You didn't think I would just let you read this and forget it, did you?) The following is a list of statements from some recent ads. Your job is to figure out what each of these ads really says:

> Dominos's Pizza: "Because nobody delivers better."
> SINUTAB: "It can stop the pain."
> TUMS: "The stronger acid neutralizer."
> MAXIMUM STRENGTH DRISTAN: "Strong medicine for tough sinus colds."
> LISTERMINT: "Making your mouth a cleaner place."
> CASCADE: "For virtually spotless dishes nothing beats Cascade."
> NUPRIN: "Little. Yellow. Different. Better."
> ANACIN: "Better relief."
> SUDAFED: "Fast sinus relief that won't put you fast asleep."
> ADVIL: "Advanced medicine for pain."
> PONDS COLD CREAM: "Ponds cleans like no soap can."
> MILLER LITE BEER: "Tastes great. Less filling."

PHILIPS MILK OF MAGNESIA: "Nobody treats you better than MOM (Philips Milk of Magnesia)."

BAYER: "The wonder drug that works wonders."

CRACKER BARREL: "Judged to be the best."

KNORR: "Where taste is everything."

ANUSOL: "Anusol is the word to remember for relief."

DIMETAPP: "It relieves kids as well as colds."

LIQUID DRANO: "The liquid strong enough to be called Drano."

JOHNSON & JOHNSON BABY POWDER: "Like magic for your skin."

PURITAN: "Make it your oil for life."

PAM: "Pam, because how you cook is as important as what you cook."

IVORY SHAMPOO AND CONDITIONER: "Leave your hair feeling Ivory clean."

TYLENOL GEL-CAPS: "It's not a capsule. It's better."

ALKA-SELTZER PLUS: "Fast, effective relief for winter colds."

The World of Advertising

47   In the world of advertising, people wear "dentures," not false teeth; they suffer from "occasional irregularity," not constipation; they need deodorants for their "nervous wetness," not for sweat; they use "bathroom tissue," not toilet paper; and they don't dye their hair, they "tint" or "rinse" it. Advertisements offer "real counterfeit diamonds" without the slightest hint of embarrassment, or boast of goods made out of "genuine imitation leather" or "virgin vinyl."

48   In the world of advertising, the girdle becomes a "body shaper," "form persuader," "control garment," "controller," "outwear enhancer," "body garment," or "anti-gravity panties," and is sold with such trade names as "The Instead," "The Free Spirit," and "The Body Briefer."

49   A study some years ago found the following words to be among the most popular used in U.S. television advertisements: "new," "improved," "better," "extra," "fresh," "clean," "beautiful," "free," "good," "great," and "light." At the same time, the following words were found to be among the most frequent on British television: "new," "good-better-best," "free," "fresh," "delicious," "full," "sure," "clean," "wonderful," and "special." While these words may occur most frequently in ads, and while ads may be filled with weasel words, you have to watch out for all the words used in advertising, not just the words mentioned here.

50   Every word in an ad is there for a reason; no word is wasted. Your job is to figure out exactly what each word is doing in an ad—what each word really means, not what the advertiser wants you to think it means. Remember, the ad is trying to get you to buy a product, so it will put the product in the best possible light, using any device, trick, or means legally allowed. Your only defense against advertising (besides taking up permanent residence on the moon) is to develop and use a strong critical reading, listening, and looking ability. Always ask yourself what the ad is *really* saying. When you see ads on television, don't be misled by the pictures, the visual images. What does the ad say about the product? What does the ad *not* say? What information is missing from the ad? Only by becoming an active, critical consumer of the doublespeak of advertising will you ever be able to cut through the doublespeak and discover what the ad is really saying.

The Other Canadians and Canada's Future

1   In Canada's province of Quebec, a majority, perhaps, of the inhabitants are convinced that they must act to protect their language and culture. A good section of these go much further, and seek an independent nation. On the other hand, in the English-speaking part of the country, especially in western Canada, the vast majority of people feel that the French, defeated in 1759 on the Plains of Abraham, have no claim to nationhood. This much publicized conflict was discussed by J.A.S. Evans in his article, "The Present State of Canada," in the September 1996 issue of *Contemporary Review.* These views are tempered by those of the remaining non-French and non-British Canadians—about 37.5 per cent of the population. These communities from many ethnic groups, who, with the French Canadians, form the majority of Canada's population, are to many observers an unknown force in Canadian society.

2   For nearly a half century, Canada has been living under the threat of Quebec separation. During this long period of tension between English—about 34.5 per cent—and French Canadians—about 28 per cent of the population—the immigrant minorities have been in a dilemma. Traditionally the overwhelming majority, even in Quebec, became integrated into "Anglo" society. (In Canada the "English" include a large number of Scots who have played a crucial role in the country's history.) However, in that province during the last few decades, this tendency to assimilate into dominant English culture has caused much friction, has raised concerns among French Canadians and has given rise to debates throughout Canada.

3   Amid these pressures, how do the Canadian minorities whose origins can be traced to countries from the four corners of the world see the Canada of the future? For an answer, one must travel back in history to the beginning of this [twentieth] century, when non-French and non-British Europeans in large numbers along with a few Asiatics begin to immigrate to Canada. In that period, assimilation of the minority ethnic groups, without regard to their desires, was the order of the day. In one or, at the most, two generations, the dominant Anglo-Saxon culture and language melted into its folds—not always happily— the vast majority of the sons and daughters of these immigrants.

4   No one in those days, when ethnic epithets and other derogatory terms were used to taunt immigrant groups, would ever visualize the multicultural Canada of our times where all Canadians are treated equally. Peoples of all racial origins, in today's Canada, are encouraged to romanticize their ethnic history and, hence, to feel "at home." Canadian society has become, at least on the surface, a truly cultural mosaic.

5   However, in the past, it was very different. For the early immigrants and their offspring, the coercion to assimilate into the dominant society was overwhelming. This took many forms. Prejudice, discrimination, racial slurs and subordination into the dominant English culture, all had their effects on the newcomers. In the early years of this [twentieth] century, the acceptance of diversity—people who held unfamiliar customs and values—was not even in the cards.

6   Some of the ethnic groups, like the Dutch, Germans, Scandinavians and many of the Lebanese, assimilated quickly; others, like the Chinese, Greeks, those from

the Baltic nations of Estonia, Latvia and Lithuania, and Ukrainians preserved their identity for several generations. However, all the racial minorities through interaction, but mainly through education, in no more than three generations, had totally melted into the governing English society or, to a much lesser extent, French culture in Quebec. In the process of assimilation, many members of the ethnic groups lost confidence in their identity, self-esteem and pride in their racial origin as they were absorbed into the dominant society. Even after receiving their citizenship and becoming new Canadians, usually because of their accents, many were labelled with the derogatory term DPs (displaced persons).

7   Others, if they remained visible like the blacks and Asiatics, were never accepted as true Canadians. One need only bring to mind the sad fate of Japanese Canadians during the Second World War: they had their property confiscated while their total population was interned. "Black Syrian! Black Syrian!" These epithets during my own school years were daily taunts. In those years, the school was a painful place for a child of non-British origin. To escape the daily verbal persecution, I, like the sons of many other immigrants of foreign origin, tried to hide my identity, making believe that my forefathers came from the British Isles.

8   All this changed when Canada's controversial Prime Minister, Pierre Trudeau, set the country on the road to "Multiculturalism within a Bilingual Framework" policy. His vision and that of the Liberal government at that time was this rule: "Canada's many ethnic and racial groups living in harmony while retaining, their cultures—a prop to the English-French nucleus of the country." The government believed that "multiculturalism" would bolster the equality of all Canadians, encourage participation of minorities in social institutions and strengthen the allegiance of ethnic groups to the communities in which they lived. "Multiculturalism" would co-exist with bilingualism as a "defining characteristic" of Canadian society.

9   Trudeau theorized that in a bilingual, multicultural Canadian nation the Anglo-Canadians would have to retire to their proper place, instead of interpreting Canadian identity in their own British terms. As a result, he assumed genuine power sharing would follow. Rather than the American melting pot idea of assimilation into the dominant ethnic group, Canada would become a land of ethnic pluralism—a cultural mosaic of many peoples, forging unity from diversity.

10   In 1971, a policy of multiculturalism was officially adopted, legitimizing the self-conception of Canada as resting on pluralist foundations. Government policy thereafter encouraged one country, two languages, many cultures. Legislation became an instrument to legitimize and manage a diverse population within a state apparatus. It officially formalized a multicultural nation and Canada became the world's only official multicultural society. "Ethnic diversity," "ethnic pluralism," "multi-ethnic" and "poly-ethnic" were now acceptable phrases. In 1988, Canada's multiracial and multi-lingual mélange was strengthened further by the passage of the Multicultural Act which emphasized "positive race relations." With its enactment, the country moved to the forefront of nations in dealing with ethno-racial diversity in a politically acceptable manner.

11   Among some of the ethnic groups, multiculturalism was accepted with great enthusiasm. In the 23 October 1978 issue of the Saskatoon *Star-Phoenix,* it was reported that at a Ukrainian fund-raising dinner in the city, one of the speakers stated: "Canada's unique characteristic and strength is multiculturalism."

He went on to say: "Canadians have abandoned the futile evangelism of patriotic nationalism. Instead, every Canadian can enjoy the joy and pride of his cultural roots, recognized, respected and accepted as a worthwhile contributor to Canadian society."

12   On the other hand, "multiculturalism" has proved to be a controversial social policy. From the very beginning, some groups wanted to emphasize language; others religion; while a number zeroed in on folklore. Opinion varied among the ethnic societies as to how much ethnicity and interaction among other cultural groups were to be stressed. At the inception of multiculturalism, critics said that it was a ploy by Trudeau and the Liberal Party to control and manipulate ethnic groups and was only a vote-getting gimmick. Subsidizing the ethnic groups to teach their own languages, which multiculturalism supported, would, according to many at that time, retard the immigrants' assimilation into the English or French societies.

13   In the ensuing years, many denounced multiculturalism as counterproductive, irrelevant, unworkable and an expensive frill which would impede assimilation—a guise to destroy British traditions and the English language. Some asserted that it would increase the risk of racial conflict; others described it as a cultural zoo: the zoo keeper—the government—would manipulate the inhabitants.

14   Yet, on the whole, multiculturalism, despite its critics, has had a beneficial and civilizing effect on Canada. It has shaped the country's collective identity as a generous and tolerant nation, enhancing the quality of life for all its inhabitants. It has become a system of achieving national consensus without the loss of integrity—a setup which all Canadians can buy into as equals. No country in the world has ventured as far as Canada into the field of ethnic interaction.

15   Contributing an inclusive sense of common citizenship, official multiculturalism, harnessing the power of the over ten million Canadians who are neither English nor French has defused mounting Quebec pressure on federalism; blunted American influences on Canadian cultural space; enhanced the country's cultural richness; and, with the demise of Anglo-conformity, filled the void in the Canadian cultural identity. Without doubt, it has elevated Canada to the ranks of progressive countries in the judicious management of ethnic relations.

16   By the encouragement of self-confidence, self-worth and a feeling of pride in their ethnic origin, multiculturalism has helped the immigrants succeed in their social and economic life and has made them feel at home. There is no better indication of how self-image determines the future of the country than when I visited the northern Alberta Arab community of Lac La Biche in the late summer of 1996. "I love it here! In this town we prospered and here we have established our roots." Khalil Abughoush, owner of the IGA supermarket in Lac La Biche, was full of enthusiasm when talking about his small northern city. Like his fellow countrymen—20 per cent of the town's 3,000 inhabitants are of Arab-Lebanese origin—he had come to seek his fortune in this northern Alberta resort. In Canada's multicultural society, Abughoush, like the majority of immigrants and their descendants, felt at home. As he prospered he felt no coercion to fit in, no pressure to leave his culture behind. There is no question that "multiculturalism" has succeeded, to a great extent, in making Canada's newcomers feel at home, with the exception of many of the visible minorities. For the latter, multiculturalism has been only of marginal benefit. It has failed

to combat racism and discriminatory practices. Even though today one of the major priorities of multiculturalism is the elimination of racism, unofficially, the dominant Anglo and French societies continue to see visible minorities as different, not equal, and an unstable factor in Canadian society. These visible minorities at present constitute 6.3 per cent of the population—expected to rise to 10 percent by the year 2000. In the large urban centres, they have become an important segment of the population. The non-Anglo population of Vancouver is 30 per cent and that of Toronto 60 per cent—20 per cent of which are visible minorities.

17   Even more forgotten by multiculturalism are Canada's "First Nations Peoples." Even though there is a widespread consensus that the country's Indigenous Peoples have been treated unfairly, they remain as the bottom stratum in Canadian society. To them, multiculturalism has brought very little benefit. In the Canada of today, for Asiatics, Africans and Aboriginals, skin colour acts as a substantial barrier to integration. The question, asked in the 2 September 1979 issue of the *Toronto Daily Star* by its columnist Richard Gwyn, persists: "How many nonwhites will prove too many for the stability of Canadian society?" Even more pointedly, Stella Hryniuk, in *Twenty Years of Multiculturalism,* quotes a Canadian of French and Haitian descent as asking, "Am I a Canadian when I feel Canadian, or when others say I am a Canadian?"

18   Nevertheless, for the majority of immigrants, multiculturalism, costing the government annually a mere dollar per Canadian, has benefited the country. A good number of newcomers believe that government funding of multicultural events like dance-fests and ethnic centres will preserve their culture forever. Ethnic gatherings such as Caravan and Caribana in Toronto, Dragon Boat Races in Vancouver, Folklorama in Winnipeg and Heritage Day in Edmonton romanticize the newcomers' history and identity and offer them a feeling of belonging. Cultural community life is more visible in Canada today than in any other country.

19   However, ethnic ceremonies and dances do not change the reality that the Canadian power structure remains English and French, around which circumnavigate lesser satellite cultures. Assimilation still goes on apace, but in a more humane manner. The difference between the Canadian "mosaic" and American "melting pot" is not overwhelming—both have the same aim: assimilation. The preservation of ethnic cultures in both countries is still very dependent on new replenishment by way of immigration. Through education and intermarriage, the overwhelming majority have assimilated into mainly the English culture—by the third generation over 85 per cent. Unlike earlier in this century, they willingly melt into the host society as they ethnically dance themselves out of existence. Our family, whose members, in the main, live in western Canada, are an excellent example of this assimilation. Out of its eight members, only two married Arabs. Today, my nieces and nephews are Carletons, McWhirters and McCallums who know very little about their partially Arab origin. Their views about Canada and its future are those of the dominant Anglo society.

20   In western Canada, where non-French, non-British and non-Native origins constitute nearly half of the population, "English only" is supported by the majority of the inhabitants. The descendants of the "black Syrians" are now the most vocal opponents of multiculturalism. To them, all the new immigrants are taking away the Canadians' jobs and bringing a foreign element into Canadian society. The same view is held by many descendants of immigrants. They are

multiculturalism's most vocal critics. The backlash against cultural retention comes, in the main, from assimilated members of ethnic communities. Strangely, support for cultural maintenance is strongest among university graduates of British origin.

21   The views about the future of Canada among the vast majority of these descendants of immigrant groups is more "Anglo" than those whose forefathers came from the British Isles. With the passing of the third generation, the countries of their origin are, I would say, to the majority, unknown. The legacy of their fathers to Canada are a few foods like falafel, hummus, pizzas and wonton soup. However, as they disappear, because of multiculturalism, they retain their self-esteem. Overwhelmingly, their view of Canada and its future is that of the Anglo Canadians.

Amy Willard Cross

Life in the Stopwatch Lane

Amy Willard Cross is a writer who manages to divide her time between the stopwatch pace of the city and the more relaxed tempo of her other home "in the woods." The Summer House: A Tradition of Leisure (1992) is Cross's first book. In it, she examines the North American practice of escaping to the more leisurely life of a cottage or summer house. Born in Washington, D.C. in 1960, Cross currently lives in Canada. Her articles can be found in City and Country Home, the Globe and Mail, and Cottage Life, and she is currently Health Editor at Chatelaine.

Preparing to Read

This article first appeared in the Globe and Mail's "Facts and Arguments" column in 1990. In "Life in the Stopwatch Lane," Amy Willard Cross examines the trend toward dividing time into progressively smaller units and labelling different types of time. Before reading this essay, think about the concept of time and how it has changed. How is time viewed differently in different cultures? What value do you place on your time? How do you measure time and what labels do you use to identify different divisions of time?

1   If time is money, the rates have skyrocketed and you probably can't afford it. North Americans are suffering a dramatic time shortage since demand greatly exceeds supply. In fact, a recent survey revealed that people lost about 10 hours of leisure per week between 1973 and 1987. Maybe you were too busy to notice.

2   Losing that leisure leaves a piddling 16.6 hours to do whatever you want, free of work, dish-washing or car-pooling. In television time, that equals a season of 13 *thirtysomething* episodes, plus 3 1/2 reruns. Hardly enough time to write an autobiography or carry on an affair.

3   How has replacing free time with more billable hours affected society? It has created a new demographic group: the Busy Class—who usurped the Leisure Class. Easy to recognize, members of the Busy Class constantly cry to anyone listening, "I'm *soooooo* busy." So busy they can't call their mother or find change for a panhandler. Masters of doing two things at once, they eke the most out of time. They dictate while driving, talk while calculating, entertain guests while nursing, watch the news while pumping iron. Even business melts into socializing—people earn their daily bread while they break it.

4   In fact, the Busies must make lots of bread to maintain themselves in the standard of busy-ness to which they've become accustomed. To do that, they need special, expensive stuff. Stuff like call waiting, which lets them talk to two people at once. Stuff like two-faced watches, so they can do business in two time zones at once. Neither frenzied executives nor hurried housewives dare leave the house without their "book"—leather-bound appointment calendars thick as bestsellers. Forget hi-fi's or racing cars, the new talismans of over-achievers also work: coffee-makers that brew by alarm; remote-controlled ignitions; or car faxes. Yet, despite all these time-efficient devices, few people have time to spare.

5   That scarcity has changed how we measure time. Now it's being scientifically dissected into smaller and smaller pieces. Thanks to digital clocks, we know when it's 5:30 (and calculate we'll be home in three hours, eight minutes). These days lawyers can reason in 1/10th of an hour increments; they bill every six minutes. This to-the-minute precision proves time's escalating value.

6   Time was, before the advent of car phones and digital clocks, we scheduled two kinds of time: time off and work hours. Not any more. Just as the Inuit label the infinite varieties of snow, the Busy Class has identified myriad subtleties of free time and named them. Here are some textbook examples of the new faces of time:

7   *Quality time.* For those working against the clock, the quality of time spent with loved ones supposedly compensates for quantity. This handy concept absolves guilt as quickly as rosary counting. So careerist couples dine à deux once a fort-night. Parents bond by reading kids a story after nanny fed and bathed them. When pressed for time, nobody wastes it by fighting about bad breath or unmade beds. People who spend quality time with each other view their relationships through rose-coloured glasses. And knowing they've created perfect personal lives lets the Busy Class work even harder—guilt-free.

8   *Travel time.* With an allowance of 16.6 hours of fun, the Busy Class watches time expenditures carefully. Just like businesses do while making bids, normal people calculate travel time for leisure activities. If two tram rides away, a friendly squash game loses out. One time-efficient woman even formulated a mathematical theo-rem: fun per mile quotient. Before accepting any social invitation, she adds up travel costs, figures out the time spent laughing, drinking and eating. If the latter exceeds the former, she accepts. It doesn't matter who asks.

9   *Downtime.* Borrowed from the world of heavy equipment and sleek comput-ers, downtime is a professional-sounding word meaning the damn thing broke, wait around until it's fixed. Translated into real life, downtime counts as neither work nor play, but a maddening no-man's land where nothing happens! Like lining up for the ski-lift, or commuting without a car phone, or waiting a while for the mechanic's diagnosis. Beware: people who keep track of their downtime probably indulge in less than 16 hours of leisure.

10   *Family time.* In addition to 60-hour weeks, aerobics and dinner parties, some people make time for their children. When asked to brunch, a young couple will reply, "We're sorry but that's our family time." A variant of quality time, it's Sunday afternoon between lunch and the Disney Hour when nannies frequent Filipino restaurants. In an effort to entertain their children without exposure to sex and violence, the family attends craft fairs, animated matinees or tree-tapping demonstrations. There, they converge with masses of family units spending time alone with the kids. After a noisy, sticky afternoon, parents gladly punch the clock come Monday.

11   *Quiet time.* Overwhelmed by their schedules, some people try to recapture the magic of childhood when they watched clouds for hours on end. Sophisticated grown-ups have rediscovered the quiet time of kindergarten days. They unplug the phone (not the answering machine), clutch a book and try not to think about work. But without teachers to enforce it, quiet doesn't last. The clock ticks too loudly. As a computer fanatic said, after being entertained at 16 megahertz, sitting still to watch a sunset pales by comparison.

12   As it continues to increase in value, time will surely divide into even smaller units. And people will share only the tiniest amount with each other. Hey, brother, can you spare a minute? Got a second? A nanosecond?

Pat Deiter-MacArthur

Saskatchewan's Indian People—Five Generations

1   It has been about five generations since Saskatchewan Indian people have had significant contact with European settlers. The First Generation strongly influenced by Europeans were the treaty-signers. The key characteristic of this generation was their ability to have some input into their future. They retained their tribal cultures but realized that they had to negotiate with the Europeans for the betterment of future generations. They did not give up their language or religion or the political structures of nationhood. They were perceived by government as an "alien" nation to be dealt with by treaty.

2   The Second Generation (1867–1910) of Indian people was the object of legal oppression by the government. This generation lived under the absolute rule of an Indian agent, a government employee. Through the Indian Act, this generation was denied their religion, political rights, and freedom to travel off their reserves. A pass and permit system was strictly adhered to on the prairies; every Indian person required a pass to leave the reserve and a permit to sell any agricultural produce. All children were required to attend residential schools run by the churches. The goals of their schools were, first, to make Christians out of their students and to rid them of their pagan lifestyles and, second, to provide a vocational education.

3   Tuberculosis was a major killer of Indian people during this time and contributed to decimating their population in Saskatchewan to a low of five thousand in 1910. This generation was treated as wards and aliens of Canada.

4   The laws which served to oppress the second generation were in place until the early 1950s. The Third Generation (1910–1945) was greatly affected by these laws and schooling. This generation can be described as the lost generation. These people were psychologically oppressed. They rejected their Indianness but found that because of the laws for treaty Indians they could not enjoy the privileges accorded to whites. This third generation was our grandfathers' generation. Many Indians at this time could speak their language but would not because of shame of their Indianness. They were still required by law to send their children to residential schools, to send their sick to Indian hospitals, and to abide by the Indian agent. They rarely had a sense of control over their own lives. This generation was considered wards of the government and denied citizenship.

5   Our fathers' time, the Fourth Generation since treaty-signing, can be best described as the generation of an Indian rebirth. This generation (1945–1980) is characterized by a movement of growing awareness—awareness that being Indian is okay and that Indian people from all tribes are united through their aboriginality, historical development, and special status.

6   This generation saw the rise of Indian and Native organizations across Canada, the return of traditional ceremonies, and an acknowledgement of the need to retain traditional languages and cultural ways.

7   Indian people of this generation were given the right to vote in 1960. The pass and permit system was abandoned in the late 1930s. In 1956, Indian children could attend either residential schools or the local public schools. However, the

effects of this generation being raised within an institution and their parents being raised in the same way had a severe impact on these individuals. The residential school not only taught them to suppress their language but also to suppress their feelings and sense of individualism. The continued attack on Indian languages by residential schools left this generation with an ability only to understand their language, but many were not sufficiently fluent to call their Native language their first language.

8　　During the sixties, there was a rise in Indian urbanization, a trend that continues today. This generation also contributed to an Indian baby boom that is estimated to be eight to ten years behind the non-Indian baby boomers. The federal and provincial vote allowed Indian people to legally consume alcohol. Alcoholism, suicides, and violent deaths were on the rise for this generation.

9　　This was a period of experimentation by both the Indian communities and the government. Unfortunately, neither side was ready for each other. The intended government goal of assimilation was besieged with problems of racism, poverty, maladjustment, and cultural shock.

10　　Today's Indian people are part of the Fifth Generation. The fifth generation is faced with choices: assimilation, integration, or separation. Indian people are now able to intermarry or assimilate with non-Indian without the loss of their Indian status. Indian leaders across Canada are seeking a separate and constitutionally recognized Indian government. Indian government is to provide its own services within Indian reserves. Integration allows Indian people to retain a sense of their cultural background while working and living within the larger society.

11　　The fifth generation people are the first children since treaty-signing to be raised by their parents. Many of this fifth generation are not able to understand a Native language. Their first and only language is English. This generation is generally comfortable about their Indianness without strong prejudicial feelings to others. However, this generation is challenged to retain the meaning of Indian identity for their children.

Lawrence Hill

The Question

1   Canadians have a favourite pastime, and they don't even realize it. They like to ask—they absolutely have to ask—where you are from if you don't look convincingly white. They want to know it, need to know it, simply must have that information. They just can't relax until they have pinpointed, to their satisfaction, your geographic and racial coordinates. They can go almost out of their minds with curiosity, as when driven by the need for food, water, or sex, but once they've finally managed to find out precisely where you were born, who your parents were, and what your racial make-up is, then, man, do they feel better. They can breathe easy and get back to the business of living.

2   I don't have the math background of, say, an actuary, but I can manage the following calculation. I am forty-four years old. Since about age ten, I have been asked "So what are you, anyway?" and all its variations. ("Where are you from?" "Yes, but where are you really from?" "Yes, but where were your parents born?") That's thirty-four years I've been fielding The Question.

3   Let's assume I have been asked The Question once a day over these past thirty-four years. $34 \times 365 = 12{,}410$. But that would be an underestimation because it fails to factor in the two years I lived in Quebec. During those two years, I was most certainly asked The Question five times per day. (*"D'où viens-tu?" "Quelles sont tes souches?" "Tes parents sont de quel pays?"*) An extra four times per day for two years in Quebec City would add on another 2,920 questions. $12{,}410 + 2{,}920 = 15{,}330$.

4   That, ladies and gentlemen, is the absolute minimum number of times Canadians have asked me either "Where are you from?' or *"D'où viens-tu?"* or any of the multitudinous variations.

5   Minelle Mahtani, whose doctoral thesis at the University of London examined identity among mixed-race Canadian women, tells a story of how she was walking alone one day in Toronto's St. Lawrence Market area, when someone tapped on her shoulder. Minelle turned around to find a woman who seemed motivated by a particular urgency—she had obviously been watching Minelle and just had to know where she was from.

6   "Ah," you may say, "but it's just curiosity. What's wrong with people being curious?"

7   I am a patient man. So patient that my children can confidently remove a chocolate chip cookie right from the edge of my fingers, or raid my dish of French vanilla ice cream and leave nothing but the cloudy bowl, and still know that I won't lose my cool. But even this patience was exhausted some time around the 5,000 mark of the 15,330 questions I have faced.

8   What is wrong with The Question? Nothing at all—when it is asked at the right time, when it results from a genuine interest in you as a person, and when the person asking the question actually accepts the answer.

9   Let's dissect the interrogation process. Imagine me at a party, sipping mineral water. A stranger walks up.

10   STRANGER: "Do you mind my asking where you are from?" [This is code for "What is your race?"]

11   ME: "Canada." [This is code for "Screw off."]

12   STRANGER: "Yes, but you know, where are you really from?" [This is code for "You know what I mean, so why are you trying to make me come out and say it?"]

13   ME: "I come from the foreign and distant metropolis of Newmarket. That's Newmarket, Ontario. My place of birth." [Code for "I'm not letting you off the hook, buster."]

14   STRANGER: "But your place of origin? Your parents? What are your parents?" [Code for "I want to know your race, but this is making me very uncomfortable because somehow I feel that I'm not supposed to ask that question."]

15   This exchange is like the opening of a chess game. The first few moves are pretty standard: White moves Pawn to King Four, Black responds with Pawn to King Four, White answers with Knight to King Bishop Three, and Black answers with Knight to King Bishop Three. From this point on, the possibilities multiply.

16   I can give a teaser, such as "My parents came up from the States," which frustrates the questioner, who really wants to know my parents' racial background.

17   I can give it all up and explain that I have a black father and a white mother.

18   I can invent an answer, such as "My father is a White Russian and my mother is an Ethiopian Jew."

19   Or I can turn the question around, as in "Why are you asking me this?"

20   And that is the nub of the issue. Why am I always asked that question? Why do people need to know the answer so desperately?

21   Have you ever noticed that black people rarely put other people of any race through the wringer like this? That's because many of them have been asked The Question more times than they care to count. They're sophisticated enough—by virtue of their own experiences—to understand that many people resent this line of interrogation.

22   Is it truly innocent? Can The Question be chalked up to basic curiosity? I don't think so. Children are the most innocent and curious of all human beings, yet they never hammer me with these questions. As a rule, adults aren't all that curious about other people. With me, they are generally interested in just one thing: my ancestry.

23   Do you suppose that—15,330 times in thirty-four years—strangers will ask an indisputably white Canadian with a traditional Anglo-Canadian accent where he is from, where he was born, or where his parents were born? Absolutely not. Strangers will assume that he is a true Canadian, and leave that part of his identity unmolested. The offence-causing kernel at the centre of this line of interrogation is its implication: "You are not white, you don't look like me, so you're clearly not Canadian." It also suggests "Since you're clearly not Canadian, and I am, I am within my rights to ask you just exactly where you're from."

24   We grow up learning that certain questions are off-limits in polite conversation. Any properly socialized Canadian knows, by the teenage years at the latest, that it would be considered grossly impolite to walk up to strangers and ask how much money they make, how they vote, whether they believe in God, or whether they sleep with men, women, or both. These questions are deemed intrusive. But to my way of thinking, they are eminently preferable to "Where are you from?" After all, what is wrong with asking what people do or think? But to ask what they *are*, and to presume to know at least part of the answer—that they are not white and therefore are not Canadian—is very different.

EXAMPLE   **437**

25   Digging into someone's identity—especially a stranger's identity—is tricky business. Hell, people can spend top dollar on psychotherapists to figure out their own identities and still fall short of satisfaction. When I wake up in the morning, stumble to the mirror, and brush my teeth, I'm certainly not saying to myself, "Hello, black man, how are you today?" Nor am I saying, "Hello, white and black mix-up, what are you doing today?"

26   Obviously, the blackness and the whiteness within me are reflected back at me by society. But I don't care to have my identity boiled down to race. My identity may, at any given time, comprise a hundred elements.

27   I suppose the reason many of us mixed-race people find The Question offensive is not just that it makes assumptions, which are often false, about our identity, but because it attempts to hang our identity on one factor: our race.

28   Not everybody I interviewed had the same take on this issue. Interestingly, two of the strongest opposing views came from young men, both in their twenties, university-educated, and living in southern Ontario.

29   Stefan Dubowski, of Hamilton, told me The Question doesn't bother him. When he is asked about his background, he just says he is part Ukrainian, part Barbadian. "Then we get into a discussion of what they thought I was. I've had Armenian, Egyptian, Pakistani, East Indian . . . It's just a question of curiosity. I've been asked so many times. If I got mad about it every single time, I'd just be this really angry person. I certainly don't feel any anger about it when people ask me about it, but my back does go up when I read it on an application form or on a government census."

30   Tyson Brown, who was raised in Burlington and now lives in Toronto, said he takes The Question as an opportunity to educate people about issues of mixed race and blackness. "I say, 'I'm mixed, African Canadian and white Canadian.'" Tyson emerged from a largely white high school to embrace his black identity completely as a young man. He read black literature, listened to black music, wore funky black clothes, dated black women, and chose to immerse himself completely in the black student community at York University. Later, he lived with his girlfriend for a year in Barbados, and there the constant references to his race grated on him. "They called me 'red man' the whole time I was there," he complained.

31   However, my brother, Dan, described The Question as a painful experience, especially during childhood. "I was definitely asked that question a lot. And a lot of times, when I said part black, or half black, people would then decide to argue with me and tell me that no, I wasn't, 'cause I didn't look black enough. I can remember it happening a lot when I was a boy, at summer camp. When I went up to camp for the first time, I was sitting on the bus with this kid who was probably a year or two older than I was. And this kid was saying, 'You're not. You can't be.' So there I was arguing with him about this."

32   Like Dan, most of the people I interviewed—and virtually all of the women— expressed impatience with constant questions about their racial background.

33   Karyn Hood, of Toronto, said, "People think I'm everything under the flipping sun, and it drives me insane. I get North African, Moroccan, Italian, Sicilian, Greek, Spanish, Jewish . . . Whenever I meet someone, I know it's going to be 'What are you? What background are you?' I usually try to put it to bed with one answer: 'My father is West Indian, my mother's Irish Canadian.' It's annoying. But life's a puzzle, and they want to know how you fit into their world." Karyn resents being perceived as "exotic," cultivates friendships in the

black community, and prefers to date black men. "You can't live in two worlds. You have to make a choice. Saying you're white isn't really an option. So this makes it clear to people. If there's any doubt, that's the choice I'm making."

34   Natalie Wall, of Toronto, concurred. "I've been asked what I am so many times. It is the rudest question in the world. It's the basest form of labelling I've ever seen. People on the street are always guessing. 'You're Spanish, right? Indian? What the hell are you?' I tell them I'm Canadian. 'But where are you from?' 'Canada.' 'What about your parents?' 'My mom is from Nova Scotia, my dad is from Trinidad.' 'So what are you?' 'Black.' I get a surprised look. 'You *are?*'"

35   Jazz Miller, of Toronto, is so sick of The Question that when people ask her what she is, she has taken to answering "aardvark." "It is designed to embarrass the person asking the question. There's always a little bit of nervous laughter."

36   Aaron Cavon, who has a white father and a black mother, was a graduate student at Dalhousie University when I interviewed him. He said people always look astonished when he says that The Question irritates him and he won't answer it. He described the attitude of the questioner as unconsciously aggressive, a stance that suggests the person being questioned is inferior. Underneath The Question, Aaron argued, is this unarticulated belief: "It's not necessary for me to explain my origins, but it's necessary for you to tell me who you are." He told me, "The assumption behind The Question is, 'I'm just white. You are the person who answers the question because you are the one who is unknown.'"

37   Sara, one of my anonymous interviewees, fumed as she recalled the numerous times she had dealt with The Question.

38   "Sometimes I'm very rude. I don't give much information. I might just say, 'I'm from here.' Some days, if I don't feel like it, I just say, 'Africa.' And they're happy, not realizing that Africa's a continent and that there are fifty-two countries in it. It's just what they want to hear. They want to place you somewhere because it makes them feel comfortable, helps them compartmentalize you.

39   "Where the hell are they from? No one's from here unless they're First Nations peoples. But they're trying to make you feel strange. It's a displacement. They're just trying to let you know that you don't belong . . . They are not coming from a position of intelligence, asking those questions. White privilege doesn't operate from a level of consciousness. It operates from a position of privilege. Because they're privileged, they don't have to think about stuff. They really don't. Does it mean that they're not well intentioned? These can be people you love dearly, you know? But that's the way the world is. They're operating from a position of belligerent white privilege, and they don't have to look at stuff and think about stuff. So they ask these reckless questions."

The Hockey Sweater

1   The winters of my childhood were long, long seasons. We lived in three places—the school, the church and the skating-rink—but our real life was on the skating-rink. Real battles were won on the skating-rink. Real strength appeared on the skating-rink. The real leaders showed themselves on the skating-rink. School was a sort of punishment. Parents always want to punish children and school is their most natural way of punishing us. However, school was also a quiet place where we could prepare for the next hockey game, lay out our next strategies. As for church, we found there the tranquility of God: there we forgot school and dreamed about the next hockey game. Through our daydreams it might happen that we would recite a prayer: we would ask God to help us play as well as Maurice Richard.

2   We all wore the same uniform as he, the red, white and blue uniform of the Montreal Canadiens, the best hockey team in the world; we all combed our hair in the same style as Maurice Richard, and to keep it in place we used a sort of glue—a great deal of glue. We laced our skates like Maurice Richard, we taped our sticks like Maurice Richard. We cut all his pictures out of the papers. Truly, we knew everything about him.

3   On the ice, when the referee blew his whistle the two teams would rush at the puck; we were five Maurice Richards taking it away from five other Maurice Richards; we were ten players, all of us wearing with the same blazing enthusiasm the uniform of the Montreal Canadiens. On our backs, we all wore the famous number 9.

4   One day, my Montreal Canadiens sweater had become too small; then it got torn and had holes in it. My mother said: "If you wear that old sweater people are going to think we're poor!" Then she did what she did whenever we needed new clothes. She started to leaf through the catalogue the Eaton company sent us in the mail every year. My mother was proud. She didn't want to buy our clothes at the general store; the only things that were good enough for us were the latest styles from Eaton's catalogue. My mother didn't like the order forms included with the catalogue; they were written in English and she didn't understand a word of it. To order my hockey sweater, she did as she usually did; she took out her writing paper and wrote in her gentle schoolteacher's hand: "Cher Monsieur Eaton, Would you be kind enough to send me a Canadiens' sweater for my son who is ten years old and a little too tall for his age and Docteur Robitaille thinks he's a little too thin? I'm sending you three dollars and please send me what's left if there's anything left. I hope your wrapping will be better than last time."

5   Monsieur Eaton was quick to answer my mother's letter. Two weeks later we received the sweater. That day I had one of the greatest disappointments of my life! I would even say that on that day I experienced a very great sorrow. Instead of the red, white and blue Montreal Canadiens sweater, Monsieur Eaton had sent us a blue and white sweater with a maple leaf on the front—the sweater of the Toronto Maple Leafs. I'd always worn the red, white and blue Montreal Canadiens sweater; all my friends wore the red, white and blue sweater; never

439

had anyone in my village ever worn the Toronto sweater, never had we even seen a Toronto Maple Leafs sweater. Besides, the Toronto team was regularly trounced by the triumphant Canadiens. With tears in my eyes, I found the strength to say:

6   "I'll never wear that uniform."

7   "My boy, first you're going to try it on! If you make up your mind about things before you try, my boy, you won't go very far in this life."

8   My mother had pulled the blue and white Toronto Maple Leafs sweater over my shoulders and already my arms were inside the sleeves. She pulled the sweater down and carefully smoothed all the creases in the abominable maple leaf on which, right in the middle of my chest, were written the words "Toronto Maple Leafs." I wept.

9   "I'll never wear it."

10   "Why not? This sweater fits you . . . like a glove."

11   "Maurice Richard would never put it on his back."

12   "You aren't Maurice Richard. Anyway, it isn't what's on your back that counts, it's what you've got inside your head."

13   "You'll never put it in my head to wear a Toronto Maple Leafs sweater."

14   My mother sighed in despair and explained to me:

15   "If you don't keep this sweater which fits you perfectly I'll have to write to Monsieur Eaton and explain that you don't want to wear the Toronto sweater. Monsieur Eaton's an *Anglais;* he'll be insulted because he likes the Maple Leafs. And if he's insulted do you think he'll be in a hurry to answer us? Spring will be here and you won't have played a single game, just because you didn't want to wear that perfectly nice blue sweater."

16   So I was obliged to wear the Maple Leafs sweater. When I arrived on the rink, all the Maurice Richards in red, white and blue came up, one by one, to take a look. When the referee blew his whistle I went to take my usual position. The captain came and warned me I'd be better to stay on the forward line. A few minutes later the second line was called; I jumped onto the ice. The Maple Leafs sweater weighed on my shoulders like a mountain. The captain came and told me to wait; he'd need me later, on defense. By the third period I still hadn't played; one of the defensemen was hit in the nose with a stick and it was bleeding. I jumped on the ice: my moment had come! The referee blew his whistle; he gave me a penalty. He claimed I'd jumped on the ice when there were already five players. That was too much! It was unfair! It was persecution! It was because of my blue sweater! I struck my stick against the ice so hard it broke. Relieved, I bent down to pick up the debris. As I straightened up I saw the young vicar, on skates, before me.

17   "My child," he said, "just because you're wearing a new Toronto Maple Leafs sweater unlike the others, it doesn't mean you're going to make the laws around here. A proper young man doesn't lose his temper. Now take off your skates and go to the church and ask God to forgive you."

18   Wearing my Maple Leafs sweater I went to the church, where I prayed to God; I asked him to send, as quickly as possible, moths that would eat up my Toronto Maple Leafs sweater.

Stanley Coren

Dogs and Monsters

You can see Stanley Coren as a guest on numerous television shows as well as in the role of host on his weekly television show "Good Dog"; you can hear him on radio programs such as Dan Rather, Ideas, Quirks and Quarks, Basic Black, and The Osgood Report; and you can read his work in articles published in USA Today, *the* Globe and Mail, *the* New York Times, *the* Chicago Tribune, Time, People, Maclean's, Cosmopolitan, *and* Entertainment Weekly. *Coren has also published several books about dogs, including* How to Speak Dog, Why We Love the Dogs We Do, The Intelligence of Dogs, *and* Sleep Thieves. *He has published a multitude of academic and scientific writings related to his research into various areas of psychology and his current role as a professor and director of the Human Neuropsychology and Perception Laboratory at the University of British Columbia. If you wanted to meet Coren, you could register for a psychology class he teaches at UBC, you could take a course with the Vancouver Dog Obedience Training Club, or you could attend one of the many fundraising events for the SPCA in which he participates.*

Coren was born in Philadelphia in 1942 and educated at the University of Pennsylvania (undergraduate) and Stanford University (doctorate). This prolific writer and researcher now lives in Vancouver with his wife, two dogs, and a cat.

Preparing to Read

One recent cellular phone ad campaign highlights the similarities in appearance between people and the dogs they choose as pets. Do you have a dog? If so, what kind of dog do you have? What characteristics made you choose that type of dog? Generally, do you think dogs are good pets? Why or why not? How has the role of pets changed over the last century? In this essay, originally published in Saturday Night *magazine in May 2000, Stanley Coren outlines the process of bio-engineering dogs to adapt to the current technologies and needs of their human owners.*

1   Today's headlines routinely raise fears about genetic engineering. The biggest concern is that "tampering with creation" to fashion new strains of plants and animals may result in the devastation of the world by upsetting the natural balance among species. Even Prince Charles has joined the debate, claiming that genetic engineering "takes us into areas that should be left to God. We should not be meddling with the building blocks of life in this way." But the genetic manipulation of species is far from new. In fact, it began at least 14,000 years ago, when human beings created the first deliberately engineered organism—the dog.

2   The bioengineered canine was not created in a high-level biocontaintment lab; rather, its beginnings were accidental. Wolves and jackals (the domestic dog's predecessors) were attracted to human camps because primitive humans left bones, bits of skin, and other scraps of leftover food scattered near their dwellings. The wolves and jackals learned that by loitering around the settlement they could grab an occasional bite to eat without the exertion involved in

hunting. These primitive dogs were initially tolerated by humans because they functioned as de facto garbage-disposal units.

3   The dogs near the campsite provided another key benefit: security. They barked whenever wild beasts or strangers approached, removing the need for human guards to be posted at night, and thus affording the villagers more rest and increased safety. The bark was critical—the most effective guard dogs, obviously, were those with loud, persistent barks. And so a selective breeding program was begun: those dogs that barked loudly were kept and bred with other loud barkers, while those that did not bark were simply killed or chased off. In fact, one of the major distinctions between wild canines and domestic dogs today is that domestic dogs bark, while wild dogs seldom do. The persistent racket that irritates so many people is actually a human innovation.

4   It wasn't until the end of the fifteenth century, though, that the dog as a genetic creation became truly unique—almost more an invention than a species. At this point people began cross-breeding dogs, not just to cater to their changing needs, but to suit advancing technology. Typically, humans had tailored machines to suit organisms. With dogs, they began modifying an organism to fit a machine. The machine was the gun, and the organism was the gun dog.

5   The earliest gun dogs were the pointers, which appeared in Europe in the 1500s. The hunting weapon of choice at the time was the muzzle-loading musket, a primitive device that was notoriously laborious to use. On sighting his quarry, a hunter had to take out his powder horn, dump gunpowder down the barrel, followed by a lead ball wrapped with oiled paper or cloth, and tamp down the shot and powder with a tamping rod; then he had to fire the gun. The process took a minimum of thirty seconds, all in the service of a weapon with an effective range of twenty-five to fifty yards. To accomodate musket technology, the pointer was designed to be slow, silent, and patient. The pointer's job was to find a bird, then to hold its position while pointing at the bird's location for the agonizingly long time it took the hunter to load and shoot his weapon. If a lucky shot actually killed a bird the pointer was expected to go out and bring the game back as well. But the retrieval was window-dressing; the pointer's genetic value lay in its ability to stretch time out, to live in a slow-motion world.

6   As weapons technology improved, guns became easier to load, with better range and accuracy. To match this new equipment, dog breeders in the late 1700s created a new kind of dog—the setter. Setters moved much more quickly than pointers, and indicated their proximity to the prey not by the stillness of their point but by the beat of their tails. The faster a setter wagged its tail, the closer it was to the game.

7   As more land was cultivated and cities and towns sprang up, hunters were forced to turn to wilderness areas, particularly wetlands, where they hid behind blinds and waited for their quarry to come to them. These circumstances placed a premium on a dog that was not simply quiet, as the pointer had been, but that possessed an almost preternatural obedience and patience. Thus, the retriever became the bioengineered star of the next century. Retrievers were bred to wait—to do nothing: not to point, not to flush, not to run, not to bark—and retrieve. They were bred to be less, not more, which, given the physiognomy of the species, may have been the more remarkable biotechnological feat.

8   Canada is responsible for the newest and most intriguing genetic invention in the retriever group: the Nova Scotia duck tolling retriever, a handsome, auburn-hued dog that stands about twenty inches high and weighs about forty-five pounds. The need for the toller arose when duck hunters found that

they could better attract their quarry by having wooden "lures," or decoys, carved to look like ducks, floating in the nearby water. Ducks are also attracted to unusual movement and activities. This is where the toller comes in. Tolling simply means that the dog runs back and forth on the shore, spinning and making noise, or swims erratically near the shore to attract the birds. Curious ducks fly near to see what all the activity is about, and come within range of the hunter's gun. Tollers will do this for hours if needed. Of course, once the bird is shot the dog is then expected to swim out and bring it back to its lazy master.

9   Like any piece of technology—the 78 rpm record player, or the pedal-driven sewing machine—a bioengineered dog can become outmoded and obsolete. One of the most common breeds of the eighteenth and nineteenth centuries, the Spanish pointer, was so popular in its day that it can be seen in scores of early paintings of hunts. These dogs were perfect for the era of the muzzle-loading musket—slow, quiet, and the most meticulous of the pointers. Today the breed is effectively extinct. Spanish pointers were simply too slow for impatient modern hunters, with their new, superior equipment—both guns and dogs.

10   Walk into homes today, and what you'll find are dogs engineered for a wholly different piece of technology: the TV remote control. Perhaps our faith in biogenetic engineering would be improved if we recognized that for those of us who don't hunt, some dogs have also been designed specifically to be our companions—to fit the couch-potato mentality of our current, leisure-addicted era. It is a wonder to me that starting with the DNA of a wolf, we have spent 14,000 years of biotechnology and genetic manipulation in the creation of the little white beast who is right now gently snoring with his head resting against my foot.

David Foot

Boomers Dance to a New Beat

David Foot is a professor of Economics at the University of Toronto who has become very well known for his work concerning the role of demographics in determining societal and economic trends. Foot's book, Boom, Bust and Echo: How to Profit from the Coming Demographic Shift, *co-written with Daniel Stoffman, quickly became a best-seller and has made Foot a popular speaker and authority on future Canadian trends.*

Prior to the 1996 publication of Boom, Bust and Echo, *Foot had published two other books:* Canada's Population Outlook: Demographic Futures and Economic Challenges *(1982) and, with Blossom T. Wigdor,* The Over Forty Society *(1988). Foot's other publications are listed on his Web site (**www.footwork.com**).*

David Foot was born in England in 1944, grew up in Australia where he completed an undergraduate degree, and then continued his education at Harvard University where he earned a doctorate in economics. While his writing has attracted much attention for Dr. Foot, he has also been recognized for his teaching ability. He is a two-time recipient of the University of Toronto undergraduate teaching award. As well, in 1992, he received a 3M Award for Teaching Excellence from the Society for Teaching and Learning in Higher Education, which recognizes outstanding Canadian university educators.

Preparing to Read

Before you read this essay, think about different generations. To what generation do you belong? What generation are your parents a part of? What defines a generation? What is a "generation gap"? Which generation has had the most significant on our society? Why?

1   Cocooning is dead, the trend-spotters have proclaimed.

2   In the eighties, North Americans hunkered down in their house-fortresses with remote control to avoid an increasingly unsafe world. Now, this cocooning trend, first labelled by guru Faith Popcorn, is in reverse.

3   Canadians and Americans are watching less TV and going out more to movies, museums, the performing arts and restaurants. Crime rates have stopped rising and, in many jurisdictions, they are falling.

4   All forms of home entertainment are either stagnant or declining in popularity. The Internet does not seem to be catching on as home entertainment or as a shopping vehicle. There has been a resurrection of city streets and a renewed concern for communities. According to a recent *Globe and Mail* article, we are rejecting the "bland fruits of wired isolation."

5   But is all this so surprising? A careful understanding of demographic trends provides a logical and easily understood explanation. For managers and marketers, it also serves as a foundation for anticipating new trends.

6   In a person's teens and 20s, "action" is important. The downtown core of major cities provide this action. Being "grounded" by a tough parent is real punishment; moving out, usually into a city apartment, is a common goal.

7   Growing up into the late 20s and early 30s often means partnering and family formation. For many parents, the city core doesn't seem like a great place to raise kids, so they buy houses in the suburbs. This means a mortgage and other loans to purchase furniture, appliances and the minivan.

8   So it was with the baby boomer generation, which has dominated, if not determined, postwar economic and social trends in North America. The 10 million boomers in Canada, born between 1947 and 1966, comprise the biggest generation in the history of this country. Watching them can provide an understanding of these trends.

9   The first boomer became a teen-ager in 1960. So the sixties and seventies were dominated by boomers moving through their teen-age years into their 20s. They rushed into cities, stimulating massive urbanization. They rented apartments, driving down vacancies and increasing rents. They went to movies and rock concerts and they ate lots of cheap food.

10   In 1977, a significant event went almost unnoticed—the first boomer reached the dreaded age of 30. The early boomers started buying homes in the suburbs. By the mid-eighties, the new trend became an avalanche. Suburbanization took off.

11   Debt levels soared and the "echo generation" was spawned. Minivan sales took off. Young children and lots of debt put a damper on going out. Technology and TV in particular, including video rentals, became the main entertainment media. Cocooning was established.

12   So Faith Popcorn was right, but it was not because of new societal values. The biggest generation in history was leaving its action years behind and moving into its family ones. Not surprisingly, family values emerged as a new social trend. Rental housing, movie theatres and take-out restaurants experienced much slower growth and, in some cases, decline.

13   Spending growth was focused on family and home. Pet-food sales were still brisk but convenience-store sales sagged. Boomers started paying off their loans and mortgages, leaving no cash for luxuries or savings.

14   With kids to raise and careers to manage, the boomers in their 30s and 40s were running "99 Lives"—another Popcorn trend. They were trying to be good parents to their kids and good children to their aging parents. They were working overtime and competing for promotion to ever-fewer mid-management positions. Woe betide any organization that wasted their time. The "vigilante consumer" had arrived in full force.

15   But last year, another watershed was reached—the first boomers turned 50. This is mid-life crisis time. The kids are beginning to leave home and those sprained ligaments are taking longer to heal.

16   Running shoes have become walking shoes, and the treadmill purchased to replace visits to the fitness centre now induces guilt. Resting has become a pleasurable activity, especially at the cottage. Anyone ignorant of the power of demographics might think values are changing again.

17   With lower interest rates and evaporating loans, there is more discretionary income, making it possible to afford a luxury or a sports-utility vehicle, a restaurant meal, and a show.

18   The teen-age or twentysomething kids don't need babysitting any more, so going out is possible again. But the show is less likely to be a movie or a rock concert unless, of course, the Rolling Stones are back in town. Increasingly, the lavish musical, the symphony and maybe the opera hold more attraction.

19   So boomers are emerging from their cocoons. Surprise! They are watching less TV—home entertainment is dropping in popularity—they are shopping in their neighbourhoods and they are not using the Internet. Their beloved pets are aging and the vet is becoming as familiar as the doctor.

20   Their parents are also getting old and mortality has come closer to home. Aging has entered a deeply psychological, almost spiritual phase. Boomers are snapping up books on the topic, provided the print is large.

21   But the seven million "echo" kids are also having an impact. Movie attendance is rising, mainly because of the increased numbers of teen-agers. Similarly, the growth in confectionary, pop and some fast-food sales has little to do with boomers trying to relive youth. Their echo kids born in the eighties are delivering these trends.

22   The marketplace of the future is becoming more complex. While the leading boomers are killing cocooning, their kids are reigniting the trends of the sixties. Rock stars have a bright future, as does new technology. Of course, it should not be surprising to see a reversal of the downward trend in crime rates as the echo generation enters its prime crime-prone ages.

23   But will this drive the boomers back to cocoons? Hardly. They are finding time to volunteer, to give to charity and to support their communities. They are increasingly worried about pensions, investing in the market and thinking about moving out of the urban rat race. These are the trends of the future.

24   The boomer generation is predictably shifting into the next phase of life: They are beginning to move from parenthood to grandparenthood.

25   Managing this new trend is both a personal and a societal challenge, with all the associated opportunities and tribulations. Demographic analysis can provide us with a window to understand these changes, to disentangle them and to predict them. What more could the successful manager ask for?

David Arnason

A Girl's Story

The fact that the entire Spring 2001 *issue of* Prairie Fire *is devoted to David Arnason is testament to his influence on the Canadian literary community and to the range of his talents. In the introduction to this issue of* Prairie Fire, *Douglas Reimer characterizes Arnason as "prodigious in his energy for the promotion of the arts and for life itself . . ." as evidenced, in part, by his writing and publishing of plays, novels, short stories, poetry, drama, film scripts, essays, anthologies, songs, and works of criticism, by his service on various arts councils, and by his teaching at the University of Manitoba.*

Arnason was born in Gimli, Manitoba in 1940, and now makes his home both in Gimli, where he does most of his writing, and in Winnipeg, where he teaches Canadian Literature and Creative Writing and is head of the English Department and of the Department of Icelandic Language and Literature. Arnason's most recent publication is a novel entitled King Jerry *(2001); the story found here comes from* The Circus Performers' Bar, *a collection of short stories published in 1984.*

1   You've wondered what it would be like to be a character in a story, to sort of slip out of your ordinary self and into some other character. Well, I'm offering you the opportunity. I've been trying to think of a heroine for this story, and frankly, it hasn't been going too well. A writer's life isn't easy, especially if, like me, he's got a tendency sometimes to drink a little bit too much. Yesterday, I went for a beer with Dennis and Ken (they're real-life friends of mine) and we stayed a little longer than we should have. Then I came home and quickly mixed a drink and started drinking it so my wife would think the liquor on my breath came from the drink I was drinking and not from the drinks I had had earlier. I wasn't going to tell her about those drinks. Anyway, Wayne dropped over in the evening and I had some more drinks, and this morning my head isn't working very well.

2   To be absolutely frank about it, I always have trouble getting characters, even when I'm stone cold sober. I can think of plots; plots are really easy. If you can't think of one, you just pick up a book, and sure enough, there's a plot. You just move a few things around and nobody knows you stole the idea. Characters are the problem. It doesn't matter how good the plot is if your characters are dull. You can steal characters too, and put them into different plots. I've done that. I stole Eustacia Vye from Hardy and gave her another name. The problem was that she turned out a lot sulkier than I remembered and the plot I put her in was a light comedy. Now nobody wants to publish the story. I'm still sending it out, though. If you send a story to enough publishers, no matter how bad it is, somebody will ultimately publish it.

3   For this story I need a beautiful girl. You probably don't think you're beautiful enough, but I can fix that. I can do all kinds of retouching once I've got the basic material, and if I miss anything, Karl (he's my editor) will find it. So I'm going to make you fairly tall, about five-foot eight and a quarter in your

stocking feet. I'm going to give you long blonde hair because long blonde hair is sexy and virtuous. Black hair can be sexy too, but it doesn't go with virtue. I've got to deal with a whole literary tradition where black-haired women are basically evil. If I were feeling better I might be able to do it in an ironic way, then black hair would be okay, but I don't think I'm up to it this morning. If you're going to use irony, then you've got to be really careful about tone. I could make you a redhead, but redheads have a way of turning out pixie-ish, and that would wreck my plot.

4   So you've got long blonde hair and you're this tall slender girl with amazingly blue eyes. Your face is narrow and your nose is straight and thin. I could have turned up the nose a little, but that would have made you cute, and I really need a beautiful girl. I'm going to put a tiny black mole on your cheek. It's traditional. If you want your character to be really beautiful there has to be some minor defect.

5   Now, I'm going to sit you on the bank of a river. I'm not much for setting. I've read so many things where you get great long descriptions of the setting, and mostly it's just boring. When my last book came out, one of the reviewers suggested that the reason I don't do settings is that I'm not very good at them. That's just silly. I'm writing a different kind of story, not that old realist stuff. If you think I can't do setting, just watch.

6   There's a curl in the river just below the old dam where the water seems to make a broad sweep. That flatness is deceptive, though. Under the innocent sheen of the mirroring surface, the current is treacherous. The water swirls, stabs, takes sharp angles and dangerous vectors. The trees that lean from the bank shimmer with the multi-hued greenness of elm, oak, maple and aspen. The leaves turn in the gentle breeze, showing their paler green undersides. The undergrowth, too, is thick and green, hiding the poison ivy, the poison sumac and the thorns. On a patch of grass that slopes gently to the water, the only clear part of the bank on that side of the river, a girl sits, a girl with long blonde hair. She has slipped a ring from her finger and seems to be holding it towards the light.

7   You see? I could do a lot more of that, but you wouldn't like it. I slipped a lot of details in there and provided all those hints about strange and dangerous things under the surface. That's called foreshadowing. I put in the ring at the end there so that you'd wonder what was going to happen. That's to create suspense. You're supposed to ask yourself what the ring means. Obviously it has something to do with love, rings always do, and since she's taken it off, obviously something has gone wrong in the love relationship. Now I just have to hold off answering that question for as long as I can, and I've got my story. I've got a friend who's also a writer who says never tell the buggers anything until they absolutely have to know.

8   I'm going to have trouble with the feminists about this story. I can see that already. I've got that river that's calm on the surface and boiling underneath, and I've got those trees that are gentle and beautiful with poisonous and dangerous undergrowth. Obviously, the girl is going to be like that, calm on the surface but passionate underneath. The feminists are going to say that I'm perpetuating stereotypes, that by giving the impression the girl is full of hidden passion I'm encouraging rapists. That's crazy. I'm just using a literary convention. Most of the world's great books are about the conflict between reason and passion. If you take that away, what's left to write about?

9   So I've got you sitting on the riverbank, twirling your ring. I forgot the birds. The trees are full of singing birds. There are meadowlarks and vireos and even Blackburnian warblers. I know a lot about birds but I'm not going to put in too many. You've got to be careful not to overdo things. In a minute I'm going to enter your mind and reveal what you're thinking. I'm going to do this in the third person. Using the first person is sometimes more effective, but I'm always afraid to do a female character in the first person. It seems wrong to me, like putting on a woman's dress.

10   Your name is Linda. I had to be careful not to give you a biblical name like Judith or Rachel. I don't want any symbolism in this story. Symbolism makes me sick, especially biblical symbolism. You always end up with some crazy moral argument that you don't believe and none of the readers believe. Then you lose control of your characters, because they've got to be like the biblical characters. You've got this terrific episode you'd like to use, but you can't because Rachel or Judith or whoever wouldn't do it. I think of stories with a lot of symbolism in them as sticky.

11   Here goes.

12   Linda held the ring up towards the light. The diamond flashed rainbow colours. It was a small diamond, and Linda reflected that it was probably a perfect symbol of her relationship with Gregg. Everything Gregg did was on a small scale. He was careful with his money and just as careful with his emotions. In one week they would have a small wedding and then move into a small apartment. She supposed that she ought to be happy. Gregg was very handsome, and she did love him. Why did it seem that she was walking into a trap?

13   That sounds kind of distant, but it's supposed to be distant. I'm using indirect quotation because the reader has just met Linda, and we don't want to get too intimate right away. Besides, I've got to get a lot of explaining done quickly, and if you can do it with the character's thoughts, then that's best.

14   Linda twirled the ring again, then with a suddenness that surprised her, she stood up and threw it into the river. She was immediately struck by a feeling of panic. For a moment she almost decided to dive into the river to try to recover it. Then, suddenly, she felt free. It was now impossible to marry Gregg. He would not forgive her for throwing the ring away. Gregg would say he'd had enough of her theatrics for one lifetime. He always accused her of being a romantic. She'd never had the courage to admit that he was correct, and that she intended to continue being a romantic. She was sitting alone by the river in a long blue dress because it was a romantic pose. Anyway, she thought a little wryly, you're only likely to find romance if you look for it in romantic places and dress for the occasion.

15   Suddenly, she heard a rustling in the bush, the sound of someone coming down the narrow path from the road above.

16   I had to do that, you see. I'd used up all the potential in the relationship with Gregg, and the plot would have started to flag if I hadn't introduced a new character. The man who is coming down the path is tall and athletic with wavy brown hair. He has dark brown eyes that crinkle when he smiles, and he looks kind. His skin is tanned, as if he spends a lot of time outdoors, and he moves gracefully. He is smoking a pipe. I don't want to give too many details. I'm not absolutely sure what features women find attractive in men these days, but what I've described seems safe enough. I got all of it from stories written by women, and I assume they must know. I could give him a chiselled jaw, but that's about as far as I'll go.

17   The man stepped into the clearing. He carried an old-fashioned wicker fishing creel and a telescoped fishing rod. Linda remained sitting on the grass, her blue dress spread out around her. The man noticed her and apologized.

18   "I'm sorry, I always come here to fish on Saturday afternoons and I've never encountered anyone here before." His voice was low with something of an amused tone in it.

19   "Don't worry," Linda replied. "I'll only be here for a little while. Go ahead and fish. I won't make any noise." In some way she couldn't understand, the man looked familiar to her. She felt she knew him. She thought she might have seen him on television or in a movie, but of course she knew that movie and television stars do not spend every Saturday afternoon fishing on the banks of small, muddy rivers.

20   "You can make all the noise you want," he told her. "The fish in this river are almost entirely deaf. Besides, I don't care if I catch any. I only like the act of fishing. If I catch them, then I have to take them home and clean them. Then I've got to cook them and eat them. I don't even like fish that much, and the fish you catch here all taste of mud."

21   "Why do you bother fishing then?" Linda asked him. "Why don't you just come and sit on the riverbank?"

22   "It's not that easy," he told her. "A beautiful girl in a blue dress may go and sit on a riverbank any time she wants. But a man can only sit on a riverbank if he has a very good reason. Because I fish, I am a man with a hobby. After a hard week of work, I deserve some relaxation. But if I just came and sat on the riverbank, I would be a romantic fool. People would make fun of me. They would think I was irresponsible, and before long I would be a failure." As he spoke, he attached a lure to his line, untelescoped his fishing pole and cast his line into the water.

23   You may object that this would not have happened in real life, that the conversation would have been awkward, that Linda would have been a bit frightened by the man. Well, why don't you just run out to the grocery store and buy a bottle of milk and a loaf of bread? The grocer will give you your change without even looking at you. That's what happens in real life, and if that's what you're after, why are you reading a book?

24   I'm sorry. I shouldn't have got upset. But it's not easy you know. Dialogue is about the hardest stuff to write. You've got all those "he saids" and "she saids" and "he replieds." And you've got to remember the quotation marks and whether the comma is inside or outside the quotation marks. Sometimes you can leave out the "he saids" and the "she saids" but then the reader gets confused and can't figure out who's talking. Hemingway is bad for that. Sometimes you can read an entire chapter without figuring out who's on what side.

25   Anyway, something must have been in the air that afternoon. Linda felt free and open.

26   Did I mention that it was warm and the sun was shining?

27   She chattered away, telling the stranger all about her life, what she had done when she was a little girl, the time her dad had taken the whole family to Hawaii and she got such a bad sunburn that she was peeling in February, how she was a better water-skier than Gregg and how mad he got when she beat him at tennis. The man, whose name was Michael (you can use biblical names for men as long as you avoid Joshua or Isaac), told her he was a doctor, but had always wanted to be a cowboy. He told her about the time he skinned his knee when he fell off his bicycle and had to spend two weeks in the hospital because of

infection. In short, they did what people who are falling in love always do. They unfolded their brightest and happiest memories and gave them to each other as gifts.

28   Then Michael took a bottle of wine and a Klik sandwich out of his wicker creel and invited Linda to join him in a picnic. He had forgotten his corkscrew and he had to push the cork down into the bottle with his filletting knife. They drank wine and laughed and spat out little pieces of cork. Michael reeled in his line, and to his amazement discovered a diamond ring on his hook. Linda didn't dare tell him where the ring had come from. Then Michael took Linda's hand, and slipped the ring onto her finger. In a comic-solemn voice, he asked her to marry him. With the same kind of comic solemnity, she agreed. Then they kissed, a first gentle kiss with their lips barely brushing and without touching each other.

29   Now I've got to bring this to some kind of ending. You think writers know how stories end before they write them, but that's not true. We're wracked with confusion and guilt about how things are going to end. And just as you're playing the role of Linda in this story, Michael is my alter ego. He even looks a little like me and he smokes the same kind of pipe. We all want this to end happily. If I were going to be realistic about this, I suppose I'd have to let them make love. Then, shaken with guilt and horror, Linda would go back and marry Gregg, and the doctor would go back to his practice. But I'm not going to do that. In the story from which I stole the plot, Michael turned out not to be a doctor at all, but a returned soldier who had always been in love with Linda. She recognized him as they kissed, because they had kissed as children, and even though they had grown up and changed, she recognized the flavour of wintergreen on his breath. That's no good. It brings in too many unexplained facts at the last minute.

30   I'm going to end it right here at the moment of the kiss. You can do what you want with the rest of it, except you can't make him a returned soldier, and you can't have them make love then separate forever. I've eliminated those options. In fact, I think I'll eliminate all options. This is where the story ends, at the moment of the kiss. It goes on and on forever while cities burn, nations rise and fall, galaxies are born and die, and the universe snuffs out the stars one by one. It goes on, the story, the brush of a kiss.

Kate Chopin

The Story of an Hour

Kate Chopin (b. Katherine O'Flaherty, 1851–1904) began her life in St. Louis, Missouri. Her father died when she was four years old, so she was reared by three widows: her mother, her grandmother, and her great-grandmother. She was graduated from Sacred Heart convent in 1870 and then married Oscar Chopin, following him to New Orleans and later to his plantation in northern Louisiana. The mother of six children, she was widowed in 1882 and moved back to St. Louis where she began to write stories and publish in stylish literary magazines. Her novels, At Fault *(1890) and* The Awakening *(1899), shocked conservative Victorian society but are praised by modern critics. Her collections of short stories,* Bayou Folk *(1894) and*

A Night in Acadie (1897) draw on her years of experience on a Louisiana plantation among Creole people. She died of a brain hemorrhage at only fifty-three. "The Story of an Hour" caused Chopin to be shunned by both her literary club and magazine publishers at the close of the nineteenth century, but it has persevered to become especially appealing to women in the late twentieth century.

1   Knowing that Mrs. Mallard was afflicted with a heart trouble, great care was taken to break to her as gently as possible the news of her husband's death.

2   It was her sister Josephine who told her, in broken sentences, veiled hints that revealed in half concealing. Her husband's friend Richards was there, too, near her. It was he who had been in the newspaper office when intelligence of the railroad disaster was received, with Brently Mallard's name leading the list of "killed." He had only taken the time to assure himself of its truth by a second telegram, and had hastened to forestall any less careful, less tender friend in bearing the sad message.

3   She did not hear the story as many women have heard the same, with a paralyzed inability to accept its significance. She wept at once, with sudden, wild abandonment, in her sister's arms. When the storm of grief had spent itself she went away to her room alone. She would have no one follow her.

4   There stood, facing the open window, a comfortable, roomy armchair. Into this she sank, pressed down by a physical exhaustion that haunted her body and seemed to reach into her soul.

5   She could see in the open square before her house the tops of trees that were all aquiver with the new spring life. The delicious breath of rain was in the air. In the street below a peddler was crying his wares. The notes of a distant song which someone was singing reached her faintly, and countless sparrows were twittering in the eaves.

6   There were patches of blue sky showing here and there through the clouds that had met and piled above the other in the west facing her window.

7   She sat with her head thrown back upon the cushion of the chair, quite motionless, except when a sob came up into her throat and shook her, as a child who has cried itself to sleep continues to sob in its dreams.

8   She was young, with a fair, calm face, whose lines bespoke repression and even a certain strength. But now there was a dull stare in her eyes, whose gaze was fixed away off yonder on one of those patches of blue sky. It was not a glance of reflection, but rather indicated a suspension of intelligent thought.

9   There was something coming to her and she was waiting for it, fearfully. What was it? She did not know; it was too subtle and elusive to name. But she felt it, creeping out of the sky, reaching toward her through the sounds, the scents, the color that filled the air.

10   Now her bosom rose and fell tumultuously. She was beginning to recognize this thing that was approaching to possess her, and she was striving to beat it back with her will—as powerless as her two white slender hands would have been.

11   When she abandoned herself a little whispered word escaped her slightly parted lips. She said it over and over under her breath: "Free, free, free!" The vacant stare and the look of terror that had followed it went from her eyes. They stayed keen and bright. Her pulses beat fast, and the coursing blood warmed and relaxed every inch of her body.

12   She did not stop to ask if it were or were not a monstrous joy that held her. A clear and exalted perception enabled her to dismiss the suggestion as trivial.

13   She knew that she would weep again when she saw the kind, tender hands folded in death; the face that had never looked save with love upon her, fixed and gray and dead. But she saw beyond that bitter moment a long procession of years to come that would belong to her absolutely. And she opened and spread her arms out to them in welcome.

14   There would be no one to live for her during those coming years; she would live for herself. There would be no powerful will bending her in that blind persistence with which men and women believe they have a right to impose a private will upon a fellow-creature. A kind intention or a cruel intention made the act seem no less a crime as she looked upon it in that brief moment of illumination.

15   And yet she had loved him—sometimes. Often she had not. What did it matter! What could love, the unsolved mystery, count for in face of this possession of self-assertion which she suddenly recognized as the strongest impulse of her being!

16   "Free! Body and soul free!" she kept whispering.

17   Josephine was kneeling before the closed door with her lips to the keyhole, imploring for admission. "Louise, open the door! I beg; open the door—you will make yourself ill. What are you doing, Louise? For heaven's sake open the door."

18   "Go away. I am not making myself ill." No; she was drinking in a very elixir of life through that open window.

19   Her fancy was running riot along those days ahead of her. Spring days, and summer days, and all sorts of days that would be her own. She breathed a quick prayer that life might be long. It was only yesterday she had thought with a shudder that life might be long.

20   She arose at length and opened the door to her sister's importunities. There was a feverish triumph in her eyes, and she carried herself unwittingly like a goddess of Victory. She clasped her sister's waist, and together they descended the stairs. Richards stood waiting for them at the bottom.

21   Someone was opening the front door with a latchkey. It was Brently Mallard who entered, a little travel-stained, composedly carrying his grip-sack and umbrella. He had been far from the scene of accident, and did not even know there had been one. He stood amazed at Josephine's piercing cry; at Richards' quick motion to screen him from the view of his wife.

22   But Richards was too late.

23   When the doctors came they said she had died of heart disease—of joy that kills.

Katherine Govier

The Immaculate Conception Photography Gallery

An article by Heather Mallick, published in the Toronto Sun *in 1995, asks, "Why don't we give Toronto's Katherine Govier her due?" and goes on to compare Govier's writing to that of Margaret Atwood and Alice Munro. While Govier is still not as well known as Atwood and Munro, she has been the recipient of several awards for her writing, which covers a variety of genres.*

Govier was born in Edmonton in 1948 and has lived in Calgary; Toronto; Washington, DC; and London, England. Her published works include six novels and three short story collections, including The Immaculate Conception Photography Gallery *(1994), where this story is found. Govier has also edited an anthology of women's travel stories, had her radio dramas broadcast on CBC Radio, and has published many reviews and essays in most major Canadian newspapers and magazines. A graduate of the University of Alberta and York University, Katherine Govier has taught English and creative writing at York University and Ryerson University and has served as chair of the Writers' Development Trust (a charitable foundation that aids promotion and education about Canadian literature and writers) as well as as president of PEN Canada (an organization that "works on behalf of writers, at home and abroad, who have been forced into silence for writing the truth as they see it").*

1   Sandro named the little photography shop on St. Clair Avenue West, between Lord's Shoes and Bargain Jimmies, after the parish church in the village where he was born. He had hankered after wider horizons, the rippled brown prairies, the hard-edged mountains. But when he reached Toronto he met necessity in the form of a wife and babies, and, never having seen a western sunset, he settled down in Little Italy. He photographed the brides in their fat lacquered curls and imported lace, and their quick babies in christening gowns brought over from home. Blown up to near life size on cardboard cutouts, their pictures filled the windows of his little shop.

2   Sandro had been there ten years already when he first really saw his sign, and the window. He stood still in front of it and looked. A particularly buxom bride with a lace bodice and cap sleeves cut in little scallops shimmered in a haze of concupiscence under the sign reading Immaculate Conception Photography Gallery. Sandro was not like his neighbours any more, he was modern, a Canadian. He no longer went to church. As he stared, one of the street drunks shuffled into place beside him. Sandro knew them all, they came into the shop in winter. (No one ought to have to stay outside in that cold, Sandro believed.) But he especially knew Becker. Becker was a smart man; he used to be a philosopher at a university.

3   "Immaculate conception," said Sandro to Becker. "What do you think?"

4   Becker lifted his eyes to the window. He made a squeezing gesture at the breasts. "I never could buy that story," he said.

5   Sandro laughed, but he didn't change the sign that year or the next and he got to be forty-five and then fifty and it didn't seem worth it. The Immaculate Conception Photography Gallery had a reputation. Business came in from as far away as Rosedale and North Toronto, because Sandro was a magician with a camera. He also had skill with brushes and lights and paint, he reshot his negatives, he lined them with silver, he had tricks even new graduates of photography school couldn't (or wouldn't) copy.

6   Sandro was not proud of his tricks. They began in a gradual way, fixing stray hairs and taking wrinkles out of dresses. He did it once, then twice, then people came in asking for it. Perhaps he'd have gone on this way, with small lies, but he met with a situation that was larger than most; it would have started a feud in the old country. During a very large and very expensive wedding party Tony the bridegroom seduced Alicia the bridesmaid in the basketball storage room under the floor of the parish hall. Six months later Tony confessed, hoping perhaps to be released from his vows. But the parents judged it was too late to dissolve the union: Diora was used, she was no longer a virgin, there was a child coming. Tony was reprimanded, Diora consoled, the mothers became enemies,

the newlyweds made up. Only Alicia remained to be dealt with. The offence became hers.

7   In Italy, community ostracism would have been the punishment of choice. But this was Canada, and if no one acknowledged Alicia on the street, if no one visited her mother, who was heavy on her feet and forced to sit on the sofa protesting her daughter's innocence, if no one invited her father out behind to drink home-made wine, Alicia didn't care. She went off to her job behind the till in a drugstore with her chin thrust out much as before. The inlaws perceived that the young woman could not be subdued by the old methods. This being the case, it was better she not exist at all.

8   Which was why Diora's mother turned up at Sandro's counter with the wedding photos. The pain Alicia had caused! she began. Diora's mother's very own miserable wages, saved these eighteen years, had paid for these photographs! She wept. The money was spent, but the joy was spoiled. When she and Diora's father looked at the row of faces flanking bride and groom there she was— Alicia, the whore! She wiped her tears and made her pitch.

9   "You can solve our problem, Sandro. I will get a new cake, we will all come to the parish hall. You will take the photographs again. Of course," she added, "we can't pay you again."

10   Sandro smiled, it was so preposterous. "Even if I could afford to do all that work for nothing, I hate to say it, but Diora's out to here."

11   "Don't argue with me."

12   "I wouldn't be so bold," said Sandro. "But I will not take the photographs over."

13   The woman slapped the photographs where they lay on the counter. "You will! I don't care how you do it!" And she left.

14   Sandro went to the back and put his negatives on the light box. He brought out his magic solution and his razor blades and his brushes. He circled Alicia's head and shoulders in the first row and went to work. He felt a little badly, watching the bright circle of her face fade and swim, darken down to nothing. But how easily she vanished! He filled in the white spot with a bit of velvet curtain trimmed from the side.

15   "I'm like a plastic surgeon," he told his wife. "Take that patch of skin from the inner thigh and put it over the scar on the face. Then sand the edges. Isn't that what they do? Only it isn't a face I'm fixing, it's a memory."

16   His wife stood on two flat feet beside the sink. She shook the carrot she was peeling. "I don't care about Alicia," she said, "but Diora's mother is making a mistake. She is starting them off with a lie in their marriage. And why is she doing it? For her pride! I don't like this, Sandro."

17   "You're missing the point," said Sandro.

18   The next day he had another look at his work. Alicia's shoulders and the bodice of her dress were still there, in front of the chest of the uncle of the bride. He couldn't remove them; it would leave a hole in Uncle. Sandro had nothing to fill the hole, no spare male torsos in black tie. He considered putting a head on top, but whose head? There was no such thing as a free face. A stranger would be questioned, a friend would have an alibi. Perhaps Diora's mother would not notice the black velvet space, as where a tooth had been knocked out, between the smiling faces.

19   Indeed she didn't but kissed his hand fervently and thanked him with tears in her eyes. "Twenty-five thousand that wedding cost me. Twenty-five thousand to get this photograph and you have rescued it."

20   "Surely you got dinner and a dance too?" said Sandro.

21   "The wedding was one day. This is forever," said Diora's mother.

22   "I won't do that again," said Sandro, putting the cloth over his head and look-ing into his camera lens to do a passport photo. In the community the doctored photograph had been examined and re-examined. Alicia's detractors enjoyed the headless shoulders as evidence of a violent punishment.

23   "No, I won't do that again at all," said Sandro to himself, turning aside com-pliments with a shake of his head. But there was another wedding. After the provolone e melone, the veal piccata, the many-tiered cake topped with swans, the father of the bride drew Sandro aside and asked for a set of prints with the groom's parents removed.

24   "My God, why?" said Sandro.

25   "He's a bastard. A bad man."

26   "Shouldn't have let her marry his son, then," said Sandro, pulling a cigarette out of the pack in his pocket. These conversations made him nervous.

27   The father's weathered face was dark, his dinner-jacket did not button around his chest. He moaned and ground his lower teeth against his uppers. "You know how they are, these girls in Canada. I am ashamed to say it, but I couldn't stop her."

28   Sandro said nothing.

29   "Look, I sat here all night long, said nothing, did nothing. I don't wanna look at him for the next twenty years."

30   Sandro drew in a long tube of smoke.

31   "I paid a nice bundle for this night. I wanna remember it nice-like."

32   The smoke made Sandro nauseous. He dropped his cigarette and ground it into the floor with his toe, damning his own weakness. "So what am I going to do with the table?"

33   The father put out a hand like a tool, narrowed his eyes, and began to saw, where the other man sat.

34   "And leave it dangling, no legs?"

35   "So make new legs."

36   "I'm a photographer, not a carpenter," said Sandro. "I don't make table legs."

37   "Where you get legs is your problem," said the father. "I'm doing well here. I've got ten guys working for me. You look like you could use some new equipment."

38   And what harm was it after all, it was only a photograph, said Sandro to himself. Then too there was the technical challenge. Waiting until they all got up to get their bonbonnière, he took a shot of the head table empty. Working neatly with his scalpel, he cut the table from this second negative, removed the inlaws and their chairs from the first one, stuck the empty table-end onto the table in the first pic-ture, blended over the join neatly, and printed it. Presto! Only one set of inlaws.

39   "I don't mind telling you, it gives me a sick feeling," said Sandro to his wife. "I was there. I saw them. We had a conversation. They smiled for me. Now . . ." he shrugged. "An empty table. Lucky I don't go to church any more."

40   "Let the man who paid good money to have you do it confess, not you," she said. "A photograph is a photograph."

41   "That's what I thought too," said Sandro.

42   The next morning Sandro went to the Donut House, got himself a take-out coffee and stood on the street beside his window.

43   "Why do people care about photographs so much?" he asked Becker. Becker had newspaper stuffed in the soles of his shoes. He had on a pair of stained brown pants tied up at the waist with a paisley necktie. His bottle was clutched in a paper bag gathered around the neck.

44   "You can put them on your mantel," said Becker. "They don't talk back."

45   "Don't people prefer life?" said Sandro.

46   "People prefer things," said Becker.

47   "Don't they want their memories to be true?"

48   "No," said Becker.

49   "Another thing. Are we here just to get our photograph taken? Do we have a higher purpose?"

50   Becker pulled one of the newspapers out of his shoe. There were Brian and Mila Mulroney having a gloaty kiss. They were smeared by muddy water and depressed by the joint in the ball of Becker's foot.

51   "I mean real people," said Sandro. "Have we no loyalty to the natural?"

52   "These are existential questions, Sandro," said Becker. "Too many more of them and you'll be out here on the street with the rest of us."

53   Sandro drained the coffee from his cup, pitched it in the bin painted "Keep Toronto Clean" and went back into his gallery. The existential questions nagged. But he did go out and get the motor drive for the camera. In the next few months he eradicated a pregnancy from a wedding photo, added a daughter-in-law who complained of being left out of the Christmas shots, and made a groom taller. Working in the dark-room, he was hit by vertigo. He was on a slide, beginning a descent. He wanted to know what the bottom felt like.

54   After a year of such operations a man from the Beaches came in with a tiny black and white photo of a long-lost brother. He wanted it coloured and fitted into a family shot around a picnic table on Centre Island.

55   "Is this some kind of joke?" said Sandro. It was the only discretion he practised now: he wanted to talk about it before he did it.

56   "No. I'm going to send it to Mother. She thinks Christopher wrote us all off."

57   "Did he?" said Sandro.

58   "Better she should not know."

59   Sandro neglected to ask if Christopher was fat or thin. He ended up taking a medium-sized pair of shoulders from his own cousin and propping them up behind a bush, with Christopher's head on top. Afterward, Sandro lay sleepless in his bed. Suppose that in the next few months Christopher should turn up dead, say murdered. Then Mother would produce the photograph stamped Immaculate Conception Photography Gallery, 1816 St. Clair Avenue West. Sandro would be implicated. The police might come.

60   "I believe adding people is worse than taking them away," he said to his wife.

61   "You say yes to do it, then you do it. You think it's wrong, you say no."

62   "Let me try this on you, Becker," said Sandro the next morning. "To take a person out is only half a lie. It proves nothing except that he was not in that shot. To add a person is a whole lie: it proves that he was there, when he was not."

63   "You haven't proven a thing, you're just fooling around with celluloid. Have you got a buck?" said Becker.

64   "It is better to be a murderer than a creator. I am playing God, outplaying God at His own game." He was smarter than Becker now. He knew it was the photographs that lasted, not the people. In the end the proof was in the proof. Though he hadn't prayed in thirty years, Sandro began to pray. It was like riding a bicycle: he got the hang of it again instantly. "Make me strong," he prayed, "strong enough to resist the new equipment that I might buy, strong enough to resist the temptation to expand the gallery, to buy a house in the suburbs. Make me say no to people who want alterations."

65   But Sandro's prayers were not answered. When people offered him money to dissolve an errant relative, he said yes. He said yes out of curiosity. He said yes out of a desire to test his skills. He said yes out of greed. He said yes out of compassion. "What is the cost of a little happiness?" he said. "Perhaps God doesn't count photographs. After all, they're not one of a kind."

66   Sandro began to be haunted, in slow moments behind the counter in the Immaculate Conception, by the faces of those whose presence he had tampered with. He kept a file—Alicia the lusty bridesmaid, Antonia and Marco, the undesired inlaws. Their heads, their shoes and their hands, removed from the scene with surgical precision, he saved for the moment when, God willing, a forgiving relative would ask him to replace them. But the day did not come. Sandro was not happy.

67   "Becker," he said, for he had a habit now of buying Becker a coffee first thing in the morning and standing out if it was warm, or in if it was cold, for a chat. "Becker, let's say it's a good service I'm doing. It makes people happy, even if it tells lies."

68   "Sandro," said Becker, who enjoyed his coffee, "these photographs, doctored by request of the subjects, reflect back the lives they wish to have. The unpleasant bits are removed, the wishes are added. If you didn't do it, someone else would. Memory would. It's a service."

69   "It's also money," said Sandro. He found Becker too eager to make excuses now. He liked him better before.

70   "You're like Tintoretto, painting in his patron, softening his greedy profile, lifting the chin of his fat wife. It pays for the part that's true art."

71   "Which part is that?" said Sandro, but Becker didn't answer. He was still standing there when Diora came in. She'd matured, she'd gained weight, and her twins, now six years old, were handsome and strong. Sandro's heart flew up in his breast. Perhaps she had made friends with Alicia, perhaps Diora had come to have her bridesmaid reinstated.

72   "The long nightmare is over," said Diora. "I've left him."

73   The boys were running from shelf to shelf lifting up the photographs with their glass frames and putting them down again. Sandro watched them with one eye. He knew what she was going to say.

74   "I want you to take him out of those pictures," she said.

75   "You'd look very foolish as a bride with no groom," he said severely.

76   "No, no, not those," she said. "I mean the kids' birthday shots."

77   They had been particularly fine, those shots, taken only two weeks ago, Tony tall and dark, Diora and the children radiant and blonde.

78   "Be reasonable, Diora," he said. "I never liked him myself. But he balances the portrait. Besides, he was there."

79   "He was not there!" cried Diora. Her sons went on turning all the pictures to face the walls. "He was never there. He was running around, in his heart he was not with me. I was alone with my children."

80   "I'll take another one," said Sandro. "Of you and the boys. Whenever you like. This one stays like it is."

81   "We won't pay."

82   "But Diora," said Sandro, "everyone knows he's their father."

83   "They have no father," said Diora flatly.

84   "It's immaculate conception," said Becker gleefully.

85   But Diora did not hear. "It's our photograph, and we want him out. You do your job. The rest of it's none of your business." She put one hand on the back of the head of each of her twins and marched them out the door.

86   Sandro leaned on his counter idly flipping the pages of a wedding album. He had a vision of a great decorated room, with a cake on the table. Everyone had had his way, the husband had removed the wife, the wife the husband, the bridesmaid her parents, and so forth. There was no one there.

87   "We make up our lives out of the people around us," he said to Becker. "When they don't live up to standard, we can't just wipe them out."

88   "Don't ask me," said Becker. "I just lit out for the streets. Couldn't live up to a damn thing." Then he too went out the door.

89   "Lucky bugger," said Sandro.

90   Alone, he went to his darkroom. He opened his drawer of bits and pieces. His disappeared ones, the inconvenient people. His body parts, his halves of torsos, tips of shiny black shoes. Each face, each item of clothing punctured him a little. He looked at his negatives stored in drawers. They were scarred, pathetic things. I haven't the stomach for it, not any more, thought Sandro.

91   As he walked home, St. Clair Avenue seemed very fine. The best part was, he thought, there were no relationships. Neither this leaning drunk nor that window-shopper was so connected to any other as to endanger his, or her, existence. The tolerance of indifference, said Sandro to himself, trying to remember it so that he could tell Becker.

92   But Sandro felt ill at ease in his own home, by its very definition a dangerous and unreliable setting. His wife was stirring something, with her lips tight together. His children, almost grown up now, bred secrets as they looked at television. He himself only posed in the doorway, looking for hidden seams and the faint hair-lines of an airbrush.

93   That night he stood exhausted by his bed. His wife lay on her side with one round shoulder above the sheet. Behind her on the wall was the photo he'd taken of their village before he left Italy. He ought to reshoot it, take out that gas station and clean up the square a little. His pillow had an indentation, as if a head had been erased. He slept in a chair.

94   In the morning he went down to the shop. He got his best camera and set up a tripod on the sidewalk directly across the street. He took several shots in the solid bright morning light. He locked the door and placed the CLOSED sign in the window. In the darkroom he developed the film, floating the negatives in the pungent fluid until the row of shop fronts came through clearly, the flat brick faces, the curving concrete trim, the two balls on the crowns. Deftly he dissolved each brick of his store, the window and the sign. Deftly he reattached each brick of the store on the west side to the bricks of the store to the east.

95   I have been many things in my life, thought Sandro, a presser of shutters, a confessor, a false prophet. Now I am a bricklayer, and a good one. He taped the negatives together and developed them. He touched up the join and then photographed it again. He developed this second negative and it was perfect. Number 1812, Lord's Shoes, joined directly to 1820, Bargain Jimmies: the Immaculate Conception Photography Gallery at 1816 no longer existed. Working quickly, because he wanted to finish before the day was over, he blew it up to two feet by three feet. He cleared out his window display of brides and babies and stood up this new photograph—one of the finest he'd ever taken, he thought. Then he took a couple of cameras and a bag with the tripod and some lenses. He turned out the light, pulling the door shut behind him, and began to walk west.

Elizabeth Hay

Cézanne in a Soft Hat

"Cézanne in a Soft Hat" comes from Small Change *(1997), Elizabeth Hay's book of 20 linked stories about friendship told by a narrator named Beth.* Small Change *was Hay's fourth book (following a 1989 collection of short stories and two works of creative non-fiction published in the early 1990s) but the first to receive widespread attention. This book received many glowing reviews and was a finalist for the Governor General's Award for fiction, the Trillium Award, and the Rogers Communications Writers' Trust Fiction Prize.* A Student of Weather *(2000), Hay's first novel, received a similar reception; she is currently working on a second novel.*

Hay, born in Owen Sound, Ontario in 1951, grew up in small Ontario towns before attending the University of Toronto and then living in Yellowknife, Winnipeg, and Toronto while working as a broadcaster for CBC Radio. In 1982, she moved to Mexico, where she worked as a documentary maker, and then lived in Manhattan. Hay now makes her home with her husband and children in Ottawa, Ontario.

1   Soon after we moved here, I picked up a small book about Cézanne. This was in September. I opened the book to dry landscapes and cool still lifes, to late summer and early fall, to the pleasure and pain of seasonal change, the detachment of weather. This is the detachment we seek and usually fail to find in friendships—an unbegrudging, clear-eyed, undemanding, infinitely interesting and natural presence.

2   Here were pears on a table, apples in a bowl, a flowered pitcher, a leafy piece of fabric. Everything gave the impression of being aware of every other thing but in a way that transcends the human.

3   I began to read the biographical notes and came upon the description of Cézanne's friendship with Zola, a deep and long friendship that began in Aix in 1852 when Cézanne was thirteen, and ended in 1886 when Zola published a novel about a painter who hanged himself in front of the painting he couldn't complete. Everyone knew the painter was Cézanne.

4   I reread the paragraph about the end of their friendship. "Although he spoke of it to no one, it could be seen that Cézanne's grief was bitter and irremediable. Perhaps it was partly because of the sincere compassion expressed in the novel that Cézanne's grief was so inconsolable."

5   I wondered how sincere Zola's compassion was. I wondered how it was known that Cézanne's grief was inconsolable if he spoke of it to no one, and how it was known that he spoke of it to no one. I wondered about Zola's ulterior motives—his desire to hurt an old friend, his competitiveness, his honesty, his dishonesty. The book said that Zola had moved away from his Impressionist friends and no longer believed in them, having been their most valiant champion. But my main interest was Cézanne and the way he dealt with the discovery that his oldest and dearest friend considered him a failure and used him as subject matter in a book.

6   No more letters passed between them, apparently. There were no more greetings, and they did not meet again.

7   In 1886 Cézanne was forty-seven. His friendship with Zola had lasted more than thirty years. The first time Zola left for Paris and Cézanne remained in Aix, they were about twenty. Cézanne wrote to him: "Ever since you left I am tormented by grief. This is the truth. You would not recognize me. I feel heavy, stupid and slow."

8   The book has two self-portraits: an unfinished sketch in 1880 when he was forty-one, half bald, heavy forehead, dark beard, large face; then *Cézanne in a Soft Hat* ten years later, several years after the break with Zola and several years in the making. His nose and chin are more pointed than broad; his beard is white and grey; the colours of his coat, hat, and jacket are repeated in the colours of the wall; and he seems less massive—flimsier and more decorative. He is known for his persistence in the face of doubts and for how slowly he painted.

9   In early October we were beside a river with two friends. The woman was telling us that old friends of theirs had just moved away. They had moved away one morning, and in the afternoon she had walked past the empty house and couldn't believe how relieved she felt. She laughed about it and went on talking, compelled to tell us, her new friends, about these old friends.

10   She said it was the woman in the couple who had pulled away, and she had never understood why. Simply, the invitations stopped, the Christmas gifts ended, various courtesies vanished. With their disappearance arrived her confusion and sense of hurt, so that when she walked her dog past their house she was never sure whether the woman came down the steps because she wanted to say hello, or because she felt she had to.

11   She said, "I talked a lot about work with him, maybe she felt left out. And then she went through a lot of changes herself and got her own friends."

12   But none of these reasons was sufficient to explain a change so drastic, and she knew it.

13   She peeled a peach as she told the story. She avoided the words *dropped* or *dumped* or *rejected*. She said only that she didn't understand, that once there had been steady contact and then there was none, that whenever they saw each other they all enjoyed themselves, but afterwards there was nothing.

14   The peach was from the market, carried in a knapsack, a little bruised and one of eight. She peeled another, her fingers curving around the fruit, picking at the peel with her fingernail, then pulling it back. We sat on a blanket on the grass and ate tomatoes, bread, cheese, the peaches, a sausage. We ate with our hands and shared a napkin.

15   My friend dealt with being rejected by understanding and not understanding, stating and understating, avoiding certain things but staying true to the general picture. Her husband was impatient. He couldn't be bothered, he said, worrying about such things.

16   This is the refreshing thing about men. They don't brood so luxuriously about friendships gone wrong. They think about them very little, it seems, and talk about them less. Cézanne, for instance.

17   Ted said, "It's hard when one person wants the friendship and another doesn't. People change."

18   But that only rubbed salt in the wound. Our friend wasn't saying they didn't want her, she was saying they seemed to enjoy her company and this was the source of her confusion. She was unable to give up the hope that she was liked.

19   I was thinking about her again this morning when I peeled a peach. I used the fingers of my left hand, picking the skin loose at the top as you pick one page free from the page below.

20   I was thinking about a conversation with Maureen. We were in a park and it was warm, it might have been late spring or early fall. We were sitting on a stone wall and she was distributing food to the kids. (She was always much more prepared than I, never leaving the house without a variety of snacks and drinks.) She could not believe, she said, that certain friends with whom she had been

incredibly close had faded away—she mentioned a roommate in university—yet she admitted it was so with tight lips, and I knew she foresaw our own end.

21   My sympathies are with Cézanne even though I am like Zola—the realistic writer using the people he knows. What defence can Zola offer? When accused of using the life of a friend to further his artful ends, what can he say? That it was his life too? It was my life too.

Thomas King

Borders

Thomas King (1943–), born in Sacramento, California, is part Cherokee, and holds a Ph.D. in English from the University of Utah. He is currently a professor of English at the University of Guelph, in Ontario, Canada. He has written novels, among them Medicine River *(1990), and* Truth and Bright Water *(1999), as well as a collection of short stories,* One Good Story, That One *(1993), which includes "Borders." King's work reflects an interest in the stereotypes of and the social biases against Native Canadians, and has led him to become a spokesperson for Native writing in Canada.*

1   When I was twelve, maybe thirteen, my mother announced that we were going to go to Salt Lake City to visit my sister who had left the reserve, moved across the line, and found a job. Laetitia had not left home with my mother's blessing, but over time my mother had come to be proud of the fact that Laetitia had done all of this on her own.

2   "She did real good," my mother would say.

3   Then there were the fine points to Laetitia's going. She had not, as my mother liked to tell Mrs. Manyfingers, gone floating after some man like a balloon on a string. She hadn't snuck out of the house, either and gone to Vancouver or Edmonton or Toronto to chase rainbows down alleys. And she hadn't been pregnant.

4   "She did real good."

5   I was seven or eight when Laetitia left home. She was seventeen. Our father was from Rocky Boy on the American side.

6   "Dad's American," Laetitia told my mother, "so I can go and come as I please."

7   "Send us a postcard."

8   Laetitia packed her things, and we headed for the border. Just outside of Milk River, Laetitia told us to watch for the water tower.

9   "Over the next rise. It's the first thing you see."

10   "We got a water tower on the reserve," my mother said. "There's big one in Lethbridge, too."

11   "You'll be able to see the tops of the flagpoles, too. That's where the border is."

12   When we got to Coutts, my mother stopped at the convenience store and bought her and Laetitia a cup of coffee. I got an Orange Crush.

13   "This is real lousy coffee."

14   "You're just angry because I want to see the world."

15   "It's the water. From here on down, they got lousy water."

16   "I can catch the bus from Sweetgrass. You don't have to lift a finger."

17   "You're going to have to buy your water in bottles if you want good coffee."

18   There was an old wooden building about a block away, with a tall sign in the yard that said "Museum." Most of the roof had been blown away. Mom told me to go and see when the place was open. There were boards over the windows and doors. You could tell that the place was closed, and I told Mom so, but she said to go and check anyway. Mom and Laetitia stayed by the car. Neither one of them moved. I sat down on the steps of the museum and watched them, and I don't know that they ever said anything to each other. Finally, Laetitia got her bag out of the trunk and gave Mom a hug.

19   I wandered back to the car. The wind had come up, and it blew Laetitia's hair across her face. Mom reached out and pulled the strands out of Laetitia's eyes, and Laetitia let her.

20   "You can still see the mountain from here," my mother told Laetitia in Blackfoot.

21   "Lots of mountains in Salt Lake," Laetitia told her in English.

22   "The place is closed," I said. "Just like I told you."

23   Laetitia tucked her hair into her jacket and dragged her bag down the road to the brick building with the American flag flapping on a pole. When she got to where the guards were waiting, she turned, put the bag down, and waved to us. We waved back. Then my mother turned the car around, and we came home.

24   We got postcards from Laetitia regular, and, if she wasn't spreading jelly on the truth, she was happy. She found a good job and rented an apartment with a pool.

25   "And she can't even swim," my mother told Mrs. Manyfingers.

26   Most of the postcards said we should come down and see the city, but whenever I mentioned this, my mother would stiffen up.

27   So I was surprised when she bought two new tires for the car and put on her blue dress with the green and yellow flowers. I had to dress up, too, for my mother did not want us crossing the border looking like Americans. We made sandwiches and put them in a big box with pop and potato chips and some apples and bananas and a big jar of water.

28   "But we can stop at one of those restaurants, too, right?"

29   "We maybe should take some blankets in case you get sleepy."

30   "But we can stop at one of those restaurants, too, right?"

31   The border was actually two towns, though neither one was big enough to amount to anything. Coutts was on the Canadian side and consisted of the convenience store and gas station, the museum that was closed and boarded up, and a motel. Sweetgrass was on the American side, but all you could see was an overpass that arched across the highway and disappeared into the prairies. Just hearing the names of these towns, you would expect that Sweetgrass, which is a nice name and sounds like it is related to other places such as Medicine Hat and Moose Jaw and Kicking Horse Pass, would be on the Canadian side, and that Coutts, which sounds abrupt and rude, would be on the American side. But this was not the case.

32   Between the two borders was a duty-free shop where you could buy cigarettes and liquor and flags. Stuff like that.

33   We left the reserve in the morning and drove until we got to Coutts.

34   "Last time we stoped here," my mother said, "you had an Orange Crush. You remember that?"

35   "Sure," I said. "That was when Laetitia took off."

36   "You want another Orange Crush?"

37 "That means we're not going to stop at a restaurant, right?"

38 My mother got a coffee at the convenience store, and we stood around and watched the prairies move in the sunlight. Then we climbed back in the car. My mother straightened the dress across her thighs, leaned against the wheel, and drove all the way to the border in first gear, slowly, as if she were trying to see through a bad storm or riding high on black ice.

39 The border guard was an old guy. As he walked to the car, he swayed from side to side, his feet set wide apart, the holster on his hip pitching up and down. He leaned into the window, looked into the back seat, and looked at my mother and me.

40 "Morning, ma'am."

41 "Good morning."

42 "Where you heading?"

43 "Salt Lake City."

44 "Purpose of your visit?"

45 "Visit my daughter."

46 "Citizenship?"

47 "Blackfoot," my mother told him.

48 "Ma'am?"

49 "Blackfoot," my mother repeated.

50 "Canadian?"

51 "Blackfoot."

52 It would have been easier if my mother had just said "Canadian" and been done with it, but I could see she wasn't going to do that. The guard wasn't angry or anything. He smiled and looked towards the building. Then he turned back and nodded.

53 "Morning, ma'am."

54 "Good morning."

55 "Any firearms or tobacco?"

56 "No."

57 "Citizenship?"

58 "Blackfoot."

59 He told us to sit in the car and wait, and we did. In about five minutes, another guard came out with the first man. They were talking as they came, both men swaying back and forth like two cowboys headed for a bar or a gunfight.

60 "Morning, ma'am."

61 "Good morning."

62 "Cecil tells me you and the boy are Blackfoot."

63 "That's right."

64 "Now, I know that we got Blackfeet on the American side and the Canadians got Blackfeet on their side. Just so we can keep our records straight, what side do you come from?"

65 I knew exactly what my mother was going to say, and I could have told them if they had asked me.

66 "Canadian side or American side?" asked the guard.

67 "Blackfoot side," she said.

68 It didn't take them long to lose their sense of humor, I can tell you that. The one guard stopped smiling altogether and told us to park our car at the side of the building and come in.

69 We sat on a wood bench for about an hour before anyone came over to talk to us. This time it was a woman. She had a gun, too.

70   "Hi," she said. "I'm Inspector Pratt. I understand there is a little misunderstanding."

71   "I'm going to visit my daughter in Salt Lake City," my mother told her. "We don't have any guns or beer."

72   "It's a legal technicality, that's all."

73   "My daughter's Blackfoot, too."

74   The woman opened a briefcase and took out a couple of forms and began to write on one of them. "Everyone who crosses our border has to declare their citizenship. Even Americans. It helps us keep track of the visitors we get from the various countries."

75   She went on like that for maybe fifteen minutes, and a lot of the stuff she told us was interesting.

76   "I can understand how you feel about having to tell us your citizenship, and here's what I'll do. You tell me, and I won't put it down on the form. No-one will know but you and me."

77   Her gun was silver. There were several chips in the wood handle and the name "Stella" was scratched into the metal butt.

78   We were in the border office for about four hours, and we talked to almost everyone there. One of the men bought me a Coke. My mother brought a couple of sandwiches in from the car. I offered part of mine to Stella, but she said she wasn't hungry.

79   I told Stella that we were Blackfoot and Canadian, but she said that that didn't count because I was a minor. In the end, she told us that if my mother didn't declare her citizenship, we would have to go back to where we came from. My mother stood up and thanked Stella for her time. Then we got back in the car and drove to the Canadian border, which was only about a hundred yards away.

80   I was disappointed. I hadn't seen Laetitia for a long time, and I had never been to Salt Lake City. When she was still at home, Laetitia would go on and on about Salt Lake City. She had never been there, but her boyfriend Lester Tallbull had spent a year in Salt Lake at a technical school.

81   "It's a great place," Lester would say. "Nothing but blondes in the whole state."

82   Whenever he said that, Laetitia would slug him on his shoulder hard enough to make him flinch. He had some brochures on Salt Lake and some maps, and every so often the two of them would spread them out on the table.

83   "That's the temple. It's right downtown. You got to have a pass to get in."

84   "Charlotte says anyone can go in and look around."

85   "When was Charlotte in Salt Lake? Just when the hell was Charlotte in Salt Lake?"

86   "Last year."

87   "This is Liberty Park. It's got a zoo. There's good skiing in the mountains."

88   "Got all the skiing we can use," my mother would say. "People come from all over the world to ski at Banff. Cardston's got a temple, if you like those kinds of things."

89   "Oh, this one is real big," Lester would say. "They got armed guards and everything."

90   "Not what Charlotte says."

91   "What does she know?"

92   Lester and Laetitia broke up, but I guess the idea of Salt Lake struck in her mind.

* * *

93   The Canadian border guard was a young woman, and she seemed happy to see us. "Hi" she said. "You folks sure have a great day for a trip. Where are you coming from?"

94   "Standoff."

95   "Is that in Montana?"

96   "No."

97   "Where are you going?"

98   "Standoff."

99   The woman's name was Carol and I don't guess she was any older than Laetitia. "Wow, you both Canadians?"

100   "Blackfoot."

101   "Really? I have a friend I went to school with who is Blackfoot. Do you know Mike Harley?"

102   "No."

103   "He went to school in Lethbridge, but he's really from Browning."

104   It was a nice conversation and there were no cars behind us, so there was no rush.

105   "You're not bringing any liquor back, are you?"

106   "No."

107   "Any cigarettes or plants or stuff like that?"

108   "No."

109   "Citizenship?"

110   "Blackfoot."

111   "I know," said the woman, "and I'd be proud of being Blackfoot if I were Blackfoot. But you have to be American or Canadian."

* * *

112   When Laetitia and Lester broke up, Lester took his brochures and maps with him, so Laetitia wrote to someone in Salt Lake City, and about a month later, she got a big envelope of stuff. We sat at the table and opened up all the brochures, and Laetitia read each one out loud.

113   "Salt Lake City is the gateway to some of the world's most magnificent skiing.

114   "Sat Lake City is the home of one of the newest professional basketball franchises, the Utah Jazz.

115   "The Great Salt Lake is one of the natural wonders of the world."

116   It was kind of exciting seeing all those color brochures on the table and listening to Laetitia read all about how Salt Lake City was one of the best places in the entire world.

117   "That Salt Lake City place sounds too good to be true," my mother told her.

118   "It has everything."

119   "We got everything right here."

120   "It's boring here."

121   "People in Salt Lake City are probably sending away for brochures of Calgary and Lethbridge and Pincher Creek right now."

122   In the end, my mother would say that maybe Laetitia should go to Salt Lake City, and Laetitia would say that maybe she would.

* * *

123   We parked the car to the side of the building and Carol led us into a small room on the second floor. I found a comfortable spot on the couch and flipped through some back issues of *Saturday Night* and *Alberta Report*.

124   When I woke up, my mother was just coming out of another office. She didn't say a word to me. I followed her down the stairs and out to the car. I thought we were going home, but she turned the car around and drove back towards the American border, which made me think we were going to visit Laetitia in Salt Lake City after all. Instead she pulled into the parking lot of the duty-free store and stopped.

125   "We going to see Laetitia?"

126   "No."

127   "We going home?"

128   Pride is a good thing to have, you know. Laetitia had a lot of pride, and so did my mother. I figured that someday, I'd have it, too.

129   "So where are we going?"

130   Most of that day, we wandered around the duty-free store, which wasn't very large. The manager had a name tag with a tiny American flag on one side and a tiny Canadian flag on the other. His name was Mel. Towards evening, he began suggesting that we should be on our way. I told him we had nowhere to go, that neither the Americans nor the Canadians would let us in. He laughed at that and told us that we should buy something or leave.

131   The car was not very comfortable, but we did have all that food and it was April, so even if it did snow as it sometimes does on the prairies, we wouldn't freeze. The next morning my mother drove to the American border.

132   It was a different guard this time, but the questions were the same. We didn't spend as much time in the office as we had the day before. By noon, we were back at the Canadian border. By two we were back in the duty-free shop parking lot.

133   The second night in the car was not as much fun as the first, but my mother seemed in good spirits, and, all in all, it was as much an adventure as an inconvenience. There wasn't much food left and that was a problem, but we had lots of water as there was a faucet at the side of the duty-free shop.

*   *   *

134   One Sunday, Laetitia and I were watching television. Mom was over at Mrs. Manyfingers's. Right in the middle of the program, Laetitia turned off the set and said she was going to Salt Lake City, that life around here was too boring. I had wanted to see the rest of the program and really didn't care if Laetitia went to Salt Lake City or not. When Mom got home, I told her what Laetitia had said.

135   What surprised me was how angry Laetitia got when she found out that I had told Mom.

136   "You got a big mouth."

137   "That's what you said."

138   "What I said is none of your business."

139   "I didn't say anything."

140   "Well, I'm going for sure, now."

141   That weekend, Laetitia packed her bags, and we drove her to the border.

*   *   *

142   Mel turned out to be friendly. When he closed up for the night and found us still parked in the lot, he came over and asked us if our car was broken down or something. My mother thanked him for his concern and told him that we were fine, that things would get straightened out in the morning.

143   "You're kidding," said Mel. "You'd think they could handle the simple things."

144   "We got some apples and a banana," I said, "but we're all out of ham sandwiches."

145   "You know, you read about these things, but you just don't believe it. You just don't believe it."

146   "Hamburgers would be even better because they got more stuff for energy."

147   My mother slept in the back seat. I slept in the front because I was smaller and could lie under the steering wheel. Late that night, I heard my mother open the car door. I found her sitting on her blanket leaning against the bumper of the car.

148   "You see all those stars," she said. "When I was a little girl, my grandmother used to take me and my sisters out on the prairies and tell us stories about all the stars."

149   "Do you think Mel is going to bring us any hamburgers?"

150   "Every one of those stars has a story. You see that bunch of stars over there that look like a fish?"

151   "He didn't say no."

152   "Coyote went fishing, one day. That's how it all started." We sat out under the stars that night, and my mother told me all sorts of stories. She was serious about it, too. She'd tell them slow, repeating parts as she went, as if she expected me to remember each one.

153   Early the next morning, the television vans began to arrive, and guys in suits and women in dresses came trotting over to us, dragging microphones and cameras and lights behind them. One of the vans had a table set up with orange juice and sandwiches and fruit. It was for the crew, but when I told them we hadn't eaten for a while, a really skinny blonde woman told us we could eat as much as we wanted.

154   They mostly talked to my mother. Every so often one of the reporters would come over and ask me questions about how it felt to be an Indian without a country. I told them we had a nice house on the reserve and that my cousins had a couple of horses we rode when we went fishing. Some of the television people went over to the American border, and then they went to the Canadian border.

155   Around noon, a good-looking guy in a dark blue suit and an orange tie with little ducks on it drove up in a fancy car. He talked to my mother for a while, and, after they were done talking, my mother called me over, and we got into our car. Just as my mother started the engine, Mel came over and gave us a bag of peanut brittle and told us that justice was a damn hard thing to get, but that we shouldn't give up.

156   I would have preferred lemon drops, but it was nice of Mel anyway. "Where are we going now?"

157   "Going to visit Laetitia."

158   The guard who came out to our car was all smiles. The television lights were so bright they hurt my eyes, and, if you tried to look through the windshield in certain directions, you couldn't see a thing.

159   "Morning, ma'am."

160   "Good morning."

161   "Where you heading?"

162   "Salt Lake City."

163   "Purpose of your visit?"

164   "Visit my daughter."

165   "Any tobacco, liquor, or firearms?"

166   "Don't smoke."

167   "Any plants or fruit?"

168   "Not any more."

169   "Citizenship?"

170   "Blackfoot."

171   The guard rocked back on his heels and jammed his thumbs into his gun belt. "Thank you," he said, his fingers patting the butt of the revolver. "Have a pleasant trip."

172   My mother rolled the car forward, and the television people had to scramble out of the way. They ran alongside the car as we pulled away from the border, and, when they couldn't run any farther, they stood in the middle of the highway and waved and waved and waved.

173   We got to Salt Lake City the next day. Laetitia was happy to see us, and, that first night, she took us out to a restaurant that made really good soups. The list of pies took up a whole page. I had cherry. Mom had chocolate. Laetitia said that she saw us on television the night before and, during the meal, she had us tell her the story over and over again.

174   Laetitia took us everywhere. We went to a fancy ski resort. We went to the temple. We got to go shopping in a couple of large malls, but they weren't as large as the one in Edmonton, and Mom said so.

175   After a week or so, I got bored and wasn't at all sad when my mother said we should be heading back home. Laetitia wanted us to stay longer, but Mom said no, that she had things to do back home and that, next time, Laetitia should come up and visit. Laetitia said she was thinking about moving back, and Mom told her to do as she pleased, and Laetitia said that she would.

176   On the way home, we stopped at the duty-free shop, and my mother gave Mel a green hat that said "Salt Lake" across the front. Mel was a funny guy. He took the hat and blew his nose and told my mother that she was an inspiration to us all. He gave us some more peanut brittle and came out into the parking lot and waved at us all the way to the Canadian border.

177   It was almost evening when we left Coutts. I watched the border through the rear window until all you could see were the tops of the flagpoles and the blue water tower, and then they rolled over a hill and disappeared.

Alistair MacLeod

As Birds Bring Forth the Sun

After teaching literature and creative writing at the University of Windsor for 32 years, Alistair MacLeod has recently retired to a new level of international literary recognition since the publication of his first novel, No Great Mischief, *in 1999, and the republication of a collection of his earlier short stories in* Island *(2000).*

Born in Saskatchewan in 1936 and raised in Cape Breton, Nova Scotia, MacLeod's fiction focuses primarily on the often harsh lives of people living in the rural areas of Canada's East Coast who make a living through hard physical labour. Although he has worked as a miner, a logger, and a farmhand, MacLeod's primary careers have been as an academic and then as a writer.

"As Birds Bring Forth the Sun" was originally published as the title story in MacLeod's 1986 collection of stories and was also included in Island *(2000).*

1   Once there was a family with a Highland name who lived beside the sea. And the man had a dog of which he was very fond. She was large and grey, a sort of staghound from another time. And if she jumped up to lick his face, which she loved to do, her paws would jolt against his shoulders with such force that she would come close to knocking him down and he would be forced to take two or three backward steps before he could regain his balance. And he himself was not a small man, being slightly over six feet and perhaps one hundred and eighty pounds.

2   She had been left, when a pup, at the family's gate in a small handmade box and no one knew where she had come from or that she would eventually grow to such a size. Once, while still a small pup, she had been run over by the steel

wheel of a horsedrawn cart which was hauling kelp from the shore to be used as fertilizer. It was in October and the rain had been falling for some weeks and the ground was soft. When the wheel of the cart passed over her, it sunk her body into the wet earth as well as crushing some of her ribs; and apparently the silhouette of her small crushed body was visible in the earth after the man lifted her to his chest while she yelped and screamed. He ran his fingers along her broken bones, ignoring the blood and urine which fell upon his shirt, trying to soothe her bulging eyes and her scrabbling front paws and her desperately licking tongue.

3   The more practical members of his family, who had seen run-over dogs before, suggested that her neck be broken by his strong hands or that he grasp her by the hind legs and swing her head against a rock, thus putting an end to her misery. But he would not do it.

4   Instead, he fashioned a small box and lined it with woollen remnants from a sheep's fleece and one of his old and frayed shirts. He placed her within the box and placed the box behind the stove and then he warmed some milk in a small saucepan and sweetened it with sugar. And he held open her small and trembling jaws with his left hand while spooning in the sweetened milk with his right, ignoring the needle-like sharpness of her small teeth. She lay in the box most of the remaining fall and into the early winter, watching everything with her large brown eyes.

5   Although some members of the family complained about her presence and the odour from the box and the waste of time she involved, they gradually adjusted to her; and as the weeks passed by, it became evident that her ribs were knitting together in some form or other and that she was recovering with the resilience of the young. It also became evident that she would grow to a tremendous size, as she outgrew one box and then another and the grey hair began to feather from her huge front paws. In the spring she was outside almost all of the time and followed the man everywhere; and when she came inside during the following months, she had grown so large that she would no longer fit into her accustomed place behind the stove and was forced to lie beside it. She was never given a name but was referred to in Gaelic as *cù mòr glas,* the big grey dog.

6   By the time she came into her first heat, she had grown to a tremendous height, and although her signs and her odour attracted many panting and highly aroused suitors, none was big enough to mount her, and the frenzy of their disappointment and the longing of her unfulfilment were more than the man could stand. He went, so the story goes, to a place where he knew there was a big dog. A dog not as big as she was, but still a big dog, and he brought him home with him. And at the proper time he took the *cù mòr glas* and the big dog down to the sea where he knew there was a hollow in the rock which appeared only at low tide. He took some sacking to provide footing for the male dog and he placed the *cù mòr glas* in the hollow of the rock and knelt beside her and steadied her with his left arm under her throat and helped position the male dog above her and guided his blood-engorged penis. He was a man used to working with the breeding of animals, with the guiding of rams and bulls and stallions and often with the funky smell of animal semen heavy on his large and gentle hands.

7   The winter that followed was a cold one and ice formed on the sea and frequent squalls and blizzards obliterated the offshore islands and caused the people to stay near their fires much of the time, mending clothes and nets and harness and waiting for the change in season. The *cù mòr glas* grew heavier and even larger until

there was hardly room for her around the stove or under the table. And then one morning, when it seemed that spring was about to break, she was gone.

8   The man and even his family, who had become more involved than they cared to admit, waited for her but she did not come. And as the frenzy of spring wore on, they busied themselves with readying their land and their fishing gear and all of the things that so desperately required their attention. And then they were into summer and fall and winter and another spring which saw the birth of the man and his wife's twelfth child. And then it was summer again.

9   That summer the man and two of his teenaged sons were pulling their herring nets about two miles offshore when the wind began to blow off the land and the water began to roughen. They became afraid that they could not make it safely back to shore, so they pulled in behind one of the offshore islands, knowing that they would be sheltered there and planning to outwait the storm. As the prow of their boat approached the gravelly shore, they heard a sound above them, and looking up they saw the *cù mòr glas* silhouetted on the brow of the hill which was the small island's highest point.

10   *"M'eudal cù mòr glas,"* shouted the man in his happiness—*m'eudal* meaning something like dear or darling; and as he shouted, he jumped over the side of his boat into the waist-deep water, struggling for footing on the rolling gravel as he waded eagerly and awkwardly toward her and the shore. At the same time, the *cù mòr glas* came hurtling down toward him in a shower of small rocks dislodged by her feet; and just as he was emerging from the water, she met him as she used to, rearing up on her hind legs and placing her huge front paws on his shoulders while extending her eager tongue.

11   The weight and speed of her momentum met him as he tried to hold his balance on the sloping angle with the water rolling gravel beneath his feet, and he staggered backwards and lost his footing and fell beneath her force. And in that instant again, as the story goes, there appeared over the brow of the hill six more huge grey dogs hurtling down toward the gravelled strand. They had never seen him before; and seeing him stretched prone beneath their mother, they misunderstood, like so many armies, the intention of their leader.

12   They fell upon him in a fury, slashing his face and tearing aside his lower jaw and ripping out his throat, crazed with blood-lust or duty or perhaps starvation. The *cù mòr glas* turned on them in her own savagery, slashing and snarling and, it seemed, crazed by their mistake; driving them bloodied and yelping before her, back over the brow of the hill where they vanished from sight but could still be heard screaming in the distance. It all took perhaps little more than a minute.

13   The man's two sons, who were still in the boat and had witnessed it all, ran sobbing through the salt water to where their mauled and mangled father lay; but there was little they could do other than hold his warm and bloodied hands for a few brief moments. Although his eyes "lived" for a small fraction of time, he could not speak to them because his face and throat had been torn away, and of course there was nothing they could do except to hold and be held tightly until that too slipped away and his eyes glazed over and they could no longer feel his hands holding theirs. The storm increased and they could not get home and so they were forced to spend the night huddled beside their father's body. They were afraid to try to carry the body to the rocking boat because he was so heavy and they were afraid that they might lose even what little of him remained and they were afraid also, huddled on the rocks, that the dogs might return. But they did not return at all and there was no sound from them, no sound at all, only the moaning of the wind and the washing of the water on the rocks.

14   In the morning they debated whether they should try to take his body with them or whether they should leave it and return in the company of older and wiser men. But they were afraid to leave it unattended and felt that the time needed to cover it with protective rocks would be better spent in trying to get across to their home shore. For a while they debated as to whether one should go in the boat and the other remain on the island, but each was afraid to be alone and so in the end they managed to drag and carry and almost float him toward the bobbing boat. They laid him face-down and covered him with what clothes there were and set off across the still-rolling sea. Those who waited on the shore missed the large presence of the man within the boat and some of them waded into the water and others rowed out in skiffs, attempting to hear the tearful messages called out across the rolling waves.

15   The *cù mòr glas* and her six young dogs were never seen again, or perhaps I should say they were never seen again in the same way. After some weeks, a group of men circled the island tentatively in their boats but they saw no sign. They went again and then again but found nothing. A year later, and grown much braver, they beached their boats and walked the island carefully, looking into the small sea caves and the hollows at the base of the wind-ripped trees, thinking perhaps that if they did not find the dogs, they might at least find their whitened bones; but again they discovered nothing.

16   The *cù mòr glas*, though, was supposed to be sighted here and there for a number of years. Seen on a hill in one region or silhouetted on a ridge in another or loping across the valleys or glens in the early morning or the shadowy evening. Always in the area of the half perceived. For a while she became rather like the Loch Ness monster or the Sasquatch on a smaller scale. Seen but not recorded. Seen when there were no cameras. Seen but never taken.

17   The mystery of where she went became entangled with the mystery of whence she came. There was increased speculation about the handmade box in which she had been found and much theorizing as to the individual or individuals who might have left it. People went to look for the box but could not find it. It was felt she might have been part of a *buidseachd* or evil spell cast on the man by some mysterious enemy. But no one could go much farther than that. All of his caring for her was recounted over and over again and nobody missed any of the ironies.

18   What seemed literally known was that she had crossed the winter ice to have her pups and had been unable to get back. No one could remember ever seeing her swim; and in the early months at least, she could not have taken her young pups with her.

19   The large and gentle man with the smell of animal semen often heavy on his hands was my great-great-great-grandfather, and it may be argued that he died because he was too good at breeding animals or that he cared too much about their fulfilment and well-being. He was no longer there for his own child of the spring who, in turn, became my great-great-grandfather, and he was perhaps too much there in the memory of his older sons who saw him fall beneath the ambiguous force of the *cù mòr glas*. The youngest boy in the boat was haunted and tormented by the awfulness of what he had seen. He would wake at night screaming that he had seen the *cù mòr glas a' bhàis,* the big grey dog of death, and his screams filled the house and the ears and minds of the listeners, bringing home again and again the consequences of their loss. One morning, after a night in which he saw the *cù mòr glas a' bhàis* so vividly that his sheets were drenched with sweat, he walked to the high cliff which faced the island and there he cut his throat with a fish knife and fell into the sea.

20   The other brother lived to be forty, but, again so the story goes, he found himself in a Glasgow pub one night, perhaps looking for answers, deep and sodden with the whisky which had become his anaesthetic. In the half darkness he saw a large, grey-haired man sitting by himself against the wall and mumbled something to him. Some say he saw the *cù mòr glas a' bhàis* or uttered the name. And perhaps the man heard the phrase through ears equally affected by drink and felt he was being called a dog or a son of a bitch or something of that nature. They rose to meet one another and struggled outside into the cobblestoned passageway behind the pub where, most improbably, there were supposed to be six other large, grey-haired men who beat him to death on the cobblestones, smashing his bloodied head into the stone again and again before vanishing and leaving him to die with his face turned to the sky. The *cù mòr glas a' bhàis* had come again, said his family, as they tried to piece the tale together.

21   This is how the *cù mòr glas a' bhàis* came into our lives, and it is obvious that all of this happened a long, long time ago. Yet with succeeding generations it seemed the spectre had somehow come to say and that it had become *ours*—not in the manner of an unwanted skeleton in the closet from a family's ancient past but more in the manner of something close to a genetic possibility. In the deaths of each generation, the grey dog was seen by some—by women who were to die in childbirth; by soldiers who went forth to the many wars but did not return; by those who went forth to feuds or dangerous love affairs; by those who answered mysterious midnight messages; by those who swerved on the highway to avoid the real or imagined grey dog and ended in masses of crumpled steel. And by one professional athlete who, in addition to his ritualized athletic superstitions, carried another fear or belief as well. Many of the man's descendants moved like careful haemophiliacs, fearing that they carried unwanted possibilities deep within them. And others, while they laughed, were like members of families in which there is a recurrence over the generations of repeated cancer or the diabetes that comes to those beyond middle age. The feeling of those who may say little to others but who may say often and quietly to themselves, "It has not happened to me," while adding always the cautionary *"yet."*

22   I am thinking all of this now as the October rain falls on the city of Toronto and the pleasant, white-clad nurses pad confidently in and out of my father's room. He lies quietly amidst the whiteness, his head and shoulders elevated so that he is in that hospital position of being neither quite prone nor yet sitting. His hair is white upon his pillow and he breathes softly and sometimes unevenly, although it is difficult ever to be sure.

23   My five grey-haired brothers and I take turns beside his bedside, holding his heavy hands in ours and feeling their response, hoping ambiguously that he will speak to us, although we know that it may tire him. And trying to read his life and ours into his eyes when they are open. He had been with us for a long time, well into our middle age. Unlike those boys in that boat of so long ago, we did not see him taken from us in our youth. And unlike their youngest brother who, in turn, became our great-great-grandfather, we did not grow into a world in which there was no father's touch. We have been lucky to have this large and gentle man so deep into our lives.

24   No one in this hospital has mentioned the *cù mòr glas a' bhàis*. Yet as my mother said ten years ago, before slipping into her own death as quietly as a grownup child who leaves or enters her parents' house in the early hours, "It is hard to *not* know what you do know."

25   Even those who are most sceptical, like my oldest brother who has driven
here from Montreal, betray themselves by their nervous actions. "I avoided the
Greyhound bus stations in both Montreal and Toronto," he smiled upon his
arrival, and then added, "Just in case."

26   He did not realize how ill our father was and has smiled little since then. I
watch him turning the diamond ring upon his finger, knowing that he hopes he
will not hear the Gaelic phrase he knows too well. Not having the luxury, as he
once said, of some who live in Montreal and are able to pretend they do not
understand the "other" language. You cannot *not* know what you do know.

27   Sitting here, taking turns holding the hands of the man who gave us life, we are
afraid for him and for ourselves. We are afraid of what he may see and we are
afraid to hear the phrase born of the vision. We are aware that it may become confused with what the doctors call "the will to live" and we are aware that some
beliefs are what others would dismiss as "garbage." We are aware that there are
men who believe the earth is flat and that the birds bring forth the sun.

28   Bound here in our own peculiar mortality, we do not wish to see or see others see that which signifies life's demise. We do not want to hear the voice of our
father, as did those other sons, calling down his own particular death upon him.

29   We would shut our eyes and plug our ears, even as we know such actions to
be of no avail. Open still and fearful to the grey hair rising on our necks if and
when we hear the scrabble of the paws and the scratching at the door.

Bharati Mukherjee

The Tenant

1   Maya Sanyal has been in Cedar Falls, Iowa, less than two weeks. She's come,
books and clothes and one armchair rattling in the smallest truck that U-Haul
would rent her, from New Jersey. Before that she was in North Carolina. Before
that, Calcutta, India. Every place has something to give. She is sitting at the
kitchen table with Fran drinking bourbon for the first time in her life. Fran
Johnson found her the furnished apartment and helped her settle in. Now she's
brought a bottle of bourbon which gives her the right to stay and talk for a bit.
She's breaking up with someone named Vern, a pharmacist. Vern's father is also
a pharmacist and owns a drugstore. Maya has seen Vern's father on TV twice
already. The first time was on the local news when he spoke out against the selling of painkillers like Advil and Nuprin in supermarkets and gas stations. In the
matter of painkillers, Maya is a universalist. The other time he was in a barber-
shop quartet. Vern gets along all right with his father. He likes the pharmacy
business, as business goes, but he wants to go back to graduate school and learn
to make films. Maya is drinking her first bourbon tonight because Vern left
today for San Francisco State.

2   "I understand totally," Fran says. She teaches Utopian Fiction and a course in
Women's Studies and worked hard to get Maya hired. Maya has a Ph.D. in
Comparative Literature and will introduce writers like R.K. Narayan and Chinua
Achebe to three sections of sophomores at the University of Northern Iowa. "A
person has to leave home. Try out his wings."

3   Fran has to use the bathroom. "I don't feel abandoned." She pushes her chair away from the table. "Anyway it was a sex thing totally. We were good together. It'd be different if I'd loved him."

4   Maya tries to remember what's in the refrigerator. They need food. She hasn't been to the supermarket in over a week. She doesn't have a car yet and so she relies on a corner store—a longish walk—for milk, cereal, and frozen dinners. Someday these exigencies will show up as bad skin and collapsed muscle tone. No folly is ever lost. Maya pictures history as a net, the kind of safety net travelling trapeze artists of her childhood fell into when they were inattentive, or clumsy. Going to circuses in Calcutta with her father is what she remembers vividly. It is a banal memory, for her father, the owner of a steel company, is a complicated man.

5   Fran is out in the kitchen long enough for Maya to worry. They need food. Her mother believed in food. What is love, anger, inner peace, etc., her mother used to say, but the brain's biochemistry. Maya doesn't want to get into that, but she is glad she has enough stuff in the refrigerator to make an omelette. She realizes Indian women are supposed to be inventive with food, whip up exotic delights to tickle an American's palate, and she knows she should be meeting Fran's generosity and candor with some sort of bizarre and effortless countermove. If there's an exotic spice store in Cedar Falls or in neighboring Waterloo, she hasn't found it. She's looked in the phone book for common Indian names, especially Bengali, but hasn't yet struck up culinary intimacies. That will come—it always does. There's a six-pack in the fridge that her landlord, Ted Suminski, had put in because she'd be thirsty after unpacking. She was thirsty, but she doesn't drink beer. She probably should have asked him to come up and drink the beer. Except for Fran she hasn't had anyone over. Fran is more friendly and helpful than anyone Maya has known in the States since she came to North Carolina ten years ago, at nineteen. Fran is a Swede, and she is tall, with blue eyes. Her hair, however, is a dull, darkish brown.

6   "I don't think I can handle anything that heavy-duty," Fran says when she comes back to the room. She means the omelette. "I have to go home in any case." She lives with her mother and her aunt, two women in their mid-seventies, in a drafty farmhouse. The farmhouse now has a computer store catty-corner from it. Maya's been to the farm. She's been shown photographs of the way the corner used to be. If land values ever rebound, Fran will be worth millions.

7   Before Fran leaves she says, "Has Rab Chatterji called you yet?"

8   "No." She remembers the name, a good, reliable Bengali name, from the first night's study of the phone book. Dr. Rabindra Chatterji teaches Physics.

9   "He called the English office just before I left." She takes car keys out of her pocketbook. She reknots her scarf. "I bet Indian men are more sensitive than Americans. Rab's a Brahmin, that's what people say."

10   A Chatterji has to be a Bengali Brahmin—last names give ancestral secrets away—but Brahminness seems to mean more to Fran than it does to Maya. She was born in 1954, six full years after India became independent. Her India was Nehru's India: a charged, progressive place.

11   "All Indian men are wife beaters," Maya says. She means it and doesn't mean it. "That's why I married an American." Fran knows about the divorce, but nothing else. Fran is on the Hiring, Tenure, and Reappointment Committee.

12   Maya sees Fran down the stairs and to the car which is parked in the back in the spot reserved for Maya's car, if she had owned one. It will take her several months to save enough to buy one. She always pays cash, never borrows. She

tells herself she's still recovering from the U-Haul drive halfway across the country. Ted Suminski is in his kitchen watching the women. Maya waves to him because waving to him, acknowledging him in that way, makes him seem less creepy. He seems to live alone though a sign, THE SUMINSKIS, hangs from a metal horse's head in the front yard. Maya hasn't seen Mrs. Suminski. She hasn't seen any children either. Ted always looks lonely. When she comes back from campus, he's nearly always in the back, throwing darts or shooting baskets.

13   "What's he like?" Fran gestures with her head as she starts up her car. "You hear these stories."

14   Maya doesn't want to know the stories. She has signed a year's lease. She doesn't want complications. "He's all right. I keep out of his way."

15   "You know what I'm thinking? Of all the people in Cedar Falls, you're the one who could understand Vern best. His wanting to try out his wings, run away, stuff like that."

16   "Not really." Maya is not being modest. Fran is being impulsively democratic, lumping her wayward lover and Indian friend together as headstrong adventurers. For Fran, a utopian and feminist, borders don't count. Maya's taken some big risks, made a break with her parents' way. She's done things a woman from Ballygunge Park Road doesn't do, even in fantasies. She's not yet shared stories with Fran, apart from the divorce. She's told her nothing of men she picks up, the reputation she'd gained, before Cedar Falls, for "indiscretions." She has a job, equity, three friends she can count on for emergencies. She is an American citizen. But.

17   Fran's Brahmin calls her two nights later. On the phone he presents himself as Dr. Chatterji, not Rabindra or Rab. An old-fashioned Indian, she assumes. Her father still calls his closest friend, "Colonel." Dr. Chatterji asks her to tea on Sunday. She means to say no but hears herself saying, "Sunday? Fiveish? I'm not doing anything special this Sunday."

18   Outside, Ted Suminski is throwing darts into his garage door. The door has painted-on rings: orange, purple, pink. The bull's-eye is gray. He has to be fifty at least. He is a big, thick, lonely man about whom people tell stories. Maya pulls the phone cord as far as it'll go so she can look down more directly on her landlord's large, bald head. He has his back to her as he lines up a dart. He's in black running shoes, red shorts, he's naked to the waist. He hunches his right shoulder, he pulls the arm back; a big, lonely man shouldn't have so much grace. The dart is ready to cut through the September evening. But Ted Suminski doesn't let go. He swings on worn rubber soles, catches her eye in the window (she has to have imagined this), takes aim at her shadow. Could she have imagined the noise of the dart's metal tip on her windowpane?

19   Dr. Chatterji is still on the phone. "You are not having any mode of transportation, is that right?"

20   Ted Suminski has lost interest in her. Perhaps it isn't interest, at all; perhaps it's aggression. "I don't drive," she lies, knowing it sounds less shameful than not owning a car. She has said this so often she can get in the right degree of apology and Asian upper-class helplessness. "It's an awful nuisance."

21   "Not to worry, please." Then, "It is a great honor to be meeting Dr. Sanyal's daughter. In Calcutta business circles he is a legend."

22   On Sunday she is ready by four-thirty. She doesn't know what the afternoon holds; there are surely no places for "high tea"—a colonial tradition—in Cedar Falls, Iowa. If he takes her back to his place, it will mean he has invited other

guests. From his voice she can tell Dr. Chatterji likes to do things correctly. She has dressed herself in a peach-colored nylon georgette sari, jade drop-earrings and a necklace. The color is good on dark skin. She is not pretty, but she does her best. Working at it is a part of self-respect. In the mid-seventies, when American women felt rather strongly about such things, Maya had been in trouble with her women's group at Duke. She was too feminine. She had tried to explain the world she came out of. Her grandmother had been married off at the age of five in a village now in Bangladesh. Her great-aunt had been burned to death over a dowry problem. She herself had been trained to speak softly, arrange flowers, sing, be pliant. If she were to seduce Ted Suminski, she thinks as she waits in the front yard for Dr. Chatterji, it would be minor heroism. She has broken with the past. But.

23   Dr. Chatterji drives up for her at about five ten. He is a hesitant driver. The car stalls, jumps ahead, finally slams to a stop. Maya has to tell him to back off a foot or so; it's hard to leap over two sacks of pruned branches in a sari. Ted Suminski is an obsessive pruner and gardener.

24   "My sincerest apologies, Mrs. Sanyal," Dr. Chatterji says. He leans across the wide front seat of his noisy, very old, very used car and unlocks the door for her. "I am late. But then, I am sure you're remembering that Indian Standard Time is not at all the same as time in the States." He laughs. He could be nervous— she often had that effect on Indian men. Or he could just be chatty. "These Americans are all the time rushing and rushing but where it gets them?" He moves his head laterally once, twice. It's the gesture made famous by Peter Sellers. When Peter Sellers did it, it had seemed hilarious. Now it suggests that Maya and Dr. Chatterji have three thousand years plus civilization, sophistication, moral virtue, over people born on this continent. Like her, Dr. Chatterji is a naturalized American.

25   "Call me Maya," she says. She fusses with the seat belt. She does it because she needs time to look him over. He seems quite harmless. She takes in the prominent teeth, the eyebrows that run together. He's in a blue shirt and a beige cardigan with the K-Mart logo that buttons tightly over the waist. It's hard to guess his age because he has dyed his hair and his moustache. Late thirties, early forties. Older than she had expected. "Not Mrs. Sanyal."

26   This isn't time to tell about ex-husbands. She doesn't know where John is these days. He should have kept up at least. John had come into her life as a graduate student at Duke, and she, mistaking the brief breathlessness of sex for love, had married him. They had stayed together two years, maybe a little less. The pain that John had inflicted all those years ago by leaving her had subsided into a cozy feeling of loss. This isn't the time, but then she doesn't want to be a legend's daughter all evening. She's not necessarily on Dr. Chatterji's side is what she wants to get across early; she's not against America and Americans. She makes the story—of marriage outside the Brahminic pale, the divorce—quick, dull. Her unsentimentality seems to shock him. His stomach sags inside the cardigan.

27   "We've each had our several griefs," the physicist says. "We're each required to pay our karmic debts."

28   "Where are we headed?"

29   "Mrs. Chatterji has made some Indian snacks. She is waiting to meet you because she is knowing your cousin-sister who studied in Scottish Church College. My home is okay, no?"

30   Fran would get a kick out of this. Maya has slept with married men, with nameless men, with men little more than boys, but never with an Indian man. Never.

31   The Chatterjis live in a small blue house on a gravelly street. There are at least five or six other houses on the street; the same size but in different colors and with different front yard treatments. More houses are going up. This is the cutting edge of suburbia.

32   Mrs. Chatterji stands in the driveway. She is throwing a large plastic ball to a child. The child looks about four, and is Korean or Cambodian. The child is not hers because she tells it, "Chung-Hee, ta-ta, bye-bye. Now I play with guest," as Maya gets out of the car.

33   Maya hasn't seen this part of town. The early September light softens the construction pits. In that light the houses too close together, the stout woman in a striped cotton sari, the child hugging a pink ball, the two plastic lawn chairs by a tender young tree, the sheets and saris on the clothesline in the back, all seem miraculously incandescent.

34   "Go home now, Chung-Hee. I am busy." Mrs. Chatteji points the child homeward, then turns to Maya, who has folded her hands in traditional Bengali greeting. "It is an honor. We feel very privileged." She leads Maya indoors to a front room that smells of moisture and paint.

35   In her new, deliquescent mood, Maya allows herself to be backed into the best armchair—a low-backed, boxy Goodwill item draped over with a Rajasthani bedspread—and asks after the cousin Mrs. Chatterji knows. She doesn't want to let go of Mrs. Chatterji. She doesn't want husband and wife to get into whispered conferences about their guest's misadventures in America, as they make tea in the kitchen.

36   The coffee table is already laid with platters of mutton croquettes, fish chops, onion pakoras, ghugni with puris, samosas, chutneys. Mrs. Chatterji has gone to too much trouble. Maya counts four kinds of sweetmeats in Corning casseroles on an end table. She looks into a see-through lid; spongy, white dumplings float in rosewater syrup. Planets contained, mysteries made visible.

37   "What are you waiting for, Santana?" Dr. Chatterji becomes imperious, though not unaffectionate. He pulls a dining chair up close to the coffee table. "Make some tea." He speaks in Bengali to his wife, in English to Maya. To Maya he says, grandly, "We are having real Indian Green Label Lipton. A nephew is bringing it just one month back."

38   His wife ignores him. "The kettle's already on," she says. She wants to know about the Sanyal family. Is it true her great-grandfather was a member of the Star Chamber in England?

39   Nothing in Calcutta is ever lost. Just as her story is known to Bengalis all over America, so are the scandals of her family, the grandfather hauled up for tax evasion, the aunt who left her husband to act in films. This woman brings up the Star Chamber, the glories of the Sanyal family, her father's philanthropies, but it's a way of saying, *I know the dirt.*

40   The bedrooms are upstairs. In one of those bedrooms an unseen, tormented presence—Maya pictures it as a clumsy ghost that strains to shake off the body's shell—drops things on the floor. The things are heavy and they make the front room's chandelier shake. Light bulbs, shaped like tiny candle flames, flicker. The Chatterjis have said nothing about children. There are no tricycles in the hallway, no small sandals behind the doors. Maya is too polite to ask about the noise, and the Chatterjis don't explain. They talk just a little louder. They flip the embroidered cover off the stereo. What would Maya like to hear? Hemanta Kumar? Manna Dey? Oh, that young chap, Manna Dey! What sincerity, what tenderness he can convey!

41   Upstairs the ghost doesn't hear the music of nostalgia. The ghost throws and thumps. The ghost makes its own vehement music. Maya hears in its voice madness, self-hate.

42   Finally the water in the kettle comes to a boil. The whistle cuts through all fantasy and pretense. Dr. Chatterji says, "I'll see to it," and rushes out of the room. But he doesn't go to the kitchen. He shouts up the stairwell. "Poltoo, kindly stop this nonsense straightway! We're having a brilliant and cultured lady-guest and you're creating earthquakes?" The kettle is hysterical.

43   Mrs. Chatterji wipes her face. The face that had seemed plump and cheery at the start of the evening now is flabby. "My sister's boy," the woman says.

44   So this is the nephew who has brought with him the cartons of Green Label tea, one of which will be given to Maya.

45   Mrs. Chatterji speaks to Maya in English as though only the alien language can keep emotions in check. "Such an intelligent boy! His father is government servant. Very highly placed."

46   Maya is meant to visualize a smart, clean-cut young man from south Calcutta, but all she can see is a crazy, thwarted, lost graduate student. Intelligence, proper family guarantee nothing. Even Brahmins can do self-destructive things, feel unsavory urges. Maya herself had been an excellent student.

47   "He was First Class First in B.Sc. from Presidency College," the woman says. "Now he's getting Master's in Ag. Science at Iowa State."

48   The kitchen is silent. Dr. Chatterji comes back into the room with a tray. The teapot is under a tea cozy, a Kashmiri one embroidered with the usual chinar leaves, loops, and chains. "*Her* nephew," he says. The dyed hair and dyed moustache are no longer signs of a man wishing to fight the odds. He is a vain man, anxious to cut losses. "Very unfortunate business."

49   The nephew's story comes out slowly, over fish chops and mutton croquettes. He is in love with a student from Ghana.

50   "Everything was A-Okay until the Christmas break. Grades, assistantship for next semester, everything."

51   "I blame the college. The office for foreign students arranged a Christmas party. And now, *baapre baap!* Our poor Poltoo wants to marry a Negro Muslim."

52   Maya is known for her nasty, ironic one-liners. It has taken her friends weeks to overlook her malicious, un-American pleasure in others' misfortunes. Maya would like to finish Dr. Chatterji off quickly. He is pompous; he is reactionary; he wants to live and work in America but give back nothing except taxes. The confused world of the immigrant—the lostness that Maya and Poltoo feel—that's what Dr. Chatterji wants to avoid. She hates him. But.

53   Dr. Chatterji's horror is real. A good Brahmin boy in Iowa is in love with an African Muslim. It shouldn't be a big deal. But the more she watches the physicist, the more she realizes that "Brahmin" isn't a caste; it's a metaphor. You break one small rule, and the constellation collapses. She thinks suddenly that John Cheever—she is teaching him as a "world writer" in her classes, cheek-by-jowl with Africans and West Indians—would have understood Dr. Chatterji's dread. Cheever had been on her mind, ever since the late afternoon light slanted over Mrs. Chatterji's drying saris. She remembers now how full of a soft, Cheeverian light Durham had been the summer she had slept with John Hadwen; and how after that, her tidy graduate-student world became monstrous, lawless. All men became John Hadwen; John became all men. Outwardly, she retained her poise, her Brahminical breeding. She treated her crisis as a literary event; she lost her moral sense, her judgment, her power to distinguish.

Her parents had behaved magnanimously. They had cabled from Calcutta: WHAT'S DONE IS DONE. WE ARE CONFIDENT YOU WILL HANDLE NEW SITUATIONS WELL. ALL LOVE. But she knows more than do her parents. Love is anarchy.

54   Poltoo is Mrs. Chatterji's favorite nephew. She looks as though it is her fault that the Sunday has turned unpleasant. She stacks the empty platters methodically. To Maya she says, "It is the goddess who pulls the strings. We are puppets. I know the goddess will fix it. Poltoo will not marry that African woman." Then she goes to the coat closet in the hall and staggers back with a harmonium, the kind sold in music stores in Calcutta, and sets it down on the carpeted floor. "We're nothing but puppets," she says again. She sits at Maya's feet, her pudgy hands on the harmonium's shiny, black bellows. She sings, beautifully, in a virgin's high voice, "Come, goddess, come, muse, come to us hapless peoples' rescue."

55   Maya is astonished. She has taken singing lessons at Dakshini Academy in Calcutta. She plays the sitar and the tanpur, well enough to please Bengalis, to astonish Americans. But stout Mrs. Chatterji is a devotee, talking to God.

56   A little after eight, Dr. Chatterji drops her off. It's been an odd evening and they are both subdued.

57   "I want to say one thing," he says. He stops her from undoing her seat belt. The plastic sacks of pruned branches are still at the corner.

58   "You don't have to get out," she says.

59   "Please. Give me one more minute of your time."

60   "Sure."

61   "Maya is my favorite name."

62   She says nothing. She turns away from him without making her embarrassment obvious.

63   "Truly speaking, it is my favorite. You are sometimes lonely, no? But you are lucky. Divorced women can date, they can go to bars and discos. They can see mens, many mens. But inside marriage there is so much loneliness." A groan, low, horrible, comes out of him.

64   She turns back toward him, to unlatch the seat belt and run out of the car. She sees that Dr. Chatterji's pants are unzipped. One hand works hard under his Jockey shorts; the other rests, limp, penitential, on the steering wheel.

65   "Dr. Chatterji—*really!*" she cries.

66   The next day, Monday, instead of getting a ride home with Fran—Fran says she *likes* to give rides, she needs the chance to talk, and she won't share gas expenses, absolutely not—Maya goes to the periodicals room of the library. There are newspapers from everywhere, even from Madagascar and New Caledonia. She thinks of the periodicals room as an asylum for homesick aliens. There are two aliens already in the room, both Orientals, both absorbed in the politics and gossip of their far-off homes.

67   She goes straight to the newspapers from India. She bunches her raincoat like a bolster to make herself more comfortable. There's so much to catch up on. A village headman, a known Congress-Indira party worker, has been shot at by scooter-riding snipers. An Indian pugilist has won an international medal—in Nepal. A child drawing well water—the reporter calls the child "a neo-Buddhist, a convert from the now-outlawed untouchable caste"—has been stoned. An editorial explains that the story about stoning is not a story about caste but about failed idealism; a story about promises of green fields and clean, potable water broken, a story about bribes paid and wells not dug. But no, thinks Maya, it's about caste.

68   Out here, in the heartland of the new world, the India of serious newspapers unsettles. Maya longs again to feel what she had felt in the Chatterjis' living room: virtues made physical. It is a familiar feeling, a longing. Had a suitable man presented himself in the reading room at that instant, she would have seduced him. She goes on to the stack of *India Abroads,* reads through matrimonial columns, and steals an issue to take home.

69   Indian men want Indian brides. Married Indian men want Indian mistresses. All over America, "Handsome, tall, fair" engineers, doctors, data processors—the new pioneers—cry their eerie love calls.

70   Maya runs a finger down the first column; her fingertip, dark with newsprint, stops at random.

71   Hello! Hi! Yes, you *are* the one I'm looking for. You are the new emancipated Indo-American woman. You have a zest for life. You are at ease in USA and yet your ethics are rooted in Indian tradition. The man of your dreams has come. Yours truly is handsome, ear-nose-throat specialist, well-settled in Connecticut. Age is 41 but never married, physically fit, sportsmanly, and strong. I adore idealism, poetry, beauty. I abhor smugness, passivity, caste system. Write with recent photo. Better still, call!!!

72   Maya calls. Hullo, hullo, hullo! She hears immigrant lovers cry in crowded shopping malls. Yes, you are at ease in both worlds, you are the one. She feels she has a fair chance.

73   A man answers. "Ashoke Mehta speaking."

74   She speaks quickly into the bright-red mouthpiece of her telephone. He will be in Chicago, in transit, passing through O'Hare. United counter, Saturday, two p.m. As easy as that.

75   "Good," Ashoke Mehta says. "For these encounters I, too, prefer a neutral zone."

76   On Saturday at exactly two o'clock the man of Maya's dreams floats toward her as lovers used to in shampoo commercials. The United counter is a loud, harassed place but passengers and piled-up luggage fall away from him. Full-cheeked and fleshy-lipped, he is handsome. He hasn't lied. He is serene, assured, a Hindu god touching down in Illinois.

77   She can't move. She feels ugly and unworthy. Her adult life no longer seems miraculously rebellious; it is grim, it is perverse. She has accomplished nothing. She has changed her citizenship but she hasn't broken through into the light, the vigor, the *hustle* of the New World. She is stuck in dead space.

78   "Hullo, hullo!" Their fingers touch.

79   Oh, the excitement! Ashoke Mehta's palm feels so right in the small of her back. Hullo, hullo, hullo, He pushes her out of the reach of anti-Khomeini Iranians, Hare Krishnas, American Fascists, men with fierce wants, and guides her to an empty gate. They have less than an hour.

80   "What would you like, Maya?"

81   She knows he can read her mind, she knows her thoughts are open to him. *You,* she's almost giddy with the thought, with simple desire. "From the snack bar," he says as though to clarify. "I'm afraid I'm starved."

82   Below them, where the light is strong and hurtful, a Boeing is being serviced. "Nothing," she says.

83   He leans forward. She can feel the nap of his scarf—she recognizes the Cambridge colors—she can smell the wool of his Icelandic sweater. She runs her

hand along the scarf, then against the flesh of his neck. "Only the impulsive ones call," he says.

84   The immigrant courtship proceeds. It's easy, he's good with facts. He knows how to come across to a stranger who may end up a lover, a spouse. He makes over a hundred thousand. He owns a house in Hartford, and two income properties in Newark. He plays the market but he's cautious. He's good at badminton but plays handball to keep in shape. He watches all the sports on television. Last August he visited Copenhagen, Helsinki and Leningrad. Once upon a time he collected stamps but now he doesn't have hobbies, except for reading. He counts himself an intellectual, he spends too much on books. Ludlum, Forsyth, MacInnes; other names she doesn't catch. She suppresses a smile, she's told him only she's a graduate student. He's not without his vices. He's a spender, not a saver. He's a sensualist: good food—all foods, but easy on the Indian—good wine. Some temptations he doesn't try to resist.

85   And I, she wants to ask, do I tempt?

86   "Now tell me about yourself, Maya." He makes it easy for her. "Have you ever been in love?"

87   "No."

88   "But many have loved you, I can see that." He says it not unkindly. It is the fate of women like her, and men like him. Their karmic duty, to be loved. It is expected, not judged. She feels he can see them all, the sad parade of need and demand. This isn't the time to reveal all.

89   And so the courtship enters a second phase.

90   When she gets back to Cedar Falls, Ted Suminski is standing on the front porch. It's late at night, chilly. He is wearing a down vest. She's never seen him on the porch. In fact there's no chair to sit on. He looks chilled through. He's waited around a while.

91   "Hi." She has her keys ready. This isn't the night to offer the six-pack in the fridge. He looks expectant, ready to pounce.

92   "Hi." He looks like a man who might have aimed the dart at her. What has he done to his wife, his kids? Why isn't there at least a dog? "Say, I left a note upstairs."

93   The note is written in Magic Marker and thumb-tacked to her apartment door. DUE TO PERSONAL REASONS, NAMELY REMARRIAGE, I REQUEST THAT YOU VACATE MY PLACE AT THE END OF THE SEMESTER.

94   Maya takes the note down and retacks it to the kitchen wall. The whole wall is like a bulletin board, made of some new, crumbly building-material. Her kitchen, Ted Suminski had told her, was once a child's bedroom. Suminski in love: the idea stuns her. She has misread her landlord. The dart at her window speaks of no twisted fantasy. The landlord wants the tenant out.

95   She gets a glass out of the kitchen cabinet, gets out a tray of ice, pours herself a shot of Fran's bourbon. She is happy for Ted Suminski. She is. She wants to tell someone how moved she'd been by Mrs. Chatterji's singing. How she'd felt in O'Hare, even about Dr. Rab Chatterji in the car. But Fran is not the person. No one she's ever met is the person. She can't talk about the dead space she lives in. She wishes Ashoke Mehta would call. Right now.

96   Weeks pass. Then two months. She finds a new room, signs another lease. Her new landlord calls himself Fred. He has no arms, but he helps her move her things. He drives between Ted Suminski's place and his twice in his station wagon. He uses his toes the way Maya uses her fingers. He likes to do things. He pushes garbage sacks full of Maya's clothes up the stairs.

97   "It's all right to stare," Fred says. "Hell, I would."

98   That first afternoon in Fred's rooming house, they share a Chianti. Fred wants to cook her pork chops but he's a little shy about Indians and meat. Is it beef, or pork? Or any meat? She says it's okay, any meat, but not tonight. He has an ex-wife in Des Moines, two kids in Portland, Oregon. The kids are both normal; he's the only freak in the family. But he's self-reliant. He shops in the supermarket like anyone else, he carries out the garbage, shovels the snow off the sidewalk. He needs Maya's help with one thing. Just one thing. The box of Tide is a bit too heavy to manage. Could she get him the giant size every so often and leave it in the basement?

99   The dead space need not suffocate. Over the months, Fred and she will settle into companionship. She has never slept with a man without arms. Two wounded people, he will joke during their nightly contortions. It will shock her, this assumed equivalence with a man so strikingly deficient. She knows she is strange, and lonely, but being Indian is not the same, she would have thought, as being a freak.

100   One night in spring, Fred's phone rings. "Ashoke Mehta speaking." None of this "do you remember me?" nonsense.

101   The god has tracked her down. He hasn't forgotten. "Hullo," he says, in their special way. And because she doesn't answer back, "Hullo, hullo, hullo." She is aware of Fred in the back of the room. He is lighting a cigarette with his toes.

102   "Yes," she says, "I remember."

103   "I had to take care of a problem," Ashoke Mehta says. "You know that I have my vices. That time at O'Hare I was honest with you."

104   She is breathless.

105   "Who is it, May?" asks Fred.

106   "You also have a problem," says the voice. His laugh echoes.

107   "You will come to Hartford, I know."

108   When she moves out, she tells herself, it will not be the end of Fred's world.

Russell Smith

Responsibility

Russell Smith (1963–) was born in South Africa and became a Canadian citizen in 1972. He was educated at Queen's University in Ontario and at the universities of Poitiers and Paris in France. Smith has spent much of his career as a journalist writing about the urban scene in Toronto. He has published two novels, How Insensitive *(1994), and* Noise *(1998). "Responsibility" appeared in 1999 in a collection of short stories entitled* Young Men. *In it we encounter a son and his mother trying to come to terms with each other's values.*

1   "Perhaps you don't value it now, but as you get older money becomes more important," said his mother. She was sitting in the breakfast nook with her tea, looking out at the bird feeder. James too was looking out at the garden, stand-

ing at the sliding doors. Anyone who talked in the kitchen did so while looking at the garden.

2   "I'm sure that's true, but you see, believe it or not, I'm hoping to make money from my writing, eventually. I know that seems ridiculous to you and Dad." He waited for her to contradict him. "Some people actually make a great deal of money from what I . . . the kind of writing I'm trying to do. I'm talking to some people about a documentary, about my music column, it could be a book, it could . . ." He clenched his jaw shut. He felt helpless. "It could be the kind of book that would sell outside this little . . . anyway. Yes, it's a bigger risk, yes, but actually it could pay off very well, if you do something successful. So actually I'm being *more* ambitious than you and Dad were."

3   "I guess it's just the risk I worry about."

4   It was no longer surprising that this conversation came up, even that it came up on the Sunday afternoons of his visits, that it came up just as simultaneous relief and tension about the trip back to the city were growing with a mental hum, ripening in him, in his nervous and circulatory systems like some slowly developing and ultimately convulsive disease, just as they were all about to begin the bargaining about which parent in which car would drive him to the bus station and dump him in its stained limbo air and promise of metamorphosis, this was so familiar it was no longer surprising; what was surprising was how unfailingly and deeply it seared him with a fine painful clear sense of abandonment, as would some long penetrating parental angioscopic device, every time, and made him think, every time, that perhaps now, this time, was the time it would all come out, it would come clear exactly what it was about what he did that so disappointed her, and why her disappointment so irritated—no, worse, let's be honest—so hurt him. He said quickly, "And you worry about my lifestyle, that I'm not married and—"

5   "I don't care that you're not married, if you're happy."

6   "Yes you do. Don't pretend you don't. Of course you do. You'd like me to be married and have kids and a minivan and come over on Sundays and talk about eavestroughing with Dad."

7   "*I* don't think you could *handle* kids," said his mother with the restrained tone of someone producing an ace.

8   "No, I couldn't," said James.

9   She was silent for a moment. Then she said, "But when you do have children, you'll want to be able to provide for them, and I think you should think of that now."

10   He turned to her and said gently, "Mom, what would you say if I told you I might never have children? Do you think there's something wrong with that?"

11   She was silent again. She twirled a strand of hair around a finger, which meant that she was agitated. She would never sit down for so long in mid-morning unless she was upset. The tea in her cup was getting cold.

12   "You think that's somehow morally wrong, not to have children, don't you?" said James. He felt merciless; he felt this was the time to get it all out.

13   "No," she said quickly, "not at all. It's you I'm thinking of. I just think that you would be happier with children. Having children . . . it takes you out of yourself. You would stop chasing after every girl you met and—"

14   "What if I don't want to stop chasing after every girl I meet? You seem to feel that I have to at a certain point, because everybody does. Why? What if it makes me happy?"

15   "It won't make you happy forever."

16   "Will children?"

17   She was silent again. "Look, all I know is that all this tension in your life, all that awful time you had with Alison and that girl in the city when they wouldn't speak to each other and—"

18   "Yes," said James, "I know, go on."

19   "All that wouldn't happen if you had a family. You wouldn't have time for it. And all I know is that when you have a child, that's the most important thing. If your child is happy, then you're happy, it's as simple as that. And you're—what is it that Joanne Winterson always said? You're only as happy as your most unhappy child. It's true." She took quick sips at her tea, which by now was surely cold.

20   "Sounds terrific." He puffed out his cheeks. "Just remind me again why this is a better system?"

21   "Oh, don't be so snooty. You're so *arrogant*."

22   "What? Sorry. I'm not following you."

23   "Yes you are. You know exactly what I mean. You're so condescending."

24   James turned back to the garden. "I have no idea what you're talking about." But he did. He made an effort to make an effort to think about trying to be nicer. He said, "I don't mean to be nasty about anyone's choices. As long as you *make* choices."

25   "What about Jennifer? Doesn't she want children?"

26   James took a deep breath. "Well, not right now she doesn't. She's trying to get her own career going, she's in the same boat as me. We have more . . ." He stopped himself. He said, "She's just too busy, and she doesn't have the money or the stability in her life for it. She doesn't want kids right now."

27   "Well, she's over thirty now. She doesn't have much time left."

28   "So maybe she won't. Maybe she won't have time. I'm not sure, because we haven't talked about it a lot, but I think that right now at least she isn't too worried about it. She's thinking about herself, about her career. Like me."

29   "*Oh!* But . . ." His mother leaned over the table to pour more tea. She spilled the tea and said, *"Bother."* She was frowning and biting her lip; she really was agitated and maybe about to cry. He wasn't sure what it was all about and he got agitated too. He handed her a cloth. At least they were getting somewhere.

30   "But what?" He sat down at the table.

31   She wiped the table with furious speed. "What she wants, what you want," she said, shaking her head. "You people—it's always what *you* want. You just think you can play around and have fun forever."

32   "Yes. Perhaps we do. What should we do instead?" His heart was beating fast.

33   She didn't answer.

34   "What is it, exactly, Mom, that upsets you? That I don't have enough responsibilities in life? Is that it?"

35   There was a long silence and then she said in a faint voice, "Yes."

36   "I have too much fun. I don't have enough to tie me down."

37   "James, if your father and I had felt like you," she said urgently, looking at him, "then you wouldn't even *be* here!"

38   "Right." James rubbed his face with his hands. "The logic of this is growing too much for me." He sighed. "Mom. You don't understand what I'm . . . Look at it this way. Imagine you had never had me. Or Kurt. Then you wouldn't, you wouldn't feel a responsibility to us, right? Because we wouldn't—"

39   "I can't imagine that," she said in a higher voice, her indignant voice. "Lucky for you, I couldn't imagine that."

40   "That's my point, Mom. That you're not imagining what I'm—"

41   "You think," she said rapidly, "that you can just live this student life forever, have no—"

42   "Why not? Why can't I—"

43   "But it's not all fun. At a certain point you have to pay the piper. At a certain point you just have to stop fooling around and accept your responsibilities."

44   James looked at her. She was fidgeting with a doily. "What responsibilities? My family responsibilities?"

45   *"Yes."*

46   "Mom, this is what I'm trying to get at. Think about it. If I don't have a wife or kids then who do I have a responsibility to?"

47   There was a long silence. She was fingering the doily on the tray that held the salt and pepper shakers and the bowl of sugar and the tiny antique silver spoons from the ancestral Germany that was unknown to them all, moving her eyes from the doily out to the bird feeder where there were no birds and back again.

48   "What is it?" he said more gently. "Is it that you think I have a responsibility to Jennifer, or maybe to you?"

49   "No, no, not to me, certainly."

50   "Is it just that you feel I have a responsibility to *have* kids? So that I can feel a responsibility to them? This is what I mean about logical—"

51   "No, no, I'm not saying that. I'm not saying you *have* to."

52   He waited. She did not go on. "I don't have to."

53   "No."

54   "Okay, so what—why—"

55   "I don't know." Her voice sounded weak now. "I'm not sure. I'm not sure—I don't know what I mean." She played with the doily.

56   James thought about this. He looked at the doily, which she had inherited from her mother who had crocheted in it Portage la Prairie, a place he had never been, and wondered for some reason how old she had been when it had been crocheted. He had a black-and-white picture of his mother in a rather Chanel-like tweed suit, leaning against the hood of a large American car, against an unblemished sky and a flat wheaty horizon of laughably pure rural nowhere. He wondered how old she had been in that photograph; probably younger, yes, much younger than him. "Are you saying, Mom, maybe that . . . maybe it's just that you, when you were young, I mean younger, you felt you didn't . . ." He stopped himself. He wanted to say, You *didn't have a choice.*

57   "Oh, we didn't even think about it. Everyone had children. It was all—it was what we wanted."

58   "Right." He paused. He had to go very carefully here. "But have you ever thought about how, about how things might have . . . about what you might have done if you hadn't"—he took a deep breath—"had me and Kurt."

59   She stood up abruptly and stood in the window, while James thought, She never does that, never takes a moment to stare at the garden without a vacuum cleaner or a duster in her hand. Her arms were folded and her shoulders hunched. She said, "You sound as if you *want* me to think about that."

60   "No." He didn't know what she was getting at, but the safe answer was no. "No, no. I just, I'm thinking of me, in my case—"

61   "If I hadn't got married? Is that what you mean?"

62   "I don't know. Was it impossible to get married and not have children? Not that I'm saying that's what you should—"

63   "Well, I suppose it wasn't impossible. But I wanted children. Your dad wanted children. And, you know, Jamie"—she gave a small laugh—"I was very flattered, you know, that Hans wanted to marry me. He was, I knew he was going to be very successful. You didn't turn down opportunity, in those days."

64   James laughed, too. As the refrigerator began to hum unevenly, he became aware of a cloud of worry too vague to describe, forming over his head. "It meant your problems were solved."

65   "Sure. And he wanted children too, you know, it wasn't just my idea."

66   "Yes. Okay. But what, I guess I mean to ask, what if you hadn't got married?"

67   "I suppose I would have had to get some kind of job."

68   James asked slowly, "Did you want . . . to do that?"

69   "No. I suppose not." She paused. "I don't know."

70   He held himself very still. Her voice had gone small as she had said it. His worry buzzed and shifted overhead. He didn't know what was approaching them here, but it was something grey and tight. He thought of the bus station, its cigarette air.

71   "I guess you don't respect at all what I did," she said in a wavering voice. "Bringing you two boys up."

72   "Of course I do, Mom. Of course I do. I know how much work it is, how hard—"

73   "No you don't."

74   It was James's turn to be silent.

75   She said, in a voice that fluttered and broke, "There was a time when people thought it was valuable, to run a house and sew and clean and cook for two boys and a man, and educate the boys, the way I read to you—"

76   "Mom," said James, agitated, "of course I value that. Of course I respect—"

77   "No you don't. You don't think it meant—it's not important to you. You think if it's not some big career it's not difficult and it's, it's some kind of cop-out."

78   "No," said James.

79   "I've heard you say it. When you found out Alison had a child you said it was a cop-out."

80   James opened his mouth and closed it. It was true, not only that he had said it, but that he believed it. It was a cop-out.

81   "The work of about twenty-two years. A cop-out."

82   He looked at the doily, her moving hands.

83   "And you're not the only one," she said quietly. "I can tell people laugh at me. The younger wives at Dad's firm."

84   James went cold. "No they don't. They wouldn't."

85   "They think we're ridiculous, me and Joanne and . . . all of my friends. I can tell. And maybe they're right."

86   "Oh, Mom, don't be—"

87   "You know, Jamie, I was thinking about this last week. I was trying to remember all the jobs I've had in my life. All the paying jobs." She counted on her fingers. "I used to babysit, as a teenager. I must have earned less than a dollar an hour. And I was in a nursing course when I met Dad, but I worked in an office in the summers. So that was two summers, about four months' total. And then I worked at the kindergarten, where you and Kurt went, for about two years, part-time, for a little extra cash, when we were just starting out."

88   James listened to the anxious fridge.

89   "So," she said, "I counted it all up. All the money I've ever earned. Myself. And I figured it came to a total of about three thousand five hundred dollars. In my whole life. That's all I've ever earned myself. I never thought about it, until now. I guess, I guess that's all the young women see. The other things we did, what we did, it's not important to anyone any more. I guess."

90   The refrigerator grunted, shuddered and stopped humming. The kitchen was silent.

91   He said as gently as he could, "Yes it is, Mom. I don't think the money's important. I do think it was a disappointing choice for Alison, because she had her music, and her . . ." He trailed off. He did not want to imply that his mother had had nothing else to do. But it was true. "She gave up her music. But you, there were fewer opportunities at that—"

92   "And I didn't have anything I could have done? Is that what you mean? And Alison shouldn't have done the most important thing in the world?" She balled her little hand into a fist and made to punch his shoulder, but of course she didn't. "You're all so selfish." Her voice wavered again.

93   "What?" said James, alarmed. "Who is? Alison?"

94   "It's just that . . . you're all so arrogant about everything. It's just not very . . . it's not very *nice*." Her voice cracked and he realized she was in tears.

95   He stood behind her and put a hand on her shoulder. His worry was gone, and in its place he had a pure, liquid anguish, a sense that the air itself was sad, over the silent garden, that forces were moving all around him like invisible rain. He said, "What isn't nice, Mom? Tell me."

96   "I can't explain it. It's just that . . ." She sniffled. "Nice people . . ." She paused and coughed. Then she said, loud and cracking, as if in physical distress, *"Nice people don't do things for themselves."*

97   She was really sobbing.

98   He felt as if the floor of his stomach had opened, and there was darkness below it.

99   He patted her shoulder. She sobbed and shook. There was nothing else to do but pat her shoulder. He looked around the immaculate kitchen, the slate-tiled floor, the island and the overhead wrought-iron pot hooks she had campaigned so hard to have his father put in. The sandy wall, the pristine counters. The pot lids were stacked in the pot-lid rack; the utensils hung from hooks over the island. "I'm sorry, Mom," he said. *"You're nice."*

100   He tried a laugh and she giggled, too, a sniffling giggle as if she was embarrassed, and wiped her eyes and blew her nose. He exhaled in relief, for if she was blowing her nose already, the whole thing was okay. He glanced at his watch: there was a bus back to the city at 3:15.

101   He put his arm around her shoulder and they looked at the empty garden, the wrought-iron chairs. He wondered what she was going to do that afternoon, after he got back on his bus. His dad had had to go into the office. And Kurt was gone, probably gone for good now, even when he got back from Whistler he would be looking for a job in the city. James wondered for a second if he should stay, maybe take her out to the craft shops. He thought of the drive through the industrial park, the deserted highways, the hot little shops. He thought of the handmade towel racks and calico quilts and apple dolls they would look at. The photo frames in amusing shapes. If they drove out of town, they would have to stop and buy corn and squash, for it was that time, which would go into soups and preserves and pie fillings which only his dad would eat.

102   He stared at the garden. There were no birds at the bird feeder. The house was dead quiet; the whole neighbourhood was silent as a tomb. And he knew then that he wasn't nice, he wasn't a nice person, because all he wanted to do was get out, get the hell out of there.

HANDBOOK

Learning the parts of English sentences won't in itself improve your writing, but it will equip you to handle errors at the sentence level. For example, before you can identify and correct unwarranted shifts from past to present time, you need to know about verbs and their tenses. Similarly, to recognize and correct pronoun case errors, you need to know what pronouns are and how they are used. This section first covers subjects and predicates, then complements, appositives, and the parts of speech, and finally phrases and clauses.

SUBJECTS AND PREDICATES

The subject of a sentence tells who or what the sentence is about. A *simple subject* consists of a noun (that is, a naming word) or a noun substitute. A *complete subject* consists of a simple subject plus any words that limit or describe it.

The predicate tells something about the subject and completes the thought of the sentence. A *simple predicate* consists of one or more verbs (words that show action or existence). A *complete predicate* includes any associated words. In the following examples, the simple subjects are underlined <u>once</u> and the simple predicates <u>twice</u>. The subjects and predicates are separated with slash marks.

> <u>William</u>/<u>laughed</u>.
>
> <u>Mary</u>/<u>has moved</u>.
>
> <u>Sarah</u>/<u>painted</u> the kitchen.
>
> <u>The student</u> over there in the corner/<u>is majoring</u> in art.

A sentence can have a compound subject (two or more separate subjects), a compound predicate (two or more separate predicates), or both.

> The <u>elephants</u> and their <u>trainer</u>/<u>bowed</u> to the audience and <u>left</u> the ring.

Sentences that ask questions don't follow the usual simple subject–simple predicate order. Instead, the order may be reversed; or if the simple predicate consists of two verbs, the simple subject may come between them.

> When <u>is</u>/your/<u>theme</u> due? (Simple subject follows simple predicate.)

> <u>Has</u>/<u>Joan</u>/<u>walked</u> her pygmy goat yet? (Simple subject comes between verbs.)

Usage Considerations Because subjects are such important sentence elements, think carefully about each one you write so that your sentences won't be vague or misleading. Read the example below:

> *Our government* has failed to repeal the Goods and Services Tax.

This statement can be expressed more precisely:

The *House of Commons* has failed to repeal the Goods and Services Tax.

The *prime minister* has rejected proposals to repeal the GST.

Paying close attention to subjects lets you present your ideas more accurately and clearly.

EXERCISE *Place a slash mark between the complete subject and the complete predicate; then underline the simple subject once and the verb(s) twice. If a subject comes between two verbs, set it off with two slash marks.*

1. The full moon rose majestically over the mountain peak.
2. John was ill on the day of the big test.
3. The boys and girls laughed and splashed happily in the pool.
4. That man by the door is my uncle.
5. The judge revoked Rudy's parole and ordered him to jail.
6. The tall oak shaded almost the entire backyard.
7. My favourite subject is history.
8. Mr. Eames has bought a wicker chair for his living room.

COMPLEMENTS

A complement is a word or word group that forms part of the predicate and helps complete the meaning of the sentence. Complements fall into four categories: direct objects, indirect objects, subject complements, and object complements.

A *direct object* names whatever receives, or results from, the action of a verb.

The millwright repaired the *lathe.* (Direct object receives action of verb *repaired.*)

Hilary painted a *picture.* (Direct object results from action of verb *painted.*)

They took *coffee* and *sandwiches* to the picnic. (Direct objects receive action of verb *took.*)

As the last sentence shows, a sentence may have a compound direct object—two or more separate direct objects.

An *indirect object* identifies someone or something that receives whatever is named by the direct object.

Doris lent *me* her calculator. (Indirect object *me* receives *calculator,* the direct object.)

Will and Al bought their *boat* new sails. (Indirect object *boat* receives *sails,* the direct object.)

An indirect object can be converted to a prepositional phrase that begins with *to* or *for* and follows the direct object.

Doris lent her calculator *to me.*

Will and Al bought new sails *for their boat.*

A *subject complement* follows a linking verb—one that indicates existence rather than action. It renames or describes the subject.

Desmond is a *carpenter.* (Complement *carpenter* renames subject *Desmond.*)

The lights are too *bright* for Percy. (Complement *bright* describes subject *lights.*)

An *object complement* follows a direct object and renames or describes it.

The council named Donna *treasurer.* (Object complement *treasurer* renames direct object *Donna.*)

The audience thought the play *silly.* (Object complement *silly* describes direct object *play.*)

Usage Considerations   Direct objects can be revised for greater precision, as these examples show:

John sent *a gift.*

John sent *a giant colouring book as a birthday gift.*

Often, you can carry the revision one step further by adding an indirect object, subject complement, or other complement to the sentence.

John sent his *niece* a giant colouring book as a birthday gift. (Indirect object added.)

APPOSITIVES

An appositive is a noun, or word group serving as a noun, that follows another noun or noun substitute and expands its meaning. Appositives may be restrictive or nonrestrictive. Restrictive appositives distinguish whatever they modify from other items in the same class. They are written without commas.

My sister *Heidi* is a professional golfer. (Appositive *Heidi* distinguishes her from other sisters.)

I have just read a book by the novelist *Henry James.* (Appositive *Henry James* distinguishes him from other novelists.)

Nonrestrictive appositives provide more information about whatever they modify. This sort of appositive is set off by a pair of commas, except at the end of a sentence; then it is preceded by a single comma.

Anatoly Karpov, *the Russian chess player,* was interviewed on TV. (Appositive names *Karpov's* occupation.)

Todd plans to major in paleontology, *the study of fossils.* (Appositive defines the term *paleontology.*)

Usage Considerations   When a brief definition is necessary, appositives can help you improve your sentences.

John Cage wrote hundreds of pieces for prepared piano.

John Cage, *a twentieth-century avant-garde composer,* wrote hundreds of pieces for prepared pianos, *instruments with odds and ends stuck between their strings to provide unusual effects.*

However, avoid cluttering your writing with appositives that provide unneeded information; the overload will impede and irritate your reader.

EXERCISE

Identify each italicized item as a direct object (DO), an indirect object (IO), a subject complement (SC), an object complement (OC), or an appositive (AP).

1. Harry is a *student* in business administration.
2. Mr. Ames gave his *son* money for the movies.
3. The study group found Kant's philosophy *difficult.*
4. Dan lost his *umbrella* in the subway.
5. Speed Spedowski, *our best pitcher,* won twenty-three games last season.
6. Bill borrowed several *tapes* for the party.
7. The newspaper named Melissa *editor.*
8. Nelson was *overjoyed* at winning the essay contest.

PARTS OF SPEECH

Traditional English grammar classifies words into eight parts of speech: *nouns, pronouns, verbs, adjectives, adverbs, prepositions, conjunctions,* and *interjections.* This section discusses these categories as well as verbals, phrases, and clauses, which also serve as parts of speech.

Nouns

Nouns name persons, places, things, conditions, ideas, or qualities. Some nouns, called *proper nouns,* identify one-of-a-kind items such as the following:

France   Christmas
Pacific Ocean   Quebec

noun

Maurice Richard	Mona Lisa
Man Booker Prize	Stanley Cup
Canadarm	Wyandotte Corporation
Canadian Charter of Rights and Freedoms	Douglas College

Mount Everest, on the border of Tibet and Nepal, was named for Sir George Everest, an Englishman.

Common nouns name general classes or categories of items and include abstract, concrete, and collective nouns.

Abstract Nouns   An abstract noun names a condition, idea, or quality—something we can't see, feel, or otherwise experience with our five senses.

arrogance	harmony	sickness
envy	liberalism	understanding
fear	love	freedom

His *desire* to win caused him to cheat.

Mary felt great *loyalty* to her family.

Concrete Nouns   A concrete noun identifies something that we can experience with one or more of our senses.

man	desk	pillow	needle
bicycle	lemon	airplane	pan
building	piston	carton	smoke

The *air* was thin at the *peak* of the *mountain*.

The *hammer* had a broken *handle*.

Collective Nouns   A collective noun is singular in form but stands for a group or collection of items.

assembly	committee	crowd	flotilla	herd
bunch	congregation	delegation	gang	tribe
class	convoy	family	group	troop

The *jury* filed into the courtroom to announce its verdict.

The *flock* of geese settled onto the lake.

Usage Considerations   Good writing demands precise, potent nouns. If you carefully select your nouns, you can help sharpen your message. Ill-chosen nouns, on the other hand, suggest poor thinking. Note how the vague word *freedom* robs the following sentence of any specific meaning:

Our *freedom* needs to be protected.

What did the writer have in mind? Here are a few possibilities:

Our *right to free speech* needs to be protected.

Our *private behaviour* needs to be protected.

Our *national sovereignty* needs to be protected.

Even when meaning does not present problems, sentences can be sharpened by careful attention to nouns. Note the greater precision of the second sentence below:

Our *dog* has a savage bite.

Our *pit bull* has a savage bite.

EXERCISE

Identify the nouns in the following sentences:

1. Jeremy has undertaken the task of learning conversational German this summer.
2. Scrabble is a pleasant game to play on a cold, wet evening.
3. The chairperson will tell you about the decision of the committee.
4. The tree was covered with blossoms around which many bees buzzed.
5. My new apartment is in St. John's, Newfoundland.
6. His intelligence and humour make him a very popular lecturer.
7. A Rolls-Royce will provide decades of transportation for its owner.
8. Marcy Johnson jumped in her car, revved its engine, and roared off down the road.

Pronouns

Pronouns, which take the place of nouns in sentences, help you avoid the awkward repetition of nouns.

If Brad doesn't like the *book*, take *it* back to the library.

There are eight categories of pronouns: *personal, relative, interrogative, demonstrative, reflexive, intensive, indefinite,* and *reciprocal.*

Personal Pronouns   Personal pronouns refer to one or more clearly identified persons, places, or things.

Subjective	Objective	Possessive
I	me	my, mine
you	you	your, yours
he	him	his
she	her	her, hers
it	it	its
we	us	our, ours
you	you	your, yours
they	them	their, theirs

pro

Subjective pronouns serve as the subjects of sentences or clauses, objective pronouns serve as direct and indirect objects, and possessive pronouns show possession or ownership. *My, your, our,* and *their* always precede nouns and thus function as possessive adjectives. *His* and *its* may or may not precede nouns.

He bought a sport shirt. (pronoun as subject)

Donald saw *them.* (pronoun as direct object)

Simon lent *her* ten dollars. (pronoun as indirect object)

That car is *theirs.* (pronoun showing ownership)

Relative Pronouns　A relative pronoun relates a subordinate clause—a word group that has a subject and a predicate but does not express a complete idea—to a noun or pronoun, called an antecedent, in the main part of the sentence. The relative pronouns include the following:

who	whose	what	whoever	whichever
whom	which	that	whomever	whatever

Who in its various forms refers to people, *which* to things, and *that* to either people or things.

Mary Beth Cartwright, *who* was arrested last week for fraud, was Evansville's "Model Citizen" two years ago. (The antecedent of *who* is *Mary Beth Cartwright.*)

He took the electric razor, *which* needed a new cutting head, to the repair shop. (The antecedent of *which* is *electric razor.*)

David Bullock is someone *whom* we should definitely hire. (The antecedent of *whom* is *someone.*)

Montreal is a city *that* I've always wanted to visit. (The antecedent of *that* is *city.*)

Which typically introduces nonrestrictive clauses, that is, clauses that provide more information about whatever they modify.

The palace, *which* was in bad condition a century ago, is finally going to be restored. (Clause adds information about palace.)

That is typically used in other situations, especially to introduce restrictive clauses: those that distinguish the things they modify from others in the same class.

The used car *that* I bought last week at Honest Bill's has already broken down twice. (Clause distinguishes writer's used car from others.)

Interrogative Pronouns　Interrogative pronouns introduce questions. All of the relative pronouns except *that* also function as interrogative pronouns.

who	which	whoever	whichever
whom	what	whomever	whatever
whose			

What is the matter?

Who asked you?

Whatever do you mean?

When *what, which,* and *whose* are followed by nouns, they act as adjectives, not pronouns.

Which movie should we see?

Demonstrative Pronouns   As their name suggests, demonstrative pronouns point things out. There are four such pronouns:

this	these
that	those

This and its plural *these* identify recent or nearby things.

This is the play to see.

These are difficult times.

That and its plural *those* identify less recent or more distant things.

That is Mary's house across the road.

Those were very good peaches you had for sale last week.

Reflexive and Intensive Pronouns   A reflexive pronoun reverses the action of a verb, making the doer and the receiver of the action the same. An intensive pronoun lends emphasis to a noun or pronoun. The two sets of pronouns are identical.

myself	herself	ourselves
yourself	itself	yourselves
himself	oneself	themselves

My father cut *himself* while shaving. (reflexive pronoun)

The premier *himself* has asked me to undertake this mission. (intensive pronoun)

Don't substitute a reflexive pronoun for a personal pronoun.

| *Faulty* | Jill and *myself* are going to a movie. |
| *Revision* | Jill and *I* are going to a movie. |

| *Faulty* | Give the tickets to John and *myself*. |
| *Revision* | Give the tickets to John and *me*. |

pro

Sometimes you'll hear people say things like "He made it *hisself*," "They're only fooling *theirself*," or "They bought *theirselves* sodas." Such forms are nonstandard. Use "himself" and "themselves" instead.

Indefinite Pronouns   These pronouns refer to unidentified persons, places, or things. One group of indefinite pronouns consistently acts as pronouns:

anybody	everything	one
anyone	nobody	somebody
anything	no one	someone
everybody	nothing	something
everyone		

A second group functions as either pronouns or adjectives.

all	any	most	few	much
another	each	either	many	neither

Here are some examples:

Everyone is welcome. (indefinite pronoun)

Many are called, but *few* are chosen. (indefinite pronouns)

Many men but only a *few* women attend the Air Force Academy. (adjectives)

Pages 513–15 discusses indefinite pronouns as antecedents.

Reciprocal Pronouns   The two reciprocal pronouns show an interchange of action between two or more parties. *Each other* is used when two parties interact, *one another* when three or more do.

Pam and Patty accidentally gave *each other* the same thing for Christmas. (two persons)

The members of the football team joyfully embraced *one another* after their victory. (more than two persons)

Usage Considerations   Many students handle pronouns carelessly, damaging the clarity of their writing. Problems include letting the same pronoun stand for different nouns or using a pronoun where detailed, vivid language would be more effective. The following passage illustrates poor pronoun usage:

My brother loves fly-fishing. He thinks *it* is the only way to spend a summer weekend. In fact, whenever he's off work, he'll do *it*.

Rewritten as follows, the passage has been notably improved:

My brother loves fly-fishing. He thinks that *wading a stream and casting leisurely for trout* is the only way to spend a summer weekend. In fact, whenever he's off work, he *can be found up to his hips in water, offering his hand-tied flies to the waiting rainbow trout.*

EXERCISE *Identify each pronoun in the following sentences and indicate its type:*

1. This is the kind of movie that I like.
2. Everyone in the class came to the party she gave at term's end.
3. If you feel thirsty, pour yourself a glass of lemonade.
4. That is a terrible-looking chair. Who would buy it anyhow?
5. What do you think Sally and Bill bought each other for Christmas?
6. I myself will take the blame for anything that goes wrong with the experiment.
7. Don't ask me to change; I like myself just as I am.
8. The children splashed one another with water from the pool.

Verbs

A verb indicates action or existence: what something is, was, or will be. Verbs fall into three classes: *action verbs, linking verbs,* and *helping verbs.*

Action Verbs   As their name suggests, action verbs express action. Some action verbs are transitive, others intransitive. A transitive verb has a direct object that receives or results from the action and rounds out the meaning of the sentence.

The photographer *took* the picture.

Without the direct object, this sentence would not express a complete thought. In contrast, an *intransitive* verb requires no direct object to complete the meaning of the sentence.

Lee Ann *gasped* loudly.

Little Tommy Tucker *sings* for his supper.

Many action verbs can play both transitive or intransitive roles, depending on the sentences they are used in.

Kari *rode* her bicycle into town. (transitive verb)

Karl *rode* in the front seat of the car. (intransitive verb)

Linking Verbs   A linking verb shows existence—what something is, was, or will be—rather than action. Linking verbs are intransitive and tie their subjects to subject complements. Some subject complements are nouns or noun substitutes that rename their subjects. Others are adjectives that describe their subjects.

Ms. Davis *is* our new director. (Complement *director* renames subject *Ms. Davis.*)

The soup *was* lukewarm. (Complement *lukewarm* describes subject *soup.*)

The most common linking verbs are forms of the verb *to be (is, are, am, was, were, be, being, been).* Likewise, verbs such as *seem, become, appear, remain, feel, look, vbs*

smell, sound, and *taste* function as linking verbs when they do not indicate actual physical action. In such cases, they are followed by adjectives. Here is an example:

> Harry looked *angry.*

When such verbs do indicate physical action, they function as action verbs and are followed by adverbs.

> Harry looked *angrily* at the referee.

Helping Verbs Helping verbs accompany action or linking verbs, allowing them to express with great precision matters such as possibility, obligation, and time. Common helping verbs include the following:

has	been	had (to)
have	do	shall
had	does	will
am	did	going (to)
is	used (to)	about (to)
are	may	would
was	might	should
were	must	ought (to)
be	have (to)	can
being	has (to)	could

> I *should ask* my parents. (helping verb *should* with action verb *ask*)

> The driver *was being lifted* onto a stretcher. (helping verbs *was* and *being* with action verb *lifted*)

> You *have been* good. (helping verb *have* with linking verb *been*)

> The patient *will feel* better soon. (helping verb *will* with linking verb *feel*)

> We *might go* to Calgary next weekend. (helping verb *might* with action verb *go*)

Helping verbs usually appear next to the main verbs, but they don't have to.

> Ellen *will* undoubtedly *resign.*

Combinations of two or more verbs are called *verb phrases.*

Usage Considerations Energetic writing requires precise verbs. Don't take verbs for granted; revise them as necessary in order to strengthen a sentence. Note the improved precision of the second example sentence:

> I *gave* the maître d' a ten-dollar bill.

> I *slipped* the maître d' a ten-dollar bill.

EXERCISE   *Identify each verb in the following sentences and indicate its type:*

1. If Butch and Jim need transportation, my car will be available.
2. Please write your name on your quiz before you give it to me.
3. Marvin has been sitting in front of the TV all morning.
4. I will be watching the Toronto Raptors play tonight.
5. The movie offered lots of action, but the plot was poor.
6. Christine's assistance on this project has been invaluable.
7. William must have finished the yard work by now.
8. Teresa will probably be elected president of the club.

Principal Parts   Verbs change in form to show time (tense) distinctions. For every action verb, tenses are built from three principal parts: *present, past,* and *past participle.* The present is the principal part you would look up in the dictionary (*win, skip, go,* and so on). If the subject of a verb is a singular pronoun (*he, she, it*) or a singular noun, add an *s* or *es* to the dictionary form (*wins, skips, goes*). For most verbs, the past tense and past participle are identical.

	Present	**Past**	**Past Participle**
I, you, we, they	talk	talked	talked
He, she, it, Henry	talks	talked	talked
I, you, we, they	stand	stood	stood
He, she, it, the decision	stands	stood	stood

For most other verbs, the past tense and past participle are different.

	Present	**Past**	**Past Participle**
I, you, we, they	swim	swam	swum
He, she, it, the boy	swims	swam	swum
I, you, we, they	bite	bit	bitten
He, she, it, the dog	bites	bit	bitten

However, for a few verbs, the past tense and past participle are identical to the dictionary form.

	Present	**Past**	**Past Participle**
I, you, we, they	set	set	set
He, she, it	sets	set	set

If you're uncertain about the principal parts of a verb, check your dictionary.

Tense   There are six basic tenses: present, past, future, present perfect, past perfect, future perfect. They are formed from the principal parts of action and linking verbs, either alone or combined with helping verbs.

The *present tense* is formed from the present principal part of the main verb. It shows present condition and general or habitual action, indicates permanent truths, tells about past events in the historical present, and sometimes denotes action at some definite future time.

Helen *looks* beautiful in her new gown. (present condition)

John *works* on the eighteenth floor. (general action)

I *brush* my teeth each morning. (habitual action)

The earth *rotates* on its axis. (permanent truth)

On November 11, 1918, the guns *fall* silent, and World War I *comes* to an end. (historical present)

Monday, I *begin* my new job. (future action)

The *past tense* is based on the past principal part of the verb. The past tense shows that a condition existed or an action was completed in the past. The verb tense leaves the time indefinite, but surrounding words may specify it.

Paul *was* angry with his noisy neighbours. (past condition, time indefinite)

Sandy *received* a long letter yesterday. (past action, time specified by *yesterday*)

The *future tense* combines *shall* or *will* and the present principal part of the main verb. It indicates that a condition will exist or an action will take place in the future.

You *will feel* better after a good night's sleep. (future condition)

I *shall attend* the concert next week. (future action)

The *present perfect* tense is formed with *has* or *have* and the past participle of the main verb. It shows that a past condition or action, or its effect, continues until the present time.

The players *have been* irritable since they lost the championship game. (Condition continues until present.)

Jean *has driven* a United Parcel Service truck for five years. (Action continues until present.)

William *has repaired* the snow blower. (Effect of action continues until present although the action itself was completed in the past.)

The *past perfect* tense combines *had* and the past participle of the main verb. It refers to a past condition or action that was completed before another past condition or action.

He *had been* in the army two years when the war ended. (Past perfect condition occurred first.)

Vivian moved into the house that she *had built* the summer before. (Past perfect action occurred first.)

The *future perfect* tense is formed from the verbs *shall have* or *will have* plus the past participle of the main verb. It shows that a condition or an action will have been completed at some time in the future. Surrounding words specify time.

Our sales manager *will have been* with the company ten years next July. (Condition will end.)

By the end of this year, I *shall have written* the great Canadian novel. (Action will be completed.)

Each of these basic tenses has a *progressive tense* that indicates action in progress. The progressive tense always includes some form of the verb *to be* followed by a present participle, a verb that ends in *-ing*.

Present progressive	I am running.
Past progressive	I was running.
Future progressive	I will be running.
Present perfect progressive	I have been running.
Past perfect progressive	I had been running.
Future perfect progressive	I will have been running.

Page 521 discusses unwarranted shifts in tense and their correction.

Voice Transitive verbs have two voices: active and passive. A verb is in the *active voice* when the subject carries out the action named by the verb.

Barry *planned* a picnic. (Subject *Barry* performs action.)

A verb is in the *passive voice* when the subject receives the action. The performer may be identified in an accompanying phrase or go unmentioned.

A picnic *was planned* by Barry. (The phrase *by Barry* identifies the performer.)

The picnic *was cancelled*. (The performer goes unmentioned.)

A passive construction always uses a form of *to be* and the past participle of an action verb. Like other constructions, the passive may show past, present, or future time.

Amy *is paid* handsomely for her investment advice. (present tense)

I *was warned* by a sound truck that a tornado was nearby. (past tense)

I *will be sent* to Ghana soon by the Canada Corps. (future tense)

I *have been awarded* a sizeable research grant. (present perfect tense)

The city *had been shelled* heavily before the infantry moved in. (past perfect tense)

By the end of this month, the site for our second factory *will have been chosen*. (future perfect tense)

vbs

To convert a sentence from the passive to the active voice, make the performer the subject, the original subject the direct object, and drop the form of *to be*.

The treaty *was signed* by the general. (passive)

The general *signed* the treaty. (active)

Technical and scientific writing commonly uses the passive voice to explain processes since its flat, impersonal tone adds an air of scientific objectivity and authority. However, other kinds of writing avoid the passive voice except when it is desirable to conceal the one performing the action or when the action is more significant than the actor.

EXERCISE *Identify each verb in the following sentences, indicate its tense, and note any use of the passive voice:*

1. They will have arrived in Tokyo by this evening.
2. This TV program is relayed to Europe by satellite.
3. The Krause Corporation's new headquarters building will be dedicated June 30.
4. The school psychologist was asked whether she had any explanation for Tim's odd behaviour.
5. We have been told we face yet another 15 percent staff cutback.
6. Nancy bought a Garth Brooks CD.
7. The Northrups will start their vacation tomorrow.
8. Leslie works in the sales department of IBM.

Mood   The mood of a verb shows whether the writer regards a statement as a

1. fact
2. command or request
3. wish, possibility, condition contrary to fact, or the like.

English has three moods: the indicative, imperative, and subjunctive. A sentence in the *indicative mood* states a real or supposed fact or asks a question.

Nancy *graduates* from high school tomorrow.

We *lived* in Oakville when Rachel was born.

He *had been* a sailor during the war.

Has Joe *asked* anyone to the prom yet?

Most verbs are used in the indicative mood.

A sentence in the *imperative mood* delivers a command or makes a request.

Leave the room immediately! (command)

Please *turn* the CD player down. (request)

The subject of a sentence in the imperative mood is always *you*. Although ordinarily unstated, the subject sometimes appears in the sentence.

You leave the room immediately!

The *subjunctive mood* is also used

1. in *if, as if,* and *as though* clauses to express a wish, a possibility, or an action or a condition contrary to fact
2. in *that* clauses expressing orders, demands, requests, resolutions, proposals, or motions
3. with modal auxiliaries to express wishes, probability, possibility, permission, requirements, recommendations, suggestions, and conditions contrary to fact.

To express a present or future wish, possibility, condition, or action in an *if, as if,* or *as though* clause, use *were* with any personal pronoun or noun serving as the subject of the clause.

If only Stan *were* less gullible! (present wish contrary to fact)

Even if Kay *were* to explain, Mary wouldn't believe her. (future possibility)

Arthur is behaving as if he *were* a millionaire. (present condition contrary to fact)

To express a wish, possibility, or condition contrary to past facts, use *had been* or *had* plus the past participle of an action verb.

If the engine *had been lubricated,* the bearing wouldn't have burned out. (past condition contrary to fact)

Alice looked as if she *had lost* her best friend. (condition expressed in clause occurs before action of verb *looked*)

When writing *that* clauses expressing orders, demands, requests, resolutions, proposals, or motions, use *be* or the present plural form of an action verb.

I move that they *be* rewarded for their bravery.

The group proposed that Margaret *go* to the scene of the accident and *inspect* it personally.

In other *that* clauses, use the appropriate indicative form of the verb.

I know that they *were* rewarded for their bravery.

The group believed that Margaret *had gone* to the scene of the accident and *inspected* it personally.

The modal auxiliaries include the helping verbs *can, could, may, might, must, shall, will, would, should,* and *ought to*. The examples below illustrate the meanings they can express.

adj

1. Wishes *(could, would)*

   I wish I *could* shimmy like my sister Kate.
   The Conservatives wish the Liberals *would* go away and vice versa.

2. Probability *(should)*

   Because I've studied diligently, I *should* do better on my next chemistry test.

3. Possibility *(may, might, can, could)*

   Low inflation *could* cause our stock market to soar.
   I *might* stay up to watch the eclipse of the moon tonight.

4. Permission *(can, may)*

   The public *can* use these tennis courts every afternoon.
   You *may* leave as soon as you've finished filing these folders.

5. Requirements *(must)*

   The landlord has raised our rent again; we *must* find another apartment.

6. Recommendations, suggestions *(should, ought to)*

   Randy *should* see a doctor about his chest pains.
   All of us *ought* to exercise regularly.

7. Conditions contrary to fact *(could)*

   If only I *could* live my life over!

EXERCISE *For each of the following sentences, identify the mood as indicative (IND), imperative (IMP), or subjunctive (SUB):*

1. The next regular meeting should be postponed for a week.
2. Hot chocolate is an excellent bedtime drink.
3. Sally should learn to curb her sharp tongue.
4. Tell me all about last night's movie.
5. Someone in the crowd shrieked loudly at the sudden thunderclap.
6. If I were boss here, I'd raise everybody's wages.
7. The latest drop in interest rates should spur consumer spending.
8. Don't ever use that tone of voice to me again.

Adjectives

An adjective *modifies* a noun or pronoun by describing it, limiting it, or otherwise making its meaning more precise.

The *brass* candlestick stood next to the *fragile* vase. (*Brass* modifies *candlestick*, and *fragile* modifies *vase*.)

The cat is *long-haired* and *sleek*. (*Long-haired* and *sleek* modify *cat*.)

There are three general categories of adjectives: limiting, descriptive, and proper.

Limiting Adjectives   A limiting adjective identifies or points out the noun or pronoun it modifies. It may indicate number or quantity. Several categories of pronouns can serve as limiting adjectives, as can numbers and nouns.

Whose briefcase is on the table? (interrogative adjective)

The couple *whose* car was stolen called the police. (relative adjective)

This restaurant has the best reputation for gourmet food. (demonstrative adjective)

Some people have no social tact at all. (indefinite adjective)

Sally swerved *her* car suddenly to avoid an oncoming truck. (possessive adjective)

Three people entered the lecture hall late. (number as adjective)

The *schoolgirl* look is fashionable this year. (noun as adjective)

Descriptive Adjectives   A descriptive adjective names a quality, characteristic, or condition of a noun or pronoun. Two or more of these adjectives, members of the largest category of adjectives, may modify the same noun or pronoun.

The *yellow* submarine belongs to the Beatles.

He applied *clear* lacquer to the tabletop.

The *slim, sophisticated* model glided onto the runway.

The child was *active, happy,* and *polite.*

Proper Adjectives   A proper adjective is derived from a proper noun and is always capitalized.

Harwell is a *Shakespearean* actor.

Articles as Adjectives   Articles appear immediately before nouns and can therefore be considered adjectives. There are three articles in English: *a, an,* and *the. The* points to a specific item; *a* and *an* do not. *A* precedes words beginning with consonant sounds; *an* precedes words with vowel sounds, making pronunciation easier.

The right word at *the* right moment can save a friendship. (Definite articles suggest there is one right word and one right moment.)

A right word can save a friendship. (Indefinite article suggests there are several right words.)

I think I'd like *an* apple with my lunch. (No particular apple is specified.)

Sometimes the definite article refers to a class of items.

> *The* tiger is fast becoming an endangered species.

Context shows whether such a sentence refers to particular items or entire classes.

Comparison with Adjectives   Adjectives may be used to show comparison. When two things are compared, shorter adjectives usually add *-er* and longer adjectives add *more.* When three or more things are compared, shorter adjectives usually add *-est* and longer ones add *most.*

> John is *taller* than Pete. (short adjective comparing two people)
>
> Sandra seems *more cheerful* than Jill today. (long adjective comparing two people)
>
> John is the *tallest* of the three brothers. (short adjective comparing three people)
>
> Sandra is the *most cheerful* girl in the class. (longer adjective comparing more than three people)

Some adjectives, like the examples below, have irregular forms for comparisons.

> good—better—best
>
> bad—worse—worst

Don't use the *-est* form of the shorter adjective for comparing just two things.

> *Faulty*   This is the *smallest* of the two castles.

Instead, use the *-er* form.

> *Revision*   This is the *smaller* of the two castles.

Position of Adjectives   Most adjectives come immediately before the words they modify. In a few set expressions (for example, heir *apparent*), the adjective immediately follows the word it modifies. Similarly, adjective pairs sometimes appear in a follow-up position for added emphasis (The rapids, *swift* and *dangerous,* soon capsized the raft). Sometimes adjectives also serve as subject complements and follow their subjects (The puppy was *friendly*).

Usage Considerations   Some students overuse adjectives, especially in descriptions, but most underuse them. Review your sentences carefully to see where adding or cutting adjectives can increase the impact of your writing.

> My Buick is the talk of my friends.
>
> My *old, dilapidated, rusty, fenderless 1970* Buick is the talk of my friends.
>
> My *rusty, fenderless 1970* Buick is the talk of my friends.

The first sentence lacks adjectives that show why the car is discussed. The second sentence overcorrects this fault by including two adjectives that repeat the information provided by the others. The final sentence strikes the proper balance.

EXERCISE *Identify the adjectives in the following sentences:*

1. Tom is a very unhappy person.
2. Paul has an aunt who writes long, chatty letters to him regularly.
3. Sean ate an English muffin and drank a cup of black coffee.
4. Barton has an unusual sideboard in his dining room.
5. The tired carpenter tossed his tools into the red truck and drove home.
6. After buying a few gifts, Linda and Audrey took a slow stroll around the resort town.
7. Harvey ate three hamburgers and four helpings of salad at the picnic.
8. From the hilltop, the view was beautiful.

Adverbs

An adverb modifies a verb, an adjective, another adverb, or a whole sentence. Adverbs generally answer questions such as "How?" "When?" "Where?" "How often?" and "To what extent?"

The floodwaters receded *very* slowly. (Adverb modifies adverb and answers the question "How?")

My sister will visit me *tomorrow.* (Adverb modifies verb and answers the question "When?")

The coach walked *away* from the bench. (Adverb modifies verb and answers the question "Where?")

The tire is *too* worn to be safe. (Adverb modifies adjective and answers the question "To what extent?")

The teller is *frequently* late for work. (Adverb modifies adjective and answers the question "How often?")

Unfortunately, the game was cancelled because of rain. (The adverb modifies the whole sentence but does not answer any question.)

Formation of Adverbs   Most adverbs are formed by adding *-ly* to adjectives.

The wind is *restless.* (*Restless* is an adjective modifying *wind.*)

He walked *restlessly* around the room. (*Restlessly* is an adverb modifying *walked.*)

However, many common adverbs (*almost, never, quite, soon, then, there,* and *too*) lack *-ly* endings.

I *soon* realized that pleasing my boss was impossible.

This movie is *too* gruesome for my taste.

adv

Furthermore, some words such as *better, early, late, hard, little, near, only, straight,* and *wrong* do double duty as either adjectives or adverbs.

> We must have taken a *wrong* turn. (*Wrong* is an adjective modifying the noun *turn.*)

> Where did I go *wrong*? (*Wrong* is an adverb modifying the verb *go.*)

Comparison with Adverbs   Like adjectives, adverbs can show comparison. When two things are compared, adverbs add *more.* When three or more things are compared, *most* is used.

> Harold works *more* efficiently than Don. (adverb comparing two people)

> Of all the people in the shop, Harold works the *most* efficiently. (adverb comparing more than two people)

Some adverbs, like some adjectives, use irregular forms for comparisons.

> well—better—best

> much—more—most

Position of Adverbs   Adverbs are more movable than any other part of speech. Usually, adverbs that modify adjectives and other adverbs appear next to them to avoid confusion.

> Her *especially* fine tact makes her a welcome guest at any party. (Adverb *especially* modifies adjective *fine.*)

> The novel was *very* badly written. (Adverb *very* modifies adverb *badly.*)

Adverbs that modify verbs, however, can often be shifted around in their sentences without causing changes in meaning.

> *Quickly,* he slipped through the doorway.

> He slipped *quickly* through the doorway.

> He slipped through the doorway *quickly.*

Usage Considerations   You can often sharpen the meaning of a sentence by adding a well-chosen adverb.

> The student squirmed in his chair.

> The student squirmed *anxiously* in his chair.

In this example, including the adverb *anxiously* in the second sentence shows the mental state of the student. Be careful, however, not to overuse adverbs as they can bog down your writing.

EXERCISE   *Identify the adverbs in the following sentences:*

1. Harold is late more frequently than any other member of the crew.

2. After dinner, the children went outdoors and played noisily.

3. The doctor told Albert his illness, though quite serious, would respond well to treatment.

4. Lucy stepped quickly to the door and listened intently to the howling wind.

5. I often wish I could study less hard without my grades suffering.

6. The pirate ship glided swiftly and silently toward the sleeping town.

7. The tired, perspiring runner staggered wearily across the finish line.

8. You'll have to work very fast to keep up with Jody.

Prepositions

A preposition links its object—a noun or noun substitute—to some other word in the sentence and shows a relationship between them. The relationship is often one of location, time, means, or reason or purpose. The word group containing the preposition and its object makes up a prepositional phrase.

The new insulation *in* the attic keeps my house much warmer now. (Preposition *in* links object *attic* to *insulation* and shows location.)

We have postponed the meeting *until* tomorrow. (Preposition *until* links object *tomorrow* to *postponed* and shows time.)

The tourists travelled *by* automobile. (Preposition *by* links object *automobile* to *travelled* and shows means.)

Warren swims *for* exercise. (Preposition *for* links object *exercise* to *swims* and shows reason or purpose.)

The following list includes the most common prepositions, some of which consist of two or more words:

above	beside	in	out of
after	between	instead of	over
against	by	into	since
along with	by reason of	like	through
among	contrary to	near	to
at	during	next to	toward
because of	except	of	under
before	for	on	with
below	from	onto	without

Many of these combine to form additional prepositions: *except for, in front of, by way of, on top of,* and the like.

Certain prepositions sometimes occur in close association with certain verbs, forming verb units with altered meanings. When this happens, we call the prepositions *verb particles.* Here is an example:

The instructor let Jeff make *up* the test.

Note the great difference between the meaning of the foregoing sentence and "The instructor let Jeff make the test."

Usage Considerations It is easy to use a small group of prepositions over and over in your writing. This habit often results in imprecise or misleading sentences. To avoid this problem, think carefully about your choice of prepositions as you revise. Read the following example:

He walked *by* the railway tracks on his way home.

Note that two interpretations are possible.

He walked *along* the railway tracks on his way home.

He walked *past* the railway tracks on his way home.

Clearly you would use the preposition that conveyed your intended meaning.

EXERCISE *Identify the prepositions and their objects in the following sentences:*

1. I finally finished waxing the car just before the rainstorm.
2. Aloe lotion will give you instant relief from sunburn.
3. For reasons of security, this gate must be kept locked at all times.
4. Shortly after dark, the group arrived at the camp.
5. Across the street, George was working on his roof.
6. At the end of the concert, everyone in the hall stood and applauded.
7. Helen sprinkled the roast with a blend of herbs.
8. Because of an error, all of the information in the computer was lost.

Conjunctions

Conjunctions serve as connectors, linking parts of sentences or whole sentences. These connectors fall into three groups: coordinating conjunctions, subordinating conjunctions, and conjunctive adverbs.

Coordinating Conjunctions Coordinating conjunctions connect terms of equal grammatical importance: words, word groups, and simple sentences. These conjunctions can occur singly *(and, but, or, nor, for, yet, so)* or in pairs called correlative conjunctions *(either—or, neither—nor, both—and,* and *not only—but also)*. The elements that follow correlative conjunctions must be parallel, that is, have the same grammatical form.

Tom *and* his cousin are opening a video arcade. (Coordinating conjunction connects nouns.)

Shall I serve the tea in the living room *or* on the veranda? (Coordinating conjunction connects phrases.)

I am going to Europe this summer, *but* Marjorie is staying home. (Coordinating conjunction connects simple sentences.)

Amy *not only* teaches English *but also* writes novels. (Correlative conjunctions connect parallel predicates.)

You can study nursing *either* at the University of B.C. *or* at Kwantlen University College. (Correlative conjunctions connect parallel phrases.)

Friendship is *both* pleasure *and* pain. (Correlative conjunctions connect parallel nouns.)

Subordinating Conjunctions   Like relative pronouns, subordinating conjunctions introduce subordinate clauses, relating them to independent clauses, which can stand alone as complete sentences. Examples of subordinating conjunctions include *because, as if, even though, since, so that, whereas,* and *whenever.*

I enjoyed the TV program *because* it was so well acted. (Conjunction connects *it was so well acted* to rest of sentence.)

Whenever you're ready, we can begin dinner. (Conjunction connects *you're ready* to rest of sentence.)

Conjunctive Adverbs   These connectors resemble both conjunctions and adverbs. Like conjunctions, they serve as linking devices between elements of equal rank. Like adverbs, they function as modifiers, showing such things as similarity, contrast, result or effect, addition, emphasis, time, and example.

The following list groups the most common conjunctive adverbs according to function:

Similarity: likewise, similarly

Contrast: however, nevertheless, on the contrary, on the other hand, otherwise

Result or effect: accordingly, as a result, consequently, hence, therefore, thus

Addition: also, furthermore, in addition, in the first place, moreover

Emphasis or clarity: in fact, in other words, indeed, that is

Time: afterward, later, meanwhile, subsequently

Example: for example, for instance, to illustrate

The job will require you to travel a great deal; however, the salary is excellent.

Sean cares nothing for clothes; *in fact,* all of his socks have holes in their toes.

phr

Usage Considerations   You can add variety to your writing by varying the conjunctions you use. If you consistently rely on the conjunction *because,* try substituting *as* or *since.* Likewise, you may periodically replace *if* with *provided that.* When you have choppy sentences, try combining them by using a conjunction.

> You can buy smoked salmon at Sally's Seafoods. You can buy it at Daane's Thriftland as well.

> You can buy smoked salmon *either* at Sally's Seafoods *or* at Daane's Thriftland.

The revision is much smoother than the original sentence pair.

Interjections

An interjection is an exclamatory word used to gain attention or to express strong feeling. It has no grammatical connection to the rest of the sentence. An interjection is followed by an exclamation point or a comma.

> *Hey!* Watch how you're driving! (strong interjection)

> *Oh,* is the party over already? (mild interjection)

EXERCISE   *Identify the coordinating conjunctions (CC), subordinating conjunctions (SC), conjunctive adverbs (CA), and interjections (I) in the following sentences:*

1. The car was not only dented but also dirty.
2. While Roger was at the movies, his brother bought a model airplane.
3. Heavens, what's all the fuss about anyhow?
4. Either the Coles or the Thurlows will drive us to the airport.
5. Although they felt under the weather, Marie and Sally attended the dance.
6. The candidate's views matched those of his audience; consequently, he received warm applause.
7. Neither William nor his brother has ever travelled out of the province.
8. Sandra is no academic slouch; indeed, she was valedictorian of her high school class.

PHRASES AND CLAUSES

Phrases

A phrase is a group of words that lacks a subject and a predicate and serves as a single part of speech. This section discusses four basic kinds of phrases: *prepositional phrases, participial phrases, gerund phrases,* and *infinitive phrases.* The last three are based on participles, gerunds, and infinitives, verb forms known as verbals. A fifth type of phrase, the verb phrase, consists of sets of two or more verbs (*has fixed, had been sick, will have been selected,* and the like).

Prepositional Phrases   A prepositional phrase consists of a preposition, one or more objects, and any associated words. These phrases serve as adjectives or adverbs.

> The picture *over the mantel* was my mother's. (prepositional phrase as adjective)
>
> He bought ice skates *for himself.* (prepositional phrase as adverb modifying verb)
>
> The toddler was afraid *of the dog.* (prepositional phrase as adverb modifying adjective)
>
> Our visitors arrived late *in the day.* (prepositional phrase as adverb modifying another adverb)

Frequently, prepositional phrases occur in series. Sometimes they form chains in which each phrase modifies the object of the preceding phrase. At other times some or all of the phrases may modify the verb or verb phrase.

> John works *in a clothing store / on Main Street / during the summer.*

Here the first and third phrases serve as adverbs modifying the verb works and answering the questions "Where?" and "When?" while the second phrase serves as an adjective modifying store and answering the question "Where?"

On occasion, especially in questions, a preposition may be separated from its object, making the phrase difficult to find.

> Dr. Perry is the person *whom* I've been looking *for.*
>
> *What* are you shouting *about?*

Participial Phrases   A participial phrase consists of a participle plus associated words. Participles are verb forms that function as adjectives or adverbs when used in participial phrases. A present participle ends in *-ing* and indicates an action currently being carried out. A past participle ends in *-ed, -en, -e, -n, -d,* or *-t* and indicates some past action.

> The chef *preparing dinner* trained in France. (present participial phrase as adjective)
>
> The background, *sketched in lightly,* accented the features of the woman in the painting. (past participial phrase as adjective)
>
> She left *whistling a jolly melody.* (present participial phrase as adverb)

A perfect participial phrase consists of *having* or *having been* plus a past participle and any associated words. Like a past participial phrase, it indicates a past action.

Having alerted the townspeople about the tornado, the sound truck returned to the city garage. (perfect participial phrase)

Having been alerted to the tornado, the townspeople sought shelter in their basements. (perfect participial phrase)

Some participial phrases that modify persons or things distinguish them from others in the same class. These phrases are written without commas. Other phrases provide more information about the persons or things they modify and are set off with commas.

The man *fixing my car* is a master mechanic. (Phrase distinguishes man fixing car from other men.)

Mr. Welsh, *fatigued by the tennis game,* rested in the shade. (Phrase provides more information about Mr. Welsh.)

Gerund Phrases   A gerund phrase consists of a gerund and the words associated with it. Like present participles, gerunds are verb forms that end in *-ing.* However, unlike participles, they function as nouns rather than as adjectives or adverbs.

Kathryn's hobby is *collecting stamps.* (gerund phrase as subject complement)

Kathryn's hobby, *collecting stamps,* has made her many friends. (gerund phrase as appositive)

He devoted every spare moment to *overhauling the car.* (gerund phrase as object of preposition)

Infinitive Phrases   An infinitive phrase consists of the present principal part of a verb preceded by *to (to fix, to eat),* together with any accompanying words. These phrases serve as adjectives, adverbs, and nouns.

This looks like a good place *to plant the shrub.* (infinitive phrase as adjective)

Lenore worked *to earn money for tuition.* (infinitive phrase as adverb)

My goal is *to have my own business some day.* (infinitive phrase as noun)

Gerunds can often be substituted for infinitives and vice versa.

To repair this fender will cost two hundred dollars. (infinitive phrase as subject)

Repairing this fender will cost two hundred dollars. (gerund phrase as subject)

At times the *to* in an infinitive may be omitted following verbs such as *make, dare, let,* and *help.*

Kristin didn't dare *(to) move* a muscle.

The psychiatrist helped me *(to) overcome* my fear of flying.

Verbals Not in Phrases   Participles, gerunds, and infinitives can function as nouns, adjectives, or adverbs, even when they are not parts of phrases.

That *sunbathing* woman is a well-known model. (participle as adjective)

Dancing is fine exercise. (gerund)

The children want *to play*. (infinitive as noun)

If you're looking for a job, Sally is the person *to see*. (infinitive as adjective)

I'm prepared *to resign*. (infinitive as adverb)

Usage Considerations   Phrases can often help clarify or develop the information in a sentence.

Original	My brother is fishing.
Revision	My brother is fishing *for trout just below Barnes Dam on Sidewinder Creek.* (prepositional phrases added)
Original	The boat barely made shore.
Revision	The boat, *listing heavily and leaking badly,* barely made shore. (participial phrases added)

However, to avoid ponderous sentences, don't weigh them down with phrases, as in the following example:

My brother is fishing for trout just below Barnes Dam on Sidewinder Creek *near Perry Pass in the Rocky Mountains.*

EXERCISE   *Identify the italicized phrases as prepositional, participial, gerund, or infinitive and tell whether each is used as a noun, an adjective, or an adverb.*

1. *Walking the dog in the rain* made me grouchy for the rest of the day.
2. *To ride the Orient Express* was Marian's fondest ambition.
3. *Opening the door a tiny crack,* Michelle stared with horror at the scene before her.
4. Sue Ellen works *in a grocery store* during the summer.
5. Tom couldn't decide which refrigerator *to buy for his mother.*
6. Old-fashioned in every way, Chester shaves himself *with a straight razor.*
7. Dave loves *flying a crop duster.*
8. *Glaring angrily at the class,* the teacher shouted for silence.

Clauses

A clause is a word group that includes a subject and a predicate. An *independent clause,* sometimes called a main clause, expresses a complete thought and can

cl

function as a simple sentence. A *subordinate clause,* or dependent clause, cannot stand by itself. Subordinate clauses may serve as nouns, adjectives, or adverbs.

Noun Clauses   A noun clause can serve in any of the ways that ordinary nouns can.

> *What the neighbour told John* proved to be incorrect. (noun clause as subject)

> The woman asked *when the bus left for Sherbrooke.* (noun clause as direct object)

> I'll give a reward to *whoever returns my billfold.* (noun clause as object of preposition *to*)

Noun clauses normally begin with one of the following words:

Relative Pronouns		Subordinating Conjunctions
who	whoever	when
whom	whomever	why
whose	that	where
what	whatever	how
which	whichever	whether

The relative pronoun *that* is sometimes omitted from the beginning of a clause that acts as a direct object.

> Dr. Kant thinks *(that) he knows everything.*

If a clause is serving as a noun, you can replace it with the word *something* or *someone,* and the sentence will still make sense.

> Dr. Kant thinks *something.*

If the clause is serving as an adjective or an adverb, making the substitution turns the sentence into nonsense.

> The person *who wins the lottery* will receive two million dollars.

> The person *someone* will receive two million dollars.

Adjective Clauses   Like ordinary adjectives, adjective clauses modify nouns and noun substitutes.

> Give me one reason *why you feel the way you do.* (Adjective clause modifies noun.)

> I'll hire anyone *that Dr. Stone recommends.* (Adjective clause modifies pronoun.)

Generally, adjective clauses begin with one of the following words:

Relative Pronouns	Subordinating Conjunctions
who	when
whom	where
whose	why

what	after
which	before
that	

Sometimes the word that introduces the clause can be omitted.

> The chair *(that) we ordered last month* has just arrived. (pronoun *that* omitted but understood)

> The man *(whom) we were talking to* is a movie producer. (pronoun *whom* omitted but understood)

Sometimes, too, a preposition comes ahead of the introductory pronoun.

> The grace *with which Nelson danced* made the onlookers envious.

An adjective clause may be restrictive and distinguish whatever it modifies from others in the same class, or it may be nonrestrictive and provide more information about whatever it modifies.

> Flora wiped up the cereal *that the baby had spilled.* (restrictive clause)

> Harriet Thomas, *who was born in Saskatchewan,* now lives in Alberta. (nonrestrictive clause)

As these examples show, restrictive clauses are not set off with commas, but nonrestrictive clauses are.

Adverb Clauses   These clauses modify verbs, adjectives, adverbs, and sentences, answering the same questions that ordinary adverbs do.

> You may go *whenever you wish.* (Adverb clause modifies verb.)

> Sandra looked paler *than I had ever seen her look before.* (Adverb clause modifies adjective.)

> Darryl shouted loudly *so that the rescue party could hear him.* (Adverb clause modifies adverb.)

> *Unless everyone cooperates,* this plan will never succeed. (Adverb clause modifies whole sentence.)

The word or word group that introduces an adverb clause is always a subordinating conjunction. Here are the most common of these conjunctions, grouped according to the questions they answer.

> *When?* after, as, as soon as, before, since, until, when, whenever, while
>
> *Where?* where, wherever
>
> *How?* as if, as though
>
> *Why?* as, because, now that, since, so that
>
> *Under what conditions?* although, if, once, provided that, though, unless
>
> *To what extent?* than

Occasionally in an adverb clause, the omission of one or more words won't hurt its meaning. Such a construction is called an *elliptical clause.*

While (he was) making a sandwich, Garth hummed softly. (*he was* omitted but understood)

Unlike noun and adjective clauses, adverb clauses can often be moved about in their sentences.

Garth hummed *softly while (he was) making a sandwich.*

Usage Considerations Like phrases, clauses can help develop sentences as well as smooth out choppiness.

Original	The old grandfather clock ticked loudly through the night.
Revision	The old grandfather clock *that my great-aunt gave me before she died* ticked loudly through the night. (Clause adds information.)
Original	The chemistry professor insisted on lab safety. He had been hurt in a lab explosion the previous year.
Revision	The chemistry professor, *who had been hurt in a lab explosion the previous year,* insisted on lab safety. (Clause adds smoothness.)

To avoid clumsiness, avoid overloaded sentences like the one below:

The old grandfather clock that my great-aunt gave me before she died *and that I took with me to England when my company transferred me there for two years* ticked loudly through the night.

EXERCISE *Identify the italicized clauses as noun, adjective, or adverb.*

1. Why do Bill's parents always give him *whatever he wants?*
2. Steve pitched *as if a big-league scout were watching him.*
3. Gary is the only golfer *who putted well today.*
4. The dog barked loudly *because he was hungry.*
5. *Why anyone would want to skydive* is beyond me.
6. The secretary *Julie hired last month* has already received a raise.
7. I can't believe *that Beth has to work all weekend.*
8. Square dancing is an activity *that millions enjoy.*

Coordination and Subordination

Coordination and subordination are ways to rank ideas in sentences. Coordination makes ideas equal; subordination makes them unequal. To understand coordination and subordination, you need to know about four kinds of sentences: simple, compound, complex, and compound–complex.

Simple Sentences A simple sentence has one subject and one predicate. Some simple sentences consist merely of a single noun and a single verb.

> Millicent shouted.

Others can include elements such as compound subjects, compound verbs, direct objects, indirect objects, and subject complements.

> Jim and Sue have bought a car. *(compound subject, direct object)*

> Lucretia Borgia smiled and mixed her guests a cocktail. *(compound verb, indirect object, direct object)*

> Autumn is a sad season. *(subject complement)*

Most simple sentences are rather short and easy to understand. This trimness can add punch to your writing, but it can also make your writing sound childish and may waste words.

> The audience was young and friendly. It was responsive. It cheered for each speaker.

Combined into a single simple sentence, the information is easier to follow and more interesting to read:

> The young, friendly, responsive audience cheered for each speaker.

Compound Sentences A compound sentence contains two or more independent clauses, each holding the same (coordinate) rank. As a result, the idea in the first clause receives the same emphasis as the idea in the second. In some cases, a comma and a coordinating conjunction *(and, but, or, nor, for, yet, so)* link successive clauses.

> Name the baby Huey, *or* I'll cut you out of my will

> The audience was young, friendly, and responsive, *so* it cheered for each speaker.

In others, a semicolon and a conjunctive adverb *(for example, however, in fact, likewise, meanwhile, instead,* and the like) furnish the connection.

> Tod wants to see the play; *in fact,* he's talked about it for weeks.

> Today, many young women do not rush into marriage and motherhood; *instead,* they spend several years establishing careers.

Finally, a writer may omit any connecting word and separate the clauses with a semicolon.

> The sky grew pitch black; the wind died; an ominous quiet hung over the whole city.

crd

> Be sure to read this Robertson Davies novel; it shows the ramifications of a single small event.

As the preceding sentences show, compound sentences allow writers to express simple relationships among simple ideas. However, such sentences have one important limitation: It is impossible to highlight one particular idea. To do this, we need to use complex sentences.

Complex Sentences   A complex sentence has one independent clause and one or more dependent clauses. Relegating an idea to a dependent clause shows that the writer wishes it to receive less emphasis than the idea in the main clause.

> *Because the young, friendly audience was responsive,* it cheered for each speaker.

> *After the ball was over,* Arthur collapsed on the sofa.

> *Once they had reached the lakeshore,* the campers found a level spot *where they could pitch their tent.*

Unlike compound sentences, complex ones allow writers to vary the emphasis of ideas.

> While I watered the grass, I discussed stock options with Liz.

> I watered the grass while I discussed stock options with Liz.

The first sentence emphasizes the talk with Liz, the second watering the lawn. By shifting emphasis a writer can change the meaning of a sentence.

> *While his bicycle was damaged,* Pat walked to work.

> *While Pat walked to work,* his bicycle was damaged.

Furthermore, complex sentences signal *how* ideas relate. Note the various relationships in the following sentences:

> *Because she was swimming well,* Millicent did 200 laps today. *(reason)*

> The CN Tower is taller *than the Empire State Building. (extent)*

> Ms. Yoshira is the executive *for whom I am working. (relationship between persons)*

Compound–Complex Sentences   This type of sentence features two or more independent clauses and one or more dependent clauses. Here are two examples with the dependent clauses italicized:

> Ms. Harris works as an investment manager, and Mr. Williams, *who lives next door to her,* owns a jewellery store.

> *If you are to communicate properly,* your thoughts must be clear and correct; thoughts are wasted *when language is muddled.*

With compound–complex sentences writers can present more intricate relationships than with other sentences. In the following example, three sentences—one compound and two simple—have been rewritten as a compound–complex sentence. Notice how subordination improves the compactness and smoothness of the final version.

Mary hated to be seen in ugly clothing, but she wore an ugly dress with red polka dots. She had received the dress as a Christmas present. Her Aunt Ida had given it to her.

Mary hated to be seen in ugly clothing; nevertheless, she wore an ugly red-polka-dot dress that her Aunt Ida had given her for Christmas.

The second version condenses thirty-five words to twenty-six.

EXERCISE

1. **Label the independent and dependent clauses in the sentences below. Then identify each sentence as simple, compound, complex, or compound–complex.**

   a. A career in broadcasting requires good verbal skills, an extensive wardrobe, and a pleasant smile.
   b. Because its bag was too full, the vacuum cleaner backfired, leaving the room dirtier than it had been before.
   c. When Tom arrived home, his roommate asked him where he had really gone; six hours seemed too long a time to spend in the library.
   d. My apple tree blossomed last week; however, the peach trees have withered, probably because of the freeze last month.
   e. It's risky to confide in a co-worker because one can never be sure that the confidence will be kept.

2. **Using coordination and subordination, rewrite the following passages to reduce words and/or improve smoothness.**

   a. He played the piano. He played the organ. He played the French horn. He did not play the viola.
   b. Life on Venus may be possible. It will not be the kind of life we know on Earth. Life on Mars may be possible. It will not be the kind of life we know on Earth.
   c. Albert lay in bed. He stared at the ceiling. Albert thought about the previous afternoon. He had asked Kathy to go to dinner with him. She is a pretty, blonde-haired woman. She sits at the desk next to his. They work at Hemphill's. She had refused.
   d. I went to the store to buy a box of detergent. I saw Bill there, and we talked about last night's game.
   e. Tim went to the newsstand. He bought a magazine there. While he was on the way home, he lost it. He had nothing to read.

frag

Accepted usage improves the smoothness of your prose, makes your writing easier to understand, and demonstrates that you are a careful communicator. These assets, in turn, increase the likelihood that the reader will accept your ideas.

When you've finished revising the first draft of a piece of writing, edit it with a critic's eye to ensure that you eliminate all errors. Circle sentences or parts of them that are faulty or suspect. Then check your circled items against this section of the Handbook, which deals with the most common errors in writing.

SENTENCE FRAGMENTS

A sentence fragment is a group of words that fails to qualify as a sentence but is capitalized and punctuated as if it were a sentence. To be a sentence, a word group must (1) have a subject and a verb and (2) make sense by itself. The first of the following examples has a subject and a verb; the second does not. Neither makes sense by itself.

If you want to remain.

His answer to the question.

Methods of Revision   Eliminating a sentence fragment is not hard. Careful reading often shows that the fragment goes with the sentence that comes just before or just after it. And sometimes two successive fragments can be joined. Note how we've corrected the fragments (italicized) in the following pairs:

Faulty	*Having been warned about the storm.* We decided to stay home.
Revision	Having been warned about the storm, we decided to stay home.
Faulty	*After eating.* The dog took a nap.
Revision	After eating, the dog took a nap.
Faulty	Sally went to work. *Although she felt sick.*
Revision	Sally went to work although she felt sick.
Faulty	Dave bought a new suit. *Over at Bentley's.*
Revision	Dave bought a new suit over at Bentley's.
Faulty	*That bronze clock on the mantel. Once belonged to my grandmother.*
Revision	That bronze clock on the mantel once belonged to my grandmother.

Joining a fragment to a sentence or to another fragment works only if the problem is simply one of mispunctuation. If the fragment stems from an improperly developed thought, revise the thought into correct sentence form.

Punctuating Your Corrections   When you join a fragment to the following sentence, you need not place a comma between the two unless the fragment has six or more words or if omitting a comma might cause a misreading. When joining a fragment to the preceding sentence, omit a comma unless there is a distinct pause between the two items. The preceding examples illustrate these points.

Intentional Fragments   Fragments are commonly used in conversation and the writing that reproduces it. Professional writers also use fragments to gain special emphasis or create special effects.

frag

CONNECTED DISCOURSE EXERCISE   *Identify and correct the sentence fragments in the following letter:*

Dear Phone Company:

Recently I received a phone bill for over $500. While I do use the phone fairly extensively. Most of the calls I make are local ones. In this case, many of the calls on my bill were to other countries. Including a phone call to New Delhi, India. I can hardly be held responsible for these calls. Especially since I don't know anyone who lives overseas. Since the only long-distance call I made was to Sudbury, Ontario. I have deducted the charges for all the other long-distance calls from my bill and am sending you the balance. In order to prevent this type of error from happening again. Would you please have a representative determine why these charges appeared on my bill?

Sincerely,
Desperate

EXERCISE   *Twelve main clauses paired with fragments are shown below. In each case identify the sentence (S) and the fragment (F) and then eliminate the fragment.*

1. The clerk handed the package to the customer. And walked swiftly away from the counter.
2. Exhausted by his efforts to push the car out of the snowbank. Paul slumped wearily into the easy chair.
3. The dinner honoured three retirees. One of them my father.
4. After tidying up the kitchen. My parents left for the movies.
5. If Dr. Frankenstein's experiment is a success. He'll throw a monster party to celebrate.
6. Even though Ned studied very hard. He had trouble with the test.

7. The dog barked at the stranger. And chased him from the property.

8. By leaving the ballpark before the last out was made. We avoided the after-game crowd.

RUN-ON SENTENCES AND COMMA SPLICES

A run-on, or fused, sentence occurs when one sentence runs into another without anything to mark their junction. A comma splice occurs when only a comma marks the junction. These errors lead your readers to think that you are hasty or careless. Here are several examples:

Run-on sentence	Laura failed to set her alarm she was late for work.
Comma splice	Violets are blooming now, my lawn is covered with them.
Run-on sentence	Rick refused to attend the movie he said he hated horror shows.
Comma splice	Perry watched the road carefully, he still missed his turn.
Run-on Sentence	Janet worked on her term paper her friend studied for a calculus test.
Comma splice	Janet worked on her term paper, her friend studied for a calculus test.

Testing for Errors   To check out a possible comma splice or fused sentence, read what precedes and follows the comma or suspected junction and see whether the two parts can stand alone as sentences. If *both parts* can stand alone, there is an error. Otherwise, there is not.

Darryl is a real troublemaker, someday he'll find himself in serious difficulty.

Examination of the parts preceding and following the comma shows that each is a complete sentence:

Darryl is a real troublemaker.

Someday he'll find himself in serious difficulty.

The writer has therefore committed a comma splice that needs correction.

Methods of Revision   You can correct run-on sentences and comma splices in several ways.

1. Create two separate sentences.

Revision	Violets are blooming now. My lawn is covered with them.
Revision	Rick refused to attend the movie. He said he hated horror shows.

2. Join the sentences with a semicolon.

Revision   Violets are blooming now; my yard is covered with them.

Revision   Rick refused to attend the movie; he said he hated horror shows.

3. Join the sentences with a comma and a coordinating conjunction *(and, but, or, nor, for, yet, so)*.

Revision   Laura failed to set her alarm, *so* she was late for work.

Revision   Perry watched the road carefully, *but* he still missed his turn.

4. Join the sentences with a semicolon and a conjunctive adverb.

Revision   Laura failed to set her alarm; *consequently*, she was late for work.

Revision   Violets are blooming now; *in fact*, my yard is covered with them.

5. Introduce one of the sentences with a subordinating conjunction.

Revision   *Because* Laura failed to set her alarm, she was late for work.

Revision   Janet worked on her term paper *while* her friend studied for a calculus test.

As our examples show, you can often correct an error in several ways.

ro cs

CONNECTED DISCOURSE EXERCISE *Identify and correct the comma splices and run-on sentences in the following letter:*

Dear Desperate:

We are sorry to hear that you are having difficulty paying your bill, it is, however, your responsibility. Unfortunately we have no way to prevent you from making overseas calls, you have to curb your own tendency to reach out and touch your friends. Following your instructions, we are sending a technician to remove your phone. Please be home this Friday morning he will arrive then. Even though we will remove your phone, you are still responsible for the unpaid portion of your bill, it is your financial obligation. We would dislike referring this matter to a collection agency, it could ruin your credit rating.

Sincerely,
Your friendly phone representative

EXERCISE *Indicate whether each item is correct (C), is a run-on sentence (RO), or contains a comma splice (CS) and then correct the faulty items.*

1. Lee is a difficult person he becomes angry whenever he doesn't get his own way.
2. The student appeared puzzled by the instructor's answer to his question, but he said nothing more.
3. The doctor warned Allan about his high cholesterol level, he went on a high-fibre diet.
4. Sally researched her topic thoroughly and wrote her report carefully as a result she received an *A*.
5. It's nice to see you again; we should get together more often.
6. The horse stumbled and nearly fell in the backstretch, nevertheless it managed to finish second.
7. Janice thought the exercises would be easy, after finishing them she found that her whole body ached.
8. I've just started to take up chess, you can hardly expect me to play well.

SUBJECT–VERB AGREEMENT

A verb should agree in number with its subject. Singular verbs should have singular subjects, and plural verbs should have plural subjects.

> *Correct*   My *boss is* a grouch. (singular subject and verb)

> *Correct*   The *apartments have* two bedrooms. (plural subject and verb)

Ordinarily, matching subjects and verbs causes no problems. However, the following special situations can create difficulties.

Subject and Verb Separated by a Word Group   Sometimes a word group that includes one or more nouns comes between the subject and the verb. When this happens, match the verb with its subject, not a noun in the word group.

> *Correct*   Our basket of sandwiches is missing.

> *Correct*   Several books required for my paper are not in the library.

> *Correct*   Mr. Schmidt, along with his daughters, runs a furniture store.

> *Correct*   The old bus, crammed with passengers, was unable to reach the top of the hill.

Two Singular Subjects   Most singular subjects joined by *and* take a plural verb.

> *Correct*   The *couch* and *chair were* upholstered in blue velvet.

Sentences like the one above almost never cause problems. However, in sentences with subjects like *restoring cars* and *racing motorcycles,* singular verbs are often mistakenly used.

> *Faulty*   *Restoring cars* and *racing motorcycles consumes* most of Frank's time.

> *Revision*   *Restoring cars* and *racing motorcycles consume* most of Frank's time.

When *each* or *every* precedes the subjects, use a *singular* verb in place of a plural.

> *Correct*   Every *book* and *magazine was* badly water-stained.

Singular subjects joined by *or, either—or,* or *neither—nor* also take singular verbs.

> *Correct*   A *pear* or an *apple is* a good afternoon snack.

> *Correct*   Neither *rain* nor *snow slows* our letter carrier.

Finally, use a singular verb when two singular subjects joined by *and* name the same person, place, or thing.

> *Correct*   My *cousin* and business *partner is* retiring next month.
> (*Cousin* and *partner* refer to the same person.)

One Singular and One Plural Subject   When one singular subject and one plural subject are joined by *or, either—or,* or *neither—nor,* match the verb with the closer of the two.

> *Correct*   Neither *John* nor his *parents were* at home.

> *Correct*   Neither his *parents* nor *John was* at home.

As these examples show, the sentences are usually smoother when the plural subject follows the singular.

Collective Nouns as Subjects   Collective nouns (*assembly, class, committee, family, herd, majority, tribe,* and the like) are singular in form but stand for groups or collections of people or things. Ordinarily, collective nouns are considered singular and therefore take singular verbs.

> *Correct*   The *class is* writing a test.

> *Correct*   The *herd was* clustered around the water hole.

Sometimes, though, a collective noun refers to the separate individuals making up the grouping, and then it requires a plural verb.

> *Correct*   The *jury are* in dispute about the verdict.

Sentences in Which the Verb Comes ahead of the Subject   Sentences that begin with words such as *here, there, how, what,* and *where* fall into this category. With such sentences, the verb must agree with the subject that follows it.

sv agr

Correct	Here *is* my *house.*
Correct	Where *are* my *shoes?*
Correct	There *is* just one *way* to solve this problem.
Correct	There *go* my *chances* for a promotion.

CONNECTED DISCOURSE EXERCISE

Identify and correct the subject–verb agreement errors in the following letter:

Regional Accounts Manager:

One of your area phone representatives have seriously misread a letter I submitted with my bill. I refused to pay for long-distance overseas calls since neither I nor my roommate know anyone who lives overseas. Instead of deducting the calls from my bill, she sent someone to remove my phone. Now my phone, along with many of my valuable possessions, have been removed. Unfortunately the technician, whom I allowed into my apartment only after carefully checking his credentials, were a thief. He locked me in a closet and cleared out the apartment. I have called the police, but I also expect the phone company to reimburse me for my losses. There is only two choices. Either the stolen items or a cheque covering the loss need to be sent to me immediately. Otherwise I am afraid I will be forced to sue. A jury are sure to rule in my favour. In addition, I expect to find that those overseas calls has been deducted from my bill.

Sincerely,

Desperately Desperate

EXERCISE

Choose the correct verb form from the pair in parentheses.

1. The pictures in the drawing room of the mansion (has, have) been insured for twelve million dollars.
2. Every dish and piece of stainless that I own (is, are) dirty.
3. Look! There (is, are) Kathy and her friend Marge.
4. Reading novels and watching TV (takes, take) up most of Stanley's time.
5. Each of these proposals (represents, represent) a great amount of work.
6. Two hamburgers or a hot beef sandwich (makes, make) an ample lunch.
7. (Has, Have) either of the orchids blossomed yet?
8. The automobile with the broken headlights and dented sides (was, were) stopped by the police.

sv agr

PRONOUN–ANTECEDENT AGREEMENT

The antecedent of a pronoun is the noun or pronoun to which it refers. Just as subjects should agree with their verbs, pronouns should agree with their antecedents: Singular antecedents require singular pronouns, and plural antecedents require plural pronouns. Ordinarily, you will have no trouble matching antecedents and pronouns. The situations below, however, can cause problems.

Indefinite Pronouns as Antecedents   Indefinite pronouns include words such as *each, either, neither, any, everybody, somebody,* and *nobody.* Whenever an indefinite pronoun is used as an antecedent, the pronoun that refers to it should be singular.

pa agr

Faulty	*Neither* of the actors had learned *their* lines.
Revision	*Neither* of the actors had learned *his* lines.

When the gender of the antecedent is unknown, you may follow it with *his or her;* or if this results in awkwardness, rewrite the sentence in the plural.

Correct	*Anyone* who has studied *his or her* assignments properly should do well on the test.
Correct	*Those* who have studied *their* assignments properly should do well on the test.

Occasionally, a ridiculous result occurs when a singular pronoun refers to an indefinite pronoun that is obviously plural in meaning. When this happens, rewrite the sentence to eliminate the problem.

Faulty	*Everybody* complained that the graduation ceremony had lasted too long, but I didn't believe *him.*
Revision	*Everybody* complained that the graduation ceremony had lasted too long, but I didn't agree.

Two Singular Antecedents   Two or more antecedents joined by *and* ordinarily call for a plural pronoun.

Correct	Her briefcase and umbrella were missing from *their* usual place on the hall table.

When *each* or *every* precedes the antecedent, use a singular pronoun.

Correct	Every college and university must do *its* best to provide adequate student counselling.

Singular antecedents joined by *or, either/or,* or *neither/nor* call for singular pronouns.

Correct	Neither Carol nor Irene had paid *her* rent for the month.

Applying this rule can sometimes yield an awkward or foolish sentence. When this happens, rewrite the sentence to avoid the problem.

Faulty	Neither James nor Sally has finished *his or her* term project.
Revision	James and Sally have not finished *their* term projects.

Singular antecedents joined by *and* that refer to the same person, place, or thing use a singular pronoun.

Correct	My *cousin* and business *partner* is retiring to *his* condo in Florida next month.

Singular and Plural Antecedents   If one singular and one plural antecedent are joined by *or, either/or,* or *neither/nor,* the pronoun agrees with the closer one.

Correct	Either Terrence James or the Parkinsons will let us use *their* lawn mower.
Correct	Either the Parkinsons or Terrence James will let us use *his* lawn mower.

Sentences of this sort are generally smoother when the plural subject follows the singular.

Collective Nouns as Antecedents   When a collective noun is considered a single unit, the pronoun that refers to it should be singular.

Correct	The *troop* of scouts made *its* way slowly through the woods.

When the collective noun refers to the separate individuals in the group, use a plural pronoun.

Correct	The *staff* lost *their* jobs when the factory closed.

CONNECTED DISCOURSE EXERCISE *Identify and correct the pronoun–antecedent agreement errors in the following letter:*

Dear Desperately Desperate:

We were sorry to hear about the theft from your apartment. Apparently a gang of con artists recently had their base of operations in your city. It posed as repair technicians and presented false credentials to anyone expecting their phone to be repaired. Someone also must have intercepted your mail and written their own response since we have no record of any previous letter from you. Clearly neither the representative you mentioned nor the phony phone technician could have held their position with our company. Every one of our technicians must provide us with their fingerprints and take periodic lie detector tests. Further, none of our representatives will answer correspondence since it is not a part of their job description. For these reasons, we do not believe we are responsible for your losses. However, a review of our records shows that you owe $500; we have included a copy of the bill in case you have misplaced the original.

Sincerely,

Accounts Manager

EXERCISE   *Choose the right pronoun from the pair in parentheses.*

pr ref

1. If everybody does *(his or her, their)* part, the pageant should go smoothly.
2. Neither Greg nor the Snows had remembered to make *(his, their)* reservations at the ski lodge.
3. The graduating class filed by the principal and received *(its, their)* diplomas.
4. Each of the performers nervously waited *(his or her, their)* turn to audition.
5. Every boot and shoe I own needs to have *(its, their)* laces replaced.
6. Either Laurie or Alicia will show *(her, their)* slides at the party.
7. Dave and Bill loudly voiced *(his, their)* complaints about the restaurant's service.
8. Pleased with the performance, the audience showed *(its, their)* pleasure by applauding loudly.

USING EFFECTIVE PRONOUN REFERENCE

Any pronoun except an indefinite pronoun should refer to just one noun or noun substitute—its antecedent. Reference problems result when the pronoun has two or more antecedents, a hidden antecedent, or no antecedent. These errors can cause mixups in meaning as well as ridiculous sentences.

More Than One Antecedent   The following sentences lack clarity because their pronouns have two possible antecedents rather than just one:

Faulty   Take the screens off the windows and wash *them.*

Faulty   Harry told Will that *he* was putting on weight.

The reader can't tell whether the screens or the windows should be washed or who is putting on weight.

Sometimes we see a sentence like this one:

Faulty   If the boys don't eat all the Popsicles, put *them* in the freezer.

In this case, we know it's the Popsicles that should be stored, but the use of *them* creates an amusing sentence.

Correct these faults by replacing the pronoun with a noun or by rephrasing the sentence.

Revision	Wash the windows after you have taken off the screens.
Revision	Take off the screens so that you can wash the windows.
Revision	Harry told Will, "I am (you are) putting on weight."
Revision	Put any uneaten Popsicles in the freezer.

Hidden Antecedent An antecedent is hidden if it takes the form of an adjective rather than a noun.

| *Faulty* | The movie theatre is closed today, so we can't see *one*. |
| *Faulty* | As I passed the tiger's cage, *it* lunged at me. |

To correct this fault, replace the pronoun with the noun used as an adjective or switch the positions of the pronoun and the noun and make any needed changes in their forms.

| *Revision* | The theatre is closed today, so we can't see a movie. |
| *Revision* | As I passed its cage, the tiger lunged at me. |

No Antecedent A no-antecedent sentence lacks any noun to which the pronoun can refer. Sentences of this sort occur frequently in everyday conversation but should be avoided in formal writing. The examples below illustrate this error:

| *Faulty* | The lecture was boring, but *they* took notes anyway. |
| *Faulty* | On the news program, *it* told about another flood in Quebec. |

To set matters right, substitute a suitable noun for the pronoun or reword the sentence.

| *Revision* | The lecture was boring, but the students took notes anyway. |
| *Revision* | The news program told about another flood in Quebec. |

Sometimes *this, that, it,* or *which* will refer to a whole idea rather than a single noun. This usage is acceptable provided the writer's meaning is obvious, as in this example:

| *Correct* | The instructor spoke very softly, *which* meant we had difficulty hearing him. |

However, problems occur when the reader can't figure out which of two or more ideas the pronoun refers to.

| *Faulty* | Ginny called Sally two hours after the agreed-upon time and postponed their shopping trip one day. *This* irritated Sally very much. |

What caused Sally to be irritated—the late call, the postponement of the trip, or both? Again, rewording or adding a clarifying word will correct the problem.

Revision	Ginny called Sally two hours after the agreed-upon time and postponed their shopping trip one day. This *tardiness* irritated Sally very much.
Revision	Ginny called Sally two hours after the agreed-upon time and postponed their shopping trip one day. Ginny's *change of plans* irritated Sally very much.

The first of these examples illustrates the addition of a clarifying word; the second illustrates rewriting.

CONNECTED DISCOURSE EXERCISE *Identify and correct any faulty pronoun references in the following memorandum:*

TO: Director of Food Services, Groan University

FROM: Vice-President of Services

DATE: February 19, 2006

SUBJECT: Student Complaints about Cafeteria

Complaints about food quality and cafeteria hours are common but easily resolved. They can be extended by simply installing vending machines. It might not make for a nutritious meal, but it certainly will undercut some of the dissatisfaction. Of course, no matter how good the food, they will complain. Still, you can partially defuse those complaints by having students list their major concerns and then meeting them. Of course, you can always increase student satisfaction by purchasing a soft ice cream machine and offering it for dessert.

EXERCISE *Indicate whether each sentence is correct (C) or contains a faulty pronoun reference (F) and then correct any faulty sentences.*

1. Ann told Jennifer that the boss wanted to see her.
2. Because the ring hurt her finger, Ruth took it off.
3. At the farmer's market they sell many kinds of produce.
4. I like the food in Thai restaurants because it is very spicy.
5. They tell me that the company's profits have risen 5 percent this quarter.
6. Knowing that my friends like hot dogs, I grilled them at the picnic.
7. When Jeffrey rose to make his speech, they all started laughing.
8. In the paper, it told about the province's budget surplus.

pr ref

MANAGING SHIFTS IN PERSON

Pronouns can be in the first person, second person, or third person. *First-person* pronouns identify people who are talking or writing about themselves, *second-person* pronouns identify people being addressed directly, and *third-person* pronouns identify persons or things that are being written or spoken about. The following table sorts pronouns according to person:

shft

First Person	Second Person	Third Person
I	you	he
me	your	she
my	yours	it
mine	yourself	his
we	yourselves	her
us		hers
our		its
ours		one
ourselves		they
		their
		theirs
		indefinite pronouns

All nouns are in the third person. As you revise, be alert for unwarranted shifts from one person to another.

> *Faulty*   I liked *my* British vacation better than *my* vacation in France and Italy because *you* didn't have language problems.
>
> *Revision*   I liked *my* British vacation better than *my* vacation in France and Italy because *I* didn't have language problems.
>
> *Faulty*   Holidays are important to *everyone*. They boost *your* spirits and provide a break from *our* daily routine.
>
> *Revision*   Holidays are important to *everyone*. They boost *one's* spirits and provide a break from *one's* daily routine.
>
> *Faulty*   The taller the *golfer,* the more club speed *you* will have with a normally paced swing.
>
> *Revision*   The taller the *golfer,* the more club speed *he* or *she* will have with a normally paced swing.

As these examples show, the shift can occur within a single sentence or when the writer moves from one sentence to another.

Some shifts in person, however, are warranted. Read the following correct sentence:

> *Correct*   *I* want *you* to deliver these flowers to Ms. Willoughby by three o'clock. *She* needs them for a party.

Here the speaker identifies himself or herself (*I*) while speaking directly to a listener *(you)* about someone else *(she)*. In this case, shifts are needed to get the message across.

CONNECTED DISCOURSE EXERCISE *Identify and correct the unwarranted shifts in person in the following paragraph:*

Good health is clearly important to you. But it is one's responsibility to ensure our own good health. You can start with simple exercises. We would like to provide you with a low-impact aerobics videotape for only $9. We guarantee that the more out of shape the customer, the quicker you will notice the benefits. The way our bodies feel affects the quality of one's lives. Let our tape help you to a better life.

EXERCISE *Indicate whether the sentence is correct (C) or contains an unwarranted shift in person (S). Correct faulty sentences.*

1. Because many of our tour guides spoke very poor English, the tourists soon became quite frustrated.
2. We like the location of our new house very much; you are close to a couple of large shopping centres.
3. If you want me to invite Gary to the party, I'll call him right now.
4. Be sure you tell the bakery clerk that we will need the cake by tomorrow noon.
5. If you complete a degree in vocational education, anyone can expect a rewarding career.
6. Once we learn to ride a bicycle, a person never forgets how.
7. Anyone wishing to make the trip to Kelowna should make your own hotel reservations.
8. After we had finished the test, the instructor told the students she would return it on Thursday.

case

USING THE RIGHT PRONOUN CASE

Case means the changes in form that a personal pronoun undergoes to show its function in a sentence. English has three cases: the *subjective*, the *nonsubjective* (objective), and the *possessive*. The following chart shows the different forms:

Subjective Form	Nonsubjective Form	Possessive Form
I	me	my, mine
he	him	his
she	her	her, hers
we	us	our, ours
you	you	your, yours
they	them	their, theirs
who	whom	whose

The subjective case is used for subjects and subject complements, and the non-subjective is used for direct objects, indirect objects, and objects of prepositions. The possessive case shows ownership and is also used with gerunds.

The following pointers will help you select the proper pronoun as you revise.

case

We and *Us* Preceding Nouns Nouns that serve as subjects take the pronoun *we*. Other nouns take the pronoun *us*.

> *Correct*   *We* tourists will fly home tomorrow. (*We* accompanies the subject.)

> *Correct*   The guide showed *us* tourists through the cathedral. (*Us* accompanies a nonsubject.)

If you can't decide which pronoun is right, mentally omit the noun and read the sentence to yourself, first with one pronoun and then with the other. Your ear will indicate the correct form.

My mother made *(we, us)* children vanilla pudding for dessert.

Omitting *children* shows immediately that *us* is the right choice.

> *Correct*   My mother made *us* children vanilla pudding for dessert.

Pronouns Paired with Nouns   When such a combination serves as the subject of a sentence or accompanies the subject, use the subject form of the pronoun. When the combination plays a nonsubject role, use the nonsubject form of the pronoun.

> *Correct*   Arlene and *I* plan to join Katimavik. (*I* is part of the compound subject.)

> *Correct*   Two people, Mary and *I*, will represent our school at the meeting. (*I* is part of a compound element accompanying the subject.)

> *Correct*   The superintendent told Kevin and *him* that they would be promoted soon. (*Him* is part of a compound nonsubject.)

> *Correct*   The project was difficult for Jeffrey and *him* to complete. (*Him* is part of a compound nonsubject.)

Again, mentally omitting the noun from the combination will tell you which pronoun is correct.

Who and *Whom* in Dependent Clauses   Use *who* for the subjects of dependent clauses; otherwise use *whom*.

> *Correct*   The Mallarys prefer friends *who are interested in the theatre.* (*Who* is the subject of the clause.)

> *Correct*   Barton is a man *whom very few people like.* (*Whom* is not the subject of the clause.)

A simple test will help you decide between *who* and *whom*. First, mentally isolate the dependent clause. Next, block out the pronoun in question and then insert *he* (or *she*) and *him* (or *her*) at the appropriate spot in the remaining part of the clause. If *he* (or *she*) sounds better, *who* is right. If *him* (or *her*) sounds better, *whom* is right. Let's use this test on the sentence below:

> The woman *who(m) Scott is dating* works as a mechanical engineer. Scott is dating (*she, her.*)

Clearly *her* is correct; therefore, *whom* is the proper form.

case

> *Correct*   The woman *whom Scott is dating* works as a mechanical engineer.

Pronouns as Subject Complements   In formal writing, pronouns that serve as subject complements always take the subject form.

> *Correct*   It is *I.*

> *Correct*   It was *she* who bought the old Parker mansion.

This rule, however, is often ignored in informal writing.

> It's *her.*

> That's *him* standing over by the door.

Comparisons Using *than* or *as . . . as*   Comparisons of this kind often make no direct statement about the second item of comparison. When the second naming word is a pronoun, you may have trouble choosing the right one.

> Harriet is less outgoing than *(they, them).*

> My parents' divorce saddened my sister as much as *(I, me).*

Not to worry. Expand the sentence by mentally supplying the missing material. Then try the sentence with each pronoun and see which sounds right.

> Harriet is less outgoing than *(they, them)* are.

> My parents' divorce saddened my sister as much as it did *(I, me).*

Obviously *they* is the right choice for the first sentence, and *me* is the right choice for the second one.

> *Correct*   Harriet is less outgoing than *they* are.

> *Correct*   My parents' divorce saddened my sister as much as it did *me.*

Pronouns Preceding Gerunds   Use the possessive form of a pronoun that precedes a gerund.

case

I dislike *their* leaving without saying goodbye.

Ted can't understand *her* quitting such a good job.

This usage emphasizes the action named by the gerund instead of the person or persons performing it. Thus, in the above sentences, the possessive form of the pronoun signals that it's the *leaving* the writer dislikes and the *quitting* that Ted can't understand. The persons involved are secondary.

When the pronoun precedes a participle, it should be in the nonsubject case. The emphasis is then on the actor rather than the action.

Jennifer caught *them* listening to records instead of studying.

In this example, Jennifer caught the listeners, not the listening.

If you have trouble deciding between the nonsubject and possessive forms of a pronoun, ask yourself whether you want to emphasize the action or the actor; then proceed accordingly.

CONNECTED DISCOURSE EXERCISE *Identify and correct the pronoun case errors in the following paragraph:*

Between my brother and I, we are always able to pull at least five good-sized trout a day from the creek behind our house. Us rural trout fishermen just seem to have the knack. Of course, those city fishermen whom insist on employing artificial flies won't appreciate our methods even if they can't do as well as us. We just let our bait, usually a juicy worm, float downstream to the waiting trout. Of course, my brother won't let the fishing interfere with him sleeping. In fact, it was him that developed the idea of looping the line around his toe so that he would wake up when a trout took the bait. Others have told my brother and I that this method is dangerous, but neither of us has lost a toe yet. Of course, the people who we invite to dinner don't complain about our methods, and they seem to enjoy the fish.

EXERCISE *Choose the right form of the pronoun for each of the following sentences:*

1. Cherie is the one student *(who, whom)* I believe has the potential to become a professional acrobat.
2. Two students, Carrie and *(I, me),* scored 100 on the calculus test.
3. *(We, Us)* Greens pride ourselves on our beautiful lawns.
4. Ken Conwell is the only candidate *(who, whom)* I like in this election.
5. Brookfield has richer friends and a more luxurious lifestyle than *(I, me).*
6. The friendly student told *(we, us)* visitors that we were in the wrong building.
7. As youngsters, Bill and *(I, me)* used to play tag.
8. My uncle has given Sandra and *(I, me)* tickets for tonight's Bach concert.

CREATING CONSISTENCY IN SHOWING TIME

Inconsistencies occur when a writer shifts from the past tense to the present or vice versa without a corresponding shift in the time of the events being described. The following paragraph contains an uncalled-for shift from the present tense to the past:

> As *The Most Dangerous Game* opens, Sanger Rainsford, a famous hunter and author, and his old friend Whitney are standing on the deck of a yacht and discussing a mysterious island as the ship passes near it. Then, after everyone else has gone to bed, Rainsford manages to fall overboard. He swims to the island and ends up at a chateau owned by General Zaroff, a refugee from the Communist takeover in Russia. Zaroff, bored with hunting animals, has turned to hunting humans on his desert island. Inevitably, Rainsford is turned out into the jungle to be hunted down. There were [shift to past tense] actually four hunts over a three-day period, and at the end of the last one, Rainsford jumped into the sea, swam across a cove to the chateau, and killed Zaroff in the general's own bedroom. Afterward he sleeps [shift back to present tense] and decides "he had never slept in a better bed."

The sentence with the unwarranted shift in tense should read as follows:

> There are actually four hunts over a three-day period, and at the end of the last one, Rainsford jumps into the sea, swims across a cove to the chateau, and kills Zaroff in the general's own bedroom.

The time shift in the quotation part of the final sentence is justified because the sleeping has occurred before Rainsford's thoughts about it.

A second kind of inconsistency results when a writer fails to distinguish the immediate past from the less immediate past. The following sentence illustrates this error:

Faulty   Mary *answered* all thirty test questions when the class ended.

This sentence states that Mary completed all thirty test questions during the final instant of the class. This is impossible. When you detect this type of error in your writing, determine which action occurred first and then correct the error by adding *had* to the verb. In this case, the first verb needs correcting:

Revision   Mary *had answered* all thirty test questions when the class ended.

Besides adding *had,* you may sometimes need to alter the verb form.

Faulty   Before he turned twenty, John *wrote* two novels.

Revision   Before he turned twenty, John *had written* two novels.

time

CONNECTED DISCOURSE EXERCISE *Identify and correct any inconsistencies in showing time in the following passage:*

> There is no better time to go swimming than at night. The summer after I had graduated from high school, I worked for a landscaping company. After a sweaty day mowing lawns and digging up gardens, all of us who worked there would jump into the back of Dick's old pickup and rattle out to Woods Lake. It is just dark as we arrive. The moon is beautiful, reflected in that black mirror set in a frame of hills. We stumble down a small, sandy hill to the beach, where we strip off our dusty jeans and sweaty shirts before plunging into the cool reflection of stars.

mis/

EXERCISE *Indicate whether each sentence is correct (C) or contains an unwarranted shift (S) in tense. Then correct the faulty sentences.*

1. Although the alarm rang, Bob continues to lie in bed.
2. When autumn arrives, we often go for long walks in the woods.
3. John is writing his dissertation but found the job tough going.
4. When the trapeze artist fell into the net, the audience gasps loudly.
5. When I baked the cake, I ate a slice.
6. Edward walks for half an hour before he ate dinner.
7. Sarah had many friends but sees them infrequently.
8. As Elaine walked toward the garden, a rabbit scampers quickly away.

USING ADJECTIVES AND ADVERBS EFFECTIVELY

Beginning writers often use adjectives when they should use adverbs and also confuse the comparative and superlative forms of these parts of speech when making comparisons.

Misusing Adjectives for Adverbs   Although most adjectives can be misused as adverbs, the following seven, listed with the corresponding adverbs, cause the most difficulty.

Adjectives	Adverbs
awful	awfully
bad	badly
considerable	considerably
good	well
most	almost
real	really
sure	surely

The following sentences show typical errors:

Faulty	Bryan did *good* in his first golf lesson. (*good* mistakenly used to modify verb *did*)
Faulty	*Most* every graduate from our auto service program receives several job offers. (*Most* mistakenly used to modify adjective *every*)
Faulty	The speech was delivered *real* well. (*real* mistakenly used to modify adverb *well*)

Because adverbs modify verbs, adjectives, and other adverbs, and adjectives modify nouns and noun substitutes, the above sentences clearly require adverbs.

Revision	Bryan did *well* in his first golf lesson.
Revision	*Almost* every graduate from our auto service program receives several job offers.
Revision	The speech was delivered *really* well.

mis/
adj/adv

If you can't decide whether a sentence requires an adjective or an adverb, determine the part of speech of the word being modified and proceed accordingly.

Confusing the Comparative and Superlative Forms in Comparisons The comparative form of adjectives and adverbs is used to compare two things, the superlative form to compare three or more things. Adjectives with fewer than three syllables generally add *-er* to make the comparative form and *-est* to make the superlative form (tall, tall*er,* tall*est*). Adjectives with three or more syllables generally add *more* to make the comparative and *most* to make the superlative (enchanting, *more* enchanting, *most* enchanting), as do most adverbs of two or more syllables (loudly, *more* loudly, *most* loudly).

When making comparisons, beginning writers sometimes mistakenly use double comparatives or double superlatives.

Faulty	Harry is *more taller* than James. (double comparative)
Faulty	The Hotel Vancouver has the *most splendidest* lobby I've ever seen. (double superlative)

The correct versions read as follows:

Revision	Harry is *taller* than James.
Revision	The Hotel Vancouver has the *most splendid* lobby I've ever seen.

In addition, writers may erroneously use the superlative form, rather than the comparative form, to compare two things.

| *Faulty* | Barry is the *richest* of the two brothers. |
| *Faulty* | Jeremy is the *most talented* of those two singers. |

Here are the sentences correctly written:

| *Revision* | Barry is the *richer* of the two brothers. |
| *Revision* | Jeremy is the *more talented* of those two singers. |

Reserve the superlative form for comparing three or more items.

| *Correct* | Barry is the *richest* of the three brothers. |
| *Correct* | Jeremy is the *most talented* of those four singers. |

mis/ adj/adv

CONNECTED DISCOURSE EXERCISE *Identify and correct the adjective–adverb errors in the following paragraph:*

This year our football team is outstanding. Spike Jones, our quarterback, has been playing real good this past season. Stan Blunder, the most talented of our two ends, hasn't dropped a pass all season. The team can most always count on Stan to catch the crucial first-down pass. Of course, the team wouldn't be where it is today without John Schoolyard's good coaching. He has made this team much more better than it was a year ago. Only the kicking team has done bad this season. Of course, with this most wonderfulest offence, the defensive players haven't got much practice. The good news is, then, that we can sure expect to watch some terrific university football for years to come.

EXERCISE *For each of the following sentences, choose the proper word from the pair in parentheses:*

1. A person can become *(stronger, more stronger)* by lifting weights.
2. Canvasback Dunn is clearly the *(less, least)* formidable of the two main challengers for Killer McGurk's boxing crown.
3. Diane did *(good, well)* on her chemistry test.
4. *(Most, Almost)* all our salaried employees have degrees in business administration or engineering.
5. Carol wore the *(silliest, most silliest)* hat I've ever seen to the masquerade party.
6. Don was hurt *(bad, badly)* in the auto accident.
7. Brad was the *(funniest, most funniest)* of all the performers at the comedy club.
8. Clear Lake is the *(deeper, deepest)* of the three lakes in our county.

PLACING MODIFIERS CORRECTLY

A misplaced modifier is a word or word group that is improperly separated from the word it modifies. When separation of this type occurs, the sentence often sounds awkward, ridiculous, or confusing.

Usually, you can correct this error by moving the modifier next to the word it is intended to modify. Occasionally, you'll also need to alter some of the phrasing.

Faulty	There is a bicycle in the basement *with chrome fenders.* (The basement appears to have chrome fenders.)
Faulty	David received a phone call from his uncle *that infuriated him.* (The uncle appears to have infuriated David.)
Revision	There is a bicycle *with chrome fenders* in the basement.
Revision	David received an *infuriating* phone call from his uncle. (Note the change in wording.)

m m

When shifting the modifier, don't inadvertently create another faulty sentence.

Faulty	Fritz bought a magazine with an article about Michael Jackson *at the corner newsstand.* (The article appears to tell about Jackson's visit to the corner newsstand.)
Faulty	Fritz bought a magazine *at the corner newsstand* with an article about Michael Jackson. (The corner newsstand appears to have an article about Jackson.)
Revision	*At the corner newsstand,* Fritz bought a magazine with an article about Michael Jackson.

As you revise, watch also for *squinting modifiers*—that is, modifiers positioned so that the reader doesn't know whether they are supposed to modify what comes ahead of them or what follows them.

Faulty	The man who was rowing the boat *frantically* waved toward the onlookers on the beach.

Is the man rowing frantically or waving frantically? Correct this kind of error by repositioning the modifier so that the ambiguity disappears.

Revision	The man who was *frantically* rowing the boat waved toward the onlookers on the beach.
Revision	The man who was rowing the boat waved *frantically* toward the onlookers on the beach.

EXERCISE *Indicate whether each sentence is correct (C) or contains a misplaced modifier (MM). Correct faulty sentences.*

1. The boss asked me after lunch to type a special report.
2. Brenda returned the cottage cheese to the store that had spoiled.

3. The hikers tramped through the woods wearing heavy boots.
4. The movie was heavily advertised by the studio before sneak previews were shown.
5. Mark mailed a package to his friend sealed with masking tape.
6. The woman packing her suitcase hastily glanced out the window at the commotion in the yard.
7. We bought a dictionary that was bound in leather at the local bookstore.
8. Jerry bought an Inuit carving for his bedroom in Regina.

REVISING DANGLING MODIFIERS

A dangling modifier is a phrase or clause that lacks clear connection to the word or words it is intended to modify. As a result, sentences are inaccurate, often comical. Typically, the modifier leads off the sentence, although it can also come at the end.

Sometimes the error occurs because the sentence fails to specify who or what is modified. At other times, the separation is too great between the modifier and what it modifies.

> *Faulty*   *Walking in the meadow,* wildflowers surrounded us. (The wildflowers appear to be walking in the meadow.)

> *Faulty*   Dinner was served *after saying grace.* (The dinner appears to have said grace.)

> *Faulty*   *Fatigued by the violent exercise,* the cool shower was very relaxing. (The cool shower appears to have been fatigued.)

The first of these sentences is faulty because the modifier is positioned too far away from *us.* The other two are faulty because they do not identify who said grace or found the shower relaxing.

You can correct dangling modifiers in two basic ways. First, leave the modifier unchanged and rewrite the main part of the sentence so that it begins with the term actually modified. Second, rewrite the modifier so that it has its own subject and verb, thereby eliminating the inaccuracy.

> *Revision*   *Walking in the meadow,* we were surrounded by wildflowers. (The main part of the sentence has been rewritten.)

> *Revision*   *As we walked in the meadow,* wildflowers surrounded us. (The modifier has been rewritten.)

> *Revision*   Dinner was served *after we had said grace.* (The modifier has been rewritten.)

> *Revision*   *Fatigued by the violent exercise,* Ted found the cool shower very relaxing. (The main part of the sentence has been rewritten.)

Revision   *Because Ted was fatigued by the violent exercise,* the cool shower was very relaxing. (The modifier has been rewritten.)

Ordinarily, either part of the sentence can be rewritten, but sometimes only one part can.

EXERCISE *Indicate whether each sentence is correct (C) or contains a dangling modifier (DM). Correct faulty sentences.*

1. Dancing at the wedding reception, my feet hurt.
2. Working in the yard, Pete was drenched by the sudden cloudburst.
3. Looking out the window, a velvety lawn ran down to the river's edge.
4. Having mangy fur, our parents wouldn't let us keep the stray cat.
5. Because of memorizing all the definitions, Pam scored 100 on the vocabulary test.
6. Reminiscing about my school days, a run-in with my principal came to mind.
7. Unaware of what had happened, the confusion puzzled Nan.
8. At the age of eight, my father wrote a best-selling novel.

MAINTAINING PARALLELISM

Nonparallelism results when equivalent ideas follow different grammatical forms. One common kind of nonparallelism occurs with words or word groups in pairs or in a series.

Faulty   Althea enjoys *jogging, to bike,* and *to swim.*

Faulty   The superintendent praised the workers *for their productivity* and *because they had an excellent safety record.*

Faulty   The banner was *old, faded,* and *it had a rip.*

Note how rewriting the sentences in parallel form improves their smoothness.

Revision   Althea enjoys *jogging, biking,* and *swimming.*

Revision   The superintendent praised the workers for *their productivity* and *their excellent safety record.*

Revision   The banner was *old, faded,* and *ripped.*

Nonparallelism also occurs when correlative conjunctions *(either/or, neither/nor, both/and,* and *not only/but also)* are followed by unlike elements.

Faulty   That sound *either* <u>was a thunderclap</u> *or* <u>an explosion.</u>

Faulty   The basement was *not only* <u>poorly lighted</u> *but also* <u>it had a foul smell.</u>

Ordinarily, repositioning one of the correlative conjunctions will solve the problem. Sometimes, however, one of the grammatical elements must be rewritten.

Revision   That sound was *either* <u>a thunderclap</u> *or* <u>an explosion.</u> (*Either* has been repositioned.)

Revision   The basement was *not only* <u>poorly lighted</u> *but also* <u>foul smelling.</u> (The element following *but also* has been rewritten.)

EXERCISE *Indicate whether each sentence is correct (C) or nonparallel (NP). Correct faulty sentences.*

1. The lemonade was cold, tangy, and refreshing.
2. Although he had practised for several days, the scout could neither tie a square knot nor a bowline.
3. This job will involve waiting on customers, and you will need to maintain our inventory.
4. My summer job at a provincial park gave me experience in repairing buildings, the operation of heavy equipment, and assisting park visitors.
5. To maintain his rose bushes properly, Sam fertilizes, sprays, prunes, and waters them according to a strict schedule.
6. Once out of high school, Barry plans either to join the navy or the air force.
7. My favourite sports are swimming, golfing, and to bowl.
8. Janice's leisure activities include collecting coins, reading, and she also watches TV.

REVISING FAULTY COMPARISONS

A faulty comparison results if you (1) mention one of the items being compared but not the other, (2) omit words needed to clarify the relationship, or (3) compare different sorts of items. Advertisers often offend in the first way.

Faulty   Irish tape has better adhesion.

With what other tape is Irish tape being compared? Scotch tape? All other transparent tape? Mentioning the second term of a comparison eliminates reader guesswork.

Revision   Irish tape has better adhesion than any other transparent tape.

Two clarifying words, *other* and *else,* are frequently omitted from comparisons, creating illogical sentences.

Faulty   Sergeant McNabb is more conscientious than any officer in his precinct.

Faulty   Stretch French is taller than anyone on his basketball team.

The first sentence is illogical because McNabb is one of the officers in his precinct and therefore cannot be more conscientious than himself. Similarly, because French is a member of his basketball team, he can't be taller than anyone on his team. Adding *other* to the first sentence and *else* to the second corrects matters.

> *Revision*   Sergeant McNabb has made more arrests than any *other* officer in his precinct.

> *Revision*   Stretch French is taller than anyone *else* on his basketball team.

Comparing unlike items is perhaps the most common kind of comparison error. Here are two examples:

> *Faulty*   The cities in Ontario are larger than Nova Scotia.

> *Faulty*   The cover of this book is much more durable than the other book.

The first sentence compares the cities of Ontario with a province, while the second compares the cover of a book with a whole book. Correction consists of rewriting each sentence so that it compares like items.

> *Revision*   The cities in Ontario are larger than *those in* Nova Scotia.

> *Revision*   The cover of this book is much more durable than *that of* the other book.

CONNECTED DISCOURSE EXERCISE   *Identify and correct the misplaced modifiers, dangling modifiers, nonparallelism, and faulty comparisons in the following memorandum:*

TO: All Residency Hall Advisors in Knuckles Hall
FROM: John Knells, Residency Hall Director
DATE: March 13, 2006
SUBJECT: Noise in Residence Hall

Recently I received a report from a student that deeply disturbed me. Apparently, after quiet hours students still have visitors in their rooms, are playing their stereos loudly, and are even staging boxing matches in the halls. The student who wrote me desperately tries to study. However, he is often forced to leave his room disturbed by the noise. He was not the only one to complain. You should know that we have had more complaints about Knuckles Hall than any residence on campus. Since discussing this problem with you at the last staff meeting, things haven't seemed to get any better. The rules are not only poorly enforced but also they are completely ignored. Your job performance is

comp

worse than the students. If you don't improve immediately, I will be forced to dismiss you.

EXERCISE *Indicate whether each sentence is correct (C) or contains a faulty comparison (FC). Correct any faulty comparison.*

1. The houses on Parkdale Street are more modest than Windsor Terrace.
2. Maxine has more seniority than any other member of her department.
3. The finish on the dresser is not as smooth as the end table.
4. In contrast to your yard, I have an underground sprinkling system.
5. My mother's homemade jam has more flavour than any jam I've eaten.
6. The dresses sold at The Bay are much less expensive than the Tres Chic Shoppe.
7. Frontline reports show that during June our side lost fewer tanks.

comp

Articles (*a, an, the*) and quantifiers (*a few, many, some, much,* and so on) introduce nouns, which may or may not be preceded by other words. We call them **determiners** because they often determine the kind of noun that will follow (singular, plural, noncount, specific, nonspecific).

article + noun
┌─────────┐
The cloth was unusually expensive.

article + adjective + noun
┌─────────┐
An exquisite cloth covered the table.

quantifier + noun
┌─────────┐
Some cloth was needed to finish the curtains.

How to Edit Sentences When English Is Not Your First Language

One you have written your first draft, take time to look at the structure of your sentences. Use this checklist to help focus on typical problem areas:

1. *Determiners.* Do they suit the nouns they introduce? Be sure to include required articles and quantifiers, especially with singular count nouns.

2. *Subjects and verbs.* Agreement rules apply here. Singular subjects take singular verbs; plural subjects take plural verbs. Do your subjects and verbs match?

3. *Verb forms.* All the verbs in a verb phrase have to match in time, number, aspect, and voice. Make sure that your verbs match their context. Check also that you've used the right auxiliaries with your main verbs.

4. *Idioms.* When you aren't sure that the expression is just right, check a dictionary or ask a native speaker of English. Be especially careful of idiomatic verb combinations and the prepositions that go with certain verbs.

5. *Completeness.* Does each sentence contain all its essential parts?

6. *Word order.* Look at your base sentence; then consider the modifiers. Is your subject-verb order appropriate for statements or questions? Are modifiers in the right place?

7. *Word endings.* Check word endings twice. First of all, are they right for their roles as nouns (for example, *safety*), verbs (*save*), adjectives (*safe*), or adverbs (*safely*)? Use a dictionary to help you make decisions. Second, do they agree in number (singular or plural), tense and

participate form (past or present), case (subject, object, or possessive), and so on?

8. *Prepositions.* Keep a master list of idiomatic pairs. Use your dictionary or a phrase book to confirm their use.

USE *A/AN* WITH NONSPECIFIC SINGULAR COUNT NOUNS

Count nouns name persons, places, or things that can be counted numerically. They may be singular or plural: *student/students, city/cities, computer/computers.* **Nonspecific count nouns** are nouns that have not yet been specifically identified:

A computer does calculations. Computers do calculations.

As the first sentence in this example illustrates, nonspecific singular count nouns can be introduced by *a* or *an.*

1   Matching *a* with consonant sounds, *an* with vowel sounds

- Use *a* before words beginning with a consonant sound: *a book, a happy man, a pen.*
- Use *an* before words beginning with a vowel sound (*a, e, i, o, u,* or silent *h,* as in *hour*): *an apple, an episode, an impossible task, an operator, an understanding, an honour.*

2   Knowing when to use *a* or *an*

With singular count nouns, use *a* or *an* in the following situations:

- To mean "one of a certain type": *A banana will give you more energy than an apple.*

  Most moral issues have $\overset{a}{\wedge}$grey area where right and wrong become cloudy.

- To refer to "one out of many choices": *Choose an apple from this bowl.*

  I have just received $\overset{an}{\wedge}$exciting job offer.

- To mention something for the first time: *A dish* [first mention] *fell off the counter and broke. The dish* [second mention] *belonged to my grandmother.*

Exceptions: *The* is used generically with certain nonspecific singular count nouns to mean "one representative of a certain type or class."

- Classes of humans, plants, or animals: *The woolly mammoth lived in Siberia 6,000 years ago.*
- Parts of the body: *The funny bone is very sensitive.*
- Inventions and devices, including musical instruments: *The koto, a stringed instrument similar to the zither, is important to Japanese sacred music.*

NEVER USE *A/AN* WITH NONCOUNT NOUNS

Noncount nouns refer to things that must be measured, not counted, and things that cannot be made plural. They are never introduced by *a* or *an*.

- Whole groups of similar items: *baggage, clothing, equipment, food, fruit, furniture, garbage, hardware, jewellery, junk, luggage, machinery, mail, makeup, money/cash/change, postage, scenery, traffic,* and so on.

  When I return home next time, I will take only ⱥ luggage. *(one piece of)*

- Abstractions: *advice, beauty, courage, education, grammar, happiness, health, homework, honesty, importance, information, knowledge, laughter, music, news, peace, progress, sleep, time, violence, vocabulary, wealth, work,* and so on.

  On television, ⱥ violence is often presented as attractive and exciting.

- Liquids: *blood, coffee, gasoline, milk, oil, soup, tea, water, . . .*

- Solids: *bread, butter, cheese, cotton, gold, ice, iron, meat, glass, paper, silver, wood, wool, . . .*

- Gases: *air, hydrogen, oxygen, pollution, smog, steam, smoke, . . .*

- Particles and powders: *chalk, corn, dirt, dust, flour, grass, hair, pepper, rice, salt, sand, sugar, wheat, . . .*

- Languages: *Arabic, Chinese, English, Polish, Sanskrit, Spanish, Urdu, . . .*

- Fields of study: *chemistry, engineering, history, mathematics, . . .*

- Recreation: *baseball, bridge, chess, soccer, tennis, . . .*

- General activities: *driving, studying, travelling, . . .*

- Natural phenomena: *darkness, dew, electricity, fire, fog, gravity, hail, heat, humidity, lightning, rain, sleet, snow, thunder, weather, wind, . . .*

Note: Many nouns have both count and noncount uses: *Please bring us two coffees* [count noun]. *The caffeine in coffee* [noncount noun] *keeps me awake.* Your dictionary may help you distinguish between units and masses with dual nouns like these.

USE *THE* WITH NOUNS WHOSE SPECIFIC IDENTITY YOUR READERS KNOW

The definite article *the,* indicating "this" or "that," introduces a specific person, place, or thing singled out from others. Use *the* in the following situations:

- When readers know exactly what the noun represents: *I have to go to the bank to get some money.*

  Many societies have abandoned ˄ death penalty. *(the)*

- When the noun refers to a unique person, place, or thing: *Last year we visited the Vatican, but we didn't see the Pope.*
  A full eclipse of ˄*the* sun or ˄*the* moon is quite impressive to see.

- When the noun is mentioned for the second time: *Last night I went to a new restaurant* [first mention]. *They call the restaurant* [second mention] *Le Cochon Dingue.*

- When the words following the noun make its identity clear: *The student who won the chess championship was Clara Vaz.*
  In this poem, ˄*the* speaker reminds us that flowers, too, are mortal.

- When the noun is modified by a superlative adjective.

  The tallest player on the team is Nestor Wozny.
  When I finally got married, **the most relieved person in the room** was my mother.

DO NOT USE *THE* WITH MOST PROPER NOUNS AND STATEMENTS MEANING "ALL" OR "IN GENERAL"

1 Proper nouns

Do not use *the* before most singular proper nouns, including languages (*French, English*), people (*Wayne Gretzky*), organizations (*Greenpeace*), special days (*Valentine's Day*), continents (*South America*), countries (*Scotland*), provinces (*Manitoba*), cities and towns (*St. John's*), streets and roads (*Bank Street, University Avenue*), squares (*Place Ville-Marie*), parks (*Victoria Park*), individual lakes (*Canoe Lake*), bays (*James Bay*), islands (*Prince Edward Island*), and specific mountains (*Mount Robson*).

> In ~~the~~ Japanese, the saying "Look up into the sky" means "Stop and smell the roses."

Some singular proper nouns are exceptions and require *the*:

- Use *the* before phrases identifying a specific language: *the Russian language, the Portuguese language,* and so on.
- Use *the* before the names of certain countries: *the United States, the Netherlands, the Philippines, the People's Republic of China.*
- Use *the* before the names of regions (*the East Coast*), deserts (*the Sahara*), peninsulas (*the Malay Peninsula*), and bodies of water other than lakes (*the Pacific Ocean, the Mediterranean Sea, the Davis Strait*).
- Use *the* before names with *of* in the title (*the Bank of Montreal, the University of New Brunswick*) and for organizational subdivisions (*the Faculty of Music, the Department of Fisheries*).
- Use *the* before plural proper nouns, such as *the United Nations, the Himalayan Mountains, the Great Lakes, the Thousand Islands.*

2   General statements

Do not use *the* before plural or noncount nouns used in a general sense.

Students
~~The students~~ today are drinking less but smoking more.

In dangerous situations, ~~the~~ courage may not be as important as ~~the~~ patience.

3   Certain place expressions

Do not use *the* before general uses of the words *school, class, work, church, town,* and *bed.*

This term I am at ~~the~~ school only three days each week.

4   Games

Do not use *the* before the names of games: *chess* [not *the chess*], *baseball, soccer.*

5   Subjects of study

Do not use *the* before subjects of study: *economics* [not *the economics*], *history, mathematics, political science, sociology,* and so on.

When I took ~~the~~ art history, I studied both Western and Asian painters.

MATCH QUANTIFIERS WITH APPROPRIATE COUNT OR NONCOUNT NOUNS

Quantifiers are words or phrases that tell how much or how many: *two millimetres of rain, a few students.* Be sure the quantifiers match the kinds of nouns used with them.

1   Using quantifiers with singular count nouns

Use *one, each, every, either, neither,* and *another* with singular count nouns: *one apple, each student, every computer, either one, neither friend, another movie.*

2   Using quantifiers with plural nouns

To tell "how many," use numbers greater than one with plural nouns, or use these quantifiers: *both, a couple of, few/a few, many, a number of, several.* For example: *seven apples, many oranges, a number of computers.*

3   Using quantifiers with noncount nouns

Use *little/a little, much, an amount of,* and *a great deal of* with noncount nouns to tell "how much": *little news, not much snow, a great deal of progress.*

4   Using quantifiers with plural and noncount nouns

Use the following quantifiers with either plural or noncount nouns to tell "how many" or "how much" according to their countability: *all, almost all, almost no, a lot of, enough, hardly any, lots of, a majority/minority of (the), most, not any/no, plenty of, some.* For example: *all the apples, all the snow, hardly any students, hardly any progress, some computers, some fog.* When count nouns follow such quantifiers, be sure to make them plural.

universities
Some ~~university~~ make an extra effort to help international students feel at home.

5   Using articles and quantifiers together

Generally, one determiner alone will do the job of introducing a noun. If you are using a quantifier, you will probably not include an article as well:

> There was ~~a~~ plenty of food at the picnic.

> The umpire explained the ruling to ~~the~~ both teams.

At the same time, remember that many quantifiers contain articles: *a few, a little, a number of, a lot of,* and so on. It would be a mistake to leave the articles out here:

> We went skiing in the Laurentians ^*a* few years ago.

This chapter focusses on features of English verbs frequently troublesome to nonnative speakers. Features that may be troublesome to native and nonnative speakers alike are treated elsewhere in this book.

- Irregular verbs
- Specific uses of verb tenses
- Subject-verb agreement
- Dropped or confused verb endings
- The subjunctive mood for wishes and nonfactual statements
- Active and passive voice

TO EXPRESS TENSE CORRECTLY, MATCH APPROPRIATE HELPING AND MAIN VERB FORMS

1   Forming tenses

Tense literally means "time": past, present, or future. English verbs have a simple form to represent actions or states occurring *at* these three times and a perfect form for those occurring *prior to* another time or action. Each of these six tense forms also has a continuous form (a form of *be* + *-ing*) to indicate ongoing or lasting action. To form verb tenses correctly, use the following combinations of helping verbs and main verbs:

- Present: For action that takes place regularly or at any time, use the base or *-s/-es* form of the main verb: *I* **write** *often. He* **speaks.** Use the present continuous to indicate action in progress at the present time:

  I **am studying** *now. She* **is speaking.** *You/we/they* **are working.**

- Past: To represent what happened in the past, use the past tense form (regular or irregular) of the main verb: *I* **wrote** *yesterday. He* **spoke.** Use the past continuous for actions in progress at a specific past time: *I/he/she/it* **was working** *then. You/we/they* **were working.**

- Future: To show what will take place, use *will* + the base form of the main verb: *I* **will write.** *She* **will speak.** Use the future continuous for actions in progress at a specific future time: *They* **will be working** *then.*

- Present perfect: To emphasize past action with a connection to the present, use *has/have* + the past participle form of the main verb: *I* **have written** *already. He* **has spoken.** For past action continuing to the present and on to the future, use the present perfect continuous: *We* **have been working** *all day.*

- Past perfect: To emphasize the earlier of two actions occurring in the past, use *had* + the past participle form of the main verb: *She* **had spoken** *before he did.* For lasting past perfect action, use the past perfect continuous: *We* **had been working** *for an hour by the time he finally spoke.*

- Future perfect: To emphasize the earlier of two actions occurring in the future, use *will have* + the past participle form (regular or irregular) of the main verb: *She* **will have spoken** *before he does.* For lasting future perfect action, use the future perfect continuous: *We* **will have been working** *for an hour by the time he finally speaks.*

As you revise, be sure that you have used the correct combination of helping and main verbs to express tense.

  changing
She is ~~change~~ her major from biology to botany.

[The *-ing* verb form is necessary to form the present continuous, indicating present ongoing action.]

  have
Scientists ~~had~~ now demonstrated that some animals are capable of reason.

[*Has* or *have* is necessary to form the present perfect, indicating past action completed prior to the present as indicated by *are.*]

A note on tense consistency: Two or more verbs that refer to the same action must be in the same tense.

2   Avoiding inappropriate omissions
Always include verbs even when the meaning or verb tense seems clear without them.

  are
So far, they the friendliest students in my residence.

[The helping verbs *be, have,* and *do* may stand alone as main verbs. Here *are* is necessary to connect the subject *they* to its complement, *the friendliest students.*]

  has
She been a member of Amnesty International for five years.

[*Has* is necessary to create the present perfect tense.]

3   Identifying verbs that lack continuous forms
The following verbs do not generally appear in the continuous *-ing* forms.

- Verbs referring to mental states: *believe, doubt, feel, forget, imagine, intend, know, mean, need, prefer, realize, recognize, remember, suppose, understand, wish.*
  have known
  I ~~am knowing~~ the Patel family for seven years.

- Verbs referring to emotional states: *appreciate, care, dislike, envy, fear, hate, like, love, mind, want.*

- Verbs referring to the act of possessing: *belong, contain, have, own, possess. Have* in its continuous form emphasizes process instead of ownership: *She is having a baby. She is having lunch. She is having a party.*

- Verbs referring to sense perceptions: *feel, hear, see, smell, taste*. Exceptions: These verbs may appear in continuous forms with a change of meaning. For example, in *I feel the soft ground beneath my sleeping bag, feel* refers to tactile experience. But in *I'm feeling good this morning, feeling* refers to the speaker's mood.

USE -*SI*-*ES* ON PRESENT TENSE VERBS THAT HAVE THIRD-PERSON SINGULAR SUBJECTS

English adds *-s* or *-es* to third-person singular verbs in the present tense: *he works*. In your writing, take care to add *-s* or *-es* when called for—and especially following the words listed on the next page.

- Singular nouns: *Joan hikes. The baby cries.*
- Singular personal pronouns: *She hikes. He sings. It falls.*
- Indefinite pronouns, which are usually singular: *Everyone hikes. Each sings.*

He ~~try~~ *tries* to come home early, but his job often ~~keep~~ *keeps* him out late.

USE THE STANDARD ENGLISH FORMS OF *BE*, *HAVE*, AND *DO*

Use Standard English verb forms in your writing.

I Be
The eight forms of *be* (*be, am, is, are, was, were, been, being*) make it the most complex English verb.

	SINGULAR	PLURAL
First person	I am/am being/ was/have been	we are/are being/ were/have been
Second person	you are/are being/ were/have been	you are/are being/ were/have been
Third person	she is/is being/ was/has been	they are/are being/ were/have been

To use *be* in its Standard English forms, follow these guidelines:

- Use *am/was* or *is/was* with first-person and third-person singular verbs; use *are* and *were* with all others.

She ~~were~~ *was* trying to get her essay published in the campus magazine.

[*She* takes a third-person singular verb, *was*.]

- Use *am, is,* and *are* + the present participle (*-ing*) to indicate events currently in progress as well as continuous events: *she is laughing, they are studying.*

  He_{is}going to school.

  [He is on his way to school.]

  He ~~be~~_{is} going to school.

  [He is currently attending school.]

- Informally, verbs are sometimes contracted with their subjects: *I'm, you're, she's, we're, they're.* But do not omit these verbs entirely.

  I_{'m}working forty hours a week.

  That bus_{had}better be on time.

2 *Have*

Use the *-s* form *has* for the third-person singular (*John has*); use *have* for all other present tense and present perfect forms (*we have*). Do not omit *has* or *have* when these forms are used as helping verbs: *John has worked, we have lived.*

She ~~have~~_{has} come to every meeting of the drama club.

He_{has}been a successful businessperson for twenty years.

They_{have}been going to Gaspé every summer for five years.

3 *Do*

Use the *-es* form *does* for the third-person singular (*she does*); use *do* for all other present tense forms.

Merrilee ~~don't~~_{doesn't} want to go to the party this weekend.

~~Do~~_{Does} he ever consider other people's feelings?

AFTER THE HELPING VERBS *DO, DOES,* AND *DID,* USE ONLY THE BASE FORM OF THE MAIN VERB

The helping verb *do* appears in questions, in negatives with *not* or *never,* and in emphatic statements. Use the appropriate form to signal tense and number (singular or plural): *do* = the base form, *does* = *-s* form (third-person singular), *did* = past tense. Following *do, does,* or *did,* use the base form of the main verb. Do not omit *do, does,* or *did* even if the meaning seems clear without them.

- A question: *Do you have the DVD I requested?*
- A negative statement: *He doesn't* [present tense: *does not*] *know what he wants for dinner.*
- An emphatic statement: *We did* [past tense] *offer to help whenever we could.*

USE MODAL VERBS TO INDICATE YOUR ATTITUDE TOWARD THE ACTION OF A MAIN VERB

The modal helping verbs *can, could, may, might, must, shall, should, will,* and *would* express the writer's attitude toward an action. Auxiliary verbs such as *ought to, had better,* and *have to* do the same.

- Capability: *I can help you with your calculus.*
- Intention: *I will finish by tomorrow.*
- Possibility: *They might go to the party.*
- Probability: *She must have gone home already.*
- Permission: *You may leave when you finish the exam.*
- Advisability: *He should edit his writing more carefully.*
- Necessity: *We must finish the book by this weekend.*

Use only one modal before a main verb.

They might ~~could~~ take a Spanish class next semester.

1 Using present/future forms

For action in the present or future, use *can, may, might, must, should, had better, ought to, will* + the base form of the main verb. Do not add an *-s,* even when the subject is *he, she,* or *it: Next semester he will take fewer classes.*

Nadia says she _^ *will* come to the party this evening.

[The modal verb *will* expresses future action and the closing phrase, *this evening,* indicates future time.]

Tamiko assured her supervisor that she ~~cans~~ *can* finish the project by Tuesday.

[Modal verbs never take the *-s* verb ending.]

With a little encouragement, Henry may ~~volunteers~~ *volunteer*.

[The modal *may* must be followed by the base form *volunteer.*]

Lucia might ~~to play~~ *play* a Chopin sonata at her next recital.

[Following the modal *might,* the base form of the main verb *play* is required.]

2 Using past forms

For past action, use *would, could, might, used to, had to* + the base form of the main verb. Do not use any other form of the main verb: *Ernie used to smoke* [not *smoked*] *cigars.*

As she listened to their explanation, she ~~can~~ *could* understand their motives.

When I saw how pale she was, I thought she might ~~been~~ *be* sick.

3   Using past perfect forms for potential past action

For past action that did not actually occur, use *could (not) have, should (not) have, would (not) have* + the past participle of the main verb: *Sven should have covered his roses to protect them from frost.*

> With regular feeding, the fish would not have ~~die~~. *died*
>
> They should ~~waited~~ a week or two before planting the flowers. *have*

USE THE PASSIVE VOICE WHEN A SUBJECT RECEIVES THE ACTION OF A TRANSITIVE VERB

In passive voice expressions, a passive subject receives the action of a transitive verb. The subject is acted on instead of performing an action.

> a subject receiving action
>
> In ancient Ethiopia, coffee was consumed as a food rather than a beverage.

I   Confusing voice and tense

Do not confuse the passive voice with the past tense. A passive voice verb may appear in the past, present, or future. To form the passive, use the appropriate form of *be* to signal number and tense followed by the past participle of the main verb. Note that *be, being,* and *been* must be preceded by another helping verb.

> Present passive: *The music is played.*
> Present continuous passive: *The music is being played.*
> Present perfect passive: *The music has been played.*
> Past passive: *The music was played.*
> Past continuous passive: *The music was being played.*
> Past perfect passive: *The music had been played.*
> Future passive: *The music will be played.*
> Future perfect passive: *The music will have been played.*

2   Misusing the passive

- To form the passive voice, use the past participle form of main verbs, not the base or past tense forms.

  > The movie will be ~~release~~ in China early next year. *released*
  >
  > The emigrants who left Ireland in the 1840s were ~~drove~~ by famine. *driven*

- Include the appropriate form of *be* in all passive voice expressions.

  > In our culture today, too much emphasis placed on material goals. *is*

- Make sure you use a verb that can be made passive.

  > The accident ~~was~~ happened downtown.

USE APPROPRIATE VERB TENSES IN CONDITIONAL (*IF* . . .) SENTENCES

Conditional sentences usually consist of two parts: (1) an *if* dependent clause stating conditions and (2) a main clause stating results.

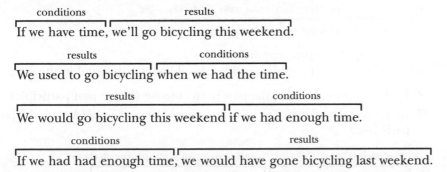

conditions   results

If we have time, we'll go bicycling this weekend.

results   conditions

We used to go bicycling when we had the time.

results   conditions

We would go bicycling this weekend if we had enough time.

conditions   results

If we had had enough time, we would have gone bicycling last weekend.

These examples illustrate three features of conditional sentences: (1) the *if* clause may appear before or after the main clause stating results; (2) not every conditional sentence contains *if;* and, most important, (3) the kind of conditional statement determines the tenses of the verbs.

1   Determining habitual past and present conditions

For conditions that occur again and again in the past or present, use the same tense in the *if* clause and the "results" main clause.

present tense (*if* clause)   present tense (*results* clause)

If we have enough time, we go bicycling on weekends.

past tense (*if* clause)   past tense (*results* clause)

When we had enough time, we went bicycling on weekends.

2   Describing possible future conditions

To predict future conditions and results:

- In the *if* clause, use *if* or *unless* + the present tense (not the future).
- In the "results" clause, use *can, may, might, should,* or *will* + the base form of the verb.

present tense (*if* clause)   *may* + base form (*results* clause)

If we have enough time, we may go bicycling this weekend.

will + base form (*results* clause)   present tense (*if* clause)

We will go bicycling this weekend unless it rains.

3   Speculating about present or future conditions

To speculate about imagined conditions in the present or future:

- In the *if* clause, use *if* + the past tense (not the present) unless you use a form of the verb *be.* In this case use *were* instead of *was,* whether the subject is singular or plural.

■ In the "results" clause, use *could, might,* or *would* + the base form of the verb.

past tense (*if* clause)   *would* + base form (*results* clause)

If the weather were better today, we would go bicycling.

might + base form (*results* clause)   past tense (*if* clause)

We might go bicycling if it stopped raining.

4   Speculating about past conditions

To speculate about what might, could, or should have happened in the past:

■ In the *if* clause, use *if* + the past perfect tense (*had* + past participle).

■ In the "results" clause, use *could have, might have,* or *would have* + the past participle.

past perfect tense (*if* clause)   *would have* + past participle (*results* clause)

If it had stopped raining, we would have gone bicycling.

could have + past participle (*results* clause)   past perfect tense (*if* clause)

We could have gone bicycling if the weather had been better.

LEARN WHICH VERBS MAY BE FOLLOWED BY INFINITIVES, GERUNDS, OR EITHER VERB FORM

An **infinitive** is the base form of a verb preceded by *to: to study.* A **gerund** is the *-ing* form of a verb used as a noun: *Studying is difficult after a full day's work.* Following certain verbs, infinitives or gerunds may appear as objects.

I   Verb + infinitive

■ Some verbs are followed by an infinitive (*to* + base form), not a gerund:

agree	come	happen	offer	seem
appear	decide	hope	plan	swear
arrange	deserve	live	pretend	threaten
claim	fail	long	refuse	yearn

The group agreed **to study** [not *studying*] in the library after dinner.

■ When used in the active voice, a related group of verbs takes an object (noun or pronoun) before the infinitive. These verbs fit in the following pattern: *We ___ her to do something.*

advise	convince	force	permit	schedule	urge
allow	enable	instruct	persuade	teach	warn
cause	encourage	invite	remind	tell	
command	forbid	order	require		

verb + noun + infinitive

We have invited Gary to join us for dinner.

verb + pronoun + infinitive

Kayla advised me to apply for a scholarship.

- A small group of verbs may be followed by either the infinitive or an object (noun or pronoun) + infinitive:

ask	dare	help	need	promise	wish
beg	expect	intend	prefer	want	would like
choose	get	mean	prepare		

verb + infinitive

The lawyer asked to address the court.

verb + noun object + infinitive

The lawyer asked the plaintiff to address the court.

- When the verbs *have* ("cause"), *let* ("allow"), and *make* ("force") are followed by a noun or pronoun + infinitive, the *to* is omitted, as it is with the "sense" verbs *watch, see, hear,* and *feel*:

Please have the carpenters **finish** [not *to finish*] their work by Thursday.

With *help,* the *to* is optional: *We helped them (to) finish it.*

2   Verb + gerund

- These verbs may be followed by a gerund (*-ing*) but not an infinitive:

admit	deny	imagine	postpone	resent
anticipate	discuss	involve	practise	resist
appreciate	dread	keep	put off	resume
avoid	enjoy	mention	quit	risk
consider	escape	mind	recall	suggest
delay	finish	miss	recommend	tolerate

Keiko recalled **leaving** [not *to leave*] her gloves in the car.

- The following expressions with prepositions may be followed by a gerund or a possessive + gerund:

account for	be jealous of	consist of
accuse someone of	be known for	delight in
apologize for	be responsible for	depend on
approve of	be tired of	disapprove of
be accustomed to	be used to	dream of
be capable of	believe in	feel like
be excited about	care about	forgive someone for
be famous for	complain about	get around to
be fond of	concentrate on	have an influence on
be interested in	consent to	help in

insist on	prevent someone from	talk about
keep someone from	recover from	think about
look forward to	stop someone from	
object to	succeed in	

For more than a year Annette and I have dreamed of travelling to Italy.
[verb + preposition + gerund]

Our success depends on his arriving on time.
[verb + preposition + possessive + gerund]

3   Verb + infinitive or gerund

- ■ Certain verbs may be followed by infinitives or gerunds with little or no change of meaning: *begin, cease, continue, hate, like, love, prefer, start.*

    Ali **loves playing** the guitar.

    Ali **loves to play** the guitar.

- ■ After the verbs *forget, remember, stop,* and *try,* the infinitive and gerund have different meanings:

    A good Samaritan is someone who **stops to help** those in need. [provides assistance]

    Concerned with his own problems, Felix **has stopped helping** those in need. [no longer provides assistance]

USE TWO-WORD VERBS CORRECTLY

A **two-word verb** (also called a *phrasal verb*) consists of a verb and a preposition-like word called a **particle.** The meaning of a two-word verb differs from the meaning of its individual words, as the following examples with *call* show:

I promised to **call up** my parents this weekend. [to telephone]

When I get the information, I'll **call** you **back.** [to return a telephone call]

Her soufflé recipe **calls for** half a dozen eggs. [to require]

The instructor **called** the student **in** for a conference. [to ask to come to a specific place for a specific purpose]

I'm going to **call on** you tomorrow. [to ask to speak, to visit]

The umpire **called off** the game because of rain. [to cancel]

I   Using a dictionary or phrase book

Because English two-word verbs are so numerous and their meanings are almost always idiomatic, use a dictionary or phrase book of idioms as you write and edit. Two reference books are the *Oxford Dictionary of Phrasal Verbs* (1993) and the *Cambridge International Dictionary of Phrasal Verbs* (1997). Check to see that you've used the correct verb + particle combination for the meaning you intend.

2   Placing objects and particles following the verb

The **particle** in a two-word verb is either inseparable or separable from the verb.

- An **inseparable particle** follows the verb immediately.

  The instructor **called on** Sergei to answer the question.

  Today's students often **drop out** of school for a few years and then return.

  Winston eventually **got over** his disappointment.

- A **separable particle** may be separated from a transitive verb according to two patterns:

  Noun objects. If the object of a separable two-word verb is a noun, place it either after the particle or between the verb and particle. *The umpire called off the game* (verb + particle + noun). *The umpire called the game off* (verb + noun + particle).

  Pronoun objects. If the object of a separable two-word verb is a pronoun, it must go between the verb and particle: *The umpire called it off* (verb + pronoun + particle).

USE WORDS IDIOMATICALLY

The term **idiom** applies to words and phrases given special meaning by native speakers of a language. Idiomatic usage has to be learned, not guessed at. For example, "Good evening" and "Good night" might look synonymous, but the first is a greeting and the second a farewell—they are not at all interchangeable. To keep things sounding idiomatic, watch for three main trouble spots.

1 Misusing individual words
Individual words are frequently used in some situations but not in others that may appear similar:

> The murderer ~~massacred~~ *killed* his victim and buried the body in the flowerbed.

[*To massacre* may mean to kill pitilessly; at the same time, it refers to mass slaughter, as in *The early Jesuits were massacred by the Iroquois.* In idiomatic English, a single victim cannot be "massacred," but is slain, killed, or even butchered.]

2 Using stock phrases
Stock phrases are verbal formulas such as *stand pat, come in handy, be on the ball, see red, travel light, make do, move heaven and earth, take stock, cut corners,* and so on. Such expressions are used in speaking, not writing, and are often overused.

3 Misusing prepositions
Prepositions (*in, by, on, with,* and so on) and preposition-like words called **particles,** which follow verbs (*agree with/to, prevent from, fight against/for, abide by,* and so on), are especially idiomatic, appearing only in certain situations and after particular words.

> Parents who really care ~~for~~ *about* their children's education provide their sons and daughters *with* many learning opportunities outside school.

[Idiomatic English calls for *care about* when concern is the issue instead of *care for,* which means "love." With *provide,* the preposition with is called for when the recipients are referred to in the sentence: *They provided the opportunity, although we provided her* **with** *that opportunity.*]

Native speakers of a language generally use words idiomatically, but nonnative speakers and writers who choose words outside their everyday vocabularies may have difficulties.

- If you're uncertain of a word or phrase, check usage notes in dictionaries.
- For stock phrases unlisted in dictionaries, refer to special dictionaries and collections of idioms in libraries or bookstores.
- For prepositions, look up the word preceding the preposition (*care* and *provide* in the above example) in a dictionary.

INCLUDE ALL NECESSARY WORDS

1   Including subjects

Except for imperatives, all English sentences require a subject. Be especially careful to include personal pronoun subjects that refer to antecedents in preceding clauses or sentences. Compare these examples:

> The Hindu god Brahma is considered equal to Vishnu and Siva. However, he has had only one temple dedicated to him, at Pushkar in India.

> Because Ray practises speaking into a tape recorder, *he* has excellent pronunciation.

> Tina is such an optimist. *She says* ~~Says~~ that problems are only clouds hiding the sun.

2   Including the expletives *it, here,* and *there*

Expletives are words used primarily for grammatical purposes. They provide a subject for a sentence that doesn't logically have one, or they introduce a subject following the verb. An expletive is usually followed by a form of *be*.

> It *is* raining again.

> delayed subject
> **There** *are* many Andean mountains higher than 6,700 metres.

Do not omit *it, here,* and *there* even though they contribute little meaning to your sentences, and be sure the verb agrees with its actual subject.

> *It is* ~~Is~~ necessary to take health precautions before travelling in tropical countries.

> [*It* is required to stand in for the subject of the sentence, *to take health precautions.*]

> Ten years ago*, there* was a severe drought on the prairies.

> [The subject of the sentence is not *ten years ago* but *a severe drought* following the verb *was. There* is required to introduce it.]

> *There are* ~~Is~~ two sides to every dilemma.

> [The subject of the sentence, *two sides,* requires the plural verb *are* to follow *There.*]

AVOID UNNECESSARY REPETITION

1   Avoiding unnecessary repetition of a subject

Do not repeat a subject within its own clause, even when the subject and verb are separated.

> American soft drink manufacturers ~~they~~ advertise heavily throughout Asia.

> *The* ~~In the~~ essay, ~~it~~ discusses the effects of acid rain on sugar maples.

2   Avoiding unnecessary object/adverb repetition

Do not repeat an object or adverb in an adjective clause beginning with a relative pronoun (*who, which, whom, whose, that*) or relative adverb (*where, when*).

Kevin is the one person whom I can always trust ~~him~~ to tell the truth.

[The relative pronoun *whom* is also the object of the verb *trust;* the objective pronoun *him* is unnecessary. Even if *whom* were omitted, *him* would be unnecessary: *Kevin is the one person I can always trust to tell the truth.*]

Marrakech sits on a high plain where the air is thin and the sun is brilliant ~~there~~.

[*There* repeats the meaning of the relative adverb *where* and is, therefore, unnecessary.]

3   Avoiding duplicate conjunctions

Coordinating conjunctions (*for, and, nor, but, or, yet, so*) link main clauses. Subordinating conjunctions (*although, because, if, when,* and so on) link dependent clauses to main clauses. Use only one conjunction to link clauses in writing.

Although credit cards are very convenient, ~~but~~ they can lead to overspending.

[The subordinating conjunction *although* links the first clause, *credit cards are very convenient,* to the following main clause, so *but* is unnecessary. To put equal emphasis on both clauses, the writer omits *although* and retains *but: Credit cards are very convenient, but they can lead to overspending.*

BEGIN DEPENDENT CLAUSES WITH APPROPRIATE LINKING WORDS

Whatever their role in a sentence, dependent clauses always begin with a subordinating word that connects them to the main clause of the sentence. Such words may be relative pronouns such as *who* or *that*, question words such as *what* or *how*, or subordinating conjunctions such as *although* or *because*. To express your meaning effectively, choose the words that fit grammatically in your sentence and that say what you intend.

The report mentioned ~~about~~ *that* students often hire tutors.

[*About* is a preposition, used for prepositional phrases; it cannot begin a clause. A subordinating word is required to begin a noun clause functioning as a direct object.]

1   Creating accurate wh- clauses

Wh- dependent clauses are headed by an interrogative word usually beginning with *wh-: who, which, whom/about whom, whose, where, when, what, why, whether,* and *how. Wh-* clauses may function as noun phrases or modifiers.

A subject	*Why she behaved that way* was a mystery to him.
An object	Peter could not predict *what his decision would be.*

A noun modifier   This is the place *where we were supposed to meet.*
A sentence modifier   People easily get sick *when work is too stressful.*

Choose the *wh-* word that best fits the meaning of the clause it begins and that links with the word in the main clause that it modifies.

It was her aunt ~~which~~ ^who^ loaned Mary the money to go to Niagara College.

[Used to refer to objects or unnamed animals, *which* is inappropriate to introduce an adjective clause modifying *aunt. Who* is best.]

The building ~~what~~ ^where^ Ina lives ~~in~~ is very old.

[*Where* is appropriate for identifying *the building.* Another option is to replace *what* with *that: The building that Ina lives in is very old.*]

2   Creating effective adverbial clauses

Adverbial dependent clauses (known as **subordinate clauses**) modify verbs and begin with subordinating conjunctions that indicate time (*after, when*), place (*wherever*), reason (*because*), comparison (*although*), and manner or condition (*as, if*). As you edit your sentences, check to be sure that subordinating conjunctions fit the clauses they introduce and that subordinate clauses contain a subject and a verb.

Josette does well on tests even ^when^ she has not studied much.

[By itself, *even* is not a subordinator. Add *though* or *if* or *when* to be idiomatic.]

I attended my political science class for three weeks before ^I began^ to feel comfortable with my instructor.

[A subordinate clause must contain a subject and verb: *I began.* As an alternative version, *before* may introduce an adverbial phrase: *before feeling comfortable with my instructor.*]

FOLLOW THESE GUIDELINES TO SUMMARIZE QUESTIONS AND SPEECH

1   Summarizing questions

Summarized questions (also called **indirect questions**) are usually part of a longer statement of fact; therefore, they follow the word order and punctuation of declarative sentences.

- After the question word (*who, which, when, why, where, what, whom, how,* and so on) that introduces the summarized question, make sure the verb follows the subject.

The panel considered where ~~is~~ air pollution ^is^ the most severe.

- Use *whether* to introduce summarized *yes/no* questions and *or* questions that pose alternatives.

whether I will
I have not decided ~~will I~~ go home for the summer or attend summer
school.

■ Omit *do, does, did* from summarized questions. Signal tense (the time of
the action) with the appropriate form of the main verb.

whether   needed
He asked me ~~did~~ I ~~need~~ help with my experiment.

[*Needed* matches the past tense form of the main verb *asked*.]

■ Punctuate summarized questions in a way appropriate to the complete
sentence.

The judge asked the jury whether it had reached a verdict~~?~~.

2   Summarizing speech

In **summarized speech** (also called **reported speech** or **indirect quotation**), a
writer restates a direct quotation in his or her own words, without quotation
marks.

■ Write the summarized speech as a noun clause within your own sentence.

DIRECT QUOTATION	SUMMARIZED SPEECH
She said, "A monsoon is a strong seasonal wind."	She said that a monsoon is a strong seasonal wind.

[*That* may be omitted from certain noun clauses.]

■ Change the present tense or present continuous of direct quotations to
the past tense or past continuous in summarized speech. An exception:
Use the present tense if the summarized speech is a general truth or
habitual action, as in the preceding example.

DIRECT QUOTATION	SUMMARIZED SPEECH
She said, "My report is finished."	She said that her report was finished.
She said, "I am finishing my report."	She said that she was finishing her report.

■ Change the past tense or present perfect of direct quotations to the past
perfect of summarized speech. Adjust adverbs accordingly.

DIRECT QUOTATION	SUMMARIZED SPEECH
She said, "They arrived an hour ago."	She said that they had arrived an hour before.
She said, "I have tried to help him."	She said that she had tried to help him.

■ With modal verbs in summarized speech, change *can* to *could, will* to *would, may* to *might, must* to *had to.*

DIRECT QUOTATION

She said, "I will call
   him next week."

SUMMARIZED SPEECH

She said that she would
   call him next week.

■ To summarize commands, use *to* + the base form of the verb (the infinitive).

DIRECT QUOTATION

She told her students,
   "Go to the lab."

SUMMARIZED SPEECH

She told her students to
   go to the lab.

CHOOSE THE CORRECT WORD ENDINGS FOR YOUR MEANING

1   Using plural forms appropriately

■ *Count nouns.* Count nouns refer to countable things and may, therefore, be either singular or plural: *apple/apples, joy/joys.* Do not omit the *-s, -es,* and other plural endings from nouns that refer to more than one countable item.

Middle Eastern cuisine makes frequent use of grape~-s~, pine nut~-s~, and

chickpea~-s~.

■ *Noncount nouns.* Noncount nouns are often generic, so they cannot be counted: *homework, equipment, furniture, news.* Do not make them plural in your writing. Keep a list of those words you should not make plural, and avoid adding *-s* when you use them.

It is important not to use ~~slangs~~ *slang* and colloquial expressions in formal writing.

[*Expression* is a count noun and should be pluralized, but *slang* is uncountable. Never use *slang* with a plural sense, for it is always uncountable.]

2   Choosing correct word endings for nouns, verbs, adjectives, and adverbs

English nouns, verbs, adjectives, and adverbs can change their forms—and often their meanings—by changing their endings. Thus, the verb *succeed* has a noun form (*success*), an adjective form (*successful*), and an adverb form (*successfully*). As you edit your writing, consider word endings to be sure each word fits your intended meaning and its grammatical function as a noun, verb, adjective, or adverb. Keep track of the words you commonly confuse, and practise using the proper endings in your writing.

I have to cancel my doctor's appointment because the time is not *convenient* ~~convenience~~.

[Because of their similarities, it is easy to confuse some adjectives and nouns. Use the adjective form if you could put *very* in front of the word, as is the case above.]

The boxer was surprised when his opponent hit him so *hard* ~~hardly~~.

[Many adverbs end in *-ly,* so it's easy to confuse *hard* and *hardly.* Use *hard* with reference to force and *hardly* when you mean *scarcely* or *not at all hard.*]

I want my instructors to respon*-d*se to my work in detail.

[This sentence confuses the noun form, *response,* with the base form of the verb, *respond.*]

SHOW POSSESSION WITH AN APOSTROPHE OR AN *OF* PHRASE

English signals a possessive noun with an apostrophe or a phrase using *of: India's president, the president of India.* In some cases, as in the preceding examples, the forms are interchangeable; often they are not.

1   Indicating possession with an apostrophe

To make a singular noun or indefinite pronoun possessive, usually add *-'s: the student's book, someone's book.* To make a plural noun ending in *-s* possessive, usually add only an apostrophe: *the students' request.* An apostrophe is generally used with nouns referring to persons and other living beings: *the editor's opinion, the lions' roar.*

2   Indicating possession with *of*

To signal possession by things, you would typically use an *of* phrase: *the body of the car, the soles of my feet.* An *of* phrase may also be used to emphasize a source rather than a possessor: *the novels of Chinua Achebe.* Do not use possessive *of* phrases with personal pronouns: *her book,* not *the book of her.*

Many par*his*ents do not consider the TV violence ~~effect~~ on their children.

Without ~~the~~ help ~~of him~~, we could not have afforded the trip.

Exceptions: The apostrophe form of the possessive appears frequently in references to time (*an hour's drive, a month's time*), natural phenomena (*the sun's rays, Earth's atmosphere*), political organizations (*the city's parks, the government's transfer payments*), and groups of people working together (*the ship's crew, the company's employees*).

USE ADJECTIVES AND ADVERBS WITH CARE

1   Forming adjectives

Adjectives modify nouns. Some languages add endings to adjectives so that they match the nouns they modify; however, in English, adjectives do not change form. Indeed, even when they look as if they should be plural because they contain a number, do not add an *-s: Dianne bought three two-dollar stamps to mail her parcel.*

Jordan wore a three-pieces suit to his interview.

2   Using participles (*-ing* and *-ed* verb forms) as adjectives

To form some adjectives, English uses the present participle (*-ing*) and past participle of verbs: *a terrifying story, a crowded street.* Both kinds of participles may appear before a noun or following a linking verb: *The terrifying story is true. The story is terrifying. The terrified child could not speak. The child was terrified.* But present and past participles may not be used interchangeably.

■ Use **present participle adjectives** (ending in *-ing*) to describe something going on or stimulating an experience: *The survivors told a terrifying story to their fearful listeners* [the story caused terror in the listeners].

They jumped in surprise at the sound of ~~broken~~ glass.
                                           breaking

■ Use **past participle adjectives** (ending in *-ed, -d, -en, -t*) to describe a person or thing undergoing an experience: *The listeners were terrified by the survivors' story* [the listeners experienced terror].

I felt ~~embarrassing~~ when my instructor read my paper aloud.
        embarrassed

3   Arranging cumulative adjectives

Cumulative adjectives are two or more adjectives that are not separated by commas and that modify the whole phrase following them: *the large round Persian rug.* To use cumulative adjectives correctly, arrange them in this order:

1. Article, possessive, or quantifier: *the, my, Teresa's, some, four, . . .*
2. Comparative and superlative: *younger, older, best, worst, least, . . .*
3. Evaluator (a word that can be preceded by *very*): *beautiful, courageous, responsible, . . .*
4. Size: *large, small, gigantic, tall, . . .*
5. Length or shape: *long, round, oval, square, triangular, . . .*
6. Age: *young, old, new, antique, modern, twentieth-century, . . .*
7. Colour: *green, yellow, violet, . . .*
8. Nationality: *Peruvian, Iranian, Polish, American, . . .*
9. Religion: *Baptist, Buddhist, Christian, Hindu, Muslim, Protestant, . . .*
10. Material: *wood, walnut, metal, gold, wool, . . .*
11. Noun used as an adjective: *guest* (as in *guest room*), *history* (as in *history class*), *. . .*
12. Noun modified: *room, class, truck, table, . . .*

Compare these examples:

Four old wooden clocks will be sold at the auction.

The baby was being entertained by her older ~~two~~ sisters.
(two inserted above "two")

A note on adjective series: Avoid long series of adjectives. Generally use no more than two or three between an article, possessive, or quantifier and the noun it modifies: *an old Hindu temple, Alan's famous buttermilk pancakes, several well-known European scientists.*

4   Placing adverbs

Adverbs used to modify verbs may appear at the beginning, at the end, or in the middle of a sentence. However, do not place an adverb between a verb and a direct object. Compare these examples:

Carefully, she took her daughter's hand.

He turned the dial **carefully.**

He walked **carefully** along the ledge.

To complete my art history project, I examined ~~carefully~~ Mayan architecture.
(carefully inserted above)

CHOOSE THE APPROPRIATE PREPOSITION FOR YOUR MEANING

English prepositions can be especially troublesome to speakers of English as a second language, no matter what their first language. There are many prepositions to remember, their meanings are often idiomatic, and certain prepositions seem glued to some words but not to others.

Mark is so busy with school and work that he can scarcely keep track the time.
(of inserted above before "the")

Mountain biking has inspired new trends ~~to~~ clothing.
(in inserted above)

Although Mila is surely in love, she is not yet ready to make a commitment ~~with~~ Brian.
(to inserted above)

I   Using reference sources to choose prepositions

To choose prepositions appropriately, see the guidelines for two-word verbs on pages 546–47, consult an English dictionary to look up the meaning of the word preceding the preposition, or check reference sources on English idioms and prepositions, such as *The Ins and Outs of Prepositions* (Barrons Educational Series, 1999). Eventually, however, your effective use of prepositions will depend upon the powers of your memory.

2 Choosing prepositions to indicate place

- Use **at** before a specific location, meeting place, the edge of something, the corner of something, or a target: *arriving at school, seated at the table, turning at the corner, living at 73 Queen Street, aiming at the bull's eye.*

- Use **in** before an enclosed space or geographic location: *growing in the garden, standing in the phone booth, hiking in the mountains, living in Mexico City.*

- Use **on** before a surface or street: *lying on the table, hanging on the wall, walking on Dalhousie Street.*

3 Choosing prepositions to indicate time

- Use **at** before specific expressions of time: *She arrived at 2:30. They left at dawn.*

- Use **in** before a month, year, century, period of time, or part of a twenty-four-hour period: *in May, in 1865, in the twentieth century, in the morning.*

- Use **on** before a day or date: *on July 20, on Thursday.*

4 Positioning place and time phrases

In most English expressions, place comes before time: *My relatives arrived at my house in the early morning.* However, a prepositional phrase of time often appears at the beginning of a sentence: *In the early morning, my relatives arrived at my house.*

5 Using prepositions that match verbs idiomatically

Many verbs require specific prepositions to follow them:

add [something] to [something]
agree on [something]
agree with [someone]
apologize for [something]
apologize to [someone]
argue about [something]
argue with [someone]
arrive at [a specific location]
arrive in [a general area]
ask for [something]
ask [something] of [someone]
be composed of [something]
be made of [something]
belong to [someone/something]
blame [someone] for [something]
blame [something] on [someone]

borrow [something] from [someone]
comment on [something]
compliment [someone] on [something]
congratulate [someone] on [something]
convince [someone] of [something]
count on [someone/something]
decide on [something]
defer to [someone]
deprive [someone] of [something]
explain [something] to [someone]
fight against [someone/something]
fight with [someone] about [something]
hear from [someone] about [something]
hope for [something]

introduce [someone/
   something] to [someone]
lend [something] to [someone]
listen to [someone/something]
participate in [something]
pay [someone] for [something]
pay [something] to [someone]
prefer [something] to
   [something]
provide [someone] with
   [something]
provide [something] for
   [someone]
question [someone] about
   [something]
reason with [someone] about
   [something]
rely on [someone] for
   [something]

remind [someone] about/of
   [something]
remind [someone] of [someone]
search for [someone]
send for [something]
separate [something] from
   [something]
substitute [something] for
   [something]
subtract [something] from
   [something]
sympathize with [someone] about
   [something]
talk to [someone] about [something]
tamper with [something]
vote for [someone/something]
wait for [someone/something]
wish for [something]
work for [someone/something]